TEXTUAL SCHOLARSHIP

GARLAND REFERENCE LIBRARY
OF THE HUMANITIES
(VOL. 1417)

TEXTUAL SCHOLARSHIP
An Introduction

D.C. Greetham

GARLAND PUBLISHING, INC. • NEW YORK & LONDON
1994

Library of Congress Cataloging-in-Publication Data

Greetham, D. C. (David C.), 1941–
    Textual scholarship : an introduction / D.C. Greetham.
        p.   cm. — (Garland reference library of the humanities ; vol. 1417)
    Includes bibliographical references (p.) and index.
    ISBN 0–8153–0058–1 (hardcover : acid-free paper). — ISBN
0–8153–1791–3 (paperback : acid-free paper)
    1. Bibliography, Critical.   I. Title.   II. Series.
Z1001.G7   1994
010'.44—dc20
                                                                    94–9786
                                                                    CIP

Cover design by Patti Hefner

Printed on acid-free, 250-year-life paper
Manufactured in the United States of America

In Memory

of

My Mother

Contents

Preface

This book has been a long time a-borning and its gestation period has seen enormous changes in the way the field of textual scholarship is perceived by its practitioners. When I first began circulating (about fifteen years ago) the idea for a general treatment of the enumeration, description, transcription, editing, and annotation of texts, there was no acceptable term to encompass all these activities, and my proposal (as I recall) was for a book awkwardly titled "Paleography, Bibliography, and Textual Criticism"—with the implicit admission that even this clumsy trivium did not adequately represent the range of my subject. Since then, there has been a moderately successful attempt to co-opt the term "textual scholarship" for the procedures of enumerative bibliographers, descriptive, analytical, and historical bibliographers, paleographers and codicologists, textual editors, and annotators—cumulatively and collectively perhaps a field somewhat like the old "philology" of an earlier dispensation, the technical and conceptual recreation of the past through its texts, and specifically the language of those texts. In part, the employment of the term "textual scholarship" in this general sense is a recognition (as G. Thomas Tanselle put it in his inaugural address to the Society for Textual Scholarship in 1981) that "textual criticism" is associated with the "great tradition of classical and biblical [studies, and] forms but one branch of textual scholarship as a whole" ("Presidential Address" *Text* 1 [1984]: 2). In part, it is a recognition that the various contributions of paleographers, codicologists, bibliographers, editors and so on are related to what elsewhere Tanselle has called "the single great enterprise" (*Rationale of Textual Criticism*. Philadelphia: U of Pennsylvania P, 1989: 46) common to them all—the historical investigation of texts as both artifactual objects and conceptual entities, and the reconstruction of those stages in the transmission that have not survived.

It is with such concerns that I founded the Society for Textual Scholarship and began publishing (with my colleague W. Speed Hill) its journal *Text*: as encouragement of the interdisciplinary and intellectual acceptance of this "single great enterprise" and acknowledgment of the interdependence of its component practices. And it is with such concerns that this book has been written, to emphasize the continuities and reciprocations in the several parts of textual scholarship, and to present the field in terms of a single narrative—a sequence from the discovery and enumeration of the text, to the history of its production as a physical artifact and a technical description of its concrete form, to its transcription and rendering into another medium (usually the modern typeset page or electronic storage), to its critical or non-critical editing, and its elucidation by annotation and commentary.

All of these processes, even the most technical, can also be seen as aspects of the "textuality" of textual scholarship, the problematization and conceptualization of the ontology of text, work, edition, and the consequent re-examination of the status of author, scribe, compositor, redactor, and editor. And that is the other major change in the last fifteen years: the apparently purely empirical nature of textual scholarship, and especially its association with fixity, historical demonstration, and positivism, has been increasingly seen as just one of several available rhetorical modes; textual scholars have thus come to interrogate the very practices that they might earlier have thought to be inevitable or natural to the discipline, and thus textual scholarship has begun to theoretize itself, largely under the auspices of a Kuhnian shift in paradigm from intentionality to, for example, reception history and materialism. This shift is most apparent in the later stages of this book dealing with editorial theory, but there are signs that even the supposedly "theory-proof" areas of "hard" bibliography, like description and analysis, will become susceptible to this interrogation.

For the moment, however, I can present this book to its anticipated readership of neophyte textuists and non-specialist literary scholars as an introduction to a field which, while confronted by theory, still relies upon an accumulated body of historical data that seems to have all the traditional surety of the demonstrated fact. Such readers will, therefore, be able to get a quick, and I hope accurate "fix" on a discipline, that, in the very process of identifying itself as a single enterprise, is questioning the premises on which that enterprise is constructed.

My aims for the book are large and ambitious, and its success depends therefore upon the contributions of many people whose advice and guidance—and sometimes very practical assistance—have enabled me to cast such a wide net. My textual colleagues in the Society for Textual Scholarship and contributors to its journal *Text* have had their experience and opinions appropriated, as have the collaborators in the volume on scholarly editing that I have recently compiled (*Scholarly Editing: A Guide to Research*. New York: MLA). I have been the grateful recipient of specific advice on the text of this book from my colleagues A. S. G. Edwards and W. Speed Hill, both of whom read the entire typescript and made innumerable suggestions for improvement. I am also in debt to my editorial confrères (and especially M. C. Seymour) on the Trevisa and Hoccleve editions, where I was initiated into the mysteries of textual scholarship: many of the bibliographical and textual examples in this book are drawn from work on these two editions, and the figures of Trevisa (and his source Bartholomæus Anglicus) and Hoccleve therefore appear more prominently in this book than their status in the literary canon might otherwise justify. I make no apologies for this: textual scholarship is a learned skill, and whatever competence I may have is to some extent derived from the *practical* experience of editing. Besides, most of the canonical authors also join in the parade of texts—from Homer and Virgil to Chaucer and Langland, Shakespeare and Milton to Wordsworth and Byron, Emerson, Dickinson, and Twain to Yeats, Joyce, Eliot, and on to Fowles and Stoppard.

In various guises, various parts of the book have been tried out on my students at the City University of New York Graduate Center, and I am grateful not only that they were willing guinea-pigs, but also that through their helpful responses they became accomplices. Jeffrey Jaso and Bennett Graff read drafts for an early version of the index, and Thane Doss worked through the entire text, checking for consistency and fact-checking various parts of the bibliography. The original typescript was expertly entered on computer by Donja Joseph, and large parts of the final text subjected to a rigorous editorial reading by my wife Eva Resnikova, whose judicious eye and critical sensitivity made the book much more accessible than my scholarly prose would otherwise have allowed. Finally, I am grateful to Gary Kuris, Phyllis Korper, and Rita Quintas of Garland Publishing, whose advice was invaluable both before and during production. Being able to work in camera-ready copy (and thus typeset the book myself) gave me one great advantage and responsibility: since I controlled the production of text, I can now express with specific validity the authorial formula that all errors remaining are purely my own. And since one of the dicta of textual scholarship is that all texts do indeed contain errors (in fact, it is that which keeps us textual scholars in business), I would be grateful to any readers who can point out errors to me.

Preface to Corrected Reprint

I have taken the opportunity of this reprint to make various corrections in the text, and I am accordingly grateful to those readers and reviewers who spotted them (including my students in courses where I have used the book as basic text). I have also substantially enlarged and comprehensively updated the selected bibliography for the whole book (with the exception of Chapter 1, where this would have been beyond the scope of a reprint). I have also added occasional updated references in the rest of the text, where I felt new citations would be helpful to a reader pursuing research in the field—for example, in the discussion of electronic editions in Chapter 9. Otherwise, the text is unaltered from the original edition.

D.C.G.

Acknowledgments

For permission to reprint copyright material, I am grateful to the following:

American Philosophical Society: Fig. 3.
Ares Publishers Inc.: Figs. 49–69, 71, 74.
Athlone Press: Fig. 143.
Basic Books: Figs. 115, 125.
Beinecke Library: Fig. 142.
Boston Public Library: Fig. 84.
The British Library: Fig. 126.
William C. Brown Publishers: Figs. 122–23.
University of California Press, Frederick Goudy, TYPOLOGIA. Copyright © 1940 renewed 1968 Regents of the University of California: Figs. 6–7, 75, 120.
Cambridge University Press: Figs. 105, 121.
Constable Publishers: Figs. 35, 37–39.
Dover Publications: Figs. 1, 76–80, 127.
The Council of the Early English Text Society: Fig. 126 (b).
Edinburgh Bibliographical Society: Fig. 40.
Folger Shakespeare Library: Figs. 70, 106, 129–32, 135–36.
Garland Publishing: Figs. 157–59.
HarperCollins Publishers: Figs. 9–10, 30, 32, 34, 36, 73, 118.
Harvard University Press: Figs. 12–14, 88–96, 100, 109–10, 112, 117, 119, 155.
Huntington Library: Figs. 133–34.
The Master and Fellows, Magdalene College, Cambridge: Fig. 137.
Malone Society: Figs. 137–42.
Modern Language Association of America: Fig. 160.
University of Missouri Press: Fig. 156.

W. W. Norton & Co.: Figs. 150–51.

Oxford University Press, Philip Gaskell, *A New Introduction to Bibliography*, 1972 © Oxford University Press, by permission: Figs. 16–17, 44–45, 98.

Penguin Books Ltd.: Figs. 11, 41–43, 97–99, 101, 103, 107–08, 111, 113–41.

Philadelphia Museum of Art: Fig. 33.

Scarecrow Press: Fig. 8.

M. C. Seymour: Fig. 40.

Spencer Collection, The New York Public Library, Astor, Lenox and Tilden Foundations: Figs. 4–5.

Taplinger Publishing Co. Inc.: Figs. 2, 48, 63–64, 72, 81–83, 85–86.

University of Toronto Press: Figs. 102–04.

University Press of Virginia: Figs. 144–49.

Albert von Frank: Fig. 156.

Yale University Press: Figs. 151–54.

Pages 340, 358–60 have previously appeared in slightly different form in my essay "Textual Scholarship," *Introduction to Scholarship in Modern Languages and Literatures*. Ed. Joseph Gibaldi. New York: MLA, 1991.

Illustrations

Introduction

Textual studies is a discipline drowning in a sea of terms: enumerative bibliography, systematic bibliography, descriptive bibliography, analytical bibliography, historical bibliography and textual bibliography, textual analysis and textual criticism, textual editing, documentary editing, and social textual criticism—to say nothing of such older dispensations as epigraphy, paleography, codicology, and diplomatics, philology and historical criticism, higher and lower criticism, all of which may still be invoked by textuists. And, as if this cacophony were not loud enough, the recent annexation of the "text" by literary theorists and critics abandoning authors, works, and history has introduced more ambiguities and another struggle over ownership of the terms. A post-structuralist journal like *Glyph* can proclaim itself concerned with *textual* studies, and Stanley Fish can ask *Is There a Text in This Class?* without any fear of his audience thinking he is about to talk of incunabula or stemmata, imposition or watermarks, substantives or accidentals. The vocabulary of the text and its study is obviously in need of clarification, and perhaps simplification. The terms are out of joint. This book attempts to set them right.

One way of approaching the terminological and disciplinary confusion might be to take on the post-structuralists in a direct struggle for the body of the text. This approach has been tried by G. Thomas Tanselle in an examination of deconstruction and textual criticism in which he finds the practitioners of deconstruction unable or unwilling to write clearly or consistently about what they mean by such basic terms as "text" or "work" ("Textual Criticism and Deconstruction"). In other publications I have tried another approach: a deliberate co-option of literary theory (and specifically deconstruction) to illuminate some of the conceptual assumptions and methodologies of contemporary textual scholarship (Greetham: "[Textual] Criticism and Deconstruction," "Textual and Literary Theory," *Theories of the Text*). Either approach can be useful in the continued negotiation with literary theory, but the present book is less concerned with such external negotiation than with setting our own house in order, by describing the various components of textual scholarship, here defined as the general term for all the activities associated with the discovery, description, transcription, editing, glossing, annotating, and commenting upon texts. Textual scholarship thus has a wider reference than "textual criticism" (that part of the discipline concerned with evaluating and emending the readings of texts), and may involve any of the technical fields listed in the opening sentence.

This book proceeds under two basic principles. The first is that all of these fields reflect a *historical* bias. Whether studying an author's single or multiple intentions, a scribal hand, a compositor's role in the setting of a hand-printed book, the transmission of a text from manuscript to print, the social reception and revision of a text, or the machine collation of a quarto to discover press-variants, textual scholars are deriving evidence from the previous history of the discipline and are placing their own work in the context of that historical perspective, thereby filling out the features of what is essentially a *narrative* argument (a story—a history—with discoverable events in their proper sequence). Textual scholars study *process* (the historical stages in the production, transmission, and reception of texts), not just *product* (the text resulting from such production, transmission, and reception). The second principle is that the various activities of the scholars practicing paleography, bibliography, textual criticism, and so on in the several subject fields where these skills are apparent—literature, history, music, etc.—are in fact related, despite an observable tendency toward both technical specialization and toward the guarding of disciplinary territorial rights which has become the expected norm in too much modern scholarship.

This belief in the disciplinary interrelatedness of all aspects of the study of the text of a book motivates and explains the purpose, strategy, and shape of *this* book. It is not a popular opinion, for some of the disciplines have long and distinguished histories (e.g., biblical and classical textual criticism) with clearly defined principles of scholarly procedure evolving out of centuries of theory and practice; while some have been perhaps too confident of the technical proficiency of their new methodologies and thereby too eager to dismiss earlier textual experiences. For example, a proponent of textual analysis once characterized "all systems before Greg as rules of thumb for ignoring the evidence" (Dearing: 13); a well-known "conjecturalist" Latin textual critic has maintained that the "conservative [textual] critic is a professed patron of error" (Willis: 11); and one of the founders of analytical bibliography, complaining that most literary critics seemed to "believe that texts are discovered under cabbage plants (or in bulrushes)," then disdainfully observed that "many a literary critic has investigated the past ownership and mechanical condition of his second-hand automobile, or the pedigree and training of his dog, more thoroughly than he has looked into the qualifications of the text on which his theories rest" (Bowers, *Textual and Literary Criticism*: 3, 5). The passions have been high, and the debates or the debaters not known for their restraint or decorum even within a given discipline. To an outsider, indeed, it might seem that the more apparently trivial the issues raised, the greater the emotional and critical commitment to the specific textual cause: one of the most vociferously argued questions among Anglo-American literary scholars in recent years has been the treatment of the so-called accidentals (the spelling, punctuation, capitalization, etc.) of a text, which to the non-specialist, unfamiliar with the ramifications of the arguments, might seem to be a remarkably minor issue.

But when "conjecturalists" and "conservatives" are fighting their holy wars, when "analogists" and "anomalists" are accusing each other of misrepresenting the history of the texts, when "social textual critics" from one ideological perspective and "New Scholars" from another both accuse "eclecticists" of having falsified the meaning of a text's history, and when the eclecticists in response claim that their accusers, in making such charges, are practicing literary criticism, not textual criticism, then these various camps (all of which will be dealt with later in this book) are at least speaking to each other—or *about* each other, anyway. They are familiar with one another's arguments—indeed, they seem to spend a good deal of their time, in print and in conference, refuting them, point by point. The greater danger is not in these often stimulating debates, but in the lack of debate—in fact, lack of contact of any sort—between textualists of different fields. The historians do not speak to the musicologists, nor the musicologists to the literary editors, nor the literary editors to the art historians, and so on.

Similarly, even within these broad subject-areas, there are clear divisions of ignorance. Practitioners of particular types of approach to the text or book know very little about what their colleagues are doing: the paleographers working on ancient manuscripts do not usually share their problems with the epigraphers working on inscriptions, and neither would dream of consulting an analytical bibliographer working on compositorial techniques. The national and period affiliations are equally well entrenched, for it would be rare to find a French textual scholar who was aware of the major questions dominating the recent history of Anglo-American bibliography (and vice versa, of course); and it is just as rare to find a medievalist who is *au courant* with the advances made in the textual scholarship of Renaissance literature—and so on.

I believe that this state of affairs severely harms the practice of textual scholarship, for the discipline has a wide range of jurisdiction and encompasses many different skills: textual scholars therefore need all the help they can get, from colleagues in their own periods or fields and from experienced researchers elsewhere. Properly endowed textual scholars will probably have the editing of the text as their ultimate aim (although many prominent textual scholars have been content to work only in non-editorial aspects of the discipline or to remain theorists rather than practitioners). To accomplish this end they must have developed a system for checking that they have access to *all* the appropriate documents (enumerative bibliography); they must have a methodology for listing and adequately describing these documents (descriptive bibliography); they must be familiar with the technical processes by which the documents were created, whether they be manuscript or printed (codicology and analytical bibliography respectively); they must have both a theoretical *system* for transcribing texts and an acute eye in accurately representing a transcript of a document (paleography and diplomatics); they must be able to establish the relative priority and probable descent of the documents and thereby chart the history of the transmission of the text (stemmatics or textual analysis); they must have a rationale for types and levels of emendation, based in part upon the principles used for the selection of a copy-text or base-text upon which all other variant texts will be collated, or compared (textual criticism or textual editing); they must have a proper formula for representing this collation and the results of emendation in a consistent and readable manner (apparatus and historical collation); they must know which parts of their texts need to be annotated for the reader and must have a comprehensive system for representing this annotation; and they must often have the necessary linguistic skills for the preparation of a glossary or lexicon.

All of this is, of course, in addition to the obvious historical, biographical, literary, or other research which must be undertaken before an edition can even be contemplated; for it must be emphasized that editing and textual scholarship are not simply technical skills, which, once learned, can be easily transferred from one field or period to another, without the editor's having developed any historical training in the new area. Editing depends upon textual scholarship, but textual scholarship is not merely method or technique; it is judgment and criticism, evaluation and discrimination, encompassing historical and cultural learning as well. This book will concentrate on method, but with the assumption that the budding textual scholar is already an expert in the specific field within which the texts are to be edited. It will take the student through the various stages that a textual scholar must master before this editing can begin in earnest.

But what of the tangle of terms with which this introduction began? Can they be ignored and simply superseded by the larger concept of textual scholarship? Do they still have value for defining some of the technical areas in which textual specialists in fact conduct their most important work? The answer is clearly no to the first question and yes to the second, and it is also clearly necessary that the student should at the very least be aware of what others mean when they refer to these apparently arcane studies. Here, then, is a brief guided tour of the terms before beginning the more detailed history in the chapters to follow.

Introducing the terms in the approximate order that they would be used by the student, we first encounter *enumerative,* or *systematic, bibliography.* The two terms are often used virtually synonymously, and both refer to that aspect of "bibliography" most familiar to the general reader—the listing of books. The term *enumerative* obviously emphasizes the listing above all other considerations, whereas the use of *systematic* does at least suggest that even a list must have some organizing or limiting principle, for the days when bibliographers sought to prepare a universal catalogue of every book ever written are long over. Thus all bibliographies are to some extent "selective" and therefore all use some system of selection and description. Enumerative bibliography has one peculiarity among the members of the "bibliography" family: it is the only one of the bibliographical terms which is commonly used to refer to manuscript as well as printed materials. Clearly, one may make a bibliography of almost anything—of musical scores, diaries, letters, papyrus rolls, films—and this material need not have been produced by the printing press or its descendants. All the other branches of bibliography, however, are normally restricted to describing printed matter. There is no etymological, theoretical, or practical reason why this should be so, for the term *bibli-ography* literally means "the writing of books" and has come to refer to various writings *about* books. But the limitation does exist, and therefore reflects the type of division already noted, and textual scholars are stuck with it for now.

The study of manuscripts as artifacts, as material objects carrying a text, is called *codicology*, although properly this term should be restricted only to the examination of the "codex" (the familiar folded, stitched book), as opposed to the "roll" which preceded it. There is no term paralleling *codicology* for the study of rolls as a separate class, unless they are made of papyrus, when the discipline becomes *papyrology*. Since most ancient rolls (unlike medieval ones) were indeed made of papyrus, this term works well enough, but it implicitly omits rolls made of other materials (animal skin, paper), unless they happen to be charters, contracts, or other legal documents, when their study is called *diplomatics* (from the Latin *diploma*, meaning document, and unconnected, except by professional association, with diplomacy). However, diplomatics is more commonly concerned with the actual writing on the documents than with the writing materials, and thus parallels, or is a part of, *paleography* (or "ancient writing"), the examination of handwriting. Even here, as the etymology suggests, there are problems, for no term exists which can do justice to the study of handwriting which is *not* ancient, *calligraphy* normally being reserved for deliberately "fine" writing, of whatever date, and hardly suitable for the illegible jottings of modern poets, now acquiring literary (and financial) value to the repositories of Europe and America. Furthermore, paleography is in practice often used to comprehend the entire study of manuscripts—writing, medium, and all—thereby partially usurping the province of codicology. Then there are the other non-print materials. If textual scholars concentrate on the writings on the wall, they are students of *graffiti* (or "scratches"), and if they are interested in inscribed writing in general (most familiarly on monumental arches, tombstones, and the like, but also in more humble circumstances), they are epigraphers studying *epigraphy*. If the medium is a coin and the "writing" denominations of value, likenesses of the local head of state, and a rough date, then the discipline is *numismatics*, and if the scholars are more drawn to the rubble and garbage heaps of past civilizations, and favor scraps of pots and the messages carved thereon, they are studying *ostraka* (potsherds). These are by no means all the specialist terms encountered in the territorial divisions of the non-print school (materials such as bronze, lead, and clay have not even been mentioned), but they give a general idea of the range, and of the terminological inconsistencies and confusions. The same will be found in looking at the post-Gutenberg school.

After having made a list of sources in an enumerative bibliography, the textual scholar will wish to get hold of as many of them as possible, and to examine them as artifacts. They are products of a particular manufacturing or technical process, and the study of that process for printed texts is usually called *analytical bibliography*. This term is often used synonymously with *new bibliography*, and its newness (in the mid-twentieth century) was consciously seen as a "scientific" reaction to the older enumerative, book-collectors' bibliography, as well as to the impressionistic, non-scientific editorial methods of an earlier period. (The term might also be seen as an antidote to the then-omnipresent, and non-historical, school of New Criticism among the literary critics, although it is ironic that both New Bibliography and New Criticism, despite their different attitudes toward history and intention, preferred the single, unitary text of the "well-wrought urn" to the multiple, contradictory, fragmentalist texts of their successors, post-structuralism in literary theory and textual revisionism in textual scholarship.) Analytical bibliography begins as a form of "history of science" or "history of technology" and involves the consideration of all those stages of printing (from paper, ink, and type manufacture to the habits of the compositor, the presswork, the binding and so on) that might tell us something about *how* the text reached its present condition. It is therefore closely related to *historical bibliography* on the one hand (sometimes referred to as the "biology of books," the study of them as part of a Darwinian evolution of a manufacturing process) and *descriptive bibliography* on the other, which uses the information gained in the practice of analytical and historical bibliography to prepare an account of the "bibliographical nature" of the book. Conventionally, descriptive bibliography will address the so-called *ideal copy* of the book (that version intended by the printer for release after all determined corrections had been made) and will list not only the contents but also the format (folio, quarto, etc.), and the collation (the make-up of the folded gatherings of the book), together with any peculiarities—e.g., canceled leaves, misnumbering, etc. It therefore stands in a sense between enumerative bibliography (for descriptive bibliographers will in practice produce a list of books) and analytical, whose technical information it employs. The last stage in the strictly bibliographical process is *tex-*

tual bibliography, the employment of the technical information derived from analytical or descriptive bibliography in charting and evaluating the effect of the technical history on the text itself.

Some bibliographers would regard all of this as an end in itself, but most textual scholars see paleography, codicology, analytical and descriptive bibliography as merely a prelude to the "real" business of textual scholarship: the reconstruction of an author's intended text and/or the production of a critical edition displaying this intention or some other version of the text. In the traditional disciplines of classics, biblical studies, medieval studies, and the like, this skill is normally called *textual criticism*, since, as the medievalist Eugène Vinaver put it, textual criticism implies a "mistrust" of texts (352), and consequently a desire to set them to rights. The findings of textual criticism (sometimes referred to as the *Lower Criticism*, emphasizing its fundamental, basic qualities) are therefore used in the so-called *Higher Criticism*, a phrase used initially in biblical studies to differentiate the "critical" science of the examination of biblical texts as works susceptible to interpretation and critical evaluation, rather than as articles of faith or dogma.

In addition to using the paleographic, codicological, and bibliographical information already mentioned, the textual scholar/bibliographer may also have to arrange the extant (and almost by definition, corrupt) remains of the text in some sort of order of relative authority. This will obviously occur only where the work exists in several editions (or several different versions of a single edition) or in multiple scribal copies. Among manuscript editors this practice has usually been known as *recension*, and makes use of a genealogical system of arrangement (similar to a family tree) called *stemmatics*. Recently, among editors of printed texts, a similar process of establishing textual descent through the charting of error and variance has been referred to as *textual analysis*, in an attempt to distinguish the history of the medium (the book) from that of the text contained within it.

After recension or textual analysis has been completed, editors will then turn to emendation and, if competent, diligent, and lucky, may produce a worthy edition of a text, thereby making them successful practitioners of *textual* or *scholarly editing*. The term "textual editing" (and its sub-species *critical editing*) has been the cause of some animated argument of late, particularly when it is opposed to *documentary editing* (the type of editing usually involving single rather than multiple documents, and often associated therefore with historical rather than literary editions). I mention the distinction here, not because the term "textual editing" is fixed, but because it is the focus for some significant conceptual disagreements among textual scholars. (The other sense of the phrase, to distinguish the scholarly construction of a critical text from the non-critical compilation of texts in an anthology or other type of collection or the reproduction of a previously established text, emphasizes the joint technical and critical skills involved in textual scholarship.) Another passionate area of argument is that associated with *New Scholarship*, whose practitioners claim that eclectic or critical editing's concentration on a single, uniform "final intention" is a chimera, and that a textual editor would be better employed describing the "process" rather than the apparent "product" of literary composition. *New Scholarship* has largely been abandoned as a textual term, but some of its supporters have remained in often heated disagreement with adherents of *social textual criticism*, which denies the automatic priority traditionally given to authors' intentions, preferring instead to regard textual creation and transmission as a collaborative, social act. Perhaps paradoxically, despite their advocacy of completely opposed first principles, both the New Scholars and the social textual critics tend to emphasize process over product and they can both be considered as components of the more general movement of *revisionism*, whether it appear as *versioning*, *genetic editing*, *textology*, or *hypertext editing*, all of which are dealt with in Chapters 8 and 9.

These are some of the major terms that are currently used to describe the several branches of textual scholarship. But textual scholarship itself is ultimately a product of the much broader historical discipline of *philology*, defined, under its nineteenth-century German auspices (often with the name *Altertumswissenschaft*, "the science of ancient times"), as the study of historical perspective, of seeing a past culture whole and trying to re-create its ethos in one's scholarly writing. A principal method in such an attempt was the study of language as an evolving process, a diachronic medium, and the success and dominance of this *historical linguistics* in the nineteenth century (later to be superseded by the synchronic methods of *structuralist linguistics*) gradually gave the term "philology" a more specifically scientific, linguistic bias. Within this wider historical dispensation, the study of literature was in practice almost always a function of *historical criticism* (i.e., source study, dating, influence, and the like) rather than of close critical analysis. Historical criticism was thus much more closely related to textual scholarship than was, say, the later New Criticism of the mid-twentieth century which avoided any such historical perspective. But, as already observed, successful textual work must also employ evaluation and critical judgment in addition to purely historical, technical information, judgment in which bibliographical (in all senses), critical, historical, linguistic, and textual skills all meet. Textual scholarship is one of the few areas of modern scholarship where philology, in its older, wider meaning, is still practiced.

The organization of this book follows the narrative of terms just described, for it attempts to lead the student through the several skills that the successful textual scholar will use, in the order of their likely employment. Thus, before being able to evaluate or annotate a text, scholars must have texts; and they will not have valid texts if these are not the product of the judgment of textual criticism and the technical information of bibliography. Furthermore, the practice of bibliography (analytical and descriptive) is itself dependent on a systematic bibliographical listing of all the resources that will be necessary in an examination of the text and the medium. The first stage, then, is "finding" the text (using the resources of archival research and enumerative bibliography), and this is where the book—and the process—begins.

The comprehensiveness of the terminologies and the fields they represent might suggest that this brief survey of an enormous subject will quickly equip the student to practice textual scholarship as a professional. But while it is my hope and intention to stimulate students to become practicing textual scholars (for there are still many valuable texts in all disciplines awaiting the attentions of competent researchers) it would be unrealistic and actually misleading to suggest that this book comes anywhere near to outfitting the would-be paleographer, bibliographer, or textual critic. It will provide, as the title suggests, only an introduction to textual scholarship, and will therefore point the interested student in the appropriate direction for more detailed study.

What specifically should a reader expect to gain from consulting this book?

1. An awareness of the *process* of textual scholarship, from discovery to editing and annotating, so that each stage can be observed as following out of, and depending upon, the skills developed in the previous one. This is, of course, particularly true of the last stage, editing, which requires a cumulative and comprehensive expertise.

2. An ability to recognize in practice the major classes of identification described throughout the book, in fields from enumerative bibliography to editing. While I would not, for example, expect readers

to be able confidently to date a gothic manuscript from merely reading the section on paleography, I would expect them to know that it *was* gothic, or secretary, or Caroline, or copperplate (or, in certain circumstances, an imitation of such a style). Similarly, the sections on descriptive and analytical bibliography are much too brief to enable readers to produce a full bibliographical description of any and all books; but I would hope that readers surviving its technical rigors might be able to interpret fairly simple collation formulae appearing in bibliographies, and might be able to distinguish the basic formats from each other, just as, after reading a later section of the book, they should be able to discriminate between genuinely "critical" as opposed to "non-critical" editions, and therefore know how to deal with and interpret the texts contained therein.

3. A familiarity with the basic vocabulary of textual scholarship and a sense of the appropriate domain of each of the skills represented by the terms. Students should, therefore, be able to tell a conjecturalist from a conservative by reading the editorial introduction to a text; they should know what to expect from a firm believer in stemmatics or an espouser of eclecticism. And while I would not suppose that the long array of technical terms very quickly glossed in, for example, the account of the printing press would remain perfectly in recall, students should at least know where to look (in this book or elsewhere) when confronted with "friskets," "quoins," or "platens."

4. Finally (and almost in despite of what I said earlier), through the active reading and criticism of textual editions and an understanding of the principles whereon they are constructed, a student might be able to produce a reputable scholarly edition of a short work, with well-defined documentary limits.

There are two final caveats which ought properly to be mentioned.

1. While there *is* a narrative to this book, I do not necessarily suppose that the text will be read complete or in order. Each chapter therefore has to stand on its own, and there is consequently some overlap and even some repetition. For example, important figures inevitably occur in more than one place—for example, Gutenberg, in Chapter 3, on bibliography of printed books, and in Chapter 6, on typography, or Greg and his influential copy-text theory in Chapter 8, on textual criticism, and in Chapter 9, on editing. Similarly, the conventional collation formulae occur both in the account of imposition (from the printer's and the binder's points of view) and in the outline of bibliographical description (from the bibliographer's point of view). Omission in either case would have made the individual chap-

ters incomplete.

2. I referred earlier in this introduction to the various national and subject loyalties as being very difficult to overcome. As founder of the interdisciplinary Society for Textual Scholarship, I have made some attempt to bring together in conference and in the Society's journal *Text* the textual theories and practices of the national camps (Anglo-American, French, German, Slavic, Oriental, etc.) and those of the subject-disciplines (literature, history, music, philosophy, etc.). But this brief book cannot attempt such a broad canvas, and its focus is frankly parochial, the "parish" being primarily literature (or at least texts written largely in linguistic as opposed to other symbolic systems—e.g., music or art history or mathematics) *and* materials written in English. Since the book is itself written in English, it is not improper to suppose that most of its readers will feel more comfortable with texts in English rather than in other languages, and this practical limitation has inevitably imposed itself at several points in what follows. While some chapters (e.g., on paleography or on the history of textual criticism) would severely misrepresent their disciplines if they were to ignore non-English traditions and practices, these other areas are discussed primarily to provide the necessary background to the later, English-language focus of the chapter. Most of the examples drawn upon in, say, the chapter on editing are works (and/or editions) in English, which will presumably be more accessible to the student reading this book. *This* book is, if you will, *vertically* integrated (showing the interrelatedness of various stages of a *process*). I have much to say on interdisciplinary (or *horizontal*) textual scholarship, but that is for another occasion and another book.

1

Finding the Text:

Enumerative and Systematic Bibliography

As noted in the introduction, the term "bibliography" has become a rather slippery one of late, and its scope is by no means yet fixed. But most bibliographers agree that its central meaning must involve a study of the physical form of books, both manuscript and printed. Some bibliographers, particularly those practicing the "hard" bibliographies (analytical or descriptive, and so called because they deal with the material aspects of books, not necessarily because their technical vocabulary is inscrutable), would regard textual criticism and textual editing as merely an offshoot of bibliography so conceived. Others would exclude the study of mere enumerative bibliography from bibliography proper, since it seems to lack sufficient technical rigor. However, since there are several points (particularly in the study of early printed texts and manuscripts) at which the listing, the description, and the analysis of books have overlapped, and when a technical training in the enumerative bibliographer is not only desirable but necessary, it seems unwise to ignore enumerative bibliography entirely. Therefore, although this book will not in general be concerned with enumerative bibliography as a special field or with the work of such modern enumerative bibliographers as Theodore Besterman (even though his *Early Printed Books: A Bibliography of Bibliographies* does deal with the central subject matter of this chapter), this section of the coverage of textual scholarship will touch on enumeration as it relates to the history of the book as artifact or as tool for textual criticism and editing broadly construed. By the currently common extension of the term "enumerative bibliography," the raw materials for enumerative bibliographies of the book and manuscript will include publishers' catalogues, sales catalogues, the accession lists of certain libraries, and private book collections, but enumerative bibliography will not usually involve library science or cataloguing, except where the history of such disciplines bears on the growth of "bibliography" in the more technical sense.

Scholarly Libraries

The first Western library which was important to the growth of enumerative bibliography as a discipline was that founded by the Ptolemies in the fourth century B.C. at Alexandria, and the first bibliographer of note was Callimachus of Cyrene (ca. 310–240 B.C.), who may have succeeded Zenodotus of Ephesus in the position of chief librarian. As bibliographer, Callimachus compiled 120 volumes of a catalogue describing the contents of the library in eight divisions: drama; epic and lyric; law; philosophy; history; oratory; rhetoric; and "miscellaneous." His methods of cataloguing were, however, inconsistent. Drama was ordered by date, Pindar and Demosthenes by the subjects of their works, Theophrastus and the "miscellaneous" entries alphabetically. Each book was quoted by its *incipit* (or opening words), by author, and by title. The importance of this pioneer work is not only that it tells us a good deal about the contents of the most famous library of the ancient world (even though the actual catalogue is lost and its contents survive only in later references), but also that it shows an early attempt—in fact, several attempts—to arrive at the "system" which must underlie all enumerative bibliography.

A later head librarian at Alexandria, Aristophanes of Byzantium (ca. 257–180 B.C.), began the fixing of the canon of Greek writers. This "selective" bibliography was to be extremely influential, for—along with the similar efforts of other Alexandrian and Byzantine scholars—it largely determined which authors were to be copied and passed down to the medieval scribal tradition. Many of those who did not make Aristophanes' lists have perished. In poetry, for example, there were five recognized epic poets (Homer, Hesiod, Peisander, Panyasis, and Antimochus), five tragic poets (Æschylus, Sophocles, Euripides, Ion, and Achæus), three iambic poets, four elegiac poets, and so on. As the canon was handed down through the centuries, the number of authors selected grew smaller and smaller, until it was gradually reduced to the most "popular" Greek writers—the only ones still read, studied, and performed today.

The reason the efforts of the Alexandrian bibliographers were so significant (a significance recently recognized by plans announced by the Egyptian government to rebuild a version of the library) is that one of the major purposes of the library was to gather several manuscripts of the same work to be used as the basis for "collation" (the comparing of different copies of the same work) and textual criticism. Those authors included in the "selective" bibliographies became those studied by the textual scholars and linguists, and therefore those whose texts were preserved. But even the inclusion of the "great" authors in these bibliographies could not prevent the destruction or deterioration of their works through carelessness and time: of the 330 plays reportedly written by Æschylus, Sophocles, Euripides, and Aristophanes, only 43 survive today. Nearly all of the Alexandrians' lyric poetry has vanished, and of the authors mentioned by the fifth-century anthologist Stobæus, 75 percent have disappeared without a trace.

The Roman libraries, both public and private, inherited the bibliographical system of Alexandria (and, to a lesser extent, that of its rival, Pergamum): there was a similar "fixing" of the canon, especially once the "classical" age of Virgil, Ovid, and Horace had driven out an interest in earlier, more "primitive" authors like Ennius. This fixing of the canon was transmitted to the medieval textual tradition during the various periods of enthusiastic copying of Roman classics, such as the Carolingian. In regard to the growth of enumerative bibliography, which depends so much upon the accumulation of works in large public depositories, Roman library stewardship was not as fruitful as Alexandrian. Unlike the Ptolemies of Egypt, each Roman emperor founded his own private library (the Ulpian by Trajan being probably the most famous), and wealthy Roman families emulated the practice. While this no doubt fostered literary culture, it did not encourage the growth of the universal "system" which enumerative bibliography requires. The situation was not dissimilar to that of Europe in the sixteenth to eighteenth centuries, where the great private collectors (Sloane, Harley, Cotton) built up very fine individual collections, which were only later to arrive at public depositories. Fortunately, the private collections of this later period were well documented (by, such bibliographers as Humfrey Wanley), but the contents of their Roman antecedents are generally undescribed.

During the medieval period, private libraries were very rare. The most famous—and no doubt very uncharacteristic—was that of Richard of Bury, Bishop of Durham, whose *Philobiblon* gives a detailed analysis of the fifteen hundred books in the collection. Alcuin of York listed some of the contents of the library at York in his poem in praise of the city, although the inclusion of certain authors (Aristotle, Cicero, Pliny, Virgil, Statius, and Lucan) may have been at least partly determined by metrical and cultural desiderata rather than bibliographical accuracy. Modern scholars such as Neil Ker have been able to reconstruct the contents of many important medieval libraries by tracing bequests, wills, and other evidence of present and former provenance.

In addition to York, Jarrow, and Westminster in England, the best libraries of the early medieval period were at those monasteries founded by Irish or Anglo-Saxon monks (e.g., Fulda, St. Gall, Reichenau, Bobbio). The first stimulus to book collecting, however, had occurred quite independently, in the sixth-century Benedictine foundation of Monte Cassino and the "Vivarium" of Cassiodorus. But the term "library," with its associations of order and system, is probably misleading. It was not until the fifteenth century that special rooms began to be regularly allotted for the preservation and reading of all the institution's books. Until then, while some religious fraternities observed more bibliographical coherence than others (the Cistercians, for example, seem to have used a small book-cupboard located between the church and the chapter-house), the books would often be distributed among several different monastic buildings, with service books in the chapel, school books in the school, books to be read during meals in the refectory. This was a perfectly practical organization, of course, but it was hardly a system. It was dictated by convenience, not by a coherent taxonomy.

It is doubtful, therefore, that even the largest of medieval monastic libraries (e.g., the two thousand volumes of Bury St. Edmunds and Canterbury, or the fourteen hundred volumes of Syon) followed any strict pattern of bibliographical arrangement. If the horrified stories of Renaissance humanist book collectors are to be believed, conditions toward the end of the Middle Ages were even worse. Boccaccio and Petrarch claim to have found the books in the monasteries they visited strewn about in haphazard fashion, piled in corners or buried under refuse, with leaves missing (stolen as love-tokens by the monks), contents incorrectly described, and generally with little evidence of any bibliography as an ordering discipline. But the humanists had a particular axe to grind, and while some monasteries in their decline were probably less careful of their textual riches than they should have been, the evidence of others, for example, the *Catalogus librorum angliæ* in the thirteenth century (a location list of various books) and the bibliographical guide of John Boston of Bury in the fifteenth century (prepared for the reorganization of the library of Bury St. Edmunds) shows that there was some emerging sense of a need for systematic classification and description. The late-medieval university libraries must inevitably have reflected this sense, for with the division into "faculties" (medicine, theology, etc.) and with certain universities being primarily known for the study of a particular discipline (e.g., Bologna for law), there was a built-in taxonomy by subject.

The founding of the Sorbonne library in the thirteenth century; Duke Humphrey's library at Oxford (later refounded by Bodley in 1610 with two thousand books after the depredations of Edward VI's commissioners had robbed it of much of its original "heretical," i.e., Roman Catholic, contents); Charles IV's academic library at Prague, founded in 1348; the Lambeth library of Archbishop Bancroft; Francis I's library at Fontainebleau (organized by the distinguished scholar Guillaume Budé and later the basis for the Bibliothèque Nationale); Cardinal Borromeo's founding of the Ambrosian library at Milan in 1609; the re-founding of the Vatican library by Pope Nicholas V after virtually nothing had survived of the medieval library of the popes at the Lateran; the Laurentian library of the Medici: all these semi-public, or at least incipiently public, institutions were augmented by the private libraries of the new humanist scholars, and in the following centuries by the collections of Arundel, Harley, Sloane, Cotton, and Rawlinson in England, and by Lenox, Arents, Folger, Carter Brown, Huntington, and Pierpont Morgan in America. Some of the public collections were to become the core of the great national libraries of a later period. Some of the private libraries were donated to, or purchased by, the public depositories (Sloane, Cotton, Arundel, and Harley to the British Library; Rawlinson to Bodley; Lenox and Arents to the New York Public Library; Spencer to the John Rylands; Lilly to Indiana). Others, while built up as the private collection of one person, and therefore reflecting a personal taste in bibliography, were to become in all other senses "public" collections (Folger's Shakespeare library in Washington; Huntington's library in San Marino, California; Pierpont Morgan's library in New York).

Systematic Bibliography

But was there any bibliographic organizing principle, any system of enumerative bibliography, in all this explosion of book collecting, this accumulation of documentary riches?

Certain collections (e.g., Folger's Shakespeare) had a built-in organizing principle of inclusion and exclusion: anything generally connected to Shakespeare or Elizabethan England was in; almost everything else was out. Others (e.g., Pierpont Morgan's great collection of incunabula and other early printed editions), while of a more general nature, at least betrayed some central concerns, as, for example, in the concentration on English and American literature of the nineteenth and twentieth centuries in the Berg Collection of the New York Public Library. Some were extremely specialized (e.g., Arents on tobacco); others, such as the so-called cabinet collections of Grolier and H. Y. Thompson, applied an external principle (the selection of the one hundred best books in a particular field), and by judicious evaluation and rejection brought their collections into line with this principle by removing one "inferior" book each time a "superior" one was added. Even those collections with a well-defined basic interest (e.g., Cotton's library of medieval manuscripts) could be internally organized by the most fanciful methods: the reference numbers of certain Cotton manuscripts (Cotton Vitellius A.xv for *Beowulf*, Nero A.x for *Sir Gawain and the Green Knight*, *Pearl* etc.) derive from the name of the Roman emperor whose bust was placed in the alcove where the manuscript happened to be situated.

It was with Gabriel Naudé's theoretical treatise *Avis pour dresser une bibliothèque* (1627) that a true systematic enumerative bibliography as related to the organization of book collections got under way. Put in charge of the Mazarine library in Paris in 1642, Naudé began the subject-cataloguing of a large general collection according to principles of practical enumerative bibliography which were to be highly influential in both the cataloguing and the very raison d'être of private and public libraries alike in the next two centuries. John Evelyn translated Naudé's treatise into English, and its principles of subject organization were put into effect in, for example, the Pepys library later in the seventeenth century, and now at Magdalene College, Cambridge. In Germany, G. W. Leibniz, after absorbing Naudé's system in Paris, together with the new philological and paleographical research of the Maurists and Jesuits, undertook to emphasize the function of the enumerative bibliographer and library cataloguer as a facilitator of that easy and open access to research materials which is the basis for all scholarship. Refined by such later works as J. C. Brunet's *Manuel de librairie* (1814), Naudé's subject system led to its most familiar modern equivalents, the Dewey decimal system (1876), the Library of Congress (LC) classification by letter rather than number (1904), and the Universal Decimal Classification (UDC, 1899).

But while systematic library cataloguing as one aspect of enumerative bibliography may grow out of such treatises as Naudé's, enumerative bibliography as an *independent* discipline—that is, concerned with more than the description of actual collections—needed a theoretical base of its own. While it is true that Dewey and Library of Congress can be (and are) used to designate the identity of a particular book before it is placed in a specific depository, and therefore can be said to have a theoretical ground as well as practical implications, as classification systems these descendants of Naudé are still primarily associated with the internal organization of actual libraries, whose librarians may decide to use one of these general systems, or may invent their own idiosyncratic methods (as, for example, in the British Library, where books are organized according to size).

Fredson Bowers ("Bibliography") recognizes four alternative "systems" for enumerative organization: general, formal, subject, and author. The first class will rarely be truly "general" in these days of mass distribution of printed or electronic materials, for there will usually be some limitation: by time (e.g., the famous Pollard and Redgrave *Short-Title Catalogue . . . 1475–1640*, and its revision), by place (e.g., the various national bibliographies), or by language. "Formal" bibliographies will list only certain types or classes of document, for example, pamphlets, manuscripts, newspapers, dissertations; "subject" bibliographies may devote themselves to materials in literature, history, science, philosophy, or to any subdivision within each large class (in this sense, they are rather like the LC or Dewey "library" systems, but focused on a particular area); and "author" bibliographies, while not strictly speaking a separate class from the other three, are such a convenient and common method of organization that they have achieved a practical independence.

Enumerative bibliography in this theoretical sense—as opposed to the description of the holdings of specific libraries—begins with the work of Konrad von Gesner (1516–65), whose author and title lists (with subdivisions by subject) in his *Bibliotheca universalis* of 1545 were the first attempt to bring Callimachus up to date by cataloguing all writers of the past. Written in Latin, Greek, and Hebrew, it was followed by a second part (listing twenty thousand works), *Pandecta-rum sive partitionum universalium*, in 1548. On a more local, or national, level, John Bale's antiquarian researches resulted in the three biographical catalogues of English writers, beginning in 1548 with *Illustrium majoris britanniæ scriptorum summarium* and continuing (with slightly varying titles) in subsequent expanded editions. Bale's work, idiosyncratic and avowedly nationalistic and Protestant, was continued in a less polemical vein by, for example, Andrew Maunsell's *Catalogue of English Printed Books* (1595), by Bodley's classified catalogue of the Stationers' Company books, by Pits's *Relationum historicarum de rebus anglicis* (1619), by Thomas Tanner's *Bibliotheca britannico-hibernica* (1748), and by the several early-nineteenth-century bibliographies of Thomas Dibdin.

Gesner's attempt at a universal (rather than a national) bibliography was emulated in the eighteenth century by Johann Fabricius (1668–1736), who published four series of catalogues: the *Bibliotheca latina* (1697), the *Bibliotheca græca* (1705–26), the *Bibliotheca antiquaria* (1713)—dealing with Hebrew and early Christian writings—and the *Bibliotheca latinæ mediæ et infimæ ætatis* (1734–36), on medieval Latin authors.

As a result of the growth of philological studies and of an interest in the national literary, religious, and political heritage, these enumerative bibliographies inevitably encouraged not only the investigation of the books themselves (thereby leading eventually to descriptive and analytical bibliography, see Chapters 2, 3, and 4), but also to the publication of major series of ancient texts in nationally sponsored programs: in England, the *Rerum britannicorum medii ævi scriptores* (known as the Rolls Series), 1858–91; in France, the *Rerum gallicarum et francicarum scriptores*, 1738–1904; in Germany, the *Monumenta Germaniæ historica*, begun in 1819 and continued under several series, the longest-running being the ongoing *Scriptores rerum germanicorum in usum scholarum ex monumentis Germaniæ historicis recusi*, 1840 (commonly referred to as the *Scriptores* of *MGH*); and, for patristic literature, Migne's *Patrologia latina* and *Patrologia græca*, 1844–66, the *Corpus scriptorum ecclesiasticorum latinorum* (*CSEL*), 1866ff., and the *Corpus christianorum*, 1951ff.

These vast multi-volume projects often made available to historians and other scholars many documents which had until then been available only in manuscript form. The problem with these various outgrowths of national pride and of the enthusiasms of enumerative bibliographers was that the texts presented were often uncritically edited, if edited at all, from a single manuscript, and that there was rarely any evidence of the documentary "state" of the original having been examined with a bibliographical eye. This omission is less true of those volumes published in more recent years (in fact, such series as *CSEL* were initiated in part to rectify the corrupt texts presented in such projects as the otherwise laudable *Patrologia* of Migne). It was with this problem that descriptive and analytical bibliography was to be concerned, although the twin disciplines first surfaced in the study of vernacular, post-medieval literatures.

The principles and practices of descriptive and analytical bibliography will be discussed in the account of printing below (Chapters 3 and 4). For the moment, we are concerned only with the growth of the discipline out of the efforts of the later enumerative bibliographers to codify and standardize access to research materials.

As might be expected, the division between enumerative and descriptive bibliography is not always perfect. No doubt, when Humfrey Wanley, otherwise a reliable bibliographer, could claim that the *Beowulf* manuscript (with its story of monster-slayings) contained an account of the wars between a Danish hero and the Swedes, it is clear that descriptive bibliography—even of contents—was not yet a science. On the other hand, when George Thomason, a seventeenth-century London bookseller, collected twenty-three thousand books and pamphlets printed during the years 1640–61 as a record of the political dissensions of the Civil War, he was not only putting together a collection as a research tool, not only organizing it according to two of the basic systems of enumeration (by subject and by form, as well as by date), but he was also, by giving exact details of date of publication, printer, state of the text, and so on, coming close to providing some of the fundamental requirements of descriptive bibliography, albeit in a somewhat primitive, non-technical manner.

Similarly, when Pollard and Redgrave's original *Short Title Catalogue of Books . . . to 1640* appeared earlier this century, it was obviously giving the researcher into early English printed books a highly significant enumerative bibliography, and in the revised edition (completed in 1991), the *STC* was itself founded upon bibliographical investigation of individual copies of specific books (wherever copies remained accessible), and was thus a product of part of the activities associated with descriptive bibliography. As was noted in the Introduction, enumerative bibliographers need not have seen actual copies of books listed in their bibliographies: this was not true of the revised *STC*.

Since descriptive bibliography and analytical bibliography as twin disciplines arose out of a detailed study of the physical form of early printed books (English Renaissance drama in particular), the history of the documentation of such books is obviously important to an analysis of these disciplines, and this documentation will often be seen to occupy a medial position between purely enumerative and descriptive tendencies. The example of the bibliography of incunabula can readily demonstrate just how various may be the methods assumed by scholars trying to reduce a fairly well defined body of printed material to a manageable system.

The term "incunabula" (literally "swaddling clothes") refers to those books printed on or before 31 December 1500, that is, in the "infancy" of printing. The date is obviously arbitrary and severely misrepresents the history of printing, for techniques did not suddenly change with the beginning of the sixteenth century. But the word and concept have stuck, and have been adopted in other languages (French *incunable*, Italian *incunaboli*, German *Wiegendrucke*). As a theoretical historical limitation, the term "incunabula" was first used by J. Saubertus in his 1643 description of the Nuremberg library; as a general term for early printed books, it was first employed by Philippe Laube in 1653, the arbitrary date of 1500 being fixed by Cornelius Beughem when he offered "incunabula" for sale in 1688.

Thereafter, the bibliographers of incunabula approached the topic from a number of different directions, some more patently "descriptive" than others. Panzer's *Annales typographici ab artis inventæ origine ad annum MD* (1793–97) gave an alphabetical listing of cities in which books were printed, with chronological order of printing within each city. Hain's *Repertorium bibliographicum in quo libri omnes ab arte typographica inventa usque ad annum MD* (1826–38) was organized around authors, listed in alphabetical order, and was given an index of printers by Konrad Burger in 1891. Burger was also among those responsible for the organization of incunabula by type-forms (particularly important, since so many incunabula contain no clue as to printer or place of publication). His *Monumenta Germaniæ et Italiæ typographica* appeared in 1892–1913, and is complemented by Holtrop for the Netherlands (1868), Thierry-Poux for France (1890), Haebler for Spain (1901), and Gordon Duff for England (1896). An arrangement by type-form was hardly enumerative in the traditional sense (for it depended upon the physical characteristics of the book—its technical history—and not upon its contents, title, author, or date of publication), but it indicated a tendency toward descriptive, formal, or technical analysis rather than simple enumeration, culminating in the work of Robert Proctor, whose *Index* (1898) to the incunabula of the British Library (then the British Museum Library) and the Bodleian Library was founded on an examination of individual copies of specific books. Haebler's *Typenrepertorium der Wiegendrucke* (1905–24) continued the same method of physical description. Finally, there is the yet-incomplete *Gesamtkatalog der Wiegendrucke*, begun in 1925 and not likely to be finished in the lifetimes of even its present contributors, and, the most technologically up-to-date of attempts to codify and describe incunabula, Lotte Hellinga's database *Incunabula Short Title Catalogue*, now in progress at the British Library.

What emerges from this brief account of incunabula bibliographies is that, even within a comparatively small area, with well-defined limits, the systems of analysis used by enumerative bibliographers may vary. Each new arrangement of basically the same materials changes the focus of study in the field. Several bibliographical methods, as they become more concerned with the examination of specific copies, and more dependent upon an awareness of the technical history of the book and its manufacture, begin to promote the study of descriptive and analytical bibliography proper, rather than simply the listing of books.

Any textual scholar must therefore practice both descriptive and enumerative bibliography, employing the latter first, partly as a means of gaining access to the basic materials upon which an edition will depend (i.e., knowing which depositories are most likely to contain the primary textual sources), and partly as a device for systematizing these materials, reducing them to a list-format that will represent their nature and their relationship with each other (e.g., identifying different editions or states of the text, or manuscripts written in the same hand or in the same scriptorium). It is in this latter area that enumerative bibliography (in its most systematic form) will approach most closely some of the other textual disciplines to be considered later in this book—for example, descriptive and analytical bibliography or paleography and codicology.

Resources for Scholarly Research

A. *General Guides*

Nonetheless, we begin the second practical part of this chapter on enumerative bibliography at a more fundamental level, with those research resources with which every scholar should be familiar before embarking on any serious intellectual work, textual or otherwise. Most readers of this book will presumably already be acquainted with the various basic primary and secondary bibliographical resources in their own disciplines: for example, in English and American literature, the Modern Language Association of America's annual *International Bibliography*, the Modern Humanities Research Association's *Annual Bibliography of English Language and Literature*, *The Year's Work in English Studies*, *The New Cambridge Bibliography of English Literature*, the bibliographies in the several volumes of the *Oxford History of English Literature*, and the similar (and similarly outdated) bibliographies in Robert E. Spiller's *Literary History of the United States*, Jacob Blanck's *Bibliography of American Literature* (now revised under sponsorship by the Bibliographical Society of America), Clarence Gohdes's *Bibliographical Guide to the Study of the Literature of the United States*, and Matthew J. Bruccoli's *First Printings of American Authors*, together with such bibliographies of bibliographies as Patricia P. Havlice's *Index to American Author Bibliographies* and Theodore Besterman's *Literature English and American: A Bibliography of Bibliographies*.

Similarly, there are general research guides which can provide an entree into research at large, and therefore into the archives where the primary materials will be available. Such guides include Eugene P. Sheehy's *Guide to Reference Books* for American materials and its British equivalent, Albert J. Walford's *Guide to Reference Material*, along with which should probably be mentioned the French parallel, Louise-Noëlle Malclès's *Les sources du travail bibliographique*. Other useful books at this general level include Marion Bell and Mary Neill Barton's *Reference Books: A Brief Guide for Students*, Frances Cheney and Wiley Williams's *Fundamental Reference Sources*, and, on an even more basic level, Agnes Ann Hede's *Reference Readiness: A Manual for Librarians and Students*. Then there are the bibliographies of bibliographies, the best known of which is undoubtedly the now very outdated *A World Bibliography of Bibliographies* (1965) of Theodore Besterman, which should be supplemented by *Bibliographic*

Index: A Cumulative Bibliography of Bibliographies (1937ff.). In the literary field, there is T. H. Howard-Hill's *Index to British Literary Bibliography* (1969ff.), Charles H. Nilon's *Bibliography of Bibliographies in American Literature*, the journal *Bulletin of Bibliography* (1897ff.), and William A. Wortman's *A Guide to Serial Bibliographies for Modern Literatures*.

There are several manuals on research methods specifically useful to students working in the humanities. For example, Jacques Barzun and Henry F. Graff's *The Modern Researcher* is particularly good for historians, while for literature students, Richard D. Altick and John J. Fenstermaker's *The Art of Literary Research* is sound, if occasionally a little polemical. George Watson (the editor of the *New Cambridge Bibliography*, cited above) has written two fairly basic but stimulating books on literary research: *The Study of Literature* and *The Literary Thesis: A Guide to Research*. James Thorpe's MLA volume *The Aims and Methods of Scholarship in Modern Languages and Literatures* (with essays by various scholars) has been superseded by Joseph Gibaldi's *Introduction to Scholarship in the Modern Languages and Literatures*, also published by the MLA in a revised second edition. The three volumes may be cumulatively useful to students interested in textual matters, for the essay in the Thorpe volume is by Fredson Bowers, that in the Gibaldi first edition by G. Thomas Tanselle, and in the second edition by the present writer, and as a series they present related but somewhat differing perspectives on the subject. It is significant, for example that Bowers (in 1970) called his essay (and his subject) "Textual Criticism," whereas Tanselle (in 1981) called his "Textual Scholarship." Another significant difference is that the latest revision has expanded coverage from six to sixteen essays—a comment on the explosion of research fields in the last few years. David Beasley's *How to Use a Research Library*, a guide to research method using the holdings of the New York Public Library as examples, is a good, practical account of specific research problems, as is Thomas Mann's *Guide to Library Research Methods*, written from the perspective of a research librarian.

The two best known of the introductory literary research guides (essentially bibliographies, annotated or otherwise, on literary scholarship) are Richard D. Altick and Andrew Wright's rather brief but sensible, if now outdated, *Selective Bibliography for the Study of English and American Literature* and James L. Harner's *Literary Research Guide* (essentially a revision of the book by Margaret C. Patterson with the same title), a much more comprehensive manual than Altick and Wright's, but unfortunately prone—at least in the original Patterson version—to a somewhat effusive style of annotation. F. W. Bateson and Harrison T. Meserole's *Guide to English and American Literature*, Donald F. Bond's *A Reference Guide to English Studies*, Arthur G. Kennedy and Donald F. Bond's *A Concise Bibliography for Students of English*, and Robert C. Schweik and Dieter Riesner's *Reference Sources in English and American Literature* should also be mentioned, although all of them are now showing their age. For literature in English, the most comprehensive recent addition to the field is Michael Marcuse's *Reference Guide for English Studies*.

B. *Library Catalogues*

Having acquired an appropriate method for literary or other research, and having dealt with the basic research guides, the student will presumably want to get into the library itself and begin to check the actual resources at hand. For the United States, the prime authority is the *National Union Catalogue, Pre-1956 Imprints*, in 685 volumes with supplements bringing it up to 1980, published (rather ironically) by the British firm of Mansell. Other national library catalogues for the U.S. include the *National Union Catalog: A Cumulative Author List Representing Library of Congress Printed Cards and Titles Reported by Other American Libraries*, (1958ff.) which is a microfiche cumulative continuation of the Mansell series, available each month and cumulatively by quarter, year, and five-year periods; the similar *Library of Congress and National Union Catalog Author Lists, 1942–1962, A Master Cumulation*; *A Catalog of Books Represented by Library of Congress Printed Cards Issued to July 31, 1942* (with a supplement to 1947); *Library of Congress Author Catalog: A Cumulative List of Works Represented by Library of Congress Printed Cards, 1948–1952*, the last three of which have been effectively superseded by the Mansell series, and continued by the *National Union Catalog . . . 1953–57*, which is itself updated by *NUC: Books*, published from 1983 as a monthly Register, and quarterly Name, Title, and LC Series Indexes, with annual cumulations.

One additional very useful U.S. catalogue is the *Library of Congress Catalogs. Subject Catalog*, 1950ff., again on microfiche, and available in quarterly, annual, and five-year cumulations. While providing access in fields where authors or titles may not be readily available, it covers only the period from 1950 on. The *Main Catalog of the Library of Congress: Titles . . . through 1980* is available on microfiche, but essentially it duplicates materials from the catalogues already listed. Electronic access to union catalogues can be made via *REMARC* (LC books from 1897 to 1980) and *MARC* (English books from 1968, French from 1973, German, Spanish, and Portuguese from 1975, and other European languages from 1976). Both *RE-MARC* and *MARC* can be accessed through the *Online Computer Library Center (OCLC)* and the *Research Libraries Information Network (RLIN)*. Most university and public research libraries belong to one or both of these systems. In addition, researchers can use *BRS/SEARCH*, which includes the *Arts and Humanities Index*, *Books in Print*, and the *Guide to Microforms in Print*; among other data bases, *DIALOG*, which has a large offering of data bases, including *Books in Print* and *British Books in Print*, the *American Library Directory*, the *Book Review Index*, and *Who's Who*; and *WILSONLINE*, which includes the *Bibliographic Index*, the *Book Review Index*, the *Humanities Index*, and the *Reader's Guide to Periodical Literature*. *INFOTRAC* covers the last four years of a number of popular journals, including *The New York Times*, *The Wall Street Journal*, *The Washington Post*, and *The Los Angeles Times*.

For the United Kingdom, the major sources are the British Library *General Catalogue of Printed Books*, in 263 volumes (1965), with supplements to 1975. This has been revised as the British Library's *General Catalogue of Printed Books to 1975*, in 360 volumes, with multi-volume supplements to 1986 (as of writing). Subject indexes are R. A. Peddie's *Subject Index of Books Published . . . to . . . 1880* and the *British Library General Subject Catalogue*, covering the period from 1881. Electronic access is provided through *BLAISE-LINE*, which includes several data bases (e.g., *British Books in Print*, the *Incunabula Short Title Catalogue*, *UK MARC*—the online *British National Bibliography*—and the *LC MARC*). In France, the Bibliothèque Nationale's *Catalogue général des livres imprimés de la Bibliothèque Nationale, Auteurs* (1897–1981) is available in 231 volumes, together with a separate twelve-volume catalogue, including anonymous authors, for the period 1960–65. This five-year supplement is superseded by a ten-year cumulation (up to 1969), and there are microfiche supplements to 1979—so far.

Beyond the holdings of such "national" libraries (the Library of Congress, the British Library, the Bibliothèque Nationale) there are, of course, hundreds in the United States and Britain which are likely to yield textual materials of value to the scholar. They cannot all be covered here. Several important libraries (e.g., the Folger) have published their catalogues of library cards, which may therefore be consulted without an on-site visit. However, not all libraries have been quite this generous with their lists of holdings, and in these cases the scholar must either consult the library catalogue *in situ* or work from published catalogues of some of the collections within the library (e.g., the Douce, Rawlinson, or Ashmole for the Bodleian). Another approach is to consult special published bibliographies or catalogues describing one particular type of holding within a given library (e.g., again for the Bodleian, Margaret Crum's excellent *First-Line Index of English Poetry 1500–1800 in Manuscripts of the Bodleian Library*, 1969).

Still another approach is to work initially from the most general of research guides, then go to the national or formal bibliographies, and then to the libraries themselves. For example, even Altick and Fenstermaker's elementary *Art of Literary Research* has a brief chapter on the typical holdings of the major British and American libraries, so that a student would learn, for instance, that Yale is famous for its so-called factories of editions, specializing in eighteenth-century figures—Walpole, Boswell, Johnson, Franklin; that Texas has recently acquired a large number of manuscripts of contemporary writers; that Buffalo specializes in the manuscripts of "works in progress," and that Harvard's Widener Library has the famous F. J. Child collection of folklore materials. With this general information in mind, the scholar-student could consult a national bibliography such as de Ricci's *Census of . . . Manuscripts* or Goff's *Incunabula . . . Census*, or, for some early printed books, the several *STC*s, which list selected major libraries holding copies of each entry. Where possible, a published library catalogue could then be consulted for confirmation or additional bibliographical information.

C. *National Bibliographies*

These catalogues are based on actual collections in the national libraries (including, for the Mansell, references to holdings in other libraries). Therefore, they are not, strictly speaking, national bibliographies, in the sense of an attempt to cover all books published in a particular country, no matter where the books are currently held. General guides to national bibliographies include Barbara Bell's *An Annotated Guide to Current National Bibliographies*, Friedrich Domay's *Bibliographie der nationalen Bibliographien*, and Marcelle Beaudiquez's *Inventaire général des bibliographies nationales rétrospectives*, with an account of the history of national bibliographies in Leroy Linder's *The Rise of Current Complete National Bibliography* (to 1959). Attempts at a genuine national bibliography would have to include (for the United States) *Books in Print* (1948ff.); the *Cumulative Book Index* (1898ff.); Robert B. Downs's *American Library Resources: A Bibliographical Guide*; the National Historical and Public Records Commission's *Directory of Archives and Manuscript Repositories in the United States* (1988), superseding Philip Hamer's *Guide to Archives and Manuscripts in the United States*; Albert Robbins's *American Literary Manuscripts: A Checklist of Holdings in Academic, Historical, and Public Libraries . . . in the United States*; G. Thomas Tanselle's *Guide to the Study of United States Imprints*; Frederick Goff's *Incunabula in American Libraries: A Third Census*; Seymour de Ricci's *Census of Medieval and Renaissance Manuscripts in the United States and Canada*; the machine-readable *North American Imprints Program (NAIP)* for pre-1801 books, to be extended to 1877; Charles Evans's monumental *American Bibliography: A Chronological Dictionary of All Books . . . in U.S. from . . . 1639 . . . to . . . 1800* (with its several supplements, indexes and so on); and Joseph Sabin's *Bibliotheca Americana: A Dictionary of Books Relating to America* (1868–1936), with an author-title index published in 1974, and Lawrence S. Thompson's *New Sabin*, which is, however, restricted to items available in microform.

For the United Kingdom, the equivalent sources for national bibliography would be such volumes as *British Books in Print* (1874ff.), *British National Bibliography* (1950ff.), the *Index of English Literary Manuscripts* by P. J. Croft, Theodore Hofmann, and John Horden, and Robert B. Downs's *British and Irish Library Resources: A Bibliographical Guide*, together with the several "short-title catalogues," the original Pollard and Redgrave and its recently completed revision by Pantzer, Jackson, and Ferguson, for the years 1475–1640, Donald Wing's *STC* for 1641–1700 (with its revision, now complete except for indexes), and the ongoing eighteenth- and nineteenth-century *STCs*, for details of which see the bibliography. In addition, there are various ancillary series making use of *STC* information, for example, the index to *STC* microfilms in *Accessing Early English Books, 1641–1700*, A. F. Allison and V. F. Goldsmith's *Titles of English Books* (although its usefulness is limited because of the exclusion of anonymous works, and its omission of much material from the *STC* revisions), Paul G. Morrison's *Index of Printers, Publishers, and Booksellers in . . . Wing*, and Wing's *Gallery of Ghosts: Books Pub-*

lished between 1641–1700 Not Found in . . . STC.

Another usual source for the earlier period is Edward Arber's *Transcript of the Registers of the Company of Stationers . . . 1554–1640*, which provides a list and description of all books licensed to be published during the period. This should be supplemented by Greg's *Bibliography of the English Printed Drama to the Restoration* (which was being updated and continued by Fredson Bowers's *Bibliography of the English Printed Drama, 1660–1700*, until his death in 1991), by Greg's *Companion to Arber . . . A Calendar of Documents*, by Greg and E. Boswell's *Records of the Court of the Stationers' Company, 1576 to 1602*, William Jackson's *Records of the Court of the Stationers' Company, 1602 to 1640*, Hyder Rollins's *Analytical Index to the Ballad-Entries (1557–1709) in the Registers of the Company of Stationers*, and Briscoe Eyre et al.'s *Transcript of the Registers of the . . . Stationers from 1640–1708.* An index of printers, publishers, authors etc. (for 1640–1708) is compiled in William P. Williams's *Index to the Stationers' Register.*

Literary Research

This survey of the national holdings in the United Kingdom and the United States is only the first stage of entry into research with primary documents. The various bibliographical guides already mentioned (e.g., the MLA bibliography and Harner's *Literary Research Guide*) can provide additional information for textual scholars, but it might be useful here simply to give some brief account of the range of primary sources for the documentary study of English and American literature, with the understanding that the list is merely representative and should be supplemented by consultation of the bibliographic guides. The account is limited to catalogues of primary sources only, and does not therefore include general bibliographies for each period; but since textual scholars will (one hopes and assumes) be working from original documents wherever possible, this is an appropriate limitation in a book like this.

A. *English Literature*

For example, in the Old English period N. R. Ker's *Catalogue of Manuscripts Containing Anglo-Saxon* is a basic tool for research, and can be supplemented by Angus Cameron's introductory "List of Old

English Texts" for the *Plan* of the *Dictionary of Old English*. The ongoing *Dictionary*—first volume, fascicle *D*, published in 1987—is (like its great predecessor the *Oxford English Dictionary*) based directly on Old English manuscripts and can thus be another helpful access, complemented by derived studies such as Venezky and Healey's microfiche *Concordance to OE* and Venezky and Butler's *Microfiche Concordance . . . The High-Frequency Words*. For the Middle English period, N. R. Ker's *Medieval Manuscripts in British Libraries* covers public collections outside the major depositories (e.g., the British Library and Bodley), and is complemented by de Ricci's *Census of Medieval and Renaissance Manuscripts in the United States and Canada*. The various incunabula catalogues already discussed cover printed books to 1500. The *Middle English Dictionary* in progress from the University of Michigan gives lexical access to Middle English texts. Medieval drama is fully documented (down to the shopping lists for productions) in the *Records of the Early English Drama* (*REED*), published by Toronto, in progress since 1979. For poetry, there is Brown and Robbins's *Index of Middle English Verse* (with supplement), and for prose the *Index of Middle English Prose*, in progress since 1977, with a general index of printed Middle English prose and several *Handlists* of holdings in individual libraries already available.

For the Renaissance, the two volumes of the Croft, Hofmann, and Horden *Index of English Literary Manuscripts*, (1450–1625 and 1625–1700) provide—as the title suggests—lists of specifically literary manuscripts, and should be complemented for printed books by the various early-period *STC*s already mentioned, whose scope is obviously much broader. Comprehensive linguistic research for the period will eventually be possible through the *Early Modern English Dictionary*, which, like its equivalents for Old English and Middle English, is based on an historical analysis of primary sources. In the meantime, the *Michigan Early Modern English Materials* (*MEMEM*) offers citations from early modern texts, supplemented by Richard Bailey's *Michigan Early Modern English Materials* and *Additions and Antedatings to . . . 1475–1700*. Greg's and Bowers's bibliographies cover the drama of the period, and W. A. Ringler's *Bibliography and Index of English Verse . . . 1476–1558* is a first-line index to its poetry.

In the Restoration and Eighteenth Century, the third volume of the Croft et al. *Index of English Literary Manuscripts* takes us down to 1800, and the already mentioned *Eighteenth-Century STC* deals with

printed books. This can be supplemented by Arber's *Term Catalogues, 1668–1709*, a transcript of booksellers' lists. Beasley's *Check
List of Prose Fiction, 1740–1749*, McBurney's *Check List of English
Prose Fiction, 1700–1739*, Robert Mayo's "A Catalogue of Magazine
Novels and Novelettes, 1740–1815" (*English Novel in the Magazines,
1740–1815*), and James Raven's *British Fiction, 1750–1770* cover fiction; drama is catalogued in *The London Stage, 1660–1800* and in
Milhous and Hume's *Register of English Theatrical Documents,
1660–1737* (together with Bowers for the Restoration). Guides to
primary sources for poetry include D. F. Foxon's *English Verse,
1701–1750* and J. R. Jackson's *Annals of English Verse, 1770–1835*.

In the Nineteenth Century, the fourth volume of Croft et al.'s *Index of Literary Manuscripts* (1800–1900) is useful, complemented by
the *Nineteenth-Century STC*, with the proviso, however, that this *STC*
is based solely on library catalogues (some of which are already published separately), and not on examination of individual books. The
error-rate is therefore much higher than in the revised versions of
*STC*s for earlier periods. Periodicals published in the century are listed in Fulton and Colee's *Union List of Victorian Serials*, William
Ward's *Index and Finding List of Serials . . . 1789–1832*, Wolff,
North, and Deering's *Waterloo Directory of Victorian Periodicals*,
the Houghton and Slingerland *Wellesley Index to Victorian Periodicals*, and Ward's *Literary Reviews in British Periodicals,
1798–1820 . . . 1821–1826*. Fiction is covered in Michael Sadleir's
XIX Century Fiction (based on his own extensive collection), Grimes
and Daims's *Novels in English by Women, 1891–1920* (with a volume
on 1781–1890 to come), Wendell Harris's *British Short Fiction in the
Nineteenth Century*, Lucien Leclaire's *General Analytical Bibliography of the Regional Novelists of the British Isles, 1800–1950*, J. Don
Vann's *Victorian Novels in Serial*, and Robert Lee Wolff's *Nineteenth-Century Fiction* (based on his own collection). Drama in the
period is accessed through Donohue and Ellis's *London Stage,
1800–1900* and Kurt Ganzl's *British Musical Theatre*. While there is
no single authoritative listing of primary sources for poetry in the
nineteenth century alone, such general compilations as *Granger's Index to Poetry* can be used in conjunction with guides to research like
Frank Jordan's *English Romantic Poets: A Review of Research and
Criticism*, Frederic Faverty's *Victorian Poets: A Guide to Research*,
Donald H. Reiman's *English Romantic Poetry, 1800–1835: A Guide
to Information Sources*, although these concentrate on secondary rather than primary materials. The same can be said for nineteenth-cen-

tury prose, where David DeLaura's *Victorian Prose: A Guide to Research* and Wilson and Hoeveler's *English Prose and Criticism in the Nineteenth Century* have a similar bias.

For twentieth-century British literature, Elgin Mellown's *Descriptive Catalogue of Bibliographies of Twentieth Century British Poets* is a good introduction, although it should be supplemented by T. H. Howard-Hill's *Index to British Literary Bibliography* and the *Bibliographic Index*. Manuscripts can be located through the *Location Register of Twentieth-Century English Literary Manuscripts and Letters* and printed works through *British Books in Print* and the *British National Bibliography* described earlier. As was the case for the nineteenth century, information on primary sources for twentieth-century British fiction and poetry may also have to be researched indirectly in general guides—such as A. F. Cassis's *Twentieth-Century English Novel: An Annotated Bibliography of General Criticism*, Thomas Jackson Rice's *English Fiction, 1900–1950*, Robert J. Stanton's *Bibliography of Modern British Novelists*, Paul L. Wiley's *British Novel: Conrad to the Present* (i.e., 1971), Vinson and Kirkpatrick's *Contemporary Poets*, and Martin Gingerich's *Contemporary Poetry in America and England, 1950–1975*, used in conjunction with the *Poetry Index Annual* (from 1982). Primary research on drama can be done through J. P. Wearing's *London Stage, 1890–1929* (with further volumes to come), supplemented by reference to such general guides as Charles Carpenter's *Modern Drama Scholarship and Criticism, 1966–1980*, the same author's *Modern British Drama*, Kimball King's *Twenty Modern British Playwrights*, and Vinson and Kirkpatrick's *Contemporary Dramatists*. Since there is no specifically primary catalogue of non-fiction prose, Brown and Thesing's *English Prose and Criticism, 1900–1950* can be used to find lists of primary works.

B. *American Literature*

For American literature, the chronological range of primary sources is obviously much less than for British. After consulting the general bibliographical guides mentioned earlier in this chapter (e.g, Gohdes or Nilon), the textual scholar could turn to J. Albert Robbins's *American Literary Manuscripts: A Checklist of Holdings* for information on the manuscripts of twenty-eight hundred authors in six hundred institutions. Other useful guides to manuscripts include Cripe and Campbell's *American Manuscripts, 1763–1815* (a record of auctions and other book sales), John W. Raimo's *Guide to Manu-*

scripts Relating to America in Great Britain and Ireland, and Hinding and Bower's *Women's History Sources: A Guide to Archives and Manuscript Collections*. For printed books, the standard work is the Blanck *Bibliography of American Literature* mentioned earlier, now revised under the editorship of Michael Winship and Virginia Smyers. Linguistic research on the American language can be done through the *Dictionary of American Regional English* (two volumes published to date), the *Dictionary of American English on Historical Principles* by Craigie and Hulbert (modeled on the *OED*), and the *Dictionary of Americanisms on Historical Principles* by Mitford Mathews. The "notorious" *Webster's Third New International Dictionary of the English Language* (because of its omission of "correct" or "incorrect" usage labels) is nonetheless the most comprehensive of American dictionaries for contemporary literature, but should be supplemented by the 1934 edition (*Webster's Second*) for words which have since become obsolete.

There is no single listing of primary materials for poetry or fiction, so information has to be gleaned from such general guides as Gerstenberger and Hendrick's *The American Novel, 1789–1959* and Roy Harvey Pearce's *Continuity of American Poetry*. Drama and prose, however, are better served. For drama, there are George Odell's *Annals of the New York Stage*, Stephen Archer's *American Actors and Actresses: A Guide to Information Sources*, Don B. Wilmeth's *American Stage to World War I*, Carl J. Stratman's *American Theatrical Periodicals, 1798–1967*, the same author's *Bibliography of American Theatre Excluding New York City*, and Carl F. W. Larson's *American Regional Theatre History to 1900*, (supplemented by documentary information contained in Walter J. Meserve's *Drama of the American People*, of which the first two volumes—*Emerging Entertainment* and *Heralds of Promise*—to 1849, have been published so far). And for prose, there are Arksey, Pries, and Reed's *American Diaries . . . 1492–1980*, and Louis Kaplan's *Bibliography of American Autobiographies* (supplemented by Mary Louise Briscoe's *American Autobiography, 1945–1980*).

For ethnic literature, basic sources include the *Dictionary Catalog of the Schomburg Collection of Negro Literature and History*, Kallenbach's *Index to Black American Literary Anthologies*, Bakish and Margolies's *Afro-American Fiction, 1853–1976*, the ongoing *Afro-American Novel Project* on electronic data base, Dorothy Chapman's *Index to Poetry by Black American Women*, William P. French's *Afro-American Poetry and Drama*, Russell C. Brignano's *Black Americans in Autobiography* . . . *since the Civil War*, Walter Schatz's *Directory of Afro-American Resources*, Littlefield and Parins's *Biobibliography of Native American Writers, 1772–1924*, the same authors' *American Indian and Alaska Native Newspapers and Periodicals, 1826–1985*, David Brumble's *Annotated Bibliography of American Indian and Eskimo Autobiographies*, and King-Kok Cheung and Stan Yogi's *Asian American Literature: An Annotated Bibliography*. Primary materials are also to be found in general bibliographical guides (e.g., Darwin T. Turner's *Afro-American Writers* and Margaret Perry's *The Harlem Renaissance*, Barbara and Cordell Robinson's *Mexican American: A Critical Guide to Research Aids*, Ernestina Eger's *Bibliography of Criticism of Contemporary Chicano Literature*, Martinez and Lomeli's *Chicano Literature: A Reference Guide*, and Ira Bruce Nadel's *Jewish Writers of North America: A Guide to Information Sources*).

Primary materials relating to the documentary study of colonial literature are covered in, for example, Evans and Sabin (see above). Another approach is taken by Alden and Landis's *European Americana: A Chronological Guide to Works Printed in Europe Relating to the Americas*. Other primary sources are listed in Clarence Brigham's *History and Bibliography of American Newspapers, 1690–1820* (with a *Tabular Guide* by Edward Lathem), Jayne Kribbs's *Annotated Bibliography of American Literary Periodicals, 1741–1850*, Nelson Adkins's *Index to Early American Periodicals to 1850*, E. W. Pitcher's *Fiction in American Magazines before 1800: An Annotated Catalogue*, Frank Hill's *American Plays Printed, 1714–1830*, Leo Lemay's *Calendar of American Poetry* . . . *through 1765*, and Oscar Wegelin's *Early American Poetry* . . . *1650–1820*. Further information on primary sources occurs in such guides as Yanella and Roch's *American Prose to 1820*, Scheick and Doggett's *Seventeenth-Century American Poetry*, Patricia Parker's *Early American Fiction: A Reference Guide*, and Levernier and Wilmes's *American Writers before 1800: A Biographical and Critical Dictionary*.

For the nineteenth century, the relevant sections of the *American Book Publishing Record* (beginning in 1876) can be consulted for primary sources, together with O. A. Roorbach's *Bibliotheca Americana* . . . *1820 to* . . . *1861*, James Kelly's *American Catalogue of Books* . . . *1861, to* . . . *1871*, Shaw and Shoemaker's *American Bibliography: A Preliminary Checklist for 1801–1819*, and Shoemaker, Cooper, Bruntjen, and Rinderknecht's *Checklist of American Imprints for 1820–1886*. Periodicals are covered in *Poole's Index to Periodi-*

cal Literature (with five supplements to 1907, a *Cumulative Author Index . . . 1802–1906* by Edward C. Wall, a key to *Titles, Volume, and Dates* by Vinton Dearing, and a *Date and Volume Key* by Bell and Bacon), in Houghton and Slingerland's *Wellesley Index,* and in Daniel Wells's *Literary Index to American Magazines 1815–1865.* Nineteenth-century American fiction is listed in three volumes (1774–1850, 1851–1875, and 1876–1900) of Lyle H. Wright's *American Fiction: A Contribution toward a Bibliography,* with continuation into the twentieth century on a data base at the William Charvat Collection of American Fiction at Ohio State University (*American Fiction, 1901–1925*). Drama is dealt with in *Dramatic Compositions Copyrighted in the United States, 1870 to 1916,* and there is much useful primary information in Walter J. Meserve's *American Drama to 1900: A Guide to Information Sources,* as there is for prose in Elinore Hughes Partridge's *American Prose and Criticism, 1820–1900: A Guide to Information Sources.*

Twentieth-century American literature is listed in such standard references as *Books in Print* (and *Books out of Print*), and authors since 1945 in Gary Lepper's *Bibliographical Introduction to Seventy-Five Modern American Authors.* The two-volume *Contemporary Authors: Bibliographical Series* (volume one on American novelists and volume two on poets, by James Martine and Ronald Baugham respectively) is useful for its lists of primary works. Other sources for documentary study include McPheron and Sheppard's *Bibliography of Contemporary American Fiction, 1945–1988,* Raymond McGill's *Notable Names in the American Theatre,* Samuel Leiter's *Encyclopedia of the New York Stage, 1920–1930,* William McPheron's *Bibliography of Contemporary American Poetry, 1945–1985: A Checklist,* Lloyd Davis and Robert Irwin's *Contemporary American Poetry: A Checklist* (to 1983), the *Index of American Periodical Verse* (from 1971), and Reardon and Thorsen's *Poetry by American Women, 1900–1975.* In addition, primary sources are covered in such general research guides as Brier and Arthur's *American Prose and Criticism, 1900–1950: A Guide to Information Sources,* Martin Gingerich's *Contemporary Poetry in America and England, 1950–1975* (cited earlier), *Contemporary Theatre, Film, and Television: A Biographical Guide . . . in the United States and Great Britain,* Wildbihler and Volklein's *The Musical: An International Annotated Bibliography,* Richard Harris's *Modern Drama in America and England, 1950–1970: A Guide to Information Sources,* James Woodress's *American Fiction, 1900–1950: A Guide to Information Sources,* and

Edward Chielens's *The Literary Journal in America, 1900–1950: A Guide to Information Sources.*

C. *Ancillary Materials*

This survey of bibliographies and guides to primary sources is limited to English and American literature (it does not, for example, cover Irish, Welsh, Scottish, or Anglophone post-colonial literatures). But even with this limitation, the coverage is inadequate for the textual scholar, for, apart from the *STC*s and general imprint catalogs, all of the listings in this brief account deal only with literary material. But a textual scholar is also an historian, a sociologist, a culture critic, and a linguist, and must therefore know where to look for guidance in establishing the context for literary works in these various other fields.

One way is through the standard multi-volume histories such as the *Oxford History of England* (ed. George N. Clark, 16 vols, 1936–86) or through consulting research manuals like Francis Prucha's *Handbook for Research in American History: A Guide to Bibliographies and Other Reference Works*, R. C. Richardson's rather brief *The Study of History: A Bibliographical Guide*, Helen J. Poulton's *The Historian's Handbook: A Descriptive Guide to Reference Works*, or the *American Historical Association's Guide to Historical Literature* by George Howe. Similarly, the standard literary histories (such as the *Oxford History of English Literature*, ed. F. P. Wilson et al., 15 vols., and the *Literary History of the United States* or the newer—and more controversial—*Columbia Literary History of the United States*, ed. Emory Eliott and the *New Cambridge History of American Literature*, ed. Sacvan Bercovitch) do contain some historical context. A particularly useful series in this regard is the *New Pelican Guide to English Literature*, ed. Boris Ford, 9 vols., in which each volume has a survey of the social and cultural milieu. Another approach is to employ a standard chronology such as E. B. Bryde's *Handbook of British Chronology*, in which the researcher may find, for example, a listing of all government office-holders, church leaders, parliaments, etc., from the earliest times.

Then there are the various indexes through which the researcher can gain access to fields other than literature. The most general are the *Humanities Index* and the *Social Sciences Index* and their predecessor, the *Social Sciences and Humanities Index*; the *British Humanities Index*; the *Essay and General Literature Index*; and the *New York*

Times Index and the [London] *Times Index*.   An electronic version of these newspaper indexes is *NEXIS*, based on listings in *The New York Times*, *The Washington Post*, *The Los Angeles Times* and representative European newspapers, with the limitation, however, that it covers only the last ten years or so.   The best directory to serials including non-literary material is the annual *Ulrich's International Periodicals Directory: A Classified Guide to Current Periodicals, Foreign and Domestic*, supplemented by Ulrich's directory of *Irregular Serials and Annuals*.   The complete national (or "union") lists for serials are the *Union List of Serials in Libraries of the United States and Canada* (1965), supplemented by *New Serial Titles . . . after Dec. 31, 1949* (1953), with monthly additions, and the *British Union-Catalogue of Periodicals*.   See also the *Reader's Guide to Periodical Literature*.

Other ancillary materials which might be useful for background historical or social information or for beginning work on annotation include the *Dictionary of National Biography*, for British subjects, and the *Dictionary of American Biography* for American, together with the *Dictionary of Literary Biography* (1978ff.), and the Oxford histories of England and the United States (see above).   For the relations between literature and other disciplines, Jean-Pierre Barricelli and Joseph Gibaldi's survey for MLA, *Interrelations of Literature*, is generally useful, although, strangely, it omits history, perhaps the discipline most closely related to literature!

With the published guides and catalogues exhausted, the scholar then becomes a detective, following a work down through its history until (one hopes) finding it uncatalogued but now available.   This will very often be the case when editing unpublished material like correspondence, where the recipient of each letter (or a descendant) will have to be contacted for information on the current whereabouts of the document in question.   Or the scholar may follow the provenance of a particular book in the records of sales, auctions, or bequests (in, for example, *Book-Auction Records*, *Book-Prices Current*, or de Ricci's *English Collectors of Books and Manuscripts* or Carl L. Cannon's *American Book Collectors and Collecting*).   Sometimes the search may prove fruitless, either because the work does not really exist, but its listing is the result of an error in describing or cataloguing a collection (a so-called bibliographical ghost), or because it does exist but is inaccessible.

One of the most famous examples of the latter is Lord Rosebery's manuscript of the Mill *Autobiography*, which he would not allow to be seen, writing to a scholar who wished to consult it that one of the major pleasures of owning a manuscript was the knowledge that therefore other people could not use it! A few years ago, when working on the text of Trevisa's *On the Properties of Things*, I and the other editors had a similar experience, for Trevisa had completed the fair copy of the book while working as chaplain in Berkeley castle in Gloucestershire. The castle still exists, is still inhabited, and might therefore hold a copy of Trevisa's text in its muniments room; but the castle is one of the few left in England still privately owned, and the current incumbent would not allow access to the family records in the muniments room to a group of mere medievalists. Trevisa's text may still be there, but our critical text—a speculative attempt to reconstruct Trevisa's original—was, perforce, based on corrupt scribal copies. There are many similar stories in the annals of textual scholarship: the Trinity College Cambridge manuscripts of Tennyson, which were denied to editors until the Ricks edition; the notorious recalcitrance of Buffalo and Rosenbach in making Joyce materials available; the Hispanic Society of America's refusal to co-operate with the new Alcalá Cervantes edition; and the efforts of some executors (of Housman and Lawrence, for example) either to retain copyright beyond the usual legal limits, and thus to prevent editorial "tampering," or even to suppress documentary materials. There is perhaps an inevitable institutional conflict between the conservation instincts of the repository and the research access desired by the textual scholar, and this can be exacerbated by personal antagonism and feuding, even by outright intransigence. It was not until after the death of Alban Berg's widow, who retained absolute control over his manuscripts for decades after the composer's death and claimed to be in direct spiritual contact with her deceased husband, that the score of the third act of his opera *Lulu* could be seen by scholars so that a performing edition could be prepared and eventually performed. Of late, the best-known example of an institutional cabal seeking to control the dissemination of important scholarly materials has been the Israeli attempt to restrict access to the Dead Sea Scrolls to an approved list of scholars, a restriction that was eventually overcome by the Huntington Library's decision to make the complete set of photographs of the scrolls available to any reputable researcher (see Wilford).

As a last resort, after having exhausted the repositories, the catalogues, and the published finding lists, the scholar may turn to others, either privately, by consulting specialists who might know where to find the document, or publicly, by a public appeal for help in such journals as *TLS* (*The Times Literary Supplement*), *The New York*

Times Book Review, *The New York Review of Books* or specialized journals in each field.

D.　Textual Research

Having assembled the primary materials and having considered the historical and social context of the work to be studied, the textual scholar will presumably want to consult the experiences of those who have already done textual research in the field. An excellent introduction to the general problem of archival research and accessioning documents toward the production of scholarly editions is Mary-Jo Kline's *Guide to Documentary Editing*, written under the auspices of the Association for Documentary Editing, and therefore especially valuable for American historians faced with the enormous task of sifting through the voluminous papers of the Founding Fathers and their successors. The "literary" equivalent of Kline, Williams and Abbott's *Introduction to Bibliographical and Textual Studies* has some information on access, but its focus is, perhaps quite properly, more on textual bibliography than enumeration. At the moment, the fullest bibliographical guide to textual and documentary editing is Beth Luey's *Editing Documents and Texts* (like Kline, sponsored by the ADE), but its coverage is uneven and should be supplemented by reference to the encyclopedic articles by Tanselle in *Studies in Bibliography* (collected under the titles *Selected Studies in Bibliography* and *Textual Criticism Since Greg: A Chronicle*), by the pamphlets published by the Center for Editions of American Authors and the Committee on Scholarly Editions, by the bibliographies in the collections by Brack and Barnes and by Gottesman and Bennett, by Falconer and Sanderson's "Bibliographie des études génétiques littéraires," by the bibliographies in the essays on "Textual Scholarship" by Tanselle and Greetham for Gibaldi's *Introduction to Literary Research*, by the suggestions for further reading in *Scholarly Editing: A Guide to Research* (ed. Greetham), by the references in the Toronto series of volumes on editorial problems, and for the earlier period, by the cumulative bibliographies in *Studies in Bibliography*.

One further possibility is to turn for assistance to one of the professional organizations concerned with textual or bibliographical matters, including the Committee on Scholarly Editions of the MLA, the Association for Documentary Editing (a group largely identified with the editing of American historical documents), and the Society for Textual Scholarship (an interdisciplinary organization). Another route is to look through recent articles on textual matters published in the standard journals (this might also prevent a scholar beginning a textual project that has already been undertaken by others). The basic journals for textual study are *The Library* (published by the Bibliographical Society [London]), *Papers of the Bibliographical Society of America*, *Studies in Bibliography* (published by the Bibliographical Society of the University of Virginia), *Analytical and Enumerative Bibliography* (published by the Bibliographical Society of Northern Illinois University), *Documentary Editing* (published by the Association for Documentary Editing), and *Text* (an interdisciplinary journal published by the Society for Textual Scholarship).

E. *Some Specific Research Tools*

I have mentioned a large array of bibliographical aids for the textual scholar, and I obviously hope that their likely value is already fairly clear. However, it might be helpful if I gave a few specific examples of the actual data the scholar can obtain from these various reference works. What can they do to make the researcher's job easier, and what sorts of particular information do they contain? Herewith a few illustrative examples.

For example, at the general bibliography level, the MLA's *International Bibliography* is available for electronic online retrieval "using free-text searching or on the basis of classification headings, document authors, and other elements of citation" for the years 1963–89 (with plans to add all bibliographical data back to 1921), and is also available in CD-ROM (compact disk-read only memory) for 1981–89. The CD-ROM version is menu-driven on "the premise that not all users will be experienced in search techniques" and therefore offers "a choice of searching strategies" to "enhance novices' use of the file." The electronic search is obviously much more efficient of time than is the printed version, but even this latter does give some idea of the range of possibilities. For example, the subject classifications for "Editor" or "Book Trade," "Book Production," "Textual Editing," and "Manuscript Study" list all publications for the given year in which such topics are covered.

In the electronic version, of course, the researcher can combine such classifications to see what manuscript studies have been done on Milton, or investigations of the book trade in the Middle Ages, just as in the CD-ROM version of the *Oxford English Dictionary* the researcher can use the flexible "parsing" facilities to link various categories, to discover, say, what words of Arabic origin entered the language in the seventeenth century, or what head-note citations for Shakespeare involve a change of usage from noun to verb, or what archaized words were first used by Spenser (always given, of course, that the record of citation in *OED* is correct). Once the *New Oxford English Dictionary*, a completely new electronic version, is published (rather than the current electronic version of the old *OED*), then records of citations can be kept continually up-to-date without separate book publication.

Another particularly sophisticated type of database of value to textual scholars is the recently announced *English Poetry Full-Text Database* (on CD-ROM and magnetic tape), which provides a complete record of all poetic works listed by authors in the *New Cambridge Bibliography of English Literature* (*NCBEL*) up to 1900. Like many such databases, it uses the Standard General Markup Language (SGML) for coding the texts, to break down the full text into its structural elements so that these can then be searched or manipulated separately or together, employing Boolean operators AND, OR, AND-NOT. According to its promotional literature, the database can therefore present, for example, "the number of times a poet or group of poets has used a particular word or phrase, the source of a specific quotation, all poems before 1800 that have epigraphs, the speeches of a particular character in a dramatic poem, or all nineteenth-century poems in which the words 'love' and 'death' occur together." The scholar can search by poet, by place and date of publication, by publisher, by volume and page reference, by title keyword or text keyword(s).

As with many primary-source databases, however, the textual evidence of *English Poetry* is ambivalent: the texts of the poems are not necessarily drawn either from modern critical editions or from contemporary manuscripts or first editions (the text of Coleridge's *Dejection: An Ode*, for example, comes from the Pickering edition of the *Poetical Works* of 1834), and to my knowledge there are no multiple text citations or collations. And with the exception of certain landmark anthologies such as Percy's *Reliques of Ancient English Poetry*, poems published only in journals or miscellanies or newspapers are not included, nor are unpublished poems. Therefore, despite the obvious usefulness of the database, it still needs careful control and discrimination by the scholar. And such electronic aids do not come cheaply: the full text *English Poetry*, scheduled for completion by March 1994, sells for $54,000 on CD-ROM and $72,000 on magnetic tape, although three separate chronological divisions will be available for smaller amounts.

In old-fashioned print format, and at the level of national bibliography, any of the *STC*s can provide detailed publication information on individual works. For example, the revised Wing *STC* (1641–1700) lists each separate edition of works by such authors as Dryden or Congreve or Behn. Under "Congreve" we find three editions of *The Mourning Bride* (entries 5856, 5857, and 5858), each printed "For Jacob Tonson" (the publisher/bookseller), and each in quarto (4°, see Chapters 3 and 4 for explanation of format). We are given the location lists of all three editions, and can thus discover where we can do research on actual copies of the books (the *STC*s use a series of letters to indicate the place, e.g., L = London [British Library], N = New York [New York Public Library], O = Oxford [Bodleian Library], Y = Yale, and so on). We can also see that the editions have some peculiarities: the first edition is dated 1697, but the second edition reads "1679," clearly an error, by transposed digits, for "1697," which Wing provides in square brackets [1697] (see Chapter 4 for principles of bibliographical description, including the use of editorial square brackets). Furthermore, there is another edition, also of 1697, claiming to be the second, although actually the third, and Wing thus places this claim in quotation marks, "Second" edition. In this way, an *STC* can give the researcher detailed primary bibliographical information on the printing history and current availability of the works under study.

A different sort of national bibliography is G. Thomas Tanselle's *Guide to the Study of United States Imprints* which, through its comprehensive listing of regional bibliographies, genre bibliographies (including everything from Accounting Books and Almanacs to Welsh Americana, via Chemistry Books, Cookery Books, Etiquette Books, Indian Captivity Narratives, Jest Books, Murder Literature, Outlaw Literature, Regimental Histories, and Sporting Books), copyright records, catalogues, and book-trade directories, provides a cumulative history of printing and books in the United States. Unlike the *STC*s, which are general indexes of all primary materials, the Tanselle listing contains only bibliographies; it is therefore a good example of an effective bibliography of bibliographies, specifically related to the history of the book in a particular country.

Another approach is exemplified in the Brown and Robbins *Index of Middle English Verse*, which is obviously organized by both language and genre, but presents its materials not by author (like an *STC*) or by genre or region (like the Tanselle national bibliography) but by first-line of the medium—verse. In Middle English, there are good reasons for so doing, since many poems are unattributed and many lack titles. The first line (*incipit*, see Chapter 2) is thus the best way of identifying them. What is probably the most famous poem in Middle English, *The Canterbury Tales*, therefore appears as "Whan that Aprill with his shoures soote" (number 4019), with an entry divided into four sections: Perfect texts (the complete *Tales*, although not all in the same order), Imperfect texts, Fragmentary texts, and Separate texts, with location lists for each manuscript of each type. Within these lists, Brown and Robbins indicate if a manuscript has changed hands and was formerly known by a different name: thus Fitzwilliam Museum McClean 181, now in the Cambridge University Library, was once the Ingilby manuscript, and Huntington El.26.C.9 (in San Marino, California) was once officially the Ellesmere manuscript, under which title it is still popularly known. The fact that manuscripts do still change hands means that scholars using such indexes as the Brown-Robbins must always check sales catalogues, auction records etc. for recent information on manuscripts no longer in the repository cited in the index consulted.

Indexes of the Brown-Robbins type attempt a comprehensive listing of all documents within a specific medium or genre. A more limited bibliographical aid is the listing of all documents within an individual repository—like Margaret Crum's *First-Line Index of English Poetry 1500–1800 in Manuscripts of the Bodleian Library*, which has the same principle of organization as Brown-Robbins (again, for obvious reasons), but, as already mentioned, concentrates only on poetic manuscripts within a single library, although its chronological scope is not confined to one period. The various indexes to Crum (authors, names cited, translated authors or works, composers, and tunes) enable the researcher to discover all manuscripts of Crashaw (105 citations) or Donne (102 citations) or all references to the Duke of Marlborough (51 citations) or translations of Boethius (20 citations) or Catullus (22 citations) or settings by William Byrd (31 citations) or by Henry Purcell (83 citations) or uses of such tunes as "The Vicar of Bray" (5 citations) or "God Save the King" (3 citations). In this way, the Crum volumes give several different types of entry into the field.

And finally, using an historical index like the *Annals of English Literature*, the researcher can gain some immediate insight into the cultural and literary milieu of a specific year. For example, we can discover that in the year that Wordsworth and Coleridge published their "revolutionary" volume *Lyrical Ballads* (1798) there were also publications by Cowper (*Two Poems*), Edgeworth (*Practical Education*), Godwin (*Memoirs of Mary Wollstonecraft* and an edition of *Posthumous Works of Mary Wollstonecraft*), Lamb (*Blank Verse* and *Tale of Rosamond Gray*), Landor (*Gebir*), Malthus (*Principle of Population as it Affects the Future of Society*), Walpole (*Works*, ed. by Berry), and various other works by minor authors: clearly, it was a banner year.

The Rewards

But even with the different types of bibliographical aid offered by these indexes and catalogues (together with the host of other references mentioned earlier in this chapter), since all bibliographies and research tools (and even scholarly articles) are in their very nature inaccurate and obsolete (as the example of *ghosts* shows), and since all the help derived from bibliographical resources has to be regarded as contingent and incomplete rather than definitive and exhaustive, there is no substitute for old-fashioned bibliographical drudgery. And sometimes riches await the careful researcher. For example, the only example of an entire language, Old Saxon, was found being used to strengthen the binding of a book in the Vatican Library; and only a few years ago, the Byron editor Leslie Marchand, refusing to accept the records of the John Murray publishing house that many of Byron's letters had, at his request, been burned, discovered many new documents that had been considered lost (although others, for example, Byron's letters to Thomas Moore and the journal for 1813–14) had disappeared since an earlier publication. Recently, the lost holograph manuscript of the first part of Mark Twain's *Huckleberry Finn* was rediscovered, necessitating the re-editing of that volume in the Twain edition, and a trove of T. S. Eliot letters and poems (in his *Practical Cats* mode) was unearthed in an attic (see Whitney). And, in what must surely be one of the greatest short-term profits in the discovery and sale of documents, a fine copy of the *Declaration of Independence* (printed on the day of signature, July 4, 1776) was sold at auction for $2,420,000 after having been found in the frame of a cheap painting purchased at a flea market for $4 two years earlier (see Blau).

Of course, it is not the aim or hope of most literary researchers to make such personal fortunes or to enlarge the canon of major authors, but only to make sure they have the basic materials on which further critical or textual work can continue. Nonetheless, such tales of discovery do point to the fact that not everything is safely catalogued and described, and there are many valuable documents waiting to be added to our knowledge. Some of the oldest libraries already had huge collections before modern methods of data input and retrieval became available, and it will be many years (if ever) before the new systems of enumerative bibliography catch up with the old depositories. For example, while new accessions to the Pierpont Morgan Library are recorded on electronic database, the Library has no hope that the whole of the earlier card catalogue will ever be entered into the database. The problem, of course, is that the collections keep growing as they are in the process of being catalogued, so the process is never-ending. Even some of the most recent academic libraries, without a long history of accessioning (such as Texas) have mountains of uncatalogued documents, and these mountains do not seem to get any smaller very quickly. In the explosion of documentary and bibliographical riches of the last few generations (making a twentieth-century *STC* virtually unthinkable), the days are long gone when a nineteenth-century gentleman-scholar like M. R. James could wander from college to college at Cambridge University and calmly produce reliable, authoritative catalogues of their manuscripts. Such a "gentleman-scholar" is, in enumerative bibliography as in so many other areas, receding before the advance of the computer, which may be the only means for scholarship to quantify, let alone describe, the documentation which literature, history, philosophy, music, science, linguistics, and so on have produced in this century. But while computers can indeed bring a level of access and a flexibility of manipulation undreamed of in the days of the Alexandrians, the enumerative and systematic bibliographer still needs a sense of discrimination, an ability to make critical decisions about the value and status of documents that has not changed much since Zenodotus of Ephesus took on his job as Chief Librarian. It is this same critical attitude that we will find in all the stages of textual scholarship yet to be described.

2

Making the Text:

Bibliography of Manuscript Books

The term "manuscript book" should first be defined. "Manuscript" is no problem; it means written by hand (although these days it is often paradoxically used to mean the opposite—written by machine, or at least typewriter or computer printer). But what is a "book"? In its most general extent, this term might refer to almost any portable material with handwriting on it: metal, stone, wax, clay, potsherds, or official articles like coins and seals. In the chapter on paleography, even walls are included as a medium for writing, since Pompeiian graffiti are the best-preserved remnants of certain Roman cursive styles. Walls, however, do not ordinarily qualify as "books," nor, for the purposes of the students for whom *this* book is intended, do the various tablets and other portable but basically non-literary objects on which writing may happen to occur. The discussion of books here is limited to those in the two most familiar forms: the roll, from which, through the Latin *volumen*, we now speak of "volumes," and the codex, or folded and stitched book (from *caudax*, the trunk or bark of a tree). And the focus here will be almost entirely on the writing of such books in the West.

The Copying of Manuscript Books:
Scribal Duties and Methods

A fairly reliable account of scribal practices can begin only in the Latin West, for it is only in the Roman and medieval periods that there is much information about scribal methods, and even that is somewhat ambiguous. Of the scribal practices employed by, for example, the Alexandrians, almost nothing is known, and there are no holograph manuscripts of any Greek *or* Roman author: all extant documents are copies, usually very far removed textually and chronologically from the authorial fair copy—or the manuscript written out by the author and released for distribution.

The Roman emperor Diocletian's offer of a prize for copying may testify both to the esteem given a scribe's responsibilities and, by implication, to the generally low level of performance. Both Cicero and Martial complained about the widespread incompetence of scribes, and the complaints have never stopped. According to Cicero, the great bulk of *librarii*—a term which could probably cover indiscriminately both copyists and booksellers, who were, in any case, most likely often the same persons—took little pride in their work and consequently produced inaccurate, unreliable texts. It was for this reason that he commissioned as his publisher Atticus, a man who took charge of the copying, distributing, and actual editing (in the commercial sense of preparing the book for sale rather than the textual sense of establishing the text) of books. There are stories of Cicero's trying to correct errors in "proof" only to find that the "edition" had already been made public. Martial's claim was simply that the scribes were so interested in turning out books as fast as possible that their writing became careless and illegible as a result. In common with almost all other periods, the Roman era allowed its formal book scripts gradually to become informal, cursive, and illegible as speed became more important than monumental exactness; and it is easy to appreciate Martial's argument, especially if the "books" he referred to were written in the truly cursive style (for examples, see Chapter 5).

That the Roman book trade was in general a healthy one can be shown not only by the numerous imperial and private libraries mentioned earlier—all of which disappeared in the fall of the Empire—but also by the extensive trade in papyrus recorded in Pliny the Elder, and by the survival of the names of several famous families of booksellers and of individuals in the trade: the Sosii, Tryphon, Atrectus. There were well-known bookshops in the Argelitum and the Vicus Sandalarius, each one bearing lists of the books for sale posted on the doors.

Even though it is likely that the greater part of the actual copying was done by educated slaves, there was little distinction between those who physically copied the books and those who sold them. This can be shown by the decree of Justinian giving scribes property in the materials they used. "Copyright" therefore was in the concrete form of the book, which simply "included" its contents. There were, of course, no royalties to the author. Even as late as the sixteenth century, Erasmus was offended by the charge that he had actually been paid by the printer of one of his books. Patronage of an author or a scholar was one thing, the commercial sale of one's works to the general public by a bookseller was quite another.

In the non-commercial world of the medieval monastery, where most copying was done in the early Middle Ages, standards were, at least in theory, much higher than in ancient Rome. This was reflected in, for example, the dedication of a scriptorium: "Vouchsafe, O Lord, to bless this workroom of Thy servants, that all which they write therein may be comprehended by their intelligence and realized in their works" (Putnam 1. 61). These high hopes have been continually challenged by generations of textual critics, who have accused the medieval scribes of willful disobedience, or cheerful unconcern for the law charging that they should reproduce exactly what they saw in the exemplar (even if it looked like an error), or with plain stupidity. James Willis finds most medieval scribes to have been "not wildly ignorant of Latin nor deeply versed" and therefore as copyists "very dangerous." According to Willis, their worst virtue, as far as the textual critic is concerned, was their "pernicious desire to do good" (3).

It was taken for granted that scribes, pernicious or otherwise, were absolutely essential to the aims of the monastic movement. While the sixth-century Benedictine Rule, the first and most successful of the Western monastic systems, made no specific reference to the actual copying of books, it is clear that reading, and therefore copying, of books was necessary to the successful monastery, since the monks were supposed to be read to during meals in the refectory. This assumes that somebody in the monastic community must have been responsible for producing the books to be read. The same practice of reading during meals was incorporated into Cassiodorus's foundation at Vivarium in 540, where a reference to the physical form of the books and the enthusiasm for their copying were more overt. "By copying the divine precepts [the scribe] spreads them far and wide, enjoying the glorious privilege of silently preaching salvation to mortals by means of the hand alone, and by thus foiling with pen and ink the temptations of the devil, every word of the Lord written by the copyist is a wound inflicted on Satan." The Rule of St. Ferreol is even more specific: "He who does not turn up the earth with the plough ought to write the parchment with his fingers" (Putnam 1.

63). While it could be argued that there is a faint suggestion here of the old dictum that "those who can, do; those who cannot, teach," it does at least regard the work of copying as the equivalent of manual labor.

That scribes were therefore valuable and often highly esteemed can be shown at the very end of the Middle Ages by Erasmus's complaint that there were not enough professional copyists in England and more should be trained, and at the very beginning of the period by the Irish *wergild*, or compensation, law, that the loss of a scribe by violence was to be considered as equal to the loss of a bishop or an abbot. In Scotland, a bishop proudly added the title "scriba" to his name as a mark of honor. God's especial favor to scribes is illustrated by two stories told in Putnam's *Books and Their Makers in the Middle Ages*. The first is that the "writing" hand of a scribe at Wedinghausen was miraculously preserved, while the rest of the body fell into corruption. The second is that a particularly carnal and sinful monk was saved from damnation by the presentation before the Judgment seat of a huge folio volume he had written out. Each letter was used to offset a specific sin, and at the end of the calculations, there was just *one* letter left over. And it was, the story remarks, "a *very* big book" (1. 65).

During the great periods of monastic copying—which was essentially an internal book trade, since the books copied were normally for the use of other monks—most scribes were, of course, anonymous. But the occasional *explicit*, or closing remarks at the end of a manuscript (developing in the early days of printing into the often highly informative printer's colophon, a halfway stage to the title-page), could often allow some personal expression. In addition to the expected pious thoughts, there could be an admission of weariness or relief at having finished the arduous task of copying: "Finis succrevit, manus et mea felsa quievit" or "Lassa manus calamusque simul cum fine quievit." There might be hopes of appropriate reward for the work: "Promisso pretio sum dignus jure peracto," or there could even be a totally irrelevant but very human jest, which catches the sense of release from the drudgery perhaps better than the formal complaints. One of the most famous of such comments is: "Jesus mercy, Lady helpe/For Cutt my dogge is a parillus welp" (Madan, "Explicits").

Some of these *explicits*, especially where they give the name of the scribe, the time taken to complete the work, and the place of the copying, are valuable in providing the provenance of the manuscript, and can therefore be useful evidence in the study of both paleography and textual transmission. Such scribal subscripts must, however, be distinguished from an authorial colophon, which is indigenous to the text, and not a comment on the copying of a specific document of that text. Authorial colophons may be used in dating and placing composition; for example, John Trevisa writes at the end of his *De proprietatibus rerum* that the work was completed "at Berkeleye [castle, home of his patron, Thomas of Berkeley] the sixte day of Feuerer, the yere of our lorde a thousande thre hundrid foure score and eiytetene" (2. 1396) and this colophon is repeated in all subsequent manuscripts of the work, even though the date was obviously not applicable to the later copying. Trevisa's comment might therefore be evidence about the author, but is completely inappropriate to the dating of specific manuscripts or the habits of certain scribes.

Without the assistance of genuine *scribal* subscripts, the identification even of general scriptorial styles, let alone the work of individual scribes, would be immeasurably more difficult than it is. For while there is, in the later Middle Ages, an occasional autograph manuscript (e.g., that of Robert of Gloucester's *Chronicle* in 1265, and of several works by the professional scribe and part-time poet Thomas Hoccleve in the early fifteenth century), tracing the productions of individual copyists can be an uncertain business. Some scriptoria do seem to have developed specific identifying habits at particular times (Exeter and Winchester in the eleventh century, St. Albans in the thirteenth); and there are some general rules which may be used with caution (for example, most medieval university manuscripts appear to have favored a double-column page, whereas the Cistercians among the monastic orders preferred a three-column layout).

But the evidence is not always consistent, and there are other problems besides. For instance, it might be a mistake to assume that all scribes always wrote in a single uniform hand. In the Elizabethan period it was normal for an educated person to be able to write in both the old-fashioned "secretary" and the new "italic" script, and the same variety was also often the case in the Middle Ages. Matthew Paris wrote in both "free" and "set" styles, and in the later period, when professional scribes took over the book trade from the monks, a scribe might very well change his style according to the nature of the book being copied. Furthermore, different types of book demanded different scripts: there could be a "liturgical" script, a "court" script, a "text" script, and a "vernacular" script all emanating from the same shop at the same time, and while no doubt certain copyists would have specialized in one script over the others, it would have been an inefficient scribe who could not have done as Queen Elizabeth I was to do, and change the style with the nature of the document.

The use of paid scribes as distinct from monks goes back even to the period of monastic copying, where *librarii* could be brought in for hack work, *rubricatores* for illumination and decoration, and *notarii* for various legal documents. By the mid-fourteenth century, professional scribes were regularly employed by individual wealthy patrons for private copying (the author of *Philobiblon* takes their existence for granted); and by the early fifteenth century, occasional manuscripts occur, usually on paper rather than parchment, which have obviously been written by literate amateurs for their own personal use, such as scientific or medical tracts to be employed for domestic reference. The existence of a class of non-monastic clerks was no doubt encouraged by the growth of the universities and by the immense amount of clerical work demanded by the ever-growing governmental and ecclesiastical chancelleries and baronial households. By the end of the thirteenth century, most such households could produce any book except perhaps a large *édition de luxe*.

Eventually, of course, this movement changes the very meaning of the word "clerk," from a member of a religious body (cleric) to somebody who earns his living by writing, whether in or out of religious orders. Legal, historical, theological, medical, and philosophical manuscripts were produced for the universities at Bologna, Paris, Naples, and Oxford, where in 1373 statutes were passed governing the activities and prices charged by the *stationarii*, or semi-official booksellers. A similar set of regulations had been issued by the University of Vercelli in 1228. The system of parceling out work at the universities was called the *pecia*, whereby a specific scribe might be responsible for producing a number of copies of the same section of a larger work, the other parts being given out elsewhere. Such practices are indications of a genuine book trade, as opposed to the monastic copying of books for internal purposes. The *pecia* can be useful in establishing the provenance of a manuscript, since practical details varied from university to university and stationer to stationer: for example, Oxford quires, or gatherings of sheets brought together for stitching, were usually of twelve leaves, Bolognese of ten. And it can also be employed in the study of textual transmission, for different identifiable scribes might have been given different exemplars of the same work.

The value of this trade to the university and to the government can be seen in the specific exemption of scribes from jury duty in London in 1357; in the organization of the Worshipful Company of Scriveners and the issue of their *Common Paper*, or list of members, beginning in 1340; in the appeal of the Stationers Company for its own ordinances in 1403; and, of course, in the actual records of payment to scribes. In the early fourteenth century, the normal rate of pay was about a half-pence per day in England. This could add up to a sizable amount for a large book: in 1380, John Prut, canon of Windsor, received 75 shillings and 8 pence for writing and illuminating a *Textus Evangelis*. (As a comparison, in the same period a well-qualified doctor would charge a minimum of 100 shillings for a successful cure; a sergeant-at-arms to the king might receive 12 pence—one shilling—per day; and the poor members of a guild would be pensioned at 7 or 8 pence per week.)

Heavily illuminated work and other special orders doubtless involved greater expense, but in general it seems likely that the scribe's stipend would account for perhaps 30 percent of the total cost of a book, with meals (and in private households, lodgings) accounting for another 30 percent on a book taking about four months to copy. In 1469, William Ebesham produced a copy of Hoccleve's *Regement of Princes* for 3 shillings and 9 pence, "aftir a peny a leaf, which is right wel worth" (Madan: 52). As was the monastic practice, when a quaternion—a quire, or gathering, of four sheets—had been finished in a secular workshop, it might be compared with the original by a "corrector," and then given to the "rubricator" for its decorated initials and rubrics, and, if it was a particularly sumptuous edition, to the "illuminator" for illuminated miniatures, which reached a high level of technical and artistic success in such commissioned works as the Duc de Berry's series of books of hours, illuminated in the International Style by the Limbourg brothers and other artists.

The second most expensive part of the book was the parchment on which it was written. In addition to the payment to John Prut quoted above, the sponsor of the *Textus evangelis* had to pay 12 shillings and 8 pence for nineteen quaternions of parchment; other costs included a half-pence for ink, 9 pence for vermilion, 4 shillings and 3 pence for illumination, and 3 shillings and 4 pence for binding. While modern research has corrected the earlier impression that parchment was inordinately expensive, it was no doubt the cost of the material, and its peculiar ability to be scraped down in order to bear a superimposed second text, which encouraged the use of *palimpsests*—documents containing two texts, one superscribed over erased earlier text—even though there were various statutes forbidding the destruction of earlier works in this fashion. A particularly famous example of a palimpsest is shown in Fig. 1, where the only surviving text of Cicero's *De republica* is the "lower" text in a manuscript overwritten with Augustine's *In psalmos*. Perhaps for fear of removing important precedents from the record, notaries and lawyers were expressly forbidden to use "old" (i.e., previously used) parchment.

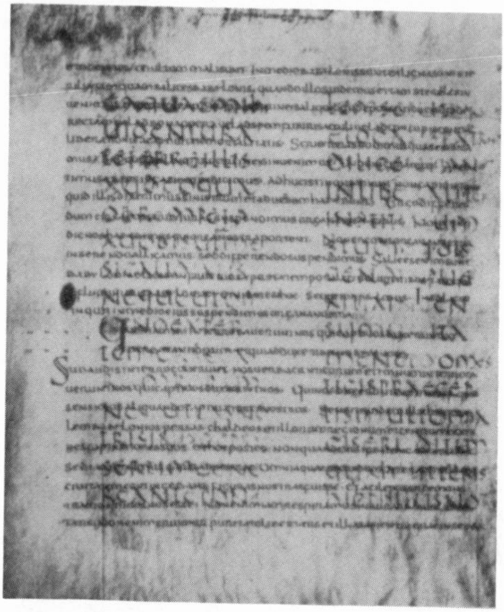

Fig. 1. A palimpsest of Cicero's *De republica* (lower text) and Augustine's *In psalmos* (upper text).

The costliness of books, and the difficulty of replacing copies stolen from depositories, public or private, also provide other opportunities for observing the personal touch in the numerous anathemas pronounced on those who might make free with the hard-won treasures of a library. Book thieves were regularly compared unfavorably to Judas, Ananias, or Caiaphas, and in a manuscript now in the Bodleian Library (safely guarded, one trusts) there occurs this imprecation: "This book belongs to S. Mary of Roberts Bridge; whoever shall steal it, or sell it, or in any way alienate it from this house, or mutilate it, let him be anathema maranatha. Amen." The present Bodleian curators are presumably not disturbed by the curse on those who would "alienate" the volume from its home, but, as Putnam reports, the curse did trouble an earlier owner of the book, who in an avowal of his honest ownership has added below the anathema: "I, John, Bishop of Exeter, know not where the aforesaid house is, nor did I steal the book, but acquired it in a lawful way" (1. 73). Again, such comments may be useful in tracing the provenance of a manuscript.

What were conditions like in the original monastic scriptoria and their secular successors, and what were typical scribal methods? (For a contemporary representation of the process of book-making, see Fig. 2, which shows the sheet of parchment being given to the scribe, the ruling of the sheet, the scribal copying, and the illumination.)

That copying a book was considered both spiritually ennobling and laborious was assumed by both lay and clerical scribes. Hoccleve complained bitterly of the physical discomfort (backache particularly), the lack of appreciation from superiors, the poor salary (often unpaid, if Hoccleve is to be believed), and the loss of faculties, especially eyesight, in the service of government.

> Wrytyng also doth grete annoyes thre,
> Of which ful fewe folkes taken heede
> Sauf we our self; and thise, lo, they be:
> Stomak is on, whom stowpyng out of dreede
> Annoyeth soore; and to our bakkes, neede
> Mot it be greuous; and the thrid, our yen,
> Vp-on the whyte mochel sorwe dryen . . . .
> And yen moost it greueth trewely
> Of any crafte that man can ymagyne:
> ffadir, in feth, it spilt hath wel ny myne. (*Regement* 1016ff.)

Five hundred years earlier, Othlo of Tergensee anticipated Hoccleve's complaint by almost losing his eyesight after a lifetime of copying, and a monk of St. Gall wrote a similar liturgy of pain: "He who does not know how to write imagines it to be no labor, but although the fingers only hold the pen, the whole body grows weary" (Putnam 1. 64).

The physical discomfort could even be used as a means of penitence, though it hardly compares to the self-chastisement of those Irish monks who would stand for hours on end in icy water to subdue the flesh. Putnam quotes the testimony of one Jacob, who had been set to copying as a penitential exercise and claimed that he had written "a certain portion of this book not of his own free will but under compulsion, bound by fetters, just as a runaway and fugitive has to be bound" (1. 64). The "one hundred lines" punishment beloved of

English public-school masters obviously has a long history, and literacy was not always a blessing—or so it appeared to some of those cursed with such abilities.

There can be little doubt that conditions were indeed uncomfortable for scribes in medieval monasteries. There was no heat, and usually no artificial light, for fear of damaging the precious manuscripts. If, as in Gloucester Abbey, the copying was done in the cloisters, it

Fig. 2. The manufacture of the medieval book. Parchment being stretched and given to the scribe (*top left*); ruling the sheet (*top right*); scribal copying (*bottom left*); illumination (*bottom right*).

must have been a drafty job. While conditions in the later commercial or private scriptoria were probably a little less harsh, the writing, especially that of some of the more ornate gothic scripts, must have been very arduous and boring. Let anyone, even in a modern, sloppy, cursive longhand, begin to copy out a full-length novel, and see how tedious it becomes!

Silence was demanded in the monastic scriptorium, not just for reasons of piety, but to ensure concentration. Once copying was under way, no-one was allowed to enter the room to indulge in idle conversation. The rule of silence required an elaborate series of signs or gestures to be used if references were needed: a cross for a psalter, a feigning of vomiting for "inferior" or secular works, and scratching the ear like a dog if a pagan work was needed. Lectionaries could be indicated by a pretense of wiping away grease, and a general inquiry by turning the imaginary pages of a book.

Copying might take place in a specific room in the monastery, or, as mentioned above, in the common cloisters. But though a particularly fortunate monk might perhaps be given a carrel of his own, the concept of taking the exemplar back to one's cell to copy it there in solitude seems to have been unknown. The brother in charge of the copying done in the monastery was called the *armarius*. His job it was to make the materials available, including the borrowing of exemplars from other institutions, and to maintain the rules of silence and accuracy—though the second of these must have been much more difficult to enforce than the first. Such a person, if he did his work intelligently, would almost inevitably develop a knowledge of where the "best" texts of certain books might be found, especially when defective copies in the monastery's possession needed to be emended by comparison with a different exemplar. One of the most famous of such *armarii* was Abbot Odo of Tournai, who helped to create and maintain the standards of one of the highest-regarded scriptoria of the Middle Ages, and would regularly seek out manuscripts from all over Europe in order to correct or improve troublesome readings in the documents owned by Tournai itself. The *armarius* would often function as librarian, and therefore be particularly aware of bibliographical gaps in the monastery's holdings.

Finally, it is still debated whether the *armarius* or some other delegated person actually dictated to the copyists, who might all be seated together in a group, or whether the scribes worked visually, with individual exemplars propped up before them. H. J. Chaytor claims that many errors can be explained only by oral methods of copying (14), which would certainly have been more efficient and were apparently used in Roman times, by notaries in the Middle Ages, and possibly in some of the commercial scriptoria of the later period, but not, it seems in Cassiodorus's Vivarium. Others have declared that oral methods were atypical, and Falconer Madan, for example, notes that when Alcuin used the term *dictare* in describing the scribe's work, he should be understood to have meant "compose" (according to the rules of the *dictamen*, or rhetoric) rather than "dictate" in our modern sense (41). It may be that even when "oral" errors appear to exist, they can be explained by the habit, which persisted until the Renaissance, of always reading aloud, even when alone. It is certainly the case that far greater numbers of errors can be traced through paleography (e.g., the confusion of minuscule *c* and *t* in several gothic scripts; see Chapter 5) than by an appeal to oral methods.

The Materials of Manuscript Books

A. *Form*

Early Chinese books, made from wood or bamboo strips and sewn together with cords, although of much greater antiquity than Western survivals—the earliest date from ca. 1300 B.C.—do not seem to have had any influence on the development of the Western book and are thus not dealt with here. Similarly, the earliest form of alphabetic writing in the West—on stones, wax tablets, potsherds, or metals—belongs properly to the realm of epigraphy and therefore lies outside the scope of this study. As noted earlier, the concern here is only with books in a rather conventional sense, that is, with a series of separate leaves either glued together to make a continuous roll or stitched together at their folds to make a codex. There is, however, some evidence that the first practical codices, usually for legal, military, or administrative purposes, were indeed on tablets, and that holes were bored through the two or three "leaves" to bind them together in a rough anticipation of the familiar codex form. These may even have been used as a model for the later codices of parchment or papyrus.

Certain historians of Greek civilization have claimed that papyrus books—that is, rolls—must have existed in Greece from the Homeric period (eighth to ninth centuries B.C.), with leather rolls going back to an even earlier time. However, the earliest surviving rolls of papyrus date from only the fourth century B.C. One of the most famous of survivals from this time is the carbonized papyrus roll discovered at Derveni in 1962, the oldest "book" from the Greek peninsula. But almost all rolls from this period are from Egypt, where a combination of a hot, dry climate and centuries of neglect have preserved perhaps thirty thousand, often having lain under heaps of accumulated garbage for hundreds of years. The very word for book in Greek, *biblion*, comes from the material *byblos* (papyrus), just as the Latin word for roll, *volumen*, has given us the modern "volume,"—as mentioned earlier. The famous Dead Sea Scrolls are, of course, in roll form, but the more recently discovered Nag Hammadi Gnostic Gospels are in codex. Both forms have been preserved by similar climatic and cultural conditions. (The word *volumen* is ultimately derived from the verb *evolvere*, "to roll up," and the *explicit* of a book means literally "it is unrolled," that is, it has been read, from *explicitus est liber*, and is not, strictly speaking, the closing equivalent of an *incipit*, or the opening words of a book.)

The roll form of books, associated almost wholly with papyrus (although the Dead Sea Scrolls are on leather), must have been very difficult to read for several reasons. Constructed of between twenty and fifty glued sheets, the average roll was perhaps thirty or forty feet in length—although some could go up to a hundred feet—and about nine or ten inches in height, with each column about three inches wide, giving approximately thirty-eight Greek letters per line. Since usually only one side was written on, and since referring to a specific passage was almost impossible, the roll was both a bulky and an inconvenient way of storing information. But it was certainly a textual improvement over the earlier, oral method of transmission—by actor, orator, rhapsode, or lecturer—which must have been the norm until perhaps the fifth century B.C.

It was in Rome that the wax tablet "books" mentioned above were replaced by the parchment leaves, or *membranæ*, referred to in Martial. There were several virtues to this new type of codex. First, a text written in codex could be easily cited, a convenience quickly realized by Christian authors and scribes, who perhaps took over the codex form under the influence of Roman lawyers: ease of reference was important to both legal and patristic scholarship. Second, the codex could receive writing on both sides of the leaf. Third, it was compact and could therefore store much longer texts. Fourth, it was more easily storable, requiring only shelves, not the elaborate system of boxes or pigeonholes needed for rolls. This last advantage does not, however, seem to have been fully exploited for some time, since the earliest illustrations of codices show them lying flat rather than stored upright. It was not until the end of the Middle Ages that the modern practice of storing codices spine outward with the title on the back rather than written on the leading edges was first used. Given the far greater number of rolls than codices that must have been required to store a typical text (it has been suggested that the traditional division of the Homeric poems into twenty-four books each was a direct reflection of the amount of material which could be stored on one roll), the claim of the Alexandrian library to have had 750,000 or more rolls must not be interpreted as meaning 750,000 *books*, or works, in our modern sense, but rather 750,000 sections of books.

The codex form of the book was taken up very quickly by Christians, and soon only pagan works were still written in roll form. Perhaps it was the advantage of having an entire Bible, or at least a testament or commentary, in one volume; perhaps, as already suggested, it was the ease of reference to particular sections for citation; or perhaps it was the sheer "difference" from the pagan form that attracted the Christians. Whatever the reasons, by the third century the roll was in decline, as was pagan literature itself, and by the early Middle Ages only legal documents, papal bulls, leases, charters, and suchlike continued to be written on rolls, in some instances surviving in this form until the nineteenth century. In fact, the continued use of so-called legal-size paper and the still-frequent stapling of smaller legal documents, such as contracts and leases, at the top rather than the side of the paper are testimony to the bibliographical conservatism of the law.

Both codices and such vestiges of rolls are now gradually succumbing to the new bibliographical medium of electronic storage. This change is dealt with in the section on printed books in the next chapter.

B. *Materials*

Papyrus: A "recipe" for making papyrus rolls from the plant growing near the banks of the Nile occurs in Pliny's *Natural History*. The inner ring of the plant was cut into long thin strips. These were laid out horizontally side by side, then backed with a transverse set of strips. It was because the front and back strips lay athwart each other (as they would have to be if a sheet were to be formed) that only one side could be used for writing: the vertical strips on the back would interrupt the flow of writing from side to side, and therefore only the horizontal strips on the front could bear a text. Soaked in Nile water (according to Pliny, though probably any water would have done), the papyrus exuded a glue that welded the strips together into a single, solid surface. After having been dried and hammered out, the papyrus could be polished with ivory or shell, and then glued into a continuous roll, or *scapus*—a standard commercial length. There were various grades of papyrus, depending upon the individual qualities of the plant and the part used in manufacture. The best grade was made from the central portion of the plant and was called *charta hieratica* (later changed to *charta Augusta*, in honor of the emperor); the grades descended through several stages, down to the cheapest commercial types of *charta emporetica*. The first sheet of the roll was called the *protokollon* and the last the *eschatakollion*. The *protokollon* could occasionally, especially in Rome, serve as the colophon was later to do in codices, listing the place of manufacture and the name of the papyrus maker.

Parchment: In its early days, the codex could be written on either papyrus or parchment, but although parchment was more expensive, the difficulties of bending and sewing the brittle papyrus into quires soon enabled the newer material to outpace its rival. Parchment has always been traditionally associated with Pergamum, in Asia Minor, the great intellectual and bibliographical competitor of Alexandria. Allegedly, Eumenes II of Pergamum was forced to turn to a new material for copying when the Ptolemies, in an attempt to prevent the Pergamanians from catching up with the riches of their library, forbade the export of papyrus from Egypt. Both Greek and Latin words for parchment—*pergamine* and *charta pergamena*, with the general sense of "materials from Pergamum"—emphasize this connection, and the story might just have some truth to it, though it is likely that parchment would have overtaken papyrus eventually without this commercial and academic quarrel. Although it was much more expensive than papyrus—it depended, after all, on the death of an animal rather than on the harvesting of a naturally abundant plant—it was much more durable, and therefore particularly attractive to Christians, who wanted to preserve the sacred scriptures. Parchment had the added advantage of being capable of re-use, with a rescraping of the surface to produce a palimpsest. The text on papyrus could be rewritten while the ink was still wet, when a rag could remove any errors, but as the ink dried, it became more difficult to alter the text. And papyrus could certainly not take the harsh scraping that was necessary to produce a genuine palimpsest.

Some bibliographers and codicologists would preserve a distinction between vellum (calf or lamb) and mere parchment (sheep or goat), but the terms are generally interchangeable today. The finest grade of vellum was "uterine," obtained from an aborted calf, since this was inevitably the most pliable and the whitest.

To prepare parchment, the skin was washed thoroughly, soaked in brine or lime, and de-haired, then stretched on a frame to be scraped, rubbed, and polished, first with pumice and then with chalk. In general, it would be reduced to about half its original thickness in this process. The leaf sizes were more or less fixed according to the type of book, with the largest for psalters or other volumes that would be read from a lectern and the smallest for portable books of hours. Charters, which were not usually folded and stitched into a codex, could be very large indeed. Although the actual hairs of the animal could be removed, the follicles remained, and this gave a peculiarly spotted appearance to the surface of the "hair" side. In order to keep the "opening" (a spread of two opposite pages) as esthetically consistent as possible, leaves were arranged so that the two "hair" sides would always face each other, as would the two "flesh" sides. Obviously, bibliographical "disturbances" in a book—where the scholar suspects that the physical makeup has been changed—can often be detected by inconsistencies in this practice.

Before the parchment could be written on, it was ruled. This was done by pricking the skin—first with an awl or spoked wheel, then with a dry-point stylus. Later, the dry-point stylus was abandoned in favor of ruling with lead. Since dry-point methods varied a good deal—Greek and Roman techniques with respect to hair- and flesh-side ruling were completely opposite—ruling can often be used to establish provenance.

Early parchment—i.e., up to ca. A.D. 1000—was sometimes stained or painted in rich colors, most often purple, and decorated with gold lettering. St. Jerome denounced this practice with some vigor, but for seven hundred years his denunciation was cheerfully ignored. The earliest parchment was probably somewhat coarser than that produced by the third or fourth centuries, when the new material had settled in as the dominant material. In later periods it varied significantly in quality, though certain general regional distinctions can be noted. For example, in southern Europe a very white polished surface was preferred. This looked "hard" and beautiful, but it had the unfortunate effect of resisting absorption, so that in time the ink might flake off. Northern Europe favored a softer, more pliant type of parchment.

While parchment almost totally displaced papyrus in the West, the traditional methods of making papyrus were still employed in Egypt as late as the tenth and eleventh centuries. And, according to some historical bibliographers, the two- or three-column arrangement of a codex page may owe something to the influence of the typical column widths used in writing on papyrus rolls.

Paper: Produced in China during the first century A.D. and made from a diverse range of materials, including rags, nets, bark, and general waste, paper was particularly suitable to the Chinese style of calligraphy (with strokes made by a brush of camel's hair) and had spread to Japan by the seventh century. In A.D. 751, it is reported that the Arabs repelled an attack by the Chinese in Samarkand and took prisoners who were skilled in papermaking. By the ninth century, Arab manuscripts were being made of paper, with flax as the major ingredient. Spreading to Egypt by the tenth century, and shortly afterward probably to Spain (though still imported), it was first made in Europe in the twelfth century and was known as *charta bombacina*, a name derived from the mistaken belief that paper was manufactured like silk (*bombax*). In 1246 there was a paper mill in Italy at Fabriano; in 1348 in France at Troyes, but the first paper mill in England was not set up until 1495, when John Tate of Hertford produced the paper used by Wynkyn de Worde to print the *editio princeps* (first edition) of Trevisa's *De proprietatibus rerum*. While Tate's mill does not seem to have been a commercial success, elsewhere the invention of printing stimulated the growth of the paper industry, for the new process of making books required abundant supplies of a relatively cheap material, although some early printed books—for example, copies of Gutenberg's 42-line Bible—were still produced on parchment.

Until the eighteenth century, all paper was made by hand. The major technical distinction of paper from both parchment and papyrus is that, although a "natural" product, it does not occur in nature in anything approaching its final useful form, for its raw materials must first be disintegrated and reintegrated in water. The "raw" rags were boiled to remove the fat and dye (apparently, storing them in a damp cellar for a month could produce the same effect), then beaten with mallets to a pulp, to which water was added to form a cream-like suspension. The pulp was poured into a rectangular frame crisscrossed with wires (the longitudinal ones being very thin and close together, the transverse heavier and farther apart). Over this was another frame, or "deckle," the height of which determined how much pulp there would be in the mold, and hence the thickness of the paper. The term "deckle" is often also used to refer to the rough edge of a sheet of handmade paper; if it still genuinely exists (rather than having been created artificially to imitate the hand-made look), then it proves that nothing has been cut down by binding. The pulp, shaken equally in all directions, was stretched out on a "couch," with intermediate layers of felt, until a "post," or one hundred sheets, had been attained. Applying pressure to squeeze out the water, the paper-maker would then hang the sheets over poles to dry. However, at this stage the paper would still be "waterleaf," or capable of absorbing moisture. In order to bear writing or printing in ink, it had to be sized in animal gelatin. (Machine-made paper is discussed in Chapter 3, in the section on later technical developments in the age of printing.)

One of the most important bibliographical results of the "wet" method of manufacture that the new writing material required was that the frame of wires on which the pulp rested produced an impression on the sheet of paper, since the pulp would be slightly thinner at the point of contact with the wires, and therefore a little more translucent. The effect of this on hand-made "laid" paper is to create so-called wire lines where the pulp rested on the thin, close wires and "chain lines" in the other direction. This characteristic can be important to the bibliographer, especially when considered in conjunction with the "watermark," the maker's device woven into the wires of the mold. Appearing in Italy in the late thirteenth century, the watermarks could be either trademarks of the paper manufacturer or an identification of the size of the mold employed. Since they could be used over a very long period, they are somewhat unreliable in dating. Various symbols, including hands, jugs, and crowns, were used as watermarks, and because they would have originally been in the top center of the sheet of paper as it came out of its mold, their position on the folded page of a book can usually indicate how many times the sheet has been folded, and hence the book's "format," an important term of identification in the description of printed books (see Chapter 4).

C. *Writing Instruments*

Different types of material need different types of instruments to make marks on them, and the relationship between the two will often determine the major characteristics of the letter-shapes. Chinese paper was particularly suitable to receive the brush-strokes of Chinese calligraphy; the chisel and stone of Roman inscriptions produced a very square, straight, and solid letter-form, with few curves; the combination of papyrus and reed pen promoted a more fluid style of writing (see Chapter 5 for illustrations of these differences). At another time and place, the Vikings of northern Europe made use of a stiff, angular runic alphabet without horizontals, since these would have been indistinguishable from the horizontal grain of the wood on which they were carved. For the wax and clay tablets which, bound together in several leaves, anticipated the book form of the parchment codex, a stylus was used, frequently with an oblique, rather than a flat or square, edge. The Greeks invented a hard reed pen (*calamus* or *arundo*) which, split at the top and kept continually sharp, was in great contrast to the Egyptians' preference for a soft reed, although both could be used for writing on papyrus.

From about the sixth century in Western Europe, the use of a quill (Latin *penna*, Old English *feder*, Middle English *penne*) became more common, displacing the reed for most purposes by the eleventh century. It used to be thought that the reed lost favor because of the growth of the angular gothic script, to which the reed was arguably less suited than the quill; however, the all-round versatility of the quill would probably have displaced the reed no matter what script was in vogue, for it dominated Western writing—on parchment, paper, or papyrus—until the invention of the steel pen in the early nineteenth century. Unlike papyrus, wax, clay, and other earlier writing materials, parchment had the great virtue of being amenable to writing instruments cut and held in various ways, straight or oblique, and it is probably fair to say that it influenced the letter-forms less than other writing surfaces and therefore encouraged greater variety of expression in the calligrapher.

The most common quill was a goose feather. If the feather was cut straight with a square edge and held obliquely, then the diagonal strokes would be the thinnest and the vertical strokes the thickest. If cut and held obliquely, then the diagonal strokes would be much thicker. If cut straight and held parallel to the ruling, then the horizontal strokes would be the thickest. The capacity of parchment to take any of these styles of nib and writing position contrasts markedly with the constrictions that would have been placed on a similar instrument by the glued strips of papyrus, which favored pen-strokes made in the same direction as the papyrus strip, and made it comparatively more difficult to write *across* the series of strips.

D. *Inks*

The basic constituents of ink are a pigment or dye and a liquid to carry it (the vehicle). Up until ca. A.D. 300, inks were usually of the carbon variety; that is, they consisted of lampblack or fine soot, which was then mixed with gum to give it body and water to give it fluidity. This ink was a strong, lustrous black, and since it was not proof against water, it could be fairly easily removed with a wet sponge: an advantage to the careless copyist but a problem for the librarian wishing to preserve the text permanently. (Examples of this type of ink were found in a still-liquid state at Pompeii.)

When parchment took over from papyrus as the characteristic writing medium, a more permanent variety of ink was required. This was produced by using iron-gall (sulphate of iron and "oak-apples" — growths, or "galls," on diseased trees), again mixed with gum and water. While the new ink was eminently suited to parchment as far as permanence was concerned, it was brownish rather than black and had the disadvantage of fading after a time and of occasionally eating into the parchment by the chemical action of gallic acid. The best-quality medieval ink was usually called *atramentum* and was blacker than the cheaper varieties. By the fourteenth century, copperas was often added, which with oxidation turned the ink greenish-blue, in contrast to the characteristically "faded" reddish-black inks of the previous century. Other colors were made from a number of different substances—animal, vegetable, and mineral. Most were fairly commonly available, but others were extremely rare. For example, the lapis lazuli employed in the making of the deepest blue pigments (and often associated with the Virgin Mary) came from Afghanistan. Used in the Lindisfarne Gospels, it must have been extremely expensive by the time it reached Anglo-Saxon England, as of course, was the gold, which was used to decorate manuscripts, either in powder form or as gold-leaf.

With the invention of printing (and the paper which was its normal medium), a type of ink had to be devised which would be absorbed by the paper without smudging under the pressure of the new process. The inks suitable for the generally hard, imporous parchment would not work for printing, and Gutenberg created a new ink made from lampblack with a varnish of linseed oil and resin. This ink was less fluid than writing ink—closer to the constituency of paint—and faster drying, both qualities necessary for successful printing.

The Format and Binding of Manuscript Books

A. *Format*

Rolls: The papyrus or parchment roll had, strictly speaking, no "format" in the bibliographical sense; it was simply rolled or unrolled and tied with cords. Some rolls might be stored in cylindrical caskets specially made for them, but there were no immediate "bindings" as such. However, different methods of joining the sheets themselves could be used. For example, if the sheets of each roll were glued head to foot to make one long roll, this was, in the Middle Ages, known as "Chancery" fashion; if they were sewn together side by side, this was "Exchequer" fashion. The only other distinction to be noted in describing a roll is the reference to its front or back, the *recto* and *dorse* respectively. But since rolls, especially of papyrus, were almost always written only on the front, or *recto*, it is rare for the bibliographer to have to deal with the *dorse*.

Codices: Once the codex was invented, there had to be some system of folding the parchment, or occasionally papyrus, which was to be bound into the book. Although theoretically it would have been easiest simply to stitch all the single sheets together, this would not make the stitching very secure, as the parchment would be more likely to rip under the pressure of opening the book. If the sheet of parchment was folded once and stitched along the fold, it was called a folio (a term which eventually became applied to the type of book in which such simple folds were found, and eventually to the typically large size of such books.) These folios were from the earliest medieval times usually not stitched individually—this would have made the back of the book very bulky with stitches and very difficult to open—but rather collected in gatherings or quires of fours. As noted earlier, these groups of four sheets were called *quaternions* (a word used later to mean rather vaguely a gathering of whatever makeup). The four sheets would therefore yield eight leaves, or "folios," and sixteen pages, although a system of pagination did not become common until the fifteenth century. Foliation, or the numbering of folios, was fairly consistently used from about the thirteenth century, and the bibliographical citation for the system is to distinguish between front—*recto* (or *r*)—and back—*verso* (or *v*). The numbers *1* and *2* may sometimes be used in place of *r* and *v*. However, the scribes themselves often numbered only the recto (corresponding to the right page of an opening, or the odd numbers of the modern pagination method), leaving the verso blank.

Because of the folding of sheets into gatherings of four or more leaves, a single sheet of parchment could contain sections of text from widely separated areas of the book being copied—as the illustration in Fig. 3 of an eight-folio gathering shows. This could involve problems in scribal distribution of labor, and in calculating the correct amount of text from the exemplar that would fit onto each leaf of the copy, since only two leaves of the copy would normally have continuous text. These issues are even more complex with printed books, and are therefore dealt with in more detail in Chapters 3 and 4.

If there were problems of space at the end of a gathering, the scribe had a great deal of latitude through the use of abbreviations. If there was not enough space for the whole text to be written out in full, he could use a greater density of abbreviations; if there was more space he could write out *in extenso*, or even fill the lines with decorative matter. Like the early printers, especially in vernacular languages in which spelling had not yet become standardized, the scribe could also vary the lengths of the words to be copied by adopting a longer or shorter form as required. All of this is not to suggest that the amount of text would not be calculated in advance and the appropriate number of folios assigned to it, but rather that it was less critical to the scribe working in a comparatively simple format than it was to become to the printer using multiple foldings. Under such systems as the *pecia*, the accurate counting-off of text per scribe and gathering would have been even more critical than in the monastic scriptoria— indeed, absolutely necessary to ensure the correct "fitting" of all the parts once they came in from the workers contracted to produce their individual sections.

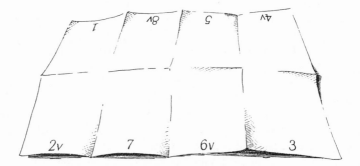

Fig. 3. Folding for a single gathering.

At need or desire, an additional work could always be added to the volume, for the concept of a book (with the exception of the Bible and other religious works) as a complete bibliographical and esthetic unit is a comparatively late one, and many medieval manuscripts are essentially "anthologies" rather than individual works. These anthologies were not always intended or written as such—by author or scribe—for materials already copied in a different gathering might be added to another series of quires previously stitched together at rebinding; but the very act of combining works in a single volume can tell us a good deal about the taste of the owner of the manuscript and about the conditions of the book trade. For example, several of the Latin manuscripts of Bartholomæus Anglicus's *De proprietatibus rerum* are lacking section fifteen, on geography, while several other manuscripts contain only this section. Obviously, the encyclopedia was not considered a sufficiently "complete" work to prevent what was essentially an extract being published as an independent volume. On the other hand, several of the manuscripts of Hoccleve seem to be conscious attempts to bring together his *opera omnia*, or complete works, for they contain numerous short poems in addition to the major works. The famous series of anonymous lyrics brought together in the Harley collection is another example of the same "anthologizing" tendency.

There was theoretically no reason why the system of folding could not be taken further, with more folds in the original sheet, resulting in smaller leaves and fewer total stitchings. If folded twice (instead of the once in a single fold to produce a folio), the sheet would yield four leaves, or eight pages (a quarto); if folded three times, then eight leaves, or sixteen pages (an octavo). But because of the comparative rigidity of parchment, these smaller sizes (and the technical terms describing their differences) are characteristic only of paper and therefore mostly of printing. In such smaller formats, the printer had a far greater problem than the *armarius* when it came to estimating the amount of space needed for a section of text, for a sheet could obviously be printed only as a flat piece of paper, not when it had already been made up into gatherings.

As previously noted, an attempt was always made to ensure that the "hair" side of the parchment matched with another "hair" side, and "flesh" with "flesh," in the opening of a manuscript book, and where this does not happen, there may have been a bibliographical "disturbance" in the book. Similarly, a single leaf with no "conjunctive," or attached leaf, on the "opposite" part of the gathering may indicate either an addition or an excision of a passage or work. All of these matters, which are generally of more concern to analytical bibliographers than to codicologists, are discussed at greater length in the next chapter. However, it is important to emphasize that while the analytical bibliography of printed books has of necessity developed an extremely sophisticated technical means of evaluating these physical features, codicologists are just as much concerned with problems of the book as physical artifact—hence the link in title between this chapter and the next.

B. *Binding*

Once the quires had been stitched, they then had to be collected together to make a single codex. As some assistance to the binder, manuscripts might contain either "catchwords" (the first word of the next leaf or gathering written on the last page of the previous leaf or gathering to ensure continuity) or "signatures"—a series of symbols, usually following the alphabet, with added numbers (e.g., Ai, Aii, Aiii, etc.), to serve the same purpose. However, the use of signatures in manuscript books was not as uniform as it was to become in printed books, where it was absolutely essential for the correct makeup. Both of these practices are therefore discussed in greater detail in the section on printing (Chapters 3 and 4).

The earliest fully bound extant codices (i.e., where the contents are still an integral part of the original binding) are the so-called Gnostic Gospels found at Nag Hammadi in Egypt. Of the thirteen volumes, eleven are in the original covers. Written on papyrus, they are in single-quire codices of up to seventy-six leaves (not in quaternions, as was later to be the norm). As Paul Needham observes in his account of these early bindings, the Coptic method of binding was essentially similar to stapling a modern single-quire pamphlet (7). In the Coptic method four holes were made through the folded quires, through which a leather thong was passed and then secured to the cover-spine. The boards (covers) of the codex were attached to the made-up book by "pastedowns," or sheets of papyrus linking the boards directly to the outer quires of the book. The more typical medieval method was to use cords attached directly to the boards, through which holes were bored for the purpose, which made for a more secure joining of board and quire. The individual quires were stitched not directly to each other but to cords running at right angles to the folds of the quires. This meant that the strain when the book was opened was largely passed on to the sturdier cords rather than to the thinner quire threadings, giving a much more solid construction.

The boards themselves were normally made of wood and covered with leather, which could be highly decorated. These decorations can be used to establish the provenance of the contents, too—if the work has not been rebound. While Cassiodorus in his account of the activities of the Vivarium speaks of the necessity of the monastery's books being "clothed in fine garments" and of the hiring of skilled artisans to accomplish this, it is unlikely that his books or those in most medieval monasteries of a later date had particularly fine or expensive bindings on any but their most public or ceremonial works, such as psalters. The sumptuous medieval "treasure bindings" are really in a class apart, for they probably descend from the "consular diptychs" of the Roman period and were hardly bindings in the modern sense. Frequently the motifs figured in the wrought ivory and precious metals and jewels had comparatively little to do with the contents of the books themselves. They were added to the pre-existing basic binding and were therefore capable of what Needham discreetly calls "migration." In fact, it is rare today for any book before the fifteenth century to be still bound between its original covers, and one of the problems of the bibliographer of manuscript books (codicologist) is, of course, to discover what happened as a result of rebinding: what was possibly lost, what added, what cut down.

In an introductory chapter like this, I cannot discuss at length the complex subject of binding decoration, with its blind and gold tooling, its designs of *dentelles* and *fleurons*, its various identifiable styles, often named after a famous book collector (Grolier, Harley, Maioli, Jansenist). But it is important to note that a description of both the type of leather used, its quality and state, and of the decoration, is a necessary part of manuscript description, which is covered in greater detail in Chapter 4. Two fairly representative styles of binding are shown in Fig. 4 (an ornate, highly individual Italian binding of the early Renaissance, with a fanciful version of a cardinal's hat as its centerpiece, presumably indicative of ownership) and Fig. 5, an English "trade binding," more practical (note the metal clasps), with only minimal decoration, and with little sign of having been made for a specific bibliophile.

Fine—or less than fine—bindings are one of the features of bookmaking that carry over from the manuscript to the printed book, for it was not until the late eighteenth or early nineteenth centuries that it became the norm for virtually all books to be sold in publishers' bindings. Until then, while some commercial booksellers would distribute

Fig. 4. A Renaissance bookbinding.

books already bound, a book purchaser would typically buy books gathered and sewn, and would then have his own binding added to the book, which (as explained in Chapter 3) thus preserved the look of the manuscript book. The practice also allowed a collector to have uniform volumes in his personal library.

Script in the Age of Print

I emphasize this sort of continuity between manuscript and printed book because the inevitably classical and medieval concentration in this chapter might otherwise suggest that manuscripts simply disappeared with the invention of printing. On the contrary, while the ef-

Fig. 5. An English "trade binding."

ficiency and comparative uniformity of print was attractive to authors with books seeking wide circulation (political and religious works, history, philosophy, science, and most literature), manuscript dissemination was still favored for more intimate or limited (or controlled) "publication." As is well known, barely half of Shakespeare's plays had appeared in print before the First Folio collected edition in 1623; the others remained in manuscript, circulating only among players, prompters, and the like. It is conceivable—though obviously unthinkable for our bardolatrous culture—that without the Folio of Heminge and Condell we might otherwise have scattered and incomplete records of half the canon of our major dramatist, for only *Pericles* has been added to that canon independently of the Folio edition. Another pertinent example from the same period is "coterie" poetry, typically

lyric, sophisticated, and erotic, which, as its name suggests, circulat-
ed at first among a small group of "cognoscenti." That the very
medium of such circulation was different in kind from print can be
shown in the varying punctuation of Donne's poems in manuscript
and in the 1633 first edition (Pebworth). In the former, the punctuation is "rhetorical," that is, it gives visual instruction to the reader on
how the poems should be breathed and phrased as spoken aloud, in
the manner of most medieval manuscript punctuation. In the latter, it
provides guidance to the syntactic relations of the sentence—a more
intellectual, visual, and personal system than the semi-public oral
expectations of rhetorical punctuation. Syntactic punctuation is, of
course, the system we are now used to in printed books and which we
regard as "normal," often introducing it back into texts where it is
quite inappropriate. (See Harold Love, *Scribal Publication*, for a full
critical and historical analysis of seventeenth-century manuscript dissemination.)

So manuscript culture did not end with the printed book, although
the two media were clearly different in mode and expectation. What
did change was that the manuscript *book* as the preferred means of
transmission of culture gradually yielded to the printed book. Manuscripts in the sense of "collected papers" even proliferated during the
print period, or at least, the evidence of their survival is greater. One
of the chronological ironies of textual scholarship is that virtually
nothing in the hands of medieval English authors survives, but that as
we move down into the nineteenth and twentieth centuries, we are
swamped by the personal documentary materials—drafts of poems and
fiction, memoranda, letters, diaries and journals, corrected proofs.

In the later periods, there are too many manuscripts rather than too
few, for Hoccleve's "shopping list," in which he reminds himself to
buy clean linen, is rare for a medieval author, whereas we have a su-
perfluity of such personal items for many authors of the last couple of
centuries, much of the material still lying uncatalogued in the vaults
of academic and scholarly libraries. Thomas Wolfe's voluminously
stuffed packing cases at the Houghton library, the 11,500 Gertrude
Stein manuscripts at the Beinecke, the millions of items by contemporary authors at the University of Texas (Nabokov, Greene, Kerouac,
Arthur Miller, Tennessee Williams, etc.)—all of these manuscript
riches and many, many more are the typical products of the "post-
manuscript" period, and they have engendered much polite and impo-
lite debate among textual scholars on their literary value and validity:
is a corrected proof "better" evidence than a fair copy or a draft man-

uscript or a copy in a letter or journal, or are they all of equal status? But these manuscript remains are not usually manuscript *books*, except in a purely adventitious manner, and thus fall outside the scope of this chapter on the material book.

Similarly, as Chapter 5 shows, scribes (and therefore manuscripts) flourished in such fields as law, business, and commerce for centuries after the introduction of printing, disappearing only with the advent of the typewriter and later the word processor. Which brings us to one last *caveat* in this survey of the manuscript book: as electronic storage and transmission have replaced scribes and print, we are now beginning to lose the manuscript evidence of those drafts and revisions and memoranda of the last couple of centuries. Unless separate hard copy is kept of every stage of a poem's or novel's gestation and development on the computer, as textual scholars we receive only "fair copy," the final intentions of an author, for publication and release. In other words, the electronic age is beginning to look very much like the classical and medieval manuscript age in terms of its access to the finished product alone rather than to the process of composition. The pre-book manuscript riches of recent times may turn out to have been a brief anomaly in the history of textual evidence, as we return to the more limited transmission of an earlier period, when the manuscript book proper was the medium for such transmission.

3

Making the Text:

Bibliography of Printed Books

The Elements of Printing: Some Definitions and Problems

Like many of the important terms covered in this manual ("bibliography," "book," "text"), the word "printing" can be somewhat ambiguous. In the West, the term is most often associated with Gutenberg's invention and can be regarded as consisting of three separate components: a relief type (letterpress), movable parts (the type pieces), and a press to imprint the negative impression of the type onto paper to produce a positive text. This restricted definition would exclude fifteenth-century wooden block books, for though they did have relief, they had no movable parts, since each page was cut as a single block. It would also exclude modern computer typesetting, which has neither relief nor movable parts. But while the three components are unsatisfactory to cover all types of material that we would conventionally accept as "printed," they make a useful touchstone for charting the early development of letterpress printing in Europe.

All three had existed before Gutenberg. Wood blocks in relief had been made by the Chinese for at least seven hundred years, but without employing a mechanical press—the paper was simply rubbed from behind with a dry brush. Separate or movable parts had also been anticipated in China from the eleventh century, and later in Korea, where types dating from the fifteenth century are still extant. And screw presses—for the production of oil, wine, linen, or other agricultural, domestic, or manufactured products—had been in use in Europe since Roman times. Evidently Gutenberg "invented" very little! But it was he who brought the three elements together. It was he, too, who made the act of printing practicable by creating an ink suitable for the new process and by devising the matrix, the female "die" of a letter made by punching brass with a relief form of the letter desired, from which any number of replicas, or "types," could be cast, using an alloy of tin and antimony, which could produce types accurately.

Since some of the necessary elements of printing existed in China long before they appeared in the West, it is tempting to believe that the idea of printing followed the same route as the introduction of paper—from China via the Arabs. But while Chinese wood blocks undoubtedly traveled the camel routes from the East and were generally available in Europe before Gutenberg, there is no evidence that the combination of the three essential elements—letterpress, movable type, and the screw press—was anything but a Western invention.

Printing will be dealt with here under two headings: first, the story of the early European printers and the spread of printing as a business and as an art; second, the technical history of the actual process of printing. The first topic will concentrate almost entirely on the initial two or three hundred years, for by the end of the eighteenth century, the publisher had taken over from the printer virtually all decisions as to format, print run, type, illustrations, etc., so that the history of nineteenth- and twentieth-century publishing thus lies outside the scope of this book, which is primarily concerned with printing as a technical medium rather than as a commercial enterprise. It is significant that in most modern books, the printer is rarely even mentioned, and certainly not on the title-page. Only small private presses continue the tradition of the printer as publisher, compositor, designer, illustrator, and sometimes even author, and these presses are therefore discussed in the section on typography (Chapter 6).

Conventionally, the term "printing" has been seen as a process involving the cutting in relief of letter-forms (types) and the transference of the image by ink to the flat surface of a sheet of paper. But this form of printing, known as letterpress, is only one of three basic methods, for the image may instead be incised into wood, metal, or some other surface (an intaglio process, as in engraving) or may be transferred planographically (as with the various photographic, chemical, and xerographic processes). In fact, the strict limitation of printing to letterpress, while it would do justice to much of the history of the art and science, would hardly represent the conditions of the trade today, where very little printing is still done by this method. In modern printing, the photographer and the computer keyboard operator have taken over from the compositor for most mass-produced books.

With the decline of letterpress has come the concomitant decline of movable type, so that this element too is no longer necessary to the definition of printing. Everybody used to know exactly what printing meant, but it is probably better these days to assume only that it should involve the transfer of an image onto a receiving material. Such experimental modern methods as spray printing, although done by machine rather than by hand, come perilously close to the process of writing, for the ink is sprayed directly onto the paper in the desired letter-shape, without type, without photography, without intaglio—in fact, without any recognizable "source" at all, except for the operator's copy-text. Even a simple device like a typewriter (as its very name suggests) betrays a similar ambiguity; it can be looked upon as a one-person printing press, for it certainly uses relief types and transfers an image by ink and some pressure. But the typewriter was a mechanical replacement not for professional book scribes (they had already been put out of business by Gutenberg) but for handwriting clerks, who now used keyboards instead of pens. Typewriting does not (without carbon paper) produce multiple copies from one original as the printing press had done, and is therefore not basically more efficient than a scribe, except in producing the first copy. The typewriter's great virtue is uniformity, and therefore legibility. Every stroke of an individual letter-key will produce an identical image without scribal idiosyncrasy. The same is true of its derivative, the computer printer, which may use relief (daisy-wheel and dot-matrix printers) or planography (laser printers).

Therefore, although we may not know what printing is, we can certainly recognize it when we see it. Or can we? Shown photo facsimiles of an incunable (a fifteenth-century book) in gothic type and a "textura" manuscript (see Chapter 5 for an illustration) produced in the late Middle Ages, many untrained eyes would not be able to tell which was printed and which written by hand. Closer bibliographical investigation would determine which was which, but the early printers certainly tried to make their books look as much like manuscripts as possible.

So where can the distinctions be made? If the term "handwriting" is limited to the direct reproduction of an image by the use of a non-mechanical object (quill, pen, reed, chisel) held in the hand, then it is at least possible to know what printing is *not*. The first remove from this direct reproduction by hand would be the cutting of a model in relief and the manual inking and/or manual pressing of this relief onto a receiving material. This method was used from the earliest times on seals and coins, and can therefore be regarded as the prototype of the making of the female dies from which the actual type was cast. A related method of printing, with paper and brush, was used in China, by tradition from the year A.D. 594. An image in relief would be inked, and then a piece of paper pressed against it from behind with a soft brush. The Chinese also engraved in stone, as a means of ensuring the textual incorruptibility of the writings of Confucius. The earliest surviving printed item is a Buddhist charm from Japan, dating from the late eighth century and said to have been printed from metal plates in an "edition" of over a million copies. Furthermore, from the eleventh century, the Chinese were experimenting with movable types cut from clay and later from tin. The Koreans were using metal type in the fourteenth century, but the problems of cutting an entire font for any ideographic script were obviously enormous.

It used to be thought that block books (see Fig. 6), made up from a number of blocks, or designs and texts cut into wood or metal, preceded books printed with genuinely movable type. But there is no datable block book before Gutenberg, and while the basic idea of printing from blocks very likely antedated the Mainz printers, it is probable that block books and printed movable-type books existed side by side in the mid-fifteenth century. Individual blocks (i.e., not made up into books) must have been available earlier, for there is a Saint Christopher block picture dated 1423 (Fig. 7). But block *books* are quite another matter.

In addition to movable type, the other necessary components of Gutenberg's "invention" were the press, the paper, the ink, and the adjustable mold capable of holding matrices for both wide letters like W and thin ones like *i*. These matrices were probably made of lead in the fifteenth century, and later of copper. The male "punches" which formed a mirror impression in the soft metal of the die evolved naturally out of the goldsmith's art (Gutenberg was a goldsmith, and many early printers had similar backgrounds). Punches of copper, or even wood, could be used to form an impression on lead dies, but iron or steel would have had to have been employed once the matrix was made from copper. The point is that the punch had to be of a harder material than the matrix.

The legend goes that Gutenberg first got the inspiration for a printing press from watching a wine press in operation. But he would have had any number of available models, all of them with a considerable history. Presses had been used since ancient times, not only

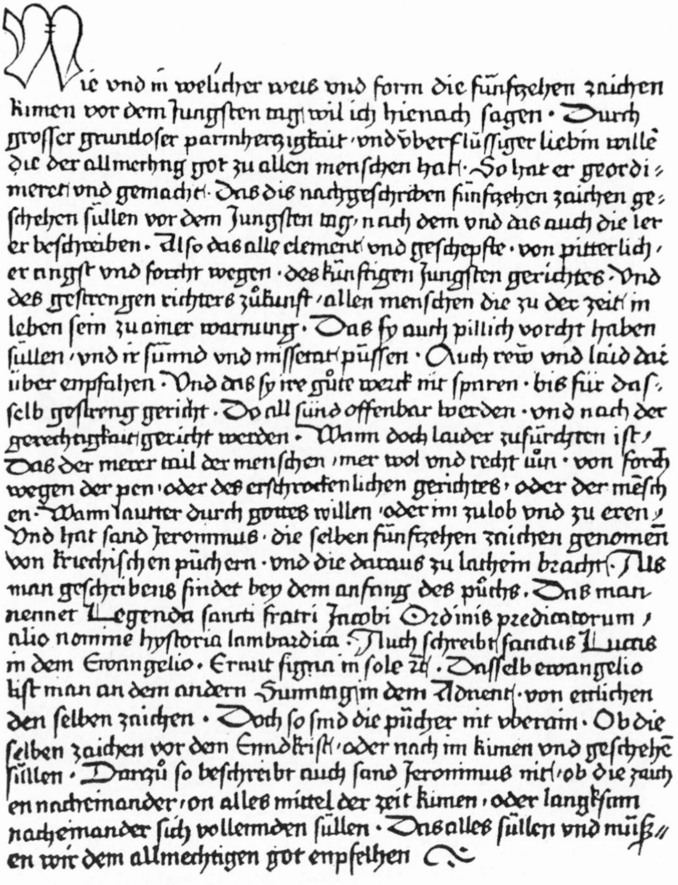

Wie vnd in welicher weis vnd form die fünfzehen zaichen
kimen vor dem Jungsten tag wil ich hienach sagen · Durch
grosser grundloser parmherzigkait vnd vberflüssiger liebin wille
die der allmechtig got zu allen menschen hat · So hat er geordi-
meret vnd gemachet · Das die nachgeschriben fünfzehen zaichen ge-
schehen sullen vor dem Jungsten tag nach dem vnd aus auch die ler-
er beschreiben · Also das alle element vnd geschepfte · von pitterlich
er angst vnd forcht wegen · des künftigen jungsten gerichtes Vnd
des gestrengen richters zukunft allen menschen die zu der zeit im
leben sein zu ainer warnung · Das sy auch pillich vorcht haben
sullen vnd ir sünd vnd misserat püssen · Auch rew vnd laid dar-
über empfahen · Vnd das sy ire güte werck mit spuren · bis für das
selb gestreng gericht · Do all sünd offenbar werden · vnd nach der
gerechtigkait gericht werden · Wann doch lauder zufürchten ist
Das der merer tail der menschen mer wol vnd recht tün · von forch
wegen der pein oder des erschrockenlichen gerichtes oder der mensch
en · Wann lauter durch gottes willen oder im zulob vnd zu eren
Vnd hat sand Jeronimus die selben fünfzehen zaichen genomen
von kriechischen püchern · vnd die daraus zu lathein bracht · Als
man geschribens findet bey dem anfang des püchs · Das man
nennet Legenda sancti fratri Jacobi Ordinis predicatorum
alio nomine hystoria lambardica · Nuch schreibt sanctus Lucas
in dem Euangelio · Erut signa in sole etc · Dasselb ewangelio
list man an dem andern Suntag im dem Advent · von etlichen
den selben zaichen · Doch so sind die pücher mit vberain · Ob die
selben zaichen vor dem Enndkrist oder nach im kimen vnd geschehe
süllen · Darzü so beschreibt auch sand Jeronimus mit ob die zaich
en nacheinander on alles mittel der zeit kimen oder langksam
nacheinander sich vollermden süllen · Das alles süllen vnd müß-
en wir dem allmechtigen got empfelhen

Fig. 6. German block book, ca. 1450.

for wine but for oil, linen, and other commercial purposes. The difference in Gutenberg's press was that a single sharp impression was
needed, as opposed to the continuous pressure required in earlier
models for other uses. The screw in a printing press had to recoil, or
"unscrew," quickly after the impression had been made, rather than
being held in place for a specific time like the screws on other types
of press.

Despite a prejudice against its lack of durability, paper was being
used for manuscript books in the West for two centuries before Gutenberg, because of its comparative cost (see Chapter 2 on manuscript
books). But while paper might have made manuscripts slightly less
expensive, it was absolutely essential for the successful introduction

Fig. 7. Earliest dated wood block (1423).

of printing, which required a constant supply of a relatively cheap material that could be produced in sufficiently large quantities. Printing worked as an economic proposition only if many pages could be pulled from a single form of type. Although early editions—typically about 250 copies in the fifteenth century—are very small by modern standards, without paper even this number could not have been printed, and the new process would have foundered for want of a suitable receiving material.

Finally, printing needed a new, special ink that would adhere to the metal types, withstand pressure, not smudge on the paper, and dry

Fig. 8. Earliest known depiction of a printing press (1499), a *Danse macabre*, with compositor, pressman, and bookseller being carried off by Death.

quickly, so as not to interrupt the printing sequence. As noted in the section on manuscripts (Chapter 2), the ink used for manuscript copying and for wood blocks was unsuitable for printing, so Gutenberg created an ink from lampblack mixed with a varnish of linseed oil and resin.

Press, paper, mold, and ink: only the last two can be described accurately as Gutenberg's invention, and even the ink had a prototype in Flemish painting. It was Gutenberg's genius to bring them all together, though there is little doubt that, given the availability of the elements, given the increased literacy which produced a larger reading public, and given the propaganda values of mass-produced books for church and state, some form of printing by movable type would certainly have evolved eventually had Gutenberg never existed.

Characteristics of Early Printers

That Gutenberg is not mentioned by name in several of the incunabula catalogues described in Chapter 1, but occurs only as "The printer of the 42-line Bible," illustrates the first of the major charac-

Fust and Schöffer   *Nicolaus Jenson, succs*   *Aldus Manutius*

Johann Froben   *Lucantonio Giunta*   *Erhard Ratdolt*

Christopher Plantin   *William Caxton*   *Bernhard C. Breitkopf*

Firmin Didot   *William Morris*   *Joaquim Ibarra*

Fig. 9. Printers' devices, including those of Caxton, Manutius, Fust and
Schoeffer, Jenson, and Plantin.

teristics of the early printers: they are often anonymous, or at least so
in the books produced by their shops. Caxton and some other early
printers were known by their devices (see Fig. 9), but others remain
mute in their books. That is, just as scribes rarely signed their names
in colophons, so many incunabula contain no hint as to where, or by
whom, the book was printed. Early printed colophons tended to be
similar in content and appearance to those in manuscript books, with

information on the date of completion, the excellence of the work (although the "weariness" topos of the scribe seems to have been abandoned), and perhaps the place of manufacture. They might also make some reference to the very novelty of printing itself, as does the first known dated colophon, in Gutenberg's *Catholicon* of 1460, which unfortunately for us omits the name of the printer—the very piece of information we would most like to have. No surviving printed work from Gutenberg's shop bears his name.

The second important characteristic of the early printers was that during the initial spread of the art and trade of printing through Europe, they were often (at least from the point of view of their adopted countries) foreigners—except, of course, in Germany, where printing had begun. Printing was one of the fastest-traveling of human inventions, moving outward from Germany via itinerant craftsmen and tradesmen: Sweynheym and Pannartz in Italy; Martin Crantz, Ulrich Gering, and Michael Freiburger at the Sorbonne; the Ravensberg agents Lambert Palmart, John of Salzburg, and Paul Hurus in Spain; Johann Trechsel, Johann Klein, and Sebastian Greyff in Lyon. The Frenchman Nicolaus Jenson worked in Venice, and his compatriot Plantin in the Low Countries. The Estienne family moved back and forth from France to Switzerland as political conditions changed. Even Aldus Manutius, although an Italian (Theobaldo Manucci), was to the Venetians a "foreigner," since he came from Rome. And while Caxton was obviously English (both in character and in his choice of vernacular literature for his press), he received his training as a printer and published his first books abroad. Dietrich Rohde (Theodoric Rood) at Oxford, John Siberch (of Siegberg, near Cologne) at Cambridge, and Wynkyn de Worde (of Worth in Alsace) at Westminster and later London were all Germans, and Richard Pynson at London was French.

This foreign involvement in, or ownership of, native printing could cause some bad feelings, for while foreign printers were specifically exempted from an English act of 1484 which otherwise forbade imported labor (printing was apparently just too important a trade, both to government and to church, to suffer restriction, and was unavoidably dependent upon skills learned abroad), when the act was repealed in 1534, the foreign printers were included in those classes banned from practicing in England.

But perhaps the single most important characteristic of the early printers was that they were not just printers. Today a publisher will employ or commission designers, compositors, printers, and binders as separate vendors to produce a book and will have ultimate authority over all aspects of the book's appearance, contents, and distribution. The first printers, however, not only printed the books, they selected which books were to be published, they edited the work (frequently in collaboration with some of the greatest scholars of their day); they might commission, translate, or even write the books themselves; they cut their own type, had their own foundries; sometimes they even made their own paper. They designed the books, advertised them, and sold them. There is some argument as to whether they commonly bound the books themselves. Some seem to have bound only copies intended for local distribution and "published" others in sheets, with the binding to be specially commissioned by the purchaser.

As printing spread, all of these various activities began to become specialized enterprises (see Fig. 10). Apart from the paper manufacturers, the type-cutters were the first to assert an independence, for it became too expensive for individual printers to have their own foundries.

Fig. 10. Type-founder, printer, and book-binder.

Claude Garamond in Paris and Jacob Sabon in Lyon were the first type-cutters to achieve fame without also being printers, although others, notably Nicholas Wolf of Brunswick, had set up as type-founders in Lyon before turning to printing. Garamond, however, was never a printer, and his entire career was devoted to just one stage of what had formerly been the printer's responsibilities.

While conditions varied from country to country and from press to press, it was in general the booksellers who next grew independent, becoming in effect what we would call publishers. The first recognizable non-printing publisher was probably Johann Rynmann of Augsburg (d. 1522), who never printed a book himself, preferring to hire others to handle the technical production and instead concentrating on distribution and sales.

Until the end of the seventeenth century, the three main responsibilities—printing, publishing, and marketing (where they were still performed by different people)—could appear together on a title-page, according to the formula: "Printed by x (printer) for y (publisher), and are to be sold by z (bookseller)." This implied, of course, that the bookseller was a direct offshoot of the publisher, or vice versa, and that the printer was essentially the manufacturer providing the materials for their trade. Eventually, with the growth of a large retail market in books, the mention of a specific bookseller became unnecessary, and both bookseller and printer were dropped from the title-page, leaving the publisher in control.

Another important characteristic of the early printers was that they tended to be middle-class tradesmen or craftsmen. Manuscript copying had become a trade by the early fifteenth century anyway, and a trade which had begun to show a movement toward mass production. Vespasiano da Bisticci had over fifty scribes in his commercial scriptorium in Florence, and this tendency obviously helped to create, and in part to satisfy, the taste for books on which printing was to capitalize. Whenever we know anything about the social background of early printers, it usually shows roots in the merchant middle class. Caxton was the head of the English "nation" of merchants at Bruges; Gutenberg was, as noted, a goldsmith; and Fust was a banker-lawyer. But printers could be elevated in society as a result of the success of their businesses. Caxton had the patronage of nobility both on the Continent and in England; Koberger married into the Nuremberg aristocracy and served on the city council; and very occasionally a printer-publisher has in modern times been knighted, as were Allen Lane of Penguin Books and Stanley Unwin of the publishing house bearing his name (George, Allen, and Unwin).

Since printing was a commercial business, there were in the early days rarely any amateurs—spiritual descendants of that bishop who had proudly signed himself *scriba*. Precisely because it was a vulgar "business," in fact, some aristocratic book collectors refused to allow the presumptuous new method of manufacture into their libraries. It was the binders, with their ability to make the printed book look indistinguishable from the manuscript book on the shelf, and to cater to the sumptuous tastes of their patrons, who finally overcame the prejudice against printed books as a "lowly" form of art. As an indication of aristocratic snobbery toward the printed book, and as a magnificent, but ultimately futile, attempt to reverse history, Wendelin de Spire's 1472 printed edition of Appian's *Civil Wars* was turned back into a manuscript by a diligent and very talented scribe on a special commission from Cardinal Giuliano della Rovere.

But although printing was the first mass-produced mechanical commercial activity, it should not be assumed that all early printers were financially successful. The general history of early printing is the history of financial failures. Even the most productive of printing houses were left with large stocks of unsold books, and while the last few decades of the fifteenth century show printing springing up in hundreds of small towns all over Europe, by the centenary of the invention it had become concentrated in a few large towns where a substantial reading public could be found. The smaller towns, where new printing presses had been so eagerly set up, could not provide the large market which mass production required, and press after press failed. Even Mainz, the birthplace of printing, could not support a press once Gutenberg and his immediate successors had gone out of business, and it was supplanted by Nuremberg as the printing center for southern Germany. Of small German university towns, only Wittenberg (which had the good fortune to number the prolific author Martin Luther among its citizens) was able to sustain a press throughout the period.

Itinerant peddlers (*colporteurs*) could carry books out to the provinces, but the predominance of large cities—Paris, Nuremberg, Venice, Rome, and London—was unassailed. Even the larger firms were not immune from financial risks. The mighty Estienne organization, despite its longevity and generally careful management, never fully recovered from the printing expenses of the superb five-volume folio edition of the *Thesaurus linguæ græcæ* in 1572; and it did not take long for Caxton's successor Wynkyn de Worde to realize that financial security lay in the cheap grammar books and large public of London rather than in the rich tastes, expensive folios, and small print-runs of the court at Westminster. Leonard Holle of Ulm, the printer of Ptolemy's *Cosmographia* in 1482, and Gunther Zainer of Augsburg, who produced the first illustrated Bible in 1475 and a sumptuously illustrated *Legenda aurea* with 131 woodcuts in 1471–72, were only two in a long line of printer-publishers who went bankrupt in the fifteenth century, having overestimated the capacity of the reading public to repay the large capital investment which printing required. The problem was that the publisher needed to tie up considerable sums of money in advance and often could not expect a return for many years, as book sales—particularly of lavish volumes—were typically sluggish. The over-expansion of university presses in the mid-twentieth century, and the subsequent decline in demand as university populations decreased and the prices of books soared, offers a parallel to the inherent dangers of the enthusiastic optimism of the first practitioners of the art five hundred years before.

But there was equally no doubt that printing as a medium was a demonstrable success. It is estimated that some twenty million books were printed before 1500 (many more, of course, than all the manuscript books made since the dawn of writing). Venice was the most successful center, accounting for 1.125 million copies of some 4,500 editions. In the same period, there were ninety-nine editions of Thomas à Kempis, ninety-four editions of the Latin Vulgate Bible, plus many vernacular translations (e.g., fifteen German translations, eleven Italian). In the sixteenth century, the works of Luther were phenomenally successful: there were approximately four hundred editions of his translation of the Bible published in his lifetime, including sixty-six pirated editions which appeared within two years of its completion. Like all other authors of the period, Luther did not, of course, receive any royalties on the sales.

According to a bishop writing at the end of the fifteenth century, as a result of the invention of printing, books now cost only one-fifth of their former price. Books were available almost everywhere—even in grocery stores—and they had become a common property, which made them both useful to authority and a potential danger to it (as Luther's tracts had shown). Both ecclesiastical and secular powers were quick to realize the importance of the discovery and to attempt to control it. The private press of Louis XIII of France became in the seventeenth century the Imprimerie royale and further continued the tendency for printing (and other cultural and social phenomena) in France to be centralized and licensed by government. On 6 July 1618, Louis issued an ordinance with the intention of bringing all printing and the entire French book trade under royal regulation. In England, the Stationers Company (although theoretically an independent guild of craftsmen), had by the late sixteenth century, through its licensing of publication, become in effect an organ of the government to track down unauthorized, and possibly seditious, works.

The success of printing therefore ensured a continual struggle between the printer and the censor. The most famous example of this contest was certainly the Roman Catholic *Index librorum prohibito-*

rum, first published in 1559 on orders of Pope Paul IV and until 1966 the arbiter of Catholic reading. But most secular and ecclesiastical rulers have tried to control printing in one way or another, though none with the comprehensive pretensions of the *Index* or of modern totalitarian regimes. Henry VIII anticipated the *Index* by some thirty years when, in 1529, he published a list of banned books and, nine years later, refused to allow English books that had been printed abroad (and were obviously more likely to contain sedition or heresy) to be imported into England. Augsburg was eventually shut down as a printing center because of pressures from the Imperial censor, and Lyon, as a center of Protestantism, suffered a similar fate in France.

By the end of the eighteenth century, the Frankfurt Book Fair, at one time the major market in the European book world, had been so constricted by Jesuit censorship that its pretensions to being able to represent the international book trade were completely untenable. The decline of Augsburg and Frankfurt may be compared with the general success of printing in the Netherlands, where a relatively liberal administration allowed many books to be published there which would not have been tolerated elsewhere. Dutch printers, sometimes using a fictitious imprint for safety, published works by Hobbes, Aretino, Montesquieu, and Rousseau which could not have been produced with impunity in their authors' native lands.

The problems of Frankfurt and the *Index* are still with us, as vetting of Western publications in various Eastern European book fairs so potently showed—until very recently, anyway. And there is no doubt that UNESCO'S on-again, off-again attempts to issue "passes" to "responsible" journalists (i.e., those who report only the official government line), and the Nixon administration's attempt to invoke "prior restraint" in the famous Pentagon Papers case, would both have been fit targets for the most eloquent defense of "the liberty of unlicensed printing," Milton's *Areopagitica*, published (without license, of course) in 1644.

As a postscript to the previous era of hand-written books, and as an unfortunate comment on the success of the new medium, there is the sad account of Rolfe Hegge, who in 1663 noted, "Since the art of printing was invented, whereby man after a more cheap way could attaine to some superficial Learning; old manuscripts were bequeathed to the *Mothes*; and *Pigens*, and *Jackdaws* became the only students in Church libraries." Manuscripts became superfluous, useless, unappreciated, once their contents had appeared in a printed edition. The record of destruction perpetrated by the scholar-printers who thought they were preserving the classical heritage is quite appalling. Far from enhancing the textual transmission, the printing of texts edited by humanist scholars often robbed textual criticism of irreplaceable manuscript sources. When a manuscript book had to be produced by long, arduous hours in the monastic or commercial scriptorium, there was at least some sense of its value as a product of much labor. But when a text could be printed in hundreds of copies by the new craft, the manuscript upon which the edition was based lost any independent authority or value and was frequently discarded. The careers of even the most scholarly of humanist-printers, Aldus Manutius included, are darkened by accounts of manuscript books that entered their shops never to be heard of again, and by the knowledge that the printer-editors' "correcting" of the texts they printed, even when countenanced by the best academic advisers of the day, cannot but have destroyed a very important stage in the transmission of the classics. Ironically, it has proven better for modern scholarship when fifteenth-century printers used *bad* manuscripts as their exemplars (and destroyed them), rather than when they used good ones—which thereafter became unavailable in the charting of textual transmission.

The Early History of Printers and Printing

A. *Germany*

The clear and uncontested emergence of Johann Gensfleisch zum Gutenberg (ca. 1399–1468) as the first printer from movable type is comparatively recent. Until modern Dutch bibliographers refuted the claim, the legend of Laurens Coster of Haarlem as the first printer provided an alternative to the German origin of the art. The so-called *verbyldung*, or "anticipation," of the Mainz invention has now been laid to rest, and it appears that the mysterious Coster (who, so the story goes, cut wooden types for his children while out on a walk) was a xylographer, or carver of block books. The survivals of this proto-printing (or *Costeriana*) offer no serious challenge to Mainz as the birthplace of printing.

The various complicated business deals and lawsuits in which Gutenberg was perennially involved will not be rehearsed in detail here. While a persistent litigant, he was usually unsuccessful; and while an equally persistent borrower, he does not appear to have been able to make good his debts. The banker Johann Fust (fl. 1450–66) foreclosed on one such loan in 1455, probably in order to acquire Gutenberg's effects, for the 42-line Bible must have been sufficiently advanced by then for Gutenberg to have been capable of repaying his debt shortly afterward if he had been given the chance. But Fust wanted the press, the types, and the Bible rather than the money, and in an early example of corporate head-hunting he invited Peter Schoeffer (fl. 1449–1502), who had been Gutenberg's foreman, to set up in business with him. Since Gutenberg's name appears nowhere on any of the printed books credited to him, the ascription of any extant piece to his shop is inevitably speculative; but even though the books themselves might have been printed elsewhere, the bulk of the credit must go to Gutenberg. In addition to the 42-line Bible, and possibly the 36-line Bible, there are several other works which probably either antedate the Fust lawsuit of 1455–56 or were produced after Gutenberg had most likely recovered some of his equipment or acquired new presses through Konrad Humery. A dated copy of an Indulgence of Nicholas V (1453), a *Turkenkalendar* of 1454, a Donatus grammar and the *Catholicon* of 1460—all of these have been attributed to the Gutenberg press by modern historians.

Whatever the share of credit, the partnership of Fust and Schoeffer, with Fust as financier and business manager and Schoeffer as craftsman, prospered as Gutenberg's firm had not. Their two most famous productions were the Mainz Psalter of 1457 and the 48-line Bible of 1462. The Bible is the first printed book to bear a date, and the Psalter has a special technical interest, since it was the first book to contain color prints—an experiment not taken up again with any success until modern times. The Psalter had red and blue initials, which were inked separately but then locked into the form and printed in a single pull. The use of color was undoubtedly an attempt to compete with and imitate manuscript technique, as in a sense were the blank spaces left in the Psalter to allow local liturgical uses to be added by hand to the printed copy. Fust and Schoeffer also produced editions of Cicero's *De officiis* in 1465 and 1466, and the *Liber sextus decretalium* in 1465 for Boniface VIII.

Schoeffer the technician advanced his social position by marrying the boss's daughter Christina (about 1466) and continued the business very successfully after his father-in-law's death, publishing another 130 books beyond the twenty-five produced by the partnership. He built up a considerable international trade and was probably the first printer to exhibit at the Frankfurt Book Fair. He had agents and depots (sometimes shared with other printers) all over Europe—in Paris,

Lübeck, and Basel.

The family firm was continued by two sons, Johann (ca. 1468–1531) and Peter II (fl. 1510–47). The first is best known for having published Erasmus and other humanists, and for printing a number of Latin first editions. But his most memorable text is the short Preface to an edition of Livy (1523), in which he confirms that Gutenberg had indeed invented printing, but adds that the art had been "improved" by Fust and his father. Peter II was not only a type-founder and punchcutter but also the printer of Tyndale's English translation of the New Testament in Worms (about 1526). Considering the large international business and sound finances of the Schoeffers, it is perhaps surprising that the firm closed (and left Mainz without a press) upon Johann's death. But Peter II's movements from Mainz to Worms to Strassburg and Venice emphasize the decline in importance of the early centers of printing.

After Mainz and Gutenberg and the Fust-Schoeffer dynasty, there are several important German printers and printing centers. The Strassburg printer Johann Mentelin (fl. 1458–78) brought out a smaller (and therefore cheaper) version of the Gutenberg Bible in 1460, and followed this with the first Bible printed in German (1466). With this move into the vernacular, Strassburg became noted for its "popular" presses and enjoyed the commercial as well as spiritual benefits of publishing the various tracts associated with the Lutheran reformation. Johann Amerbach of Basel (1443–1513) inherited the humanist attitudes of his adviser and teacher Johann Heynlin, who had helped to set up the first printing press at the Sorbonne. In partnership with Johann Petri (d. 1511) and Johannes Froben (1460–1527), Amerbach was the most significant printer-publisher of Basel, producing eleven editions of the Latin Vulgate Bible, and a Latin dictionary, and he was at work on a monumental edition of the four Doctors of the Church when he died.

Froben continued the business and has perhaps the best claim to be regarded as the German equivalent of Manutius, for like his Italian rival he concentrated on classical texts (Latin, Greek, and Hebrew) and employed the greatest scholars of the age to edit them, including Beatus Rhenanus and Erasmus, who worked briefly as press-corrector for Froben, and whose Latin translation for his Greek New Testament Froben published in 1516. Froben also published a number of works by Luther, including the first collected editions (1518–20) of the Latin tracts, and he used the Holbein brothers to produce decorated borders, initials, and illustrations.

Anton Koberger (1440–1513) was one of the most successful of early German printers, beginning work in 1470 and taking advantage of Nuremberg's favorable position as a great commercial center, based upon its principle of the free exchange of goods. He not only had twenty-four presses of his own (a figure rivaled during the first two centuries of printing only by Plantin in the Netherlands) but also commissioned other printers, so large was his business. Its expansion was aided by a network of sales agents as far afield as Budapest and Warsaw, Vienna, Lyon, and Paris. Koberger had his own bindery for books to be sold locally, but exported others in sheets to be bound at their destinations. The one hundred compositors, pressmen, and proofreaders in his employ produced over two hundred titles, many of them large folio editions. His first dated book is the Alcinous *Disciplinarum Platonis epitome* of 1472, and his most famous are the so-called *Nuremberg Chronicle*, with its 1,800 woodcuts, published in 1493, and his edition of the *Apocalypse*, in both German and Latin versions, with woodcuts probably by Dürer (1498). However, even Koberger's success was not permanent. The firm—as in so many cases where the personality of one man seems to have held the business together—closed down within a few years of his death; and there were unsold stocks of his books left in cities as far distant from one another as Prague, Venice, Como, Florence, and Budapest. It is another story of apparent financial security being unable to sustain itself.

Christopher Froschauer of Zürich (fl. 1521–64), a keen partisan of the Protestant faith, brought out a vast number of religious works (some five hundred of his total of nine hundred). He had a monopoly on the writings of Zwingli (including his complete German Bible of 1524–29 in six volumes), and published a decidedly Protestant annotated edition of the Latin Bible, undertaken by Conrad Pellikan in seven volumes (1532–37). Froschauer's Protestant leanings meant that of the twenty-seven Bibles printed at his press, only ten were in Latin: the others were in German or English (the 1550 Coverdale Bible). With its promise of easy access to the Scriptures for the laity, the vernacular was beginning to take over as the language of Protestant Christianity. Froschauer also published the first volume of Gesner's *Bibliotheca universalis* in 1545.

Of the army of German printers who set up printing shops in the century after Gutenberg, two should be mentioned here. Erhard Ratdolt (1447–1527) published in Augsburg the first genuine title-page (1476), the first sheet of type specimens (1486; with fifteen typefaces

ue maria
gra plena
dominus
tecu bene
dicta tu in mulierib'
et benedictus fruct'
uentris tui : ihesus
christus amen.

Gloria laudis resonet in ore
omniu Patri genitoqz proli
spiritui sancto pariter Resul
tet laude perhenni Labori
bus dei vendunt nobis om
nia bona. laus:honor: virtus
potetia: 7 gratiaz actio tibi
christe.Amen.

Viue deu sic 7 vines per secula cun/
cta. Prouidet 7 tribuit deus omnia
nobis. Proficit absque deo null9 in
orbe labor. Illa placet tell9 in qua
res parua beatu. Ode facit 7 tenues
lururiantur opes.

Si fortuna volet fies de rhetore consul.
Si volet hec eadem fies de cosule rhetor.
Quicquid amor iussit no est cotedere tutu
Regnat et in dominos ius habet ille suos
Vita data e vreda data e sine fenere nobis.
Mutua:nec certa persoluenda die.

Usus 7 ars docuit quod sapit omnis homo
Ars animos frangit 7 firmas dirimit vrbes
Arte cadunt turres arte leuatur onus
Artibus ingenijs quesita est gloria multis
Principijs obsta sero medicina paratur
Cum mala per longas conualuere moras
Sed propera nec te venturas differ in horas
Qui non est hodie cras minus aptus erit.

Non bene pro toto libertas venditur auro
Hoc celeste bonum preterit orbis opes
Precaueatis animi est bonis veneranda libertas
Seruitus semper cunctis quoque despicienda
Summa petit liuor perflant altissima venti
Summa perunt dextra fulmina missa iouis
In loca nonnunqu am sicas arentia glebis
De prope currenti flumine man ac aqua

Quisquis ades scriptis qui mentem forsitan istis
Vt noscas adhibens pronius istud opus
Nosce: augustensis ratdolt germanus Erhardus
Litterulas istos ordine quasqz facit
Ipse quibus venera libros impressit in vrbe
Multos 7 plures nunc premit atqz premet
Quique etiam varijs celestia signa figuris
Aurea qui primus nunc monumenta premit
Quin etiam manibus proprijs vbicunqz figuras
Est opus:incidens dedalus alter erit

Nobis benedicat qui trinitate viuit
7 regnat Amen: Honor soli deo est tribuendu
Aue regina celor mater regis angelo-
rum o maria flos virginum velut rosa
velitium o maria : Tua est potentia tu
regnis domine tu es super omnes gen
tes da pacem domine in dieb' nostris
mirabilis deus in sanctis suis Et gloria
osus in maiestate sua orb' panthon kyr

Quod prope sacce diem tibi fum conuiua futurus
forsitan ignoras at fore ne dubites
Ergo para cenam non qualem sloecus ambit
Sed lautam sane more creenaco
Manque duas mecum florente etate puellas
Adducam quarum balsama cunnus olet
Vernula sola domi sedeat quam nuper habebas
Si nondum cunnus vepulbus borruerit
Sunt qui nimulent 7 auari crimen amica
O bicant facto rumoz vrsile cadat Hec Philelphus

Punc ades mira quicunq uolumins querns
Arte uel er animo pressa fuisse tuo
Seruer iste nbi:nobis iure fotores
Incolumem seruet usqz rogare licet

Est homini uirtus fuluo preciosior auro: æneas
Ingenium quondam fuerat preciosius auro.
Miramurq magis quos munera mentis adornat:
Quam qui corporeis emicuere bonis.
Si qua uirtute nites ne despice quenquam
Ex alia quadam forsitan ipse nitet

Nemo sue laudis nimium letetur honore
Ne ullis factus post sua fata gemat.
Nemo nimis cupide sibi res desiderat ullas
Ne dum plus cupiat perdat & id quod habet.
Ne ue cito uerbis cuiusquam credito blandis
Sed si sint fidei respice quid moneant
Qui bene proloquitur coram sed postea praue
Hic erit inusus binia q ora gerat

Pax plenam uirtutis opus pax summa laborum
pax belli exacti præcium est præcuiumque pericli
Sidera pace uigent consistunt terrea pace
Nil placitum sine pace deo non munus ad aram
Fortuna arbitris tempus dispensat ubi
Illa rapit iuuenes illa serit senes

ΚΛιω Τευτερτην τε θαλεια τε μελπομενη τε
Τερψιχορη τερατω τε πολυμνεια τουρανιη
τε καλλιοπη θελη προφερεστη εστιν απα
σαωυ ιεσυσ χριςουσ μαρια τελοσ.

Indicis characteζ diuersaζ mane/
rieru impressioni parataru: Finis.

Erhardi Ratdolt Augustensis viri
solertissimi:preclaro ingenio 7 miri
fica arte:qua olim Venetijs excelluit
celebratissimus. In imperiali nunc
vrbe Auguste vindelicor laudatissi
me impressioni dedit. Annoqz salu-
tis.M.LLLL.LXXXVI.Kale.
Aprilis Sidere felici compleuit.

in the three families of roman, gothic, and greek, see Fig. 11), and the first printed geometrical diagrams (in his first edition of Euclid's *Elementa geometriæ* 1482). Ulrich Zell of Cologne (fl. 1466-1507), countered what was to happen in the humanist and Protestant presses of other German cities in the sixteenth century by producing a large number of theological tracts representing the strict Thomist orthodoxy of the university faculty. Unlike almost every other major printer, Zell published no books at all in the vernacular. In his conservative, Catholic output, Zell was the anomaly in Germany, for from the mid-sixteenth century until the eighteenth, printing became a virtual Protestant monopoly in Germany, although Catholic texts were obviously published elsewhere. From Germany, printing quickly spread all over Europe, and by the end of the fifteenth century only Russia was without a printing press.

B. *Italy*

The partnership of Conrad Sweynheym and Arnold Pannartz (fl. 1465-73) brought printing to Italy in 1465. They were, inevitably, Germans, but it was not long before a native Italian, Johannes Philippus de Lignamine, took up the trade, bringing out an edition of Quintilian at Rome in 1470. Sweynheym and Pannartz set up their first printing shop in the Benedictine Santa Scolastica at Subiaco, just outside Rome, and in 1467 moved to Rome itself, in the Palazzo Massimi. The Lactantius *Divine Institutes* of 1465 is the first dated Italian book (and the first successful use of greek type), but it was probably preceded by an edition of Cicero's *De oratore* and an edition of a Donatus, of which no copy now exists. In Rome, the partners continued to concentrate on classical and patristic works, producing editions of Apuleius, Cæsar, Virgil, Augustine's *De civitate dei*, a two-volume edition of the letters of Jerome, and Torquemada's *Meditationes*. But even though the firm was located at the center of Western Christendom and produced a total of some twenty-six works in forty-eight volumes (usually published in very modest print runs of about 275 copies), there were still unsold stocks, and the partnership was dissolved in 1473. Sweynheym tried to keep the business going for a while alone, but failed, and Pannartz turned to engraving as a more profitable enterprise.

Elsewhere in Italy, Venice became the next important center for printing—indeed, the most important in Europe at the end of the fifteenth century, with over 150 presses operating in 1500. The first printers in Venice were Johann and Wendelin de Spire, who started a shop in 1467. They published an edition of Cicero's *Epistolæ ad familiares* and were also responsible for the first book to be printed in Italian—Petrarch's *Canzoniere* in 1470. An Italian translation of the Bible appeared from the Spire press in 1471. The next major Venetian printer was another foreigner—this time a Frenchman, Nicolaus Jenson. More famous for his typography than his publishing (perhaps unjustly so), Jenson was sent by Charles VII of France to Mainz to learn the new art—and presumably to bring it back to Paris—only to have his patron die when he had mastered it. Accordingly, he moved to Venice and set up a house which was a worthy precursor of the *Neakademia* of Aldus Manutius. Jenson published over seventy books, the bulk of them classical editions, of which the Pliny *Natural History* of 1472 is the best known. While his classical editions (Cæsar, Suetonius, Quintilian in 1471, Eusebius, Justin, Cicero's *Epistolæ ad Brutum* in 1470, Virgil in 1475) were printed in the appropriate "roman" typeface, his edition of the Vulgate Bible in 1476 used a gothic type, since it was considered a "modern" rather than a "classical" work.

The most eminent of all Venetian publishers was certainly Theobaldo Manucci (1450–1515), more famous under his Latinized name, Aldus Manutius. Aldus started his business in 1490 and from the very beginning had a very clear idea of his audience—the educated humanistic *conoscenti* and *dilettanti* eager to get easy and cheap access to those classical texts (especially Greek) which would confirm their humanist credentials. Taking advantage of the pre-eminence of Venice both as a center for Greek studies (it was the port of entry for many exiles from the recently defeated Byzantine Empire) and as the major commercial *entrepôt* of the Eastern Mediterranean, Aldus could obtain the two elements necessary to the successful publishing of classical texts: money and manuscripts. The first he acquired through the good offices of Pico della Mirandola and the second through the library of St. Mark set up by Cardinal Bessarion—a depository particularly rich in imported Greek manuscripts from the East, bought or otherwise obtained during the foraging expeditions of Italian humanists during the fifteenth century when it became clear that Byzantium would not last long.

Using the best Greek and Latin scholars of his day as editors—and insisting that they stay in his house while working for him—Aldus began the series of pocket-sized octavo "Aldine" editions, which were so successful that they were widely imitated (and even pirated) elsewhere. Fifty-nine "Aldines" were printed in conscious plagiarism from 1501–26 in Lyon, a situation partially assisted by Manutius's typographer, Griffo, agreeing to provide the Lyon presses with punches for the types. From 1540 Johannes Sturm of Strassburg issued a series of reprints, and in the seventeenth century the Elzevir family published a duodecimo series of classics at a price below that of the original Aldines. So famous did the Manutius press become for its classical editions that scholars from all over Europe would send Aldus manuscripts from their own collections for printing by the Venetian house. Beginning in April 1501, when the Virgil appeared, a new Aldine classic was published approximately once every two months for the next five years—a remarkable record of scholarship and industry.

Erasmus lived with Aldus while seeing his *Adagionum collectanea* through the press in 1508; the Aldine foreman, Yannis Gregoropoulos, was a permanent resident; and another Greek, Marcus Musurus, became responsible for many of the Greek first editions while a member of the household. Hieronymous Avantius was the editor of the Aldus Lucretius in 1500, joining perhaps the most distinguished scholarly house ever associated with a "commercial" activity. That Aldus took all of this scholarly publishing very seriously can be demonstrated by his founding in 1500 of the *Neakademia*, where all proceedings were conducted in Greek, with fines for anyone who lapsed into the vernacular. But he did not neglect vernacular publishing. He brought out Petrarch's *Canzoniere* in 1501 and Dante's *Divina commedia* in 1502, both of them edited by Pietro Bembo. His two most important publications were, however, a Greek, five-volume Aristotle from 1495 to 1498, and his italic edition of Virgil in 1501. It was the use of Griffo's italic face (with its lateral compression yet legibility) which enabled Aldus to publish in a small format and therefore to bring the classics within reach of a much wider audience. This is reflected by his average editions of one to two thousand copies, quite unusually large for the time.

The fortunes of the Manutius firm were later to be associated more with Rome than with Venice, for the high standards of scholarship demanded of a true Aldine edition were not kept up by Aldus's brothers-in-law after his death. It was through Aldus's son Paulus (1512–72) and grandson Aldus II that the tradition of scholarship continued. Paulus directed the Tipografica del popolo romano and Aldus the Typographia apostolica vaticana, both of them official presses rather than viable private commercial operations.

Of other Roman printers besides the later Manutius branch, only two need be mentioned here. Ludovico Arrighi (fl. 1510–27) was a "writing master" and author of the manual *La operina*. This was published in Rome in 1522 and was the first printed specimen book of humanist handwriting. Arrighi printed a number of books in his fine italic type, including another manual, *Il modo de temperare le penne* (1523), and Trissino's *Canzone* (1523/4). His typeface, of course, followed Griffo's cutting of an italic for Manutius, the most influential sloping style of the period. Antonio Blado (1490–1567) was one of the beneficiaries of Arrighi's experiments, acquiring a cursive sloping type probably designed by Arrighi about 1526, and using it in 1535 to print Leone Hebreo's *Dialoghi d'amore* and in 1539 for Paolo Giovio's *Vita Sfortiæ*. Blado was the official printer to the Holy See and therefore produced the first *Index librorum prohibitorum* in 1559. However, his responsibilities to the Roman ecclesiastical hierarchy do not appear to have inhibited his publishing, for he printed works as diverse (and polar) as Machiavelli's *Prince* (1532) and Loyola's *Spiritual Exercises* (1548).

C. *France*

Again, it was the Germans who brought printing to France, as they did to other European countries. Martin Crantz, Ulrich Gering, and Michael Freiburger were invited to the Sorbonne in 1470 by Johann Heynlin and Guillaume Fichet. From the start, it was clear that in France the institution and the publisher were in charge, not the printers. The Sorbonne specified the type (roman) and the books to be printed—Latin classics to be used as rhetorical models. The three Germans were hired artisans rather than independent merchants like Fust and Schoeffer, Koberger and Manutius. Eventually both Heynlin and Fichet were lured away to other centers—Heynlin to the press of Johann Amerbach in Basel, Fichet to Rome. Soon after, the Sorbonne press was disbanded.

From this point, French printing was taken over by French nationals, most notably Jean Dupré and Antoine Vérard. Dupré (fl. 1484–97) set himself up as a classical printer of the Froben-Manutius type, but in addition to publishing such works as Juvenal's *Satires* (1470), he also printed extensively in the fields of law, theology, and practical grammar. His most important publication was *La mer des hystoires* of 1491. Antoine Vérard (fl. 1485–1512) is chiefly remembered for his elaborate editions of Books of Hours. He published almost two hundred such editions, with special versions printed on vellum and hand-illuminated for royalty. Unlike other French publishers of the time (whether he actually operated the presses himself or worked solely as a publisher is unclear), he produced much work in the vernacular, the most famous being the *Grandes chroniques de France* of 1493, which boasted nearly a thousand woodcut illustrations. As with his Books of Hours, this edition was also produced in a special presentation version, with the printed woodcuts replaced by hand-painted illuminations. Vérard's Books of Hours and Dupré's *éditions de luxe* (such as the *Legenda aurea* of 1489) were both conscious imitations of the richness of late-medieval manuscripts.

In fact, some of Vérard's special editions occupied a rather ambiguous position between manuscript and printed book. The subject matter was similarly medieval, as were the romances and chronicles produced in the Vérard manner by such French printers as Philippe Pigouchet (fl. 1488–1515), Thielman Kerver (fl. 1497–1522), and Guy Marchant, whose *Danse macabre* of 1499 contains the first representation of a printing press, with the printers themselves being carried off by the figures of Death (see Fig. 8). In the early years of the sixteenth century a greater interest in humanist literature began to show itself in France, beginning with the publications of Jodicus Badius Ascensius (1462–1535), who printed the work of the famous Greek scholar Guillaume Budé, first in Lyon and then, after 1499, in Paris.

It was his successor, Henri Estienne (fl. 1460–1520), also known by his Latinized name, Henricus Stephanus, who founded the great scholar-printer dynasty that was to make France pre-eminent in humanist book production for a hundred years. Estienne used the major talents of his time as advisers, both scholarly and technical—Jacques Lefèvre d'Étaples, the philologist and the greatest Greek scholar in France, and the designer Geofroy Tory (1480–1533), who provided many of the woodcut initials and type decorations for Estienne. The scholarly tradition was continued first by Simon de Colines, who married Henri's widow, and later by Robert Estienne (1503–59), the heir through marriage to both the Stephanus and Badius presses. Using Garamond as typographer (in, for example, the *Isagoge* of Jacques Dubois, 1531), the firm of Estienne, Colines, and Tory made the reign of Francis I the greatest period of French printing. It began when Robert—royal printer in Hebrew, Greek, and Latin—and his son Henri II (1528–98) used the Aldine model, both domestic and commercial, for their classical editions, with a houseful of resident scholars aiding in the editing of cheap but reliable texts. For example,

Robert's edition of a Greek New Testament in 1550 was based on no fewer than fifteen manuscripts, a far cry from the days when a printed edition was simply the "correcting" of the evidence of a single manuscript. Robert printed first editions of Eusebius, Dionysius of Halicarnassus, Dion Cassius, and Appian, Latin grammars for school use—and Bibles.

In addition to the Greek New Testament mentioned earlier (which was itself a third edition and was responsible for the modern practice of subdividing biblical chapters with verses for easy reference), the Estiennes produced in a comparatively short time several important editions of the Bible: a Latin Vulgate in 1527–28, a Hebrew Old Testament in 1539–41 (with a second edition in 1544–46), and a specially sumptuous folio Bible in Hebrew, Chaldee, and Latin, printed on vellum. The Estiennes' Bibles were, however, attacked by the Sorbonne faculty, and Robert was accused of heresy on several occasions. As a Protestant, Robert needed the protection of Francis I, and on the king's death in 1547, Robert had to move the press to Geneva, leaving the Paris branch in the charge of his brother Charles (1504–64), who was evidently a much poorer businessman than the other members of the family, for the Paris press did not prosper.

In Geneva, Henri II and François (1557–82) maintained the Aldine standards with a number of Greek and Latin first editions (including the *History* of Thucydides, 1588; Anacreon, Diodorus Siculus, and Plutarch). Henri also inherited the Estienne interest in lexicography: his father, Robert, had published a famous Latin thesaurus in 1531, followed by a Latin-French dictionary in 1538 and 1539–40. Henri II added to this list a very influential *Thesaurus linguæ græcæ* in five folio volumes (1572), a monumental work which set the family fortunes back considerably. The Estienne tradition of working with great scholars was continued by Henri II's son Paul (1557–1627), who collaborated with Isaac Casaubon, generally acknowledged to be (after J. C. Scaliger) the finest textual critic of his time. Although Paul's branch of the family firm was later to return to Paris, and although his son Antoine, a Roman Catholic, became "Imprimeur du roi," the line of Estiennes as printers expired with Antoine's death in 1674. Meanwhile, Henri II's brother Robert II, who had remained a Roman Catholic like his uncle Charles, inherited the Paris press from Charles before Paul's return from Geneva and was Royal Printer from 1564–71.

The history of French printing from the mid-seventeenth century on is very largely the story of the Imprimerie royale, for the increas-

ing centralization of French government and society meant that printing, like all other social activities, was kept very much in the eye of
the king. Louis XIII's private press of 1620 in the Louvre became the
official Imprimerie royale under Richelieu in 1640. With Grandjean
as its most important typographer, the Imprimerie concentrated on
works appropriate to the neo-classical mission of French culture,
combined with the French tradition of *éditions de luxe* going back to
Vérard in the fifteenth century. Of the one hundred titles produced in
the first ten years of the Imprimerie, many were expensive and monumental folio editions, including an edition of the Greek fathers and
an eight-volume Vulgate Bible in 1642. The first book published by
the Imprimerie set the tone—a Thomas à Kempis in 1640. Other mag-
isterial multi-volume sets to follow included the complete works of
Bernard of Clairvaux in 1642, a collection of Church Councils in
thirty-seven volumes, Byzantine authors in twenty-nine volumes, ancient authors in sixty-four volumes, and a Polyglot Bible in ten volumes, printed by Antoine Vitre in Armenian, Chaldee, Coptic, Samar-
itan, and Syrian.

D. *The Netherlands*

In the late sixteenth and early seventeenth centuries, the Netherlands began to become important in the commercial and technical history of printing, with the Frenchman Christopher Plantin (ca.
1520–89) dominating the Catholic south in Antwerp, and the Elzevir
family the Protestant north. Plantin's ambiguous situation as a
Frenchman in the Low Countries is shown by his heavy reliance on
fine French models of typography (particularly Granjon and Sabon) in
his early work and the gradual intrusion of the more solid Dutch style
in his later publications (see Chapter 6 for examples of the different
styles). Plantin was at first a binder, one of the earliest to introduce
gold tooling and inlaid binding into the Netherlands. He continued to
employ binders for his editions after he began publishing his own
books, the first of which was Giovanni Bruto's *La institutione di una
fanciulla nata nobilmente*, a dual-language edition in Italian and
French, in 1555.

Of his approximately fifteen hundred editions (an enormous number for the period), his Polyglot Bible, printed under the patronage of
Philip II of Spain, was undoubtedly the greatest. But in common with
several other Dutch-based printers, he also produced a large number
of atlases and scientific works. However, these special extravagances

were partially financed by the monopoly on liturgical books which he had acquired for Spain and its colonies. Missals and breviaries were the economic staple of his press. His promotion of copper engravings instead of the usual woodcuts (and his patronage of such designers as the Wiericx brothers, François Huys, and Pierre van der Borcht) helped to ensure the ascendancy of the new method, although Plantin continued to employ woodcuts as decorative devices. Throughout his career he supplied his own paper, but he bought the matrices for his type (to be finished and cast in Antwerp and Ghent) on periodic visits to the Frankfurt Book Fair. Plantin's son-in-law Moretus took over the business upon his death.

While the Elzevirs can almost match the Estiennes in longevity as printers, they were not scholars in any sense. The first Elzevir, Louis, worked with Plantin in Antwerp before setting up in Leiden in about 1580. However, he was at first only a binder and a bookseller, and did not publish on his own account until 1592, when he brought out an edition of Eutropius. Even then, he did not actually do his own printing but acted as publisher for the University of Leiden, commissioning several printers to do the technical work for him. The Elzevirs were most famous for two long-term projects which combined good workmanship, an informative and entertaining text, and a reasonable price. The first was a series of imitation Aldines in duodecimo, pocket editions of French and Latin literature selling for the bargain price of one gilder for an edition of five hundred pages. The second was the series of "Little Republics," thirty-five monographs each describing a foreign country for the enquiring armchair traveler or potential tourist—a sort of seventeenth-century Baedeker.

The family actually entered printing in 1618, when Louis's grandson Isaac started up a press in Leiden, although it was Louis's son Bonaventura (1583–1652), together with a nephew Abraham I (1592–1652), who made the "Officina Elzeveriana" well known. The typeface for the Elzevir classics was cut by Christoffel van Dijck and became the "model" Dutch face, highly influential in France and England. Various members of the family started branches of the firm—in, for example, Amsterdam, The Hague, and Utrecht. The best-known production of these branches was a Dutch New Testament by Daniel (1626–80), Bonaventura's son. Upon Daniel's death in 1673, the family took over the van Dijck foundry and sold the types and matrices, which ultimately passed on to the famous Haarlem firm of Enschede. The last active member of the family, Abraham II (1653–1712), had his headquarters in Leiden. The business was sold in 1713, shortly after Abraham's death.

The Elzevirs acted more as book brokers (somewhat similar to modern "packagers") than as craftsmen-printers and would often undertake a particular commission for a foreign publisher. For example, they produced two thousand copies of Grotius's *De veritate religionis* for a publisher in London in 1675. Of the Elzevir output, 80 percent was in Latin, 10 percent in French, 4 percent in Greek, and the rest divided among Flemish, German, Italian, and Oriental languages.

E. *The Rest of Europe*

The general movement of the centers of printing in Europe was from Germany (Gutenberg, Fust and Schoeffer, Froben, Koberger) in the mid-fifteenth century to Italy (Sweynheym and Pannartz, Jenson, Manutius) in the late fifteenth and early sixteenth centuries, to France in the late sixteenth (Garamond, Granjon, Estienne) and early seventeenth centuries, and then to the Low Countries (Plantin, the Elzevirs) in the mid-seventeenth century.

Other European countries—with, for the English reader, the exception of England—are inevitably somewhat peripheral and can be very briefly sketched in here. Printing reached Valencia in Spain in 1473 (again via German immigrants: Lambert Palmert of Cologne, Johann of Salzburg, and Paul Hurus of Constanz). Spanish printing is, like English, notable for its concentration on the vernacular. The first book in Spanish was Diego de San Pedro's *Carcel de amor*, published by Johann Rosenbach in Barcelona in 1493, with a second edition by another German printer, Frederick Eid, in 1496. Other vernacular texts followed in quick succession. Jacob Cromberger's press in Seville was known for its editions of the classics, supervised by Elio Antonio de Nebrija. Cromberger was also responsible for the first American book, having sent Juan Pablo to Mexico in 1539 to publish *Doctrina christiana en la lengua mexicana e castellana*. But the main centers for classical learning in Spain were Salamanca and Alcalá. In Alcalá, Cardinal Ximenes secured the appointment as university printer of Arnão Guillen de Brocar of Pamplona, whose greatest achievement was the vast Complutensian Bible of 1514–17 (issued in 1522) printed in four languages: Hebrew, Chaldee, Greek, and Latin.

Printing spread to Denmark in 1482, to Portugal in 1489, to Sweden in 1495, and finally to Russia in 1552, when Christian III of Denmark responded to Ivan the Terrible's request for a printer by sending Hans Missenheim of Copenhagen to instruct the Russian Ivan Feodorov into the mysteries of the new art. An earlier attempt by Bartholomæus Gothan of Lübeck to introduce printing into Russia was frustrated when Bartholomæus was murdered in 1496 before having printed any Russian books.

F. *England*

The story of Caxton is, to the English-speaking reader, the most familiar of printers' biographies. After a prosperous career as a merchant and governor of the "English Nation" at Bruges, Caxton accepted the patronage of Margaret of Burgundy, the sister of Edward IV of England, and turned his attention to literature, beginning a translation of the *Recueil des histoires de Troye*. He was in Cologne at the time of the printing of an edition of Bartholomæus Anglicus's *De proprietatibus rerum* (1471–72) and probably learned about printing during this trip. Certainly the Middle English translation of Bartholomæus by Trevisa was one of the works which Caxton intended for his Westminster press, as it was printed by his successor Wynkyn de Worde very shortly after his death, in an act of discipleship and homage to a former master. De Worde specifically mentions that Caxton had printed the Latin original at Cologne, although this may simply mean that Johann Veldener had taught Caxton the principles of printing. It was from Veldener that Caxton received seven of the eight gothic and bastard types he was later to use in his own editions. At Bruges in 1474 Caxton began printing the *Recuyell*, the first book printed in English. He also published the French original of the same work and *The Game and Playe of Chesse*, translated via French from the Latin of Jacobus Cessolis. In Bruges, Caxton entered into some sort of business agreement with Colard Mansion, the nature of which is still debated, though it is likely that Mansion was Caxton's employee rather than the other way round.

With the retirement of Margaret, his patroness, Caxton moved to Westminster and set up a press there in 1476. He no doubt printed some minor works, including an Indulgence, before the first dated book produced in England, the *Dictes or Sayengis of the Philosophres* of 1477. Of the one hundred surviving editions from his press, some seventy-three are in English, a quite remarkable percentage for the period and a testimony to his acceptance (and active promotion) of the vernacular as a proper medium for the press. These English publications included two editions of Chaucer's *Canterbury Tales*, and the same author's *Parliament of Fowls, House of Fame, Troilus and Criseyde,* and translation of Boethius's *Consolation of Philosophy*; Lydgate's *Temple of Glass* and *Life of Our Lady* and his translation of *The Pilgrimage of the Soul*; Gower's *Confessio Amantis* and Malory's *Morte Darthur*—in other words, all of the major works of literature in English at the end of the Middle Ages (with the exceptions of *Piers Plowman* and the works of the Gawain-poet, both rather special cases, since they were written in the "old-fashioned" alliterative meter rather than the more popular rhymed verse of Caxton's time).

Caxton's achievement was not, however, limited to publishing books. From the very beginning he saw himself in the role of translator and author. While he was not a trained scholar, there can be no doubt that he was a very conscious "editor" even of works he did not translate. His version of Malory's *Morte Darthur* was the only one known until the discovery earlier this century of the Winchester manuscript, and the argument still persists among critics as to whether Caxton "improved" his original. His two other main contributions to his publications were his colophons and prefaces, which became little essays in their own right, commenting on the esthetic, historical, and cultural qualities of the work, and his adoption of London English as the standard form for his publications. While his spelling was by no means consistent, the appearance of so many books in English at the very time that Middle English was becoming Modern English may have helped in the process of "fixing" the language in its literary, written form. Pronunciation was to move further away from spelling in the centuries ahead, but Caxton was one of the main influences in making the written medium of the language comprehensible and orthographically static.

Wynkyn de Worde (fl. 1477–1530) may have come with Caxton to England in 1476. He was certainly Caxton's chief assistant at the Westminster press, and he inherited its direction upon his master's death in 1491. De Worde's early work is still very much in the Caxton manner, exemplified by his edition of Trevisa's translation of *De proprietatibus rerum* about 1495 (i.e., a large, important book in English, in the tradition of Caxton's *Canterbury Tales* and *Morte Darthur*). This edition can also be used to demonstrate the further progression of Middle English into Modern English. While argument over de Worde's copy-text manuscript for the edition continues to this day, there can be no doubt that the manuscript he used was written at least half a century before the *editio princeps*. But instead of merely reproducing all of its readings in fidelity to the text, de Worde consistently modernizes—changing, for example, *clepede* to *called*, *wende* to *go*, *wone* to *dwell*, *ydedled* to *divided*, *fonge* to *receive*. In almost every change he introduced, it is de Worde's "modern" version which has survived, and this substitution tells us a good deal about the passing of one stage of the language into another.

After 1500, de Worde moved his press to Fleet Street—into the City of London and away from Westminster Abbey and the court. It is no accident that "Fleet Street" (in the City) as metonymy has become synonymous with journalism as opposed to "book" publishing, for, once independent of Westminster and of Caxton's influence, de Worde began to issue practical, cheap textbooks rather than the literary masterpieces of the earlier period. His was probably the first publishing house in which the school textbook division (grammars, primers, etc.) became the most profitable part of the organization. But he did continue to experiment in typography. He was the first printer in England to use italic type, the first to use type ornaments, and the first to print greek and arabic typefaces.

De Worde's early-sixteenth-century English contemporaries can be dealt with fairly briefly. Richard Pynson (fl. 1490–1528) was French (another foreigner) and held the title of King's Printer from 1508. The following year he became the first printer in England to use roman type, importing it from Paris for his edition of *Sermo fratris Hieronymus de Ferraria* and for a speech by Petrus Gryphus of Pisa. He printed an edition of the Berners translation of Froissart's *Chronicles* in 1523–25 and Lydgate's translation of Boccaccio's *Falles of Princes* in 1494; and as King's Printer, it was Pynson who in 1521 published Henry VIII's *Assertio septem sacramentorum*, the orthodox Catholic defense of the sacraments against the Lutherans, which earned from the pope the title of "Defender of the Faith" for the future despoiler of the Catholic Church (and, more profitably, the Catholic monasteries), a title still borne today by Britain's Protestant monarchs.

Thomas Berthelet (fl. 1528–55) was another King's Printer and is chiefly remembered for printing the first Latin Bible in London and the second edition (1535) of Trevisa's *De proprietatibus rerum*. It is in a copy of this Berthelet edition that the forged signature of "William Shakespeare His Book" occurs, contributing to the reputation of the work as "Shakespeare's Encyclopedia." Berthelet also printed Elyot's Latin dictionary in 1538, Lily's Latin grammar in 1540, and some translations of Erasmus. Edward Whitchurch (d. 1562) and Richard Grafton (d. 1572) were responsible for bringing the so-called

Matthew Bible to England. This text, a version of the Tyndale and Coverdale translations, had originally been printed in Antwerp, and it was only after the Paris edition had been interrupted by the French Inquisitor-General (and Whitchurch and Grafton had fled to England) that an English printing was undertaken. Cranmer supervised the editing of the Bible in 1540, and Whitchurch and Grafton's connection with the Tudor ecclesiastical and secular establishment was confirmed when they were given not only the patent to print Edward VI's *Book of Common Prayer* in 1549, but also the authority to impress other printers so that sufficient copies of the work would be available for use in churches throughout the country.

Outside London and Westminster, printing was in England a very uncertain enterprise, and the two university towns of Oxford and Cambridge were the only places with any success (if such it can be called) with the new medium. Unlike the capital city, both universities had to rely upon Germans to bring the invention to them. Theodoric Rood was in Oxford between 1478 and 1486 (not from 1468, or MCCCCLXVIII, as the colophon of his first book would have us believe, in error for MCCCCLXXVIII), and his only distinction was to have printed the first classical edition in England, Cicero's *Pro milone* (1486). By 1483 Rood was in partnership with Thomas Hunte, the university's official stationer, but three years later he was out of business. Thereafter Oxford was without a press for thirty years.

Cambridge was even less fortunate, for again it was a German, John Siberch (1476–1554), who introduced printing—but not until 1519, many years after the most provincial of cities in Germany had acquired (and often lost) their presses. Siberch (or Johann Lair, as he was born) managed to get a university-chest loan to begin printing on what seems to have been a very small scale—and has therefore been often cited as the precursor of the Cambridge University Press, just as Rood has for Oxford University Press. Both claims are a little fanciful, for despite the slight administrative or financial links with the universities, neither printer can be said to have had any formal contract for printing the "publications" of the institution. Siberch had a gothic (textura) type, a cursive minuscule greek, and a roman—the last two probably cast for him by Froben. But it appears that the greek was never used, and of the fourteen pieces ascribed to him, all are totally insignificant works. Siberch left Cambridge in 1523, and the famous university did not feel the need for another press until 1583. In both cases, this is a disgraceful record for two of the major universities of Europe, but it points again to the commercial necessity of having a large town with a substantial reading public if printing is to succeed. Mere scholars have never been able to keep a press going without additional financial support.

The late sixteenth and seventeenth centuries were not a great period in English printing, and there are no English printer-publishers to compare to Plantin or Elzevir. John Day was among the most successful of English printers, for although suffering persecution under Queen Mary, he became one of the chief agents of the Elizabethan Protestant settlement, working under Archbishop Parker to produce the Anglo-Saxon font for Ælfric's *Homilies* (1567). He also printed Parker's *De antiquitate britannicæ ecclesiæ* (1572). Both of these works were intended to show that the Protestant revolution in England was in fact merely a return to the original principles of the Anglo-Saxon church. Foxe's *Acts and Monuments* (1563) and Latimer's *Sermons* served a similarly political Protestant purpose. During the seventeenth century, while certain individual books (the Shakespeare First Folio of 1623, the King James Bible of 1611, Milton's *Paradise Lost* in 1667, Bunyan's *Pilgrim's Progress* in 1678) are important to the history of literature and society, there are few English monuments to the printer's art.

In fact, seventeenth-century printing in England and throughout Europe was marked by a decline in layout and typography. The introduction of the famous "Fell types," bequeathed by John Fell to Oxford University in 1686, is one of the few signs that an interest in typography and book design was still extant in England at this time. Bought from van Dijck and Jacques Vallet, the fonts for the university included type by van Dijck himself, as well as by Garamond, Granjon, and Haultin. A Greek New Testament was among the works printed with the new types soon after they arrived in England, but the university obviously did not fully appreciate the gift, for the types fell out of use for over a century. The most popular books of the period, apart from religious or political tracts, were two emblem books (collections of quotations from Scripture or other "improving" literature, with accompanying woodcuts and doggerel verses as morals), by the Puritan George Wither and the Anglican Francis Quarles. Quarles, later known derisively as "the darling of our plebeian judgements," survived well into the eighteenth century as a very popular author, but none of the editions of Quarles's or Withers's *Emblemes* has any typographic merit.

The same general esthetic comments can be made about printing in the English colonies. In 1638, Stephen Daye set up the first printing press in New England at Cambridge, Massachusetts, and produced *The Freeman's Oath* as the initial offering of his press. The first genuine book from Daye's press was *The Whole Booke of Psalmes*, usually called the Bay Psalm Book. In 1663 Marmaduke Johnson started up another Cambridge press, where John Eliot's translation of the Bible into the local Indian language was printed. Johnson broke the Cambridge monopoly on printing when he opened a shop in Boston in 1674. Philadelphia and New York received their first printing presses in 1685 and 1693, respectively, both run by William Bradford of London. However, none of the products of these presses can be called in any way distinguished, and it was not until Benjamin Franklin, an enthusiast for the typographic innovations of Caslon and Baskerville (see Chapter 6), began printing in Philadelphia that the history of American printing acquires any dignity. After a number of false starts, Franklin became official printer to the colony of Pennsylvania in 1730. In 1744 he printed the first novel in America—Richardson's *Pamela*—and in the same year produced his masterpiece, an edition of Cicero's *Cato Major*. That he always considered printing one of his prime interests can be seen in his beginning his Will with the words, "I, Benjamin Franklin, Printer . . . ."

By the mid-seventeenth century the functions of printer and publisher were becoming separate almost everywhere; a century later, the printer as an independent selector, editor, and distributor of books was an anomaly. The most significant figures for the student of English literature of the period are the two Jacob Tonsons, the first of whom began as a bookseller in 1677 and started buying up the copyrights to the major authors of the day, becoming intimately associated with Dryden, although not always amicably. Dryden regarded some of the printers used by Tonson as incompetent fools, and was not shy of telling his publisher, "The Printer is a beast, and understands nothing I can say to him of correcting the press" (qtd. Thorpe: 141). Tonson and his nephew, also called Jacob, published the early work of Pope (until Pope gradually became his own publisher, taking complete control of format, typography, and distribution), and other members of the family continued to publish throughout the eighteenth century. Other important eighteenth-century English publishers were Bernard Lintot (1675–1736), Edmund Curll (1675–1747), and Robert Dodsley (1703–64). In Scotland there was the firm of Robert and Andrew Foulis, which was an exception to the general rule of the separation of functions, since the two men ran their own printing shop, edited the texts they published, and also had their own booksell-

ing business. The great contribution of the Foulis brothers was toward the modern development of the title-page: simplification was
the rule, with no lower case, no italics, and a single size of capitals
for each line.

Two other methods of seventeenth- and eighteenth-century publishing should be briefly touched on here: the "subscription" and the
"conger" or co-operative association. The most famous early example of a publishing co-op in England was that conger of four publishers—William Jaggard, Edward Blount, John Smithweeke, and William Apsley—who in 1623 collaborated in William Shakespeare's
First Folio. Considering the less-than-enthusiastic response to the
first major attempt at a folio edition of plays (Ben Jonson's self-lauda-
tory *Workes* of 1616), the publishers might indeed have felt that they
needed the financial security of a consortium to make the venture successful. But this time they were, of course, well rewarded for their
investment. In the following century, the system became more common, with publishers actually holding shares in the enterprise. Seven
publishers formed a conger to publish Johnson's *Dictionary* (which
brought its author the vast sum of £1,575, as compared with the mea-
ger £5 which Milton received for *Paradise Lost*); and thirty-six booksellers joined the association which collaboratively sponsored Johnson's *Lives of the Poets*.

Books published by subscription were, in effect, commissioned by
the readers themselves, who supported the authors while they completed the work and saw it through the press. In a sense, it was a
form of advance royalties paid to the printer-publisher on the author's
account by the reading public. Through this system, Pope's 1720 *Iliad* netted him £5,320; other well-known works published in this way
were John Minsheu's 1617 *Guide to Tongues* (the first English book
published by subscription) and Thomas Roycroft's six-volume folio
Polyglot Bible, appearing in 1653–57, and printed for the Bishop of
Chester. Both methods were devices for lessening some of the risk
involved in floating possibly unprofitable works, but the tendency
toward the end of the eighteenth century was for large family firms to
emerge out of careful investment in congers and for publishing to
become centralized again. Several of the firms which still dominate
English publishing (Longman, Murray) were begun in this way.

But why stop the account in the eighteenth century? Why not follow the printer-publishers through to the present day? The answer is
simple, and reflects the changing economic and cultural climate after
the first three centuries of printing: apart from the small "private

presses" discussed in the section on typography (Chapter 6), there are no families of printer-publishers in the later period to compare to Estienne, Elzevir, Manutius, or Caxton. The small private presses of Horace Walpole at Strawberry Hill, William Blake, and William Morris are anomalies, not the rule. This brief outline of the first three hundred years has been concerned with the general cultural history of the art and craft only insofar as it is necessary for the student to be aware of the role of the printer in determining the type of work to be published. Once printers no longer typically exercised their original function, once they became essentially hired artisans, once they could no longer decide which books were to be published, what manuscripts they were to be based on, and how and by whom they were to be edited; when the format, type, page size, print run, and distribution were dictated by the publisher; and when printers no longer sold the books themselves—then the role of printer becomes a purely technical one, with very little influence over the cultural issues discussed in this section of the book. The parallel change from hand-press to machine-press, with its requirements of greater capital expenditure and a larger market, contributed to the decline of the printer's independence. What was left—typography and technical improvement—falls under a different aegis and is dealt with elsewhere. What remains to be discussed in this chapter, therefore, is the technical processes during the period when the printers did still exercise some control: the first three hundred years.

Printing Techniques: The First Three Centuries

After the provision of the basic materials (paper and ink), the punch-cutter was the first link in the mechanical process which produced the early printed book, and he was one of the first craftsmen to become independent from the printer-publisher. The punch was a male relief model of the type to be cast. As its name suggests, it was used to punch out the shape of the type into the softer material from which the type would be cast (the matrix), and thus was made of hardened metal—iron or steel. The "punch" was cut with those tools typically used by goldsmiths and engravers: files, gravers, oil-stones, and gauges. The punch-cutter's job was perhaps the most delicate of all those crafts associated with printing, and it was no accident that several of the most famous punch-cutters had already been trained in the exacting profession of goldsmith: Griffo, Lautizio of Perugia,

Cennini of Florence, and van Dijck were all goldsmiths, and Caslon had been an apprentice engraver in an armorer's shop.

The printer usually received from the punch-cutter not the punches themselves but the unfinished copper matrices, or "strikes," though some punch-cutters actually did cast type and even printed their own books (Jenson, John Day, and the Le Bé family). Later, when independent foundries had been set up, entire fonts (or sets of type characters) in different sizes would be sold rather than the matrices.

As noted earlier, one of Gutenberg's major contributions to printing was the invention of an adjustable mold capable of accommodating the various matrices for a font of type. Through experimentation, the alloy to be poured into the matrix to cast the type became standardized as a mixture of lead, antimony, and tin, with the lead as the "base" metal. The antimony made the lead harder, and the tin made it more easily meltable. The main qualities sought in the metal used in type-founding were that it should melt at a temperature low enough not to damage the matrices and that it should expand slightly when hardened, so that the mold's shape would be firmly represented in the resulting type.

The type itself was cast with a "jet" or "tang" (a wedge-shaped extension), which was then broken off before the type (see Fig. 12) was actually used. All type had to be of exactly the same height from "foot" (the base of the piece of type) to "face" (the surface which actually came into contact with the paper) to ensure an equal impres-

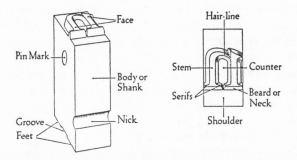

Fig. 12. A piece of type ready for use. Note the "nick" to show the compositor which way up the type is to be held.

sion on the printing surface (today this is fixed at 23.317 mm in most English-speaking countries, although there are still some aberrations, the Clarendon Press of Oxford University retaining the so-called Dutch height of 23.851 mm). The type had to be large enough for the hand-compositor to grasp between thumb and finger, and had a nick along the base line or front of the type so that the compositor could feel which way up the type should go (although in early years there was no nick, so that the compositor would have had to visually inspect each sort before placing it in the stick). Another important standard measurement is point-size, the vertical dimension of a typeface. For several centuries after the invention of printing this measurement lacked any uniformity, with only descriptive names like Gros Oeil, Paragon, Cicero, Gros Romain, Augustin as guide (see Chapter 6 for some examples). When Fournier and later Didot did fix the point system (first at 0.349 mm, then at 0.376 mm per point), it was based on a purely arbitrary calculation, one point being 144th the size of the king's foot. The text of this book is composed in Times Roman 10-point.

A font of type was stored in two cases, the "upper case" containing the capital letters and the "lower case" the small letters. The "lay of the case," or arrangement of the type within the cases (see Fig. 13) was not fixed, for not all types would be needed with the same frequency in every language and in every publication. But the illustrations of cases in Joseph Moxon's *Mechanick Exercises*, 1683, can probably be taken as a general guide to typical practice. Here, the compartment towards the center of the lower case contained those letters needed most often (in English, *e* obviously had a much larger compartment than others), while types used least (e.g., *x*, *z*) were located toward the edges of the case. Working with the two cases, compositors would take their composing-stick in one hand (usually the left) and, consulting the copy before them, select the appropriate type, placing it in the stick upside-down. Inserting spaces between each word, they would proceed until they reached the end of the line. Later composing-sticks were calibrated in 12-point *ems* or *ens* (the width of a capital *M* and *N* respectively in 12-point), but it is unlikely that early compositors had such conveniences to guide them. A complete font of letterpress types is shown in Fig. 14. Modern compositors typically do not use composing sticks at all, except in the few hand-presses still working. Instead the compositor is a keyboard operator and will select characters from a computer "character set" such as the ASCII conversion chart (Fig. 15), which shows the codes for

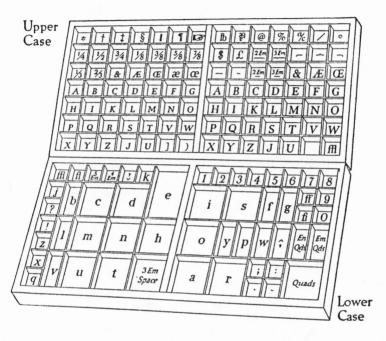

Fig. 13. The lay of the case. Note the "capital" letters in the "upper case" and the small letters in the "lower case," and the large compartments for frequently used letters like *e* and *i*.

accessing special characters like æ, Æ, and £. Different sorts of books will require different character sets, and this book was partly composed in Ventura Math (since I needed technical characters like the Greek χ in the chapter on descriptive bibliography) and partly in Roman-8 (since I needed Anglo-Saxon characters like þ and ð in the chapter on paleography).

Sometimes, the end of a line would correspond with the end of a word, but more often, in order to make the right-hand margin consistent, the compositor would have to "justify" the line-endings by varying the amount of space between words. To early printers, however, there was another alternative—to vary the spelling of the words themselves or to use contractions. A simple suffix like *-less* could be spelled *-les*, *-less*, or *-lesse*. For this reason, it is dangerous to infer

ROMAN

Capitals: A, B, C, D, E, F, G, H, I, J, K, L, M, N, O, P, Q, R, S, T, U, V, W, X, Y, Z, &, Æ, Œ.

Small capitals:[1] A, B, C, D, E, F, G, H, I, J, K, L, M, N, O, P, Q, R, S, T, U, V, W, X, Y, Z, &, Æ, Œ.

Lower case: a, b, c, d, e, f, g, h, i, j, k, l, m, n, o, p, q, r, s, t, u, v, w, x, y, z, æ, œ, ff, fi, fl, ffi, ffl.[2]

Accented letters: á, à, â, ä, é, è, ê, ë, í, ì, î, ï, ó, ò, ô, ö, ú, ù, û, ü.

Figures: 1, 2, 3, 4, 5, 6, 7, 8, 9, 0.

Marks of punctuation: - , ; : . ? ! — ' [ ] ( ).

Marks of reference: *, †, ‡, §, ‖, ¶, ☞.[3]

ITALIC

Capitals: *A, B, C, D, E, F, G, H, I, J, K, L, M, N, O, P, Q, R, S, T, U, V, W, X, Y, Z, &, Æ, Œ.*

Lower case: *a, b, c, d, e, f, g, h, i, j, k, l, m, n, o, p, q, r, s, t, u, v, w, x, y, z, æ, œ, ff, fi, fl, ffi, ffl.*

Accented letters: *á, à, â, ä, é, è, ê, ë, í, ì, î, ï, ó, ò, ô, ö, ú, ù, û, ü.*

Figures: *1, 2, 3, 4, 5, 6, 7, 8, 9, 0.*

Marks of punctuation: *- , ; : . ? ! ( ).*

Spaces: en quadrat, and 3 to em, 4 to em, 5 to em, 6 to em, and hair spaces, used to separate words.

Fig. 14. Letterpress font. Note the sets of small capitals, the accented letters, and the comparatively few remaining ligatures.

spelling usage (either authorial or compositorial) from early printed books, unless all bibliographical possibilities have been considered. In fact, some modern bibliographers have concluded that some apparently unusual spellings (say, the interconsonantal *e* in such words as *amongest*) depended upon the compositor's having to avoid setting two consecutive letters with overlapping "kerns" (parts of a type projecting beyond the body of the type proper, like the tail of *Q*, though not in this type-face) and should not be construed as representing a "normal," or pronounced, spelling. If the page was to be "leaded" (by placing blank strips between the lines of type) the compositor would add the leading (which could be of wood rather than lead) under the line of type, and then proceed to the next line. Leading is almost universal in modern hand-set books, since it makes the lines of print more legible, but it seems not to have been very common in the early years. "Quads" (as the name suggests, originally square spaces,

Dec	Hex	Mnem	Ctrl	Char		Dec	Hex	Mnem	Ctrl	Char
000	00	NUL	^@			016	10	PLE	^P	►
001	01	SOH	^A	☺		017	11	DC1	^Q	◄
002	02	STX	^B	●		018	12	DC2	^R	↕
003	03	ETX	^C	♥		019	13	DC3	^S	‼
004	04	EOT	^D	♦		020	14	DC4	^T	¶
005	05	ENQ	^E	♣		021	15	NAK	^U	§
006	06	ACK	^F	♠		022	16	SYN	^V	▬
007	07	BEL	^G	•		023	17	ETB	^W	↨
008	08	BS	^H	◘		024	18	CAN	^X	↑
009	09	HT	^I	○		025	19	EM	^Y	↓
010	0A	LF	^J	◙		026	1A	SUB	^Z	→
011	0B	VT	^K	♂		027	1B	ESC	^[	←
012	0C	FF	^L	♀		028	1C	FS	^\	∟
013	0D	CR	^M	♪		029	1D	GS	^]	↔
014	0E	SO	^N	♫		030	1E	RS	^^	▲
015	0F	SI	^O	☼		031	1F	US	^_	▼

Dec	Hex	Char		Dec	Hex	Char		Dec	Hex	Char		Dec	Hex	Char		Dec	Hex	Char
032	20	(SP)		077	4D	M		122	7A	z		167	A7	º		212	D4	╘
033	21	!		078	4E	N		123	7B	(		168	A8	¿		213	D5	╒
034	22	"		079	4F	O		124	7C	|		169	A9	⌐		214	D6	╓
035	23	#		080	50	P		125	7D	)		170	AA	¬		215	D7	╫
036	24	$		081	51	Q		126	7E	~		171	AB	½		216	D8	╪
037	25	%		082	52	R		127	7F			172	AC	¼		217	D9	┘
038	26	&		083	53	S		128	80	Ç		173	AD	¡		218	DA	┌
039	27	'		084	54	T		129	81	ü		174	AE	«		219	DB	█
040	28	(		085	55	U		130	82	é		175	AF	»		220	DC	▄
041	29	)		086	56	V		131	83	â		176	B0	░		221	DD	▌
042	2A	*		087	57	W		132	84	ä		177	B1	▒		222	DE	▐
043	2B	+		088	58	X		133	85	à		178	B2	▓		223	DF	▀
044	2C	,		089	59	Y		134	86	å		179	B3	│		224	E0	α
045	2D	-		090	5A	Z		135	87	ç		180	B4	┤		225	E1	β
046	2E	.		091	5B	[		136	88	ê		181	B5	╡		226	E2	Γ
047	2F	/		092	5C	\		137	89	ë		182	B6	╢		227	E3	π
048	30	0		093	5D	]		138	8A	è		183	B7	╖		228	E4	Σ
049	31	1		094	5E	^		139	8B	ï		184	B8	╕		229	E5	σ
050	32	2		095	5F	_		140	8C	î		185	B9	╣		230	E6	μ
051	33	3		096	60	`		141	8D	ì		186	BA	║		231	E7	τ
052	34	4		097	61	a		142	8E	Ä		187	BB	╗		232	E8	Φ
053	35	5		098	62	b		143	8F	Å		188	BC	╝		233	E9	Θ
054	36	6		099	63	c		144	90	É		189	BD	╜		234	EA	Ω
055	37	7		100	64	d		145	91	æ		190	BE	╛		235	EB	δ
056	38	8		101	65	e		146	92	Æ		191	BF	┐		236	EC	∞
057	39	9		102	66	f		147	93	ô		192	C0	└		237	ED	φ
058	3A	:		103	67	g		148	94	ö		193	C1	┴		238	EE	ε
059	3B	;		104	68	h		149	95	ò		194	C2	┬		239	EF	∩
060	3C	<		105	69	i		150	96	û		195	C3	├		240	F0	≡
061	3D	=		106	6A	j		151	97	ù		196	C4	─		241	F1	±
062	3E	>		107	6B	k		152	98	ÿ		197	C5	┼		242	F2	≥
063	3F	?		108	6C	l		153	99	Ö		198	C6	╞		243	F3	≤
064	40	@		109	6D	m		154	9A	Ü		199	C7	╟		244	F4	⌠
065	41	A		110	6E	n		155	9B	¢		200	C8	╚		245	F5	⌡
066	42	B		111	6F	o		156	9C	£		201	C9	╔		246	F6	÷
067	43	C		112	70	p		157	9D	¥		202	CA	╩		247	F7	≈
068	44	D		113	71	q		158	9E	₧		203	CB	╦		248	F8	°
069	45	E		114	72	r		159	9F	ƒ		204	CC	╠		249	F9	∙
070	46	F		115	73	s		160	A0	á		205	CD	═		250	FA	·
071	47	G		116	74	t		161	A1	í		206	CE	╬		251	FB	√
072	48	H		117	75	u		162	A2	ó		207	CF	╧		252	FC	η
073	49	I		118	76	v		163	A3	ú		208	D0	╨		253	FD	²
074	4A	J		119	77	w		164	A4	ñ		209	D1	╤		254	FE	■
075	4B	K		120	78	x		165	A5	Ñ		210	D2	╥		255	FF	
076	4C	L		121	79	y		166	A6	ª		211	D3	╙				

Fig. 15. ASCII Conversion Chart for desktop publishing. The special characters are usually accessed through the alt key and the decimal codes.

Fig. 16. An octavo form on the imposing stone.

though the word is now used in the looser sense of any width of word-divider) could be employed to fill out lines of verse or to leave a line-space in setting stanzaic verse.

Once the composing-stick held six or eight lines of type, the type would be placed in a "galley," or tray holding a complete page of type. When a page was complete, it would be tied with page-cord and stored until there were enough pages set in type to print an entire sheet, when the type-pages would be laid in a form (or forme) on the imposing stone for printing (see Fig. 16).

In the "hot-type" composing common until comparatively recently, it was usual to proof the text from "long galleys" (i.e., before the matter was "made up" into separate pages), but it is unlikely that this proofing occurred often in early printing, and if so, printed copy would not necessarily be checked against manuscript but rather inspected for broken types, faulty lineation and other technical and esthetic matters, not textual accuracy. In computer typesetting, the norm these days, proof is read from first-pass "pages," although second proof is often still separately referred to as "page proof," and some traditional publications, e.g., Bowers's *Studies in Bibliography*, are still proofed in long galleys—and still printed by letterpress (Linotype). Once all the pages were assembled, or "imposed" in the correct order for a gathering, a metal "chase" would be fitted around the pages to make a form, complete with its "furniture," the various nontextual spaces used to fill up the pages, and the whole secured by locking the "quoins," or wedges driven into the form to make it a solid piece which could be lifted without any of the type or furniture falling out.

Now the presswork began (see Fig. 17). The form would be placed on the bed, or "coffin," of the press, which could slide under the "platen," a flat wood and/or iron plate which pressed the paper onto the inked surface of the form by means of a bar-operated screw. The inking was done from an ink-covered stone with two ink-balls, usually of leather with cotton or hair inside, one held in each hand. To prevent the furniture from also being inked by accident, a "frisket," or light hinged frame, was attached to the "tympan," the iron frame covered with parchment on which the paper was placed. The frisket would be secured to a sheet of paper with holes cut in it, which allowed the type-pages to show through but not the furniture. When the form was printed, it had to be hung up for the ink to dry before the other side of the sheet could be printed. To make sure that the positions of the pages on the other side of the sheet corresponded exactly with those on the first side (or were in perfect "register"), two points were attached to the tympan-sheet to make pin-holes in the paper as a guide. Once all the required sheets of paper had been printed from a form, the form would be washed to clean it of ink, "unlocked" to remove the furniture, and the pages tied up again preparatory to folding and stitching. The types would then be "distributed," or replaced into their appropriate compartments of the case, by the compositors, who probably each had a particular case as his own responsibility.

The process of imposition is a complex one. The following description is from the point of view of the printer; another account, as an aspect of bibliographical description, may be found in Chapter 4. For both accounts the reader is referred to the diagrams in Figs. 18–28, which provide some visual assistance.

The simplest "format" of printing is where one sheet contains only one page of matter, with no folding required. These "broadsheets" or "broadsides" (bs. or 1 to the bibliographer, see Fig. 28) were often used for proclamations to be posted on a wall and were therefore

Fig. 17. Parts of a printing press.

printed on only one side. But they were hardly "books" in the sense we are using the term here. The next degree of complexity is where a single sheet is folded once, to make a folio (fol. or 2 to the bibliographer, see Fig. 19). The outer side of the sheet would contain pages 1 and 4 and thus be known as the outer form (forme in British usage, and so designated in the illustrations) and the inner sheet would contain pages 2 and 3 and be called the inner form. The same principle holds for all formats: the outer form prints page 1 and the inner form page 2. However, as with manuscripts, printed folios in the early period would normally be sewn not individually but in groups, or "gatherings" or "quires," the most common form being three sheets, or a folio in six leaves (and therefore called a folio in sixes, with simi-

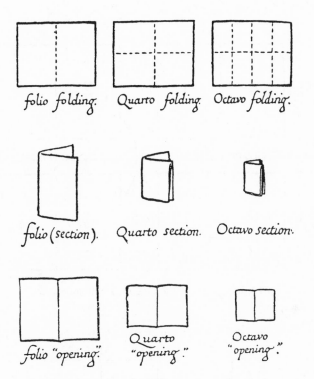

Fig. 18. Folding for folio, quarto, and octavo.

lar terms for the other smaller formats, where the number of leaves determines the designation within the format, e.g., a quarto in fours or eights, an octavo in eights or sixteens, see Figs. 23–24, 26–27). Folios in sixes continued to be common until the eighteenth century, when quiring was largely discontinued and folios were gathered by single sheets, despite the extra sewing this would involve (see Figs. 20 and 21 for imposition and folding for a folio in sixes, and see Chapter 2 for the manuscript book equivalent). The problem for the printer, as for the scribe, was that since these sheets had to be printed flat rather than after they had been sewn together into a gathering, a form would not (except for the innermost pages) contain consecutive matter. In a folio in sixes the text for pages 1 and 12 would have to

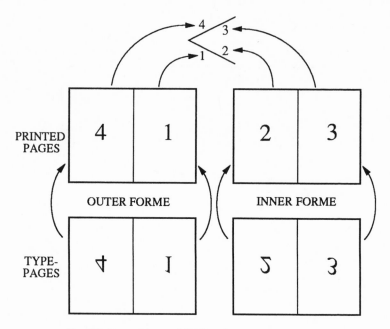

Fig. 19. Imposition and folding for single folio sheet.

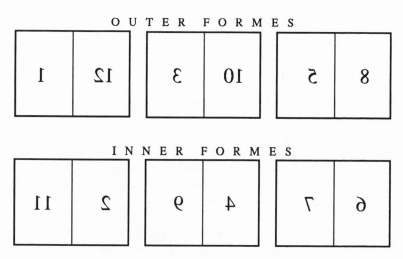

Fig. 20. Type-pages for folio in sixes.

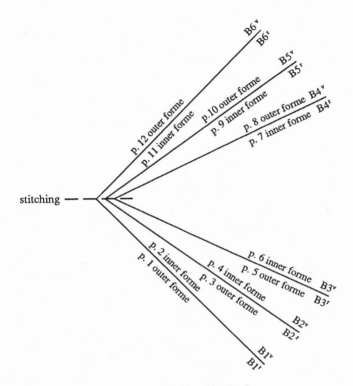

Fig. 21. Folding for folio in sixes.

be set at the same time, and only pages 6 and 7 would have continuous copy on the same form. This meant that the amount of type for every page after the first (which would not necessarily be printed first) would have to be estimated in advance. The number of forms that could be set up before printing began would, of course, be determined by the availability of type in the same font, so that there were practical limitations on the number of sheets in a gathering.

Folio volumes were large, cumbersome books reserved for only the most monumental works (hence the derision poured on Ben Jonson when he dared to publish mere plays—or "works" as he affectedly called them—in folio). The more common format was the quarto, a book made up of sheets folded two times (4°, 4to, Q, or Q^{to} to the bibliographer; see Figs. 22 and 23 for imposition and folding for a single-sheet quarto). All of Shakespeare's plays printed before the great First Folio of 1623 were in quarto. The quarto was a smaller,

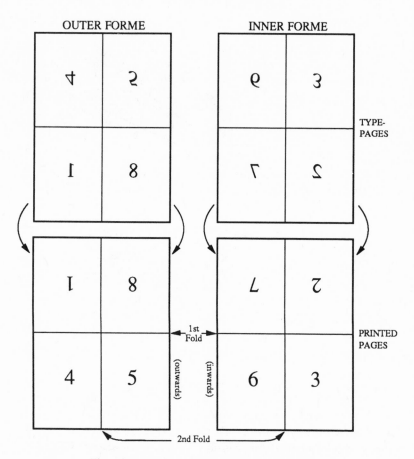

Fig. 22. Imposition for a single sheet of quarto.

more easily handled book, but it increased the problems of imposition yet again, especially since, like the folio, it would in the early period often consist not of a single sheet but of several sheets folded together, one inside another, to produce, say, a quarto in eights (see Fig. 24). The convenience of multiple folding (it involved less sewing) meant that the number of intervening text-pages between the two outer pages of the gathering increased yet again, for in a quarto in eights pages 1 and 16 would be imposed at the same time, and only pages 8 and 9 would have continuous copy set on the same form.

An added result of quarto folding was that some of the folds re-

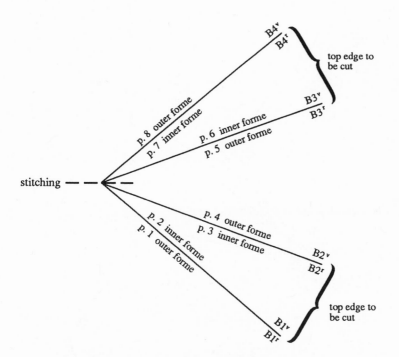

Fig. 23. Folding for a single sheet of quarto.

mained on the top edges of the book and that these would have to be cut (usually by the purchaser) before the book could be read. In a quarto in eights, the top edge between pages 2 and 3, 6 and 7, 10 and 11, and 14 and 15 would need to be cut. If a book still remains in this condition, it is called "unopened" (the term "uncut" being used to refer to a book which has not been trimmed down from its original dimensions). These same basic principles of multiple foldings and the resulting increased separation of copy to be set at the same time become more complex as the formats decrease in size (i.e., as the broadsheet is folded more times to produce more and smaller pages). Thus octavo (see Fig. 25 for imposition of a single sheet and Fig. 26 for folding of a single sheet) was folded three times, and represented as 8°, or 8vo, with eight pages on one form. Pages 1 and 16 would be set at the same time and only pages 8 and 9 would have continuous copy on the same form. An added complication with octavo was that folds would remain on both top and fore-edges, and that, for a single sheet octavo, the top folds between pages 4 and 5, 12 and 13 (and the

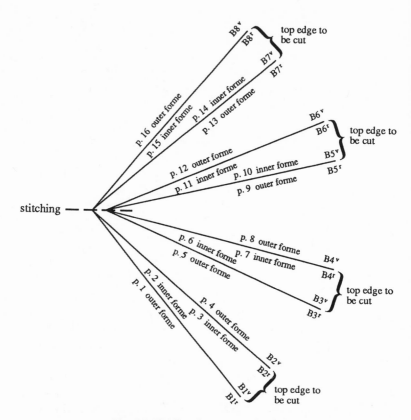

Fig. 24. Folding for a quarto in eights.

top folds between pages 1/2 and 7/8 and 9/10 and 15/16), plus the fore-edges between pages 10 and 11 and 14 and 15, would all have to be cut. Again, octavo might in the early days of printing be sewn in gatherings or quires of multiple sheets (although this is not common after the fifteenth century), so that the distance between the outer pages of the gathering would increase yet again (see Fig. 27 for an octavo in sixteens, where pages 1 and 32 would be set at the same time, and only pages 16 and 17 would have continuous copy set at the same time on the same form). Top and fore-edges would again have to be cut as in the diagram.

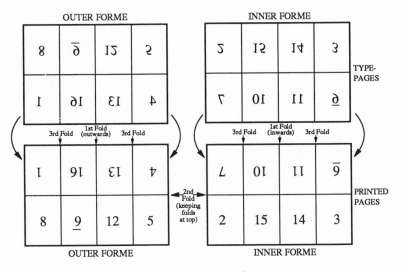

Fig. 25. Imposition for single-sheet octavo.

As the formats get smaller still, the imposition complexities increase, from sextodecimo, or sixteenmo (folded four times, and represented as 16° or 16mo), with sixteen pages per form; tricesimosecundo or thirtytwomo (folded five times and represented as 32° or 32mo), with thirty-two pages per form, and even to sexagesimoquarto, or sixtyfourmo (folded six times, and represented as 64° or 64mo), with sixty-four pages per form. There were two common intermediate formats (duodecimo and twentyfourmo, represented by 12mo and 24mo respectively), which were formed by folding twice across the longer dimension of the sheet and three times across the shorter, and removing the "offcut" of four leaves and folding it inside the eight-leaf remainder of the sheet, to make the total of twelve leaves (duodecimo), and doubling the folding and leaves for twentyfourmo. An alternative method to whole-sheet imposition was "half-sheet imposition" in which a half-sheet was imposed in a single form, the paper then turned after one side had been printed, and the other side then printed from the same form, the sheet being cut to produce two identical copies. The advantage of half-sheet imposition was that it would halve the number of pages the printer would have to keep in

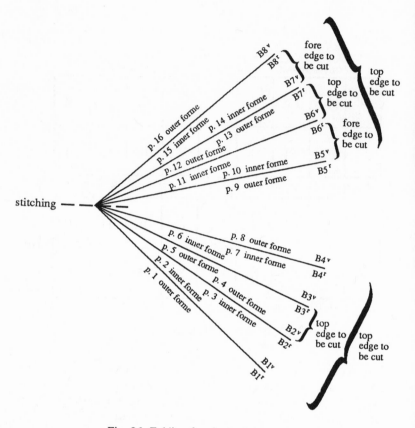

Fig. 26. Folding for single-sheet octavo.

type at one time, and thus cut down on the most expensive part of the printing process, standing type.

How may the bibliographer discover which format (folio, quarto, etc.) was used for a book? To some extent, the size and proportions may be a guide: folio books are large, octavo are small; folios and octavos tend to be taller and thinner than quartos (although cutting and binding may obscure these distinctions). But this is in any case a very imprecise method of analysis. Short of ripping apart the binding and taking the gatherings apart, the bibliographer may employ a number of other tests to determine the format of a book. Many of these tests are too complicated to be discussed here, but one may be described in general outline: the use of the watermarks and chain lines to determine the format (see Fig. 28, and also see Chapter 2 for an

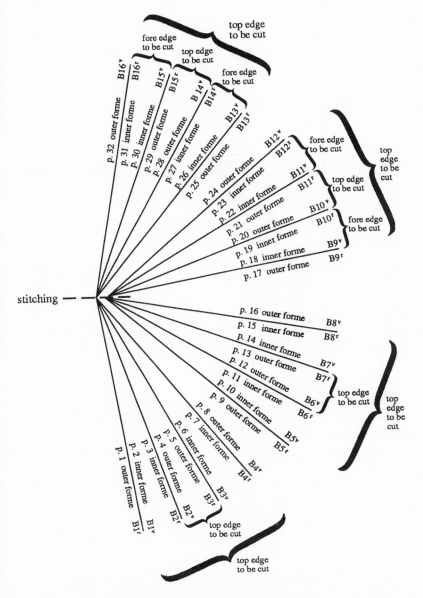

Fig. 27. Folding for an octavo in sixteens.

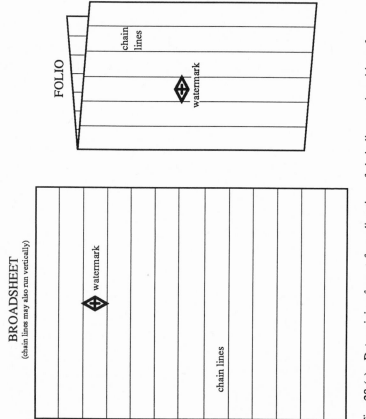

Fig. 28 (a). Determining format from direction of chain lines and position of watermark: broadsheet and folio.

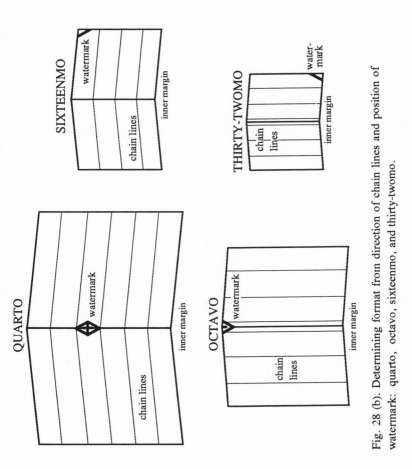

Fig. 28 (b). Determining format from direction of chain lines and position of watermark: quarto, octavo, sixteenmo, and thirty-twomo.

account of how watermarks and chain lines are produced.) In a broadside, the watermark will be in the top center of the sheet, and the chain lines will be horizontal. Once this sheet is folded (folio), the watermark will appear in the center of the first leaf of the folded sheet, and the chain lines will be vertical. In a quarto, the watermark will be split by the stitching, appearing half in the first leaf of the folded sheet and half in the last sheet, with the intermediate sheets bearing no watermark (i.e., the watermark will appear on leaves 1 and 4 or pages 2 and 3, depending upon the imposition). The chain lines will again be horizontal. In an octavo, the watermark will be quartered, appearing in the top inner margins of four leaves (1, 4, 5, and 8, or 2, 3, 6, and 7), with the chain lines vertical. The system is not perfect, for half-sheet imposition could change the direction of the chain lines, and in some of the smaller formats the watermark may have disappeared altogether into the binding.

Describing imposition and format verbally, especially in the abbreviated manner of the last few pages, is not likely to make this aspect of bibliography appear a model of simplicity and clarity, although the diagrams should help to visualize the process. The best way to demonstrate the descriptions outlined above is to become a temporary printer and binder—that is, to follow the directions for imposition and gathering oneself. Take, for example, Figs. 20–21 showing the imposition of type pages and the folding for a folio in sixes. Fold three sheets once each and gather them in a quire of sixes as shown in Fig. 21, and then number them in the order they will appear to the reader, from page 1 to page 6. Ignore, for the moment, the "signatures" B1, B2, etc. (these will be explained in the next few pages). Then separate the sheets again to see how that numbering scheme will appear to the printer before binding (you should get a layout for imposition like that in Fig. 20). Do the same for quarto (folding the sheet or sheets twice), for octavo (three times), and for the position of watermarks and chain lines, beginning with the single broadside sheet. In this way, the theoretical complexities of format should become a good deal less forbidding and more comprehensible. Printing is, after all, an eminently practical craft, and the complications were introduced not for their own sake but to make the resulting manufacture of books cheaper, easier, and quicker.

When the separate sheets to be made up into the printed book arrived at the binder, some guidance was obviously necessary as to how they should be stitched together to form the completed volume. Thus came about the "signature," a letter or other symbol appearing at the bottom of a page to indicate which gathering it belonged to. While theoretically the entire alphabet from A to Z was available for signatures, in practice only the twenty-three letters of the latin alphabet were employed, with I but not usually J, V but not usually U, and with W omitted. A complete sequence of alphabetical signatures would therefore consist of twenty-three gatherings: A, B, C, D, E, F, G, H, I, K, L, M, N, O, P, Q, R, S, T, V, X, Y, Z. Furthermore, although in practice often unsigned, the "preliminaries" of a book (dedication, title-page, etc.) could sometimes be regarded as the A gathering, and the actual signatures might therefore begin with B. In an embarrassing example of the text beginning with the B gathering is Lady Mary Wroth's *Urania* (1621), where the printer began the text with B on the assumption that laudatory introductory materials from noble personages would arrive for the A gathering, only to have none turn up, and thus to do without an A gathering or any prelims. Unsigned preliminary gatherings are represented in bibliographical description by the symbol *pi* [π]. Signed preliminary gatherings may have as a signature any of several other symbols not easily confused with actual letters of the alphabet: # or $ or * or § or ‡.

Once a single alphabetical run was exhausted, the letter system could be repeated by doubling (AA, BB, CC, etc. or Aa, Bb, Cc), then by tripling (AAA, BBB, CCC, etc. or Aaa, Bbb, Ccc, etc.), and so on. The bibliographer represents a complete run of signatures by the bibliographical formula A–Z, that is, twenty-three gatherings, in the order of the modified alphabet listed above. If there are any abnormalities in the signature run (e.g., the use of both I and J, or U and V, or of W, or the omission of any letter usually included), these are noted in the formula. Thus, the formula A–I, J, K–T, U, V, W, X–Z is the bibliographical equivalent of an entire "modern" alphabet from A to Z. The formula A–D, F–Z would show that the expected signature E has been omitted from the sequence, but that everything else is as normal.

The repeated alphabets are usually not given in the actual signature form of multiple letters, but in a reduced formula. For example, 2A means the second gathering of "As," no matter how it may actually be signed (as AA, Aa), 3A means the third gathering of "As," etc. The number of leaves in each gathering is indicated by a supralinear number (e.g., $A-Z^4$ means there are twenty-three gatherings, each with four leaves). Just as in the listing of the alphabetical symbols, the bibliographer should note in the formula any abnormalities or irregularities in the number of leaves. Thus, $A-E^4$, F^6, $G-Z^4$ shows that the F gathering is alone in having six leaves, all twenty-two others having four. Within each gathering, the printer would number each *recto* (the right-hand page in an opening) in numerical sequence: B1, B2, B3, etc. Strictly speaking, it would have been necessary for the printer of, say, a folio in sixes, to have printed signatures only as far as the third recto, leaving the rest unsigned. This would have been sufficient to show that there was no additional sheet to go inside the B3 and B4 "conjugate" (or joined) leaves. In practice, however, a printer's habits might be quite erratic, with sometimes fewer, sometimes more than the requisite number of rectos being signed.

Even when pagination is included in an early printed book, the descriptive bibliographer will prefer to use the signature system as a more accurate guide to the makeup of the book, and even as a reference to individual pages. As in manuscript description, the use of a supralinear ^{r} (for recto), and ^{v} (for *verso*, or left-hand page in an opening) indicates the pages in a gathering. Thus, $B3^r$ means the recto side of the third leaf of the B gathering in the first alphabetical sequence of gatherings. Given that there is no A gathering, this will normally correspond to what would be "page 5" in a modern book (see figures for additional examples within typical B gatherings in various formats). Should there be alphabetical repetitions, the formulas $2B3^r$, $3B3^r$, etc., could be employed.

Note that in these cases, we cannot tell what the "page-number" equivalent would be without knowing from the full bibliographical formula how many leaves there are in each gathering and how many gatherings in a sequence of signatures. For a perfectly regular folio in sixes, with twelve pages in each gathering, and with twenty-two gatherings per alphabetical sequence and no irregularities in number of leaves per gathering, $2B3^r$ (the recto page of the third leaf of the B gathering in the second sequence of alphabetical sections of the book) would probably be page 269 ($22 \times 12 + 5 = 269$) if there were no paginated or signed A gathering in either sequence. If there were regular A gatherings in both sequences, then $2B3^r$ would correspond to page 293 ($23 \times 12 + 12$ [second A gathering] $+ 5 = 293$). Finally, while a raised ^{a} ($=^r$) and ^{b} ($=^v$) may also be used to refer to specific pages of a gathering, this could be somewhat confusing, since in books (and especially manuscripts) in two columns, the ^{a} and ^{b} can refer to the column rather than the page, so that 2^b would mean the right-hand column of the recto page of the second folio (for manuscripts), or gathering (for printed books).

A full bibliographical description of a book will always contain an account in the "collation" section of the "register of signatures," according to the formulas listed above. This will normally come immediately after the format and the quasi-facsimile title-page transcription (see Chapter 4, for a fuller account of bibliographical description) and will include a listing of signed and unsigned leaves, any indication of foliation or pagination, and running-titles.

In modern books the signature may not appear. If the printer does not want the signature to clutter up the bottom of the page in the bound volume, he may place it so low on the page that it will be trimmed off by the binder in making up the book. Alternatively, black-step collation marks may be used instead of signatures as a guide to the binder. These are quad marks printed on the back of a gathering between the first and last pages, graduated down the page in such a way that when the sections are brought together, any error in gathering can immediately be seen. Since the collation marks are covered by the spine when the book is bound and covered, they cannot be seen by the reader.

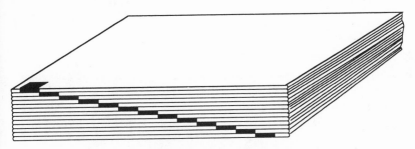

Fig. 29. Black step collation marks.

The process of printing has now been followed up to the point of stitching the gatherings together. Next, the book had to be bound. Binding practices did not greatly change in the first three hundred years after the invention of printing. The binding was still considered as separate from the book itself and thus the one area in which the idiosyncrasies of the individual owner could be indulged. For this reason, the reader may still use the section on manuscript binding as a rough general guide to the subject. Some early printers did their own binding, but it was probably the normal practice for the purchaser to commission the binding separately from the book itself. This is demonstrably so in England in the late sixteenth century, where the association of a binding with a particular press (through, for example, a printer's device) seems to disappear, although cheap "publishers' bindings" were used in the seventeenth century for the less expensive smaller formats. Books sold by subscription in the eighteenth century were delivered in sheets, roughly sewn. Since the book was hardly readable in this condition, the publisher began to provide a temporary binding, which gradually led to the conventional cloth-covered boards of the early nineteenth century, and ultimately to the "hardback" book of today.

This account covers the *text* of the early printed book. But books were often lavishly endowed with illustrations, as were their manuscript predecessors, and something should be said here of how such illustrations in printed books were typically produced during the first three centuries of printing. As already noted, there are three basic methods of printing—letterpress, intaglio, and planographic—and any of these may be used to produce book illustrations. In practice, however, the first two, or relief methods, were most commonly used in the first three hundred years. The earliest illustrations were relief woodcuts (xylography), cut with the grain of the wood.

Fig. 30. Woodcut from first printed book with illustrations, *Der Edelstein*, Albrecht Pfister, Bamberg, 1461.

Fig. 31. Woodcut from *The Nuremberg Chronicle*, 1493.

The illustrator followed essentially the same method as the punch-cutter, cutting away everything except the parts of the illustration that were to appear printed on the paper. The great advantage of this technique was, therefore, that a woodcut could be printed in the same way, and at the same time, as the text proper. This made printing an illustrated book comparatively easy, for a single "pull" at the press (from the motion necessary at the handle of the press-screw to lower the platen onto the paper) could provide both words and picture, instead of having to print them separately. And woodcuts soon became widely used in incunabula printing, as evidenced in the 1,800 woodcuts included in Koberger's famous *Liber chronicarum* (better known as the *Nuremberg Chronicle*), a survey of the world with many illustrations of places and people (see Fig. 31).

In contrast to the letterpress method of the woodcut, the wood engraving is an intaglio method. The engraver works on the end of a

Fig. 32. Wood engraving by Thomas Bewick, 1790.

block of wood, cutting into it the lines which are to be printed.

Wood engraving was not perfected until the eighteenth century in the work of Thomas Bewick (see Fig. 32), whereas woodcuts were popular from the very earliest days of printing, attracting some of the finest artists of the time, amongst whom Dürer was probably the most prominent. Woodcuts did, however, lose some ground to the finer work that could be produced by copper engravings (another intaglio process) in the late seventeenth and eighteenth centuries. The copper engraver used a sharp burin to engrave in the metal, and much greater pressure was needed to pick up the fine lines engraved into the metal than was used in letterpress. Because copper is a relatively soft metal, these fine lines were easily worn down by repeated printings; thus, the earlier the print, the better the quality. As a result, steel was adopted as the medium for engravings at a later date. Other developments in the history of book illustration will be considered at the end of this chapter.

Later Technical Developments in Printing

A. *Paper-Making*

As mentioned earlier, it was not until the end of the eighteenth century that the old system of paper-making by hand began to change. Nicolas-Louis Robert patented a long-wire cloth machine in 1799, later improved by Bryan Donkin and the Fourdrinier brothers. Steam power was added by Crompton in 1821, and, as newspapers started to require web-fed rather than sheet-fed paper for their increasingly mechanized printing presses, the continuous roll of paper began replacing sheets for most large-scale commercial uses. A modern machine for newsprint like a Canadian "papriformer" can produce web paper at a speed of five thousand feet of paper per minute (as compared with the most recent version of the Fourdrinier process, at three thousand feet per minute).

Machine-made paper, often called "wove" (although the term is somewhat ambiguous, since a "wove" effect was introduced in the mid-eighteenth century, before the paper-making process had been properly mechanized), can be distinguished from "laid" or hand-made, paper by its very even, fine mesh, lacking the chain-lines of hand-made—although these features can be introduced artificially in modern machine-made paper. Furthermore, if a circle of hand-made paper is dropped into water, all the edges will turn up uniformly, whereas with machine-made paper, only two sides will turn up. Finally, wove paper will tear easily in one direction but will resist tearing, producing a ragged edge, in the other direction.

Modern paper must pass through a series of machines, each with rather violent or painful names: the thrasher, cutter, devil or whipper, the duster, digester, washer, drainer, beater. The "half-stuff" solution of soaked rags (about 97 percent water) is pumped onto a moving belt of tightly woven screen wire. The pulp, kept in place by "deckle-straps," gradually moves from the "wet end" to the "dry end" of the machine. A "dandy-roll" then compresses the pulp. After passing through the press-rolls, which squeeze out the remaining water, the paper is then dried and given a smooth finish by the "calendars;" (glossy finishes are produced by "supercalendaring").

B. *Types and Typesetting*

While even today some of the more fanciful display types may still be cut by hand, the invention of the Benton punch-cutting machine in 1884 in Milwaukee enabled multiple copies of the same punches to be engraved. The Benton machine, which used a revolving cutting tool to trace around an enlarged outline of a model of the type, spurred the invention of mechanical typesetters, which obviously needed an ample supply of identical punches if they were to run efficiently. The Benton also encouraged the growth of "families" of type (bold, condensed, etc.) of basically the same design.

The earliest machine for casting type was invented in 1822 by William Church. This machine was capable of casting up to three thousand sorts (or individual pieces of type) per hour by placing the type cast directly into a magazine, from which it could be set up by keyboard instructions rather than manually. However, the Church machine still needed two or three workers to operate it, and in labor productivity it was therefore not particularly efficient. After a number of improvements to the method in the early nineteenth century, the first casting machine to produce type which could be used without any additional finishing was introduced by the firm of Foucher in 1883.

Stereotyping is the process of casting a duplicate plate of the original page from a molded matrix taken from the type-page. The advantage of this method is that it saves wear on the original and avoids having to re-set the pages for a reprint. The stereotype is thus a solid-metal duplicate relief-printing surface. The matrix for a stereotype is made of "flong," which may be wet paper pulp, plaster of paris, clay, plastic, or other malleable materials. The casting produced by the molten metal poured into the matrix is often hardened by plating with nickel or other materials to increase its durability. The term "stereotype" was first used by the Didot firm in the late eighteenth century, but this was only after a hundred years of earlier experiments, the progress of stereotyping having been hindered by opposition from printers and typefounders. The best-known early experimenter, William Ged (1690–1749), died a pauper. Ged had used plaster of paris molds to cast the printing plates in 1727, as did Alexander Tilloch and Andrew Foulis in a patent of 1784. The first stereotype plates had been cast by the German Johann Müller at the very beginning of the eighteenth century. The other major advantage of the papier-mâché or plaster-of-paris mold was that it could be curved and thus produce printing plates to fit onto a printing cylinder. This was first done by William Nicholson in 1816, in experiments which led in 1886 to the use of stereotypes on the rotary press of *The Times* newspaper in London.

In 1886 Ottmar Mergenthaler introduced the Linotype machine in New York. This machine, which combined the three stages of composing, casting, and justifying, and needed only a single operator, could produce a complete line of type, or "slugs" from brass matrices circulating through each stage and back again. After each use, the lead slugs were melted down and the same process was repeated. While the production of type-pages was made much more efficient by the Linotype machine, proof correction became more expensive, since an entire line had to be re-cast in order to correct even a single letter. Moreover, in the correcting, another, different error could very well be introduced, and so on.

The Monotype machine, invented by Tolbert Lanston in 1885, offered an alternative for more expensive book printing (Linotype was at first used primarily for newspapers). The Monotype machine, as its name suggests, cast individual types, which, like those used in Linotype, could be melted down after use. The pneumatic Monotype keyboard produces perforations in a roll of paper, which acts as a code for the casting and justifying mechanism. (The Elektron version of Linotype is also operated by tape.)

Similar to the stereotype is the electrotype, a duplicate printing surface, again formed from pressure-molding, of wax, lead, or plastic. The mold is dusted with graphite to make it electroconductive, and then coated with a thin shell of copper. This is often backed by lead and given a hardened face of nickel or chromium. Nickeltypes are produced in basically the same manner.

All of these systems—stereotyping, electrotyping, Linotype, and Monotype—are sophistications of the letterpress, or relief, method of printing. With the growth of photography and related planographic practices, and with the addition of computers as an aid to both composing and printing, the use of letterpress declined greatly during the last half-century, and has now virtually disappeared, except for fine printing at private presses.

Lithography was the earliest (or at least, the first documented) employment of an essentially planographic system for printing and illustration. The term means "printing from stone," and it was Aloysius Senefelder of Munich who in 1796 began producing relief-engravings from drawings on local stone. Gradually, it occurred to him that the relief was not necessary, for the stone could absorb water, in contrast to a greasy design, which would repel water but attract a similarly greasy ink. This was the beginning of the concept of chemical printing. Nowadays, stone has been largely abandoned in large-scale lithographic printing, and specially prepared zinc or aluminum plates are used instead. Because most modern lithography is produced by the "offset" method of printing (see below), the two terms, separately or in combination, are often used synonymously. Offset lithography is properly a printing process in which a planographic surface is used to produce an inked impression on a rubber-blanketed cylinder, which in turn transfers this impression to the receiving surface.

Fig. 33. Early lithograph on stone by Géricault.

Photo-offset is a form of offset in which the planographic plate is prepared photographically.

Phototypesetting or filmsetting uses not a relief matrix but a trans-
parent, plane surface, from which the model letters are produced on
film or paper for printing by a photographic process. William Friese-
Greene patented the first photographic composition method in 1895,
but the invention was not successful commercially. Later, the Dutch

Hadego headline machine photographed hand-composed lines of plastic matrices of display type, but the first filmsetting machine for general use was Intertype's Fotosetter, developed in 1947, in which entire lines (as in Linotype) were composed on film from characters photographed from negatives in separate matrices. Linotype's Linofilm, Monotype's Monophoto, and many other different models, representing different systems of using photography, quickly followed. Some of these were essentially modifications of existing hot-metal principles, but others began to dispense with any mechanical system, a process enhanced by the introduction of computer assistance.

The great advantage of computer typesetting is not only that insertions, deletions, justification, pagination, indexing, typeface changes, and the like can be easily accomplished without having to re-set, but that the "text" of the work can be economically and conveniently stored as data on tape or disk for future editions in different formats, typefaces, and sizes, since the data are merely a series of codes which can be reinterpreted according to instructions given to the composing machine. With advances such as Donald Knuth's *TEX* typesetting system (see Hofstadter), individual authors can (theoretically, at least) exercise complete control over the typesetting of the work as it is being "composed" (in both senses). It is no accident that two of the most important recent books on textual criticism, Jerome J. McGann's *A Critique of Modern Textual Criticism* and Peter Shillingsburg's *Scholarly Editing in the Computer Age* (see Chapter 8), had their typesetting programs written by their authors. Even this present book is an example of "desk-top" publishing, for the text was entered on a conventional computer keyboard, and then typesetting commands (e.g., typeface and "family,"—roman, italic, bold, bold italic—point size, leading, running heads) added through a typesetting program (Hewlett Packard Type Director) compatible with the software (Wordstar 6.0) and a laser printer (Hewlett Packard LaserJet II).

C. *Printing Presses*

The history of printing as a technical process during the last two hundred years is largely the account not only of mechanical changes to the press itself but also of the widening use of non-letterpress methods in the printing of typographic copy. Printing presses before the nineteenth century were all essentially of the platen type—that is, they were machines which used a flat printing surface and a flat form, brought together by pressure. Improvements to these presses were

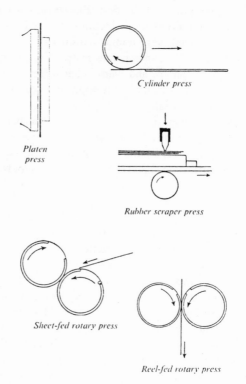

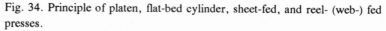

Fig. 34. Principle of platen, flat-bed cylinder, sheet-fed, and reel- (web-) fed presses.

mostly concerned with the introduction of lighter and more powerful (and eventually screwless) presses made of iron in place of the slow, cumbersome, wooden ones, which could produce only about 250 sheets per hour. The first iron press was made by Wilhelm Haas of Basel in 1772, but it was the designs of Earl Stanhope and the work of his engineer Robert Walker in the late eighteenth and early nineteenth centuries which brought the iron press proper recognition. The compound levers of Stanhope's presses added greatly to the power of the screw, improved by George Clymer of Philadelphia in his Columbian press (ca. 1813), by Dingler in his Washington press (1820), and by R. W. Cope in his Albion press (1822). The simplicity and strength of the iron-platen hand press ensured its success throughout the century, and small jobbing presses are often still of a basically platen type.

In the meantime, however, there were experiments to overcome an inherent limitation in the platen press: that its mechanical principles were in conflict, with a horizontal movement needed to place the printing surface in position, but a vertical movement needed for the actual printing. These two could be combined in a cylindrical method of inking (in much the same way as a rotary engine in an automobile avoids the transference of a reciprocal motion to a circular one in the conventional internal combustion engine), and as William Nicholson had realized as early as 1790. By 1811, Friedrich König, who had been living in England since 1806, had produced a steam-driven flat-bed cylinder press which could print eight hundred copies an hour. In 1814, two of these machines were purchased by *The Times* of London to produce (at eleven hundred sheets an hour, on one side) the "first newspaper printed by steam," as the editors announced to their astonished readers.

Much of the subsequent improvement in printing-press technology occurred first in newspapers, and very often at *The Times*. These changes were a reflection of the need to produce high-quality large-scale printing at great speed. For example, by 1827, Augustus Applegath and Edward Cowper had improved the printing rate of the flat-bed cylinder press to five thousand impressions an hour by 1827. But the flat-bed cylinder press still involved a reciprocal action: the printing surface was flat and horizontal, whereas the plate cylinder had to roll back and forth. Richard Hoe's true rotary press—in which both impression cylinder and plate cylinder rotated and could therefore move continuously, without having to stop and roll back—was introduced in 1845, employed in a Philadelphia newspaper in 1847, and taken up by *The Times* in a form modified by Applegath the following year. Ten years later, an improved version of the Hoe press, with an increased number of impression cylinders, was adopted at *The Times*.

The rotary press needed continuously fed paper to work to its maximum efficiency. Experiments in "web-fed," as opposed to "sheet-fed," presses had been made by Rowland Hill in 1835, but William Bullock's press in Philadelphia (1865) and *The Times*'s Walter press (1866) were the first successful applications of the continuous roll of paper for printing in a rotary press. The Walter press could print twenty-five thousand sheets, on both sides, per hour. It was the offset principle which made the rotary press even more efficient. In offset there is no direct contact between the form and the

Fig. 35. Drypoint engraving by Dürer, *St. Jerome*, 1512.

sheet, the impression being carried by a "blanket" (usually of rubber). As suggested above, offset is most commonly associated with plano-graphic lithography, although offset presses for intaglio and letter-press have been invented.

Finally, one of the most popularly used forms of reproducing doc-uments, xerography, should be considered briefly. This is, in fact, not really a printing process, for there is no impression and no ink. The image is transferred photoelectrically, with powders that adhere only to areas of the receiving surface that remain electrically charged. The "ink" is thus really powder (called "toner"), and the "impression," or rather image, is made permanent by heat, not pressure.

D. *Other Developments in Illustration*

What follows is only a brief selection of some of the most important methods of illustration beyond those already covered earlier in this chapter—wood-cut, wood engraving, and lithograph. There is no attempt to cover the field comprehensively, but simply to define some of the more common terms which the student is likely to encounter.

In its widest sense, the term "gravure" can be used to describe any process for making an intaglio printing surface by incision. After Bewick's work on wood engraving in the late eighteenth century (mentioned earlier in this chapter), the most significant developments

Fig. 36. Meisenbach's first half-tone, 1882.

in this process were dry point, mezzotint, and photoengraving.

Drypoint (see Fig. 35) is an engraving made with a needle rather than a burin. The engraving is carved directly into the metal (i.e., there is no acid used, as in etching), and the burr thrown up is not removed (as in regular copper or steel engraving) but retained, to produce the soft lines which are typical of this sort of print. A "half-tone" (so-called because for the first time, an image could be produced effectively displaying the grays or "half" tones between black

Fig. 37. Mezzotint by Ludwig von Siegen, portrait of Elizabeth of Bohemia, 1642.

and white) is a photoengraving, and therefore a "mixed" or "semi-mechanical" method. The image is photographed through a screen made up of a dense lattice of horizontal and vertical lines. During engraving, the details are reproduced by thousands of dots, heavier ones producing the darker areas, and finer, more diffused ones the

Fig. 38. Etching by Piranesi, *Carceri*, 1750.

lighter areas. The first successful half-tone was produced by Meisenbach in 1882 (see Fig. 36). Mezzotint (see Fig. 37) is an engraving produced on an already roughened copper or steel plate, in which the patterns of light and shade are created by a gradual burnishing of the rough places. "Line-cuts," which use lines of varying thickness, grain, dots, stipples, and cross-hatching, are another form of photo-engraving.

Unlike engraving, the term "etching" should properly be restricted to processes in which a "ground" covers the plate and is then incised with a metal tool and/or acid. A "soft ground" is usually made of a tallow or grease mixture and can produce various textured effects. During a series of separate "bitings" in the ground, the artist "stops out" particular areas at different depths, resulting in a print with graded shades of dark and light. An aquatint (see Fig. 39) is a partic-

Fig. 39. Aquatint, *La ménagère*, by Jean-Baptiste Le Prince.

ular form of etching in which the ground is made grainy by adding sand or powdered rosin. A stopping-out varnish is used in the earliest biting for the white areas, and in further bitings, gradations of shade, each containing the grainy effect of the sand or rosin, produces a print looking rather like a watercolor (hence its name). The process was invented by Jean-Baptiste Le Prince (1734–81).

We have now investigated the physical make-up of books both manuscript and printed (codicology and historical/analytical bibliography), with some consideration of the cultural and social circumstances in which they are produced. The next stage in the evolving narrative of textual scholarship is to employ this technical information in describing the book as artifact (descriptive bibliography), and to this subject the next chapter is devoted.

4

Describing the Text: Descriptive Bibliography

Having examined the physical history of the book as artifact, the textual scholar must then have some system for describing the book. In dealing with printed books, bibliographers have used the concept of "ideal copy" to represent a state of the text that, while recognizing the physical differences in individual copies, attempts to describe a form of the book as intended for "publication" by the printer. The codicologist, however, works only from specific manuscripts and usually describes each of them (when dealing with texts with multiple copies) rather than reconstructing an ideal version. Otherwise, the process of description—even the basic terminology and formulae—used by descriptive bibliographers of manuscripts and printed books is quite similar. Some of the practical differences are simply the result of the separate histories of manuscripts and printed books. For example, the "quasi-facsimile" title-page transcription is very important in the descriptive bibliography of printed books but virtually unknown for manuscripts, because title-pages hardly occur in manuscripts (and only rarely in incunabula) but are the primary means of identifying printed books from the sixteenth century on.

Manuscript Description

In describing manuscripts, the following information (technical details of which can be found in Chapter 2) should normally be noted:
1. The title of the manuscript (i.e., its accession number, catalogue number, etc., in the library where it is currently housed).
2. The number of folios, expressed by the formula "Ff."

3. The material (papyrus, parchment, vellum, paper, including any watermarks if on paper). Any change in materials should be given.

4. The general condition of the material.

5. The folio size and the size of the writing block (page or column), expressed in millimeters.

6. The number of lines per writing block, as well as stanzas or other divisions where appropriate.

7. The date and type of binding, with a description of all tooling and other decoration. Any traces of chaining or fastening should be mentioned.

8. The "collation" (i.e., the make-up of the gatherings or quires, beginning with the number of quires in a specific series and the type of gathering—in folios of four, eight, etc.). If the system of foliation or pagination is not obvious from the collation, it may be given separately. Any excisions or additions (of leaves, not necessarily text) should also be noted, as should catchwords and signatures. (Sometimes, the collation may be difficult to establish in a tightly bound book.)

9. The contents, with folio numbers and any omissions or other peculiarities. If there is no title, the *incipit* (first words of text) should be used, or the first words of the extant text if the actual beginning is lacking. *Explicits* or colophons (closing remarks by the scribe) should be given where available. If any of the text of this particular manuscript has been printed (not just the text of the work, which may be extant in several different manuscripts), it should be noted here.

10. Decoration, describing typical floreations or historiated initials, and so on. Coats of arms, miniatures, and illuminations in general should be noted.

11. The probable date and place of writing, followed by the general style of script, with specific indicators (characteristic letter-forms especially). Any idiosyncrasies or changes in the hand are to be noted. As in the description of the contents, any printed facsimiles should be mentioned. If the manuscript is pre-1200, the method of ruling may be given here.

12. Evidence of the manuscript's history from coats of arms, signatures of ownership, sales catalogues, catalogues of libraries, etc. Some speculation may be in order here.

13. Printed notices, including descriptions or other references to the manuscript in bibliographical works.

1. B.M. MS. ARUNDEL 38

Ff. 99. Vellum, slightly wormed. 285 × 185 mm. Frame 185 × 92 mm., containing 28 long lines in 4 spaced stanzas. 19th-c. binding of brown morocco.

COLLATION: 1-11⁸, 12⁸ (wants 3), 13⁶ (wants 4, 5). Catchwords on ff. 8ᵛ, 16ᵛ, 95⁵, no signatures.

CONTENTS:

    f. 1 Hoccleve, *Regiment* (2229). Lacks ll. 4990-5042 through excision of one leaf after f. 90. Stanzas 1-16, 139-148, 267-301, 598-622, 695-713, printed by Seymour. Stanzas 280-3, 297-301 (ll. 1954-81, 2073-2107) printed by Hammond, pp. 74-5.

    f. 99 Blank, apart from scribbles in late 15th-c. and 16th-c. hands.

DECORATION: f. 1 foliate tinted and gilded borderwork, including the royal arms of England differenced for the Prince of Wales. Similar borderwork introduces the major sub-divisions of the text on ff. 39ᵛ, 45ᵛ, 55, 60ᵛ, 63, 66, 71, 73, 75, 81ᵛ, 87, 88 and, less ornately, on f. 98. Alternate tinted and gilded initials introduce each stanza. On f. 37 a large tinted drawing depicts Hoccleve's presentation of the book to Prince Henry, and the borderwork includes the arms (Gu. lion rampant argent) borne by the FitzAlans, Earls of Arundel. On f. 65 in the lower margin a tinted drawing depicts a man hauling into place, with a rope, stanza 512, which is written in the margin by the scribe, having been previously, it seems, omitted in error. On f. 71 are arms (Sa. lion argent crowned or), perhaps borne by the Segrove family. On the leaf excised after f. 90 a tinted drawing of Chaucer undoubtedly occurred.

SCRIBE: written in London, probably before Henry V's accession (21 March 1412/13), and carefully corrected in dry-point (ff. 2, 11, 14, 18, etc.). *Cursiva formata* hand: headless *a*, ascenders of *d*, *l* looped and of *b*, *h* hooked, open and closed *e*, short *r*, kidney-shaped final *s*, dotted *y*, open-tailed *g*. Facsimiles of the tinted drawing on f. 37 may be found in *Facsimiles of Manuscripts and Inscriptions*, Palæographical Society, 1873-83, ii, plate 251; M. Rickert, *Painting in Britain: the Middle Ages*, 1954, p. 185, plate 169c; *Schools of Illumination*, part iv, 1922, plate 11, etc.

HISTORY: the FitzAlan arms on f. 37 suggest that this may have been a presentation volume of the *Regiment of Princes* given to a member of the FitzAlan family, perhaps Thomas FitzAlan (d. 1415) or Joan, Countess of Hereford (d. 1419), for whom Hoccleve wrote the *Letter of Cupid* in 1402. Subsequently owned by Thomas FitzAlan, Earl of Arundel (d. 1646), whose grandson Henry, Duke of Norfolk (d. 1684), presented the family library to the Royal Society in 1667, whence it passed to the B.M. in 1831. On f. 99 occur the names of Jane Roden, Jenet Colfox, Margarete Talbut, and Phelep Ratkelff in 15th-c.–16th-c. hands.

PRINTED NOTICES: Bernard, ii, 75, item 2937. *Catalogue of the Arundel and Burnley Manuscripts*, 1834-40, p. 9.

Fig. 40. Manuscript description, BL Arundel 38 of Hoccleve's *Regement of Princes* (M. C. Seymour/Edinburgh Bibliographical Society).

Bibliographical Description of Printed Books

A brief outline of the most basic formulae used in bibliographical description has already been given in Chapter 3. However, that account is part of the history of printing and is therefore told largely from the printer's point of view. The concern in this chapter is with the means whereby the bibliographer may achieve an accurate description of the make-up of actual books. The most useful form of bibliographical description, while based on such an investigation of specific copies of a work, results in the description of "ideal copy," defined by Gaskell as "the most perfect state of a work as originally intended

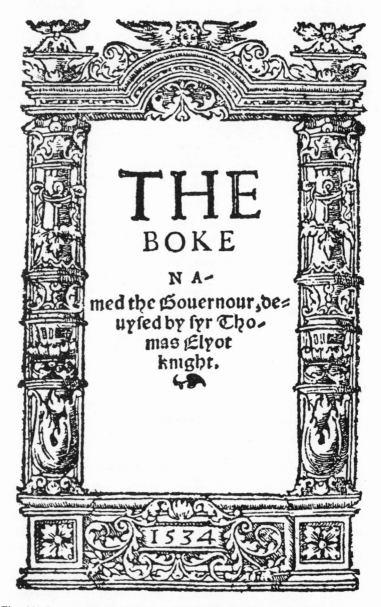

Fig. 41. A compartment, title-page of Sir Thomas Elyot, *The Boke named the Gouernour*, first published 1531, reprinted by Thomas Berthelet, 1534.

by its printer or publisher following the completion of all intentional changes" (321). Tanselle similarly emphasizes intention, in declaring that ideal copy excludes "alterations that occurred in individual copies after the time when those copies ceased to be under the control of the printer or publisher," although he does admit variants made by the printer "from design or accident" ("Concept": 46). Tanselle further stresses general over particular in noting that the "reconstruction [of ideal copy] thus encompasses all states of an impression or issue" (46). The amount of information necessary to describe ideal copy may vary according to Madan's "degressive principle" (of adjusting description to period and means of production), avoiding a "degree of specificity . . . so high as to make every copy of a book (or every sheet or forme) a variant state" (Williams and Abbott: 28).

A. *Quasi-facsimile title-page transcription*

As already noted, the title-page is, to all intents and purposes, an invention of the age of printing and in many ways is therefore the equivalent in bibliographical description of the incipit used to identify a manuscript. In fact, many incunabula retained the manuscript preference for an incipit rather than a title-page (much to the chagrin of bibliographers, who must therefore use other means to discover the information about author, printer, publisher, etc., that would normally be contained on a title-page). In these cases, the incunabulum must be treated rather like a manuscript and, in addition to the incipit, the explicit and colophon (where available) used as a source for descriptive data. Inevitably, there will be many blanks and conjectures in the description of incunabula; these and any other scholarly additions should be placed in square brackets—for example, a putative date of publication would be expressed thus: [1483]. (If there is considerable doubt, a question mark should also be used—i.e., [1483?].) Place names are still usually given in their English versions (*Venice*, not *Venezia*, *Cologne*, not *Köln*), but this testament to Anglo-American parochialism may eventually give way, as recent atlases and gazetteers for English speakers begin to recognize the local spelling as authoritative. Where, however, a printer-publisher became known in a Latinized or other form of his local name (Theobaldo Manucci was always known as Aldus Manutius in his printed works), it would be pedantry and bad history to insist upon the native form.

Incunabula aside, what may one expect to learn from a quasi-facsimile title-page? The information about publisher, printer, place

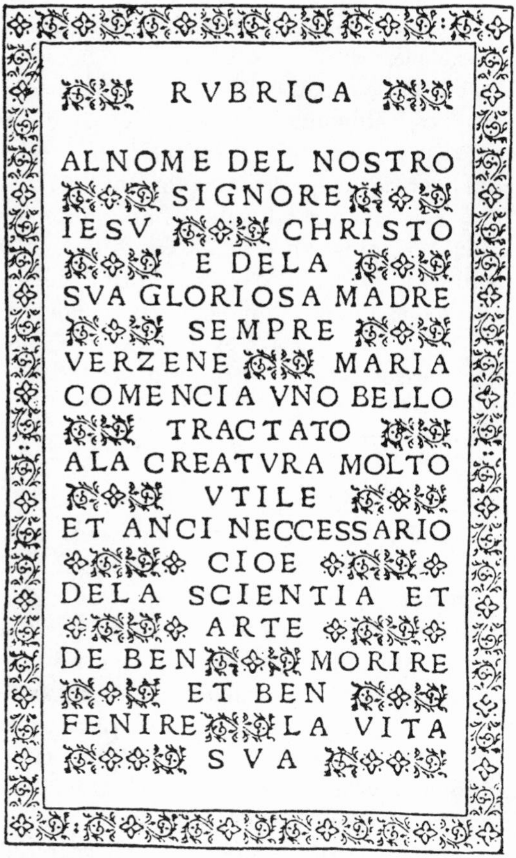
RVBRICA

ALNOME DEL NOSTRO SIGNORE IESV CHRISTO E DELA SVA GLORIOSA MADRE SEMPRE VERZENE MARIA COMENCIA VNO BELLO TRACTATO ALA CREATVRA MOLTO VTILE ET ANCI NECCESSARIO CIOE DELA SCIENTIA ET ARTE DE BEN MORIRE ET BEN FENIRE LA VITA SVA

Fig. 42. A frame of rules and ornaments (printers' flowers), *Arte de ben morire*, printed by Giovanni and Alberto Alvise, Verona, 1478.

of publication, etc., could be found in a regular enumerative bibliography like the *STC* (see Chapter 1). What distinguishes the quasi-facsimile transcription from a simple bibliographical listing is that it will usually enable the bibliographer to tell one type-setting from another (although there is a caution: the transcription only distinguishes roman, italic, and gothic type, not varieties of type within these three broad categories, except for two sizes in the same line; see the other caveats in Foxon's *Thoughts on . . . Bibliographical Description*). The transcription of a quasi-facsimile title-page is neither a photocopy of the original nor merely a list of facts gleaned from the title-page itself: it is more a means of identifying than simply recording, and, theoretically, the bibliographer should in almost all circumstances be able to recognize a particular edition from a consultation of the quasi-facsimile transcription. Confirmation of the identification and information provided in the transcription can, of course, now be easily obtained through a collating machine, by which even the tiniest typographic divergence will be immediately apparent by a mechanical/optical direct comparison of two pages from two books at the same time.

The first item on the quasi-facsimile transcription is a description of the borders, under three categories:

1. "Compartments," or pieces specially cut to form the type-frame into which the title-page information will be placed (see Fig. 41). These may be cast or engraved as a single block, or made up of separate pieces.

2. "Frames," which usually consist of separate pieces (often type ornaments) that the printer has built up to make a frame for the letter-press (see Fig. 42).

3. "Rules," which are simply lines (vertical and/or horizontal) used by the printer to form a rough border (see Fig. 43).

The conventional description of borders would therefore be: "[within a compartment/frame, a x b mm, description of piece]" or "[within single/double/triple rules]."

The second item on the quasi-facsimile transcription is the information within the compartment, frame, or rules—that is, the "letterpress." The most general principle for the transcription of the letterpress is a combination, or balance, of fidelity and consistency. The bibliographer should decide what form the "transliteration" (for that is essentially what is involved) should take, and how the reader of the facsimile will best be able to avoid ambiguity or outright confusion. This principle means that spelling, capitalization, punctuation, and contractions or other abbreviations must be transcribed as is, with a vertical line [|] used to mark line-endings. Therefore, such features as digraphs [œ], tailed letters [ɳ], the long *s* [ʃ], "swash" italics (floreated, curlicued letters) [𝒳], two *V*s used instead of a *W*, wrong fonts, and any special characters or diacriticals [e.g., *, ~ , ^] must appear in the transcript exactly as they do on the title-page, and/or with appropriate annotation. Misprints must, of course, be transcribed exactly and not corrected, although a note may supply a possible conjectural emendation. Broken letters and wrong fonts should also be annotated at the end of the transcript. There is some disagreement on how to represent ligatures, with Gaskell, for example,

```
      THE
Pilgrim's Progreſs
    FROM
  THIS WORLD,
      TO
That which is to come:

Delivered under the Similitude of a

DREAM
   Wherein is Diſcovered,
The manner of his ſetting out,
His Dangerous Journey; And ſafe
   Arrival at the Deſired Countrey.

I have uſed Similitudes, Hoſ. 12. 10.

      By John Bunyan.

Licenſed and Entred according to Order.

      LONDON,
Printed for Nath. Ponder at the Peacock
  in the Poultrey near Cornhil, 1678.
```

Fig. 43. A border of rules, title-page of first edition of John Bunyan's *Pilgrim's Progress*, published by Nathaniel Ponder, London, 1678.

claiming (325) that they are best noted by a link drawn over the two joined letters [e.g., publiſhed], but with other descriptive bibliographers ignoring them. Two or more different sizes of capitals in the same line should be noted, as should the distinction among roman, italic, and gothic types; but it is generally recognized as impractical to aim for greater discrimination than these broad divisions. Some bibliographers would suggest that the type distinctions should actually be drawn in (i.e., the transcriber should imitate an italic typeface and a set of small caps), but the technique of using underlining (single for italic and/or gothic, with an appropriate note; double and triple for two sizes of capitals) is obviously easier to produce on the conventional typewriter or computer printer lacking italic or gothic. As Gaskell (327) notes, however, where underlining is also used to show color (if not by reference to the National Bureau of Standards centroid color charts), there will be some ambiguity if a word is both italic (or gothic) and red or blue. He suggests underdotting the gothic in this case, thereby preserving the underlining for the type-size and color distinctions.

Any illegible or mutilated copy should be placed within pointed brackets <   >, with a conjectural reading inserted if possible. Editorial comments or explanatory material should be placed within square brackets (e.g., [type ornament a x b mm]) and omissions noted by dots within square brackets [. . .]. Square brackets should therefore be used to describe rules, ornaments, and printers' devices. Finally, any manuscript additions to the title-page (e.g., signs of provenance or ownership) should be noted.   Here is an example of these principles in practice, with Gaskell's typescript quasi-facsimile transcript (325) of the Shakespeare First Folio (see Figs. 44 and 45).

Among the points to be noted are the distinction between the two sizes of capitals (*M* and *R*) in the first line; the use of the vertical line [|] to mark all line-divisions; the ignoring of the difference in size of the capitals *between* lines (i.e., there is no special notice of the much larger type-size of "SHAKESPEARES," since the letters all occur on a single line); the editorial description (in square brackets) of the copperplate engraving, with the dimensions (vertical by horizontal) of both the engraving itself and the plate-mark (the lines depressed into the paper by the engraving during printing), which cannot, of course, be observed without an examination of the book itself; the use of a single underline to mark the italics of *Martin Droeshout*, etc. and *LONDON*; and the noting (again, in square brackets) of the swash italics in *LONDON*.

B. *Collation Formula*

The second part of the conventional bibliographical description of a book consists of formulae designed to describe the collation, which comprises the statement of format, the statement of gatherings, the statement of signings, foliation, and pagination, the statement of plates and insets, and the statement of press figures.

Fig. 44. Title-page of Shakespeare First Folio, 1623.

Mʀ. VVILLIAM | SHAKESPEARES | COMEDIES, | HISTORIES, & | TRAGEDIES. | Publiſhed according to the True Originall Copies. | [copperplate portrait, 188 × 157 mm., signed '*Martin · Droeshout · ſculpſit · London ·*', plate-mark 195 × 164 mm.] | *LONDON* | Printed by Iſaac Iaggard, and Ed. Blount. 1623.

Here is the same transcription prepared for reproduction from typescript:

MR. VVILLIAM | SHAKESPEARES | COMEDIES, | HISTORIES, & | TRAGEDIES. |
Publiſhed according to the True Originall Copies. | [copperplate
portrait, 188 x 157 mm, signed 'Martin • Droeshout • fculpsit • London •',
plate-mark 195 x 164 mm] | LONDON [swash N, D, N] | Printed by Iſaac
Iaggard, and Ed. Blount. 1623.

Fig. 45. Typeset and typescript quasi-facsimile transcript by Gaskell.

1. *Statement of format:* As noted in Chapter 3, format can be determined by an examination of imposition, page size, and folding. For example, the direction of chain lines and the relative position of the watermark (if observable) can assist the bibliographer in deciding a book's format. In the period of the machine-made book, however (as opposed to the hand-press and hand-made-paper period), it may be impossible to determine the original size of the paper before folding. The formats are as follows: unfolded (broadsheet/broadside), 1° or bs or b.s.; folded once (folio), 2° or f. or fol.; folded twice (quarto), 4° or 4to or Q or Q^{to}; folded thrice (octavo or eightmo), 8° or 8vo; folded four times (sextodecimo or sixteenmo), 16° or 16mo; folded five times (tricesimosecundo or thirtytwomo), 32° or 32mo; folded six times (sexagesimoquarto or sixtyfourmo), 64° or 64mo.

There are in addition the two intermediate formats (duodecimo or twelvemo: 12° or 12mo; and vigesimoquarto or twentyfourmo: 24° or 24mo). (For a slightly fuller description of how these formats are achieved by the printer, executed by the binder, and determined and analyzed by the bibliographer, see the account of printing practices in Chapter 3.)

2. *Statement of gatherings:* The statement of gatherings is the heart of the collation and uses a technical vocabulary (or, rather, sigla and formulae) which can often be very perplexing to the beginning student in literature. (For a highly simplified introduction to the basic principles of gatherings, see Chapter 3.)

Gaskell defines the collation formula as "a shorthand note of all the gatherings, individual leaves, and cancels as they occur in the ideal copy" (328). What this means is that every page (which translates into every leaf) of the book must be accounted for in the formula, so that the reader could theoretically construct a copy of the book being described, with every leaf placed in the correct position, with its actual or inferred signature, and some sense of its contents (or, at least, where it fits into the contents).

As noted earlier, the collation formulae in early books used the twenty-three-letter Latin alphabet (with *I* or *J* but not both, and with *U* or *V* but not both, and with *W* omitted). Thus, the formula A–Z would assume twenty-three gatherings in appropriate alphabetical order, with gatherings signed by numbers similarly represented in the formula (e.g., 1–23 would be twenty-three gatherings regularly signed). Wherever possible, the bibliographer should reproduce the symbols actually used by the printer as signatures, whether they be letters, numbers, or arbitrary symbols (e.g., \$, *, ~), and should also observe distinctions between upper and lower case (at least in the first alphabetical sequence of letters).

Where duplicate runs of signatures occur (e.g., two or more alphabetical sequences), the normal contracted formula for regular signings in these sequences does not usually observe this distinction: thus the "longhand" formula $A-Z^8$, $AA-ZZ^8$ (or $Aa-Zz^8$)—i.e., combinations of upper- and lower-case letters in the second type of duplicate series—could be abbreviated $A-2Z^8$. Where only the duplicate or triplicate series is being cited (rather than the entire register of gatherings), then the appropriate number before the signature-letter indicates which series is being referred to: for example, 2A–2Z would be the second sequence, 3A–3Z the third, and so on.

Unlike the transcription of title-pages, the collational formula does not distinguish among roman, italic, and gothic type in signatures, although greek and other non-roman alphabets are noted. Any interruptions, breaks, or additions to the alphabetical or numerical sequence must be noted. Thus, if both *I* and *J* or *V* and *U* were to appear, the formula must accommodate this. The formula A–I, J, K–Z would note the unexpected appearance of both *I* and *J*, as would A–U, V, W–Z for the inclusion of both *V* and *U* in addition to *W*. The formula A–B, D–Z would note the omission of the expected C gathering. If certain leaves or sheets are not actually signed, this creates no problem in a regular alphabetic sequence. In fact, as noted in Chapter 3, within a specific gathering it would be unnecessary for the printer to sign the second part of the gathering as long as there was a signature on the conjugate leaf. However, in some cases an entire gathering may be unsigned; and where this occurs, the bibliographer must try to infer the appropriate letter or number. In a sequence A–E [unsigned gathering] G–Z, it is fairly clear that the unsigned gathering is the F, and can therefore be represented (usually in italics) in the formula: A–E, *F*, G–Z. If the unsigned gathering contains the preliminaries (a common practice), then it is arbitrarily assigned the symbol for *pi* [π]; but if the preliminaries, although unsigned, can be inferred to require a regular letter in the alphabetical sequence, then this letter would be used instead of *pi*. Thus, if the regular series begins with *B*, then an italic *A* would be used as an inferred signature for the preliminaries: *A*, B–Z.

Elsewhere in the sequence of gatherings, after the preliminaries, an unsigned gathering is represented in the collation formula by the symbol for *chi* [χ]. Thus, an unsigned gathering in the sequence A–K [unsigned gathering] L–Z could obviously not be K, L, or *pi* and is therefore denoted by the symbol *chi*: A–K, χ, L–Z. A similar addition within, rather than between, gatherings is indicated by a plus-sign at the appropriate position: thus, A–F (F2 +1) represents a single leaf added after the second leaf of the F gathering. If two "disjunct" (unconnected) leaves have been added, the formula would be +1,2; if two "conjugate" (joined) leaves have been added (to make a single fold), the formula would be +1.2. Each of these additional leaves is called a "cancellans," and a similarly omitted leaf is called a "cancellandum" (the word "cancel" to refer to either or both of these conditions is now out of favor as being too ambiguous). The cancellandum is, quite logically, represented by a minus-sign: so, for example, the formula A–F (–F3) G–Z would show the cancellation of a leaf from the F gathering. Straightforward substitutions (of a cancellans for a cancellandum) obviously require both the + and the –, as in the formula A–H ($\pm$H2) I–Z, showing that the original second leaf of the H gathering has been excised and replaced by another.

Throughout these various alphabetical or other sequences, interruptions or substitutions, a supralinear numeral indicates the number of leaves in each gathering: A–Z^4 would therefore represent a regular sequence of twenty-three gatherings, each with four leaves. As with the formulae for signatures, the supralinear figure must record any aberrations in the number of leaves: A^4, B^2, C–Z^4 shows that, alone among this sequence of gatherings, the B gathering has two leaves instead of four.

3. *Statement of signatures:* The statement of signatures indicates exactly which leaves are signed in each gathering. The symbol $ is used to mean "all the gatherings," so that the formula A–K^4, [$3 signed] would show that in each gathering, the first three leaves are signed. Any aberrations are noted with the plus and minus signs: thus A–Z^4, [$3 (+BCD4) signed] would show that in gatherings B, C, and D, the fourth leaf is signed as well as the three common to the other gatherings, and the formula A–Z^4, [$3 (–M2, N3) signed] would show that the second and third leaves of the M and N gatherings, respectively, are unsigned, but the first three leaves of all other gatherings are signed regularly. If a leaf is missigned, this is noted: A–Z^4, [$3 (M2 missigned M3) signed], where the expected "M2" on the second leaf of the M gathering appears erroneously as "M3." Note, however, that this does not mean that the actual leaves have been misbound and are in the wrong order; it means only that the printed signature is wrong.

Included as an addendum to the statement of signatures is a list of foliation or pagination. This list must, of course, agree with the collation formula already given. For example, with the conventional twenty-three-letter alphabet, the total number of leaves in a book will be 23 x the number of leaves in each gathering (e.g., A–Z^4 would produce 23 x 4 = 92 [leaves, not pages]). Again, any aberrancies should be noted, as, for example, misprinted numbers (which are parenthetically noted after the pagination), and actual disturbances to the sequence, which should appear in the pagination formula itself: for example, 92 leaves, ff. 1–92 (misprinting 15 as '13', 101 as '110') and 92 leaves, pp. 1–10, 12–22, 25–187. As with signatures, inferred pages or folios are listed in italics. Where the missing numbers cannot be inferred from their position in the numerical sequence, only the total number of pages or folios in the missing part can be listed—in square brackets. Thus, the formula 92 leaves, pp. 1–10, *11–12*, 13–184 shows that one leaf between pages 10 and 13 is not numbered, but can be confidently assigned the page numbers 11 and 12, whereas the formula 92 leaves, pp. 1–10, [*20*], 11–164 shows that a twenty-page section between the numbered pages 10 and 11 bears no pagination and cannot therefore have its page numbers inferred.

4. *Statement of plates and insets:* Where not included in the collation proper, plates and other insets should be mentioned in the technical notes. The number, location, and technical process should be indicated (e.g., Plate I [opp. H4^v; copper engraving]), and some description of the subject might be included.

5. *Statement of press figures:* Press figures appear at the bottom of a page (not usually on a page already bearing a signature) in some books of the late seventeenth to early nineteenth centuries, marking the form as the work of a specific press or pressman. They are noted by position: thus, press figure: 2 (A4^r). Errors (or "miscatchings") in catchwords may also be noted. (A catchword is the first word of the next page appearing at the bottom of the previous one to assist the printer in ensuring that type pages were in the correct order.)

C. *Contents*

As with the statement of signatures and foliation or pagination, the list of contents must take account of every page in the book, whether or not it "contains" anything. Where consistent pagination occurs, references may be to page numbers; otherwise, the signature reference (described above) should be used. In post-incunabula books, the contents may include half-title, title, dedications, epistles to the reader, table of contents, prefaces, the text, indices, glossaries, and so on. All blank pages must be recorded.

Beyond these three major areas (title-page transcription, collation, and contents), there are several other features of the book which might be commented on in an especially full bibliographical description. For example, there might be information about the paper, the watermark, or the chain lines, or about variant impressions, issues, or states. An edition can be defined in bibliographical terms as "all copies of a book that are printed from one setting of type, whether directly from the type or indirectly through plates made from it" (Williams and Abbott: 22). How much of the type has to be reset in order to qualify the resetting as a new edition may be open to dispute, but the resetting should obviously involve substantial sections of the entire text, and not be limited to the correction of individual errors. Moreover, within an edition, several separate printings (impressions) may occur, and an impression may thus be defined as all copies of a book printed at one time. Before stereotypes (see Chapter 3), each edition would normally consist of only a single impression, since it would be too expensive to keep a book in standing type until it was determined whether a new impression were needed. After the introduction of stereotypes, different impressions might very well have few or no changes in the type, making the bibliographical determination of separate impressions difficult to determine without additional evidence from paper stocks or changes in gathering, gutter margins and so on. However, damage to or shrinkage of plates may assist in making such determinations. Within an impression, there may be two or more issues (for example, the difference between an expensive "limited edition" and a "trade" issue). Issues are thus determined by a difference in "unit of sale" (Williams and Abbott: 23)—with variant title page, paper, date, or publisher but otherwise identical settings—rather than by any physical change to the body or text of the book.

Before the early nineteenth century, bindings were not normally regarded as part of the manufactured book (see Chapter 3), but were commissioned specially by the purchaser. Thus, binding is not usually considered part of ideal copy and not included in bibliographical description until the period in which books began to be sold in edition binding or publishers' bindings. Such bindings (including endpapers) were produced in cloth with an identifiable pattern (wavy lines, diagonals etc.) and are included in the description, together with reference to any stamping or printing on the front, spine, or back, to the treatment of the sheet-edges (e.g, gilded, sprinkled, trimmed), and to dustjackets and endpapers.

Within each published state identified by the bibliographer, the full descriptive bibliography may also designate the specific typeface(s) employed, going beyond the three-family distinction of the quasi-facsimile title-page transcription. The bibliographer might also list the actual copies consulted, as well as any pertinent information from authors' or publishers' correspondence or other records (for example, on print runs and copies sold in each state, prices, copyright details, contemporary references)—in sum, anything that might help to clarify the book's history as an artifact, without engaging in esthetic criticism of the contents or the physical make-up. With all of this material at hand, the student should then be able to make positive identifications of specific copies of books (at least as far as edition is concerned, if not always impression or issue) and, having mastered the basic formulae, will be able to move from the book lists of enumerative bibliography to the close technical analysis of descriptive bibliography.

Reading the Text: Paleography

This and the following chapter describe the development of the latin alphabet (first in its hand-written, then in its printed forms) over
the last two millennia. Non-latin alphabets (e.g., greek, cyrillic, se-
mitic) and non-alphabetic writing (e.g., Chinese ideograms) are not
dealt with here. Even though several of these other systems of writing have been remarkably conservative when compared with the latin
alphabet's various transformations and reformations, it would be impossible here to give them anything but the most superficial treatment.
In any case, it is anticipated that the typical reader of this book will be
working with Western European or American documents, which employ the latin alphabet almost exclusively. Those few symbols borrowed from other systems (e.g., the runic "thorn" [þ] of medieval
English manuscripts, now represented by *th*; the arabic numerals; the
abbreviated *x̄p̄s*, which represents "Christus" in the *nomina sacra* of
religious documents) can be briefly mentioned without seriously qual-
ifying this basic limitation. The other major restriction in this section
is that the term "paleography" is used primarily in the sense of the
reading of the latin alphabet, and specifically the reading of that alphabet on papyrus, parchment, or paper rather than on walls, potsherds, or coins. The act of writing (and printing) this alphabet is
covered in the section dealing with the making of the book in Chapter
2, along with the practices of scribes and printers in general in Chapter 3. Inevitably this division will break down (where, for example,
specific writing surfaces or implements may have influenced the form
of the letters read by the paleographer), but the distinction remains
useful nonetheless.

The present chapter begins with an historical account of the major styles of handwriting since the Roman period, with each script placed in its cultural or social context, where appropriate. Complementing this account is a series of illustrations giving examples of each script discussed, with paleographical notes pointing out the major characteristics to be looked for in the representative manuscript. Certain related problems (e.g., the dating of manuscripts by paleographical evidence, the scribal use of numerals and abbreviations) are then covered briefly. Since this book is obviously intended for an English-speaking audience, wherever possible manuscripts written in English have been chosen to illustrate a handwriting style, although obviously this cannot be done for periods or areas which are non-Anglophone (e.g., Roman monumental capitals or Caroline minuscule).

Paleography: Definitions

There are several major divisions of handwriting. First, there is the distinction between a "two-line" script, in which all letters are of the same height, confined within two imaginary (or sometimes real) horizontal lines, and a "four-line" script, in which certain letters extend above or below these two lines.

The first class of script is sometimes called "capital" (ABCD, etc.) but since this term can also refer to letter-forms rather than to letter height, the class should properly be called "majuscule". The second class of script, in which the vertical strokes of the "ascenders" and "descenders" in letters like *b*, *d*, *f*, and *q* project beyond the body of the line, is called "minuscule." The familiar terms "upper case" and "lower case," which do not necessarily reflect the same formal distinctions, should properly be used only of typographical styles, since the words refer to the two cases, or trays, from which a compositor selects type in letterpress printing (see Chapter 3).

Another major division of handwriting concerns the purpose or occasion of the writing. If a text has been written for formal, monumental, or consciously esthetic purposes, the scripts will tend to consist of letters carefully and separately formed, with few ligatures (joining of letters by a medial stroke), and often with many individual strokes, or "ducts" per letter. This style is usually called "book" or "text" script, since it is normally employed in literary or religious works, and, after the advent of the codex (or book of folded, stitched leaves), is associated with this book form rather than with the roll, which was still the favored medium for charters and other legal doc-

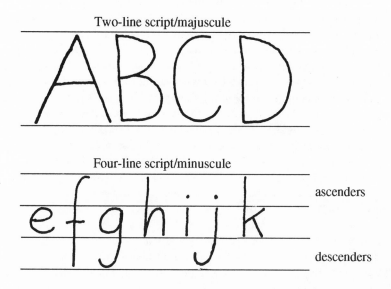

Fig. 46. Two-line (majuscule) and four-line (minuscule) scripts.

uments (see Chapter 2). If a text has been written for private, commercial, or other quotidian activities, the scripts usually encourage a faster, more economical style, with much joining of letters, so that the pen did not have to be lifted from the writing material more often than would be necessary to refill it with ink. These scripts are called "cursive" or "court" or "current," the first term deriving from the continuity of pen strokes rather than from the rounded letter-forms (though these letter-forms are sometimes characteristic of cursive styles), the second from the use of these scripts in legal or royal administrative courts, and the third from the fluid or "running" (Latin *curro*) quality of the scripts. A further subdivision within the cursive group can be made between "set" scripts, which are more carefully calligraphic in nature, and "free" scripts, which, as the term suggests, are somewhat idiosyncratic and, as a result, often very illegible. The distinction between cursive and book scripts is, however, not always clear or valid, for there are some periods, in certain countries, in which there is virtually no difference between the two styles, and other periods in which a third style, or "bastard," may evolve out of a mixture of the two. But the terms do at least have an important descriptive function, though they must be used with care.

Further, while usage is by no means fixed in this matter, it is probably better to restrict the term "hand" to the work of a specific scribe, and "script" to a style of writing identifiable in a particular place or period. Thus, a manuscript may be written in several "hands," all belonging to basically the same "script"; conversely, a particular scribe may be able to write in more than one script (e.g., italic and "secretary" in the English Renaissance; see Chapter 2).

While the study of ancient handwriting was in many ways the forerunner of historical scholarship in general (especially in the perception that scripts could be arranged in a linear development as they progressed from one style to another and could thus be dated by an identification of these styles), there is also a counteracting movement in the progression of scripts. This movement can probably best be seen as a "re-cycling" of scripts. The characteristic process seems to be that a highly formal "book" or "text" script gradually becomes less formal, more cursive, and eventually so sloppy and illegible that there is a call to return to earlier standards of purity, balance, and clarity. Thus, in the chart (Fig. 47) showing the development of Western scripts, Renaissance humanistic roman (and to a lesser degree, italic) are conscious attempts by handwriting reformers of the period to repudiate the contemporary thick, black gothic and its impenetrable court equivalent "secretary" in favor of a return to the clear, formal lines of Caroline minuscule. But Caroline was itself an attempt to replace the contemporary Merovingian script (laterally condensed and increasingly illegible) and to go back to the orthographic standards of Roman scripts. Then, in the twentieth century, reformers in England and the United States, offended by the decadent remains of copperplate and its nineteenth-century offshoots, deliberately resuscitated the roman and especially the italic of the humanistic period.

In this way, scripts can come and go, as a yearning for the past and its supposed virtues of clarity and fine distinction reclaims old scripts in a new way. Usually, the imitation of the old script is not exact, and there is thus little difficulty in distinguishing modern italic from humanistic. But sometimes the replication is almost perfect, and some early Renaissance versions of Caroline look disturbingly like "the real thing." Against this dual movement of change and revision, there is one solid and reliable element to be observed, and that is the remarkable continuity and tenacity of Roman square capitals, where Western paleography essentially begins. At almost every period in the history of Western writing, the massive, monumental, and very

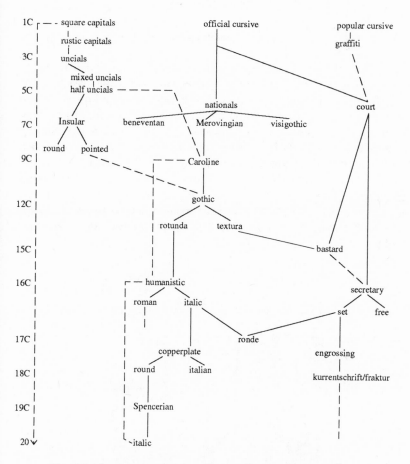

Fig. 47. The descent of scripts (from a diagram by the author).

legible letters of Roman square capitals appear somewhere: they may not be used as a genuine book script, but they will surface in titles, in chapter headings, in rubrics, or on the facades of modern buildings. One result of this continuity is that it may be easier for the modern eye to read a third-century manuscript text of Virgil than a seventeenth-century manuscript text of Shakespeare, and bearing this reliability and continuity in mind, it is thus appropriate that we begin this survey with Roman square capitals, for we still know them best.

Roman Scripts

A. *Roman Majuscule* (?First century-fifth century)

The handwriting of Roman documents may be divided first into majuscule and minuscule styles. Within the majuscule class, another division is traditionally recognized, between square and rustic capitals on the one hand and uncials on the other. However, since rustic capitals may be regarded as a less formal version of square capitals and uncials as a similarly less formal version of rustics, it is probably better to treat them all together as variants within one class.

1. *Square capitals* (?First century-fifth century): As the name suggests, square capitals (or *capitalis quadrata*) were used for the large, angular inscriptions of Roman monumental writing and properly belong more to epigraphy, or "inscribed" writing, than paleography.

Fig. 48. Roman inscribed square capitals (Trajan inscription, ca. A.D. 114).

The strong solid shapes of the letters, with as few curves as possible, their forms dependent on the chisel rather than on the reed or quill, were very suitable for the *scriptura monumentalis* of triumphal arches, temple inscriptions, and commemorative plaques. (See Fig. 48, an inscribed square capital alphabet, and note, for example, the finials on the feet of the *A*, the straight-line composition of such letters as *E*, *F*, *M*, and *N*, and the restriction of curves to those letters—*B*, *C*, *O* and so on—where they are unavoidable. Note that the *L* and *O* are shown on their sides in line 2.)

For writing on soft materials, however, their cumbrous size, the difficulty of their execution, and the sheer wastefulness of space inevitably restricted their use. Each large letter, written independently with no linkages to surrounding letters, had to be formed in several distinct strokes and then finished off with delicate "serifs" or "finials." Certain letters, such as *L*, might on occasion rise slightly above the majuscule format, but the two-line system was otherwise determinedly obeyed. With the necessity of such care and arduous composition, only the most serious of literary works could be honored with this formal script in actual manuscripts. Virgil is the only author to have survived in the few extant leaves written entirely in *capitalis quadrata*, and these leaves are of a date (fourth century-fifth century) when square capitals had already been superseded by less rigid scripts.

(See Fig. 49, and note, for example, the general two-line form of the script and the straight-line construction—in several independent strokes—of letters like *A* and *E*, but the tendency of *L* in line 1 to rise *above* the two-line form, and the slight rounding of such letters as *M*.)

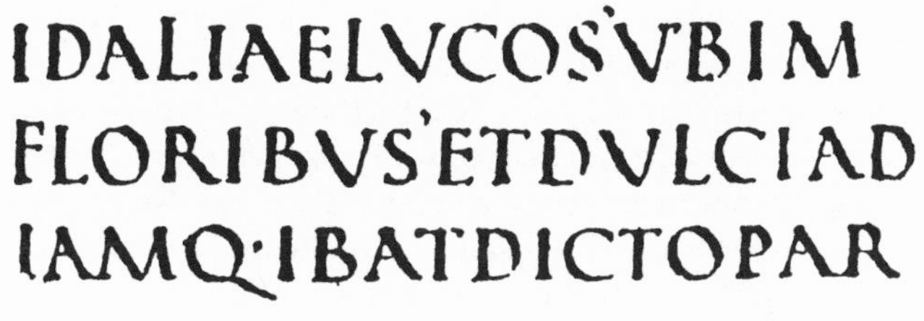

IDALIAELVCOSVBIM
FLORIBVS'ETDVLCIAD
IAMQ·IBATDICTOPAR

Fig. 49. Roman manuscript square capitals (Virgil, fourth or fifth century).

As the acknowledged classic of Latin literature, a Virgil text could be preserved in a style which would normally have been regarded as out of date. In this way, Virgil exerted a similar influence on handwriting as that of the classics of Christian and Greek literature—the Bible and Homer—which were also copied in very conservative scripts. In other manuscripts, square capitals are used only for titles, but the relegation to an almost decorative function has not prevented the formal Roman majuscule from continuing as the standard for carefully constructed "capitals" down to the present day. We all know what such capitals look like: they resemble those leaves of Virgil, and we find them on banks, government buildings, and other edifices aspiring to a Roman (or Virgilian) seriousness. As noted above, of all the handwriting styles discussed in this book, the square capital is certainly the most easily recognized by the modern reader, for the majuscule Roman alphabet embodied in these bold, formal letters has outlasted all other fashions and variations and therefore, despite its age, looks very familiar.

2. *Rustic capitals* (First century-seventh century): The extant documents in rustic capitals antedate those in square capitals by some four centuries, but it is likely that the rustic form developed out of the square, rather than the other way around. Rustics were a true majuscule script, with the letters held within two, not four, lines and can be viewed as the genuine "book" or "written" (as opposed to inscribed) version of square capitals. Rustics represent a stylistic relaxation resulting from the use of a broad pen, held somewhat obliquely. This type of pen produces a script with a much greater contrast between the thick and thin ducts than in square capitals, the diagonal strokes being the heaviest and the vertical the lightest. Right angles become curves, and the letters are not "finished off" by the addition of the finials typical of square capitals. This distinction, together with the extremely short horizontal strokes and the small bows of letters such as *P* and *R*, encouraged a lateral compression of letter-forms. At their most formal, rustic capitals are, despite their pejorative name, very carefully constructed, each letter requiring the pen to be lifted several times. They are not in any sense a cursive style and, being unsuitable for business, were, like square capitals, eventually restricted to formal subjects, usually Virgil or other major texts.

(See Fig. 50, and note the distinction between thick and thin strokes throughout, the small bows on *R* [line 1], the increasingly rounded form of, e.g., *V*, and the tendency toward fluidity by the dropping of the bar in *A*, thus allowing the letter to be formed in two

VOIVITVRATERODORTECTISTV
INTVSSAXASONANIVACVAS
ACCIDITHAECEESSISETIAMTO
QVAETOTAMIVCTVCONCVSSIT

Fig. 50. Roman rustic capitals (Virgil, fourth century).

connected strokes without removing the instrument from the writing surface.) By the early sixth century, the better rustic capitals were no longer being employed for entire texts and continued only in titles and other ornamental writing, or in consciously conservative copying (such as the ninth-century Utrecht Psalter).

3. *Uncials* (Third century-eighth century): Since neither square nor rustic capitals could be used by those who wanted a faster style of writing, a cursive majuscule script called uncials (meaning "inch-high") developed in the third century (probably in Africa, and possibly under the influence of patristic authors writing in Greek), in which the pen would not have to be lifted as often. It was this quality which made the script "cursive," rather than its rounded letter-forms, which remained basically majuscule. For example, the uncial *E* [Є] could be made with only two strokes, instead of the four necessary in earlier scripts. However, the cursive tendency of uncials did not extend to the formation of ligatures or the fusing of letters themselves, for uncials still retained something of the monumental nature of early capitals and were by no means suitable for the day-to-day activities of the business world. The characteristic letters of uncial script are *a*, *d*, *e*, and *m* [∂ , δ , Є , ɰ], and the developing differences in their letter-forms can be used in dating manuscripts. For example, the first limb of *m* is usually more vertical in early uncials, becoming more rounded as the style progressed, and the cross-stroke of *e* was always rather high early on, varying a good deal in later manuscripts.

Uncials did tend to become less solidly majuscule than square or rustic capitals, for certain letters (noticeably those with pronounced ascenders or descenders, like *b*, *d*, *h*, *q*) strayed above or below the strict two lines of the majuscule format. Although uncials were un-

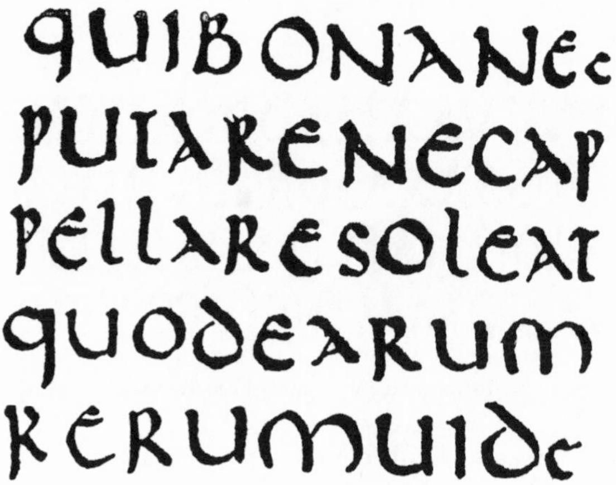

qUIBONANEc
PUTAKENECAP
PELLAKESOLEAT
qUOdEARUM
KERUMUIOc

Fig. 51. Uncials (Cicero, *De republica*, fourth century).

doubtedly more efficient of time than square or rustic capitals, they were not usually more efficient of space. This can be demonstrated clearly in those manuscripts which have been used twice, the earlier uncial script having been almost obliterated and a later, smaller script written on top. These palimpsests (see Chapter 2), which in earlier centuries often involve a Christian work being substituted for a pagan one, show that the enormous letters and narrow columns of uncials could be very wasteful indeed when compared with the tiny scripts of later periods.

(See Fig. 51 and note the characteristic rounded forms of *a*, *d*, *e*, and *m*, the tendency of *d*, *l*, and *q* to extend beyond the two-line and to anticipate what we would now call "minuscule" shapes, confirmed by my having to use lower case type to refer to them; and note the large, expansive size of the letters.)

B. *Roman Minuscule* (Fifth century-seventh century)

1. *Mixed uncials* (Fifth century-seventh century): It would be misleading to suggest that there is an absolute distinction to be observed between majuscule and minuscule writing of the Roman period. The third type of majuscule (uncials) had already displayed certain tendencies toward minuscule mannerisms, which were taken up with greater freedom as the strict uncial style became too formal for many occasions. Ascenders and descenders became more pro-

nounced, and the letters bearing such strokes (particularly *b*, *d*, *q*) became more recognizably minuscule as well as cursive, as the four-line system took over from the two-line. But the letter-forms themselves were for a time mixed, until the true half-uncials had developed a distinctive style. Majuscule and minuscule forms could inhabit the same line, with the ends of a line proving to be the weakest points, where minuscule forms were more likely to dominate.

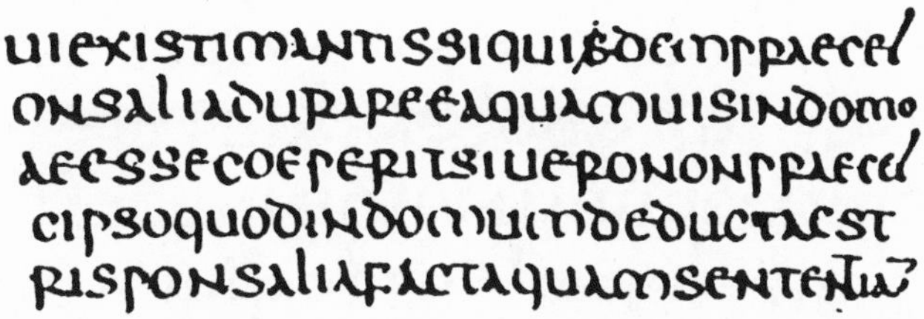

Fig. 52. Mixed uncials (*Pandects*, sixth or seventh centuries).

(See Fig. 52, and note the basic two-line conformity but with *q*, *p*, and *R* extending considerably below the line and *d* above and with the "weak" ends of each line allowing a much greater upward extension.)

It was a process of infiltration rather than conquest, for literary manuscripts could be invaded by minims (the short vertical ducts of *i*, *u*, *m*, *n*), and the presence of these minims gradually pushed the handwriting toward a more defined minuscule form, although some of the majuscule equivalents (e.g., *N* instead of *n*) were often retained as alternatives—as is the case in Fig. 52.

2. *Half-uncials* (Fifth century-eighth century): Since the very concept of "half"-uncial, or "half-inch," script implies that the body of the line has been reduced to accommodate the minuscule tendencies of certain letters, it is only proper to regard the settled half-uncial as more essentially minuscule than majuscule. This settled form seems to have been originally most popular in southern France and northern Italy and to have been characterized by a greater reliance upon ligatures and minims. It was therefore a more pronounced cursive script than the uncial, as well as being decidedly minuscule. Furthermore, there were certain letter-forms which became symptomatic of half-uncial. For example, uncial [ε] became *e*, the short *s* turned into the long [ʃ], [∂] became *a*, and *G* became [ʒ]. Other letter-forms (*h*,

m, u) retained their uncial shapes but were now written as minuscules. While the degree to which half-uncials actually displaced uncials as a text script is still debated, there can be little doubt that the combination of cursive and minuscule in the half-uncial and the anticipation of some of the letter-forms of Caroline script made the transitional status of half-uncial of great importance in the history of Western writing.

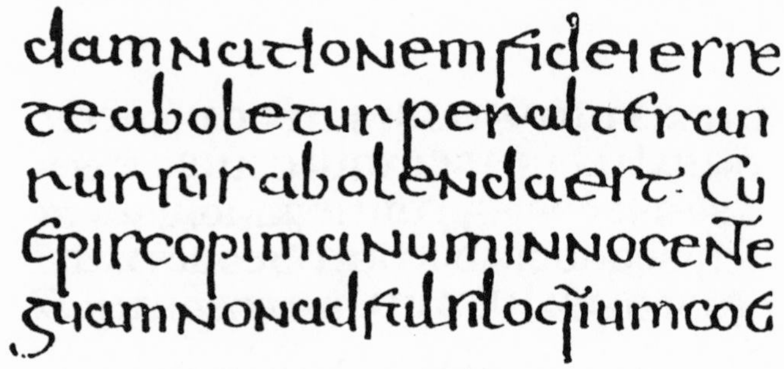

Fig. 53. Half-Uncials (St. Hilary On the Trinity, before A.D. 509–10).

(See Fig. 53 and note the frankly four-line, "minuscule" format, with the initial *d* in line 1 and the *b* and *l* of line 2 with firm ascenders and the *p* in line 4 and *q* in line 5 with descenders; note that majuscule *N* is retained but that some ligatures—e.g., between *a* and *m*, *t* and *i*, *e* and *m*, in the first word *damnationem*—are appearing.)

C. *Roman Cursive* (?First century-thirteenth century)

1. *Popular cursive* (?First century-sixth century): Given that cursive characteristics have already been observed in uncial and half-uncial scripts, it may seem unsound to designate another, competitive style as specifically "cursive." However, as already noted, all the scripts discussed so far have been to one degree or another "text" or "book" scripts, although the more debased forms of half-uncial could possibly have functioned in a business context. But the Roman world was not only literary and monumental; it was also practical and utilitarian. This side of its activities needed a script with no pretensions to calligraphic style, a script which was ephemeral, idiosyncratic, economical, and easily written. This is the "popular" style of Roman cursive. The first-century *terminus a quo* of popular cursive repre-

sents only the accidental riches of Pompeiian graffiti and other scrib-blings. But since much later popular cursives discovered in Dacia (modern Romania) and elsewhere have quite similar forms, it would be illogical to suppose that the Pompeiian versions mark the actual beginnings of such attempts at a business writing medium. For as long as houses and slaves had been sold, as long as love messages and satirical attacks had been scratched on walls or tablets, some form of popular cursive must have been available. Unlike the book scripts of Virgil and the Bible, popular cursive was never intended for posterity; if it reached its target immediately, that was enough—and, true to its purpose and character, it has in general not survived.

The more formal versions of this cursive style can be regarded merely as a hastily written degeneration of book-script. The quill, brush, or stylus was lifted from the writing material less often, but the letter-forms remained more or less distinct. However, the influence of the medium (particularly when it was a wall and the script therefore "graffiti") could lead to remarkable changes in letter formation. Thus, the regular majuscule *M* might be transformed into four vertical strokes with no horizontal connectives [*M* = IIII]; the *O* might change from a rough circle into two separate concave strokes, since the con-cave shape is much easier for a right-handed person to scratch on a wall than a convex shape [*O* = (( ].

The necessity for speed further compounded the problems of legi-bility, as some letters were actually "broken" by the tendency toward ligature: the first part of a letter might get attached to the previous one, and the second to the subsequent one. The uncial "open" [*Є*], for example, decayed into two slightly rounded vertical strokes rather like a *u* [(( ]; and the very form of *e* could depend upon how it was linked to surrounding letters. These characteristics—the idiosyncratic letter-forms as a result of the writing medium, the tendency toward ligature and the consequent dismembering of the medial letter—can make the tiles, tablets, papyrus scraps, and wall scribblings of popular Roman cursive extremely difficult to read. There is much confusion of letter-forms (*A* with *R*, *B* with *D*, *C* with *O*, *C* with *P*, *C* with *T*, *E* with *U*), and it is unlikely that this style of writing will ever be the perquisite of any but the most experienced paleographers, although it can have great value for the social and cultural historian.

(See Fig. 54, and note the three-vertical-line form of *m* in the first word *communem*, together with the *u*-like form of *e* [in this word and in *censio*, the first word of line 2, where the characteristic broken *o*, two concave strokes, can be seen]; note, however, that some letters

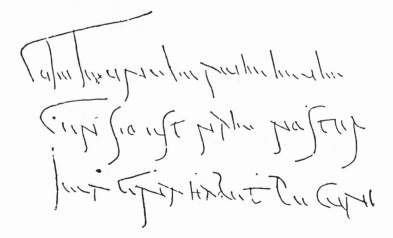

Fig. 54. Roman popular cursive (wall inscription, Pompeii, first century).

are still quite legible and unbroken, e.g., the majuscule *N* in both *communem* and *censio*.)

2. *Official cursive* (?Fifth century-thirteenth century): It might be expected that once a cursive style was taken up by government, whether secular or ecclesiastical, it would tend to become stereotyped, formulaic, and clearer; but this seems not to have been the case with Roman cursive, nor, indeed with many of the official or court cursives of later periods. For example, the style known as Imperial Rescript (from its use by the imperial government) provided paleographers with great problems, for it combined the compounding of letterforms of popular cursive with a flourished extravagance and a greater calligraphic freedom resulting from the medium of ink on papyrus. There might also have been other, more insidious, reasons. The scripts of lawyers have many times been condemned and proscribed by various well-meaning legislators as being too deliberately esoteric for the general reading public (to say nothing of the denseness of legal language). When he banned Imperial Rescript from southern Italy, the emperor Frederick II was only one of a long list of secular rulers to attempt the suppression of lawyers' script as impenetrable and therefore anti-social. In the fifth and sixth centuries, the Papal Chancery version of official cursive could even be employed as a semiformal book script, but the apparently inevitable degeneration of these court styles into complicated, illegible, and corrupt scrawls intelligible only to other professionals eventually rendered it unsuitable for

the book trade. The literary script of the Caroline reformation based much of its minuscule indirectly on Roman cursive but only through a strict standardization of letter-forms, eliminating the idiosyncratic and stressing the formal and the legible.

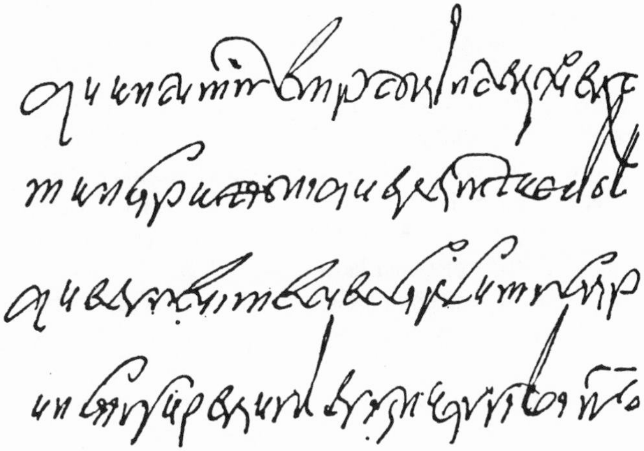

Fig. 55. Official Roman cursive (Deed of Sale, A.D. 572).

(See Fig. 55, and note both the extravagant flourishes above the line—e.g., the *c* of *unciis* at the beginning of line 4—and the similar extensions below, e.g., the initial *q* in both line 1 and 3; note the general lateral compression and fluidity of strokes, with many ligatures, more rounded than in popular cursive but retaining some of the broken letter-forms, e.g., the *a* looking like a *u*—third letter of line 1 *quantum*—with a ligature to the following *n*.)

National Scripts

Just as the breakdown of the Latin language produced the Romance languages of the Mediterranean Middle Ages, so the late Roman cursive scripts, when written by scribes now distant from any central authority and speaking these embryonic new languages, degenerated (or developed) into the so-called national scripts. The term "national" has to be treated with some care, however, for the territories of these new scripts by no means corresponded with then-current (or modern) linguistic or political boundaries. The Spanish, or Visigothic, variety is fairly distinct, geographically and paleographically but could often be influenced by Frankish forms. The Italian national, formerly known as Lombardic (before the great seventeenth-century paleographer Mabillon, a term used almost indiscriminately of most types of medieval handwriting), is better labeled as Beneventan, emphasizing its largely southern provenance, centered on the monastery of Monte Cassino, near Naples. The Frankish defeat of the Lombards in northern Italy served, in fact, to keep north and south Italian styles quite separate. The Merovingian script of the Franks themselves is now usually divided into a series of related sub-styles, each one associated with a particular monastic center. And finally, the English and Irish Insular scripts, while certainly geographically identifiable, do not develop from Roman cursive at all but are much more closely related to Roman half-uncial. With these and other reservations (which will become clearer in the following sections), the "nationals" can be briefly described.

A. *Beneventan* (Seventh century-thirteenth century)

The symptomatic "broken" vertical ducts of the Beneventan national have at times encouraged a belief that the gothic script of the high Middle Ages was anticipated in southern Italy. But the similarity is largely coincidental, for the Beneventan style was essentially the old Roman cursive formalized and made more consistently vertical, becoming a book script with cursive tendencies. This formality was demonstrated in each minim's being written in two strokes rather than one (i.e., [?] not [ı]), and it is this characteristic which gave the script its broken look (which extended to other letters, for example, the broken-backed *e* [*ℓ*]). The cursive quality of the new minuscule was apparent in its frequent use of ligatures (e.g., in the long *i* ligature after *e, f, g, l, r, t*) and in the splitting of the open *a*, which, formed out of two concave strokes (as in Roman cursive, [⟨⟨]), could look remarkably like a modern double *cc* and might occasionally find its two constituent parts attracted by ligature to the surrounding letters. The Beneventan script, no doubt because of its provenance, was surprisingly tenacious and resisted not only the Caroline reformation of handwriting in the ninth century but also the later standardization into gothic—at least until the thirteenth century, although it survived both of these movements only in a very debased and often illegible form. In this determined isolation from the calligraphic novelties of the rest of Europe, it was similar to the national consistency of the

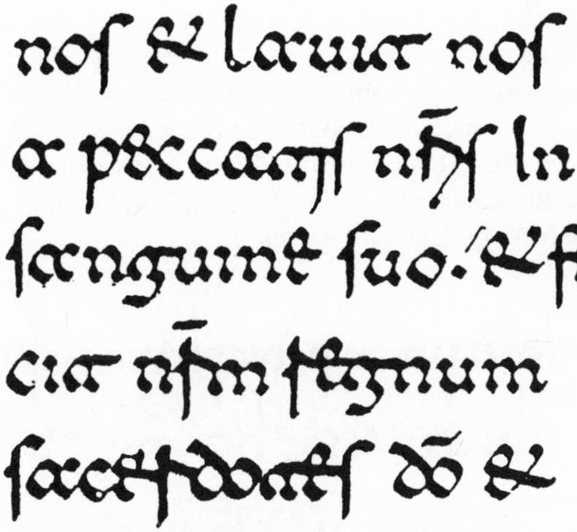

Fig. 56. Beneventan (Lectionary, Monte Cassino, 1058–87).

Insular scripts in the far north, both Irish and English varieties.

(See Fig. 56, and note the "broken" forms of all minims—e.g., the initial *n* in line 1—the broken-backed *e* and the double-*c* form of *a* in *peccatis* [second word of line 2], together with the ligature between *t* and long *i* in the same word.)

B. *Visigothic* (Seventh century-twelfth century)

The Spanish Visigothic national did not develop the single characteristic identifier of the broken Beneventan style and was often influenced by Frankish forms—for example, in the "clubbing" of ascenders. Similarly, the early Spanish tendency to slant backwards was largely overcome by Frankish influence in the ninth century. However, Visigothic scribes did have a number of distinctive habits which help to identify their scripts. Spanish abbreviations were remarkably different from those used in the rest of Europe: the old (originally Hebraic) method of suppressing the vowels in the *nomina sacra* was more prevalent throughout this period in Spain, as was the abbreviation [ꝓ] for *per* (which elsewhere equals *pro*) and [ꝙ] for *qui* (which elsewhere equals *quod*). The use of *qu* instead of *c* in such words as *quum* (for *cum*) and *quur* (for *cur*), of *c* instead of *h* in, e.g., *nicil* (for *nihil*) and *mici* (for *mihi*), and of *b* instead of *v* in, e.g., *salbator* (for *salvator*); the development of a *q*-like form of *g*, the prosthetic *i* in such words as *iscribo* (for *scribo*), and its opposite, in such words as *stius* (for *istius*)—all of these habits, even though they may only rarely be found together in a single manuscript, help to confirm the *lettera toletana* (or "writing from Toledo," as Visigothic was often known at the time) in its status as the national style of Spain. Note, however, that several of the distinctive features enumerated above may be the result of a linguistic (that is, phonological) as well as a merely paleographical nationalism.

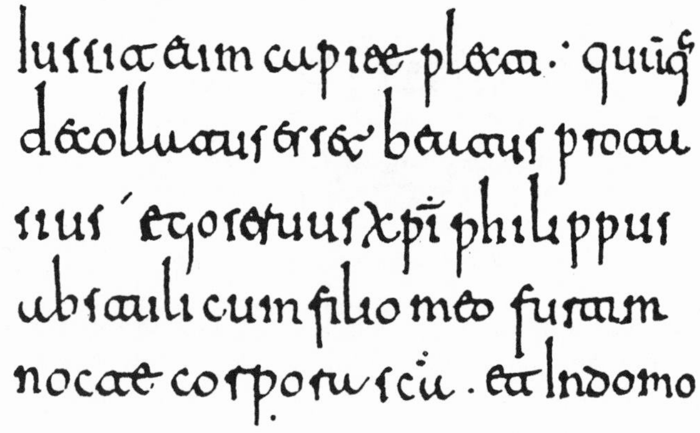

Fig. 57. Visigothic (Martyrology, Burgos, A.D. 919).

(See Fig. 57, and note the slight clubbing of ascenders of *l* throughout, the *q*-like form of *g* in *ego* [line 3, second word], the *quu-* instead of *cu-* at the end of line 1, and the general squareness and thinness of letter-forms.)

C. *Insular* (Sixth century-eleventh century)

As mentioned earlier, unlike the Continental scripts, the handwriting of Ireland and England in this period descended not from Roman cursive but from half-uncials. The famous "round" scripts of the *Book of Kells* and the *Lindisfarne Gospels* had disappeared by the ninth century, but the "pointed" version of Insular, a laterally compressed derivative of the round style, successfully resisted the uncial and rustic capitals brought to England by the Roman mission of Saint Augustine of Canterbury. Even though the clearly uncial hand of the well-known *Codex Amiatinus* was probably written in Northumbria about 700, it was not typical of that period or area; it was possibly composed by foreign scribes. Indeed, not only did it preserve its own territorial sovereignty, but, through the Irish and Anglo-Saxon missions to Europe, the Insular script was carried to such newly founded centers as Luxeuil, in France, St. Gall, in Germany, and Bobbio, in Italy, during the seventh and early eighth centuries—though the extant manuscripts from these places display only Insular "symptoms" (signs of having been influenced by, or copied from, documents written in Insular), rather than having an Insular script themselves, and it is likely, therefore, that the direct effect of the imported style was rather short lived.

Later, the Insular script kept its identity against the powerful influence of the Caroline calligraphic reform, particularly in Ireland, and, while eventually yielding to gothic as the book script for literary and religious works in the high Middle Ages (in England anyway), gradually emerged as the basis for the English court scripts. These court scripts were, in combination with the gothic text scripts, to produce the bastard styles which were used for medieval English vernacular literature. Down to the eleventh century, however, there was no consistently formal distinction between literary and charter scripts, and during the early English Middle Ages the various versions of Insular pointed could be used for almost any purpose—secular, religious, literary, or legal.

The Irish and English variants of Insular can usually be distinguished by experienced paleographers (although, since the early English monasteries were founded by Irish monks, the distinctions are perhaps somewhat arbitrary). But it is more important to trace the paleographic division between the round and pointed versions of Insular. The round script was a conservative, highly formal, and ornamental manifestation of Roman half-uncial. In fact, it was often so ornamental that the letter-shapes became fantastic and extravagant, more a part of the artistic design of the page than a unit of the individual word. At its most exuberant, this tendency can be seen in the entire pages devoted to the tracing of single words or phrases in the *incipits* (or first lines) of a text. Just as the shapes of the figures represented in these highly schematized *incipits* became abstract, overpowered by the interlacings and trellis-work of the design, so the letter-forms were not to be "read" as a part of the text but observed as a part of the page-format.

The fantasy of the round script could obviously not be used for the ordinary business of writing, and the more cursive pointed style was the normal book-script of both Ireland and England in the early Middle Ages. Like its Merovingian neighbor, it tended toward lateral compression, but unlike the Merovingian, its ascenders were not usually "clubbed" (carrying instead the characteristic lozenge-shaped finials), and it retained a number of special letter-forms: *f* as [ꝼ], *r* as [ꞃ], *g* as [ᵹ] (becoming [ȝ] ["yogh"] in Middle English texts), *w* as [ƿ] "wyn" (which, as the regularized *W*-form, not found in the original latin alphabet, was exported to France and Germany in the eighth century), *th* as [þ] ("thorn") or [ð] ("eth"). Wyn and thorn were borrowed from the runic alphabet. Both wyn and eth were to disappear in early Middle English documents, but thorn survived (since it represented a very common sound in the English language, and one which was not logically or easily denoted by any of the letters of the latin alphabet—certainly not by *th*). By the fifteenth century, thorn had unfortunately become virtually indistinguishable from *y*, so that the early printers often did not feel it necessary to cut a special type for the character. I should emphasize, however, that *ye* or [ẏ] for *the* (as in "Ye Olde Coffee Shoppe") was never pronounced as *ye*, but always as *the*.

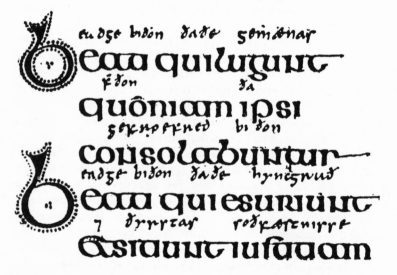

Fig. 58. Round Insular with pointed Insular glosses (*Lindisfarne Gospels*, ca. A.D. 700).

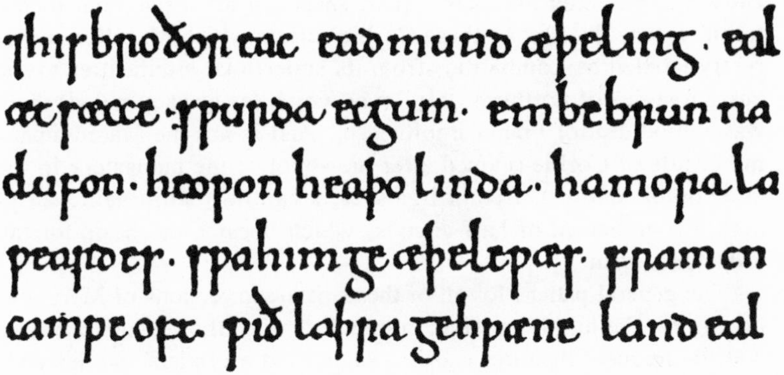

ꝥhıꞃbꞃoðoꝥ ꞇꞩc ꞇꞽdmuno æꝥeᶅınᵹ· ꞇꞷl
æꞇꞃꞩꞇꞇ·ꞃꝛuꝛða ꞇꞃᵹum· ꞇmbꞇbꝛun na
duꞃon· hꞽꞷpon hꞇaꝥo ᶅınða· hamoꝛaᶅa
pꞇaꝛꞷꞇꞃ· ꞃꝛahımᵹꞇ æꝥeᶅꞇpæꞃ· ꞃꝛamꞽn
ꞇampꞇoꝛꞇ· pıð ᶅaꝥꝛa ᵹꞇhpænꞇ ᶅanð ꞇal

Fig. 59. Pointed Insular (*Anglo-Saxon Chronicle*, ca. 1045).

(See Fig. 58 for the round script with pointed interlinear glosses
and Fig. 59 for the pointed script in a vernacular manuscript. Note,
in the former, the tendency of virtually all letters to become perfect
circles, not only the *o* of *quoniam* [line 2] but the *a* and *t* of *beata*
[line 1]; even the *b* of *consolabuntur* [line 3] and the *q* of *quoniam*
and *p* of *ipsi* in line 2 are virtually circles with slight identifying clubs
or descenders. Note, in the pointed script of 59, the lateral compression and verticality as compared to the round script and note the characteristic letter-forms of *f* and *r* [*fram*, penultimate word of line 4], *g*
in *ecgum* [fourth word of line 2], *ash* [= æ] in *æt* [first word of line
2], *wyn* in *swurda* [next word], *thorn* and *ash* in *æpeling*, [line 1,
word 5], and *eth* in *broðor* [line 1, word 2].)

D. *Merovingian* (Seventh century-eighth century)

Because of the sheer size of the Merovingian territory in Europe,
it would be unrealistic to expect a uniform script during a period of
great experimentation. The early "compressed" style, which showed
a close relationship to late Roman cursive of the official variety, fairly
quickly developed into a number of different book scripts. These

used to be thought of as highly local versions of Merovingian; but, for example, the so-called Luxeuil script is now considered to have been more regional than local. The monastery of Corbie seems to have had three distinct sub-scripts of its basic parent form (the *ab*, *az*, and *en*, named after the characteristic shapes of these symptomatic letters). It was the first of these Corbie scripts which Mabillon incorrectly labeled as Lombardic, from its superficial similarities to the current styles of northern Italy, over which (as already noted) there was a good deal of Frankish influence. And it was the Maurdramnus minuscule of Corbie (named after the abbot of the monastery in the late eighth century), free of ligatures, a careful, calligraphic script highly reminiscent of half-uncials, which became the basis for the Caroline reform.

The general pattern for all of these different versions of Merovingian is for the highly cursive, cramped style of the seventh century, with its frequent ligatures and its exaggerated ascenders and descenders, to become more formal as it progressed into a book script. Partially under the influence of half-uncial, late Merovingian dropped its ligatures and gradually acquired the rounded forms associated with the pre-Caroline scripts of the late eighth century.

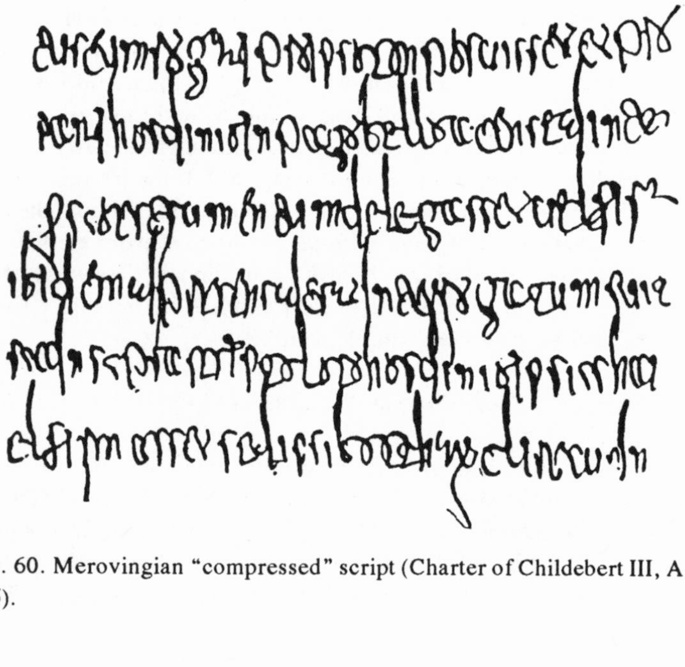

Fig. 60. Merovingian "compressed" script (Charter of Childebert III, A.D. 695).

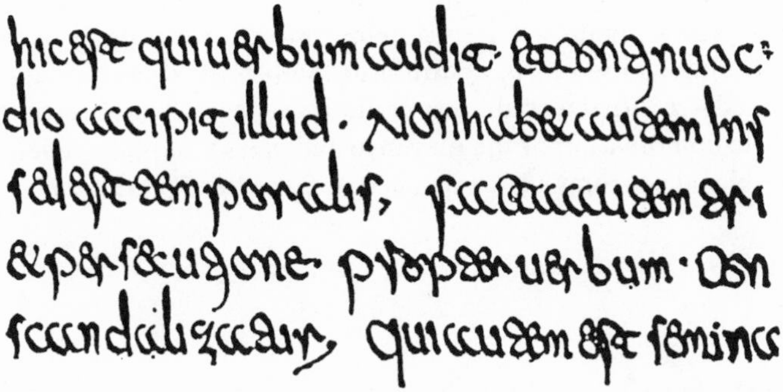

Fig. 61. Luxeuil script (Lectionary, A.D. 669).

(See Fig. 60 for an example of the earlier "compressed" Merovingian script from the seventh century, and note its lateral, cramped, and disfigured style, with very long ascenders and descenders joining (even overlapping) lines. Note the lack of word division and the large number of ligatures, e.g., the *bi* of initial *ibid* [line 4]. Compare this with Fig. 61, the Luxeuil script, and note the more rounded letter-forms of Luxeuil, its comparatively fewer ligatures and clearer word-division, and its generally greater legibility, e.g., *hic*, first word of line 1. Note, however, that some forms of the broken cursive style are retained, e.g., the *a* as a double *c* in *accipit* [line 2, word 2].)

Caroline Scripts

In 789, Charlemagne published a decree requiring that liturgical works be copied with the greatest possible care and expedition. This decree—and the political power behind it ("nostra auctoritate constabilimus"), together with the invitation to Alcuin of York to take charge of the production of books at Tours—has often been credited with inaugurating the reformation of calligraphy which was to dominate Europe for the next three centuries. On purely paleographical grounds it can be shown that the influence of half-uncials at Corbie and elsewhere had already begun the transformation of the straggling, undisciplined roman cursive national scripts into the neat, round Caroline style sometime before this. But there can be little doubt that Charlemagne's interest in the project, coupled with the spread of the

Cluniac monastic reform movement, helped the dissemination of the new (or, rather, old) clear script throughout the Frankish Empire and beyond. The stimulus given to copying—which was soon extended to secular, classical works in addition to the liturgical texts originally mentioned—required a script that could be economical yet easily legible. The combination of the elegance and clarity of half-uncial with the speed and economy of roman cursive provided the medium.

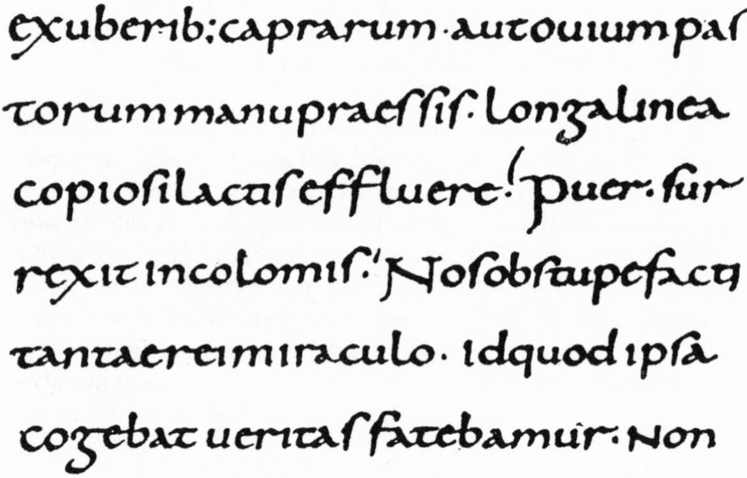

Fig. 62. Caroline minuscule (Sulpicius Severus, early ninth century).

(See Fig. 62 and note the general clarity and breadth compared with Merovingian; the general lack of ligatures and clear separation of minims [*ouium*, line 1]; the uncial *a* and closed *e* throughout; the retention of capital *N* [*Nos*, line 4, *Non* line 6]; the long sloping *s* [*ʃ*] (even at the end of words) and *f* [*praeʃʃiʃ*, line 2, *effluere*, line 3]; the slight clubbing of *b*, (straight) *d*, and *l* [*cogebat*, line 6, *quod*, line 5, *longa*, line 2].)

There has been some argument among paleographers as to whether the "perfected" Tours style of Caroline should properly be looked upon as a "debased" half-uncial or an "elevated" cursive. The debate has some historical interest, but it is important here only in that it emphasizes the quality of compromise that characterizes the script.

INCIPIT LIBER
EXODVS

ʌ ϵ c ѕ υ ɴ т (
ɴ o м ɪ ɴ ʌ
f ɪ ʟ ɪ o ʀ ū
ɪ ѕ ʀ ʌ ♭ ϵ ʟ
q υ ɪ ɪ ɴ ç ʀ ϵ ѕ
ѕ ɪ ѕ υ ̃ т . ɪ ɴ
ʌ ϵ ç ʏ p т ū
c υ м ɪ ʌ c o ʙ
ѕ ɪ ɴ ç υ ʟ ɪ
c υ м ∂ o м ɪ
ʙ υ ѕ ѕ υ ɪ ѕ
ɪ ɴ т ʀ o ɪ ϵ
ʀ υ ̃ т

Ruben. ſymeon leui luda. iſſachar zabulon
etbeniamin. danetnepthalim. gad etaſer
Erantigitur omneſ animae eorum quae egreſ
ſae ſunt de femore iacob. ſeptuaginta quinque
Joſeph autem. in aegypto erat Quomortuo et
uniuerſiſ fratribus eiuſ omniq; cognatione ſua.
filii iſrt creuerunt. et quaſi germinanteſ multi
plicati ſunt ac roborati animiſ impleuerunt terrã

Fig. 63. The hierarchy of scripts (*Grandval Bible*, Tours, ca. 840), Roman square capitals, uncials, and Caroline minuscule.

The long, sweeping *s*, the frequent use of the majuscule *N*, the disappearance of almost all ligatures—these and similar symptoms gave the script the breadth and clarity necessary for formal book work. But the Caroline reform also penetrated the worlds of business and government: by the ninth century, most "court" roman cursives had given way to the new style, although the papal curia held out until the twelfth century, and southern Italy for a century longer.

The script was not absolutely consistent. The heavy clubbing of ascenders gave way almost universally, the uncial [$\mathcal{E}$] took on its closed form *e* (or cedillared, as [$\mathcal{C}$]), and the uncial [$\mathfrak{a}$] overcame the "open" [$\mathcal{a}$] of cursive, avoiding the confusion with *u* or *cc*. But straight *d* might alternate with uncial [$\mathfrak{d}$]—though not usually in the same hand—and the minuscule form of *n* could frequently alternate with majuscule *N*.

Along with the revival of the classical minuscule script came a similar revival of, for example, rustic capitals. The majuscule revival followed much stricter models, so on paleographical grounds it is almost impossible to distinguish some Caroline rustic capitals from the original Roman versions. The minuscule was essentially a hybrid, but the majuscules were much purer, no doubt because they were less widely used, being still largely confined to ornamental and monumental purposes. In this sense they were a part of a "hierarchy" of scripts, all of which could theoretically occur together in the same manuscript: square capitals could be employed for headings, rustics for explicits, uncials for rubrics and first lines, and Caroline minuscule for the body text (Fig. 63). This feeling for formal fitness of appearance to function is close to the principles practiced in modern printing and demonstrates the Caroline sense of the "book" as a total artifact.

Gothic Script

One of the recurrent fashions in interdisciplinary criticism has been to find (or try to find) esthetic similarities among the various art-forms of a given period. Usually these attempts strain after resemblances which evaporate upon closer inspection. This is probably true of any comprehensive theory linking Caroline script to contemporary romanesque architecture on the one hand, and gothic script to the architecture of the twelfth to fifteenth centuries on the other. But some useful distinctions can be made. As we have seen, the Caroline script is basically a round style, stressing breadth and solidity, just as romanesque architecture emphasizes the round, not the pointed, arch and a solid, occasionally even squat, denseness. But gothic script is broken (hence its name *littera fractura*) and in its perfected form promotes the vertical line, not the curve, just as the architecture of its time is renowned for its broken arches and its generally perpendicular

design. Stretching the similarities further than these superficial resemblances would be merely facile, but the resemblances do provide
us with a standard by which the aberrations can be judged.

It was from the mid-eleventh century, and particularly in the
twelfth-century Renaissance, that the breakdown of the Caroline monopoly became noticeable. The growth of the universities, the rise of
a class of professional (and even amateur) scribes outside the monastic
scriptoria, the documentary requirements of the greatly expanded secular governments—these changes encouraged an increase in production, a national and local reaction against the omnipresence of the
Caroline system, and a great deal of individual experiment. (See Fig.
64 for the development of gothic from Caroline, and note the gradual
compressing of the letter-forms and the loss of rounded clarity as the
script becomes more angular and broken into separate strokes.)

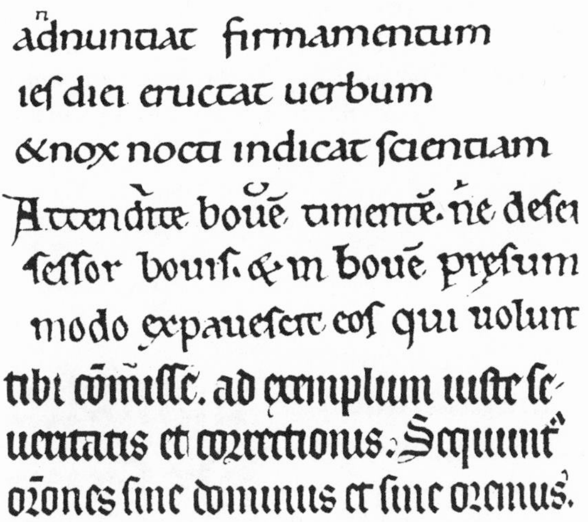

Fig. 64. Development of gothic from Caroline (mss. from tenth, twelfth, and
fourteenth centuries).

Inevitably, this means that gothic is more difficult to describe and
classify than Caroline, for there were many more local variations,
many more occasions for writing, and many more scribes involved in
the act of copying.

But there were identifiable symptoms. Gothic substituted angles for curves, breaking each letter into a series of straight lines (e.g., *o* is written not as a circle but as four, or six, separate strokes [O]); gothic emphasized the difference between light and heavy strokes, with the light becoming virtual hairlines and the heavy thickly, even grossly, written; it encouraged ligature, and even the actual fusing of letters, with a central vertical duct acting as the last stroke of one letter and the first stroke of the next (e.g., [ထ]); in its movement toward a very tight compression (e.g., in fused letters) it also produced closed rather than open letter-forms (by the thirteenth century the open [a] had often closed its bow to [B], and similar changes occur in the forms of, e.g., [6], [ꞃ], and [ꟑ]). All of these tendencies were very different from Caroline practice. At their most extreme, in liturgical manuscripts of the thirteenth century and later, these practices could result in a dense lattice-work of strokes (the so-called picket-fence effect), where the individual letter-forms, particularly of the minims in *i*, *u*, *m*, *n*, were subordinated to the desire for uniformity and equalization of spacing. This *littera textura* (or "woven writing") had completely forgotten the Caroline desire for clarity and legibility. The lozenge-shaped feet of *textura quadrata*, compared with the flat feet, resting squarely on the line, of *textura prescissus* (see Fig. 65) further exacerbated this movement toward a thick, heavy denseness.

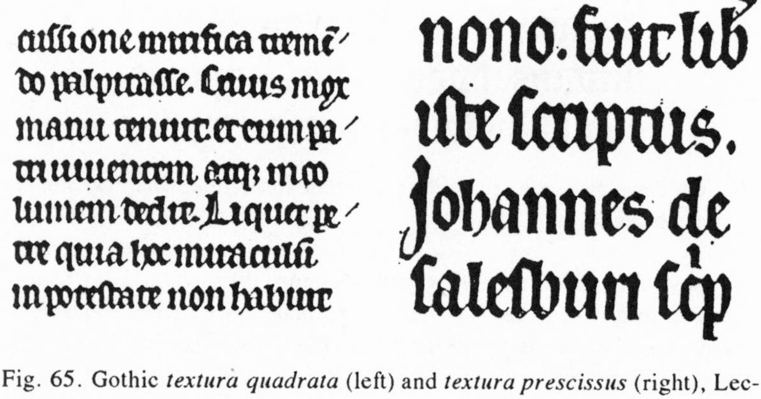

Fig. 65. Gothic *textura quadrata* (left) and *textura prescissus* (right), Lectionary, written by the English scribe, John of Salisbury, 1269.

The promotion of uniformity (especially in letter size and spacing), the lateral compression, and the angular and perpendicular tendencies caused a number of characteristic confusions of letter-form (most important, of *c/t*, *c/e*, and all the minim letters). It can be best seen in thirteenth-century documents, where a tiny script (probably in part the result of a new call for "pocket Bibles" which could be easily portable and accessible) took over from the monumental, large hands typical of service books of the twelfth century. In the later Middle Ages, the letter-forms began to be more carelessly written, especially in vernacular manuscripts, and to take on cursive tendencies, producing the bastard styles of the fifteenth century. A good deal of the most significant Middle English literature was preserved in manuscripts written in such bastard scripts.

In addition to these chronological developments, there were also a number of geographical distinctions to be noted. It is often possible for the experienced paleographer to determine not only the country but the specific town where a gothic manuscript was produced, just as Corbie, Luxeuil, and other pre-Caroline monastic centers had created their own styles in another period of great experiment. The gothic script began in northern France in the eleventh century and, although dominating Europe in one form or another for four hundred years, was always more consistently used in northern countries. The full, "perfected" gothic style is therefore essentially a northern European phenomenon, and pure textura is rare in Mediterranean countries. Since the textura style was particularly associated with the liturgy, and therefore with Latin, even at a comparatively late date it could be found in northern manuscripts alongside a hand using the bastard script, based on cursive, for the vernacular: the *lettre batarde* versus the *lettre de forme*. The same process was seen in Fig. 58, where the round hand of the Latin text is glossed by a pointed Insular hand (though in this case, the pointed is a later addition).

Another northern—and, at first, specifically Flemish or Burgundian—development was the sloping heavy form of bastard (see Fig. 66) used in vernacular literature in the late Middle Ages and taken over by Caxton and other printers of this literature in the fifteenth century. Perhaps its most characteristic feature was the long, strongly written, and sloped *s*, which greatly contrasted with the square, formal *s* of textura. In southern Europe, especially Italy, the angularity of gothic was modified by a tendency to soften the broken lines with curves, producing a style appropriately known as rotunda (see Fig. 67). While displaying the gothic features of fusion and the heavy shading

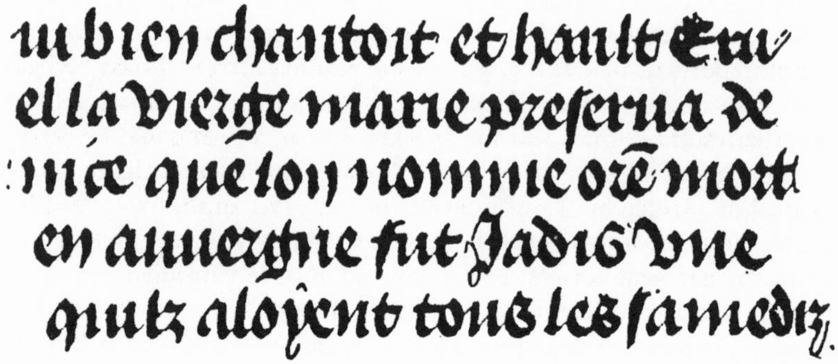

[Gothic bastard script specimen — five lines of manuscript text]

Fig. 66. Gothic bastard script (*Miracles de Nostre Dame*, written for Philip the Good of Burgundy, ca. 1450).

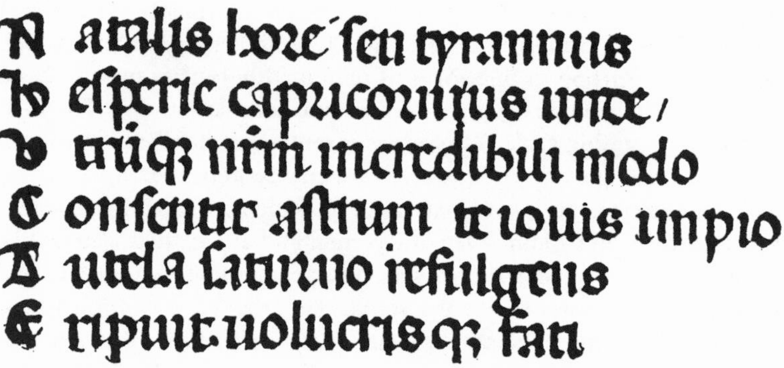

[Gothic rotunda script specimen — six lines of manuscript text]

Fig. 67. Gothic *rotunda* (Horace, written in Cremona, 1391).

of strong strokes, this *littera bononiensis* can with some justice be seen as bearing a similar relationship to the early humanist scripts of the Renaissance as the pre-Caroline experiments of Corbie had to the Tours Caroline style. To write in a humanistic style was simply a smaller step to take for an Italian scribe than for a northern European.

Court Scripts

Both Caroline and gothic scripts were formed for book work, although the imperial growth of the former and the documentary ubiquity of the latter inevitably ensured that their influence would extend into charters, legal documents, and business records usually written in court script. At certain periods the two types of writing—book and court—are virtually indistinguishable (e.g., eleventh-century English charters may often be written in a late version of the Insular pointed book script), and at other times the two produce a third bastard style which combined the formality of book script with the letter-shapes of court. Furthermore, general cultural tendencies are sometimes observable in both types. When, for instance, thirteenth-century book scripts became tiny and compressed, so too the court equivalents were reduced in size, possibly for a similar reason (i.e., the great amount of clerical work in government necessitated a more economical use of materials, just as the proliferation of Bibles as a result of the preaching movement of the friars necessitated a smaller, more portable format and style).

While there was obviously always a good deal of variety in individual court hands (if anything, they tended to be even more local and idiosyncratic than book hands), there are certain characteristics which can in general be delineated. First, since speed was more important than elegance, a court script tended to be more cursive than a contemporary book version, especially in the free rather than the set variety. It has been argued that no true cursive existed before the fifteenth century, but from the time of the first-century Roman cursive used for commercial transactions in Pompeii, the scribe of a business script tried to reduce the number of pen-lifts to the minimum consonant with the demands of letter-form. Second, since speed could, even in fairly formal scripts, easily result in carelessness and decay of orthography, court scripts often look more illegible to the untrained eye. This is no doubt partly the result of our modern writing and printing having developed out of the humanistic book script rather than out of the chancery styles of the papal or imperial courts; but court script frequently seemed illegible to its contemporaries—witness the numerous decrees (including Frederick II's banning of Imperial Rescript referred to above) from the age of Justinian down to the papal ban on the use of the arcane and fanciful *littera Sancti Petri* in 1879. Third, the cursive tendencies of court script, when allied to the commemorative nature of the documents produced, often promoted an indulgence in long, floreated, and extravagant ascenders and descenders (see Fig. 68), sometimes notched or otherwise decorated (and apparently therefore contradicting the general rule of speed as a requisite), resulting frequently in much more broadly spaced lines than was typical of contemporary book script. While this tendency is not universal (sixteenth-century secretary script can be very densely packed indeed), it

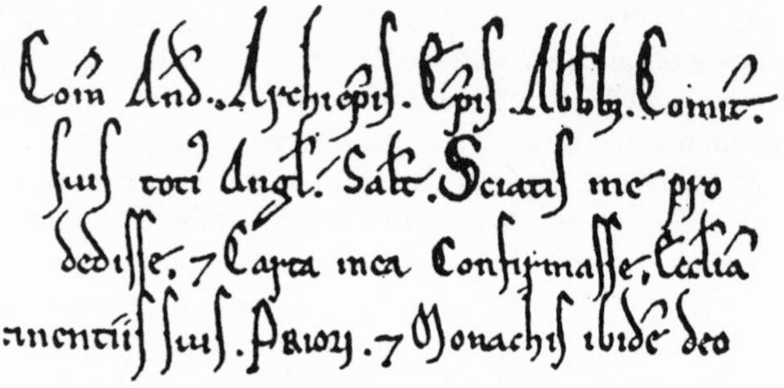

Fig. 68. English court script (Charter of Henry II to Bromfeld Priory, 1155).

appears in documents dating from the *littera beneventana* of the ninth-century papal chancery, through the business version of the Caroline style, down to many charters, grants, leases, etc., of the later Middle Ages. Business scripts were often flourished, notched, and extravagant even when book scripts were uniformly dense and tight.

All of the examples of court script in Figs. 68–70 have these characteristics of the court style to one degree or another. But it should also be remembered that, just as a book style might degenerate into a cursive, hastily written form suitable for business use, so a court script might become formal enough to be used for literary purposes. The handwriting of the vernacular manuscripts of the later English Middle Ages has been characterized by Denholm-Young as a "slightly formal court hand written in a book hand spirit" (36). The letter-forms in these documents usually descended from court models, but the script itself could achieve a clarity in its bastard style which lent itself to literary work. While the flourished extravagance was muted, and the letters themselves were more carefully written, the origins of the script are clear.

(See Fig. 69 and note the general gothic book script shape of the letters, especially in minims, but the rounded, floreated effect of court script, reducing the angularity of the script compared to the thicker strokes of contemporary textura.)

The other court-derived script which is of particular interest to students of English literature is secretary (see Fig. 70), in its various special (and often highly personal) forms, growing out of the free small scripts of the early Tudors and succeeding the more formal set scripts by the mid-sixteenth century for general business purposes.

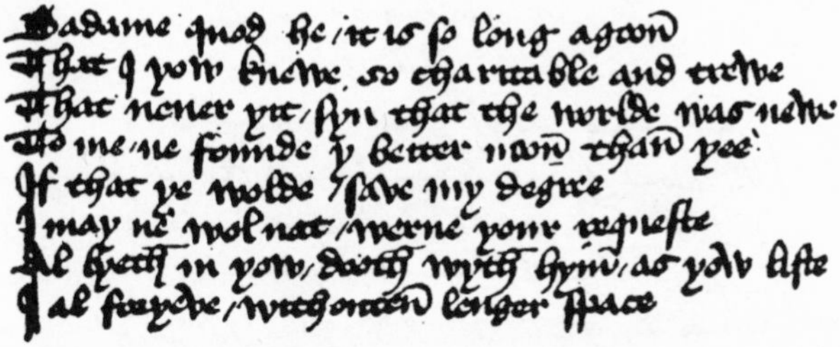

Fig. 69. Gothic bastard: English *cursiva formata* (Chaucer, *Legend of Good Women*, mid-fifteenth century).

But there are two problems, both the product of the invention of printing. First, since professional scribes were no longer necessary for literary works, the naturally idiosyncratic character of the court script became more pronounced, for it lacked the corrective of a formal text script, at least until secretary was overcome by the Italian cursive version of humanistic in the seventeenth century. Second, since the literary works were actually printed using a type-face (whether "black-letter," i.e., gothic, or roman or italic) very different from the secretary scripts employed by the authors in their manuscripts, and since so many of these manuscripts, especially of dramatic texts, were simply destroyed as of no further use once the book had been printed, theoretical or practical access to the putative manuscript form of any printed letter, work, or line of text is often quite tenuous. This problem is taken up in the section on textual bibliography (Chapter 7), but it is worth mentioning here as an indication of how the later English court script of the sixteenth and early seventeenth centuries is not as directly related to contemporary typography (and therefore does not necessarily give as much help in charting textual transmission) as the bastard scripts of the late Middle Ages in the textual criticism of vernacular literature.

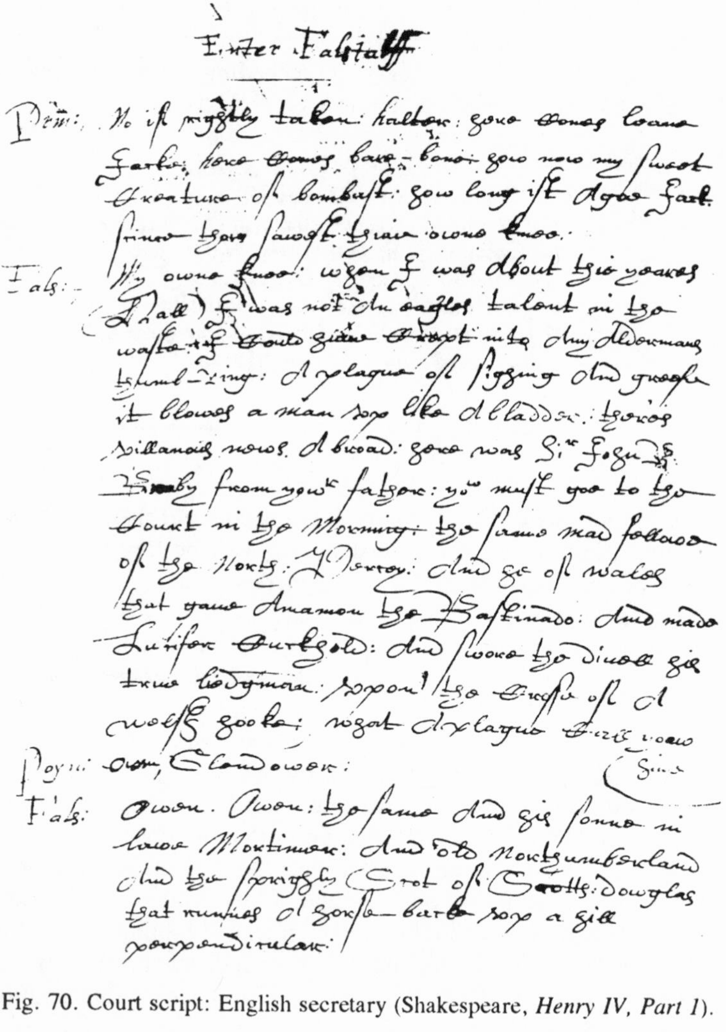

Fig. 70. Court script: English secretary (Shakespeare, *Henry IV, Part 1*).

Humanistic Scripts

In the survey of geographical variations on the basic gothic script, it was noted that the Italian version (rotunda) never indulged in the extreme angularity of northern forms. It was consequently very much easier for humanists like Poggio Bracciolini, prompted by the "pre-humanist" hands of Petrarch, Boccaccio, and Salutati (all of whom frequently complained about the illegibility of gothic), to modify rotunda by eliminating all traces of gothic straightness and denseness, by stressing the roundness of the letter-forms—in short, by imitating the *littera antiqua* of the Caroline minuscule (itself an imitation of roman half-uncial), as if the High Middle Ages had never existed. (See Fig. 71 for a particularly conservative replication of Caroline minuscule, even to the extent of retaining the long *s* in final positions.) Gradually losing the letter-fusions, decreasing the shading, making the angles and broken verticals round, Poggio's "new" script was a conscious attempt to recreate the legibility and harmony of the Caroline reform.

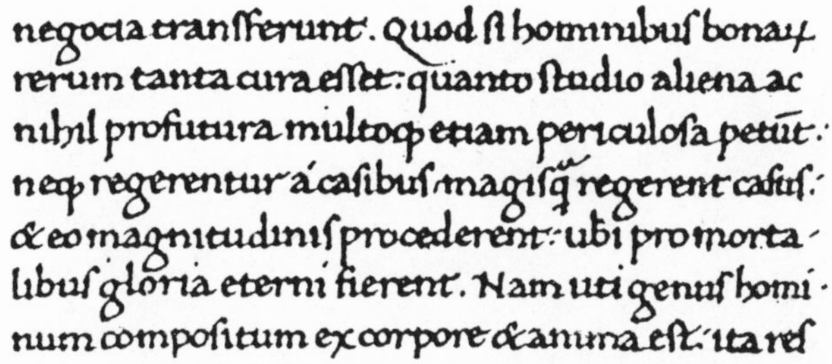
negocia tranſferunt. Quod ſi hominibuſ bonaꝝ
rerum tanta cura eſſet: quanto ſtudio aliena ac
nihil profutura multoq; etiam periculoſa petūt:
neq; regerentur a caſibuſ magiſq̄ regerent caſuſ:
& eo magnitudiniſ procederent: ubi pro morta-
libuſ gloria eterni fierent. Nam uti genuſ homi-
num compoſitum ex corpore & anima eſt: ita reſ

Fig. 71. Humanistic revival: Caroline minuscule (Sallust, Florence, 1466).

But there were some distinctive traits in its "modern" incarnation: the dotted *i*, the round *s* and *r*, the long *t*, the pointed initial *v*—all of these features of humanistic (see Fig. 72) mark the continued presence of gothic influences, as does the retention of the typical gothic abbreviation system in some of the early versions of the humanistic script.

Beginning in Florence in the early years of the fifteenth century, the new/old script had reached most areas of Europe within a hundred years, though England and Germany held out longer than some other countries. Indeed, once the black-letter gothic became enshrined by German printers in its native land, no foreign script could make much headway there until the twentieth century. But while humanistic can be seen as yet another reform of writing by the resuscitation of ancient models, there is a difference. Within a little over a half-century after Poggio had "invented" the new roman script, the craft of formal

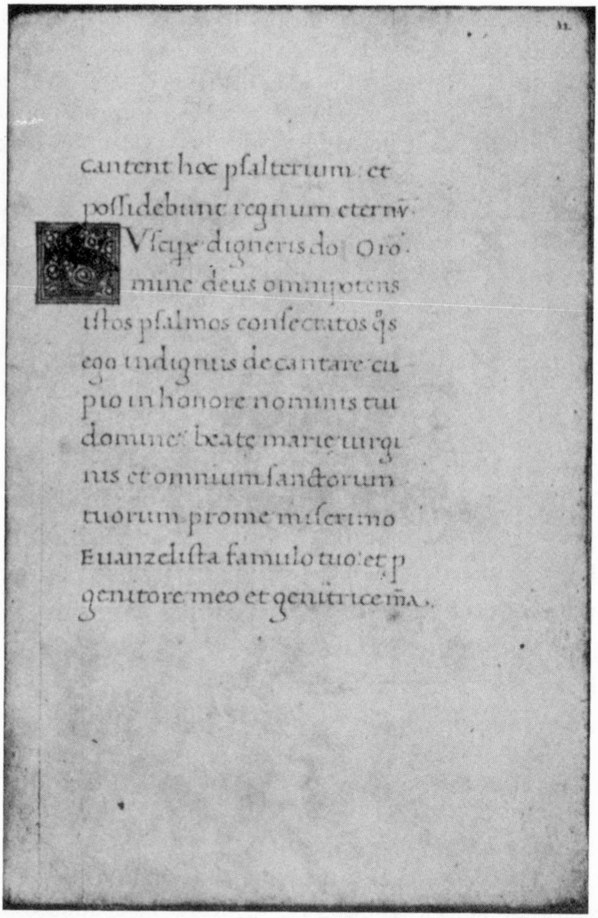
cantent hoc pſalterium: et
poſſidebunt regnum eternū.
Vſque digneris do. Oro
mine deus omnipotens
iſtos pſalmos conſecratos q̄s
ego indignus decantare cu
pio in honore nominis tui
domine: beate marie uirgi
nis et omnium ſanctorum
tuorum pro me miſerrimo
Euanzeliſta famulo tuo: et p
genitore meo et genitrice mā.

Fig. 72. Humanistic revival: roman minuscule (Italian, late fifteenth century).

handwriting in books was rendered obsolete by the invention of printing. Literary text-hands were no longer necessary, though calligraphic handwriting for other purposes would still be needed. Thus it was ultimately the cursive or "italic" (see Fig. 73), rather than the formal or "roman," version of the humanistic script which enjoyed the longest influence in writing and is still the basis for most calligraphic styles today. This cursive modification seems to have been first used by Niccolo Niccolì at about the same time that Poggio was experimenting with *littera antiqua*. Unlike earlier attempts at cursive,

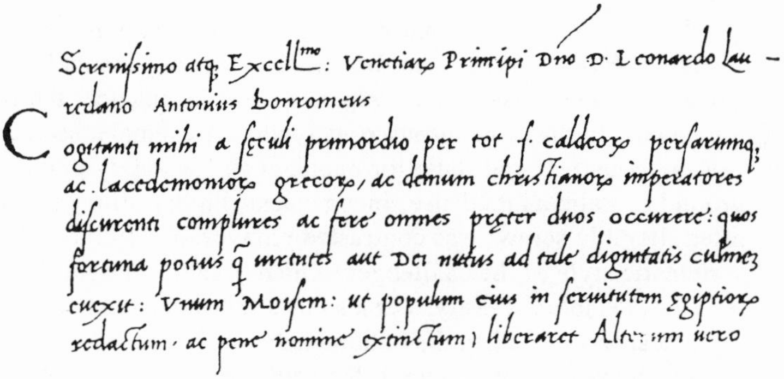
Serenissimo atq; Excell.mo: Venetiarum Principi Dno D. Leonardo Lau-
redano Antonius Bonromeus
Cogitanti mihi a seculi primordio per tot s. caldeorum persarumq;
ac lacedemoniorum grecorum, ac denum christianorum imperatores
discurrenti complures ac fere omnes preter duos occurere: quos
fortuna potius q virtutes aut Dei nutus ad tale dignitatis culmen
euexit: Unum Moysem: ut populum eius in servitutem egiptiorum
redactum ac pene nomine extinctum liberaret Alterum uero

Fig. 73. Humanistic cursive (italic) as a book script (Venice, 1521).

which had linked letters together only at the cost of distorting the letter-forms through complicated ligatures (remember that roman cursive *e* depends for its shape on the type of letter it is linked with), the new humanistic cursive had built-in linkages in the basic form of the letter itself—in much the same way that an italic typewriter or computer printer face would today. It is in this sense that the italic humanistic script can be regarded as the first real cursive ever used. Apart from the linkages in the italic, formal and cursive forms of the new experiments were not otherwise dissimilar in letter-shape, except that the closed *a* was used in italic, and the open a in roman, a distinction which survives in this present type-face.

A further development occurred when italic began to be used as a business script, first by the papal chancery in the mid-fifteenth century (hence the name *littera cancelleresca*), and later, through the influence of "writing masters" like Lodovico Arrighi, as a personal and official script for almost all occasions. Arrighi's manual *La operina*, printed in 1522, became a standard authority for the italic style that was so influential that even in England, where the native secretary was very healthy, it was considered socially necessary for an educated person to be able to write in both italic and secretary. As noted in Chapter 2, Queen Elizabeth was proficient in different scripts (as were most other upper-class writers of the day), for she had been taught italic by her tutor Roger Ascham and by Italian writing masters specially imported by Henry VIII for the purpose. Both Catharine Parr and Lady Jane Grey could write a competent italic hand, and in 1554, the new style entered the middle classes, for from this date italic signatures begin to appear in the *Common Paper* (the roll of members) of the Scriveners Company.

Jean de Beauchesne and John Baildon's *A Booke Containing Divers Sortes of Hands* (1570), the first English writing manual, kept the two styles, foreign and native, separate. But in practice, the two began to appear in the same manuscripts (with, for example, secretary used for the body text and italic for quotations). Secretary gradually lost ground to italic as its dense, inconsistent, highly idiosyncratic, and often illegible scrawl was contrasted unfavorably with the clear and systematic style of the challenger, which became recognized not only as a fashionable necessity, but also as a more obviously all-purpose, practical script. When the oblique italic way of holding the pen was adopted by writers of secretary, the battle was over. By the mid-seventeenth century, the native gothic, now in a very decayed state, had given way to the Continental humanistic for most business and personal occasions, though various forms of a degenerate "engrossing" gothic were to be used by, for example, lawyers for another two centuries. (See Fig. 74, and note the retention of the floreate ascenders of late court script, together with the thick, black and angular strokes of gothic.)

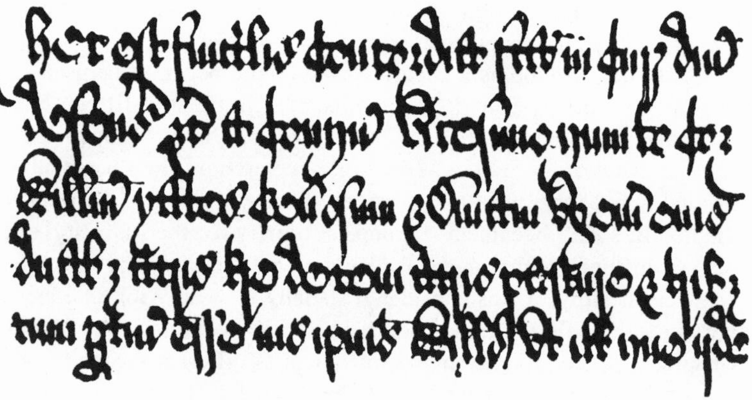

Fig. 74. Engrossing script (Final Accord, 1673).

The Writing Masters and Later Calligraphic Styles

A. *Early Writing Manuals*

Arrighi's *La operina* has already been cited as standardizing the humanistic cursive script that came to dominate handwriting in the later sixteenth and the seventeenth centuries. Thereafter, specific changes of style were more and more dependent upon the activities and publications of these writing masters, whose clients were interested either in a convenient business script, employable in those professional areas where printing had not made appreciable inroads, or in a more purely calligraphic script which could be used for personal purposes by the now "amateur" scribe. Research into letter form and format had been going on at least since the time of Ciriaco of Ancona and Feliciano of Verona, whose work during the fifteenth century in collecting, transcribing, and commenting on the shapes of ancient inscriptional alphabets was, for example, incorporated into frescoes by Mantegna. Luca Pacioli's *De divina proportione* (1509), with its geometric analysis of letter-making; Fanti of Ferrara's expansion of this system to include gothic letter-forms (1514); Geofroy Tory's development of Pacioli's geometric method in his *Champfleury* (1529); Jaugeon's scheme for construction of "perfect" roman capitals (Fig. 75): all of these works and the experiments which they encouraged (e.g., the modification of gothic *cursive françoyse* to produce the French business script *civilité*; the *lettres de fantaisie* with their characteristically extravagant, flourished abandon) promoted an interest in a calligraphic style which would demonstrate the user's culture and awareness of the new humanism.

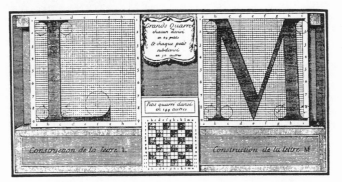

Fig. 75. Jaugeon's roman capitals (Paris, 1693).

Parallel to this concern was the more practical one of creating scripts which professional clerks could adopt. Inevitably, some professions (and some countries) were more conservative than others, Germany and the law being generally the most reactionary. It was not until after the Second World War that the late gothic cursive of *Kurrentschrift*, with its more formal equivalent *Fraktur*, was superseded in Germany by more modern styles based on roman/italic. And this was only achieved after Hitler had banished the printed black-letter gothic as being of "Jewish origin," in a re-writing of paleographic history. Extremely fanciful versions of late gothic cursive (including the upright "engrossing script" developing out of secretary) were used by lawyers' clerks in England and elsewhere well into the eighteenth century, and for certain types of document, even into the nineteenth.

The survival of the gothic *Whereas* and *This Indenture* (not reproducible in this type-face) in otherwise roman printed law documents is a further testimony to this conservatism. Debased forms of gothic cursive for regular business use existed in most Western European countries outside Italy until the mid-seventeenth century, when a form of humanistic italic began to be preferred.

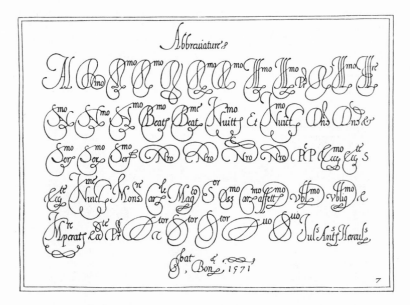

Fig. 76. Hercolani, *Essemplari di lettere cancelleresche* (Bologna, 1570).

While Arrighi's pure italic was sometimes the model for these reforms, a rival occurred in the influence of A. G. Hercolani's *cancelleresca testeggiata*, first appearing in his manual *Essemplare utile* (1570), see Fig. 76. Hercolani engraved his scripts on copper rather than cutting them on wood, and this use of the engraver's burin encouraged extremely fine ascenders and descenders (but characteristically finished with an ugly blot or angular serif). Hercolani's style was carried into Spain by Yciar and into England by Edward Cocker (see Fig. 77), whose late seventeenth-century manuals can be compared with the more decidedly gothic models of Martin Billingsley's *The Pen's Excellencie* at the beginning of the century (1618), though even at this early period, testeggiata was being used for private correspondence in England. (See Jonathan Goldberg, *Writing Matter: From the Hands of the English Renaissance*, for a provocative poststructuralist analysis of the cultural significance of English writing manuals.)

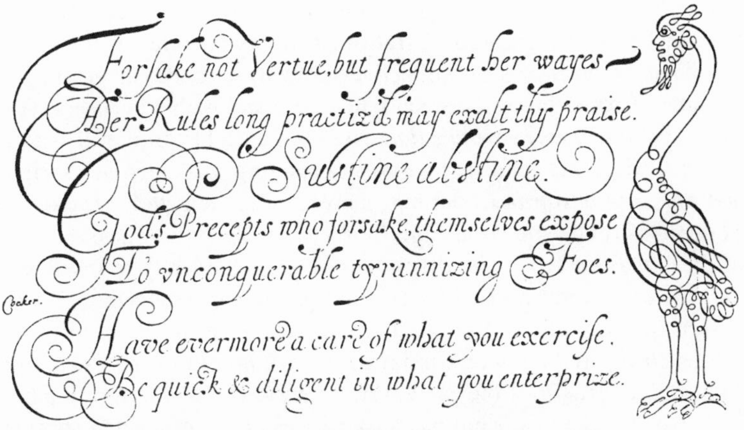

Fig. 77. Edward Cocker, *The Pen's Triumph* (London, 1660).

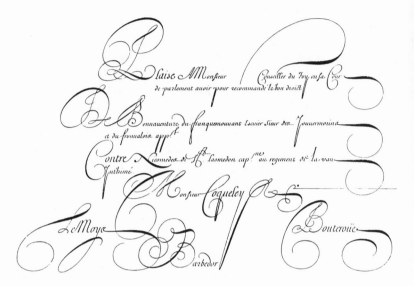

Fig. 78. Louis Barbedor, *Les écritures financières et italienne bastarde* (Paris, 1659).

In France, the influence of the Italian reformation of handwriting was felt through Louis Barbedor's *Les écritures financières et italienne bastarde* (see Fig. 78). In his mid-seventeenth century overhaul of French royal administration, Colbert introduced three new scripts based on Barbedor, collectively known as ronde (displaying, as a whole, a compromise between humanistic and gothic cursive). The three versions were: *écriture financière* (an upright script still betraying several gothic features), *coulée* (a running, or "current" script), and *italienne-bastarde* (a sloping, more humanistic style). The ornate example of ronde shown in Fig. 78 is a particularly flourished version of the *italienne-bastarde*, displaying ronde's tendency to indulge in the sort of fanciful play of letter-construction depending more on the design of the plate as a whole than on any hope of communicating information, in a manner similar to that of the round Insular script. This characteristic of the early writing masters, in reaction to printing's having taken over normal book-text work, is what often survives in modern calligraphic styles, where extravagant whorls and floreation, and ornamentation for its own sake, confirm the function of calligraphy as extraneous to the content of text.

By the end of the seventeenth century, the various forms of humanistic, in modified or purer states, had virtually replaced gothic
cursive outside Germany and the law.

B. *Copperplate, the Later Manuals, and the Twentieth Century*

With the brief exception of the export of Insular scripts to the
Continental monasteries founded by Irish and Anglo-Saxon monks,
the history of English paleography is very derivative, almost passive.
England received its scripts ready-made from elsewhere. The one
major exception was the "copperplate" reaction against the extravagances of the testeggiata flourish. John Ayres's late seventeenth-century manuals (Fig. 79) and George Bickham's mid-eighteenth-century
collection of models in *The Universal Penman* (Fig. 80), together
with John Seally's later *The Running Hand*, helped the development
and acceptance of copperplate, but its success internationally was
more directly a reflection of the spread of English commercial power
from the late seventeenth to the nineteenth centuries.

Fig. 79. John Ayres, *A Tutor to Penmanship* (London, ca. 1698).

On Promissory Notes.

A Promissory Note mentioning Order *is indorsible from one Person to another; which is done by the present Possessor's writing his Name on the Back of it, and delivering it up to the Party, to whom he intends to assign over his Property therein.*

It is unnecessary to have a Promissory Note payable to Bearer *indorsed, if you are satisfy'd the Note is good: And if a Note be indorsed, it is necessary to write a Receipt thereon, to prevent its being negociated, after it is paid and deliver'd up.*

If the Drawer of a Note refuses Payment, the Note is good against the Indorser. The delivering up a Promissory Note to the Person who sign'd it is a sufficient Voucher of its being paid, nor is there any Occasion of writing a Receipt thereon.

Promissory Notes, and Book-Debts, if not legally demanded in six Years, cannot be recover'd by Law: And if you keep a Promissory Note upon Demand, in your own Hands above three Days, and the Person it's upon should fail, the Loss will be your own; but if he fail within the three Days it will light on the Person that paid it you. Let all Notes be made for Value receiv'd, and in the Form of these that follow.

G. Bickham Fecit.

Nº. XXXV.   MD CCXXXVIII

Fig. 80. Commercial copperplate: George Bickham, *The Universal Penman* (London, 1743).

Known as *lettres anglaises*, *lettre inglesa*, or *littera inglese*, copperplate was the only genuinely English national style of handwriting to have reached (and dominated) Europe and beyond, although it was no doubt influenced by earlier Dutch experiments in the mid-seventeenth century. It was divided into two styles—a "round" version used for business and a lighter "Italian" version for personal occasions. The Italian was supposed to be particularly suitable for women. Monopolizing European and American commercial script until the invention of the typewriter, the business version of copperplate was in effect the last triumph of the professional calligrapher/scribe. Thereafter, the combination of the printer and the typewriter so reduced the prerogative of handwriting that calligraphers and calligraphic manuals catered almost wholly to a personal rather than a professional clientele. Teachers were still expected to instruct the young in the acquisition of a fluent, legible script, but these students did not then become scribes for a living.

Because of this dual displacement by printer and typewriter (and now by computer printer), the work of most nineteenth- and twentieth-century calligraphers thus lies outside the specifically textual focus of this book; that is, calligraphy becomes primarily a branch of the fine (or applied) arts rather than a vehicle for the transmission of verbal texts, and the bibliographer or editor is much more likely to encounter a modern text produced either by mechanical or electronic means, or scrawled in a highly idiosyncratic hand without any pretensions to calligraphic style. Nonetheless, it may be useful briefly to sketch in the major movements.

Probably the most significant new theory during this period was that advanced by Joseph Carstairs in 1809, claiming that the entire forearm (rather than the wrist) should control the motions of the pen. The models produced by this theory were very popular in England and in the United States, where Platt R. Spencer's chain of business colleges promoted the Spencerian style, a script strongly contrasting fine and thick strokes. The invention of the steel pen in the early nineteenth century further accentuated the tendency of copperplate towards extremely delicate, thin lines, but this was modified in the late nineteenth and early twentieth centuries, not only by the Spencerian "contrastive" school, but also by the work of William Morris, M. M. Bridges, Rudolph von Larisch, Rudolf Koch, Edward Johnston, and Graily Hewitt in promoting various versions of pre-copperplate and frankly humanist or gothic scripts.

Morris, for example, actually began to use a form of a humanistic round cursive in his own correspondence, and through his founding of the Kelmscott Press, promoted the status of several revised versions of gothic. Bridges resuscitated a different style of humanistic—the professional writing-masters' cancelleresca of the sixteenth century. Von Larisch, working in the Austrian Chancery, published his *Unterricht in ornamentaler Schrift* in 1906, after having been convinced that the standards of contemporary handwriting compared poorly with the manuscripts he was accustomed to dealing with in the Chancery. Koch, working like many modern calligraphers in both handwriting and type-design, was to Germany what Morris had been to England, for he emphasized the close connection of all aspects of arts and crafts, letter-design being only one of the activities covered in his workshop community, the Offenbach Penmen.

"Durham Book" hand (copy).

abcdefghijklm nopqrstuvxyz:

Modernized Half-Uncial (I.).

Fig. 81. Revival of uncial and half-uncial scripts: Johnston, *Writing, & Illuminating, & Lettering*, 1906.

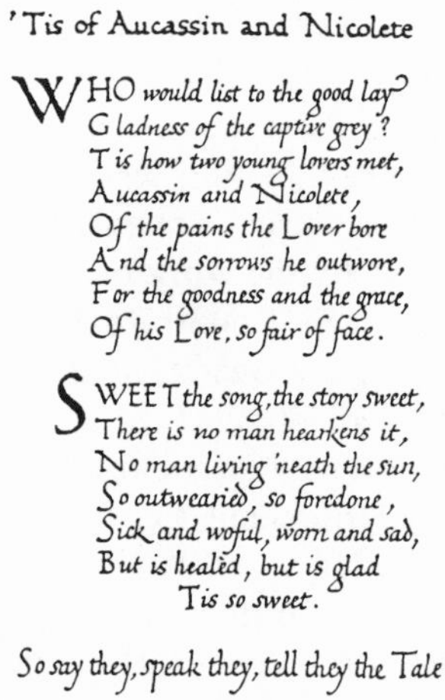

'Tis of Aucassin and Nicolete

WHO would list to the good lay?
Gladness of the captive grey?
T is how two young lovers met,
Aucassin and Nicolete,
Of the pains the Lover bore
And the sorrows he outwore,
For the goodness and the grace,
Of his Love, so fair of face.

SWEET the song, the story sweet,
There is no man hearkens it,
No man living 'neath the sun,
So outwearied, so foredone,
Sick and woful, worn and sad,
But is healed, but is glad
Tis so sweet.

So say they, speak they, tell they the Tale:

Fig. 82. Italic revival: Edward Johnston.

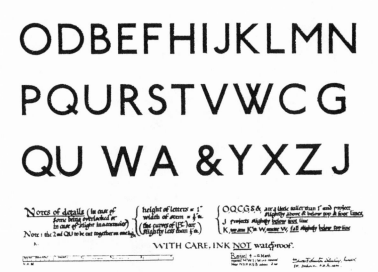

Fig. 83. Johnston's sans-serif alphabet for London Transport, 1916.

Johnston's rebellion against the decadent end of copperplate took the form of his promotion of a broad rather than thin pen, and in his reworking of several medieval (Fig. 81) and humanistic (Fig. 82) scripts, most notably in the extremely influential *Writing, & Illuminating, & Lettering* (1906), which is still in print. For London Transport, Johnston also designed the first successful sans-serif alphabet (Fig. 83), a design which is still in use on London's buses and trains. The sans-serif was a simplification of the letter-form, without the finials that distinguish it from Roman square capitals. It cannot be used in continuous book text, for the lack of serifs make it difficult for the eye to rest on the letter-shapes, but it has been very influential on display type in the twentieth century (see Chapter 6).

Hewitt, a student of Johnston, can (together with Alfred Fairbank and Jan van Krimpen) be regarded as the author of the modification of cancelleresca adopted as the standard for modern italic (see Fig. 84). This latest (perhaps last) modern calligraphic movement to counterbalance the potentially insipid and thin qualities of nineteenth-century copperplate has been adopted as a standard by a number of English (and to a lesser extent, American) schools.

But the later twentieth century can hardly be said to possess a dominant calligraphic script (in the sense that, say, the thirteenth century is dominated by gothic and the eighteenth by copperplate). De-

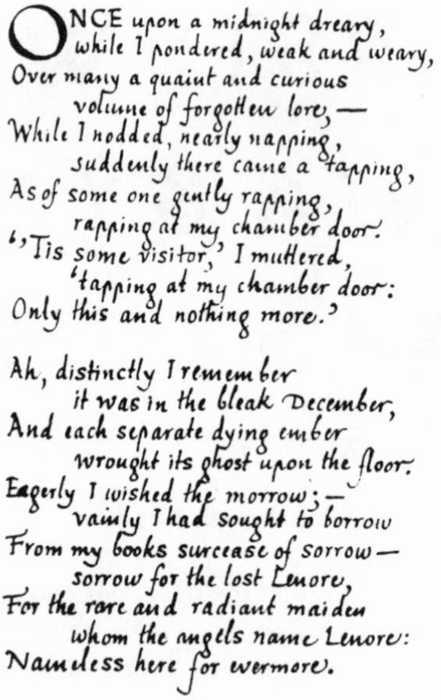

> ONCE upon a midnight dreary,
>   while I pondered, weak and weary,
> Over many a quaint and curious
>   volume of forgotten lore, —
> While I nodded, nearly napping,
>   suddenly there came a tapping,
> As of some one gently rapping,
>   rapping at my chamber door.
> 'Tis some visitor,' I muttered,
>   'tapping at my chamber door:
> Only this and nothing more.'
>
> Ah, distinctly I remember
>   it was in the bleak December,
> And each separate dying ember
>   wrought its ghost upon the floor.
> Eagerly I wished the morrow; —
>   vainly I had sought to borrow
> From my books surcease of sorrow —
>   sorrow for the lost Lenore,
> For the rare and radiant maiden
>   whom the angels name Lenore:
> Nameless here for evermore.

Fig. 84. Modern italic in literary use (Poe, *The Raven*, by Jan van Krimpen).

spite the efforts of the Arts and Crafts movement and its successors (see Chapter 6 on typography), a calligraphic hand is no longer a cultural necessity among literate classes, for, like Hamlet, we seem to

> ...hold it, as our statists do,
> A baseness to write fair, and labour much
> How to forget that learning.

With handwriting almost a completely amateur activity, we are in personal correspondence and the other remaining remnants of scribal functions faced with a variety of scripts (and hands), each peculiar to the user and the occasion. We can still generally recognize the "families" of script (roman, italic, gothic, etc., see Fig. 85), and there are many experienced and gifted calligraphers at work, such as Donald Jackson. It is also still possible to identify German, American, English, or French styles—for the teaching of handwriting in schools still

Fig. 85. The families of script (Donald Jackson).

follows basic national guidelines—but once the writer has reached maturity, the hand may very quickly become irrelevant or degenerate into an illegible scrawl comprehensible (if at all) only by the user. While that old Roman square capital alphabet is still very much alive for monumental purposes, often in modern versions of its original inscribed form (see Fig. 86), in our own personal writing we are back in Pompeii.

Fig. 86. Inscribed Roman square capitals (Eric Gill, 1903).

Abbreviations

One of the major difficulties in reading roman, medieval, and even early humanist scripts is the great number of abbreviations employed by the scribes. Not all periods used the system to the same extent. Caroline scripts generally employ comparatively few abbreviations, gothic rather more. Some areas developed their own systems: early Insular scribes had a peculiar set of abbreviations which can therefore be used to identify their manuscripts, and abbreviations may be similarly used in dating.

No doubt one of the reasons for the growth of the abbreviation system was the desire to save space in writing on expensive materials like vellum (coupled with the necessity of aligning or "justifying" the right-hand margins by varying the length of words). But even the most sumptuous gothic scripts in *éditions de luxe* often used a dense pattern of abbreviations, and stylistic considerations as well as economy must have been part of the explanation. That tradition exerted a great influence can be shown by the early printers' use of the same complex system of abbreviations, when the difficulties of cutting so many unnecessary types were not mitigated by the advantages of economy and justification to the same degree (that is, unlike vellum, paper was not expensive, and a printer could justify margins by other means).

The historians of abbreviations (Traube, Chassant, Lindsay, Capelli) recognize essentially two basic methods—by "suspension" (by using a period or other mark to show that the word is incomplete, even by giving just its initial letter, for example, *M.* = *Marcus, Cæs.* = *Cæsar*) and by "contraction" (by omitting vowels or other parts of the word, with a macron or other sign to show that omission has taken place, for example, $\widehat{DS}$ = *Deus*, $\widehat{XPS}$ = *Christus*). The first type seems to have arisen from the practice of Roman lawyers, who could thereby indicate entire phrases by suspension (e.g., *C.D.E.R.N.E.* = *cuius de ea rea notio est*), the so-called *notæ juris,* and the second probably stems from the Greek (and ultimately Hebrew) unease at naming the deity (the *nomina sacra*). The difference between the two systems can be shown today in the British/American debate over the period in the abbreviations *Mr.* or *Dr.* Since *r* is the last letter of the abbreviated words, the suspension mark (.) is strictly speaking incorrect, for it is not the conclusion of the word which has been omitted but the middle, and thus the abbreviation should have a contraction mark rather than a suspension. There is a similar problem with *Mrs.*

(for "Mistress"), where internal letters have in part been omitted, but not with *Miss* (also standing for "Mistress"), although here a suspension period is rarely used, if ever. The created form *Ms.* is a special case, for the form is not an abbreviated version of any other longer orthographic entity and should not, therefore, be regarded as either contraction or suspension, and should not take an abbreviation mark, although by convention it does, perhaps to make it seem of the same class and status as *Mr(.)*.

In addition to the two basic systems of suspension and contraction there were special shorthand signs which could stand for entire words or parts of words (e.g., [÷] = *est.*, [Ⱶ] = *enim*), the so-called Tironian signs named after Tiro, Cicero's freedman secretary. Finally, there were suprascript signs or letters (and occasionally infrascript) used to show omission (e.g., a supralinear [~] over a vowel usually to indicate a following nasal *m* or *n*; *autẽ = autem*).

The abbreviation system was developed for the convenience of scribes producing Latin manuscripts. When writing in the vernacular, some scribes tried to use the same system, but since it was so dependent on the Latin language, its usefulness was limited, and in general vernacular manuscripts tend to have many fewer abbreviations. Where they do occur, their meaning often becomes vaguer, thus [ꝑ] could mean *par*, *per*, *por*, *pur*, *pour* (or almost any combination of *p* and a vowel plus *r*), or even *puis*.

Some typical suspension marks/*notœ juris* are H.S.E. = *Hic situs est*, TM. = *testa-mentum*, D.M. = *Dolum malum*, R.P. = *Res publica* or *res privata*, A.U.C. = *Ab urbe condita*, C. = *consul*, Tr. pl. = *tribunus plebis*, F. = *fecit* or *familia* or *fides*, FF. = *filii* (upside down if feminine—the Roman world was unabashedly sexist), and perhaps best known of all, S.P.Q.R. = *Senatus populus-que Romanus* (the Roman senate and people).

Note that the meaning of several of these suspended letters or phrases could be ambiguous, and this led to several attempts to standardize, or ban completely, the use of *notœ juris*. Where R.P. could mean either *res publica* or *res privata*, only the lawyers could untangle the documents.

Some typical contraction marks/*nomina sacra* include D̄S̄ = *Deus*, d̄io = *divino*, s̄p̄s = *spiritus*, s̄c̄s = *sanctus*, d̄n̄s = *dominus*, ep̄scs = *episcopus*, ec̄lsa = *ecclesia*. Note that when *spiritus* is used in the sense of "breath" and *dominus* in the sense of a secular lord, the contraction mark is not normally used in early manuscripts. This confirms the religious origin of this class of abbreviation.

Some typical *notæ communæ*—usually contractions, or modified contractions—are: ẳ = *alia*, ãñn = *annus*, ãñ = *ante*, ap̃ = *apud*, ã = *autem/aut*, bñ/bẽ = *bene*, c̃r = *cetera*, c̃c̃ = *circum*, c̃ = *cum*, d̃d̃ = *deinde*, d̃m̃s = *dicimus*, d̃c̃a = *dicta*, dĩ = *dicit*, ec̃ = *ecce*, eĩ = *enim*, eg̃ = *ergo*, eẽ = *esse*, gĩa = *gloria*, hĩ = *habet*, h̄ = *huius*, h^c = *hoc, hæc, hunc*, iẟ = *ideo*, -ĩ- = *id est*, ig̃ = *igitur*, ĩiq = *itaque*, mg̃ = *magis*, m^i = *mihi*, m^o = *modo*, n^c = *nec*, nĩ = *nihil*, ñs = *nisi*, nõm = *nomen*, ñ = *non*, õ = *omnis*, ⟋ₚ = *per*, pĩs = *populus*, p̃ = *pre (præ)* or *post*, p^o = *primo*, ꝓ = *pro* (Spanish mss. = *per*), pp̃ = *propter*, q̃s = *quasi*, rƀ = *rebus*, s̃ĩ = *satis*, s̃c̃l = *scilicet*, s̃c̃d = *secundum*, s̃ = *sed* or *sive*, sp̃ = *semper*, sm̃ = *simul*, sr̃ = *super*, tm̃ = *tamen*, ĩi = *tantum*, tõ = *tota*, ĩr = *trans*, t^c = *tunc*, ữ = *ubi*, uñ = *unde*.

Some of the special signs are: ⁊ = *con*, ƺ = *-bus* or *-que* or *-m* or *et*; Ჽ or ẕ = *-rum*, *-tur*, *-us*, or a general suspension sign with various meanings; ꝑ = *is* or *es*; ⁊ or ꝛ = *et*; ⁊̃ = *etiam*; ꝑ = *ser* or *secundum*; ÷ = *est*; ⸗ or ꝫ̃ = *et*; ƙ = *autem*; ᴣ = *eius* (may also be regarded as *notæ communæ* or suspension); ≈ = *esse*; ꞁ = *uel*; θ = *obiit*. Examples of these and other special signs functioning within words are ⁊ *stat* = *constat*, littor ƺ = *littoribus*, diciẕ = *dicitur*, regꝑ = *regis*, patꝛ = *patet*, ꝑuantur = *seruantur*.

Some of the common supralinear marks are: ~ or ‾ = a following nasal *m* or *n*, (e.g., autẽ = *autem*), ~ or ꞁ = *r* plus vowel/vowel plus *r* (e.g., dic~e = *dicere*), ꞁ or 9 = a following *-us* (e.g., man9 = *manus*). Supralinear vowels indicated an *r* with the vowel (e.g., c^imen = *crimen*); a supralinear vowel with *q* indicated an omitted *u* (e.g., q^o = *quo*, q^i = *qui*, q^d = *quid*). The supralinear contraction mark ~ indicated general omissions, usually of vowels (e.g., õro = *oratio*, sĩr = *similiter*, vĩ = *videlicet*). See the *notæ communæ* for other examples.

Numerals

Since Roman numerals could also be used as letters of the alphabet, they were frequently distinguished by being placed between periods. Thus · VI · = 6, not a form of *vis*, and · MIX · = 1009, not an abbreviated form from *misceo*. The representation of 4, 9, 40, and 90 as iv, ix, xl, and xc respectively was largely a Renaissance convention. Earlier, the forms iiij, viiij, xxxx, lxxxx were more usual, with the last minim lengthened to j.

Multiples of 20, 100, and 1000 could be expressed either by the supralinear number as a sign of multiplication (e.g., iiii = 4 x 20 = 80, viii = 8 x 100 = 800, ii = 2 x 1,000 = 2,000) or, in the case of 1000, by a supralinear stroke: ii = 2,000. Subtraction of half a unit could be indicated by a transverse stroke (e.g., iiij = 3½, x = 9½ etc.).

From the late twelfth century, Arabic numerals are occasionally found, but they were at first largely restricted to mathematics treatises, and were only rarely employed with complete consistency. A scribe might begin with one system and change to another quite arbitrarily. 1, 2, 3, 8, and 9 were usually very similar to their modern forms; 4 appeared as [⊂], 5 as [ʔ], 6 as [G], and 7 as [ʔ]. The zero often had a vertical or horizontal stroke, i.e., [Φ] or [θ], not dissimilar to the modern computer printer zero.

Dating by Paleography

This account of the development of Western handwriting since the Roman period should have demonstrated that attempting to date a manuscript by studying its paleography alone is a foolhardy enterprise. Even the greatest of paleographers have been forced to admit that there are very few reliable rules and that uncertainty or downright ignorance are the norm. Lowe, Bischoff, Foerster, Watson, Traube and other accomplished paleographers, especially those like Lowe and Watson who have made dating a specialty, are all agreed that because of the general cycles of imitation and repetition, plus the force of individual scribal idiosyncrasy, dating by paleography is hazardous at best.

With so many imitations and revivals, conservative reactions and idiosyncratic mannerisms, the letter-forms are themselves only rarely reliable enough for exact dating. Paleographers will normally be as much interested in binding, in signs of ownership, in illumination, format (including ruling and gathering), the type of writing materials, the ink, the variants in Latin spelling or the forms of vernacular dialect as they will be in letter-shapes. All of these matters, together with other assistance in dating, are discussed in Chapter 2 on codicology. But, despite these reservations, there is assistance available, and there are some important generalizations to be made. First, it is always best to begin by studying a manuscript which has been dated exactly (e.g., one with a date of completion in the explicit), and then to work outwards into undated manuscripts, using these few dated examples as standards for judgment. The manuscript genealogy of a given work may be of some help here, for a *codex descriptus* (a manuscript derived from another extant copy) must obviously be later than its source. The method of comparative dating by fixed standards may occasionally cause problems: for example, a conservative manuscript might retain forms (orthographic or linguistic) which could make it appear to be very much earlier than it is; scribes might move from one area to another, or reach an advanced age while still writing in the style of their youth and birthplace. An explicit might possibly be copied automatically by a thoughtless scribe using a completely different script—though this was no doubt rare.

The paleographer may test the handwriting of a specific manuscript by reference to the several handbooks and illustrated guides mentioned in the bibliography. One of the best of such current guides is Andrew Watson's *Dated and Datable Manuscripts*, published by the British Library. A detailed study of the paleographic illustrations (together with their descriptive analyses) in this present book will help to fix the most general styles, so that it should be possible for a student to tell the difference between, say, a Beneventan manuscript of the eighth century and a northern gothic of the twelfth century. Within particular periods (e.g., the High Middle Ages, 11th-14th centuries), certain more detailed features may be noted: small *s* takes over from long [ʃ] in final positions at the end of the thirteenth century (to resurface in conservative imitations of Caroline minuscule in the fifteenth century; the cedillared [ȩ] disappears in the twelfth century; the cross-stroke of [7] is broken by the vertical stroke [*t*] in the fourteenth century; minuscule double *ff* begins to be used in place of initial majuscule *F* in the mid-thirteenth century; the fused letters of gothic appear from the early thirteenth century; the open [a] becomes closed [a] by the mid-thirteenth century; W appears in the eleventh century (gradually replacing the Anglo-Saxon "wyn" in vernacular manuscripts).

A general principle (which cannot be invoked when dealing with gothic manuscripts) is that northern manuscripts will usually tend to be more conservative than southern.

Punctuation

There was no universal system of punctuation in the classical or medieval periods, and even Renaissance texts were often highly idiosyncratic (with, for example, the colon frequently used for the minor pause where modern practice would prefer the comma). Early Roman practice was to use a point (or sometimes a slash) to indicate word-division, a method derived from inscriptions, but this was not uniformly carried out. One of the major problems in the textual criticism of early manuscripts is that without either word-division or punctuation, the chances of scribal error in copying were enormously increased. As the paleographical illustrations demonstrate, word-division does exist in, for example, Caroline manuscripts, but does not become the universal rule until late gothic, and punctuation remains arbitrary and idiosyncratic until the eighteenth, or even the nineteenth century, and there are still local or national variants, with British and American practice being quite different in regard to, say, punctuation within or outside quotation marks. (This book has supposedly been "translated" from British to American usage, but there may very well be certain examples of my past habits remaining.)

In medieval manuscripts, there were theoretically three levels or degrees of punctuation, represented by three symbols. There is still some disagreement among paleographers about the exact arrangement of the hierarchy, but most would agree that it proceeds in the following manner: first the slight pause, where additional material was expected, indicated by a forward-slanting line, or "virgule" [/]; second, a median pause, where additional material could be expected, but not demanded, indicated by a point [·]; and finally, a period or conclusion to the sentence, indicated by a combination of point and comma, looking like a transposed semi-colon [⁏]. The point could also be used as an infrascript mark of expunction, rather than messily crossing out the deleted letters or words.

The actual practice of medieval scribes was, however, far removed from this neat theory (some manuscripts have only virgules, some virtually no punctuation at all), and it was rare for a scribe to employ any of these signs with complete consistency. In general, medieval punctuation was very light, and did not reflect the syntactic organization of a sentence, but the pauses necessary for rhetorical delivery (that is, breathing-spaces rather than units of grammatical logic).

Recent research has suggested that even before the invention of printing, fifteenth-century Chancery scribes had begun to evolve a uniform system for both spelling and punctuation. One scribe in the Privy Seal, Thomas Hoccleve (who is encountered in various guises in this book), evolved for himself a particularly rigorous system of orthographic distinctions (Greetham, "Normalisation"), but this may have been out of personal taste rather than bureaucratic necessity, and there is still considerable debate on how wide this practice of normalization was; and if it did exist at all it was employed only at the very end of the Middle Ages. It can be assumed that it was largely left to the printers to mandate a coherent system for punctuation and spelling.

The most conservative editorial approach to the problem of manuscript punctuation and word-division is, of course, to reproduce all the characteristics of the copy-text, no matter how inconsistent they may be. Some modern textual scholars of medieval texts have tried to introduce the practices of the "strict and pure" bibliographers of later periods into the representation of the "accidentals" (or surface features, including the punctuation) of a medieval text, but there is still a good deal of argument over the validity of this approach, and many editors simply begin modernizing the punctuation and word-division at the initial stages of transcription, assuming that medieval (and classical) punctuation has no inherent value or interest to the modern reader. Perhaps they are right for most such readers, but the committed textual scholar must at least investigate the punctuation and spelling practices of the copy-text before coming to such conclusions. (See M. B. Parkes, *Pause and Effect: An Introduction to the History of Punctuation in the West*, for a full account of this subject.)

6

Reading the Text: Typography

The function of this chapter is obviously very similar to that on paleography—to provide the student with an overview of the history of the actual appearance of the text in a book. This will involve not only demonstrating the evolution of styles of typography from early black-letter to modern display types, but also providing evidence to help in the actual bibliographical investigation which one hopes will follow a reading of this introductory survey. As in the chapter on paleography, the same caveat must be made: in such a brief account, it is impossible to mention every development in the history of the printed word. This obviously means that a reading of the chapter will not, by itself, provide the information necessary, for example, to date or make a correct ascription of any typeface found in a printed book. It will, however, demonstrate how certain styles evolved out of their predecessors (by imitation, corruption, or conscious reformation) and will place all the major typographic movements within the broad history of Western printing.

General Principles

The art of printing (especially in the design of type) began as a consciously inferior or imitative process. The first types were specifically designed not to draw attention to themselves as manifestations of the new medium, but, on the contrary, to reassure the reader that nothing much had changed. The old, familiar late-gothic letters of contemporary fifteenth-century manuscripts and the lack of title-page and of pagination, the removal of information about the printing of the book to the colophon at its end—all of this demonstrated that printers were trying to make their books look as much like manuscripts as possible (even, on occasion, using parchment rather than paper, in an ironic denial of the cost-saving per copy which was from the beginning one of the major desiderata for printing as opposed to scribal copying). Thus, it is virtually impossible for the untrained eye to distinguish in facsimile between a mid-fifteenth-century manuscript and a early printed book (given, that is, the printer's use of a black-letter font and the scribe's employment of a similar formal book-script).

This close esthetic connection between type and script was not to last consistently for more than the first generation of printing. While it is true that the invention and development of "new" styles like humanistic roman and italic are equally noticeable in manuscript and printed forms, and while it is also (paradoxically) true that the calligraphic paradigms for most of the sixteenth- and seventeenth-century writing masters were fixed in *printed* manuals (from which hand-written copies were then to be produced), by the time of, say, the first printing of most English Renaissance drama, the putative authorial manuscripts on which these first editions were based would doubtless have been written in a debased form of English secretary, unlike the contemporary formal gothic type, and completely dissimilar from a contemporary roman or italic. Furthermore, while the writing-masters produced many printed manuals during the long hegemony of English copperplate in the eighteenth and nineteenth centuries, and while most European clerks (there were no longer any real "scribes") and private persons wrote therefore in various derivative versions of this copperplate, the history of typography during the same period shows no such uniformity, ranging from the "classical" reformations of Caslon and Baskerville, through the polymorphous extravagance of the early nineteenth century, down to the medieval-inspired typographic experiments of William Morris's Kelmscott and other Victorian private presses.

In the twentieth century, the separation is almost complete, for both "book" and commercial handwriting has virtually vanished with the ascendancy of the typewriter, word processor, and telephone, leaving only the consciously calligraphic movements (like the italic revival mentioned in the previous chapter) as possible inspiration for typographic forms. In fact, most twentieth-century typographic developments have been prompted not by parallel symptoms in calligraphy but by either a complete re-thinking of type-forms (e.g., the sans-serif type-faces of Eric Gill and Edward Johnston) in a deliberately "modern" medium or a careful re-working of earlier styles to reflect contemporary needs (e.g., the refurbishing of roman in Stanley Morison's Times New Roman, one of the most successful of modern typefaces, and one—quite appropriately—created for a newspaper (*The [London] Times*) which prided itself on its patrician dignity and yet required an efficient and highly legible type). In one sense, Morison's Times New Roman is therefore the twentieth-century equivalent of Griffo's italic for Manutius, except that Morison's typographic experiments were not as closely linked to any similar general revival of roman handwriting at the popular level. To call the relative history of handwriting and typography the story of a close marriage which became a legal separation is merely to reflect the gradual sense of independence which typography and printing achieved from their scribal origins. The divorce is not yet complete, for the same *divisions* of styles still obtain in both script and print (roman and italic, for example), but since handwriting except as a formally calligraphic exercise may have vanished by the early part of the next century, it is difficult to imagine any written equivalent for the vast range of type-styles which modern printers have (and will have) at their disposal. In fact, as typesetting from the personal computer becomes more of a reality, the border between professional typography and private writing will inevitably become vaguer, and may perhaps disappear entirely.

This was not always so: there is some irony in that several of the later "paleographical" samples cited in the history of Western *handwriting* in Chapter 5 occurred in the form of *printed* books. The letters were cut as "types" rather than being produced by a pen, although it was often the intention of type-designers to make their handiwork look as much as possible like its handwritten models. This paradox (should Arrighi's *La operina*, the first *printed* manual for scribes, be included in a history of writing or a history of printing?) points to another overlap: that early printed books tended to look identical to the manuscripts upon which they were presumably based. Especially in the gothic style, they reproduced the complicated ligatures and abbreviations of the medieval manuscript. They even left space for a rubricator to add the decorated initials and other individual touches which made a book unique (like a manuscript) rather than uniform (like a printed book). In order to achieve this sense of visual continuity, Gutenberg must have used close to three hundred different type sorts, compared with the seventy-five or eighty normal in a modern font (or set of types in one style and size). The invention of printing, even though its separate elements had been known for some time, may have been revolutionary, but at first typography was quite conservative, and only very cautiously evolutionary. For example, that flourish of the scribal art the long *s* [*ʃ*] was not dropped from the printer's armory of types until the late eighteenth century (and continued as an alternative in some fonts and in formal handwriting for a century more). So while it is certainly true that type-founders began to assert their independence from scribes towards the end of the fifteenth century, it is equally true that all of the three great families of type (gothic, roman, and italic) were founded upon calligraphic models. And the concentration on this sense of continuity in this chapter emphasizes that the purely visual aspects of typography are the main focus here, and are not relegated to a separate bibliographical section simply because the letter-forms happen to be printed. The discussion of printing as a *technical* (rather than an esthetic) medium is dealt with in Chapter 3, on the "making" of books. This concern for the appearance of typography also means that this chapter will not be restricted to "pure" typography (which, strictly speaking, should consider only "types," or the metal relief blocks used in letterpress printing): any form of printed letter, no matter how it got on the page—by press, photograph, or computer—is part of the subject of this chapter.

One of the paradoxes of the history of typography (and its vocabulary) is that roman type (which is not of Roman origin, but was first cut in Strassburg) looks to the twentieth-century eye much more modern than does gothic, which these days is largely reserved for the *incipits* of legal documents and the mastheads of pretentious newspapers. In the fifteenth century, of course, gothic (which was not given this clearly derogatory name until the humanists Valla and Vasari decided that it stood as a corrupting and embarrassing barrier between their own times and the standards of the classical age) was the most dominant contemporary script and therefore—as we have seen—the logical choice for the first type-faces of the age of printing. To the humanists, gothic was a reminder of the very recent past and of the tenuous hold of the new esthetic and cultural standards on the present; therefore, the roman type-face (like its offshoot italic) was seen as a manifesto of the moderns (perhaps even the avant-garde), who, again paradoxically, liked to think of the *new* script and type as "antiqua," thereby emphasizing its continuum with the Roman past. So the ultra-modernists of the fifteenth century, in their disgust for the present decadent medievalism, fondly re-created an ancient style as the form which was ultimately to be recognized as the standard for all modern writing and printing in the West from the mid-Renaissance on. In Europe proper, only Germany held on to type-faces that were resolutely medieval (fraktur and schwabacher), finally to acknowledge roman supremacy during the Third Reich.

Why did a type-face like gothic, which was so clearly old-fashioned, which lacked small capitals, and which became almost illegible in a word printed all in capitals, manage to retain its ascendancy in Germany, Scandinavia, and the Slavic countries for so many centuries? Much of the answer depends upon the origins of printing, for even when this German invention was exported, it was usually taken to foreign countries by native Germans, who therefore brought their tradition of gothic type with them. While printing in Italy (by Germans) used roman type from the very beginning, England (and to a lesser extent France) initially both succumbed to versions of German gothic. In Eastern and Northern Europe, where German political and cultural hegemony was more difficult to resist, German typography was just a reflection of the similar presence of, for example, the German language. And perhaps most significant, gothic was associated in the popular mind with a particular type of book—theological and ecclesiastical, rather than classical and humanist. Even outside Germany, it was not unusual to find Bibles and other religious works printed in gothic, and even in Germany, some classical works were printed in roman. But it was the predominance of theological controversy in the Holy Roman Empire, and the late arrival of the humanist Renaissance there, which probably doomed German printing to its four-hundred-year entanglement with a typographic leftover from the Middle Ages.

History of Typography

A. *Early German Printing*

1. *Gutenberg and Gothic:* Because the first books to be printed were Bibles and other religious works, they appeared in a printed

---

Fig. 87 (*overleaf*). The first page of Genesis in a copy of Gutenberg's 42-line Bible. Note the angular textura style type-face, the retention of large numbers of abbreviations (e.g., *dicim9* = *dicimus* in line 2 of first column), the hand-illumination and decoration of the page—all to suggest the appearance of a typical contemporary manuscript.

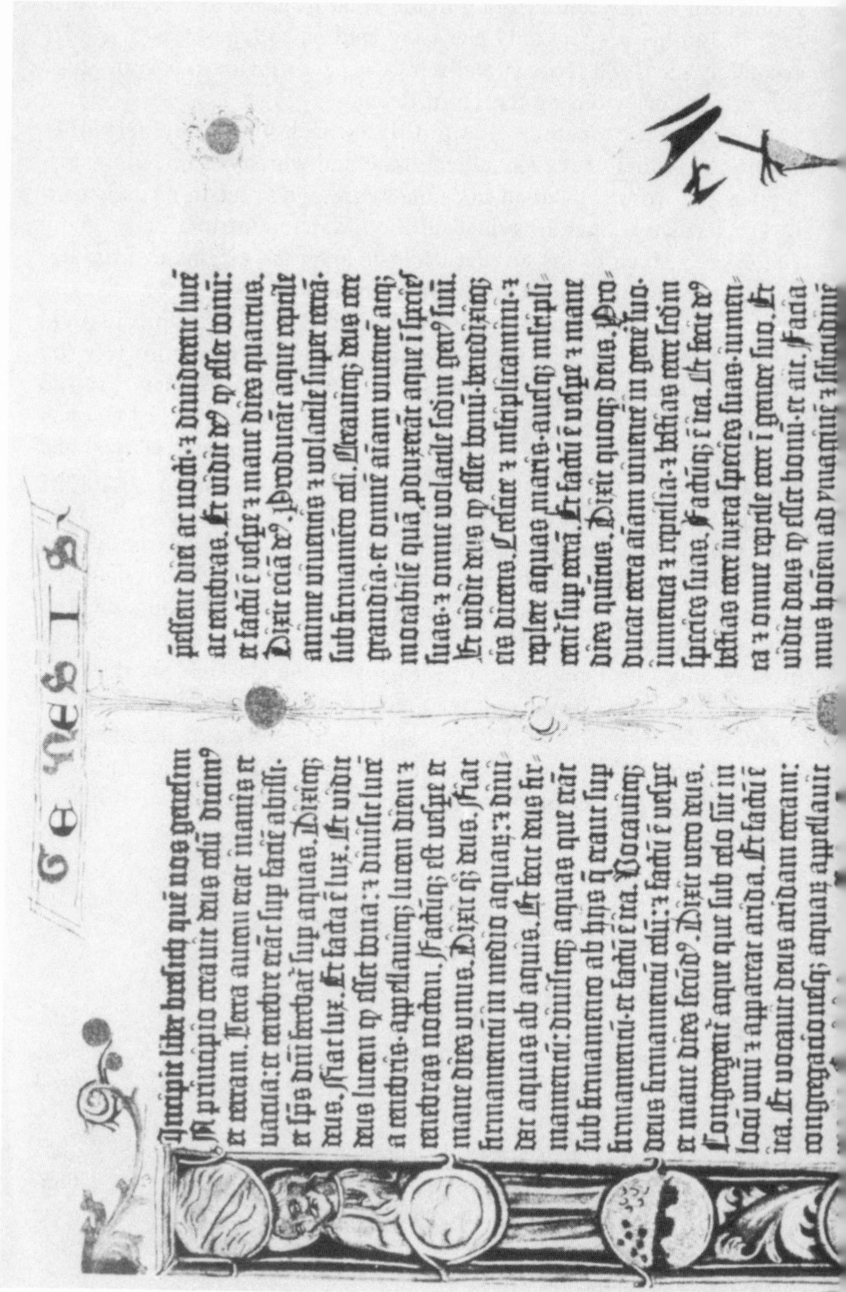

GENESIS

Incipit liber bresith quem nos genesim dicimus. In principio creauit deus celum et terram. Terra autem erat inanis et uacua: et tenebre erant sup facié abissi. et spus dñi ferebat sup aquas. Dixitq; deus. Fiat lux. Et facta é lux. Et uidit deus lucem qp esset bona: et diuisit lucem a tenebris. appellauitq; lucem diem et tenebras noctem. Factumq; é uespe et mane dies unus. Dixit qq; deus. Fiat firmamentü in medio aquarü: et diuidat aquas ab aquis. Et fecit deus firmamentü: diuisitq; aquas que erant sub firmamento ab hiis q erant sup firmamentü: et factü é ita. Vocauitq; deus firmamentü celü. Et factü é uespe et mane dies secüdus. Dixit uero deus. Congregentur aque que sub celo sunt in locü unü: et appareat arida. Et factü é ita. Et uocauit deus aridam terram:

pissarüt dies ac noctem: et diuiderent lucé ac tenebras. Et uidit deus qp esset bonü: et factü é uespe et mane dies quartus. Dixit etiam deus. Producant aque reptile anime uiuentis et uolatile super terram sub firmamento celi. Creauitq; deus cete grandia: et omné aiam uiuenté atq; motabilé quá produxerat aque in species suas. et omne uolatile scdm genus suü. Et uidit deus qp esset bonü: benedixitq; eis dicens. Crescite et multiplicamini. et replete aquas maris: auesq; multiplicentur sup terrä. Et factü é uespe et mane dies quintus. Dixit quoq; deus. Producat terra aiam uiuentem in genere suo. iumenta et reptilia: et bestias terre scdm species suas. Factumq; é ita. Et fecit deus bestias terre iuxta species suas: et iumenta et omne reptile terre in genere suo. Et uidit deus qp esset bonü: et ait. Faciamus hominem ad ymaginem et similitudinem nostram:

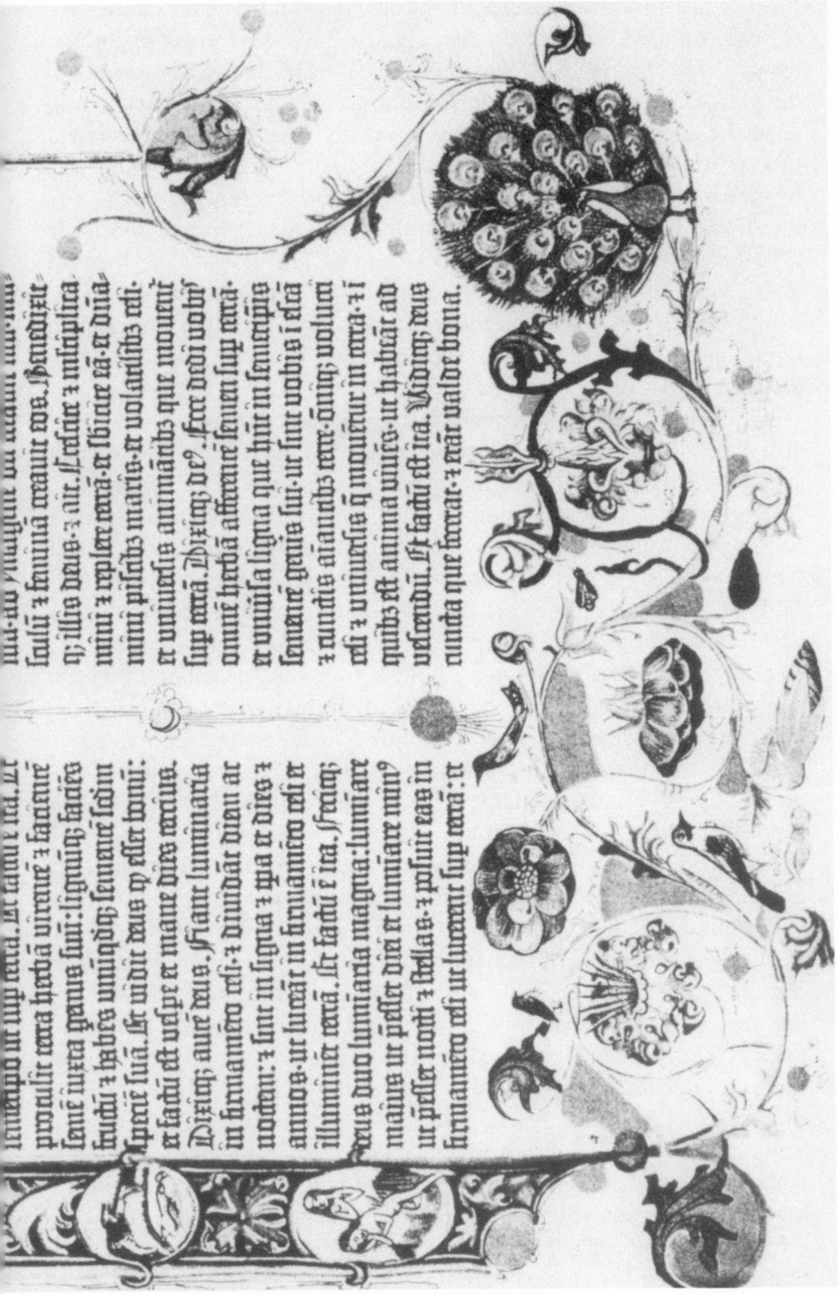

form of the "liturgical" script of textura, the conservative, dense variety of gothic which held its own against the experiments of the humanists, the flourishes of the court scribes, and the bastard scripts of the vernacular texts. As Steinberg has pointed out, "the lawyer who needed a copy of the Decretals knew exactly what the Decretals ought to look like because he had handled it all his life" (29). The same rule of familiarity applied to the ecclesiastic (and, increasingly, the layman) who wanted a copy of the Bible. Even when roman and italic type-faces were used for other books (e.g., the classics), a form of gothic was still employed for the scriptures. This was true in seventeenth-century England, and it was true of the "inventor" of roman type himself, Nicolas Jenson, whose Vulgate of 1476 is alone among his published works in using a gothic face.

The gothic type of Gutenberg and his descendants possessed virtually all of the formal characteristics already noted of its hand-written equivalent, textura. It had the same dense lattice work of angular, lozenge shapes, the same clubbed feet and heads, the same solidity and uncompromising darkness. It was this quality which has given it the name "black-letter," for compared with roman (or especially italic) type, its vertical lines are remarkably thick and oppressive. One additional (and perhaps unexpected) characteristic is the retention of so many of the scribal signs for contraction and suspension. These special sorts might perhaps have helped slightly with right justification, but otherwise they were a complete anachronism in the age of printing on cheap, readily available paper. Their retention is undoubtedly yet another testament to the desire of the first printers to make their texts look as much like manuscripts as possible.

The comparatively short descenders and ascenders, the strong angularity of the vertical lines of each letter, the tendency to break up even rounded letters (like *o* and *d*) into a series of separate lines—all of these qualities were familiar from the textura script of the late Middle Ages. Printing could not, of course, easily indulge in the actual fusion of strict textura (e.g., of ⮭⮭) without specially cast ligatures or kerns for the letter-combinations or overlapping types. Ligatures were generally restricted to the joining of letters at their points of contact rather than overlapping of the letter-strokes themselves. The fact that several of the early printers were goldsmiths (like Gutenberg), or had connections with the goldsmiths in their typefounding, probably reinforced the acceptance of the angular gothic script as a form easily reproducible in metal, for the lines of textura were particularly suited (or at least "comfortable") to the metalworkers' file

and burin. As printing advanced, particularly with the introduction of
the imitations of humanist script, the difference between the technical
origins of type-cutting and the actual types produced became greater;
and it is similarly arguable that the "roman" type-faces of the fifteenth-century printers show a greater freedom from their models than
do the gothic faces developed from textura.

None of this should suggest that the textura form of gothic was the
only type-face favored by even the earliest printers. Roman (and later
italic) faces appeared very quickly, and even within the gothic family
there were looser, freer styles employed for different occasions.   The
colophon of the Gutenberg *Catholicon* is one of the best known examples of this less strict, less angular, more rounded form,

Another famous variant on Gutenberg's gothic was the series of
"bastard" types used, for example, by Caxton in his press at Westminster. As already seen in the chapter on paleography, the bastard
script is (as its name suggests) a compromise or balance between the
"court" and "book" versions of gothic, having the basic regularity of
the book script and some of the informality of the court script. It was
ideally suited for the northern European (and particularly English)
vernacular literature, where it became almost the dominant form, and
it was therefore quite logical that Caxton should use a type-face (or,
more properly, a series of type-faces) based on this successful bastard.

The bastard type-face is typically lighter and rounder than Gutenberg gothic, for while it still possesses the same tendency toward
"broken" letter-forms and still has a similar strong contrast between
thin and thick strokes, its ascenders and descenders are often flourishes in the manner of the court script, and its lower-case letters have a
roundness unknown to textura gothic.

Fig. 88. Alphabet of fifteenth-century fraktur used by Neumeister, Mainz,
1479.

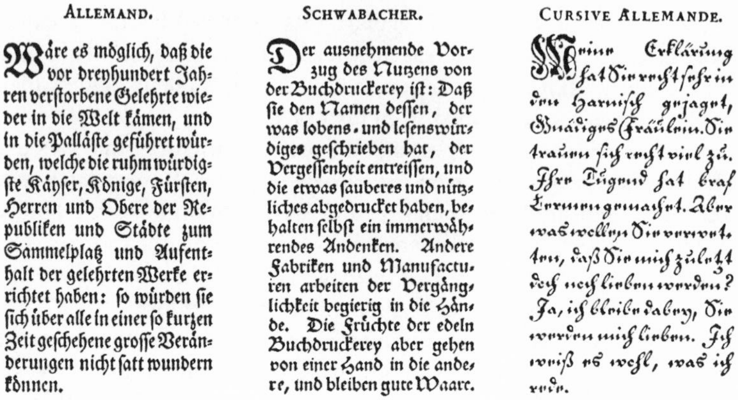
ALLEMAND.
Wäre es möglich, daß die vor dreyhundert Jahren verſtorbene Gelehrte wieder in die Welt kämen, und in die Palläſte geführet würden, welche die ruhmwürdigſte Käyſer, Könige, Fürſten, Herren und Obere der Republiken und Städte zum Sammelplatz und Aufenthalt der gelehrten Werke errichtet haben: ſo würden ſie ſich über alle in einer ſo kurzen Zeit geſchehene groſſe Veränderungen nicht ſatt wundern können.
SCHWABACHER.
Der ausnehmende Vorzug des Nutzens von der Buchdruckerey iſt: Daß ſie den Namen deſſen, der was lobens- und leſenswürdiges geſchrieben hat, der Vergeſſenheit entreiſſen, und die etwas ſauberes und nützliches abgedrucket haben, behalten ſelbſt ein immerwährendes Andenken. Andere Fabriken und Manufacturen arbeiten der Vergänglichkeit begierig in die Hände. Die Früchte der edeln Buchdruckerey aber gehen von einer Hand in die andere, und bleiben gute Waare.
CURSIVE ALLEMANDE.
Meine Erklärung hat Sie recht sehr in den Harnisch gejagt, Gnädiges Fräulein. Sie trauen sich recht viel zu. Ihre Tugend hat brav Lermen gemacht. Aber was wollen Sie verwetten, daß Sie mich zuletzt doch noch lieben werden? Ja, ich bleibe dabey, Sie werden mich lieben. Ich weiß es wohl, was ich rede.

Fig. 89. Development of fraktur, schwabacher, and cursive by Fournier Le Jeune, ca. 1766.

Even in Germany, typographically the most conservative of Western European nations, there were at least two different grades of gothic. Fraktur (based upon the script of the Imperial Chancellery, see Fig. 88), which was given its final form in Nuremberg by Neudorffer and Hieronymus Andreæ, by the early sixteenth century had become the standard printed equivalent of a "text," or "book," script, and thereby displaced the earlier schwabacher type, a more cursive-looking face which has frequently been regarded as bearing to fraktur the same relationship that italic bears to roman. While it can be claimed that schwabacher was a little less rigid than fraktur, it completely lacked the fluidity and grace of italic and was insufficiently differentiated from the formal book face to have achieved the dignity of a separate standing.

Finally, it should be noted that gothic seems to have been regarded in Germany as a "national" type-face (as, in practice, it was to become by default and as it was regarded by non-Germans, who cut gothic-style faces as conscious imitation of German practice, see Fig. 89). "Foreign" works (including, as already noted, the classics) appeared in antiqua. Since its rejection by modern Germany, gothic has lost its stature as a reading type-face and has become essentially a "display" type, used to arrest the eye momentarily.

2. *The Germans Abroad:* As mentioned above, to the modern eye, the gothic or "black-letter" type looks old-fashioned, and it is the

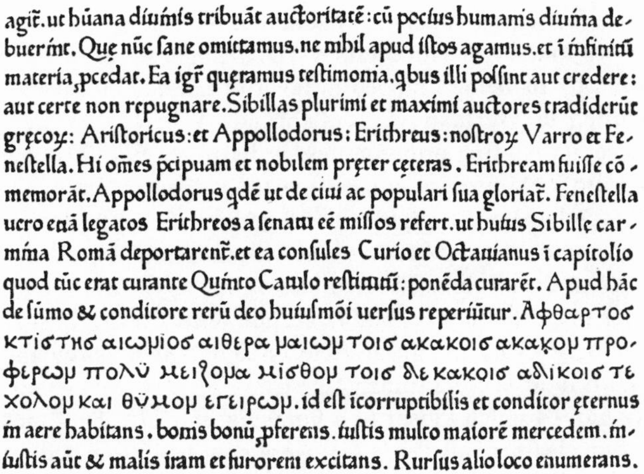

agit.ut hūana diuīnis tribuāt auctoritatē:cū poctus humanis diuīna de-
buerint.Quę nūc fane omittamus.ne nihil apud istos agamus.et i īnfinitū
materia,pcedat.Ea igr quęramus testimonia.qbus illi possint aut credere:
aut certe non repugnare.Sibillas plurimi et maximi auctores tradidērūt
gręcoy: Aristoricus:et Appollodorus: Erithreus:nostroy Varro et Fe-
nestella.Hi omes pcipuam et nobilem pręter cęteras. Erithream fuisse cō-
memorāt.Appollodorus qdē ut de ciui ac populari fua gloriāt. Fenestella
utro enā legatos Erithreos a fenatu eē missos refert.ut huius Sibille car-
mina Romā deportarent.et ea consules Curio et Octauianus i capitolio
quod tūc erat curante Quinto Catulo restituit:poneda curarēt. Apud hāc
de fūmo & conditore rerū deo huiusmoi uersus reperiūtur. Αφθαρτος
κτιστης αιωριος αιθερα μαιωρ τοις ακακοις ακακομ προ-
φερωμ πολυ μειξομα μισθορ τοις δε κακοις αδικοις τε
χολομ και θυμομ ετειρωμ.id est icorruptibilis et conditor ęternus
in aere habitans. bonis bonū,pferens.fustis multo maiore mercedem.in-
fustis aūt & malis iram et furorem excitans. Rurfus alio loco enumerans.

Fig. 90. First type used in Italy: Sweynheym and Pannartz, Subiaco, 1465.

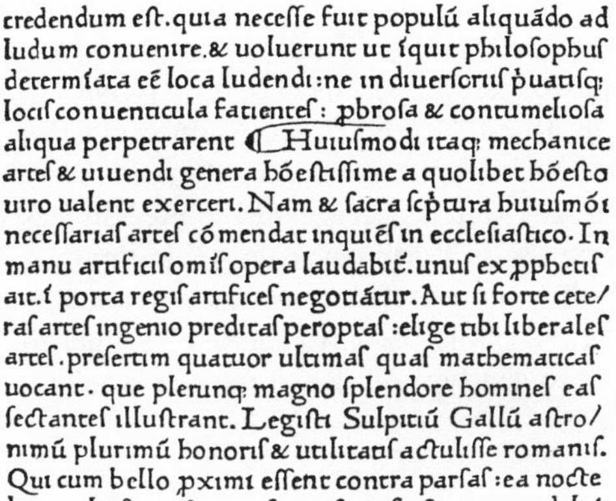

credendum est.quia necesse fuit populū aliquādo ad
ludum conuenire.& uoluerunt ut squit philofophuf
determinata eē loca ludendi:ne in diuerforisp uatisq;
locisconuenticula facientes: pbrofa & contumeliofa
aliqua perpetrarent ⸿Huiusmodi itaq; mechanice
artes& uiuendi genera hōestissime a quolibet hōesto
uiro ualent exerceri.Nam & facra scptura huiusmoi
necessarias artes cōmendat inquit es in ecclefiastico. In
manu artificis omis opera laudabit.unus ex ppbetis
ait.s porta regis artificis negotiātur.Aut si forte cete/
ras artes ingenio preditas peroptas:elige tibi liberales
artes.presertim quatuor ultimas quas mathematicas
uocant. que plerunq; magno splendore homines eas
fectantes illustrant.Legisti Sulpitiū Gallū astro/
nimū plurimū honoris & utilitatis actulisse romanis.
Qui cum bello pximi essent contra parsas:ea nocte
luna eclipsata est. quo figno stupefacti romani deli/

Fig. 91. Second type of Sweynheym and Pannartz, Rome, 1467.

roman type which we regard as typical of our age. But in the mid-fifteenth century, exactly the opposite point of view obtained, for gothic
was the contemporary letter-form, and the humanist roman was ancient (antiqua), although the roman faces (except perhaps for capitals)
never had more than a tenuous relation with the actual scripts used in
the Roman period.

Present-day German terminology, in still referring to roman type as "antiqua," preserves the theoretical origins of the humanists' experiments, for it was under this name that the "new" face was most often known in the fifteenth century. The national status of gothic was emphasized by its being dropped in favor of antiqua by several of the most influential German printers abroad. When Sweynheym and Pannartz set up the first printing press in Italy (see Fig. 90), they published Cicero's *De oratore* in a recognizably "roman" face. That is, the new face lacked the angularity of gothic: its round letters were genuinely round, and its verticals bore only traces of a broken appearance (e.g., in the slightly clubbed feet of minims). But the face was still rather thick and heavy, and in certain letters (e.g., *e*) it showed its gothic origins by the great difference between heavy and light lines. With their second roman face (see Fig. 91), Sweynheym and Pannartz moved much closer to a humanist model. The lines were generally much finer, all the letters were now truly rounded, and except for the slight "foot" on the second vertical of *n* (which might properly be regarded as a decorative serif rather than a decayed remnant of gothic *littera quadrata*), the angularity had almost completely vanished.

Just as these two German printers in Italy, the home of humanism, used a humanist-based font for the classics published in Subiaco and later in Rome itself, so the first German printers in France, under instruction from their humanist employers at the Sorbonne, used an antiqua font when they were commissioned to publish Gasparinus Barzizius's *Epistolarum libri,* a handbook on writing correct and pure Latin—although they used a gothic *lettre batarde* type for works in French (see Fig. 92). But there was gradually emerging a firm connection between roman type-faces and the classics, or works dependent on the classics.

Ꞁꞓꝰ premier cꞕappitre parle cõ ment les francois descenbirẽt des tropens.

Batre cens et qua tre ans auant que Romme fuſt fõbee regna priant en trope ſa grant. il enuoia paris laiſne be ſes filꞩ en grece pour rauoir la ropne Helaine ſa femme au rop Menelaus pour ſop ꝟenger bu

ne Honte que les grecꞩ lui auoiẽt faitte. les greiois qui mouſt furent courouciez be cefte cHoſe fefmeurent et Binbrent affieger trope. a ce fiege qui.y.ans bu ra furent occiꞩ tous ſes filꞩ au rop pri ant. mais-que Bng appelle eſenus il et ſa ropne ecuſa ſa femme. ſa cite fut ar fe et beſtruicte le peuple et ſes Barons occiꞩ·mais aucuns eſcHapperent be cefte peſtilence et pluſieurs bes princes feſpã birent en pluſieurs et biuerfes parteis bu mõbe pour querre nouuelles Habita cions cõme eſenus encas antHenoret

Fig. 92. Lettre batarde in first book published in French: *Croniques de France*, Bonhomme, Paris, ca. 1477.

B. *Jenson, Caxton, and Griffo*

1. *Jenson:* It was not until the Venetian press of Nicolas Jenson, a Frenchman who had learned his trade in Mainz, and had set up his press in 1470, that a universally recognized "perfected" roman type appeared. This new type (see Fig. 93) took the transitional type of Sweynheym and Pannartz and, through the use of generally finer lines, and slimmer and longer ascenders and descenders, created a roman lower case which feels comfortable to the modern eye. In fact, fonts based on Jenson are still very much in use as book-faces today—without, of course, the ligatures and abbreviations which still characterized Jenson's roman. Jenson's capitals achieved the same sense of breadth as his lower case, but they were generally thicker, stronger, and squarer (close, indeed, to Roman square capitals), while his lower case was rounder and lighter.

qui omnibus ui aquarum fubmerfis cum filiis fuis fimul ac nuribus mirabili quodā modo quafi femen huāni generis conferuatus eſt:quē utinā quafi uiuam quandam imaginem imitari nobis contingat:& hi quidem ante diluuium fuerunt:poſt diluuium autem alii quorū unus altiſſimi dei facerdos iuſtitiæ ac pietatis miraculo rex iuſtus lingua he⁄ bræorū appellatus eſt:apud quos nec circuncifionis nec mofaicæ legis ulla mentio erat . Quare nec iudæos(poſteris eni hoc nomen fuit)neqʒ gentiles:quoniam non ut gentes pluralitatem deorum inducebant fed hebræos proprie noīamus aut ab Hebere ut dictū eſt:aut qa id nomen tranfitiuos fignificat.Soli qppe a creaturis naturali rōne & lege īnata nō fcripta ad cognitionē ueri dei trāfiere:& uoluptate corporis cōtēpta ad rectam uitam pueniſſe fcribunt:cum quibus omibus præclarus iłle totius generis origo Habraam numerādus eſt:cui fcriptura mirabilem iuſtitiā quā non a mofaica lege(feptima eīm poſt Habraā generatione Moyfes nafcitur)fed naturali fuit ratione confecutus fūma cum laude atteſtatur.Credidit enim Habraam deo & reputatū eſt ei in iuſtitiam. Quare multarum quoqʒ gentium patrem diuina oracula futurū:ac in ipfo benedicēdas oés gentes hoc uidelic& ipfum quod iam nos uideūs

Fig. 93. Jenson's roman type-face, *De præparatione evangelica*, Venice, 1470.

2. *Caxton:* Jenson also used a gothic type, to produce ecclesiastical works, and in countries where a vernacular printing was particularly strong (e.g., France and England), a form of gothic was the norm for non-classical works. A roman type did not appear in England until 1518 (by Richard Pynson), and italic not until 1524 (by Wynkyn de Worde). No doubt, this apparent conservatism of England was the result of its first printer, William Caxton, having lived much of his commercial life in the Burgundian-dominated Low Countries, where the semi-cursive bastard script was favored for vernacular works (see Fig. 94). Thus, when he returned to England, he naturally used a form of this bastard (see Fig. 95) in his printing of vernacular works, for which he is most celebrated.

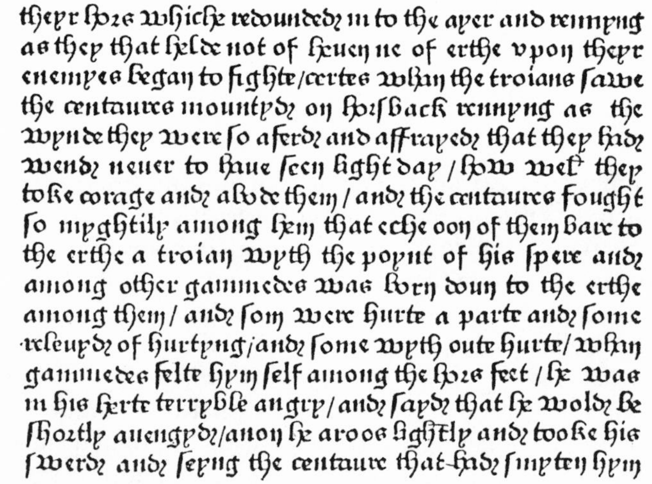
theyr hors whiche redounded in to the ayer and rennyng
as they that helde not of heuen ne of erthe vpon theyr
enemyes began to fighte/certes whan the troians sawe
the centaures mountyd on horsback rennyng as the
wynde they were so aferd and affrayed that they had
wend neuer to haue seen light day / how wel they
toke corage and abode them / and the centaures fought
so myghtily among hem that eche oon of them bare to
the erthe a troian wyth the poynt of his spere and
among other gannimedes was born doun to the erthe
among them / and som were hurte a parte and some
releuyd of hurtyng/and some wyth oute hurte/whan
gannimedes felte hym self among the hors feet / he was
in his herte terryble angry/and sayd that he wolde be
shortly auengyd/anon he aroos lightly and toke his
swerd and seyng the centaure that had smyten hym

Fig. 94. Caxton's Type 1: *The Recuyell of the Historyes of Troye*, first book printed in English, Caxton and Mansion, Bruges, ca. 1475.

Caxton's jobbing work—the indulgences, missals, etc. (see Fig. 96), that provided him with much of his business, and other semi-commercial works—were printed in a type closer to strict textura, though never approaching the denseness and compression of the Gutenberg 42-line Bible. But even in "classical" works (e.g., his edition of Cicero's *Of Old Age*) Caxton used a bastard type, not a roman, and there can be little doubt that it was this style which was most typical of the bulk of his publications. Just as the handwritten bastard was

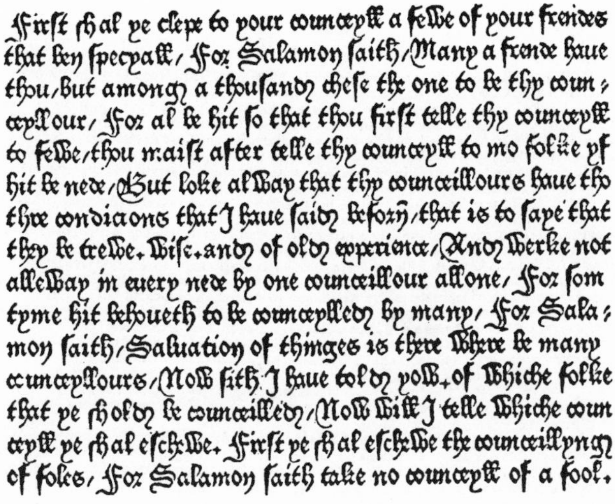

Ffirſt ſhal ye clepe to your counceyll a feſſe of your freindes
that ben ſpecyall/ ffor Salamon ſaith / Many a frende haue
thou / But among a thouſand cheſe the one to be thy coun-
ceyllour / ffor al be hit ſo that thou firſt telle thy counceyll
to feſſe / thou maiſt after telle thy counceyll to mo folke yf
hit be nede / But loke alway that thy counceillours haue tho
thre condicions that J haue ſaid before / that is to ſaye that
they be trewe. Wiſe. and of old experience / And werke not
alleway in euery nede by one counceillour allone / ffor ſom
tyme hit behoueth to be counceylled by many / ffor Salamon ſaith / Saluation of thinges is there where be many
counceyllours / Now ſith J haue told yow yow. of whiche folke
that ye ſholder be counceilled / Now will J telle whiche counceyll ye ſhal eſcheſe. Firſt ye ſhal eſcheſe the counceillyng
of folks / ffor Salamon ſaith take no counceyll of a fool.

Fig. 95. Caxton's Type 2: *The Dictes or Sayengis of the Philosophres*, first
book printed in England?, Westminster, 1477.

characterized by its long swooping *s* and by its intermediate position
between strict gothic and cursive court script, so Caxton's printed bastard had the same qualities. The English bastard types perhaps tended
to be more angular and less fluid than those used by such contemporary French printers as Jean Dupré and Guillaume de Roy, whose
fonts approximate the *written* bastard styles of the country more closely (see Fig. 97). But Caxton's practice (and that of his successor de
Worde) was governed largely by the nature of the work itself, as the
difference between Figs. 95 and 96 illustrates.

3. *Griffo:* Jenson's roman type held the field until the scholar and
merchant Aldus Manutius commissioned Francesco Griffo to cut two
new fonts which would be particularly adapted to the special format
of the so-called Aldine classics. Aldus, in common with many other
publishers of his day, seems to have over-estimated the popular enthusiasm for the classics and to have been left with large unsold stocks
on his hands, but there can be no doubt about the success of Griffo's
new fonts. His greek font has not found much favor among historians
of typography (greek fonts as a whole seem to have been rather too
ornate, cursive, and clumsy in comparison with their roman counterparts), but Griffo's great invention was the italic, a sloping, compact
type based on the "cancelleresca" cursive script, and ideal for the new

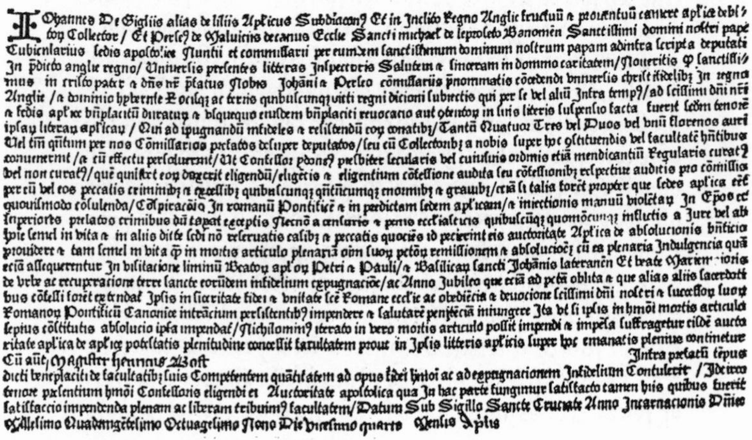

Iohannes De Gigliis alias de liliis Apricus Subdiacon⁹ Et in Inclito Regno Anglie fructuu̅ n̄ prouentuu̅ camere aplic̄e debli⁹ to̅₉ Collectoꝛ / Et Preseꝛ₎ de Waluicino decanus Eccle̅ Sancti michaet̄ de leproleto Banomē Sanctissimi domini nostri pape Cubienlarius ledio apostolic̄e Nunfii et commissarii p̅ eum̅m sanctissimu̅m dominum nostrum papam adintra scripta deputati In pdicto anglie regno/ Uniuerse presente₎ litteras Inspectorio Salutem n̄ sinceram in dommo caritatem/Nouericio ꝙ sanctissi⁹ mus in trislo pater n̄ d̅n̅e n̅r̅ platus Notho Iohāni n̄ Perleo commissario pronmmatio cōardendi vniuerlio chrilt fidelib₎ In regno Anglie /n̄ dominio bptʒrnse Eorsg₎ ac sterio qunbulcunq₎ virti regni dicioni subrectio qui p̅ se bel alii Intra temp⁹/ad scissimi d̅n̅i nr̅i n̄ sedis aplic̄e bñiplacitu̅ duratu₉ n̄ biqueq₎ eorum eiusdem bñiplaciti ruocano aut ofentoꝛ in sur₎ literio suspensio facta fuerit seom senio₉ ipsa₉ literas aplicay / Qui ad ipugnandu̅ mforeles n̄ relistendu̅ eog̅ conatib₎/Tantã Quatuoꝛ Tres bel Duos bel bnii florenos auri Uel ti̅ qiitum p̅ nos Commissarios presadaos te̅super teputadao/leu cu̅ Collectonb₎ a nobis super ho̅c osfituendio bel facultatē bñtibus conuenerit /n̄ cu̅ effectu persoluerent/Et Confessoꝛ ponns⁹ presbiter secularis bel cuiusluis ordinio etiã mendicantiu̅ Regularis curat⁹ bel non curat⁹/que̅ quislibt eog̅ dugerit eligendu̅/eligerio n̄ eligentiu̅m cōelsione audita seu cōfelsionib₂ respectiue auditio pro cōmillus p̅ eu̅ bel eos peccatio criminid₂ n̄ quelibt₂ qunbulcunq₂ qñficunq₂ enormib₂ n̄ grauib₂/era̅ si talia foret propter que sedes aplic̄a ess quouismoto colulenda/Colpieacdio In romanu̅ Pontificē n̄ in perdictam sedem aplicam/n̄ iniectionio manuu̅ biolēta₉ In Epoo et superiorto prelatao crimibus du̅ topat teceptio Nec̅m n̄ peno ecclesiastcio qunbulcuiq₂ quomodocuiq₂ influtio n̄ Iure bel ab ipse semel in bita n̄ in alio diste sedi nō reseruatio calib₂ n̄ peccatio quocies io pecierint eis auctoritate Aplic̄a te absolucionis bñficio prouidere n̄ tam semel m bita ꝙ in morte articulo plenarã oim suoꝝ pctõu̅ remisltonem n̄ absolucioē₂ cu̅ eis plenaria Indulgencia quã eia̅ asequerentur In bisitatione liminu̅ Weatoꝝ apt oꝝ Petri n̄ Pauli/n̄ Basilicaꝝ sancti Iohānis laterancn̅ Et brate Marien̅ ioꝝis de bcbe ac recupᵉratioe itere sancte eoriitem infidelium ꝛqpugnaciōe/ac Anno Iubileo que era̅ ad pctã oblita n̄ que alia₂ alio sacerdoti bus cōtelli foret n̄ tendat Ipsio in sircitate sidei n̄ bnitate sce Romane ecclesie ac obedieria n̄ deuocione scilsimi d̅ñi nostri n̄ sucestoꝛ suoꝝ Romanoꝝ Pontificis Canonice inteacium presistentib⁹ impendere n̄ salutare penitēciã imungere Ita bt si ipsis in hmōi mostis articula sepius cōtitutis absolucio ipsa impendat/Nichilomin⁹ iterato in bero mostio articulo possit impendi n̄ impela suffragetur tisdē aucta ritate aplic̄a de apl̄ice potestatis plenitudine conceslit tarulfatem prout in Iplis litteris aplic̄io super hoc emanatio plenius continetur Cu̅ aut₂ M Agustr hennus₉ ꝛ₎ost   Intra prelacti tepus dicti beneplaciti de faculfatib₂ luis Competentem quãtifatem ad opus idei binoi ac ad ꝛqpugnarionem Infidelium Contulerit /Ideireo tenoꝛe presentium hmōi Confelsoꝛio eligendi ei Auctoritate apostolica qua In hac parte fungunrur satisfacto tamen hiis quibus fuerit satisfacrio impendenda plenam ac liberam tribuim⁹ facultatē₎/Datum Sub Sigillo Sancte Crucats Anno Incarnacionis D̅ñie Millesimo Quadringētelimo Octuagelimo Nono Die brensmo quarto Menlis Aplis

Fig. 96. Caxton's Type 7 (jobbing type): *Indulgence*, Westminster, 1489.

Aldine classics (see Chapter 3) because of its compactness and legibility. It first appeared in the 1501 edition of Virgil's *Opera*. Like its hand-written equivalent invented by Niccolo Niccolì, its letter-forms were not markedly distinct from the upright roman, nor did it have a special set of capitals: the capitals from the roman face were used until quite late. But it could afford to be printed very small without a great loss of legibility and was not tiring to the eye, as gothic inevitably was.

Griffo's roman type, by returning more securely to the pre-Caroline, and therefore more "roman," scripts as a model, produced a style which, first used in the Aldine edition of Bembo's *De Ætna* in 1495, became the source for a long line of "old-face" roman types, from the French printers of the sixteenth century, to the Dutch of the seventeenth, the English of the eighteenth, and so on, down to modern times. Following the experiments of Sweynheym and Pannartz and Jenson, it was Griffo who can be said to have invented the school of "old-face roman" fonts.

Legende de faint Barnabe.

B

Arnabe feuite fut du lignaige
de cypze/τ fut lun des feptāte
τ deup difciples de nrēfeigneur
Et eft loue en moult de manieres furhaul
ce en fpftoire du fait des apoftres:car il fut
treſbien infoime τ oidōne quāt a foy:quāt
a dieu τ quāt a fon prochain. Quāt a foy
il fut oidōne felō trois chofes:ceftaffauoir
raifōnaſle:couuoiteuſe:τ preuſe. Jl eut foz
ce raifonnaſle en lumiere de congnoiſſāce
Dōt il eft dit au fait des apoftres au piii
chapitre. Jfʒ eftoient en leglife qui eftoit
en antioche prophetes τ docteurs entre lef
quelʒ Barnabe τ fymon eftoient. Seconde

Fig. 97. Jean Dupré's French bastard type for Jacobus de Voragine's *Legenda aurea*, Paris, 1489. Note the space left for hand-illumination of the initial letter *B*.

mus; quas adolescentes, non possumus :
quo in consilio nobis diutius permanen
dum esse non puto: nam ut interdum nó
loqui moderati hominis est; sic semper
silere cum eo , quem diligas, perignaui :
neq; Hercule; si in officio permansimus

Fig. 98. Griffo's roman type, Pietro Bembo, *De Ætna*, Venice, 1495–96.

P·V·M·AENEIDOS LIBER
SECVNDVS.

Onticuere omnes , intentique ora
tenebant,
Inde toro pater Aeneas sic orsus
ab alto,
Infandum Regina iubes renouare
dolorem,
T roianas ut opes, et lamentabile regnum
E ruerint Danai, quáeque ipse miserrima uidi,
E t quorum pars magna fui· quis talia fando
M yrmidonum, Dolopum ue, aut duri miles Vlyssi
T emperet à lachrymis? et iam nox humida coelo
P ræcipitat, suadentq; cadentia sydera somnos·
S ed si tantus amor casus cognoscere nostros,
E t breuiter Troiæ supremum audire laborem,
Q uanq animus meminisse horret, luctuq; refugit,
I ncipiam· Fracti bello, fatisq; repulsi
D uctores Danaum, tot iam labentibus annis,
I nstar montis equum diuina Palladis arte
A edificant, sectaq; intexunt abiete costas.
V otum pro reditu simulant, ea fama uagatur·
H uc delecta uirum sortiti corpora furtim
I ncludunt cæco lateri, penitusq; cauernas
I ngenteis, uterumq; armato milite complent.
E st in conspectu Tenedos notissima fama
I nsula, diues opum, Priami dum regna manebant,
N unc tantum sinus, et statio male fida carinis·
H uc se prouecti deserto in littore condunt.

Fig. 99. Griffo's italic type, Virgil, *Opera*, Venice, 1501. Note space left for
initial letter.

C. *France: Tory, Granjon, and Garamond*

1. *Tory:* The Aldine influence of Griffo's new types was felt everywhere in Western Europe except Germany. But it was in France that Griffo's models were taken up with greatest enthusiasm, thereby extending the domain of roman type even into service books, which had previously been the monopoly of gothic. Geofroy Tory's *Champfleury* (1529, see Fig. 100), the first manual of type design (which ironically, while being influenced by the early Italian experiments with humanist type-faces, later became a familiar source-book for Italian developments in both calligraphy and typography), helped to promote not only the roman and italic, but also his own use of accent and cedilla, which can be regarded partially as a necessary adjunct to French pronunciation, but also as an aspect of the general French tendency towards decoration, ornamentation with "flowers," and an interest in the *éditions de luxe* over the practical characteristic of, say, German and English printing.

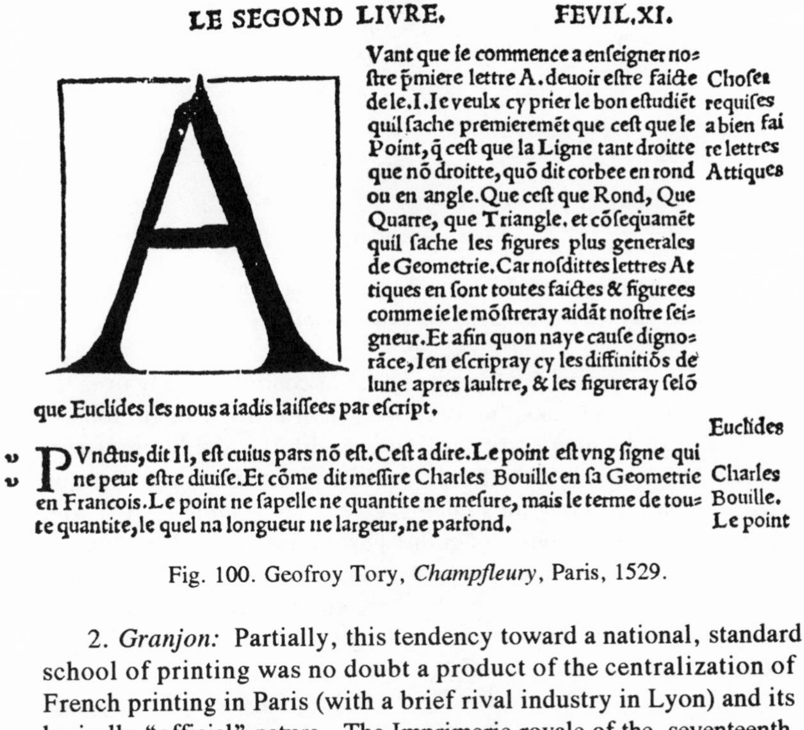

LE SEGOND LIVRE. FEVIL.XI.

Vant que ie commence a enſeigner noſtre p̃miere lettre A. deuoir eſtre faicte de le. I. Ie veulx cy prier le bon eſtudiẽt quil ſache premieremẽt que ceſt que le Point, q̃ ceſt que la Ligne tant droitte que nõ droitte, quõ dit corbee en rond ou en angle. Que ceſt que Rond, Que Quarre, que Triangle. et cõſequamẽt quil ſache les figures plus generales de Geometrie. Car noſdittes lettres Attiques en ſont toutes faictes & figurees comme ie le mõſtreray aidãt noſtre ſeigneur. Et afin quon naye cauſe dignorãce, Ien eſcripray cy les diffinitiõs de lune apres laultre, & les figureray ſelõ que Euclides les nous a iadis laiſſees par eſcript.

Choſes requiſes a bien faire lettres Attiques

Euclides

PVnctus, dit Il, eſt cuius pars nõ eſt. Ceſt a dire. Le point eſt vng ſigne qui ne peut eſtre diuiſe. Et cõme dit meſſire Charles Bouille en ſa Geometrie en Francois. Le point ne ſapelle ne quantite ne meſure, mais le terme de toute quantite, le quel na longueur ne largeur, ne parfond.

Charles Bouille. Le point

Fig. 100. Geofroy Tory, *Champfleury*, Paris, 1529.

2. *Granjon:* Partially, this tendency toward a national, standard school of printing was no doubt a product of the centralization of French printing in Paris (with a brief rival industry in Lyon) and its basically "official" nature. The Imprimerie royale of the seventeenth

Fig. 101. Robert Granjon: first *civilité* type, Jean Louveau, translation of Innocent Ringhier's *Dialogue de la vie et de la mort*, Lyon, 1557.

century was typical of French governmental control not only over the content of French books, but even over their actual esthetic appearance, so that the elegant book of hours with the highly decorative borders and somewhat fanciful design, the *civilité* of Robert Granjon (first used in Jean Louveau's *Dialogue de la vie et de la mort*, Lyon, 1557, see Fig. 101), with its gothic cursive origins making it seem more like an ornate handwritten style than a printed one—all of this can be considered as a part of the same esthetic tradition. Granjon also provided numerous type-faces (along with Garamond) for Plantin and Moretus (see Figs. 102–03).

3. *Garamond:* The greatest figure in this period of French typography is Claude Garamond (see Fig. 104), who is historically impor-

Vraye Auguftine Curfiue.

Cleanthes. *Cuidam reprehendenti Arcefilaum , quod officia vitæ tolleret: Define, inquit , hominem vituperare. Nam ille licet dictis tollit officia, tamen factis commendat. Id audiens Arcefilaus : Non moueor , inquit , adulatione. Hic Cleanthes: Scilicet, inquit, adulor tibi, dicens te aliud loqui , aliud facere. Cleanthes mitigauit dictum obtrectatoris, fed ita vt à crimine inconftantiæ non liberaret Arcefilaum : turpißimü enim eft philofopho fecus docere , quàm viuit. Si vita proba eft, cur docet diuerfa ? Si doctrina fana eft , cur eam fecus viuendo refellit ?*

Fig. 102. Granjon's *Vraye Augustine Cursiue* (ca. 1562–74) for Plantin's *Folio Specimen*, 1585.

Courante fur le vray Text.

Les autres ont deploré tous les longs iours de leur vie, les calamitez humaines , & ont accompaigné leurs pas de larmes , comme vn Heraclite: fe perfuadant que tout ce qui fe peuft contempler foubz la concauité des cieux , n'eft autre chofe qu'vn vray Theatre de mifere, digne de continuelles plainctes & perpetuelle compaffion.

Fig. 103. Granjon's *Courante sur le vray Text* (1567) for Plantin's *Index characterum*, 1567.

tant as the first independent type-founder. (Actually, Nicholas Wolf of Lyon had worked independently as a type-founder in 1493, but Garamond was the first to offer a large-scale inventory of punches and matrices for general sale, in which he was followed by Granjon.) The early printers had been type-founders, printers, and publishers all in one, and the breaking up of the single craft into several was a reflection of the generally poor financial record of most printers. Garamond could provide type-faces for many printers, most of whom would not have been able to retain the services of a type-founder within their own businesses. The era of specialization had begun. Garamond based his roman font on Griffo and his italic on Arrighi, and

III. TVSCVL.

Sàpienti malum videri
nullum videri poteſt, quod
vacet turpitudine:aut ita pa
rum malum , vt id obruatur
ſapientia , vixque appareat:
qui nihil opinione affingat,
aſſumatq; ad ægritudinem:
neque id putet eſſe rectum:
ſed , quammaximè excru‐
ciari luctuque confici , quo
prauius nihil eſſe poteſt.

B 2

Fig. 104. Garamond's *Gros Canon Romaine* (1560) for Plantin's *Index char‐acterum*, 1567.

until the further codification of French type-faces under the seven-teenth-century Imprimerie royale, his fonts dominated French printing and were to be the medium whereby Griffo's styles were passed on to subsequent centuries.

With Garamond and Granjon, the period of typographical experi-mentation comes to an end. While there may be other, historical, rea-

sons for the retention of 31 December 1500 as the demarcation between the "primitive" (incunabular) period of printing and its subsequent history, as far as type-design is concerned, the mid-sixteenth
century was the important watershed. All subsequent type-faces, with
the exception of some of the more fanciful display faces of the twentieth century, can be regarded as dependent upon one or another of the
styles employed by printers in the first century of printing.

D. *The Late Sixteenth and Seventeenth Centuries*

Historians of typography generally agree that the second half of
the sixteenth century and the great bulk of the seventeenth century
were marked by a slackness of invention and execution in type and
book design. The examples in the illustrations will bear this out better than any description could. Compared to the care, authority, and
vigor of Gutenberg and the fifteenth-century printers, the likes of
Nathaniel Ponder (the printer of Bunyan's *Pilgrim's Progress*; see
Fig. 43) could hardly seem to set a line straight, and their work
lacked the sense of printing as an art, a belief which had motivated
even the most commercial of early printers. One brief anecdote will
illustrate the problem. The first (quarto) edition of Shakespeare's
Love's Labour's Lost (see Fig. 105) is notoriously badly printed (it

Fig. 105. First (quarto) edition of Shakespeare's *Love's Labour's Lost*,
1598.

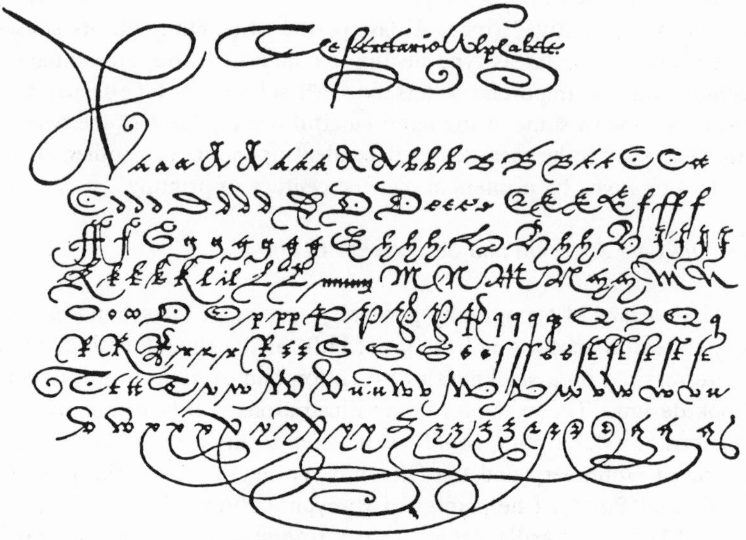

Fig. 106. Secretary alphabet, 1571.

was, after all, only a play, by a then comparatively little-known author), and one of its printing anomalies is that all surviving copies of the quarto have different readings for some passages. This phenomenon does not seem to have been the result of a licentious desire for determined variation on the part of correctors, but rather of the printer having failed to "lock" his type properly, so that actual pieces of type fell out while the book was being printed, thereby producing the respective readings *wil*, *wi*, and *w* in three copies of *LLL* in the British Library; Trinity College, Cambridge; and the Bodleian Library.

Apart from such sloppy workmanship, one additional factor in the general sense of decline might have resulted from the fact that fifteenth-century printers had the carefully copied textura or bastard manuscripts of professional scribes to set copy from: if, therefore, they were to produce a pleasing esthetic imitation of these manuscripts, they had to be equally careful. But the printers of seventeenth-century vernacular texts (perhaps especially of apparently ephemeral matter like plays) were more than likely working from so-called foul papers, which, even if fairly close to what we might call fair copy, were almost certainly written in the highly informal "free" scripts of the secretary style, in which no successful commercial font seems to have been cut (although printed alphabets—see Fig. 106—and writing

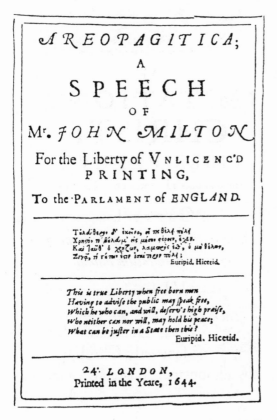

Fig. 107. Milton's *Areopagitica*, 1644. Note wrong (roman) font in "GL" of *ENGLAND*.

manuals in secretary were produced). In part, this slippage of standards was also a product of the democratization of the printer's art. Used for pamphlets, broadsheets, political manifestos, and popular collections of rough ballads and ephemeral literature, these late gothic forms perhaps inevitably declined and spread to other, more respectable works. Milton's *Areopagitica* (Fig. 107) was not, in literary terms, an ephemeral or unsubstantial work; but its occasion was certainly ephemeral (Milton was himself to become a censor in his career), and its political purpose—seditious and radical—was manifest in part by its typographical irregularity. One does not look for fine calligraphy or fine typography in an age characterized by the polemics of the gutter press and the political atmosphere of the *samizdat*.

DE
IMITATIONE
CHRISTI
LIBER PRIMVS.
Admonitiones ad ſpiritualem vitam vtiles.

Caput I.
De imitatione Chriſti, & contemptu
omnium vanitatum mundi.

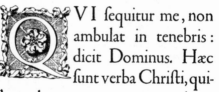

VI ſequitur me, non
ambulat in tenebris :
dicit Dominus. Hæc
ſunt verba Chriſti, qui-
bus admonemur, quatenus vitam

A

Fig. 108. First book published by the Imprimerie royale, Thomas à Kempis, *De imitatione Christi*, Paris, 1640.

But the democratization and irregularity were at least partly checked by seventeenth-century French neo-classicism and a desire for uniformity and decorum. The Imprimerie royale (see Fig. 108), established by Louis XIII in 1640, undertook the scientific redrawing of letter-forms under a mandate from Louis XIV in 1692. The mandate was an extremely strict one: on a square divided into 2,304 equal parts, a commission drew a series of "ideal" letters according to purely mathematical principles. The committee had replaced the individual, and, as William Morris was to say of the nineteenth century, the engineer replaced the calligrapher. But this was, fortunately, only theory. The types were actually cut by Philippe Grandjean (1666-1714), who, while accepting the commission's general desire for a

dans l'Isle de Saint-Amand, & battit encore huit cens chevaux fortis de
Doüay. Aprés quoy il fe campa entre cette Ville & Bouchain, & porta la
terreur dans tout le Pays, qu'il fourragea jufques aux portes de Cambray.
Enfin il marcha vers Condé, & ayant pris d'abord le fauxbourg de l'Efcauld, il fit faire un logement fur la contrefcarpe ; de forte que le jour
mefme, 25 d'Aouft, le Gouverneur fe rendit à la feconde fommation. Le
Comte demeura aux environs de cette Place jufqu'au mois de Septem-
bre, & cette entreprife n'ayant efté faite que pour amufer les Efpagnols,
ou pour les attirer à un combat, il abandonna Condé avant la fin de la
Campagne, & prit Maubeuge en revenant.

C'eft le fujet de cette Médaille. On y voit Pallas, tenant un Javelot
preft à lancer ; le fleuve de l'Efcauld effrayé s'appuye fur fon Urne. La
Légende, HISPANIS TRANS SCALDIM PULSIS ET FUGATIS,
fignifie, *les Efpagnols défaits & pouffez au-delà de l'Efcauld.* L'Exergue,
CONDATUM ET MALBODIUM CAPTA. M. DC. XLIX. *prife de
Condé & de Maubeuge. 1649.*

Fig. 109. Grandjean's *romains du roi* (roman), Imprimerie royale, Paris,
1702.

clear, refined style, did not rely upon their actual drawings. It was
Grandjean's *romains du roi* (see Fig. 109), in twenty-one different
sizes, which took over from Garamond and provided, in their great
regularity and precision, an antidote to much of the technical and esthetic sloppiness observable elsewhere. Intended initially for use only
by the Imprimerie royale, the Grandjean designs were quickly copied
in France and abroad, providing most of Europe with its punches and
matrices. The line from Grandjean extended to the *modèles de
caractères* (see Fig. 110) of Pierre-Simon Fournier (1742) and the
Didot family of printers, who were later to be influenced by the English revival in Baskerville.

The other important seventeenth-century school was the Dutch,
made most famous in the English-speaking world by the Dutch fonts
of van Dyjck, chief supplier to the Elzevirs, which Dr. Fell of Christ
Church presented to the Oxford University Press (see Fig. 111) in
1675, together with others modeled after Granjon. Even when actually located outside Holland (as in the case of the "Luther" foundry at
Frankfurt), the type-faces produced under Dutch influence were
known as *holländische Schriften.* The other major influence of the
Dutch school was on William Caslon (1692-1766, see Fig. 112).
Caslon was the first Englishman to make his fame as an independent

AUTRE PETIT PARANGON.

L E cruel Neron fit mourir fa me-re, Antonie fa tante, Britannicus, Senecque, Corbulon un de fes Capitaines, & plufieurs autres de fes proches ; & tua lui-même d'un coup de pied Poppée fa feconde femme.

S Aint Pierre, Saint Paul, & les autres Chrétiens furent aussi les innocentes victimes de fa fureur, il leur fit fouffrir les plus cruels tourmens & inventa pour cela tout ce que la rage & la cruauté ont de plus ingenièux-

AUTRE GROS ROMAIN.

O N revêtit les uns de peaux de bêtes fauvages, & enfuite on lâcha contre eux des chiens affamez ; on en expofa d'autres aux lions dans l'amphithéatre ; & on attacha les autres à des poteaux, ou ils furent tous brulez vifs.

P Eu de tems après les hommes, & le ciel même étant lassez de la cruauté de ce monstre, il fut lui-même fon propre bourreau ; & lorsque le Senat fe préparoit à en délivrer la terre, il s'arracha une vie qui étoit en exécration à tout l'univers.

Fig. 110. Fournier Le Jeune: *modèles de caractères*, Paris, 1742.

type-cutter but, unlike his later compatriot John Baskerville (and Garamond), was a success from the beginning, with his famous *Specimen Sheet* of 1734. Although his first commission was to cut an arabic font, his greatest achievement was the modification of Dutch type to a thinner, more elegant style, with greater contrast between the thick and thin strokes. His type-face was thus a little heavier than Garamond but somewhat lighter than the rather squat and solid Dutch. This legibility and utility of the compromise Caslon type ensured the virtual monopoly in England of his type-faces from 1726 on, when William Bowyer used a Caslon for an edition of John Selden, until the early nineteenth century, when they fell into disuse, to be revived in the later part of the century and to become one of the standard "old-face" styles of the present day. Caslon was especially popular in America, where his type-faces were used by Benjamin Franklin and for the printing of the Declaration of Independence.

A
SPECIMEN
OF THE
SEVERAL SORTS
OF
LETTER
GIVEN TO THE
UNIVERSITY
BY
Dr. JOHN FELL
LATE
LORD BISHOP of OXFORD.

To which is Added
The LETTER Given by Mr. *F. Junius.*

OXFORD,
Printed at the THEATER *A.D.* 1693.

Fig. 111. Fell types, roman and italic: Oxford University Press, 1693.

Two Lines Great Primer.

Quouſque tandem
abutere Catilina, p
Quouſque tandem a-
butere, Catilina, pa-

Two Lines Engliſh.

Quouſque tandem abu-
tere, Catilina, patientia
noſtra? quamdiu nos e-
Quouſque tandem abutere
Catilina, patientia noſtra?

Two Lines Pica.

Quouſque tandem abutere,
Catilina, patientia noſtra? qu
Quouſque tandem abutere, Ca-
tilina, patientia noſtra? quam-

Fig. 112. William Caslon: roman and italic specimen sheet, 1763.

ORLANDO
FURIOSO

D I

LODOVICO

ARIOSTO.

TOMO TERZO.

BIRMINGHAM,

Da' Torchj di G. BASKERVILLE:

Per P. MOLINI Librajo dell' Accademia
Reale, e G. MOLINI.

M. DCC. LXXIII.

Fig. 113. John Baskerville: Ariosto, *Orlando furioso*, Birmingham, 1763.

E. *The Eighteenth Century and Modern Face*

1. *Baskerville:* By common consent, the greatest English type-founder of the period was John Baskerville of Birmingham (see Fig. 113). Baskerville went back to the methods of the old printers, who had been responsible not just for the type-face but for the selection of the paper and ink and the general design of the page. Beginning as a writing master, and having made his fortune in japanning, Baskerville lost it all in his experiments with design and ended up bankrupt, his widow having to sell his matrices and punches to Beaumarchais. Baskerville preferred a strong contrast between the type and paper, which he produced by using a highly glossed, very white paper, and inventing a special black ink. He thus drew attention to the type itself and rejected all other devices—borders, decorative illustrations etc., in favor of a rather severe new classical style. His wide margins, wide spacing, and very elegant type-faces certainly caught the mood of the neo-classical esthetic, but he was greatly criticized in England,

so that even though he was printer to Cambridge University and produced his acknowledged masterpiece for them (the folio Cambridge
Bible of 1763), his enterprise was not otherwise successful in England. His first book, a quarto Virgil in 1757, was the first in a series
of classical editions which were to be most influential on the Continent; for while authors like Pope had tried to introduce the new classical style of pure roman into their texts (in, for example, his translation of Homer, with its duodecimo popular style and its simultaneous
serious quarto edition), the native English method of merrily mixing
italic with roman virtually indiscriminately, of using capitals equally
capriciously, was to defeat Baskerville's attempts at an elegant and
systematic clarification of the hierarchies of type.

Norcia, piccola Città d
Italia nell' Umbria, nel
Ducato di Spoleto. Ab-
benchè soggetta alla san-
ta Sede, forma nondime-
no una specie di Repub-
blica, ed elegge quattro
Maestrati. San Benedet-
to nacque in questa Cit-
tà, e vi ebber pure i lo-
ro natali Giambat. Lalli,
e Monsignor Querenghi.

Fig. 114. Bodoni, *Manuale tipografico.*

2. *Bodoni and Modern Face:*   Giambattista Bodoni took up Baskerville's principles of page design, rejecting the fanciful "flowers" of
the *éditions de luxe* in favor of a neo-classical typographical austerity.
The apparent simplicity of his type design is often regarded as the
beginnings of the "modern" school (as opposed to the old-face style
typified by Caslon).   The terms no longer have any historical or
chronological significance, but refer rather to the tendency of fonts to
reflect either the more solid, highly serifed style of the Caslon type or
the simple, starker, and thinner lines of the Bodoni type—best exemplified in his *Manuale tipografico* (Fig. 114) of 1818.   The differences can be shown effectively by reference to Fig. 115 (printed using
Donald Knuth's *Metafont* program, and by gradual calibrations in design moving the text of *Psalm 23* from old face to modern face: see
Hofstadter: 241).

The LORD is my shepherd;
        I shall not want.
He maketh me to lie down
              in green pastures:
        he leadeth me
              beside the still waters.
He restoreth my soul:
        he leadeth me
              in the paths of righteousness
              for his name's sake.
Yea, though I walk through the valley
              of the shadow of death,
        I will fear no evil:
        for thou art with me;
              thy rod and thy staff
              they comfort me.
Thou preparest a table before me
              in the presence of mine enemies:
        thou anointest my head with oil,
              my cup runneth over.
Surely goodness and mercy
              shall follow me
              all the days of my life:
        and I will dwell
              in the house of the LORD
              for ever.

Fig. 115. Old and modern face in Donald Knuth's *Metafont* program.

The differences between old and modern face are summed up suc-
cinctly in Glaister's *Glossary*:

> *Old face* types preserved the alternating thick and fine
> strokes and the slanting distribution of the centres of
> gravity of the curves as occurring in the manuscript.
> Serifs are bracketed, but more flexible and finer than in
> the roman of the fifteenth century. . . . *Modern
> face[s]* . . .[have] a tendency to a more geometric type
> with a pronounced vertical construction. . . . Character-
> istics are contrasting thick and thin strokes, serifs at
> right angles, and curves thickened in the centre (288).

F. *Nineteenth and Twentieth Centuries*

1. *Mixed Styles:* The first part of the nineteenth century was a period of typographical anarchy, not dissimilar to the late sixteenth and
early seventeenth centuries. For example, in contrast to the simple,
austere concentration of a Baskerville title-page, the Victorian printer
preferred an enthusiastic display of type-faces, mixing styles, sizes,
and fonts with little care for the unity of the page (see Fig. 116 for an
early version of this tendency, Isaiah Thomas's *Holy Bible*, 1791, and
note the use of gothic in *Out of the Original Tongues, United States
of America, Worcester,* and *London*; italic in *APOCRYPHA, England,
Appointed to be read in Churches*; small capitals at several places,
including *AND* fourth line, *FORMER, COMPARED,* and *REVISED* in
line 11; the shaded type of *TESTAMENTS*, the roman capitals of
INDEX, and an engraved version of late textura in *HOLY BIBLE*—and
most of these in *different* sizes as well.) The neo-classical restraint of
Baskerville was replaced by a delight in variety for its own sake—in a
manner rather similar to the exuberant decorative fancy which created
such Victorian architectural manifestos as St. Pancras Station and the
Albert Memorial in London.

2. *Mechanization and the Private Presses:* Two developments
curtailed this tendency in the latter part of the nineteenth century.
One was the substitution of mechanical methods of composition
through the invention of the Linotype and Monotype machines; the
other was the efforts of William Morris and others in the Arts and
Crafts movement to return to the techniques of an earlier period. The
technical advances, which are discussed in greater length in the chapter on printing history, meant that it was now too expensive for a

T H E

CONTAINING THE

O L D AND N E W

TESTAMENTS:

W I T H   T H E

A P O C R Y P H A.

T R A N S L A T E D

Out of the Original Tongues,

A N D

With the FORMER TRANSLATIONS diligently COMPARED and REVISED,

By the fpecial Command of King JAMES I, of *England.*

W I T H   A N

I   N   D   E   X.

Appointed to be read in Churches.

V O L.   I.

United States of America.

PRINTED AT THE PRESS IN *WORCESTER,* MASSACHUSETTS,
By   I S A I A H   T H O M A S.

Sold by him in *Worcester* ; and by him and Company, at FAUST's STATUE, No. 45, NEWBURY STREET, *Bofton.*

MDCCXCI.

Fig. 116. Mixed styles: Isaiah Thomas, *Holy Bible*, 1791.

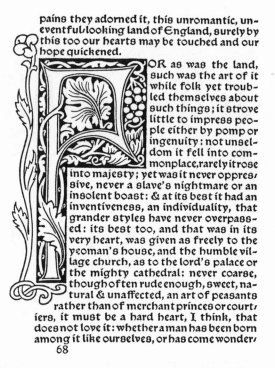

pains they adorned it, this unromantic, un-
eventful-looking land of England, surely by
this too our hearts may be touched and our
hope quickened.

OR as was the land, such was the art of it while folk yet troubled themselves about such things; it strove little to impress people either by pomp or ingenuity: not unseldom it fell into commonplace, rarely it rose into majesty; yet was it never oppres/ sive, never a slave's nightmare or an insolent boast: & at its best it had an inventiveness, an individuality, that grander styles have never overpassed: its best too, and that was in its very heart, was given as freely to the yeoman's house, and the humble village church, as to the lord's palace or the mighty cathedral: never coarse, though often rude enough, sweet, natural & unaffected, an art of peasants rather than of merchant princes or court/ iers, it must be a hard heart, I think, that does not love it: whether a man has been born among it like ourselves, or has come wonder/

68

Fig. 117. William Morris: Chaucer type, Kelmscott Press.

printer to carry a large number of fonts, several of which might be used very rarely. Some standardization was therefore inevitable. The Morris movement is traditionally supposed to have been set in motion when he attended a lecture at the Arts and Crafts Exhibition of 1888, at which Walker Emery showed lantern slides of early typefaces. The movement ushered in the private presses of the late nineteenth and early twentieth centuries, and the movement is still comparatively healthy, largely because its competition is not with large-scale commercial houses, but with itself.

Obviously, these private presses—the Kelmscott (with its eighteen thousand copies of fifty-two books published between 1891 and 1896), and the Doves and Ashendene, could never reach a wide audience, for with the hand-cut types, the hand-made paper, the hand stitching and binding, Morris and his confreres were consciously returning to the laborious, if esthetically pleasing, practices of an earlier period, before mass-production. But the effect on typographical design was significant. The very names of the "new" types invented by these presses show where they turned for inspiration: Chaucer (see Fig. 117), Subiaco, Jenson. And their esthetic effects on mechanical composition can be similarly shown by the new faces created for the Monotype, Linotype, and other improved mechanical methods of composition (see Fig. 118), for example, Plantin (in fact, based on Caslon), Trajan (based on the roman capitals of Trajan's column), Garamond, Bembo (based on Aldine roman), Baskerville, Arrighi, and so on. There was even some direct effect on the commercial book industry, when J. M. Dent adopted Morris's principles for the title-pages and page layout of its Everyman reprint series.

Garamond

Based on types of the Imprimerie Nationale, not in fact cut by Garamont but by Jean Jannon (Mrs. B. Warde *Fleuron* No. 5) Monotype 1922. 12 pt

ABCDEFGHIJKLMNOPQRST UVWXYZ abcdefghijklmnopqrs tuvwxyz 1234567890
ABCDEFGHIJKLMNOPQRS TUVWXYZ abcdefghijklmnopqrst uvwxyz 1234567890
ABCDEFGHIJKLMNOPQRSTUVWXYZ
ABCDEFGHIJKLMNOPQRSTU VWXYZ&ÆŒ abcdefghijklmnopq rstuvwxyzæœfiflffiffiflff 1234567890

Janson

Originally cut by Nicholas Kis, *c.* 1690, and re-cut by C. H. Griffiths for Linotype, 1937. 12 pt

ABCDEFGHIJKLMNOPQRSTU VWXYZ abcdefghijklmnopqrstu vwxyz 1234567890
ABCDEFGHIJKLMNOPQRSTU VWXYZ abcdefghijklmnopqrstu vwxyz 1234567890
ABCDEFGHIJKLMNOPQRSTUVWXYZ

Plantin

Based by F. H. Pierpont on a Granjon face used in the 16th century by Plantin's contemporaries but not by him. 12 pt

ABCDEFGHIJKLMNOPQRS TUVWXYZ abcdefghijklmnopqr stuvwxyz 1234567890
ABCDEFGHIJKLMNOPQRS TUVWXYZ abcdefghijklmnopqrs tuvwxyz 1234567890
ABCDEFGHIJKLMNOPQRSTUVWXYZ
**ABCDEFGHIJKLMNOPQRSTU VWXYZ&
abcdefghijklmnopqrstuvwxyz
1234567890   1234567890**

Fig. 118. Revival of old faces for commercial use.

Morris's gothic types, Troy and Chaucer, were a sort of self-in-dulgence reflecting his admiration of German incunabula; but while attractive enough in such showpieces as the Kelmscott Chaucer, they were never a considerable influence upon book-faces and can be re-garded as an eccentricity compared with the success of the resuscitated romans and italics created elsewhere. The importance of the Kelms-cott Chaucer was that, despite its typographical quaintness, it showed printers and designers what could be done in book production if con-sistent standards of typography and design were adhered to. Morris despised the thin "new" faces descending out of Bodoni (although other famous private presses e.g., Mardersteig, in a D'Annunzio edi-tion, used a version of Bodoni very effectively). Morris therefore used a very black ink and a gothic type emphasizing this blackness against the wide margins of the page. He believed that it was the "opening" (the double facing pages of a book, now called a spread in the commercial book trade) rather than the individual page which should be the basic unit of design and thus reduced the inner margins significantly so that together they would balance the effect of the out-er. Considering the "opening" as a unit he was in fact doing no more than medieval book-makers had done, when they made sure that when a book was opened, the reader was always confronted by two facing "hair" or "flesh" sides of vellum, but never with combinations of the two. It is perhaps ironic that the layout of a recent scholarly edition of Morris's letters should have been criticized for having failed to observe Morris's dictates about page design in a publication of his own work, although there was no question about the scholarship of the editor, Norman Kelvin.

The history of the private press in England and Europe is too broad to be dealt with here, but it should be noted that while many of the greatest typographers, designers, calligraphers, and illustrators of recent history were associated with such presses (Emery Walker, Edward Johnston, Graily Hewitt, and T. J. Cobden-Sanderson, with his "Jenson" type at the Doves Press—see Fig. 119, a deliberate at-tempt to counteract the thick incunabular and Germanic qualities of Morris's types with a finer, more Italianate style based on Jenson's roman face—Hewitt with the Ashendene; Walker, Johnston, and Eric Gill with the Cranach; Gill at the Golden Cockerel and St. Dominic's; Goudy at the Village Press; Jan van Krimpen with Enschede, van der Velde with Drugulin; Rudolf Koch at the Klingsor foundry), much of the most significant and influential work in the revival of typography and book design was undertaken by artists working for large corpora-

between the seen and the unseen, the finite and the
infinite, the human and the superhuman, and is a
monumental work of the eighteenth as distinguished
from the seventeenth century, the century of the
Bible and of Milton. Finally, in the nineteenth century, Sartor Resartus, the Essays of Emerson, and
Unto this Last, are related & characteristic attempts
to turn back the Everlasting Nay of scepticism into
the Everlasting Yea of affirmation, & in the presence
of the admittedly inexplicable & sublime mystery of
the whole, to set man again at work upon the creation
of the fit, the seemly, and the beautiful. Browning's
Men & Women, now in the press, conceived about
the same time, is a more direct presentment of the
same positive solution.
⁋ These Books printed, as a first essay, the whole
field of literature remains open to select from. To-day
there is an immense reproduction in an admirable
cheap form, of all Books which in any language have
stood the test of time. But such reproduction is not
a substitute for the more monumental production of
the same works, & whether by The Doves Press or
some other press or presses, such monumental production, expressive of man's admiration, is a legiti-
mate ambition and a public duty. Great thoughts
deserve & demand a great setting, whether in building, sculpture, ceremonial, or otherwise; & the great
works of literature have again and again to be set
forth in forms suitable to their magnitude. And this

3

Fig. 119. Doves Press type, based on Jenson.

tions—Morison for the Monotype Company, Cambridge University
Press and *The [London] Times* newspaper; Goudy for Lanston Monotype; Dwiggins for Knopf and Linotype; Bruce Rogers for Riverside
and Oxford University Press. Goudy in particular (see Fig. 120),
with over one hundred different type-designs to his credit, must certainly be counted among the most prolific and influential of type-designers of any period, and Morison's Times New Roman (see Fig.
121) of 1932 (based on the Dutch letter-cutters' designs for periodicals, with its deceptively large appearance in a relatively narrow compass) has, among all this experimentation and renovation, proved to
be the most durable and successful of all twentieth-century type-faces.

TYPOLOGIA

1 : By Way of Explanation

MY STUDY of type design and type founding was begun almost forty years ago. At that time, little instructive, constructive, or accurate information was easily available with regard to the various steps involved in the making of a face of type; and this dearth of precise information, it seems, has persisted from Gutenberg's time to the present. That section of Moxon's *Mechanick Exercises* [1683] which relates to the subject of type cutting and founding is somewhat out of date; at best, it is not of any great value to the beginner seeking information on present-day methods. Until a few years ago, Fournier's *Manuel Typographique*, a much more interesting treatise, was obtainable only in French. Other works on type making are too general in their scope, or provide too little material in concrete form, to be of much use.

Within the past few years, articles on the cutting of punches for driving matrices have appeared here and there, in articles which in themselves are admirable enough but which are likely

[1]

Fig. 120. William Goudy: University of California Old Style, *Typologia*, 1940.

A modified version of Morison's type-face is used in the desk-top publishing program for this book. The activities of these typographers, whether in the private presses or in their commercial work, were chronicled in mid-century by a series of distinguished (and now highly sought-after) journals of fine printing, including *The Fleuron*, *The Dolphin*, and *Imprimatur*.

The Arts and Crafts movement and its aftermath was, of course, more recuperative or restorative than it was innovative. That Times

The plague of frogs,   EXODUS 7, 8   *of lice, and of flies*

smite with the rod that is in mine hand upon the waters which are in the river, and they shall be turned to blood.

18 And the fish that is in the river shall die, and the river shall stink; and the Egyptians shall lothe to drink of the water of the river.

19 ¶ And the LORD spake unto Moses, Say unto Aaron, Take thy rod, and stretch out thine hand upon the waters of Egypt, upon their streams, upon their rivers, and upon their ponds, and upon all their pools of water, that they may become blood; and that there may be blood throughout all the land of Egypt, both in vessels of wood, and in vessels of stone.

20 And Moses and Aaron did so, as the LORD commanded; and he lifted up the rod, and smote the waters that were in the river, in the sight of Pharaoh, and in the sight of his servants; and all the waters that were in the river were turned to blood.

21 And the fish that was in the river died; and the river stank, and the Egyptians could not drink of the water of the river; and there was blood throughout all the land of Egypt.

22 And the magicians of Egypt did so with their enchantments: and Pharaoh's heart was hardened, neither did he hearken unto them; as the LORD had said.

23 And Pharaoh turned and went into his house, neither did he set his heart to this also.

24 And all the Egyptians digged round about the river for water to drink; for they could not drink of the water of the river.

25 And seven days were fulfilled, after that the LORD had smitten the river.

CHAPTER 8

AND the LORD spake unto Moses, Go unto Pharaoh, and say unto him, Thus saith the LORD, Let my people go, that they may serve me.

2 And if thou refuse to let them go, behold, I will smite all thy borders with frogs:

3 And the river shall bring forth frogs abundantly, which shall go up and come into thine house, and into thy bedchamber, and upon thy bed, and into the house of thy servants, and upon thy people, and into thine ovens, and into thy kneadingtroughs:

4 And the frogs shall come up both on thee, and upon thy people, and upon all thy servants.

5 ¶ And the LORD spake unto Moses, Say unto Aaron, Stretch forth thine hand with thy rod over the streams, over the rivers, and over the ponds, and cause frogs to come up upon the land of Egypt.

6 And Aaron stretched out his hand over the waters of Egypt; and the frogs came up, and covered the land of Egypt.

7 And the magicians did so with their enchantments, and brought up frogs upon the land of Egypt.

8 ¶ Then Pharaoh called for Moses and Aaron, and said, Intreat the LORD, that he

may take away the frogs from me, and from my people; and I will let the people go, that they may do sacrifice unto the LORD.

9 And Moses said unto Pharaoh, Glory over me: when shall I intreat for thee, and for thy servants, and for thy people, to destroy the frogs from thee and thy houses, that they may remain in the river only?

10 And he said, To morrow. And he said, Be it according to thy word: that thou mayest know that there is none like unto the LORD our God.

11 And the frogs shall depart from thee, and from thy houses, and from thy servants, and from thy people; they shall remain in the river only.

12 And Moses and Aaron went out from Pharaoh: and Moses cried unto the LORD because of the frogs which he had brought against Pharaoh.

13 And the LORD did according to the word of Moses; and the frogs died out of the houses, out of the villages, and out of the fields.

14 And they gathered them together upon heaps: and the land stank.

15 But when Pharaoh saw that there was respite, he hardened his heart, and hearkened not unto them; as the LORD had said.

16 ¶ And the LORD said unto Moses, Say unto Aaron, Stretch out thy rod, and smite the dust of the land, that it may become lice throughout all the land of Egypt.

17 And they did so; for Aaron stretched out his hand with his rod, and smote the dust of the earth, and it became lice in man, and in beast; all the dust of the land became lice throughout all the land of Egypt.

18 And the magicians did so with their enchantments to bring forth lice, but they could not: so there were lice upon man, and upon beast.

19 Then the magicians said unto Pharaoh, This is the finger of God: and Pharaoh's heart was hardened, and he hearkened not unto them; as the LORD had said.

20 ¶ And the LORD said unto Moses, Rise up early in the morning, and stand before Pharaoh; lo, he cometh forth to the water; and say unto him, Thus saith the LORD, Let my people go, that they may serve me.

21 Else, if thou wilt not let my people go, behold, I will send swarms of flies upon thee, and upon thy servants, and upon thy people, and into thy houses: and the houses of the Egyptians shall be full of swarms of flies, and also the ground whereon they are.

22 And I will sever in that day the land of Goshen, in which my people dwell, that no swarms of flies shall be there; to the end thou mayest know that I am the LORD in the midst of the earth.

23 And I will put a division between my people and thy people: to morrow shall this sign be.

24 And the LORD did so; and there came a grievous swarm of flies into the house of Pharaoh, and into his servants' houses, and

Fig. 121. Stanley Morison: Times New Roman, *Holy Bible*, Cambridge University Press (Times semi-bold 421, Morison's specific adaptation for this publication).

New Roman in its upper case could be traced without too much effort back to the very earliest of Western European letter-forms—Roman square capitals—is an indication of this conservative eclecticism of the twentieth century. This was doubtless because most of the great type designers of recent history have been more concerned with book faces, and consequently with legibility (and conservation) than with arresting the eye by a new, bold, and striking face. As Morison remarked: "The typography of books requires an obedience to convention which is almost absolute . . . for a new format to be successful, it has to be so good that only very few recognize its novelty" (qtd. Steinberg: 28).

3. *Display Faces:* Elsewhere, in the world of advertising, in the printing of pamphlets, brochures, and circulars—in short, any medium which does *not* require sustained reading but on the contrary demands an immediate response—the twentieth century has been remarkable for the richness of its invention. Most such jobbing faces, because of their topicality and immediacy, quickly become dated. Using only the type-face as a guide, it is easier for even an amateur to date an advertisement or brochure of, say, the Twenties or the Thirties than a book of the same period (see Fig. 122 for examples of changes in the logo of J. C. Penney since 1902, each one looking very representative of the design features of its period). Styles in the type-design of such ephemeral material have always reflected the various esthetic movements of their day—Art Nouveau, Bauhaus, Dadaism, etc., but certain type-faces of this sort have enjoyed a longevity which picks them out from the general mass. Eric Gill's Sans Serif (1927) and Paul Renner's Futura have been particularly successful, but the range is too broad for full coverage here (see Figs. 123–4).

The "script" types, with their imitation of calligraphy; the "open" types, with their letter-forms left unblackened; the "shaded," with their three-dimensional boldness; the "foliated" or "decorated" types, with their interior designs *within* the letter-shapes; the "Egyptian" or "slab" types, with their heavy, fat style; the various sans-serifs, with their plain boldness—all of these are widely used in "jobbing" printing as "display" (rather than "book") types, and all have contributed to the richness of modern typography. But the romans and italics of the early printers remain the favored styles for books, even though it is now rare for an entire book to be printed in italics (as were the Aldine classics). Italic has, in a sense, become an acceptable variant *within* a roman body text (for emphasis, titles, footnotes, running heads, etc.) in a way in which the contemporary "display" types

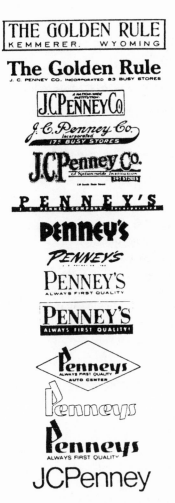

Fig. 122. Changes in the logo of J. C. Penney since 1902.

could not be used. (Imagine the shock of discovering an "Egyptian" face used in the citations of a learned article, instead of the expected italic!) But otherwise italic is probably best regarded as simply the most traditional and formal of the display types, and no longer as a book face. Nicolas Jenson's roman and its many distinguished derivatives have conquered in book typography, but are balanced by the proliferation of idiosyncratic styles used by the present-day jobbing

Ultra Bodoni Italic Optima BROADWAY *Garamond Italic* Lydian

Stymie Light **Eurostile Bold Extended** *Palatino Italic* P. T. Barnum

Franklin Gothic Condensed **Franklin Gothic Wide** *Kaufmann Script* *Brush*

Century Schoolbook *Century Schoolbook Italic* **Spartan Black** *Mistral*

BALLOON EXTRABOLD Caslon No. 540 **Caslon Bold Condensed** Engravers Old English

COPPERPLATE GOTHIC HEAVY *Commercial Script* Cheltenham Medium

Fig. 123. Modern display types.

printer. This range of differing identities for the old Roman alphabet can be shown in Fig. 125, where a series of current display styles for a single letter (A) calls into question the very identity of the letter itself. If we can somehow recognize as *A* such widely diverse variants as "Phyllis" (a highly calligraphic style) and "Block Up" (as its name suggests, almost a square block), in what sense can the letter be said to have a distinct, formal, and consistent feature? In modern typography we are very far from the ideal letter-forms of the Imprimerie royale.

Mierop Inline
Peter Max Riverside Drive
Neon
Glaser Filmsense
Bitur Graphic
Prisma Bauhaus
Glaser Babyfat Outline
Cenotaph
Delacroce Beta #1
Alien Sculpture
Chwast Art Tone
Obese
Bordanaro Grumpy Open
Rosenblum Razzamataz
Jefferson Aeroplane
Tension
Chwast Blimp
Calypso
Magnetic Ink
Julino Paperclip
Benguiat Chrisma Contour
Hobo Outline

Fig. 124. Modern display types in advertising.

	A	B	C	D	E	F	G
1	Balmoral	Cardinal	Squire	Glastonbury	Arnold Böcklin	Bottleneck	Countdown
2	Eckmann Schrift	Futura Black	Hobo	Lazybones	Old English	Revue	Park Avenue
3	Romic Bold	Tintoretto	Vivaldi	Univers 67	Airkraft	Apollo	Algerian
4	Astra	Baby Teeth	Block Up	Bombere	Buster	Calypso	Columbian Italic
5	Aristocrat	Company	Glaser Stencil	Cathedral	Good Vibrations	Le Golf	Harrington
6	Harlow Solid	Motter Ombra	Masquerade	Phyllis	Pluto Outline	Process	Primitive
7	Magnificat	Quicksilver	Raphael	Roco	Shatter	Stripes	Sinaloa
8	Stop	Stack	Piccadilly	Neptun	Motter Tektura	Odin	Yagi Link Double

Fig. 125. Range of type-forms for a single letter, *A*.

7

Evaluating the Text: Textual Bibliography

The title of this chapter might appear to be begging (or avoiding) the question. Conventionally, textual bibliography has been defined as "textual criticism adapted to the . . . problems of editing printed texts" (Gaskell, *New Introduction*: 337), and therefore my adoption of the term defined restrictively by Gaskell might suggest that the problems of non-printed texts are somehow very different, and should therefore be treated separately, whereas they are in fact included in this chapter. Even Gaskell (who does deal only with printed texts) admits that the textual criticism of manuscripts is "analogous" to that of printed, but I would go further, and yet paradoxically limit the term more than would Gaskell and other textual bibliographers.

It is the basic position of this book that several disciplines and textual practices which have formerly been considered as unconnected could more profitably be examined together. The texts contained in manuscripts and printed books are obviously dependent upon their bibliographical "vehicles" or "carriers" for not only their appearance but also their form—and therefore frequently their content as well. A text written in an uncial script in a roll is not only going to look different from the same words written in a gothic script in a codex, it is likely to have its text modified by the actual circumstances of its physical composition and appearance. Gatherings can be displaced in a codex but obviously not in a roll (which does not have gatherings, see Chapter 2), and different types of scribal error are more or less likely in different scripts, for certain letters may or may not look similar in those scripts (see Chapter 5). So, with printed books, the methods of composition and imposition, the format, the proof-reading and so on, may all affect the actual nature of the text produced during this bibliographical process. It is therefore the study of the textual implications and results of this process of making a bibliographical artifact which I believe should most properly be called textual bibliography, whether the artifact happens to be hand-written or printed (which would in any case usually descend from a hand-written version, at least in the long period of literary composition before authors produced fair copy on typewriter or computer printer). This enlarged definition, including manuscripts as well as printed books, would still leave "codicology" as the term proper to the study of the codex as such (i.e., without necessarily any textual bias to the study); yet by restricting textual bibliography to a joint concern with both medium and text, with both artifact and contents, I would exclude from the field of the textual bibliographer those types of textual research relating *only* to the text (i.e., divorced from a consideration of the medium carrying the text). This distinction, separating "pure" textual criticism from the study of the physical object, may not be a desirable one, but we have to recognize that many textual critics have practiced such a distinction, especially those working on "textual analysis," the formal charting of the transmission and filiation of the text (see Chapter 8). This chapter can therefore afford to be much shorter than it might otherwise be, for I am concerned here only with some of the likely ways that the process and the medium of book-making, of manuscript or printed book, can affect the content of the text. The study of textual criticism at large (in its history and its current practices) is examined at much greater length in the next chapter.

Textual Bibliography of Manuscripts

First then, to the textual implications of the bibliography of manuscripts. As already seen (Chapter 2), one of the most significant bibliographical changes in the history of the transmission of texts in the West was the replacement from the third or fourth centuries of the papyrus roll by the parchment codex as the preferred vehicle for copy. Until the period of transfer, the codex had been primarily associated with Christian works. Unfortunately, we can only guess at the accidental as opposed to the deliberate changes in the texts that might have been introduced in the process. If the original roll was in good condition without major rips or *lacunæ* (physical gaps, often actual holes, in the manuscript), a competent scribe should not have had particular difficulty in copying individual words or lines. A problem would arise, however, in the different column structure between roll and codex (where errors of eyeskip could very easily occur), although there is some suggestion that the typical column-format of early codices might have in some cases emulated that on the copy-text rolls. Before the recent series of discoveries of surviving ancient papyrus rolls in Egypt and elsewhere, there was no possibility of checking the relationship between a codex and roll version of a text, since only the former was usually extant (often not in its original version, but at several removes from the first act of copying from the roll). Even now, the evidence is very sparse, and it would be rash to draw conclusions more specific than those already offered, although the current textual and bibliographical research into the newly available rolls might eventually lead to comparative textual judgments similar to those that have been accepted for some time between, say, the Dead Sea scrolls, the Septuagint and the Masoretic text of the Old Testament/Hebrew Bible (see Chapter 8). One very clear textual advantage of the new codex medium was that references, chapter, verse, and book divisions became much easier to manipulate in a folded, stitched book than in a continuous roll, and this would have encouraged not only larger bibliographical units (the roll had to be kept fairly compact if it was to be consultable and storable), but citation and more accurate quotation. But again, the comparative data between roll and codex are largely wanting. We do know, however, that determined variation did take place during the move from roll to codex—mostly excision and selection—but how far this conscious revision might also have depended on the bibliographical format of the roll being copied is again speculation.

There is one type of bibliographical change during the move from pagan to Christian literature that is measurable, and that is the *palimpsest*. Palimpsests (manuscripts containing two texts, one written over the top of an imperfectly erased lower text, see Fig. 126) are almost impossible on papyrus, for the delicate medium cannot be scraped to remove enough of the original text so that a new one can be written on the writing surface. But palimpsests are possible on the sturdier surface of parchment, and there are many interesting textual examples of a pagan (classical) text in an early script (say, uncials) having been written over by a Christian text in a later script (one of the nationals or Caroline). In cases like these, the evidence of medium (the parchment), appearance (the scripts), and content (the texts) are clearly very closely related, particularly where the old text is otherwise unavailable.

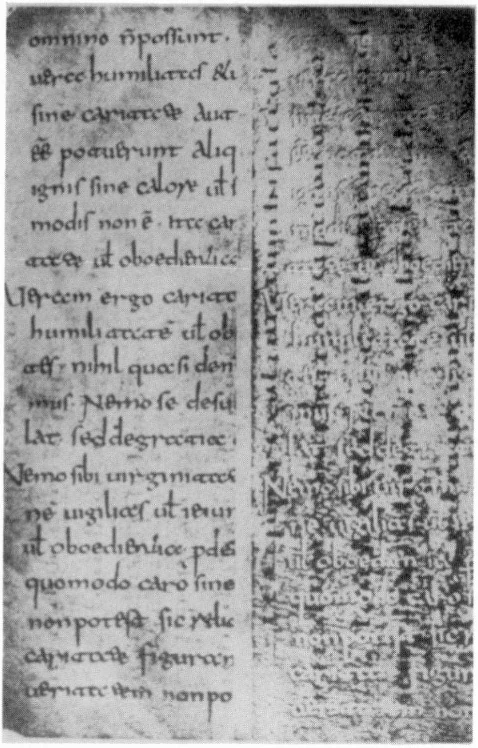

Fig. 126. Palimpsest (*Codex Sangallensis*) photographed under (*left*) ordinary light and (*right*) ultra-violet light.

Another bibliographical "disturbance," thereby suggesting that the codex has been rebound, regathered, or misbound occurs when a single opening displays both "hair" and "flesh" pages opposite each other, contrary to the usual practice. As noted in Chapter 2, since the hair side of parchment looks very different from the flesh side, most codices would be bound to avoid the sudden jolt of seeing the two together. Thus, where this does happen, the codicologist/textual bibliographer can be fairly confident that some bibliographical disjunct has occurred (leaves or even entire gatherings omitted or added, books rebound incorrectly), and these disturbances could obviously have a significant effect upon the text. Usually, such a change would be immediately noticeable, but might not be in an anthology, *florilegium*, or other compilation of bibliographically distinct originals, particularly if the disturbance occurred not in the present copy but in its (lost) exemplar. By calculating the typical page and line-size of this lost exemplar from "symptoms" in the copy (e.g., the presence of line-ending contractions, of errors in column eyeskip which could not be accounted for by the current layout), the bibliographer might be able to discover where an original flesh and hair page might indeed have faced each other, thereby suggesting a likely disturbance which could then explain a textual disruption in the copy.

Some disruptions are more noticeable than this rather sophisticated case, as when an entire gathering has simply been removed from the codex (or when a stain in an Epictetus manuscript has caused a lacuna in all its copies). The textual dislocation would presumably be manifest, as it would if a single leaf had been excised (the equivalent of a cancellandum in descriptive bibliography of the printed book, see Chapter 4), unless, of course, the leaf had been mistakenly bound into the copy. For example, the autograph manuscript of Cavendish's *Life of Wolsey* (Egerton 2402) contains a leaf lacking in all the other thirty-odd copies. Some particularly popular sections of medieval works were very prone to such excision and removal (the geography section of Bartholomæus Anglicus's *De proprietatibus rerum* is an example), and similar textual dislocations can occur where illuminations have been excised. Where a decorated initial, say, is (carefully) cut from the leaf, then the only text one might lose would be the initial itself plus whatever was on the reverse side of the leaf; if this has happened in a lost exemplar, then again, sufficient symptoms might be present in the copy to determine the extent of the loss, and perhaps also to determine the scope of the copyist's likely rationalization of the text as he peered through the hole and found the text of the next leaf staring at him! But sometimes (as in the case of some manuscripts of Hoccleve's *Regement of Princes*, where a portrait of Chaucer has been excised) the entire leaf containing the illumination has been removed, causing an even greater disruption in the text.

Not all such lacunæ or physical gaps in the manuscript leaf are as neat or as determined as these examples, however, and the damage wrought by water, fire, worms, and other natural enemies of textual scholarship are well known and often well documented. For example, the famous fire in the Cotton library damaged many unique witnesses, such as the *Beowulf* manuscript. The subsequent history of the bibliographical fortunes of the text of this manuscript (including the Thorkelin transcript made after the Cotton fire in 1731, followed by the damage of this transcript during the British shelling of Copenha-

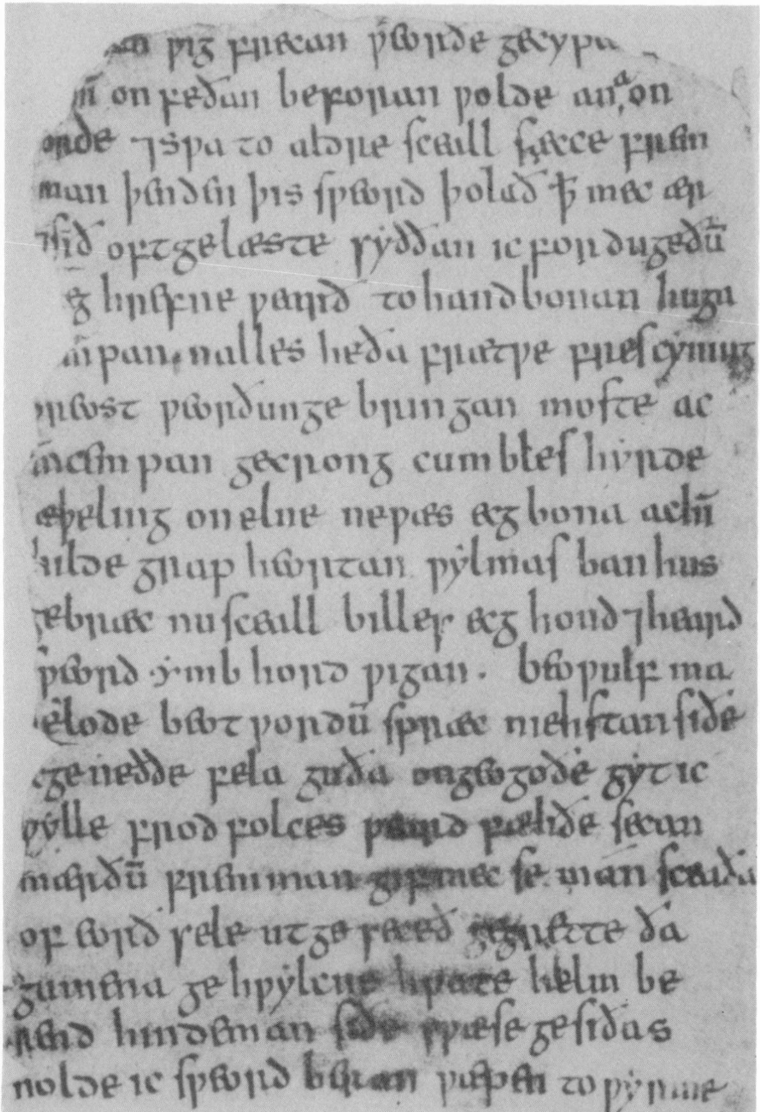

Fig. 127 (a). A page from the charred manuscript of *Beowulf* (fol. 185^v).

p. 114 = fol. 185ʳ = ll. 2496—2519.

wyrsan wig-frecan weorðe gecypan symle
ic him on feðan beforan wolde ana on
orde *ond* swa to aldre sceall sæcce frem-
man þenden þis sweord þolað *þæt mec ær   2500
5   *ond* sið oft|gelæste syððan ic for dugeðum
dæg-hrefne wearð to hand-bonan huga
cempan nalles he|ða frætwe fres-cyning
breost-weorðunge bringan moste *ac   2505
in|cempan gecrong cumbles hyrde
10 æþeling on elne ne|wæs ecg bona ac|him
hilde-grap heortan wylmas ban-hus
gebræc nu sceall billes ecg hond *ond* heard
sweord ymb hord wigan. *beowulf ma-   2510
ðelode beot-wordum spræc niehstan siðe
15 ic|ge-neðde fela guða on|geogoðe gyt ic
wylle frod folces weard fæhðe secan
mærðum fremman gif|mec se mân-sceaða
*of eorð-sele ut ge-seceð gegrette ða   2515
gumena ge-hwylcne hwate helm-be-
20 rend hindeman siðe swæse gesiðas
nolde ic sweord beran wæpen to wyrme

---

¹ *wyrsan* A, ... B; now only *an* and the bottom of *s* left ‖ *gecypan* AB ; now *n* gone, and the tops of *p* and *a* covered ‖ *symle* A, *symle* B ; now nothing left but the bottom of *s*.

² *ic* AB ; now gone ‖ part of *h* in *him* covered ‖ *an*,ᵃ : correction in the same hand.

⁵ only an inconsiderable part of the abbreviation for *ond* covered.

⁶ *dæg* AB ; now *d* gone, and a small part of *æ* covered.

⁷ *cempan* AB ; now *c* and the greater part of *e* gone, and what is left of *e* as well as the top of the first stroke of *m* covered.

⁸ *breost* AB (nothing before it) ; now the top of *b* gone, and part of what is left of it covered.

⁹ *in* AB ; now the top of *i* rubbed off.

¹¹ *hilde* AB ; now part of the first stroke of *h* gone.

¹² *gebræc* AB ; now a small part of *g* gone, and part of what is left of it covered.

¹³ part of *s* in *sweord* covered.

¹⁴ *ðelode* A, *ðeloþe* (ð altered from *d* with another ink) B ; now a great part of ð gone (but, to judge from what is left, the first letter was, doubtless, ð, not þ).

¹⁵ *ic* AB ; now the greater part of *i* gone, and the rest of it as well as part of *c* covered.

Fig. 127 (b). Zupitza's transcript of the page from *Beowulf*, noting changes since the Thorkelin transcript.

gen in 1802) aptly illustrates the tenuous evidence by which so much early literature is represented, and the continued problem of its documentary decay. For example, many readings legible to former editors or transcribers of the *Beowulf* manuscript are no longer present, as the delayed effects of fire and time continue (see Fig. 127). The same Cotton fire destroyed all but a few fragments of another Old English poem, *The Battle of Maldon*, and the work exists today only in the transcript made by Elphinstone about 1724: the only witness to *Maldon* thus post-dates its composition (in the late tenth century) by some seven and a half centuries.

This may be a long gap for most vernacular literatures, but it is, of course, not unusual in the textual transmission of biblical or classical literature. Ultra-violet light has helped the resuscitation of many formerly "lost" passages in early manuscripts, so that the admission of a former editorial fallibility in the frequent typographical formula [. . .] (for missing and irretrievable material) has in some later editions been overcome; but where there is an actual hole in the manuscript, then the textual lacuna is permanent, unless other exemplars can supply the loss. In some cases, however, the arrangement of lacunæ on the leaf may be valuable evidence as to textual transmission and provenance. For example, Anthony J. Cárdenas has shown that the translation of a work of Alfonso X can be charted bibliographically by the "tell-tale" lacunæ which were present in the exemplar in one language, to modify and limit the form of the translation into another. While, therefore, gaps in texts are not generally to be endorsed, they may have significant textual importance if carefully examined by a skilled bibliographer.

Occasionally, the bibliographical disturbance may be so extreme that the text may disappear, perhaps temporarily, to be recovered (and maybe reconstituted) only centuries later. One of the most famous examples of such a loss and recovery is the manuscript of the Old Saxon *Heliand* (the only survival of a work written in that language) found used as stiffener in the binding of a later book in the Vatican Library. In that case, there was little bibliographical reconstruction involved, but one of the Cleopatra manuscripts in the Cotton Library was actually chopped up into small fragments ("shredded" is perhaps the word), to be used as pastedowns in another volume in the library. Fortunately, it has since been reconstituted by careful bibliographical work, although it obviously looks a little strange in its new form, rather like a ransom note stuck together from separate "pieces" of text.

Scribal Variants

The final area of bibliographical evidence to be considered here is that most familiar to textual criticism—the form of the words themselves, and involves, therefore, a study of paleography. But throughout, the concern is with the textual significance of the bibliographical data. For example, the scribal use of the abbreviation system (see Chapter 5) might point to particular bibliographical problems. An editor might discover, say, that the incidence of abbreviations increases beyond the scribal norm for that document in certain places. If these increases correspond to the end of a leaf or a gathering, then the bibliographer might rightly conclude that the scribe (or his superior, the *armarius*) had erred in estimating the amount of copy that would fit the page and that the only way to accommodate the remaining text would have been to shorten it physically, by using more abbreviations than usual. This principle (and problem) is virtually identical to a scribal use of abbreviations to achieve right-margin justification and, of course, to a compositorial modification of the text after a similar error in the casting-off of copy for a printed book (see below, in the discussion of the Shakespeare First Folio).

Other types of scribal variant can be divided into the "mechanical" and the "determined," those produced by accident and those intended by the copier. Traditionally, both such variants are regarded more as a part of textual criticism (particularly where they may assist in demonstrating the relationship of witnesses according to stemmatic theory), but since they are also physical marks on a physical medium, and since they involve the effect of this physical act on transmission, they can properly be included here. My discussion is dependent upon the technical charting of the actual process of scribal copying suggested by Eugène Vinaver (see Fig. 128), and analogous therefore to studies of compositorial method by analytical bibliographers. Obviously all scribes, like all compositors or all typists, had their own idiosyncratic types of error which might serve to identify their individual involvement in a text just as effectively as might a consideration of the hand itself; but Vinaver's system is at least that—a general paradigm which can then be used to place individual errors or variations within the context of the act of copying.

Vinaver recognizes four distinct movements, during any one of which a scribal error could occur. The problem for the scribes was essentially that (as James Willis puts it), like "the amateur typist" they were working in two planes, not one, and had continually to move from exemplar to copied page and back again. There could be no "touch typing," and if there was, or rather its opposite "reading by memory" (that is, if the scribes really thought they knew the text so well that they did not need to keep looking up at the exemplar), then this confidence could itself introduce both carelessness and idiosyncratic error through contamination (the retaining of one version of a text in memory while copying another).

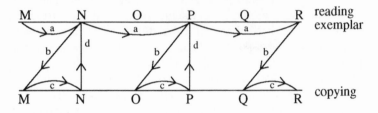

Fig. 128. Vinaver's diagram of scribal copying. The scribe follows the exemplar in movement (a) from M to N etc., then carries this information in movement (b) to the copy, reproducing the text on the copy in movement (c). Errors of eyeskip (homœoteleuton) might occur where, in movement (d) back to the exemplar, the scribe takes up the text of the exemplar at the wrong place, producing dittography or perseveration.

It could be argued that Vinaver's model shows certain flaws. For example, M, N, O, P, etc., on the exemplar line would have to be individual words, with no intervening matter, for movement b) in the *second* step not to refer back to N rather than O on the blank page. And most scribes might in any case seek the security of the *last* point actually written (N) rather than venturing on a new blank space when taking up writing again. Movement b) should therefore perhaps revert to N not O. But whatever its specific faults, the Vinaver diagram does give us a vehicle for discussion.

A. *Mechanical variants*

1. *Misreadings:* (generally in Vinaver's movement a), though held in the mind through movement b)). Lack of word-division or faulty word-division: *lof / al of, a tour / autour, fidere coeptis / fide receptis, velut imago / veluti magno, venerat ad eum / venerata deum / venerata Dominum* (where word-division has promoted a further error). Similarity of letters in certain scripts: *best / left, fecunditatem / securitatem, femina / semina* (error on original long ſ / f), *tractas /*

fractas, nummis / minimus (error on minims), *conceyued / conteyned* (error on *c* and *t* in gothic), *nyghe / nyght, mentisque / meritisque, nomenclator / nomen dator, clemente / demente* (error on *cl* and *d* in gothic). Misreading of abbreviations: *brode / brande* (nasal macron error), *lettres / hors* (plus *l* and *h* error in gothic), *fraternite / fruyte, profytes / poetes, profitable / parfyt, interimat / intimat.* Confusion of two words of similar shape and/or spelling: *bratful / bredful, tempus / corpus, signiure / segoury / synge / synnes / seruyse.* Confusion over similar meanings though different spelling: *litoribus / finibus, asseverebat / affirmabat, cognominatum / vocatum, vnclennesse / vnchaste, entendyth / thinketh, taken / vsen.* Transposition: *latera / altera, versantur / servantur, folk / flokke, cloude / colde.*

2. *Omissions:* Haplography (omission of similar letters by moving ahead too quickly on the exemplar—a movement d) error): *quidquid id est / quidquid est, geminam / illuminando geminando.* Homœoteleuton ("eyeskip" or "saut de même au même," the same word repeated within a short space and consequent omission of the space, or omission of an entire line): *Præterit tempus non legis [sed libidinis tuæ fac tamen legis]; ut succedatur decernitur; impedis et ais "habe meam rationem"; The sonne shal not beare the wyckednesse [of the fader nor the fader shall not beare the wyckednesse] of the sonne; and made mencyon [on] his tombe.*

3. *Additions:* Dittography (movement d) error, going back too far in the exemplar line): *Quod acerbum fuit ferre, [re]tulisse iucundum est; mynster / mynyster.* Contextual repetition (e.g., added materials from a gloss, marginalia, or by contextual influence): *German army / Germany army; Name and initials in block capitals* (a famous sign in the British Library); *relatu maximam / relaxatu maximam; religione Apollinem / religione Apolliginem.*

B. *Determined Variation*

Deliberate changes do not, of course, fall into Vinaver's model, for they do not depend upon a slip of hand or eye. However, they are all based upon a dissatisfaction with the exemplar line, and may be regarded as conscious changes made during the a) movement. Note, incidentally, that c) errors are not peculiar to the act of transcription, but may also occur in non-copyist writing; and that movement b) is also similar to writing since it replicates the transfer from mind to paper.

1. *Changes of subject (especially in satirical targets): Somnour /*

Squyer / Shipman; *Margaret / Maud*; *Bette / Bernard*; *tokkeris / tynkeris / tapsters / tanners / tynkelers / torners / thackers* (a series from *Piers Plowman* manuscripts, as are several of the examples in this section). 2. *Modernization or normalization: hyght / is cleped / is called, wonderly / wonderfully, ibrent / brent / burnt.* 3. *Censorship or bowdlerization: pope / peple, be crist to / anon to, so me god helpe / sothely to telle.* 4. *Emphasis: tour / ryche tour, mountayne / fayre mountayne, precious / preciousest, gode / the best.* 5. *Idiosyncratic change (virtually change for the sake of change): Cartageeus putte hadde into seruage / The hier hand hadde of hem of Cartage, xx yeer and iii of age / xxiiii yere of age.*

If there are any general tendencies to be observed in determined variation, they may be subsumed under the *lectio difficilior* principle: that scribes will usually prefer the familiar word, the easy concept, the regular metrics, and will therefore often reject both neologisms and archaic words, strikingly original expressions and nonce-words. Thus *nusquam* becomes *numquam*, *opimus* becomes *optimus*, *ycrammid* becomes *filled*, *halside* becomes *askyd*, *kenne* becomes *knowen*, and *molde*, *world*. I found this principle to be very frequent in the editing of Trevisa, for as a translator Trevisa often had to invent new words in Middle English to represent the Latin vocabulary of his source, and sometimes these neologisms would be reduced to nonsensical but familiar forms by the scribes. The examples of *conceyued* and *conteyned* in misreadings above are both scribal rationalizations of Trevisa's original *constrained*, which was his coinage but was unrecognized by the scribes.

One further ramification of the problem of charting scribal variance may be where the editor suspects that some copy has actually been omitted (with again, exact parallels in printed books), or where the presence of such possible omissions or of abbreviations is apparently not adequately explained by the current bibliographical nature of the book—i.e., it is not at the end of a current gathering in the current book. In this case, it may again be necessary to surmise that the present scribal forms are only "symptoms," inherited from an earlier stage in the transmission, and that the real bibliographical problem occurred in the exemplar or in the exemplar's exemplar or beyond, whose features the present scribe may have all-too-faithfully reproduced.

Such scribal symptoms are known to occur, for example, in the descendants of Continental books copied from exemplars written by Anglo-Saxon or Irish missionaries, and thus presumably written in a form of one of the Insular scripts (see Chapter 5). While the extant texts may not be written in Insular, the only way of explaining the types of error made by the scribe is to assume that they arise from let-ter-confusions possible in the parent script but unlikely in the copy-script. Each type of script had its own characteristic errors of copy-ing, the best-known of which is probably the minuscule gothic confu-sion among all minims—*i, u, m, n*—which would have been much less likely in the carefully separated letters of Caroline minuscule, and impossible in the entirely differently formed letters of uncial (see Chapter 5 for examples). So, while editors may be puzzled as to the paleographic causes of error within a given script, by knowing the features of the script in the putative exemplar, they may be able to decide with more bibliographical certainty the probable reading in the exemplar and ultimately in the archetype. The same principle holds, of course, for editors of printed texts, where the book itself might appear in a very dense version of textura, but where the putative man-uscript from which it was set (now undoubtedly lost) might have been in a highly decadent secretary or even in a version of italic—though this latter combination of book and manuscript styles is less likely (see Chapters 5 and 6).

Textual Bibliography of Printed Books

People make mistakes, and while scribes as a group tend to make certain sorts of mistakes, the practice of an individual copying an exemplar is often idiosyncratic enough to make the habits of these in-dividuals distinguishable from their fellows. This process of identifi-cation can, of course, be assisted in manuscript bibliography by the study of the paleography as well. Strictly speaking, this additional component is not available to the textual bibliographer of printed books, for while a compositor may indeed make idiosyncratic and codifiable errors, each compositor is presumably handling the same physical typeface within a given section of a book (and this qualifica-tion is not really modified by the likelihood of a compositor having—and being responsible for—his own specific "case" of type, see Chapter 3). However, these limitations notwithstanding, the charting of individual compositorial error is one area of the textual bibliography of printed books which is very similar to the parallel ac-tivity of the manuscript bibliographer.

Thus, all or most of the errors already noted in the section on scribes (including, it should be emphasized, the determined variants as well as the involuntary ones) can be replicated in the study of compositorial habits. Compositors might misread words or letters of similar shape, might change word order or transpose letters within a word; they might misunderstand word-division, and might be guilty of haplography and homœoteleuton and contextual repetitions—all in a manner similar to that of the scribes. In fact, Vinaver's theoretical model for scribal copying and the sort of error it is likely to produce could be adapted without too many modifications to the act of setting a text from copy onto a composing stick. (The major difference, of course, would be that the compositor does not really "see" the results of the copying—movements M to N, O to P, Q to R on Vinaver's "copying" line—for the text on the composing stick is not read as text, but only letter by letter.) Psychologically, in fact, compositors had no real "copied" text in any bibliographical sense, for they held the copy-text in their minds while choosing type for the stick, but the text was not seen as words until it had been laid in the form, or sometimes not until even later.

In the early period, compositors could show a good deal of freedom in representing the features of the text—for example, in spelling. And it is here that the individual habits can often be most easily observable, for sometimes a series of compositors working on a given book may have had characteristic spelling systems which can serve to identify their work. However, as has been frequently demonstrated by bibliographers of Renaissance books, compositors were by no means consistent in their usage patterns, and without additional information (e.g., on the methods of imposition) judgments of compositorial attribution based on spelling should be somewhat tentative. One possible modification to such a judgment may be the problems of right-margin justification, for the compositor (like the scribe) could use the comparative freedom of both spelling and abbreviation without thereby indicating a personal preference for all occasions. For example, the spelling *doe* for *do* might indeed be a personal idiosyncrasy, or it might be because the compositor needed an extra letter to justify his line. In verse, of course, one might assume a greater individual license, since right-hand justification is not necessary. After the seventeenth century, when spelling becomes more standardized (sometimes reflecting a house style but more often simply the gradual tendency toward a normalized orthography for the language as a whole), it is rarely possible to make textual or bibliographical judgments of this sort based purely on spelling.

While scribes and compositors had in some ways similar responsibilities and similar habits, the compositor had problems which the scribe did not. For example, Renaissance books were not always set in the same page order as the manuscript had been written in. In such "setting by forms" (rather than by pages, see Chapters 3 and 4) it would be necessary to "cast off" copy in advance—i.e. to estimate the amount of manuscript text that would fit onto a given number of printed pages. If the guess was correct, then all was well, but if the estimate was wrong, then the compositor had to adjust the remaining text to the space now available. The division of labor in some medieval scriptoria could present similar problems, where different sections of text from a single gathering might sometimes be assigned to different scribes, but because of the greater flexibility of script over print, a scribe might be able to overcome mistakes in estimation more easily than a compositor would. A famous (fairly detailed) example will make this clear.

Through a study of the composition of the Shakespeare First Folio (see Appendix I for the pages from the Folio illustrating the following discussion), Charlton Hinman established that the book was set as a "folio in sixes"—made up of gatherings of three leaves each folded once, with the inner leaves placed inside the outer. Since pages 1/2 and 11/12 of such a gathering would form the conjunct outer leaves, then the content of pages 11 and 12 would have to be known at the same time as that of pages 1 and 2, and only the inner pages of the innermost sheet (pages 6 and 7) of the gathering would have completely continuous matter. Hinman discovered that the compositor would in fact work from this innermost sheet outwards, so that the outer leaves of a gathering (and therefore the ones whose text would be adjacent to that on the adjoining gatherings) would be set last. Where there was more space available than text on these outer leaves, the compositor would therefore have to waste space, by introducing blank lines, giving a great deal of room between speeches or stage directions, or even (as in the example of page 95 from *Timon of Athens*) setting prose as verse, so that the lines at the bottom of the left-hand column, "What's to be thought of him? / Does the Rumor hold for true, / That hee's so full of Gold?", while looking like very "free," mature Shakespearean verse, are in fact so only visually, and were originally prose. We can immediately tell that the compositor was trying to waste space from the evidence of the double lines inserted before and after the stage direction in the right-hand column *Enter Timon from his Caue.*

Setting prose as verse uses up more space, as does breaking a verse-line into two, for example on page 40 of *Titus Andronicus*, where the last two lines on the bottom of the page read "Who marks the waxing tide, / Grow waue by waue"—a perfect iambic pentameter line set as two lines to waste space. Again, the evidence of the white space around the stage directions on this page, plus the space around *Actus Tertius* confirms the situation. The opposite condition can be seen in page 257 from *Hamlet*, where, compared with the white space around the stage directions of *Timon* or *Titus*, there is a very cramped page (note that there are no lines added around the stage directions *Enter Ghost.* etc. and that the compositor places the second syllable of the broken word *further*, line 681, at the end of the previous line rather than giving it a line to itself), ending with a fifteen-syllable line "Will sate itself in a Celestiallbed,& prey on Garbage," instead of the expected ten syllables. The lack of word-breaks between "Celestiall," "bed," and "&" (together with the use of the ampersand instead of "and") is further evidence of the desperate attempt to save space.

In many of these cases, the bibliographer has another authoritative version of the text with which to compare the cramped or spacious version. This is so with *Hamlet* where the quarto splits the fifteen-syllable line appearing in the Folio into two. A similar comparison can be made with two pages from *Much Ado About Nothing*, the cramped folio version (page 121) bearing signs of the compositor's having had to fit too much text into too little space, and the quarto version where there is no such problem. This disparity is, incidentally, to be expected, for because of the difference in folding (see Chapter 4), quartos have proportionally wider pages than folios and will thus accommodate longer lines. Signs of the cramping in the folio *Much Ado* include the use of the abbreviations "ỹ" (for "thou") and "ỹ" for "that," and the ampersand "&" for "and" (bottom of right-hand column), together with the omission of "that" in the two lines "They swore [that] you were almost sicke for me" and "They swore [that] you were welnigh dead for me" (lines 2639–40), and the fact that the play (ending at the bottom of the page), has no "exeunt" in the folio, only a "FINIS."

Such comparisons can therefore be very useful in demonstrating the effects of wasting or losing space, but, as Hinman points out, there are some plays showing similar bibliographical disturbances for which there is no other authority with which to compare. For example, in two pages from *Anthony and Cleopatra* (for which the folio is the first edition and there is no comparative quarto), page 364 is an outer page of an outer leaf of a gathering with lots of space between stage directions.   On the next page, 365, however (the first, outer page of the *next* gathering), there is no such luxury, and instead there is a great sense of a packed, cramped text, with very little (if any) white space around stage directions, e.g., *Enter Proculeius.* at the top of the left-hand column.   In this column there is even evidence for a section of text having been dropped, perhaps to make space.   The repeated speech heads "Pro." (referring to Proculeius, lines 3238 and 3241) show that there must have been something in between them, for otherwise there would be no need for the duplication; and the very sudden (and inexplicable) dramatic shift between the two speeches (with the first very conciliatory and courteous, "deere lady / Haue comfort...your plight is pittied," and the second brusque and almost violent, "how easily she may be surpriz'd; / Guard her till *Cæsar* come") confirms this suspicion.   But since there is no other authoritative text for this play, it will never be known what is missing which might explain this shift in Proculeius's tone.   Did Cleopatra say something offensive, or do something to cause Proculeius to change his demeanor, or was there a missing stage direction showing Proculeius's own duplicity?   It is impossible to tell (although virtually all modern critical editions of the play speculatively introduce a stage direction as explanation of the change), but because of the bibliographical evidence available from a study of the printing of the folio, it is at least fairly clear that *something* went wrong.

This detailed demonstration of one of the bibliographical characteristics of a very famous book shows how a knowledge of analytical bibliography may affect a decision or judgment made in textual bibliography.   One more (possibly contentious) example, again from Shakespeare.   It has long been assumed that the verse of Shakespeare's late plays, particularly the "problem" plays and the "romances" becomes very rough, free, and irregular.   However, it may be that some of this apparent irregularity (of verse-length if not of internal metrics) may in fact be the result of the setting of these verses within the much narrower columns of a folio (as compared to the relatively wider quarto columns), so that lines would have to "broken" by the compositor (just as they were in the example from *Timon*), not necessarily by the author.   And since several of these late plays (for example, *The Tempest*, *Cymbeline*, *Measure for Measure*, *All's Well That Ends Well*, and *The Winter's Tale*) had their first publication in folio, with no prior publication in quarto, there is no other authoritative text layout to compare them with—as was the case with *Anthony and Cleopatra.* This possibility has yet to be analyzed in full, but it demonstrates the potentially close link between printing history, the physical nature of the document, and esthetic judgment.

Another difference between scribal and compositorial method was that scribes simply picked up their writing implements, dipped them into ink, and began writing. They did not have to choose among many different types of ink, and run the risk of "loading" the wrong sort on to their pens. But compositors had continually to reach into the compartments of their cases in order to fill their composing sticks. If there were wrong types in a box, then they would have "foul case" (see Fig. 108 in Chapter 6) and would set errors in their sticks (unless, of course, they bothered to "feel" or actually see the type in the stick).

Beyond the work of the compositor, the text of a book could, of course, undergo changes both within an edition or impression (e.g., during proof-reading, where the "correction" of errors might also introduce new errors), and between editions or impressions. For example, while some proof correction must have been done before the first "pull" at the press, it seems to have been common in the early period to retain some uncorrected printed sheets and to include them in copies of books otherwise made up from a later (corrected) state of the text. It is from this practice that it becomes necessary for textual editors to collate a number of individual copies of an edition, for they cannot assume that all copies will be identical. Proof-reading was, in any case, a rather undisciplined affair, for the printer's proof-correction was not usually made against original copy, nor was the manuscript returned to the author for proofing against printed copy. Thus, proofing was often largely a matter of spotting self-evident errors, or of introducing modifications for purely esthetic effect. It is unclear how much the authors participated in this process.

Once stereotypes (see Chapter 3) were introduced in the late eighteenth century, the likelihood of a whole new series of errors occurring in the resetting of a new edition was lessened. That is, since the type-pages were now retained from the earlier edition, rather than having the type distributed and then the text recomposed again for a new edition, all changes would be those resulting from deliberate revisions in the stereotype plates (or from the gradual decay of the plates). In a sense, therefore, a new edition set from well-preserved plates is almost analogous to a stage of additional printer's and author's proofing in the early period. Errors can indeed be introduced, but they will usually be the result of a deliberate modification made to the text on the plates, thereby possibly resulting in accidental errors as well. Furthermore, just as in the early period, uncorrected states could be mixed with corrected within a single edition. Added to this is the possibility of stop-press corrections made during a print-run (e.g., if plates had been damaged).

All in all, therefore, while printing does arrest some parts of the process of textual corruption, it can introduce new ones. And there is no analogy in scribal practices for errors or deliberate changes introduced on the composing stick or as a result of the imposition methods. Even the newest methods of preparing a text for printing have their own built-in dangers. For example, if a text is stored on a computer disk or tape, there is the possibility of different states of the text being conflated in a manner similar to the mixing of states from stereotype plates or from corrected or uncorrected sheets. An author's corrections to hard-copy revises might, for example, be entered on a disk representing an earlier state of the text, so that the result would be a mixture of the latest version of the pre-publication text with the earliest. I suffered a particularly embarrassing example of such an electronic confusing of states of text in my role as co-editor of the journal *Text*: one of the essays we were to publish was heavily revised (with new material from recent research as well as with corrections of the earlier typescript we had already submitted to the publisher). At the time the revised version came in, the earlier state had already been typeset and had its own electronic file. However, it was a simple enough matter to open a new file for the revision, and it was the typesetting from this new file which appeared in the various stages of proof. Unfortunately, when the volume of *Text* actually appeared, mysteriously it printed, not the new, corrected and revised state, but the old, uncorrected typesetting. How did this happen, *after* proof and after the editors and the author had all checked the right version? Presumably because the new and old files had very similar names (maybe differentiated only by 1 and 2 or a and b), and the compositor mistakenly hit the wrong key at that last stage of production, after all checking had been completed—an error which could not have occurred in the days of hot type/letterpress.

Each technology thus carries with it the possibility of determined or accidental variation, for as Greg maintained, there is a principle of "universal variation" which operates whenever a text is transmitted: every act of copying introduces new errors—even the act of photocopying, as the following story will demonstrate. Again for the journal *Text*, we had received an article by the well-known Shakespearean

Gary Taylor (co-editor of the Oxford Shakespeare) for possible publication. Taylor was in England at the time, so he sent us his typescript on English (European) "A4" paper, which is a little longer than conventional U.S. "letter-size" but not as long as "legal-size." To send the article out for review by our board, I asked our secretarial staff to make some photocopies. Seeing that the A4 paper was not as big as legal-size (or perhaps quite unconsciously pressing the "letter-size" rather than the "legal-size" button on the copier), they simply copied the article on to letter-size paper. As I read down to the end of the first page of the copy on letter-size paper, all looked well, for there was an apparently perfect syntactic link between the end of page 1 and the beginning of page 2. It all seemed to make sense, except that the argument in the sentence appeared to be the opposite of what I knew to be Taylor's general position on Shakespearean revision. Suspicious, I retrieved the A4 version to discover that the photocopying had neatly cut off the bottom line of the A4 in transferring to letter-size, and that this excised line (which syntactically could be omitted from the sentence without structural harm) contained a verbal negative which completely reversed the remnant of meaning in the photocopy. Lines can, of course, be omitted in any copying, but this particular omission, and the resulting inversion of meaning, was caused only by technological means (and, admittedly a little human fallibility in the selection of the wrong-size paper).

Other types of error peculiar to electronic transmission include improper changes in typesetting commands caused by embedded codes. For example, some of the alt commands entered by a graduate assistant to access special symbols (e.g., *ü*) in early versions of the bibliography for this book were read by my typesetting program as commands to switch on or off such features as italic or boldface, so that titles of books and their authors would slip back and forth from italic to roman without any apparent logic. Of course, the combination of a visual check of the print-out with an investigation of these hidden codes identified and then removed the problem (or, at least, I hope so), but the introduction of a new type of error demonstrates that the challenge of textual bibliography has not disappeared just because of the move from print to electronic transmission. In fact, electronic transmission can even have identifying typographic symptoms: thus, an article in the *New York Times* after the failed Soviet coup in August, 1991, invented a new ethic/religious group when it claimed "the loss of its [Ukraine's] 52 million Slavs would tilt the ethnic balance of the remaining union toward the Muslim oslems of Central Asia,"

(August 26, 1991: A10). These mysterious "oslems" were presumably created when a *Times* stylist noticed the form "Moslems" (rather than the preferred *Times* style "Muslims"), but instead of striking out the entire word left the initial "M" in place and inserted "uslims," without, however, remembering to delete the offending "oslems." The sequence of error would be impossible in a non-electronic medium.

Considering such new technological means of introducing error into transmission, it is the responsibility of the textual bibliographer to be familiar with the technical characteristics of the medium (through analytical bibliography) and then to employ this knowledge in an adjudication of the likely textual results of the medium.

Just as in the textual bibliography of manuscript books, textual scholars may not restrict themselves to the clearly defined stages of actual textual transmission. The investigation of paper, ink, watermarks, binding, and provenance (according to the principles already described in the sections on analytical and descriptive bibliography, Chapters 3 and 4) is all a part of the range of evidence that might be used by the textual bibliographer. The concentration on transmission in this chapter merely reflects the textual focus of this stage of the scholarship of the text. It is assumed that the bibliographical nature of the book or manuscript has already been charted before the textual scholar turns to the contents. As noted in the chapter on textual criticism (Chapter 8), some textual theorists have declared that transmission (or "textual analysis") should be kept separate from strict bibliographical matters. But as this chapter shows, this transmission can be crucially affected by the technical medium in which the transmission takes place. Thus, the well-rounded textual scholar must be prepared to be an historian of technology and a critical interpreter of this history as well.

And the role of critical interpretation in the conduct of textual bibliography has recently been much emphasized by a growing movement in textual criticism—to be dealt with more fully in the next chapter—which seeks to show the textual and esthetic implications of the physical production of the work in what Jerome J. McGann ("What Is Critical Editing?") has called its bibliographical codes (as distinct from the "linguistic codes" of the text proper). This concentration on the "meaning" of textual bibliography has not been prominent in the practice or assumptions of traditional textual bibliographers, but it does form a valid link between the world of "strict and pure" bibliography and that of textual criticism, and thus deserves a brief discussion here.

For example, Ben Jonson's publication of his *Works* in folio in 1616 is mentioned in several places in this book as an instance of an author's attempting to determine the documentary meaning of his literary production: by taking what had been regarded as an ephemeral, almost vulgar genre (mere plays) and publishing them in a collected works in folio Jonson was actively promoting the acceptance of those plays as "literature," on a par with the theology, philosophy, and the classics which had been associated with this format. On a purely practical level, the Jonson folio could not be used as play-text, for it was simply too big, heavy, and monumental to function as prompt-book or script. And Jonson further emphasized the difference in format and genre by rewriting many of the plays for the new medium, turning them into literary texts rather than dramatic texts.

There were similar intentions behind the re-publication of Milton's *Paradise Lost* in folio, and behind the intended publication of Bunyan's *Pilgrim's Progress* in the same medium—in the latter case a remarkable change from the popular, lower-class author of the English Civil War to recognition as a national monument. Pope was very much aware of these bibliographical codes, and published his translation of Homer in two simultaneous editions—one a "traditional" edition with the old-fashioned use of italic and roman, and the other a modern scholarly edition without such features, in the manner that Baskerville was to associate with the clean and clear presentation of a classical text (see Chapter 6). Byron's *Don Juan* had a similar dual existence, with a series of expensive authorized printings of very limited print-runs (which McGann estimates at two thousand copies) on the one hand, and many cheap piracies on the other, selling in the tens of thousands.

Two final examples of the meaning given to a text by its enclosing bibliographical features will, I trust, make the connection clear. When Steinbeck handed over the text of *The Grapes of Wrath* to his publisher in 1940, he was concerned that his attack on the agricultural growers of California and on banking practices in the United States not be misinterpreted as a foreign-inspired piece of radical agitation. (He had already written and then destroyed an earlier draft which was much more overt in its criticisms.) Accordingly, he insisted that the book have in its end-papers the text and music of that patriotic song *The Battle-Hymn of the Republic*, and when the publisher initially included only the text, he responded by demanding that the whole thing be there—music as well. Thus the socially conscious book almost literally wrapped itself in the flag to protect itself against misconstrual of its meaning—except for one thing. While *The Battle-Hymn of the Republic* might have been taken by most readers as a bibliographical defense against a charge of sedition (then and now), the fact was that in the Thirties, the *Hymn* had regularly been sung at meetings of the Communist Party in the United States—as Steinbeck was well aware—so that he might have been disingenuous in claiming that his new end-papers brought only one meaning: maybe there were two, one for each audience.

Even the dustjacket can have textual-bibliographical meaning, as F. Scott Fitzgerald demonstrated when he incorporated features of the initial jacket design for *The Great Gatsby* into the text of the novel. He cabled his editor Maxwell Perkins from Paris: "For Christ's sake, don't give anyone that jacket. I've written it into the book" (see Hedges). The melancholy eyes staring out over strings of carnival lights thus become not just an additional and extraneous bibliographical element in the book but a motivating force in the text itself, confirming the close relation between the two.

Although some textual critics (Randall McLeod, under his various pseudonyms of Random Cloud or Random Clod) have made a specialty of concentrating on the meaning of the physical appearance of a book, as opposed to its verbal content, I realize that many textual bibliographers would not approve of my including such matters as electronic transmission and dustjacket design into the discussion of their craft. But as McLeod has demonstrated in a number of amusing and highly idiosyncratic articles on the role of type and layout in the production of meaning, any aspect of the physical transmission can be significant in influencing our "reading" of a book. McLeod would go further, suggesting that a literary reader must deliberately attempt *not* to read for conventional verbal meaning in order to perceive these physical features: he claims that he has been trying for years not to read the text of Harington's translation of Ariosto's *Orlando furioso* so that he can better observe the bibliographical codes in which this text is embedded. Such deliberate embedding—on the part of the author—has been described by several textual critics, notably James McLaverty in his insistence that it is the actual physical and bibliographical layout of Pope's *Dunciad* (and its bibliographical allusions to the contemporary scholarly variorum edition) which is the peculiar point of Pope's satire in the poem, and a reading for its "text" alone misses this quality. John Barnard, D. F. McKenzie, Barbara Woshinsky, G. Thomas Tanselle and others have made similar emphases in their recent work.

In stressing the materiality of text, these textual critics are drawing broad cultural implications from the technical information provided by analytical and descriptive bibliography and thus building on the work of analytical bibliographers like Carter and Pollard when they exposed the forgeries of the book-dealer and collector T. J. Wise. Carter and Pollard demonstrated that the kernless type used by Wise in his forged editions was not employed until after 1883, although the Wise editions dated from as early as the 1840s—a finding later challenged by James Mosley (vii). They similarly discovered that the esparto grass and chemical wood pulp used by Wise post-dated the ostensible publication dates of Wise's forged pamphlets. Carter and Pollard's exposure of Wise rested on a demonstrable material connection between text, appearance, and means of production, and in proving the Wise editions forgeries they obviously changed the cultural "meaning" of these works as physical artifacts, just as the cultural status of the Vinland Map purporting to show Viking colonization of North America was changed when the ink used in the map was shown to have been first used in the 1920s.

The "materialist" textual critics cited in the latter part of this chapter tend to stress the social construction of meaning out of the physical codes, but the value given to those physical codes will obviously depend to a large extent upon the general social acceptance of their authority and validity. Carter and Pollard's adjustment of this authority through bibliographical demonstration was as much a critical act as is a materialist's demonstration of the semantics of typography or the conjecturalist editor's reconstruction of a lost authorial reading. All involve both technical information and critical interpretation and one is incomplete without the other.

It is with confidence, therefore, that I can claim, here and elsewhere in this book, that all facets of a book's history and presentation and reception are ultimately connected, and I use the physical examples in this chapter—from scribal error to electronic storage—as a bridge to the treatment of textual criticism to follow in the next chapter.

8

Criticizing the Text: Textual Criticism

The documents have been discovered and enumerated, they have been described in technical detail and their physical make-up has been investigated, especially as it might affect the content of the text contained in the documents. The script or print has been read with care and appropriate transcriptions have been made. The historical and cultural circumstances of composition and transmission have been explored. What now? What do we do with all this information?

The traditional response to this question has most commonly been to prepare a scholarly edition in order to present the information in a helpful manner to a learned audience. And the procedures typically used in preparing such scholarly editions are described in the final chapter of this book, as the logical fulfillment of all the textual activities encountered so far. But before plunging into the task of editing, the student should ideally have some sense of how this task has been undertaken by other scholars faced by the same problem of interposition, of standing between author and reader, of interpreting one to the other, of clarifying and elucidating a text whose features may have been obscured by the passage of time. For the single most important characteristic of textual *criticism* (that part of textual scholarship charged with interrogating the text and preparing it for public consumption, usually in the form of a scholarly edition) is that it is *critical*, it does involve a speculative, personal, and individual confrontation of one mind by another, despite the attempts by some textual critics to turn the process into a science, and despite the frequent misunderstanding by non-textuists, who often suppose that textual criticism is merely a mechanical imposition of certain technical procedures in order to produce "definitive editions" of works that can be accepted without question and will never need editing again.

To be fair, it must be admitted that there have been periods when such confidence was encouraged by textual scholars (e.g., during the early days of the Modern Language Association's Center for Editions of American Authors, when large sums of money for scholarly editing were obtained from the federal government, via such agencies as the National Endowment for the Humanities and the National Historical and Public Records Commission, often on the promise that the resulting editions were to fix the text for all time). And, through the apparently neutral and value-free techniques learned from analytical and descriptive bibliography, it was all too tempting to assume that editions built upon such techniques would be similarly free of merely human intervention. But despite these temptations (for what E. Talbot Donaldson has referred to as the "editorial death-wish," the desire to pretend that one's handiwork as editor is invisible, [105]), most scholarly editors have rejoiced in their role as critics rather than having been ashamed of it.

Being a critic means being sensitive to another person's quirks and peculiarities; it means that the critic must by an almost phenomenological leap, "become" that other person while preparing the text for publication. And this is true whether the other person is the author or one of the text's transmitters, scribe, compositor, printer, proof-reader, or publisher's editor. It means using a critical attitude to all evidence that a text brings with it, not taking anything merely on faith and not believing that anybody is completely free from error. It means that textual criticism, through its interrogative, speculative disposition, is (as I have remarked elsewhere) the exemplary discipline for these days of a "hermeneutics of suspicion," and that far from retreating before the monstrous regiment of post-structuralists and other theorists, textual critics might do better to embrace these new dispensations and to find common ground for suspecting the documentary evidence of texts. As Eugène Vinaver, the noted editor of Malory's *Morte Darthur* put it, textual criticism is founded upon a "mistrust of texts" (352), and it is this mistrust that motivates the act of editing.

And being a textual critic, being a mistruster of texts, also means that we must bring to that suspicion all of our experience as readers of texts, and that we inevitably base our judgments as critics on this experience. We are thus part of the long tradition of such suspicious readers, and before embarking on the specific task of interrogating a text by producing a scholarly edition, it is as well if we are aware of this tradition, of those other readers who have preceded us in the role.

To this end, this chapter on textual criticism will offer a brief history of the critical reading of texts, concluding with an account of the various current camps and their attitudes to the problems of text and textuality. The survey must be somewhat cursory, for only those positions which have been most influential can be touched on, as can only those editors and textual theorists whose work has contributed to important critical principles still being employed. It is in reality a long story, told all too quickly here, but the account should at the very least provide a frame of reference for the practical editorial matters to follow in the final chapter.

Classical Textual Criticism

Textual criticism is the most ancient of scholarly activities in the West. Before the theoretical literary criticism of Plato and Aristotle, unknown Greek scholars had, by the end of the sixth century B.C., established the text (or more properly, *a* text) of the Homeric epics by an admittedly subjective reading in order to remove the errors that had crept in as a consequence of continued oral transmission. There was even a legend that Aristotle himself had prepared an edition of Homer. This sort of scholarship, while itself subject to the dictates of personal judgment, was a conscious attack on the claim of the rhapsodes, or professional reciters of poetry, to have preserved the Homeric text perfectly, and marks the first acknowledgment that any act of transmission, oral or scribal, is inherently partial to corruption. Peisistratus (560–527 B.C.) is credited with the decision to have an "official" text of Homer compiled for the Panathenea festival, although none of the features of this text have survived. But the characteristics of the early Greek book encouraged further corruption in copying: without word-division or punctuation, with verse written out as prose, subjected to the continual revision of declaimer and actor, the texts of both epic and drama presented many of the problems still encountered by editors of medieval prose or poetry and Renaissance drama. In an attempt to overcome this tendency toward textual dissolution, Lycurgus (ca. 390–324 B.C.) placed a standard copy of the texts of Æschylus, Sophocles, and Euripides in the public archives in 330 B.C. However, it is unlikely that Lycurgus's standard editions of the Greek dramatists were any more authoritative than others currently in circulation, and the deposit should be seen more as an effort to prevent further corruption than as a scholarly attempt to overcome corruptions already present in the text. The deposit did at least slow down the circulation.

Before genuine textual scholarship was possible, a large archive containing many different manuscripts of the same works was necessary. Under the advice of Demetrius of Phalerum, this step was undertaken by Ptolemy Soter, who in ca. 284 B.C. named Zenodotus of Ephesus (ca. 325–ca.234 B.C.) as the first Chief Librarian at Alexandria. The manuscripts in the Alexandrian library, in the form of papyrus rolls, might have grown to a collection of 750,000 during the next two centuries (estimates vary). Zenodotus approached his duties as scholar and archivist from two perspectives: first, through the compilation of an Homeric Glossary, an attempt to define the "hard" words in the Homeric epics, largely by context, and therefore open to some very subjective readings; and second, through editing both the *Iliad* and the *Odyssey*, after collating the many manuscripts of each work in the library. It was Zenodotus who divided the two epics into twenty-four books, who began the process of rejecting spurious lines by marking them with an obelisk, and who introduced marginal signs into the text. He transposed and telescoped problematical lines and generally tried to produce a "perfect" text from the corrupt remnants in the extant manuscripts. Unfortunately, there was no basic *theory* of reconstruction involved in Zenodotus's editing, and he was later criticized for relying too heavily on highly subjective criteria.

His successors Aristophanes of Byzantium (ca. 217–ca. 180 B.C.) and Aristarchus of Samothrace (ca. 220–145 B.C.) attempted to reduce this subjective element and to make textual reconstruction more technical and less whimsical. This movement approached a *system* of criticism only in the work of Aristarchus, for his predecessor Aristophanes, while producing "standard" critical editions of the dramatic works of Euripides and the comedies of his namesake Aristophanes, and a collected edition of Pindar, still based much of his textual judgment on purely esthetic values, rather than on paleographic or codicological characteristics as well. With Aristarchus, the first textual criticism to combine both esthetic and technical evidence began. Often cited as the "complete" critic (by, for example, Horace and Cicero), he brought to his editing a wide knowledge of grammar, etymology, orthography, and literature. The remnants of his commentaries contained in the medieval commentaries or scholiasts show him to have been a highly conservative critic, who tried to remove the layers of conjecture built up by his predecessors. He produced critical recensions, not only of the *Iliad* and the *Odyssey*, but also of

Hesiod, Pindar, Anacreon, Archilochus, and Alcæus, trying as far as possible to isolate "good" manuscripts for each of these authors. Some of his critical method is open to the same charge of circular reasoning later leveled at the Lachmannian system (see below), for he invoked such criteria as consistency and decorum (in both technical and literary senses) in the establishment of a reading. Since such judgments largely depended upon the evaluation of readings already contained in extant witnesses (which were therefore declared "good" or "bad" by their success or failure to be "consistent" or "decorous"), Aristarchus's method could in practice merely confirm his esthetic predispositions. But the technical stance was important to the direction of textual criticism as a discipline.

This reliance upon individual critical perceptions (often masquerading as "scientific" methodology) becomes, in fact, the major characteristic of the Alexandrian school of analogy. According to this theory, it is possible to re-create a genuinely "Homeric" usage out of the corrupt documentary remains simply by constructing an ideal paradigm of "correctness," involving, therefore, a critical evaluation of this documentary evidence, and an ability to recognize the "Homeric" (or "Shakespearean" or "Miltonic") reading from the merely scribal. Analogy also allows the textual critic not only to sort the authorial from the non-authorial through collation, but also to create (or reconstruct) an authoritative reading where none of the extant documents seems to represent the expected or appropriate usage. Obviously, this method can, in the hands of an able critic, produce a sensitive and discriminating text responsive to authorial intention—and can certainly take the reader much closer to this intention than could a reliance upon any one of the corrupt "remaniements" or surviving documents.

But it is equally obvious that in the hands of an enthusiastic perfecter of an author's work, a critic who values "smoothness," "consistency," and "correctness" more than documentary "authority," the analogy method can result in extreme eclecticism, subjectivism, and normalization according to the esthetic dictates of the critic, not the author. At the opposite extreme, the Pergamanian linguistic and scholarly rivals of the Alexandrian analogists invoked the principle of anomaly. This principle, dependent upon a Stoic acceptance of the inevitable corruption of all temporal, earthly phenomena as a result of man's "fallen" condition, maintains that it is impossible to create or re-create an ideal form (of grammar, a system of accidence, or of authorial usage) and that the only honest recourse is to select that specif-

ic utterance or that extant document which, on philological or other
grounds (e.g., provenance) seems best to represent authorial intention, and once having made that selection, to follow the readings of
the document as closely as possible. To the Pergamanians and their
text-critical descendants in the last two millennia, *all* utterances and
readings are anomalous, so that critical judgment is suspended once
the first leap of faith has been made. Obviously, this method can
produce very careful and very conservative texts, but it does involve a
failure of critical nerve in blindly accepting all readings of the "best
text;" and this failure (in, for example, some of the editions produced
by both late nineteenth-century Lachmannians and proponents of
Bédier's "best-text" theory, see below) has been noted and ridiculed
by those critics for whom discrimination among extant readings, no
matter where they occur, is a proper and an inevitable part of editing.
The polarities of analogy and anomaly (under different names and different dispensations) have, therefore, been present from the beginnings of textual criticism in the West, and the debate between their
constituencies shows no signs of waning.

Complementing their critical editions of standard authors (who
became standard largely by the fixing of a secure canon of authors and
works), the Alexandrian scholars produced exegetical works, lexicographical, metrical, and grammatical studies intended to enhance the
elucidation of the texts. An interest in this type of ancillary material
became associated with the Pergamanians (where, according to tradition, parchment was first used in place of papyrus, see Chapter 2),
and where the canon of literature was extended to include prose as
well as poetry. Inevitably, this accretion of scholarship began to acquire a value of its own, and from the second century B.C. variorum
commentaries (editions recording a wide range of textual and critical
annotations) were published in their own right, though usually with
lemmata (head-words to each note) linking them with the text itself.
As public interest began to shift from the primary works to the secondary commentaries and critical analyses, the continued use of such
devices as the referential lemmata (cross-references) helped to preserve the original text from further corruption, since the commentary
would "fit" only a particular edition. Today, the New Variorum
Shakespeare prints the lineation of both the Globe edition and the
Norton Facsimile First Folio to ensure the same sort of "fit."

Another change in popular taste, reflecting the general decline in
interest in classical Greek authors, is the growth from the first century
A.D. of anthologies and abridged versions. It is likely that much was

lost in the process of making these selected editions, but what remained does not seem to have undergone severe corruption. Additional loss occurred when the old papyrus roll was gradually replaced by the parchment codex in the fourth and fifth centuries (see Chapter 2), for only the most popular works would be transferred to the new expensive medium. The *Bibliotheca* of Photius (ninth century) is one of the most significant of these abridgements. Compiled by the Patriarch of Constantinople at the request of his brother Tarasius, the work is an encyclopedic effort to summarize critical responses to 280 prose works read by Photius, and it provides much information about otherwise lost material. But like the *Suda*, an historical and literary lexical encyclopedia compiled at the end of the tenth century, the sloppily edited contents of the *Bibliotheca* testify to the severe decline in Greek textual scholarship. Not until the activities of Tzetzes and the Paleologi at Byzantium (see below) was there to be any genuine textual criticism of manuscripts in Greek.

In the Roman world, there was initially no Homer to stimulate early editorial work, and the first Latin scholars therefore tend to be grammarians and linguistic researchers rather than editors and textual scholars. Crates of Mallos is usually credited with provoking the Romans to this linguistic analysis, and the linguistic rather than textual bias meant that Latin scholarship was more typically involved with etymological, grammatical, or even orthographic research, than with textual analysis. Varro's *De lingua latina*, Nigidius Figulus's *Commentarii grammatici*, Verrius Flaccus's *De orthographia* and *De verborum significatu*, Quintilian's *Ars grammatica*—these works show the general direction of Latin scholarship. The founding of the Palatine Library in 28 B.C., the appointment of Julius Hyginus as librarian, and the appearance of Virgil as the Roman national poet, balanced this linguistic interest with a concern for textual matters. Hyginus produced a commentary on Virgil, and in the first century A.D. Asconius Pedianus wrote a similar commentary on Cicero's orations, and Valerius Probus began the careful editing of the earliest available manuscripts of Latin authors.

Lexicographical and grammatical studies continued in Aulus Gellius's *Noctes Atticæ* (second century), and the later Greek indulgence for abridgments and selections was paralleled by Solinus's epitome of Pliny, the *De mirabilibus mundi*, and by Nonius Marcellus's *De compendiosa doctrina*. The exegetical tradition can be represented by Servius Honoratus's commentary on Virgil, which is determinedly scholarly in that it omits any mere literary criticism, and by the extremely influential commentary on Cicero's *Somnium Scipionis* by Macrobius. Late Latin scholarship tends more and more to the encyclopedic rather than the textual, and can be represented by three works: the fifth-century *Nuptiæ Philologiæ et Mercurii* of Martianus Capella, a "liberal arts" pedagogical arrangement of ancient learning; the sixth-century *Institutiones grammaticæ* of Priscian, the most comprehensive work on Latin grammar; and the seventh-century *Etymologiæ* of St. Isidore of Seville, a compendium of all learning and pseudo-learning, which passed on to medieval Europe the classical educational system of the declining Roman world.

Biblical Textual Criticism

Isidore of Seville was a bishop (and later a saint) as well as a scholar, but his *Etymologiæ*, while finding a place for God and theology, is essentially a product of a pagan tradition of scholarship. For example, it reflects the pagan educational system in its organization, which is based on rhetoric rather than on theological principles (i.e., God does appear, but not at the beginning of the book, which is devoted to the liberal arts). In textual scholarship as in so much else, medieval Europe was influenced by both this pagan tradition *and* by its Hebreo-Christian equivalent. The special problem for textual critics of biblical studies was, of course, that in dealing with the word of God, they had to be especially careful in the employment of the tools of textual scholarship. The fundamentally esthetic (and therefore secular) principles of Zenodotus would be impossible in the biblical scholar, and this limitation may, in fact, have discouraged some of the more arbitrary excesses typical of secular textual critics of the eclectic or analogy schools, although there can be little doubt that it also inhibited the scholarship even of textual polemicists like Jerome. In fact, it was not until the growth of the Higher Criticism (see below) in the eighteenth and nineteenth centuries that biblical textual scholarship could safely approach its subject-matter without a doctrinal apologia.

The text of the Hebrew Bible (Old Testament) was established fairly securely in a version known as the Masoretic text, at some time between the sixth and eighth centuries A.D. The Masoretes, or preservers of the biblical text, were responsible for ensuring accuracy and consistency in the vocalization, accentuation, and word-division of the consonantal Hebrew text. But while textual emendation since the establishment by the Masoretes has been minimal, a comparison of the Masoretic version with the Septuagint (the Greek translation of the Old Testament produced for Alexandrian Jews in the second century B.C.) shows that there must have been considerable textual divergence at an earlier date. But since the textual tradition of the Septuagint, while it antedates the Masoretic "fixing," is by no means clear and unequivocal itself, the Greek translation cannot always be used with confidence in emending the Masoretic version. The Dead Sea Scrolls confirmed the textual ambiguity of the two traditions, and showed that while the Masoretes undoubtedly performed a very necessary task as purifiers of the Hebrew Bible, this purification was achieved at the sacrifice of a number of rival textual traditions: in a sense, the Masoretes created a *textus receptus* for the faithful, consistent and reliable, but not necessarily displaying the greatest degree of fidelity to textual history.

However, the textual variety of the Hebrew Bible pales before the documentary superabundance of the New Testament. Most important manuscripts of the New Testament date from the second to the tenth century. Containing the most "popular" book of the period (and a book which, unlike the Hebrew Bible was far from being fixed textually), the manuscripts of the New Testament were not only especially prone to the accidental errors introduced by the thousands of scribes laboring in the endless copying of exemplars, but were also subject to "determined variation," the conscious (and no doubt pious) desire of the scribe to harmonize the text with other biblical books and to clarify dubious passages. Furthermore, in a time of sectarian feuding, of voluminous patristic commentary, and of the important work of translation, it was inevitable that all three of these activities should further exacerbate the tendency toward textual dissolution, while paradoxically contributing to the authority of the text itself. Thus, the Latin and Syriac versions of the Greek, and the textual references of the early Fathers, demonstrate that the textual variants must have been even more ambiguous than the evidence of the extant manuscripts suggests today.

What was a biblical scholar to do with this embarrassment of riches, and how could the evidence of the witnesses be disentangled and evaluated? The way had already been shown to New Testament textual critics by the work of the Old Testament scholar Origen (d. 255), who drew up in his *Hexaplar*, a comparative Old Testament text in six columns (as the name suggests), containing the original Hebrew, the Hebrew transliterated into Greek, the two Greek versions of Aquila and Symmachus, the Septuagint, and the Septuagint revision by Theodotion. This monumental collation (it was not strictly speaking an edition), which took fourteen years to produce, was in principle to be the basis for most textual criticism of the Bible throughout the medieval period and into modern times, as when Erasmus produced a Greek text of the New Testament (with a parallel Latin version) based on a careful collation of as many manuscripts as were available to him, complemented by readings from patristic sources. In the late classical world, however, the mantle of Origen was assumed with greatest authority by Jerome who, despite his involvement in political and doctrinal squabbling, seems to have been able to bring a relatively objective scholarship to his work on the text of the Bible. He was always interested in textual matters. He visited the Nazarenes of Berœa to examine their claim to hold a supposed Hebrew gospel which was the source for Matthew. He became a devotee of Origen's exegetical and collational method of investigating different versions of a work. The loyalty to Origen's theology was not to last, but the acceptance of the scholarly method was permanent. At the order of Pope Damasus, he undertook the revision of the Old Latin versions of the Gospels, which had been criticized for betraying too much divergence and for being lacking in literary style. He compared the Old Latin versions with Greek texts, and tried as far as possible to preserve familiar usage while bringing the Latin into line with that branch of the Greek textual tradition now best represented by the Codex Sinaiticus in the British Library. His work on the Old Testament began with the Psalms, of which he was to make three versions, the second of which was based on the *Hexaplar* of Origen. It was only in the third version that he translated directly from the Hebrew instead of the Septuagint, and during the fifteen years of his residence at Bethlehem, he translated the entire Old Testament from the Hebrew.

Inevitably, the same forces which had led the Greek version of the New Testament to multiplicity and corruption caused Jerome's Vulgate to require continued revision by such medieval textual scholars as Alcuin, Theodulfus, and Lanfranc. But without a secure methodology, no medieval editor was able to produce anything but an eclectic text of the Vulgate, mixing various strains of textual tradition according to the doctrinal lights of a particular sensibility. The universality of Latin hindered any genuine collational effort, for polyglots like Jerome were rare in the medieval world of Latin Christendom. The only data readily available were the accumulations of text and textual commentary, both subject to scribal error. The eight thousand surviving Vulgate manuscripts testify to Jerome's success in making his translation the accepted version of the Bible for well over a millennium, but also to the inherent problems of the act of transmission in such a popular medium. The very centrality of the text of the New Testament in Latin Europe made the possibility of producing a reliable or consistent version of that text ever more difficult.

Early Medieval Textual Criticism

As noted in Chapter 2, it was in the monastic foundations that classical literature and the newer patristic and biblical commentaries were preserved in the early Middle Ages. What sort of textual criticism was practiced in such foundations? According to the theoretical rules of accuracy required in the scriptoria and according to the obvious authority and respect given to the word of God, one might suppose that a conservative fidelity was the norm, at least for scribe and scholar. But the evidence is ambiguous at best.

Take, for example, the career of perhaps the most highly praised of medieval textual scholars—Lupus of Ferrières (ca. 805–862). Working at first under Hrabanus Maurus at Fulda, he became determined to increase the holdings of Ferrières when he was transferred there in 836. He wrote to such centers as Tours, York, and Rome to arrange for the loan of manuscripts, especially of works which his library already possessed. His purpose was to employ the Alexandrian principle of collation (which, as we have seen, attempted to reconstruct a putative original form from the comparison of variant copies), and he both marked corruptions and recorded variants just as the Alexandrians had done. He seems to have been basically conservative, for he would leave a space where a textual *lacuna* (a break in the text) was suspected, rather than risk a conjectural emendation of his own. In annotating Cicero's *De inventione*, Livy, Macrobius, and Aulus Gellius, and in producing an edition of Cicero's *De oratore* himself, he testified to the importance of the scribal and editorial duties in the monastic foundation. He stood in the main line of the medieval editorial tradition, for his master Hrabanus had been taught by Alcuin of York, and he himself taught Remigius and Heiric, who went on to have distinguished independent careers, cast very much in the mold of their master. And yet, as E. J. Kenney remarks, "to apply terms such as 'philology' to what we know of the activities even of a scholar like Lupus of Ferrières verges on an abuse of language" (3). Without the paleographic skills of the later Maurists, without a textual theory by which to judge variants, without the philological researches of the post-humanists, the only commendable recourse was the scribal fidelity, mixed with editorial speculation, that Lupus endorsed. But the best this could achieve was a temporary freezing of determined variation—it could not prevent accidental variation, and was not to have much ultimate effect upon what appears to have been a conjecturalist norm elsewhere.

The history of this norm in medieval Europe can be briefly summarized. The easy tolerance for pagan classics of a man like Isidore was, during the centuries of the Moslem encroachment upon the faded remnants of the old Roman empire, undermined by the reticence of monastic centers to undertake the active preservation and restoration of classical texts, preferring rather to erase a pagan work from a manuscript and literally superscribe a Christian one to produce a palimpsest (see Chapter 2). The *De republica* of Cicero exists only in such a palimpsest. From the copying of pagan works in the sixth century, for example, there survive only two small fragments of Juvenal, and a few pieces by the two Plinys; from the seventh century, only a fragment of Lucan; and from the eighth century, there is nothing. Bede's knowledge of the classics (perhaps via Isidore and Macrobius), and Alcuin's references to such authors as Virgil, Lucan, Pliny, and Statius in his praise of York's library were, for the time, particularly unusual.

Through the Caroline reform of handwriting and the Cluniac monastic movement, there was from the ninth century an increased attention paid to the theoretically "accurate" copying of both pagan and Christian literature. Some of the important figures are the Corbie librarian Hadoard and his work on Cicero, Sallust, the Plinys, Cæsar, Martial, Terence, and others; Sedulus Scottus of Liège, the compiler of a *Collectaneum* of excerpts intended to illustrate important rhetorical styles; Walafrid Strabo and his scrap-book compiled at St. Gall in 878; Lupus of Ferrières; Theodulfus, Abbot of Fleury and his edition of the Vulgate in the mid-ninth century (using marginal sigla to distinguish the sources of variants); Abbot Desiderius, who presided over the revival of Monte Cassino in the eleventh century and produced unique manuscripts in the Beneventan style (see Chapter 5) of, for example, *The Golden Ass* of Apuleius, Varro's *De lingua latina*, and Seneca's *Dialogues*. The new commercial book-scripts, and the commercial scriptoria in which they were produced, while hardly helping the textual purity of the works involved, did at least break the ecclesiastical monopoly on copying and therefore led indirectly to the humanist revival, with its attention to the *studia humanitatis* (grammar, rhetoric, history, poetry, and moral philosophy) and so ultimately to the philological investigations that were necessary to the successful editing of both Christian and pagan literature.

Late Medieval and Renaissance

The wide reading and the search for lost texts exemplified by a man like the "pre-humanist" Lovato Lovati (1241–1309) were an indication of the direction textual work was taking. Lovato knew Catullus, Propertius, Tibullus, and Lucretius long before these authors were "discovered" by Petrarch, Poggio, and Salutati. And it similarly was both a wide and a close reading of the text which, for example, enabled Giovanni de Matociis (fl. 1306–20) to make the first successful textual distinction between the two Plinys, and which allowed Geremia da Montagnore (ca. 1255–1321), while a compiler of a typical medieval florilegium (*Compendium moralium notabilium*), to uncover Seneca's tragedies for the later humanists proper. These considerations aside, there can be no doubt that when Petrarch (1304–74) created his own version of Livy, corrected and annotated from the fragments that had been all that the medieval scholar had been able to read of the great historian, he was attempting something different in kind from either the comparative reticence of Lupus or the enthusiastic conjectures of the typical scribe. In recording the variants of Livy in a separate note-book, in making use of the papal court at Avignon as a central repository for manuscripts from all over Europe, in discovering a copy of Cicero's *Letters to Atticus* in the Chapter Library of Verona in 1345, in mentioning no medieval works in his list of his favorite authors copied on the flyleaf of a manuscript—in all this work of discovery, enumeration, collation, and emendation, Petrarch was pushing textual criticism towards the philological and humanist bias of the new Renaissance Europe.

Boccaccio was a similarly devoted hunter for manuscripts, probably having access to Monte Cassino and bringing back to Florence a number of important Beneventan manuscripts (including one of Varro). He was perhaps less careful in making copies than Petrarch, but balanced this by an interest in publishing the lesser-known classical poets, including Martial and Ausonius. Coluccio Salutati (1331–1406) not only plundered the East for Greek manuscripts, he was lucky at home, too. While looking for a Cicero *Atticus*, his agent

Pasquino Capelli accidentally turned up a manuscript of the *Ad famil-iares* in the Cathedral Library at Vercelli. But he did not just bring manuscripts to Florence, he brought scholars. Through his invitation to Manuel Chrysoloras, Greek began to be studied seriously in West-ern Europe once more. And finally, continuing the Alexandrian tradi-tion, he was a determined manuscript collator, bringing together many copies of the same work in an effort to see how corruptions had oc-curred.

Poggio Bracciolini (1380-1459) has, like Petrarch, Boccaccio, and Salutati, already been encountered as a manuscript collector (see Chapter 2). As papal secretary, he traveled widely throughout Eu-rope—to Konstanz, Cluny, St. Gall, Cologne—and everywhere he sought ancient manuscripts of classical authors (Cicero, Quintilian, Valerius Flaccus, Lucretius, Manilius, Ammianus Marcellinus) to provide the raw materials for editing by others. His contribution to textual scholarship is therefore primarily as a bibliophile and book collector (all entertainingly set down in his letters to his patrons and fellow-bibliophiles), but, as the inventor of one of the new humanist scripts (see Chapter 5), he gave the copying of manuscripts a new tool in the clarity and legibility of scribal reform.

With the materials at hand, the serious editing could begin. And the first major humanist editor is Lorenzo Valla (1407-57), who, educated in Latin and Greek by Aurispa and Bruni and holder of the chair in rhetoric at Rome from 1450, brought a new philological in-dependence of mind to the study of both classical and Christian doc-uments. His specialty was the exposure of forgery and stupidity. He successfully criticized the *Donation of Constantine* (on linguistic and historical grounds) as an eighth- or ninth-century forgery, thereby depriving the popes of the documentary basis for their claim to tem-poral political power, since the Roman church had always cited the *Donation* as proof that the Emperor Constantine had deeded secular as well as spiritual authority to the Papacy. He correctly described the supposed correspondence of Seneca and St. Paul as a forgery; he at-tacked the scholarship of the court of Alfonso in his *Emendationes sex librorum Titi Livi*; and, using both Greek and patristic texts, began to emend the Vulgate on philological principles in an edition (the *Adno-tationes in Novum Testamentum*) printed by Erasmus in 1505.

It was Politian (Angelo Poliziano, 1454-94) however, who can be credited with the first inklings of a genealogical theory of manuscript affiliation. He showed that the *P* manuscript of Cicero's *Epistolæ ad familiares* was a copy of the *M* and that *P* was the parent of other extant manuscripts. His theory that all late manuscripts must ultimately derive from and be less authoritative than older ones was no doubt too unyielding a position (based on his disdain for humanist copying), but he articulated for the first time the principle that conjectural emendation can only begin from the earliest recoverable stage of transmission (the so-called O'—O prime, or archetype of later textual criticism).

This principle, and its corollary of the *eliminatio codicum descriptorum* (the uselessness as primary textual authority of derived copies where their exemplars are still extant) are two of the most basic arguments in the development of the genealogical, or stemmatic, system of analysis—although some recent classicists (e.g., Timpanaro "Stemmatic Method" and Reeve "Eliminatio") have questioned the value of the *eliminatio*, Timpanaro suggesting the adoption of *eliminatio codicum inutilium* ("useless") in place of *descriptorum* (187), and Reeve going further, providing "proof that establishing the exclusive derivation of one manuscript from another is not merely difficult but impossible" (1). Such conclusions would confirm Willis's view that the medieval (and late classical) tradition of copying the classics is characterized by conflation and contamination, not direct linear descent, but the axiom propounded by Maas in his defense of Lachmannian stemmatics ("If a witness, J, presents all the errors of another witness extant, F, and at least one of its own besides, then J must derive from F" §8a) has in general been widely accepted as a necessary means of sorting good (or independent) witnesses from bad.

The healthy textual skepticism and rigor of Valla and Politian was continued when Erasmus (ca. 1466–1536) produced an extremely influential (if somewhat controversial) edition of the New Testament in 1516, based upon earlier research on the text of the Bible, and particularly on his reading, in 1504, of the Valla *Adnotationes* on the New Testament. Valla had found the textual tradition of the Vulgate guilty of subjective eclecticism and had advocated a strictly philological approach to biblical textual criticism. Erasmus was impressed by these arguments (so much so that, as mentioned earlier, he published an edition of the *Adnotationes* in 1505), and began collecting manuscripts of the Greek New Testament and making copies therefrom. After the usual peripatetic and polemical interruptions characteristic of his career, he produced his edition of the Greek eleven years later, with the philological assistance of other scholars. The new text, despite inaccuracies zealously pointed out by political and scholarly enemies, generally found favor with such contemporaries as Luther, Vadianus of St. Gall, A. Karlstadt at Wittenberg, and Thomas Bilney and Robert Barnes at Cambridge. It was probably the prefaces which caused the greatest excitement.

In these prefaces Erasmus launched his famous plea for translations into every tongue, and it is here that he explained the new philological method of textual criticism, an appeal to scholarly objectivity after the whimsical or doctrinal editing of earlier centuries. To Erasmus, the Bible as a text could be treated in the same way as any other work, and although his knowledge and experience of paleography was not great and his understanding of genealogical affiliation not as developed as Politian's, it was his ideological position that texts—religious or otherwise—should be studied by scholars in the original language and edited according to philological rather than theological principles which gave respectability to the later efforts of such textuists as Scaliger, Bentley, and Lachmann.

His actual editorial work was inconsistent, for although he knew his codex B to be very old, he employed it only occasionally for collation, and actually made his own Greek translation from the Vulgate where he felt the original Greek to be too corrupt for emendation. Finally, he was unable to articulate his unease over the readings found in a forged Greek manuscript (readings which tended to reinforce later Church doctrines over those found in the original Greek) because he had no way to test the authenticity of this forgery. In other words, he was a better advocate for humanistic/philological editing than a textual critic, for he lacked the technical skills to defend positions which he sensed to be right.

In what sense was Renaissance textual scholarship of the type practiced by Erasmus and Valla different from medieval? According to the famous oration of the philosopher Ramus in 1546, not only had contemporary learning overcome the Scholastics' dependence on Aristotle, but all of the major classical authors were now being read in good editions instead of in the inherently corrupt medieval compilations. The problem with Ramus's argument is that while there was no doubt a desire to purify the text from its medieval accretions and indiscretions, most of these new Latin editions were based on manuscripts which had themselves been copied by medieval scribes. Furthermore, there was no theory of textual criticism which could adequately distinguish a good manuscript from a bad one, nor was there to be until the Maurists' work on paleography and the Lachmannian genealogical method created the first thorough-going technical system for evaluating scribal hands and textual transmission. The most that could be done was either to use a modified version of the Origen *Hex-*

aplar: i.e., to accumulate as much documentary evidence as possible and then to make eclectic decisions based upon a sense of the "rightness" of each reading—Alexandrian analogy—or to select a copy-text which seemed complete, consistent, and of good provenance, and to reproduce it faithfully (Pergamanian anomaly).

The collecting of Latin and Greek manuscripts (many in private libraries) would certainly assist both of these methods, as would the sheer proliferation of manuscripts from a desire for ownership that was as much acquisitive as it was scholarly. The increased availability of witnesses, coupled with the breaking of the Church's textual hegemony, made the practice of textual scholarship easier in the Renaissance than in the Middle Ages; and a growing sense of historical evolution, compounded by the Renaissance self-awareness as a deliberately "modern" period after the apparent sterility of the medieval mind and society, helped promote the various nascent philological disciplines (paleography, linguistics, etc.). But none of these disciplines acquired a developed methodology during the Renaissance, and all therefore depended ultimately on the personal predilections and skills of the editor. Manuscripts did indeed become more available, but the competence to deal with them was still wanting.

The Eastern Empire

It used to be thought that it was the fall of Constantinople to the Turks in 1453 which drove Greek manuscripts to the West and therefore initiated the revival of classical learning, of which textual criticism was a part. However, there is ample evidence that Italian humanists ("entrepreneurs" is almost the better word) had despoiled the archives of the decaying Eastern Empire of the Byzantines long before. Textual criticism and the preservation of the classical texts in the East had long been in decline. However, there are some important names to be mentioned. In the eleventh century, for example, there was an awakened interest in classical texts following the lectures of Michael Psellus (1018–78) on Plato and Aristotle; and while she did not give lectures, but rather lived a completely secluded life, Anna Commena similarly promoted textual study of the classics.

But it was Eustathius, Abbot of Thessalonica (ca. 1160–92), who began the serious revival of textual methodology in the East. He collated various texts of Sophocles' *Antigone* in the Alexandrian manner and produced a huge variorum commentary on Homer, in which the

discussion of the first line of the *Iliad* took some ten pages. John
Tzetzes (ca. 1110–80), with his commentaries on Aristophanes, Hesiod, and Homer, based on immense reading of primary and secondary
documents, was the last major figure of Byzantine textual scholarship
to have the advantage of the Constantinople libraries, for, in 1204,
the Fourth Crusade arrived in the Eastern capital and probably destroyed more manuscripts than did the Turkish reduction of the city
two centuries later. The later work of, for example, Maximus Planudes (ca. 1255–1305), Demetrius Triclinus (fl. 1305–20), and the
Paleologi (important for the revised *Greek Anthology*, including materials not found in the tenth-century *Palatine Anthology*) takes place in
an atmosphere of decline. Planudes is important, but ironically he
was most widely read not in Greek but in Latin, and his and Triclinus's search for early Greek literary texts—especially Plutarch—demonstrates an admirable bibliographical principle (the importance of
charting the history of transmission) but also reflects the same sense
of discontinuum which motivated the Latin humanists to begin assembling the "lost" works of their classical heritage. Planudes' complaints about the shortage of parchment are perhaps symptomatic of
the same decline.

With Planudes stands Triclinus: neither can be counted as particularly reliable editors, for Planudes simply replaced apparently corrupt
lines with his own verses when he felt the text to be intractable, and
Triclinus was a confirmed normalizer, emending metrics to produce
ideal, regular forms, but at least provided the Western world with the
text of nine otherwise unknown plays by Euripides. Without this last
stand of Byzantine scholarship, without the anthologizers, the epitomizers, and the commentators, the losses to Greek literature would
certainly have been much greater, and while the standards of editing
had declined since the great days of the Alexandrians, Constantinople
and the last Byzantine scholars proved an immensely useful reservoir
for the stimulation and continuance of textual criticism in the Latin
West.

It was this reservoir which Salutati hoped to use when, as Chancellor of the Florentine *signoria*, he specifically instructed his envoy
Jacopo Angelo in 1398 to look in Constantinople for Greek manuscripts of Homer, Plato, and Plutarch. Twenty years later, Giovanni
Aurispa came back with 238 literary manuscripts, and there are many
other similar stories. Theoretically, it was possible to argue that any
edition based on a Greek manuscript thus retrieved would be superior
to a medieval Latin translation of an Arabic version of the same origi-

nal (it was, of course, in this latter condition that the works of Aristotle were first known in the West, until William of Moerbeke began translations into Latin directly from the Greek). But, as the discussion of the Septuagint has shown, such textual assumptions cannot always be defended. In fact, since the early function of these Greek manuscripts was merely to serve as the bases for Latin translations (as in the case of Moerbeke's Aristotle), the question is moot. Even when the Greek texts were used in their own right, it would be a mistake to think of these editions as critical by modern standards. Either they were exponents of a simple "best-text" theory without the rationale or the technical requirements for best-text selection, or they were idiosyncratic and eclectic editions exemplifying the editor's esthetic disposition as much as the author's. The great achievement of the Aldine press in the late fifteenth and early sixteenth centuries was not in producing scholarly editions (though many of these texts were prepared by the most eminent humanists of the time), but in making the Greek and Latin classics available to the new audience of "conoscenti" and "dilettanti" in a cheap, easily portable form—largely through the brilliant use of Griffo's italic font (see Chapter 6).

The Rise of Philology

The achievements of the early Renaissance (e.g., of Erasmus in biblical textual criticism) are more than matched by the first great secular scholars of the modern period—the two Scaligers. The elder, Julius Cæsar Scaliger (1484–1556) is important to this survey primarily for his *De causis linguæ latinæ* of 1540, an analysis of the theory of Latin grammar. But the elder Scaliger was not primarily a textual critic, and his concern was not to produce through critical method an authoritative version of an ancient work, but rather to criticize the content, style, and philosophy of the work itself. His *Poetice*, published posthumously in 1561 was, therefore, justifiably his most popular book, for its focus is on literary criticism, conducted, however, with a strong underpinning of rhetorical theory and philological analysis. Rather, it was his tenth son, Joseph Justus Scaliger (1540–1609), who can be regarded as the founder of modern textual criticism. His greatest single achievement was his work on Manilius's *Astronomica*, published in two editions of 1579 and 1600. These two editions (a third, enlarged and corrected from Scaliger's notes, was published in 1655), can be seen as epitomizing the difference between the subjective eclecticism of earlier editors and the more conservative methodology of the new. As A. E. Housman noted, when the first edition appeared there was no good Manilius manuscript available, and consequently "the transformation which first made Manilius a legible author was the work of Scaliger's own unaided wits." But by 1600, the Gemblacensis collation was available, and the conjectures could now be confirmed or rejected according to more strictly bibliographical standards. If we are to accept Housman's judgment on the results, "no critic has ever effected so great and permanent a change in any author's text as Scaliger in Manilius" (23). Scaliger had that rare gift of a combination of good taste and immense learning, qualities all editors should possess.

From Scaliger on, the history of textual criticism can be seen to follow two apparently mutually exclusive directions. The first (predominating in the early modern period, from the seventeenth to the mid-nineteenth centuries) is to place the study of the text and the editorial restoration of authorial intentions within the broad discipline of philology, where textual criticism may often be regarded as the summit of philological work, but where it is very clearly only one aspect of a general scholarly enterprise, the restoration of the past under the auspices of *Altertumswissenschaft*, the science of ancient times. The second movement (predominating from the late nineteenth century to the present day) is to bring an increasingly specialized (and often increasingly technical) competence to the discipline of textual criticism, in fact to regard editing as partly dependent on the application of discoverable and verifiable scientific principles, which may be used to balance, or even lessen, the role of individual criticism in the construction and reconstruction of texts—with unfortunate results for the practice of this criticism. The division I have drawn between the two tendencies is somewhat simplified, for there were scholars in the earlier period whose interest was almost entirely in textual matters and who brought a technical rigor to the practice of textual criticism (Lachmann in his classical editing might fit this description). And, in the twentieth century, there have been editors who have brought a belletristic rather than a technical disposition to the tasks of textual criticism, and who have resisted the encroachments of "science" upon a tradition which (as already seen) has been as much dependent upon subjective inspiration as it has upon hard bibliographical data. But in general, the division holds.

The old dispensation of *Altertumswissenschaft* (towards which the increasingly systematic methods of the early German and English philologists were moving) finally could not sustain itself as an organized body of authority once its linguistic core, its critical medium, and its editorial practices had been attacked respectively by structuralist and transformational linguistics, New Criticism and post-structuralist literary theory, and the technical demands of analytical and textual bibliography. Thus, in the first category, language, the linguistic *donnée* of philology and *Altertumswissenschaft* was that the proper study of language is in the form of historical linguistics, the arrangement of linguistic characteristics along a linear path of predictable development through such features as sound changes: such *diachronic* assumptions of the old philology were challenged by Saussure's concentration on the *synchronic* structure of a given language, its system of current syntactic coherence rather than on its historical development, and later by Chomsky's transformational grammar, an attempted analysis of the "deep structure" of grammatical relationships supposedly common to all languages, a further repudiation of the diachronic bias of the historical linguistics of traditional philology.

And in the second category, that of critical medium, the various branches of historical criticism, concerned with the reconstruction of moments in the past and an exposure of their *alterity* or "otherness" (again dependent on a faith in predictable historical development and the mapping of this development along linear paths) were challenged first by the anti-historical bias of New Criticism, in its attempt to isolate the complexity of textual utterance from such extraneous features as author, audience, and cultural context, and later by the post-structuralist dictum that all writing (*écriture*) is "always already written," a weaving of intertextual associations seemingly denying any place for the individual authorial consciousness.

Finally, in the third category, of editorial method, the eclectic *divinatio*, or "divining" of the truth of a reading through an inspired self-identification with one's author (a method associated both with consciously belletristic editing and perhaps unexpectedly with the technically more rigorous Lachmannian system of genealogy) had to confront the new emphasis on bibliography as part of the history of technology, a view promoted by the late nineteenth- and early twentieth-century research of the analytical and descriptive bibliographers, particularly in the Anglo-American school of Pollard, Greg, and then Bowers.

As I argue at the conclusion of this chapter, the textual practitioners of the old philology and its heirs in the twentieth century need not have regarded these three-fold assaults as inimical to the business of textual scholarship and editing. I have, for example, claimed that even deconstruction and traditional textual criticism have much in common ("[Textual]"); and the technical bias of analytical bibliography, while regarded with some suspicion by more humanistic textuists like James Thorpe, could, if used in a sophisticated manner, be illuminating rather than deadening to the practice of criticism, as I hope is shown in Chapter 7, on textual bibliography. But there can be no doubt that the battle lines have been drawn around these causes (and their differences), so that when Tanselle declares in his *Rationale of Textual Criticism* that "this activity [the "questioning of surviving texts"] is necessarily a historical enterprise" (69), he is consciously aligning himself with the tradition of *Altertumswissenschaft* against the non-textual critics, those "[P]ersons not interested in taking any of the historical approaches to literature" (70).

The terms of this debate are more characteristic of the twentieth century than they are of the late Renaissance, but the seeds of the dissension are already present in the earlier period, for it is through the determined adoption of the virtues of historicity as against mere human conjecture that the philological movement (especially in Germany) became impatient with the sort of intuitive guesswork characteristic of Erasmus and leaned ever more on the historical "proof" of systems like recension and stemmatics, so much so that Housman's corrective was to accuse the German inheritors of Lachmann's ideas with having mistaken textual criticism for mathematics. "A textual critic engaged upon his business is not at all like Newton investigating the motions of the planets: he is much more like a dog hunting for fleas. If a dog hunted for fleas on mathematical principles, basing his researches on statistics of area and population, he would never catch a flea except by accident. They require to be treated as individuals; and every problem which presents itself to the textual critic must be regarded as possibly unique" (*Selected Prose*: 132–33).

This type of increased technical specialization of the textual critic has been paralleled by a concentration of editorial activity within one field—indeed by the replacement of the textual dilettante or amateur by the editing professional. As already shown, the textual work of Julius Cæsar Scaliger was in practice ancillary to his other literary interests, and even a rigorous classical textuist like Bentley was tempted to stray (with horrifying results in his edition of Milton) outside his specialized classical field. Similarly, while Johnson brought a wide scholarly training to his editing of Shakespeare, this edition was only one of a number of scholarly enterprises during his life.

Lachmann too, famous for his editing of Lucretius as well as for his codification of the stemmatic method for the textual analysis of classical works, also ventured into the vernacular (with, for example, his edition of the *Nibelungenlied*), and used an entirely different text-critical method for this vernacular project.

In the late twentieth century, however, it is now common to discover that a scholarly edition will have its several elements divided piecemeal among scholars displaying different technical training. There may be a textual editor to provide an authoritative text, an annotations editor to write the historical notes, a glossarist, an indexer, and so on. This is another manifestation of the specialization which has driven textual scholars into disciplinary enclaves from which they no longer speak either to each other or to scholars involved in nontextual activities. Finally, the wide range (by period) of the Bentleys and Lachmanns has been replaced by a concentration on a specific area. There have been some modern textual critics (Fredson Bowers is a prime example, with editions in five centuries, from Marlowe to Nabokov) who have produced editions in several different periods; there have even been scholars (Vinton Dearing, for example, in his work on Dryden and on the New Testament) who have done textual work in apparently unrelated fields. But these are the exceptions, and it is in part to propose a remedy for this situation that this book has been written.

In the account of the textual criticism of the modern period which follows, it is obviously impossible to do appropriate justice to every textual theorist or editor of the last four hundred years whose work has had an effect upon the development or the current status of textual criticism. All we can do is to use selected figures as a means of organizing the major issues which have been debated since the Renaissance. Everybody will get short shrift, but the outline of the problems which the textuists attended to will provide a necessary background to the practical questions of editing to be taken up in the next chapter.

Thus, the career of Nicolaus Heinsius (1620–81) exemplifies well the gradual loosening of the hold of both the *textus receptus* and the humanists' highly selective collation methods upon textual theory. As Kenney points out, the procedure for collation which Heinsius inherited was that "readings were recorded when they seemed to coincide with the critic's idea of what constituted an improvement, passed over in silence otherwise" (59–60). This highly subjective distinction between "good" and "bad" readings also failed to perceive that an authoritative reading might be carried by an otherwise unauthoritative witness. It was scholars like Heinsius who overcame this prejudice and who therefore turned collation into a much wider-ranging and more comprehensive practice than it had been formerly. No doubt his appointment as traveling acquisitions librarian for Queen Christina of Sweden helped him to develop this position.

Discrimination between potentially good and bad authorities is, of course, one of the major skills that a textual scholar must acquire, and (as suggested earlier), it was greatly assisted by the Maurists' investigation of diplomatics (the handwriting of official state documents), whereby the various scripts—and even the specific hands—of a manuscript could be placed on an historical continuum. In the early modern period, the major figures associated with such discriminations are Mabillon and Montfaucon, whose work on identifying forgeries gradually began to turn the practice of diplomatics into the critical attitudes of paleography: that is, a competence in accurate transcription of ancient documents led the way for a critical evaluation of the scripts themselves. In a sense, therefore, the paleographic work of the Maurists may almost be seen as the first genuinely philological (i.e. historical) discipline, for it created a secure technical basis for a branch of historical research long before historical linguistics had realized that languages could also be arranged on this linear pattern and even before the genealogy of texts themselves had been fully articulated as an analytical system. The early paleographers made mistakes (some of them famous ones), but they did at least initiate the philological approach which was to be the prevailing scholarly attitude for the next two centuries.

There are, to be sure, some notable exceptions to this general tendency towards technical proficiency and historical methodology, and it would be a misrepresentation of critical history to maintain that a philological procedure can be seen developing consistently from the seventeenth to the nineteenth centuries. Even a generally reliable, and historically persuasive, textual critic like Richard Bentley could swerve violently away from the practices he had adopted elsewhere (in the editing of classical texts) when he came to work on the vernacular. Bentley's notorious invention of the corrupting Milton "amanuensis" has brought him into disrepute among vernacular textual critics, but his *Paradise Lost* edition is not typical of his career at large. It is the Milton, however, which is most interesting to the critic of English literature, textual or literary. By postulating an amanuensis who had—perhaps deliberately—misrepresented what Milton dictated,

Bentley was able to indulge in a level of conjecture that he would never have endorsed in his classical work. The theory was that since Milton was blind he could not correct the amanuensis's errors (in fact, that he did not even know what the amanuensis had written), so that the textual critic now had to take up the poet's mantle and restore his text to a more "Miltonic" condition, in a development of the Alexandrian system of analogy at its most extreme.

Bentley's vernacular experiment is not atypical of the prevailing attitude to vernacular texts in his period, however. It is perhaps ironic, for example, that the eighteenth century's most famous textual emendation to the text of Shakespeare is Theobald's conjectural "a' babbled o' green fields" ("he babbled of green fields," in Mistress Quickly's account of the death of Falstaff in *Henry V*) in place of the apparently nonsensical "a *table* of green fields;" for Theobald was, for the period, a somewhat conservative critic, and certainly more so than his fellow-editor of Shakespeare, Alexander Pope, who unfairly made Theobald the hero of one version of his satirical *Dunciad*. Theobald's emendation has gained currency, especially in performed versions of the text, in a perfect exemplification of the growth of the authority of a *textus receptus*, for it has no documentary support and yet satisfies the editor's (and reader's) demands that the text should "make sense." It is, therefore, at this basic semantic level, an emendation that "improves" the text, and such an "improvement," while perhaps not as characteristic of Theobald as it was of Pope, who smoothed out the rough verse and imagery of Shakespeare, is virtually the norm in most vernacular scholarly editing before Johnson.

The fact that *King Lear* could be performed for a hundred years and more with a happy ending in which Cordelia survives (as does Lear himself) to marry Edgar is not directly a textual problem (for the real ending of *Lear* was still preserved in contemporary editions), but it is certainly an indication of the general indifference about authorial intention and of the assumption that Shakespeare, Chaucer, and other "natural" poets could greatly benefit from such improvement. Johnson was the first editor of Shakespeare to return the phrase "hugger-mugger" to its place in the text of *Hamlet*, for it had been banished by the neo-classical textual critics on the grounds of its bad taste.

As Donald H. Reiman's recent survey of the editing of the texts of the Romantics has effectively shown ("Four Ages"), this rather patronizing attitude toward the improvement of unlettered poets prevails even in the nineteenth century, when the textual criticism of both classical and biblical texts had long since accepted the very different dis-

pensation of Higher Criticism and Lower Criticism and modern philology, whereby the historical imagination and technical rigor of the
biblical and classical editor was to be observed in the supposedly objective treatment of the sacred texts of Western culture as essentially
secular objects, and thus susceptible to the vicissitudes of transmission
and not therefore to be easily returned to a pristine state by conscious
"improvement." But, as Reiman reminds us, such editors as W. M.
Rossetti, in his corrections of Shelley's apparent anomalous texts,
were merely carrying out a refinement which was necessitated by the
critical attitude (of, e.g., Matthew Arnold) that the Romantics did not
"know enough." Such an attitude is clearly going to promote a textual practice in the editing of vernacular texts which parallels the earlier
textual treatment of classical texts: a desire for uniformity and polish
over roughness and idiosyncrasy, and a consequent elevation of the
textual critic to the position of virtual co-author in the attainment of a
refined text purged of both historical accretions and of improprieties
in the composer.

   Until the philological bent of men like F. J. Furnivall and his various creations (e.g., the Early English Text Society) had affirmed
vernacular textual criticism as an essentially historical activity, it was
inevitable that undocumented (and undefended) conjecture should be
the prevailing practice in the editing of vernacular texts. In a recent
study ("Logic"), Lee Patterson has convincingly shown that this suspicion of mere documents is a direct growth from the Romantic and
post-Romantic rejection of the historical document in favor of the
"transcendent meaning" to which the document (even an authorial
holograph) is merely a witness. As Patterson points out, this strange
discrepancy between the nineteenth-century philology of classical editing and the "Romantic" editing of vernacular literature is perfectly
exemplified in the career of Lachmann himself, for his famous Lucretius edition is completely circumscribed by fidelity to a document (in
this case the reconstructed archetype, whose physical features Lachmann claimed to be able to delineate perfectly from the imposition of
his system of charting genealogical filiation, even to the extent of determining the exact positioning of text on the folios of this non-extant
manuscript). Beyond the archetype Lachmann would not go, and this
reticence is shown visually in his disciple Maas, who charts the various relationships that the Lachmann system can demonstrate in lower
levels of the transmission of texts, but above the archetype provides
only a speculative series of undetermined stages reaching back to the
unresolvable features of the author's fair copy, forever beyond the

grasp of the Lachmannian textual critic.

But Lachmann's *Nibelungenlied* was, according to Patterson, a testament to a "quest for origins that were by definition incapable of documentation" (83). The use of the technical discipline of stemmatics could (ironically) have enabled Lachmann to reconstruct one of the poem's two hyparchetypes (the common ancestors of "branches" of the family tree of manuscripts, at one level below the authority of the archetype itself), but as a vernacular Romantic editor he was operating under a different aegis and in the case of the national German epic preferred to reject the provable documentary compromise of the hyparchetype in favor of the unprovable but more emotionally and ethnically satisfying attractions of the distant Ur-text.

As already suggested, the gap between vernacular editing and classical is made even more apparent by considering that it was in the same early and mid-nineteenth century that the textual critics of the Bible (and particularly of the Old Testament) had, like their colleagues in classical studies, finally broken with the "quest for origins" and had learned to settle for a text that would derive its authority from a diligent linguistic and historical analysis of the extant documents rather than from an inspired leap beyond archetype or inferred manuscript. This position was best exemplified in Eichhorn's *Introduction to the Old Testament* (1780–83), and its immediate result is the realization that the Old Testament is, as a text, no different from any other which has been copied and recopied and whose original features (if there ever were any) are now irrecoverable (see Patterson 76–77).

The textual criticism of Eichhorn and his followers is therefore to be distinguished from the unquestioning acceptance of religious texts by commentators, exegetes, and critical interpreters who very much take their text "on faith." This secularization of biblical criticism became the norm for biblical textual work from the mid-nineteenth century on and can even be observed in the textual editing of a "popular" (although quite scholarly) edition of today—the *Anchor Bible*. For example, having established through a close study of the text and transmission of Revelation that the author was John the Baptist and that parts of the book (including its first three chapters) were a later "Christian" addition, the Anchor editor J. Massyngberde Ford reorders the text so that it now begins with the traditional chapter four (and with the rather nonsensical words, "After these things, I looked . . ."). The textual proof in this case renders the received, sacred text curiously fragmentary and esthetically unsatisfying, but so great is the confidence in linguistic and historical demonstration, that protecting the very integrity of the text becomes less important than proudly displaying its corruptions as a document.

This influence of the late results of secular criticism in a popular study shows that the *textus receptus* as an authority has indeed retreated in biblical textual criticism, and compares rather ironically with the unexpected opposite phenomenon in some twentieth-century editing of Shakespeare. For example, while the Oxford Shakespeare accepts the "versioning" implications of the fragmentation of *King Lear* into two different plays, and presents them as two separately edited texts, such implications are shied away from in other Shakespearean editing, for example J. Dover Wilson's New Cambridge edition of *Love's Labour's Lost*, despite the weight of bibliographical evidence that Wilson himself brings to the textual argument. He produces an elaborate analytical bibliographical demonstration (resting upon the measuring of lines in the putative authorial manuscript, and on the typical proofing methods of the time) that a section of dialogue in the play was in fact intended for excision by Shakespeare, but that the printer failed to heed the author's wishes (116–24). But such evidence notwithstanding, the pull of the *textus receptus*, and (one assumes) the presence of a bardolatrous inability to jettison anything that Shakespeare wrote, results in Wilson's retaining the canceled passage in his edition, countermanding his own proof (22). In this case, unlike the Ford edition of Revelation, the sacred text exerts its own power and maintains its esthetic integrity in the face of mere technical demonstration.

Meanwhile, back in the late eighteenth century, biblical criticism's rejection of a search for an "original" version was paralleled by a similar development in classical studies, when F. A. Wolf published his *Prolegomena ad Homerum* in 1795 and ruefully reported that the original text of Homer was (like that of the Old Testament) irrecoverable, no matter how much polishing and "improving" the textual critic lavished on the extant documents. It seems, therefore, that the confidence that the early philological discoveries of the proponents of *Altertumswissenschaft* had encouraged was now yielding to a more realistic sense of the possible rather than the ideal. (The same process, from great enthusiasm for new technological weapons to a realization that the "definitive" text is an illusion, has also characterized the late-twentieth-century employment of analytical bibliography, which began as a panacea for textual ills and gradually became just one more weapon in the textual critic's armory.) The Lachmannian system, with its clearly defined methods and its clearly limited objectives (the resuscitation of the archetype, but not the author's fair copy) was soon to reinforce this sense of limited, but achievable, editorial aims, and (at least in Germany) ossified into an orthodoxy that enshrined a conservative devotion to technical procedure over enlightened conjecture. Lachmann's great contribution to textual theory was not the *stemma codicum* (the family-tree of extant manuscripts and "inferred"—but lost—witnesses), for he never constructed one, not even for his famous Lucretius. Rather it was the theoretical separation of the two stages of approaching the text: first, *recensio* (recension) or the charting of variants (which can then translate into "true" readings and "errors"); and second, *emendatio* (emendation, often having to resort to a third stage, *divinatio*, divination), or the rectification of such error—all with the end of reconstructing the physical features of a witness that the editor does not have access to (the archetype).

The Twentieth Century

As later critics like Housman, Bédier, Pasquali, Kane, Donaldson, and others were to point out (particularly in the latter two's disdain for the false securities of recension in highly corrupt transmissions), the Lachmann genealogical arrangement of witnesses does have certain logical weaknesses and does perhaps encourage a timidity on the part of the editor. For example, the recognition of the direction that a variant moves along (from exemplar to copy and from error to correction or from correct to corrupt reading) of necessity assumes that one can easily tell which is the "error" and which the genuine reading. The problem is that this evidence (employed to determine which are "good" manuscripts and which "bad") is then used to disallow readings from the "bad" manuscripts and to welcome those from the "good," in a perfect exemplification of circular reasoning. As Housman put it, in his general disdain for the insipid logic to which late Lachmannism had fallen: "To believe that wherever a best MS. gives possible readings it gives true readings, is to believe that an incompetent editor is the darling of Providence, which has given its angels charge over him lest his sloth and folly should produce their natural results and incur their appropriate penalty. Chance and the common course of nature will not bring it to pass that the readings of a MS. are right wherever they are possible and impossible wherever they are wrong; that needs divine intervention" (36). Furthermore, once the "best" text has been determined, the Lachmann system encouraged in its less-adept practitioners a fidelity to documentary evidence that infuriated Housman, who accused the Germans of hanging onto the readings of a manuscript like hope to an anchor (53). Lachmann had wanted to go further than merely identifying the *extant* witness that stood in the "highest" position on the stemma: from comparing the reading of several such witnesses, it should be possible to arrive at the reading which certainly lay in the archetype. But since this was (by admission and design) not demonstrably the reading of the author's fair copy, Housman and other (more conjecturalist) critics of the later twentieth century have tended to find the "backtracking" of the Lachmann stemma up to the archetype as a wasted journey. Why not simply begin conjecture at a lower level on the tree, if the end-product of the construction of the stemma is still corrupt? But Housman reserved his greatest scorn for conservatives using "language less as a vehicle than as a substitute for thought," who were "readily duped by . . . 'scientific criticism' or 'critical method'" (*Selected Prose*: 37), and who consequently would not even go as far as the archetype.

Joseph Bédier's criticism of the Lachmann method was rather different: not that it was conservative or encouraged textual laziness, but that it was fraudulent. He found that the great majority of stemmata constructed by the Lachmannians resulted in a two-branch pattern, whereby the editor then simply had to choose between a "right" and a "wrong" reading, a "good" and a "bad" manuscript. He felt that the Lachmannians were deliberately avoiding the confrontation with a three- or four- branch stemma since this would destroy the apparent technical basis for their system by throwing them back on conjecture (i.e., by what system of "error" or genealogy does one deal with the radiation of multiple authorities, the production of many witnesses by the repeated copying of the same exemplar, rather than with simply the neat dichotomy of two divergent variants?). Actually, later apologists for Lachmann (e.g., Maas in his *Textual Criticism*) did include such radiating models, but it remains true that the Lachmannian system could not effectively deal, for example, with any sort of horizontal "cross-fertilization" of lines of descent (as opposed to the expected vertical dissemination of the standard Lachmannian stemma), whether by *conflation* (a copyist's working from two exemplars at the same time) or by *contamination* (a copyist's incorporation of remembered readings from one version while actually copying from another exemplar). In fact, in the more sexist climate of the Twenties, Maas was able to get away with remarking that the (impossible and unacceptable) mapping of contamination on a stemma was the genealogical equivalent of introducing female descent into family trees (!), technically a pertinent analogy but doubtless fueling some of the recent feminist dissatisfaction with the paternalistic pretensions of orthodox recension-based textual criticism, with its privileging of "correct" reading over "error" and its repudiation of variation itself as an improper corruption of direct monogeneous descent.

There is an irony, however, in Bédier's having decided that, because the genealogical system did not work honestly (or was not practiced honestly), the editorial prerogative should be curtailed. Bédier's cure for the ills of the Lachmannian system was to suggest that once having established—by linguistic, historical, codicological or other grounds—that a particular manuscript best represented the author's wishes, this manuscript (or "best-text") should thereafter be followed religiously. Bédier's position is, of course, a version of the old Pergamanian doctrine of "anomaly," except that through a perverse logic, he believes it possible to judge manuscripts by their ability to fulfill authorial preferences and yet then supposes that these preferences are otherwise unknowable, as far as emending the text is concerned. There is therefore a further irony in Bédier's "best-text" theory having duplicated (by a different intellectual and scholarly route) the "best-text" rationale which some of the more timid (or non-conjecturalist) Lachmannians had employed once the mechanics of recension had arranged rival witnesses of a complex tradition in their putative genealogical relationships: such Lachmannians (with their anchors of hope) were, as already shown, best-text editors of the Bédier stamp *avant la lettre*.

Rather than taking refuge in another form of bibliographical surety (the best text), such critics as Pasquali and George Kane and E. Talbot Donaldson have emphasized the necessarily subjective element of textual decisions, and particularly the requirement that each variation be judged on its own merits. Pasquali was uneasy about the wholesale importation of German stemmatic theory into the editing of vernacular as well as classical works, and, in his critique of the highly theoretical Lachmannism of Maas's *Textual Criticism* in the *Storia della tradizione e critica del testo* (1934), he even attacked the basic Lachmannian assumptions about error and downward or divergent variation, calling into question the value of the hierarchical structure on which stemmatics was based and pointing to the system's inability to deal with contamination. His general thesis was that history (and thus the history of transmission) is not neat and tidy as the Lachmannians would have it, but complex and human. The problems of transmission were thus not to be solved by the pseudo-scientific dogma of recension.

The work of Kane and Donaldson on the text of *Piers Plowman* takes a similar view, for after having tested the applicability of the recension method on the manuscripts of the A-text, Kane came to the conclusion that the patterns discoverable in individual variations did not match the patterns of putative affiliation for the documents conceived as complete witnesses, and thus the only solution was to edit each variant separately according to a demonstrable difference between the *usus auctoris* and the *usus scribendi*. This method, which became known as deep editing, was taken up with increasing vigor and enthusiasm in Kane and Donaldson's editing of the B-text, to much acclaim and condemnation. The problem with deep editing is its elevating of the "mistrust of texts" to a doctrine as intransigent as recension or best-text theory, as critics like David Fowler have demonstrated. Thus, believing that Langland always wrote metrically (i.e., alliterative) perfect lines, Kane and Donaldson emend a line like "And wepen whan I shulde *slepen* though whete brede me faille" to "werchen" instead of "slepen," since this emendation creates a correct three-stress accent on *w*. They always have subtle critical arguments to back up their individual decisions (in this case, that the arguably scribal "slepen" is caused by "rhyming inducement" of the previous "wepen" and by the influence of a nearby Latin tag, *lacrimæ nocte*), but these arguments themselves depend upon an acceptance of the specific sorts of distinction between authorial and scribal usage that this form of deep editing depends on anyway.

In the other direction (toward mechanical system and away from individual judgment) another reaction against the Lachmann system was initiated by Dom Henri Quentin, who, after working with the particularly intractable conditions of New Testament textual transmission, came to the conclusion that the problem lay in the apparent objectivity of the "recension" stage of stemmatics. He proposed that, instead of trying to discriminate an error from a genuine reading, the editor produce a so-called positive critical apparatus, in fact not a critical apparatus in the conventional sense at all, but an arrangement of manuscript evidence dependent upon a concordance table of readings grouped in threes. Within any three divergent readings, if two agreed against the third, then according to Quentin, the third could not stand as intermediary between the other two. Quentin's basic argument therefore replaces the critical adjudication of variants by a branch of statistics (or distributional analysis, as it was to be called).

Statistical or distributional evidence is obviously of potentially great value in editing (it has been used, for example, in David Vieth's editing of Rochester and in Harold Metz's and M. W. A. Smith's stylometric analysis of disputed Shakespeare plays). But a problem may be that the variants (particularly in Quentin's relatively unsophisticated methodology) are not given any value—they are merely counted. One of the basic principles of traditional textual criticism is that "[witnesses] should be weighed, not counted," and while the sheer volume of evidence in a system like Quentin's might, through its accumulation of the same relationships over and over again, provide statistically convincing genealogies, Quentin does not discriminate between a reading that can be produced independently (and therefore repeatedly, by accidental recurrence) and one that must demonstrate a close affinity between manuscripts sharing the same reading. Indeed, there are those who would declare that all variants are finally independent of each other and of any rigidly imposed system for charting their relations, for one can never be sure that two scribes could not have produced the same "error" from the same exemplar, only to have the exemplar's reading restored by another scribe, and in the process destroying the premises of Quentin's argument.

Two additional modifications to filiation theory or the mapping of family descent may be briefly mentioned before closing this section. The first is Greg's algebraic formulae used to chart possible filiation in his *Calculus of Variants*. Like Lachmann's and Maas's, Greg's system will not readily admit of "cross-fertilization of collaterals" (what has been called elsewhere, "horizontal" or "convergent" variation, as opposed to "vertical" or "divergent" dissemination). That is, there may be variants shared within a "variation group," all of whose members must belong to the same branch of the stemma, but not *across* the filiation pattern, from one branch (or "collateral") group to another. Greg is primarily interested in defining the concept of the "exclusive common ancestor," or the latest ancestor common to a variation group within one branch of the stemma and to no other—unless the two groups at the top of two branches also share features, in which case these features would presumably descend from the exclusive common ancestor at the head of the entire tree (what Lachmann would have called the archetype). Greg represents this idea of the exclusive common ancestor with a formula (xA') rather than by a diagrammatic position, as in the Lachmann stemma. Thus, the exclusive common ancestor of a group of two witnesses (B and C) in which readings largely agree could be expressed by the formula $xA'BC$, a formula which can then be simplified by designating this exclusive common ancestor by the Greek letter beta (β). If another variation group, comprising the witnesses B and C, can be shown to share certain features with the A of the previous formula (so that an exclusive common ancestor, designated by the Greek letter alpha (α), could be postulated for the convergence of both variation groups), then this relationship can be expressed by the formula xA'A(BC), and so on, with increasingly more complex formulations.

The great virtue of Greg's system is that it can efficiently and accurately represent relationships which might be only ambiguously traceable through a conventional geometric (i.e., stemmatic) pattern, but its weakness is its forbidding mathematical surety, from which editors seem to have retreated. Thus, while some later theorists (notably Vinton Dearing) have praised Greg for the originality of his symbolic method, and while his theory has found some advocates, I know of no practical editing which has been entirely conducted according to the precepts of the *Calculus*. Greg's book is unfortunately symptomatic of a type of textual criticism which is more enamored of the system it constructs than of the results it might create, and I can only assure the reader that my brief account, necessarily synoptic, simplifies much of the detailed algebraic demonstration upon which Greg's calculus depends.

It is indeed Greg's disciple Vinton Dearing and his *Principles and Practice of Textual Analysis* which are the last exhibits in this survey of filiation theory. Dearing attempts to construct models for filiation using the arguments of symbolic logic, but unlike Greg's and Lachmann's, his system (at least at an entry level) will support convergent variation or contamination. Thus, he postulates the "ring" as the model for such variation, a ring being defined as a "closed sequence in which all elements are intermediary" (95).

$$A—B—\overset{|}{C}D \qquad u\overset{|}{x}—vx—v\overset{|}{y}$$
$$G—F—E \qquad uz—wz—wy$$

As the diagram of a typical Dearing ring shows, what this means is that a "sequence" of witnesses (denominated by the conventional sigla A, B, C, D, E, F, and G) can be formed into a ring (rather than a simple line) because of certain shared features: thus witness A contains the reading *ux*, witness B the reading *vx*, witnesses CD the readings *vy*, witness E the reading *wy*, witness F the reading *wz* and witness G the reading *uz*. Since each one of these readings "overlaps" with readings in witnesses on either side (*u* is in both A and G, *x* in both A and B etc.), the overlapping readings form the witnesses into a circle or ring and there is no *obvious* point at which this ring can be broken. To the concept of the ring, therefore, Dearing adds that of the principle of parsimony (derived from logic), whereby the textual analyst would never rewrite two variations when rewriting one will represent the filiation, and it is this principle which Dearing then uses to break (i.e., "rewrite") the rings as lines. The concept of parsimony is similar to the "simplification" principle of Archibald Hill ("Some Postulates"), who suggests that in pure distributional theory, (where the concept of "error" should properly be replaced by the neutral "addomission," a term which simply acknowledges the variation without ascribing value to it), stemmata with complex or multiform stages of genealogy should be replaced by simplified models, so that the fewer stages of transmission that a model needs to explain the extant forms, the more efficient that model becomes. Using parsimony as his principle of simplification, Dearing is unwilling to allow the convergent variation to be sustained where it can be broken into, and the rule for the breaking of rings is that it should take place in "decreasing order of the strengths of their weakest connections" (97).

All of this sounds fine as a theoretical procedure, but rather like Quentin's arrangement of threes, it runs into the issue of the *value* of a connection. For example, if the x held in common by A and B is, say, a noun (the subject of a sentence, even), is this weaker or stronger than the u between A and G, which might be perhaps, the verb? Where and how should convergent spelling be evaluated? What do we do about punctuation? Or word-division? It is not that Dearing does not have some answers for some of these questions, but rather that the answers may very well change from text to text, according to the demonstrable authorial preferences in these matters. But these preferences are themselves (we assume) embedded in the "connections" that are to be broken, so that the argument again becomes (like Lachmann's and like the symbolic model Dearing has chosen to represent his system), a ring.

The important work of Lachmann, Quentin, Greg, and Dearing is significant in its placing emphasis upon the features of the text itself rather than upon the characteristics of the "carriers" of that text—the manuscripts and printed books from which the evidence for a calculus or a ring might be drawn. Dearing has moreover declared that this study of transmission from the internal features of the text should be separate from that of the bibliography of books and has called the study textual analysis (rather than "textual criticism"). It is a useful term, as long as it is not employed to sanctify the practice it describes as preferable to or more authoritative than other types of analysis, for textual scholarship at large must comprehend not only the content of the text but its bibliographical nature. And it is the material, hard bibliographical side of textual scholarship that has, in the last century, advanced most in vernacular scholarship, and it is that topic that must be dealt with next.

As already noted, it was largely the twin ancient disciplines of biblical studies and classics which together were in the vanguard of textual theory up to the mid-nineteenth century. The editing of vernacular texts either lagged far behind these two, borrowed from their ideologies or practices, or promoted a rival textual dispensation (e.g., "Romantic" editing, in Patterson's sense) which consciously rebelled against the traditions of the classicists and biblicists. But towards the end of the nineteenth century, an independent movement in the scholarship of English documents led to Anglo-American textual criticism taking the lead in modern textual theory.

The beginnings of this movement can be observed first in medieval studies, but by the early twentieth century the center of gravity moved to the Renaissance (particularly drama), and since then has also encompassed other fields, most notably English and American literature of the nineteenth century. These beginnings can be traced to the philological aims of F. J. Furnivall, and particularly to his plan for a new English dictionary on "historical" principles. This *New English Dictionary—NED—*(or *Oxford English Dictionary—OED—*as it was to become, and *NOED*, or *New Oxford English Dictionary* in its latest, electronic, manifestation, see Chapter 1) was to be based on a study of original documents (manuscripts and printed books) where the history of the language could be observed in practice. The plan therefore involved a vast research effort by hundreds of volunteer workers, to read the sources and to record the usages. The *OED* was therefore related to the similarly national enterprise of reproducing a number of these significant documents in generally conservative documentary editions. For history, this was the *Rolls Series* and for literature, the Early English Text Society's publications. In fact, the EETS (another brainchild of Furnivall's) was specifically intended to provide the materials on which the *OED* would be built, although it has long outlasted its original purposes. The Malone Society, with its series of diplomatic reprints of Renaissance dramatic documents, continued the work of EETS in a later field.

The inherent documentary conservatism of EETS and the Rolls

Series was not, however, paralleled elsewhere in the editing of medieval texts, which still tended to be produced either under a vaguely stemmatic dispensation or with the old mixture of editorial whimsy and enlightened conjecture. Even Furnivall could be a remarkably idiosyncratic editor, as when he selected Harley 4866 as his copy-text for his edition of Hoccleve's *Regement of Princes* because it had "the best portrait of Chaucer" (xvii). Not all nineteenth-century medievalists were quite as cavalier as Furnivall: the scholarly record of such figures as Macaulay on Gower, Henry Bradshaw, Frederick Madden, and W. W. Skeat would be enough to demonstrate the sense of discrimination and adjudication which characterized much editorial work in the century. But much of this work has (inevitably) been superseded, and finally it is in the linguistic "philological" presentation of cumulative documentary evidence in the volumes of EETS and the pages of the *OED* that the nineteenth-century medievalists made their enduring contribution to scholarship.

The major change in editorial method came from the Renaissance, and (like its medieval counterpart) it begins in enumerative and descriptive bibliography, rather than in editing itself. Two of the milestones have in fact already been mentioned in the chapter on enumerative bibliography: Gordon Duff's descriptive catalogue of the typeforms of English incunabula in 1896, and Robert Proctor's index to the incunabula of the British Museum and the Bodleian Library (1898). These enumerative/descriptive catalogues were an extension into English materials of the practices of the German incunabula bibliographers, and (together with the equally significant bibliographical work of Pollard and Redgrave in the original *Short-Title Catalogue*) promoted an attention to the physical characteristics of early printed books which was to develop into the "science" of analytical bibliography. The major editorial manifesto of this movement was R. B. McKerrow's *The Works of Thomas Nashe* (1904–10), paralleled by the contemporaneous bibliographical study of the Shakespeare texts in Alfred Pollard's *Shakespeare Folios and Quartos* (1909), and the later *Prolegomena for the Oxford Shakespeare* (1939), also by McKerrow. The publications of the Malone Society were (as already observed) one of the main vehicles for the documentary presentation of the new bibliographical evidence, and for many years (1906–39), the general editor of the Society's publications was W. W. Greg, who became the central theorist of the the editorial implications of the "new" bibliography. The basic bibliographical training required in incipient scholars of the new bibliography was enshrined in McKerrow's textbook

An Introduction to Bibliography for Literary Students (1927, first edition), which became the *vade mecum* of bibliography until it was largely superseded (or updated) by Philip Gaskell's *A New Introduction to Bibliography* (1972), which interestingly drops the "for literary students" qualification.

What all these editions, bibliographical studies, manifestos, and textbooks have in common is a concentration upon the physical form of the book in which a text appears. Using the technical information which was gradually accumulated about the history of early printing, the bibliographers of the new dispensation seemed to be moving textual studies firmly into the camp of technology. But they were not all equally sanguine about the possible results of such a move, and McKerrow in particular had serious reservations about a technological approach usurping the traditional territory of "textual criticism." His phrase "for literary students" was perhaps to be taken more seriously than one might suppose, since it betrays his assumption that while bibliography was an essential tool in textual study, the results of this study should be better, more authoritative, literary texts. All too often in the mid- and late twentieth century, one senses that analytical bibliography became an independent discipline, with no ultimate literary responsibilities (and ironically this can be paralleled by the attempts of the literary critics to make criticism equally independent of literature). Gaskell's dropping of "for literary students" is clearly a sign of the times.

In the later twentieth century, the two major apologists for the influence of analytical bibliography were W. W. Greg and Fredson Bowers. Indeed, it is quite proper to speak of a "Greg-Bowers" school of textual scholarship, for Bowers consciously saw his own work as a continuation of the principles of Greg, to whom he dedicated his authoritative *Principles of Bibliographical Description* in 1949 and whose bibliography of printed drama he was extending at the time of his death in 1991. Bowers was a great proselytizer, partly by his own example in producing editions on Greg-Bowers principles (for, as already noted, he edited works in all of the post-medieval periods) and partly by the influence of such organs as the annual *Studies in Bibliography* (which Bowers edited from its first volume in 1948 until 1991, in the latter years assisted by the eighteenth-century scholar David Vander Meulen) and through the general guiding principles of the Modern Language Association's Center for Editions of American Authors and the somewhat less restrictive attitudes of its successor, the Center (later Committee) for Scholarly Editions.

It is impossible in a few short lines to do adequate justice to the enormous output and scholarly influence of Greg and Bowers, for their positions—on copy-text, on critical editing, on the application of the principles of analytical bibliography—have been the focus of most of the scholarly debate in Anglo-American studies over the last half-century. A brief summary will have to suffice. Although he was active as editor, as bibliographer, and as textual critic, Greg's experience in editing texts with complex traditions was limited to *Dr. Faustus* and *The Masque of Gipsies*, and his single most influential contribution to textual scholarship came in a short theoretical essay he wrote towards the end of his life—"The Rationale of Copy-Text," published in Bowers's *Studies in Bibliography*. To be fair, Greg did not conceive of the essay as primarily theoretical, but rather as a practical editorial response to the documented conditions of English printing of the sixteenth and seventeenth centuries; but the essay has been used as the focus for a long debate on principle as well as practice.

Greg's basic position in this essay was to call into question a widely held textual assumption that the most authoritative copy-text for a scholarly edition should be the last edition published during the author's lifetime. This assumption rested on an undocumented (and often undocumentable) theory that it was the normal practice for authors personally to see all editions of their works through the press. It was clear that in the Renaissance this was rarely so (particularly for drama) and that when an author did assume any prerogative (as in the famous case of Ben Jonson's *Works* of 1616) this was regarded as an aberration (again, particularly for drama). To overcome this problem and to recognize the actual circumstances of publication in the period, Greg proposed that a distinction be made between what he called substantives (the actual words, or the "meaning" of a text) and accidentals (the spelling, punctuation and so on, or the "surface features" of a text). Greg suggested that wherever possible, the editor of a Renaissance work should use an authorial manuscript (presumably itself the copy-text for the first edition or of some pre-publication state of the text) as copy-text for the "accidentals," and that later states of the text (usually including the first edition) should then be consulted for substantive emendation of this copy-text, wherever it could be shown that later substantive changes had indeed been introduced by the author.

This suggestion of a "divided" authority in copy-text (one text for accidentals and possibly several others for imported substantives) then resulted in the production of "eclectic" editions bearing features from various witnesses, in what became known as the "text that never was" (but by implication, *ought* to have been, in the best of all possible worlds, since it constructed authorial intention in despite of the testimony of individual documents).   In other words, the Greg theory was a late blossoming of Alexandrian analogy, the construction of putative authorial usage out of the collation of multiple witnesses, and was a deliberate repudiation of the prevailing best-text procedures favored by other editors, including McKerrow, who was very reluctant to emend his copy-text from other sources.   This change in philosophy, coupled with the selection of copy-text for its accidentals rather than its substantives, engendered an animated, sometimes vociferous response, which is still going on.

For example, while Greg's principle was (initially) endorsed by the CEAA editions and applied by Bowers in the editing of Renaissance texts, it met stiff resistance from editors in other fields (including nineteenth-century American fiction, which had been the focus of the first CEAA editions).   While the editorial work and the theoretical essays of Bowers and G. Thomas Tanselle have promoted Greg's theory (so successfully, indeed, that much of the reaction against Greg was motivated until comparatively recently by the apparent acceptance of his essay as the current "orthodoxy" of textual scholarship, and a consequent resistance to its hegemony), there has been an increasingly vocal displeasure with the supposed expansionist aims of the Greg-Bowers school.   Some of this displeasure can be dismissed as mere ill-will, such as Edmund Wilson's notorious attack on the CEAA editions, "The Fruits of the MLA," where his ill-informed mud-slinging seems to rest largely upon his rancor at having his own proposal for a series of "reader's" editions of American classics turned down by the National Endowment for the Humanities, while the MLA's proposal for "scholarly" editions was at first well-funded.   Some measure of the general anti-academic and anti-scholarly tone of the essay can be observed in that its favorite term of abuse seems to be the word "professor."   Wilson was an amateur and proud of it, but some of the other attacks have come from professionals.   (A later irony is that Wilson's desire for an inexpensive uniform series of reprints of American literature is now very much under way—*The Library of America*—but that the direct NEH support for the MLA Committee on Scholarly Editions has disappeared, and support to the editions themselves generally dwindled.)

Thus, by the third quarter of the twentieth century, it would be fair to say that the dominant mode of Anglo-American textual criticism, institutionally and academically, was the copy-text school of eclectic editing designed to produce a reading clear-text whose features were a fulfillment of authorial intentions by the selection of authorially sanctioned substantive variants from different states of the text, and whose copy-text was selected on the basis of its accidentals being as close as possible to authorial usage (and therefore normally a manuscript rather than a later printed edition, if such a manuscript existed). The success of the eclectic method can be demonstrated by the fact that, with very few counter-examples (the Cornell Wordsworth and the Harvard Emerson), virtually all of the three hundred or so volumes endorsed by the CEAA or CSE seal of approval have been constructed on Greg-Bowers principles of eclecticism and copy-text theory. Moreover, the influence of Bowers's editions, and of his voluminous theoretical writings, can be shown on many fronts: for example, Jo Ann Boydston, current chair of the CSE, testifies that it was the authority of Bowers's essay "Some Principles for Scholarly Editions of Nineteenth-Century Authors" that led her to begin her own monumental edition of John Dewey on similar principles (*"Collected Works"*). The combined efforts of Bowers (e.g., "Greg's Rationale," "Multiple Authority,") and Tanselle (e.g., "Greg's Theory," "Editorial Problem," "Editing of Historical," "External Fact," "Recent Editorial," "Historicism," *Rationale*, *Textual Criticism Since Greg*, "Textual Criticism and Literary Sociology") in a series of comprehensive and encyclopaedic surveys of editorial problems, again enlarged the purview of the eclectic, copy-text school.

But things change, and the last decade or so has seen a major shift in the disposition of textual criticism as practiced on works in English and other European languages: indeed, much of the change in Anglo-American textual criticism has been the result of the influence, direct or indirect, of Continental theories and practices, just as has occurred in literary theory and criticism.

The Current Debate

Even within the Greg-Bowers camp. it would be a mistake to assume a monolithic orthodoxy in its adherents. Thus, while generally accepting the basic principles of dual/divided authority and eclectic editing in multiple text traditions, Tanselle has distanced himself from other features of Greg's theory, for example, finding the terms "accidentals" and "substantives" to be misleading and often untenable in

their implication of a firm distinction in all cases. Similarly, the opposition to Greg-Bowers has been far from united and represents various interests.

James Thorpe's *Principles of Textual Criticism* (1972) has become
one of the best-known "literary" (even "belletristic") rejections of
Greg-Bowers, largely on his—perhaps mistaken—assumption that the
"system" which Bowers had articulated in his *Principles of Bibliographical Description* and the "theory" which Greg had proposed in
his "Rationale" were too scientific, too technical, and too removed
from the actual circumstances of composition of literature. Philip
Gaskell's position rests less on these philosophical grounds and more
on his interpretation of the printing and publishing history of post-
Renaissance English literature. In brief, he holds that since most authors expected their accidentals to be corrected or modified or regularized by the publisher, an acceptance of the authorial manuscript as
copy-text would give us only a consciously unfinished state of intention. Thus, while Gaskell would support the use of manuscript for
copy-text in works not intended for publication (e.g., diaries, letters,
and so on)—indeed, what else is there?—he maintains that the act of
publication presupposes that the author has willingly endorsed all the
changes in his text that this involves (*New Introduction*: 339-40).
Now, it is clear that this division of opinion does result in a philosophical distinction after all, no matter how much it may appear to be
grounded in strict bibliographical data. And much of the most recent
debate has been concerned with this question of "intention" (and particularly "final intention") and how best to recognize it, represent it
or reject it in favor of other competing ideologies.

Tanselle, for example, believes that the textual critic should be
very cautious about accepting the mere facts of the subsequent history
of the text of a work as indicating that the author willingly accepted
(or even "intended") these later conditions. In his edition of Melville's *Typee*, for example, he and his colleagues Hayford and Parker
restore the first edition text containing criticism of Christian missionaries in the South Seas, even though Melville expressly agreed that
the second edition text, in which large cuts were made to remove the
criticism, was a superior work, and the cuts "beneficial." As Tanselle remarks, "There is no question that Melville is responsible for
the changes, and in this sense they are 'final'; but they represent not
so much his intention as his acquiescence. Under these circumstances, an editor is justified in rejecting the revisions and adopting
the original readings as best reflecting the author's 'final intentions';

in fact, to accept the readings which are final in chronological terms would distort that intention. . . . In the end, one cannot automatically accept such statements at face value; as in any historical research, statements can only be interpreted by placing them in their context" ("Editorial Problem": 193–94). Clearly, the concept of intention and final intention is more complex than one might imagine.

In a somewhat lighter vein, Gary Taylor confirms that apparently unambiguous protestations on authorial intention must be treated with caution. He muses that we might "hope to find reliable early testimony to Shakespeare's habits of composition. An autograph letter, for instance. 'Dear Anne, I'll be home next week, as soon as I finish revising that old play of mine, *King Lear*. Your loving Willy. London. 1 April 1610'." But as Taylor goes on to suggest, such documentation may be suspect: "Artists, after all, do, often enough, lie about their work. For all we know, 'revising *King Lear*' might have been Shakespeare's alibi, to cover an adulterous weekend" ("Revising": 296–97).

Taking on the traditional preoccupation with authorial intention, and reacting against what he perceives as an intentionalist privilege given to a Romantic concept of the solitary author creating a work in an "originary moment" of composition, Jerome J. McGann has proposed an alternative view of composition, in which the entire history of the work is a fit subject for textual scholarship, and even posthumous changes by editors, publishers, friends and relations, are to be considered a perfectly valid part of the text read as a social construct. McGann's social textual criticism, appearing in his *Critique of Modern Textual Criticism* and various other writings in the last ten years, has been the major point of contention in recent debate. Emphasizing the inevitably collaborative nature of literature (with an analogy drawn from music, another art in which the receiver is a major element in the construction of meaning), McGann's work has been seen on the one hand as an "unattributed gloss" on the Marxist Pierre Macherey's dictum that "the work is not *created* by an intention (objective or subjective); it is *produced* under determinate circumstances" (Sutherland: 581) and on the other as an exemplification of Stanley Fish's "interpretive communities," whereby textual meaning is constructed by a social contract within which the transmitted text operates, rather than by an appeal to the intentions of a now-absent author (Greetham, "Textual and Literary Theory": 11).

There is perhaps an irony in McGann's editorial reputation having been made with his authoritative edition of Byron for Oxford, an edition constructed on intentionalist rather than on social principles. Because of the inevitable delay between theory and practice, McGann is therefore in the paradoxical position of having in effect to repudiate the basic principles of his major scholarly work (although it is, of course, regarded with justifiable admiration by more traditional textual critics). It remains to be seen whether he will produce other scholarly editions on social principles, but he has expressed some caution over the possibilities of even a hypertext's being able to chart the bibliographical codes he now finds so essential to an understanding of the meaning of text (see Chapter 9). These bibliographical codes (typography, layout, format, paper etc.) are contrasted with the "linguistic codes" (the words of a text), on which most textual criticism has concentrated, and have been discussed briefly in the section of Chapter 7 concerned with the work of McGann, McLeod, McLaverty and others in showing the impact of bibliographical features on the construction of textual meaning.

McGann finds that a poem like Byron's "Fare Thee Well!" (addressed to his estranged wife) can be interpreted as a poem of "hate and revenge" or "love and broken-heartedness" depending on its bibliographical context—authorized private printing, unauthorized newspaper printing, or book publication—even though its "linguistic text . . .is quite stable" ("What Is Critical Editing?": 22). He finds similar meaning in, say, the varying tables of contents of Matthew Arnold's poems at different times in his life (16–17), as does George Bornstein in Yeats's changing views of his own poetic and political career as manifest in the differing categories and ordering of poems in his tables of contents ("Remaking Himself"). This issue is explored in some detail by Ian Jack in his essay "A Choice of Orders."

Independently of McGann, D. F. McKenzie has proposed a sociology of the text which expands the scope of traditional bibliography and takes an entire culture as "text." Working initially on orality, literacy, and print in New Zealand, McKenzie has also charted the history of Cambridge University Press (1696–1712), together with an investigation of Congreve's concern with the physical nature of his publications. But it is through his prestigious position as Reader in Textual Bibliography at Oxford, through his directing of the multivolume *Cambridge History of the Book in Britain*, and through his influential British Library lectures, *Bibliography and the Sociology of the Text*, that McKenzie has moved the center of historical bibliography away from the book narrowly conceived (and particularly the book of "literature") towards a consideration of all forms of communication in a society. Thus, the data-base for the Cambridge *Book in Britain* project is the entire *STC*, especially for the seventeenth-century, McKenzie's period, and one of the results of this decision is that deliberately anonymous, non-authorial literature assumes statistically a much more prominent role than it would have in a study of great authors. This widening is also shown in plans for the final volume of the series, where McKenzie's collaborator Ian Willison includes such "non-book" media as television scripts, film scripts (and associated records of film production) in his definition of the book.

It is possible to regard both McGann and McKenzie as Anglo-American collateral branches of the European school of *l'histoire du livre*, a movement growing out of the *annales* historical group associated with Marc Bloch, Le Roy Ladurie, and Fernand Braudel and their concentration on the detailed cultural context for past events rather than on the "great figures" who are normally the subject of a more hierarchical view of history. The *annales* school typically studies either a small cultural occurrence in multifaceted detail (e.g., Ladurie's account of the small French village of Montaillou in the fourteenth century) or an enormous canvas of interrelated social, economic, commercial, and political events (e.g., Braudel's vast portrait of the *Mediterranean and the Mediterranean World in the Age of Philip II*). The *annalistes'* rejection of major figures and their enlarging of the scope of cultural history to favor records of grain prices and peasant domestic economy over dynastic intrigue at court and international warfare is of a piece with the *l'histoire du livre*'s placing of the book as cultural artifact within the wide context of national history and with the bibliographical rejection of "literature" as a special class of writings—indeed, with the rejection of "writing" as a privileged form of discourse. The bibliographical work of such scholars as Lucien Febvre and Henri Martin (and particularly their *L'apparition du livre*) was until recently in stark contrast to the dominant Anglo-American technical emphasis on analytical and descriptive bibliography. But through the research of Elizabeth Eisenstein (*The Printing Press as an Agent of Change*) and the proselytizing of Tanselle (*The History of Books as a Field of Study*), and now through the social enlargement of bibliography as practiced by McGann and McKenzie, the Anglo-American branch has drawn closer to its European colleagues.

This can also be seen in Donald Pizer's socially conscious theory of the cultural artifact (as against the privilege of authorial intention). Pizer takes a similar position to McGann in his rejection of the "self-censorship" argument of Tanselle and the intentionalists, claiming that works like Dreiser's *Sister Carrie* and Crane's *Red Badge of Courage*, while altered by their authors under external influence, should best be read in the "censored" versions rather than original manuscript forms, since these censored texts have acquired an independent cultural value outweighing any appeal to the "originary moment." While not endorsing such a specific historical view, the evidence Philip Gaskell assembles in his *From Writer to Reader* emphasizes the social transactions that a text undertakes as it becomes increasingly public property: he demonstrates the "dynamic" of the text by showing examples of the various ways texts have undergone changes, from Harington's translation of Ariosto to Tom Stoppard's *Travesties*, and suggests that there can be no one textual method suitable for dealing with all of them.

This concentration on the variance of texts and an acceptance of their engagement with society can be seen in many textual critics working today—in Derek Pearsall's call for a loose-leaf edition of Chaucer ("Editing Medieval Texts"); in Gary Taylor's insistence on Shakespeare as inveterate reviser ("Revising Shakespeare"); Steven Urkowitz's promotion of multiple-text interpretations of, for example, *Lear* and *Hamlet*, and Michael Warren's edition of the "complete" (i.e., multiple-text) *Lear*; in Peter Shillingsburg's vision of multiple computer-created texts of nineteenth-century novels ("Limits"; "Technology"); in Donald H. Reiman's emphasis on "versioning" rather than final intentions in the editing of the Romantics; in Lafuma and Sellier's separate editing of the two states (*la Première Copie* and *la Seconde Copie*) of Pascal's *Pensées* to overcome the false sense of unity and organicism given in earlier editions by Pascal's nephew Étienne Périer; in A. Rossi's insistence that there are three, not one, authorial versions of Boccaccio's *Decameron*; in De Robertis's experimental apparatus for recording multiple authorial variants in Ungaretti's poetry; in the Soviet textology of Dmitrij Lixacev, concentrating on the layers and divergent states of text; in John Miles Foley's computer program HEURO for the continuous construction and reconstruction of Yugoslav oral epic poetry, a medium which would otherwise be arrested by editing; in Hershel Parker's designation of a "New Scholarship" which would promise a "full intentionality" drawn from the multiple, and frequently contradictory, states of many nineteenth- and twentieth-century American authors; and in Philip Gaskell and Clive Hart's publication of a reader's kit (*Review of Three Texts*) for "repairing the major faults" of *Ulysses* editions, including Hans Walter Gabler's, which is itself an example of the influence of the genetic school of editing prominent in Franco-German textual criticism (e.g., in editions of Proust, Hölderlin, Kafka, Klopstock, Flaubert, etc.). Genetic editing, uncommon in Anglo-American circles except for the Gabler *Ulysses* and the almost equally notorious Harvard Emerson edition (the focus of much of Wilson's attack on the "barbed wire" of scholarly apparatus that keeps readers away from texts) aims to present the growth and development of texts in a continuous display of variant states, rather than separating the favored "clear text" of the eclectic editions from rejected variants. It is thus a method endorsing process over product, variance and indeterminacy over final authority and the definitive edition.

What all these textual scholars have in common is a reaction against any simplistic imposition of the final intentions principles of Greg-Bowers eclecticism. Instead of postulating a single, consistent, authorially sponsored text as the purpose of the editorial enterprise, they suggest multiform, fragmentary, even contradictory, texts as the aim of editing, sometimes to be constructed *ad hoc* by the reader. In general, then, the characteristic feature of textual scholarship in the closing years of this century is its democratic pluralism: there is no longer, in Anglo-American editing, at least, any single orthodoxy among textual scholars, although it would have to be admitted that eclectic, intentionalist editions are still being produced more often than any other form, perhaps because it will take some time for practice to catch up with theory.

McGann's theoretical shift from "intention" (an authorial prerogative) to "affect" (a reader's) is symptomatic of a general shift in critical theory from a reliance on an author's imputed meaning to the free play of meaning associated with post-structuralism. This is no accident, for textual criticism participates in the ideological climate as do all other intellectual activities—history, philosophy, science, literature. As I have noted elsewhere ("Textual and Literary Theory": fn. 4 [14–15]), it was not coincidence that the hegemony of the new bibliography and eclectic editing (with its emphasis on the single consciousness of "the text itself" and on the removal of variance to a discrete part of the volume) was virtually co-terminous with that of the New Criticism, with its similar endorsement of the singular "text itself" and its similar desire to resolve tension, irony, and variance in the "well-wrought urn" that was the proper object of critical study. In this way, while not speaking directly to each other, and often seeming to represent markedly different attitudes (to, for example, history and intention), practitioners of the new bibliography of eclectic editing and the New Criticism of *explication de texte* reinforced each other's predispositions in a cultural context that favored close reading of a fixed, definitive text over the irresolution of competing witnesses and competing readers.

These days, it seems that all we have are competing texts and competing readers, and the list of textual critics accepting versions over fixed texts is emblematic of the change. There has thus been a new acknowledgment that textual criticism is not merely a dry, mechanical, tedious investigation of physical fact but, like all other intellectual activities, operates under various theoretical persuasions, which may change from time to time. Much of the important work on textual criticism in the next few years is likely to be in the further exploration of this relation between theory and text. For example, Gary Taylor is working on a study of the historical hermeneutics of editing, tentatively entitled *The Matter of Text*; W. Speed Hill on the humanist antecedents of editing in the vernacular and on the text as scripture; Joseph Grigely on textual criticism and the arts; and James L. W. West III on the editorial "construction" of authorship. The collections of essays on literary and textual theory appearing in the special issue of the journal *Critical Exchange* on *Textual Scholarship and Literary Theory* and in the volume that Philip Cohen has edited (*Devils and Angels*) will doubtless fuel the debate, as will George Bornstein's edited collection *Palimpsest: Editorial Theory in the Humanities*, Jerome J.McGann's recent collection of reprinted essays *The Textual Condition* (the title of which is taken from a paper on his social theory of textual criticism delivered at a conference of the Society for Textual Scholarship), and Oliphant and Bradford's recent editing of the proceedings of the 1989 Texas conference on *New Directions in Textual Studies*, in which the sociological and materialist aspect of text and textuality is very prominent. My own *Theories of the Text* draws all of this discussion into the conceptual and methodological matrix of contemporary theory.

Even critics primarily associated with traditional intentionalism have shown themselves alert to the challenge of theory: Tanselle's *A Rationale of Textual Criticism*, a version of his Rosenbach lectures published in 1989, is a comprehensive analysis of the ontology of text in various art-forms (cinema, painting, architecture, music, literature, dance), responding in part to F. W. Bateson's question, "If the *Mona Lisa* is in the Louvre, where are *Hamlet* and *Lycidas*?" The same question prompts Peter Shillingsburg's lengthy investigation of ontology in his article "Text as Matter, Concept, and Action," as it does

James McLaverty's article "The Mode of Existence of Literary Works of Art," the title of which is a direct allusion to Wellek and Warren's formalist view of the issue in their *Theory of Literature*. It is against this formalist, essentialist, literary, and non-material position which McLaverty argues, in his insistence that the ontology of the literary work is as much in its physical form as in its language, a persuasion independently endorsed by McGann's claim that meaning lies in the "bibliographical codes," the type, layout, format, paper, etc., just as much as it does in the "linguistic codes," on which most textual criticism, and particularly textual analysis, has concentrated ("What Is Critical Editing?").

In another important study ("The Concept of Authorial Intention"), McLaverty takes issue with both Thorpe and Tanselle's definitions of "intention"; but while citing some of the specifically textual and bibliographical critics already mentioned in this chapter (for example, Maas, Bowers, Gaskell, and Hinman), McLaverty's primary frame of reference is to philosophers, aestheticians, and literary theorists. McLaverty's thesis is that E. D. Hirsch is "much the most important figure as far as textual criticism is concerned" and proceeds to claim that neither Tanselle nor Thorpe fully account for the levels and types of intention that Hirsch's work (for example, *Validity in Interpretation* and *The Aims of Interpretation*) defines in the relations of author, text, and reader/critic/editor. Making, for example, a distinction between the "motives" (which ought not to be within the textual critic's province) and "intentions" (which might be), McLaverty declares that Dickens's "motives" in accepting the advice of Bulwer Lytton to change the ending of *Great Expectations* are beyond the power of the textual critic to question. All that matters is that we can demonstrate Dickens's "intention" to make the change, and his "expectation" that these intentions should be carried out by the publisher.

On another front—the much rarer treatment of textual matters, and specifically the problem of intention, by literary theorists rather than by textual critics—Steven Mailloux's book *Interpretive Conventions* is, like McGann, clearly indebted to Fish's concept of the "interpretive community" as the determinant of meaning—both in its title and in its reforming of some of the levels of "intention" accepted by textual critics like Tanselle. Thus, where Tanselle accepts Michael Hancher's term "active intentions" and its definition ("the actions that the author, at the time he finishes his text, understands himself to be performing in the text" [830]), Mailloux suggests that such an acceptance of "final" intentions misrepresents the circumstances of composition. He therefore proposes that "active intentions" (as far as textual scholarship is concerned) be redefined as "the actions that the author, *as he writes the text*, understands himself to be performing in that text" (97), and this redefinition throws an emphasis upon performance and process similar to that endorsed by Fish's affective stylistics. That is, even composition is thought to be primarily "processional" rather than "productive," and "final intentions" become a chimera.

Another important contributor to this debate over the processional nature of literature has been Hershel Parker (already mentioned among the list of "revisionists"), who has written a number of energetic articles (and a book—*Flawed Texts and Verbal Icons* which, like Mailloux's and McGann's lies half-way between textual scholarship and literary theory) demonstrating that Greg's copy-text theory will simply not accommodate the circumstances of much American fiction. He cites, for example, the revisions of Melville's *Pierre*, Crane's *Red Badge of Courage*, Twain's *Puddn'head Wilson*, and Mailer's *American Dream* in the conviction that the self-contradictory and changing motivation and practice of such works cannot be represented by "orthodox" Greg-Bowers copy-text theory. Parker places the focus of attention on "composition," not on product, for he believes that it is impossible to realize "final intentions" in a product that is ultimately destructive of its own motivation. Parker's avowed aim is to resuscitate what he calls "full intentionality," the acknowledgment of various levels of intention in the production of literary texts. However, as I have elsewhere remarked, I believe that his concentration on the self-contradictions in texts draws his work close to that of the deconstructors. "Parker's and Derrida's concerns, while differently motivated, are not dissimilar in their application: both tend to take the specific image, scene, or fragmentary moment in its reflexive qualities throughout the text (back and forth), to allow it to accomplish the dismantling of the logic of the text as a whole. Both are interested in the 'traces' of meaning left in a text, and both are concerned with *différance*, the reader's having continually to 'defer' a conclusive, closed interpretation of a text. To both critics, texts are embarrassments, embarrassments of narrative and of logic" ("Textual and Literary Theory": 12).

While Parker may be a deconstructor *malgré lui*, Tanselle has tackled the issue of deconstruction directly in his struggle with poststructuralism for control over the concepts of "text" and "work," specifically in the collection of essays by Hartman, Bloom, de Man,

Derrida, and Miller, *Deconstruction and Criticism*. Reversing the hierarchies of their title in his own ("Textual Criticism and Deconstruction"), Tanselle plays in the deconstructors' text with a verve hardly reminiscent of a "strict and pure" bibliographer: he cuts up their text, redefines it, contradicts it, and even rewrites it, in a manner I take ("[Textual] Criticism") to be a classic piece of deconstruction.

Textual scholars are thus confronting many of the critical issues (e.g., interpretation, meaning, authority, textuality) characteristic of other parts of the discipline. Perhaps the most provocative to date has been the attempt by some feminist scholars to interrogate not only the patriarchal canon of received texts but also the ideologies embedded in editions, for example, the status of text and apparatus as "center" and "margins" respectively (see Betty Bennett; Katie King; Brenda R. Silver; Patricia White).

Some of this speculation, especially that reversing the hierarchies of traditional textual components (e.g., truth and error, reading and variant, center and margin) may very well result in editions bearing a non-intentionalist stamp, perhaps following the examples of European geneticism, based on the principles of structuralism. Until a few years ago, the technical constraints of letterpress editions lent themselves quite naturally to the production of definitive, fixed, permanent editions, both on the page and in time, so that eclectic, final intentions editions seemed almost natural for the technical medium. But it is now possible for the textual scholar to produce fragmented, spliced, mutilated, multiform, grafted, or deconstructed texts—doubtless embodying the worst nightmares of New Critic and New Bibliographer alike—and most textual scholars now recognize that there is a natural affinity between the computer and the variable discourses of contemporary textual scholarship, an issue raised more fully in the next chapter.

Donald H. Reiman has characterized the hegemony of the Greg-Bowers method as a "brazen" age of editing "because of the too-sanguine hopes they, at least for a time, entertained about the results obtainable through systematic application of fixed principles to a wide variety of texts" ("Four Ages": 142), and contrasts this mood with the more pragmatic, less systematic work of Tanselle and other interpreters of Greg and Bowers—what he calls an "iron" age of "relatively rough and unpolished texts, allowed to reflect the vagaries of authorial behavior" (251). While he predicted that the texts of the iron age would "rust in time," when he wrote his essay on the "four ages" of editing (a decade ago) Reiman would probably not have foreseen that the spread of what he has called "versioning" would not so much rust texts as shatter them. These fragmented shards, uncollected pieces, and unfixed states are doubtless appropriate symptoms of our age (and they re-emphasize the critical role of the textuist in evaluating their relative status), but how shall we nominate this age, after those of gold, silver, brass, and iron? Borrowing from Reiman's system (itself borrowed from Peacock's account of poetic history), perhaps we might venture that the right name for this age of brief, open-ended, fissured texts should come from one of those trans-uranium elements created for milliseconds in the fierce collisions of the accelerator.

What fierce collisions may yet come in textual criticism cannot be foreseen, except that the confidence in the perfect applicability of pure technology is unlikely ever to have the seductions it once had in the early days of analytical bibliography. Technology will always be a part of textual criticism, and particularly a part of scholarly editing, as the increased use of electronic aids in everything from optical scanning of texts to indexing and typesetting so forcefully demonstrates. But the criticism aspect of textual criticism is as secure a part of the discipline as at any time since the Alexandrians—perhaps even more so. Earlier this century, A. E. Housman proposed the formula that textual criticism is "the science of discovering errors in texts, and the art of removing them" (*Selected Prose*: 131), but today, most practicing textual critics would probably insist that art and science are equally mixed in both parts of Housman's equation.

Editing the Text: Scholarly Editing

The design of this book has followed what I believe to be a natural (even an inevitable) narrative—from gaining access to the text in its various forms, to discovering its bibliographical characteristics and interpreting its surface features, to defining its transmissional history. The narrative has moved therefore from enumerative bibliography to analytical and descriptive bibliography, from paleography and typography to historical bibliography and textual bibliography, and on to textual criticism or critical bibliography. Theoretically the process could stop there (and some important theorists in textual studies have been content to do so); but the culmination of textual scholarship is in editing the text, in using all of this information to prepare a version of the author's work for presentation to a reading public. It is with this task and with the decisions and problems attending it that this book concludes.

The first major decision and distinction to be made is whether the edition is to be *critical* or *non-critical*, that is, whether it is to attempt to establish a text (based upon the sort of research described in this book), or whether it is simply to reproduce a text already in existence, and perhaps to use this text as a vehicle for annotation or interpretive criticism.

There is doubtless a place for such non-critical texts, especially where an authoritative scholarly edition of the text has already been produced by a reputable textual critic or critics, and where this text can then serve as the focus for a critical commentary which is perhaps not available in the original edition. This sort of edition ("commentary" is probably the better word) has long been a tradition in classical scholarship, where the line-by-line interpretation of the work in question is the major purpose of the book. A related form is the variorum critical commentary, where again the text is inherited from some other authority; or in certain cases may simply be the *textus receptus* as it has been established, modified, and clarified through the history of transmission. The critical variorum (e.g., of Shakespeare) does not pretend to be primarily a work of *textual* scholarship, but rather seeks to focus on the various critical responses to the text in a cogent and consistent manner (in fact, some variorums of this type do not even include a text in the "edition", e.g., the *Milton Variorum Commentary*). In these cases, there is at least no confusion over the scope and purposes of the edition and its text.

Elsewhere, unfortunately, the same clarity of intention is not observed. For example, would-be "editors" may decide simply to make use of an earlier (ideally, out-of-copyright) version of the text because they have neither the time nor the inclination to establish texts for themselves—but may then pass off the resulting editions as if they were genuinely, and newly "critical." This masquerade often occurs in so-called classroom editions, and happened recently when A. L. Rowse blithely co-opted the old (in fact, *very* old—1864) Globe edition of Shakespeare as "the most authoritative" version of the text upon which to hang his annotations. The problem (and, it seems to me, the deliberate obfuscation) here is not that Rowse decided to produce a popular annotated Shakespeare, but that he based his annotations on a text which can no longer be regarded as authoritative.

The issue may in some ways reside in the terms conventionally applied to non-critical editions. An "editor" is often thought of as simply the person responsible for preparing a text for publication (indeed, the duties of "editors" working in publishing houses consist almost wholly of acting as liaison between author and publisher/printer). It is not surprising, then, that a person who inherits a text from elsewhere, adds a few notes and a brief introduction, can be spoken of as an "editor." Even in "strict" bibliography, the term "edition" refers quite properly to the identifiably separate type-setting of *any* book, whether it is an edition in the text-critical sense or not. Similarly, the text-book "editions" of rhetorics and readers so beloved of English composition teachers are editions only in the sense that somebody selected the essays, obtained permission to reprint, and then probably wrote a student's introduction and invented some interpretive questions on each essay. (Virtually the same comments could doubtless be applied to scholarly *Festschriften* and other collections, which may occasionally be called "editions"). The printer's copy for both such editions is almost invariably the pages of the base text employed, with no further correction. Let us agree, therefore, that for the purposes of this book on textual scholarship, these editions are not genuine editions (even non-critical ones), and turn to those which are.

In addition to the textual commentaries mentioned earlier, the most important type of non-critical edition is one which seeks to present a faithful version of a single document, with only minimal textual involvement by the editor. The most faithful of all (at least theoretically) is the *photographic reprint*, which presents a technically exact—and, one trusts, unaltered and unretouched—facsimile of the original. This type of edition is for obvious reasons most commonly associated with manuscripts, where the scribal idiosyncrasies of, for example, abbreviation marks, letter- and word-spacing, letter-formation and relative letter-size could perhaps not be accurately displayed in a type-setting. The manuscripts so selected will usually have some specific interest in themselves, either textual or codicological. They may, for example, be the only or the primary documentary witness to a text (e.g., the manuscripts containing *Beowulf* or *Pearl* and *Sir Gawain and the Green Knight*), or they may represent a particularly significant stage in the textual transmission (e.g., the Variorum Chaucer facsimile of the *Canterbury Tales* Hengwrt manuscript, which provides the base-text for the textual collation in subsequent volumes of the Variorum, or, in the modern period, the edition of *The Waste Land* manuscript, reproducing both Eliot's original, and Pound's annotations and suggestions). Both of these editions usefully provide transcripts of the manuscript material. There is also a thriving interest in purely paleographic or ornamental features, represented in, for example, the popular recent series of Braziller facsimiles of medieval Books of Hours (such as the Limbourg brothers' *Très riches heures* and *Grandes heures* of Jean, Duc de Berry, produced in the richly decorative International Style of the fifteenth century), where the textual interest is clearly minimal. Printed books have also been widely photocopied in facsimile editions, especially where the book has some historical or cultural significance (e.g., the Norton facsimile of the Shakespeare First Folio, or the more recent California facsimile of Shakespeare Quartos). The major difference between a manuscript and print facsimile is that in most cases, the printed book will not be unique, whereas the manuscript will obviously always be. This distinction may allow a slightly greater editorial role in the print facsimile, where, for example, Charlton Hinman's Norton facsimile is made up of various leaves from leaves containing corrected forms from a number of copies to create a textual "ideal copy," which is available only in the facsimile, not in any of the individual extant copies. It should go without saying that, especially in manuscript facsimiles, the photocopy should not be accepted as if it were the original. The facsimile fulfils a valid purpose (esthetic, historical, even scholarly), but it is no substitute for the examination of the manuscript itself, especially where this manuscript is to be the chosen copy-text for a scholarly edition. The use of microfilm has made textual work very much easier than it used to be (especially in reducing travel to out-of-the-way repositories), but a microform edition is not the same thing as reading the manuscript, for reader or editor, who must be able to observe such features as hair-line abbreviation marks often invisible in facsimile, and must sometimes use the evidence of the bibliographical materials of the manuscript (parchment, paper, ink, binding etc.) in making textual decisions: see Chapter 7 for an account of the influence of materials and production on the text.

Next to the photographic facsimile edition in its degree of fidelity to the document stands first the *type facsimile* and then the *diplomatic transcript*. The type facsimile attempts to reproduce the actual physical appearance of the original in a different type-setting, by observing such features as the original lineation, type-size and type-face in the reprint. The diplomatic transcript, however, dispenses with any attempt at such scrupulous fidelity to appearance, and concentrates primarily on the textual content of the original, reproducing the exact spelling, punctuation, and capitalization (usually) of the *diploma* (the document), but transcribing the text into a different type-face, with different lineation (except in verse, of course) and different type-sizes.

Of late, there has been a good deal of argument over the specific editorial practices to be used in this latter form of transcription, and in part this argument rests upon another type of documentary classification. In his analysis of the various distinctions to be made between types of edition and types of document (upon which this present account is in part based), G. Thomas Tanselle notes ("Textual Scholarship") that the editor should distinguish between the treatment accorded documents intended for publication and those which are of a more private nature (for example, personal correspondence, notebooks, etc.). This distinction is a valuable one, and can work well generically in the age of print, where it is usually easy to determine the published state of the text (hastily scrawled notes are clearly private, a printed text of a novel is clearly public, as would also be the author's manuscript fair copy of the novel, or a corrected proof). Tanselle argues, quite properly, that "a scholarly editor has no right to guess what the author would have done if faced with the prospect of publishing [private documents]," and that the editor should therefore transcribe correspondence etc. *as is*, and not attempt to normalize it for the modern reader (34). This distinction is less clearly drawn, however, in the pre-Gutenberg age, where there are virtually no truly "private" documents (in the sense of personal notebooks or correspondence not intended to be read by anyone but the recipient)—and this is especially so of literary figures having otherwise no historical significance. In this period, all documents are, of course, manuscripts, and while some may be more carefully written than others, one should not assume that the more legible are the more "published." One may argue that a "presentation" copy was obviously intended by its author for publication, but the converse (that a hastily scrawled manuscript represents a non-publishable version) is less easy to maintain with any surety.

But given that a distinction between publishable and private can be arrived at, how does the argument over transcription proceed from there? The most famous debate on this issue in recent years has been that between Tanselle ("Editing of Historical Documents," representing a very strict line in transcriptional fidelity to the surface features of a private document) and a number of American historians, particularly those associated with the editing of the papers of the so-called great white fathers—Adams, Jefferson, and so on. In brief, the historians have felt it necessary to normalize, rationalize (and even modernize) authorial usage in such documents (largely to make them more accessible to a modern reading public—see Robert Taylor), whereas Tanselle and many literary editors (see Cook, "Short") have maintained that private documents should be preserved in transcript as closely as typographically possible to their original features, within the accepted limits of the diplomatic reprint, as opposed to the type-facsimile.

Non-critical editions (as representing one of the most basic of editorial choices) have been dealt with at some length largely because they raise issues which have not been adequately covered already in the previous chapter on textual criticism. (Since non-critical editions by definition do not involve any criticism of the text, their characteristics have not been in the forefront of textual theory, as have the features of critical editions.) But critical editions are clearly more difficult and more costly to produce, and the basic editorial decisions which lead to a successful critical edition should be touched on before moving on to an account of the actual procedures of editing.

As noted in the previous chapter, one of the major debates in twentieth-century textual criticism has been over the status of authorial intention and its representation in a critical text. All textual criticism is conjectural at some point, for as soon as the decision to produce a critical text has been made, the editor is faced with critical choices which will depend not only upon certain technical data (e.g., information about the format or imposition of the book) but also upon a subjective interpretation of the available evidence. It has often been assumed that conjecture is involved only when an editor reconstructs or creates a reading which is not extant in any of the witnesses; but the choice among extant variants is just as critical, and just as ultimately conjectural, as the recreation of a form which happens not to be extant in any of the witnesses. The intentionalist editor is deciding which reading is the more authorial (and is therefore interpreting intention), and in the process presumably rejecting all other readings as unauthoritative (or the cancelled first thoughts of an author). An apparently authorial variant in a document does not in all cases depend for its authority on the characteristics or existence of the document, for if this were so, then works extant in only one manuscript would never be susceptible to editorial emendation—a clearly untenable position for a critical edition, especially where the single witness is a scribal or compositorial copy and therefore inherently corrupt to one degree or another.

So a critical edition demands both criticism and conjecture—the problem is the degree and nature of that criticism. As seen already, the history of textual criticism has often moved between two extreme reactions to criticism and the discovery of authorial intention, one extreme (analogy and eclecticism) believing that correct readings are discoverable given enough information about the texts and enough intelligence and inspiration on the part of the editor, and the other extreme (anomaly and conservatism) believing that conjecture is more likely to represent editorial rather than authorial intention and that consequently the evidence of the documents—and ideally one specific document—should be placed above that of editorial judgment or taste. Both schools involve some criticism, for the analogists maintain that critical discriminations are possible among variant readings from different witnesses, and the anomalists maintain that critical discrimination is possible in selecting the witness to be faithful to. The question is: what system or what rationale may one use to make these discriminations?

As noted earlier, the most famous (and in Anglo-American literary editing, certainly the most dominant) rationale offered in the twentieth century has been Greg's, for its division of authority between substantives and accidentals, and its implied "residual authority" of copytext on those occasions where no critical discrimination among variants seems possible, allow both fidelity (to copy-text accidentals) and conjecture (in selection of variant substantives) their proper roles. The notion of residual authority is also perhaps a form of compromise, for it retains the concept of best-text without withdrawing from active interpretation and criticism of this best-text and other variant states. The degree to which Greg's rationale properly represents the actual history of compositorial and authorial practice in any period after the Renaissance is still being debated, and copy-text theory as a whole has yet to make much inroad into the editing of medieval texts. But Greg's theory (especially through Bowers's championing of it and Tanselle's explication and defense of it) has at least provided a framework or a mechanism for the active discussion of intention and criticism (even though Greg's essay did not really attend to the former of these two terms), and it is likely that the editing of English and American literature will be influenced (pro or con) by his essay for some time to come, despite the recent changes in philosophical emphasis described at the conclusion of the previous chapter. Indeed, there are even signs of its basic precepts being debated in other disciplines (for example, music, see Broude, Kallberg).

The critical edition will therefore contain emendations, and these emendations will involve one level or other of editorial conjecture. What these emendations will produce in an intentionalist edition is of necessity a degree of authorial intention unrepresented by any of the extant witnesses. But what if this intention, when discoverable, turns out to be manifold rather than single? What if it is dynamic rather than static? As observed in the previous chapter, the work of the many recent scholars (revisionists, textologists, New Scholars, versionists, social textual critics, geneticists, etc.) has focused upon those texts which either contradict themselves internally and so betray their original intentions in their subsequent revisions (e.g., Melville's *Pierre* or Mailer's *American Dream*) or are subject to external, non-authorial pressures which may be accepted by authors but which complicate or even vitiate the very concept of intentionality (e.g., Crane's *Red Badge of Courage*). But several of these new revisionist schools (especially Parker's New Scholarship and McGann's social textual criticism) have been criticized by intentionalist, eclectic critics for their failure to address in practical terms the very problems they posit: while perhaps effectively describing the textual phenomena, the revisionists have not yet produced a critical vehicle for representing them in a scholarly edition. Given the conditions of revised and contradicted and socialized and multiplied intention, should one simply not read Melville, Mailer, and Crane at all, or read them in two or three discrete versions, or read only the remnants, or what?

One type of answer has been produced by the genetic editors (more common in the scholarly editing of French and German authors than anglophone, see Chapter 8), and the best-known genetic edition of late has been Hans Walter Gabler's *Ulysses*, which provides a "synoptic apparatus" of the text(s) on the verso pages, balanced—or contradicted by—a clear-text reading version on the recto pages. The synoptic version includes all variants *within* the critical text-page, rather than critically editing a copy-text, producing a clear text, and relegating rejected readings to the apparatus. In a synoptic apparatus, there are no rejected readings (or at least, no authorial ones). The conflict between synopticism and intentionality in part explains the contention which this edition has generated (see Bates, Kidd, Rossman), for Gabler's attempted marriage of a Continental, non-authorial method and an Anglo-American, author-centered, presentation has not been fully successful, or at least not fully understood, and has exacerbated the other issues raised about the edition (for example, its failure to consult originals of primary documents, its ambivalent emendations policy, and the problematic status of some of the readings recorded only in historical collation.)

Another development of the principle of versioning and geneticism can be seen in the work of John Miles Foley, the editor of Yugoslav oral literature who, confronted by an enormous range of variants and having, for obvious reasons, no clearly defined concept of a documentary copy-text, has produced a computer-generated series of texts, each one obeying different critical requirements with regard to particular versions of particular oral formulae. In this case (as in the manipulation of the evidence documented in a synoptic apparatus), textual critics or critical readers create their own texts from the raw materials presented by the editor, in a technically more advanced but conceptually similar manner to that traditionally employed by the editor of a conventional critical edition with full historical collation. The difference between such a traditional edition and the experiments with Joyce and oral literature is largely in format, not theory. By placing the accepted reading on the textual page and relegating other readings to the apparatus or the historical collation (usually printed in smaller type, and sometimes placed in the back of the book, or even in a different volume), the editor of a traditional critical text is, in the very layout of the edition, enshrining a hierarchy of variants: those which make it onto the textual page are somehow in a different class from those which are printed in apparatus and collation. And this is rightly so, for the editor presumably believes that the text-page readings are better than those recorded elsewhere. The Foley computer selection and the Joyce synoptic apparatus may therefore be looked upon either as technical attempts to make all the information available simultaneously, or (as a result of their conscious sacrifice of the hierarchy of variants) as yet another version of Donaldson's "editorial death-wish" already encountered in Chapter 8—the futile pretense that no critical decisions are necessary in editing critical texts and that Lachmannian stemmatics, or new bibliography, or distributional analysis, or computer programs can protect the editor from having to think.

But there are some works which do not respond to the conventional interpretation of the editorial mandate to produce a single critical edition. For example, is it really possible for us to read the 1799, 1805, and 1850 versions of Wordsworth's *The Prelude* as if they were all simply "variants" of the same work? What about the F and G versions of the Prologue to Chaucer's *Legend of Good Women*, in which the bestowing of textual priority on one or the other would involve the sacrifice of much fine "Chaucerian" verse? Do we suppose that when Dickens changed the "unhappy" ending of *Great Expectations* to a "happy" one at the instigation of Bulwer Lytton he was being subjected to the same sort of literary censorship as that which caused Crane's *Red Badge of Courage* to lose its original intentions because of his editor Ripley Hitchcock's textual interference? And is it therefore possible for sensitive readers to hold *both* endings of the Dickens novel in their minds as parts of the *same* work? What of the constant revisions and additions in such works as Sidney's *Arcadia* or Burton's *Anatomy of Melancholy*, or the two versions of *King Lear* and the three versions of *Hamlet*? Is Pope's original, satiric version of *The Rape of the Lock* compatible (textually? esthetically?) with the expanded mock-epic version? Is Fowles's mature revision of his juvenile *The Magus* destructive of the original intentions of that work? And, in reference to two works already cited in a different context: does the final version of *The Waste Land* display more of Eliot or of Pound as they are represented in the manuscript? And why did it take five centuries for anybody to notice that *Piers Plowman* was not really one poem but three poems, and how has it now apparently become possible for some textual critics to regard it as one again, (when Kane and Donaldson rationalize their emendations policy for the B version by an appeal to the readings of Kane's earlier edition of the A version)?

These questions, it should be emphasized, are not peculiar to the editing and/or textual criticism of literature, for in music the changing intentions and locales of Verdi's *Masked Ball*, for example, or the protean changes—in length and content—of his *Don Carlo(s)*, the two versions of the Sibelius Violin Concerto (the first of which was released by the Sibelius family only in 1991), and the post-*Tristan* stylistic revisions of the Dresden version of Wagner's *Tannhäuser* betray a similar complexity, as does Chopin's regularly having sent off—sometimes on the same day—three radically different versions of solo piano works to his three publishers in England, Germany, and France (Kallberg). How can the reader/editor deal with such discrepancies when the authors/composers cannot seem to make up their minds about what are the work's intentions? In the case of *Tannhäuser*, the option of an embarrassment of riches seems almost always to be exercised, despite the resultant clash of two different chromatic systems—rather like printing both endings of *Great Expectations* in the same volume—but since this obeys authorial final rather than original intentions, it has a respectable rationale, since presumably Wagner was satisfied with the joining of a later style and an earlier work.

It is true that people do read Wordsworth and Dickens and they do listen to Verdi and Wagner, but it is perhaps equally true that the works they read and hear are sometimes best regarded not as single entities, with the possibility of the textual critic's being able to arrive at a single, definitive text embodying all authorial intentions.

Even with the convenience of the hierarchy of variants presentable in apparatus (a convenience not possible, of course, in the actual *performance* of temporal media like music or spatial media like painting), some works may finally destroy their own integrity, achieving or displaying what the deconstructionists like to call their *aporia*, their "central knot of indeterminacy," and may therefore have to be considered as related, but nonetheless separate works. The editorial solutions to this condition may range from a determined rejection of one or other alternative (apparently the norm with *Great Expectations*), to parallel-text editions (often used, for example, in the editing of the Chaucer *Legend*) to completely independent editions of the various versions (as in the usual modern editing of *Piers Plowman*). It is in works such as these that the discipline of textual criticism and its attendant practice of editing seem to reach their limits, as traditionally defined.

It is also true that, with changes in technology it is now possible for the recipient of the text to manipulate the textual evidence to produce variant states, not all of which may reflect authorial intention, or at least single or final intention. Thus, recent recordings of *Don Carlos* (i.e., in its original French text, not in the Italian translation, *Don Carlo*) and of *Show Boat* take advantage of CD technology and include variant versions of several arias which can then be programmed individually into the listener's desired order for the work as a whole, displacing those in the main text with the push of a button. Taking advantage of this facility, the editors/producers of a recent CD recording of Handel's *Messiah* actually provide the users with a key to re-create any of the nine distinct versions which Handel wrote: the 1741 autograph, the Dublin premiere of 1742, the Covent Garden performances of 1743, 1745, and 1750, the London Foundling Hospital performance of 1759, Handel's conducting score, with changes made to his death in 1759, and a copy produced in Dublin in 1761. Even this largesse is insufficient to chart the actual performance variation, however; for while the orchestral forces on the recording remain constant, there was a larger body of strings in 1749 and possibly no oboes in Dublin (Kenyon). Thus, only textual variance is offered, not performance variance. Moreover, what the producers do not emphasize is that the CD player is not restricted to just these nine "authorized" versions, for the individual listener can obviously "mix and match" various arias from various states to construct virtually unlimited conflated editions. It will surely not be long before it is the norm for editors of literary editions to provide similar reader-manipulated facilities in electronic editions based on the so-called hypertext principle of variant electronic storage. Such editions might properly be called post-critical, in that the editor does not establish a text nor does he or she simply reproduce a previously existing text. Such editions provide the raw materials (through hypertext) for a series of possible conflated editions, in a manner very different from the fixing of text usually associated with critical editions. The future of scholarly editing is clearly a very exciting and provocative one, as these technological possibilities become reality.

Even now, the computer is an essential and inevitable part of scholarly editing. It is in the early stages of editing, especially collation and filiation, and in the very end, concordances and indexes, that computers have proved most useful so far, with comparatively limited electronic influence on the middle stages of textual *criticism* or emendation.

For example, it is safe to say that no complete record of the fundamental units of a verbal text—its words—will ever again be done without computer assistance. Such concordances, if they are to be of textual value, will not merely list the words in a work or *œuvre* but will show a selection from the text in which they appear. There are basically two ways of making such selections—with KWIC (key-word-in-context) and KWOC (key-word-out-of-context) concordances. In a KWIC concordance, the keyword (the main entry) will be recorded as it appears in a particular lexical position, say, in the middle of a word block with five or ten words on each side—with no reference to how the word appears on the textual page (at the beginning or end of a line, for example). A KWIC concordance can be instructed to sort the keyword to the left or right of such a block, but a central position is generally more useful for observing how the word is used in its context. The KWIC system is widely used in fluid texts like prose or verse with much enjambment. The KWOC concordance, on the other hand, will position the keyword not in a particular lexical context but rather as it appears in a specific textual unit (e.g., a metrical line); in such concordances, an editor will be more interested in seeing how the word is used by an author in the *line* rather than in the word-block. Thus, a KWIC concordance for the word "impediment" in Shakespeare's sonnets (with the keyword in a central context of five words on either side) would yield an entry "marriage of true minds/Admit *impediment*. Love is not love/Which," whereas a KWOC concordance using the metrical line as its unit would record "Admit *impediment*. Love is not love." Despite the iambic pentameter of the sonnet structure, the KWIC system shows the enjambment better (although this is in part because the sample is larger). Each method has its advantages, and the concordance-maker will have to decide which better suits the textual conditions.

Other problems in computer concordances include homographs (e.g., how does the computer distinguish between "does" [third person singular of the verb "to do"] and "does" [plural of the female deer]?) and lemmatization (how does the computer recognize a word temporarily disguised by, e.g., prefixes or variant spelling: should the word "pressure" be regarded by the computer as having the prefix "pre-"?). Through morphological segmentation sub-programs, it may be possible to make these distinctions, especially in texts with typically small lexicons, like Old English, but often the entire text may need to be pre-sorted syntactically and morphemically. On a wider lexical scale—entire languages—a scholar may now do semantic, morphological, or syntactic searches (Stubbs and Tompa, Amos) through the parsing facilities of such dictionaries as the revised OED (*Oxford English Dictionary*), DARE (*Dictionary of American Regional English*), DOE (*Dictionary of Old English*), and TLF (*Tresor de la langue française*). An editor working on a Shakespeare text may determine not only whether a particularly word is ever used by Shakespeare—from the Spevack concordance to the Riverside edition—but also whether this word occurs in any other headnote citations collected in OED. An editor may also discover, say, all words entering the English language from Italian in the sixteenth century or all quotations from Shakespeare, or Milton, or Keats, or Melville, cited in the NOED. Another related form of computer assistance is in vocabulary or stylistic studies, usually concerned with forming a view of the author's idiolect, the personal imprint upon the language choices available. However, one must be very careful here to construct this imprint from neutral terms and must be very wary of context. For example, a recent stylometric study of the Pearl poet (quoted in Pearsall and Cooper, "Statistical Approach" 371–72) came up with the surprising results that the author had a high incidence of "I," "me," "she," and "her," but a very low incidence of "he," "him," "they," and "them," where a quick look at the context of *Pearl*—a dialogue between a narrator-dreamer and a vision of a young maiden—would immediately determine why this was so. Similarly, "p" is obviously a very common alliterative initial in *Pearl*, "c" a very common alliterative initial in *Cleanness*, etc. Thus, the context may pre-determine the results of stylometric studies, which ought therefore to concentrate as far as possible on unconscious selections within the idiolect, not substantive ones.

In collation of witnesses, computers can remove much of the drudgery formally associated with textual scholarship, especially when used with optical scanners such as the Kurzweil machine. However, most editorial experience suggests that scanners can be used with confidence only on printed texts of the machine-print, post 1800, era, in which there is a chartable degree of uniformity and variance in the physical appearance of type-forms, although some recent experiments on manuscripts offer the possibility of direct electronic entry of handwritten text with an accuracy rate as high as 99% (Giunta and

Hacker).

Once the various witnesses have been scanned or otherwise entered into the collation program, then the charting of variants and the mapping of filiation can proceed electronically. The current range of collation and filiation programs is very wide and will no doubt be wider in the years ahead. Some work line by line, some with blocks of a specific number of words; some can compare only two texts at a time, others up to fifty. The best known at present (Hockey, *Guide*; Oakman) include Widmann's program for *A Midsummer Night's Dream*, project OCCULT (Ordered Computer Collation of Unprepared Literary Text), the Cabaniss program, and COLLATE. Ted-Larry Pebworth and Gary Stringer's collation program, based on the Donne Variorum, is available for personal computers, as is Peter Shillingsburg's CASE (Computer Assisted Scholarly Editing) system, based on the Thackeray edition. CASE is particularly useful, since it combines nine interrelated programs which do much more than merely collate. For example, CASE can produce fair copy from a diplomatic transcription, merge variant files into a single comprehensive historical collation, sort lists of selected variants, and turn working lists of variants into files appropriate for producing textual apparatus. For filiation, Vinton Dearing has written several useful programs, including PRELIMDI, ARCHETYP, and MSFAMTRE, the latter using the data collected in PRELIMDI, and then arranging the variants according to theory of probability (Hockey, *Guide*: 158-59).

While computers have been used to research, edit, produce, and typeset *printed* critical editions, fully *electronic* texts, marketed in computer-readable form and even manipulated by the reader and used to create reader-designed critical editions, are still in the planning stage—although there is little doubt that they will come soon. The cumulative electronic storage in hypertext of *all* forms and states of text forming that text's history will assuredly provide the raw and combinatory materials for the production of reader- (or more correctly, viewer-) created editions in the near future, as suggested by Shillingsburg (*Scholarly Editing*, "Polymorphic") and others. (See McGann on D. G. Rossetti, Duggan on *Piers Plowman*, and Mosser, Robinson on *The Canterbury Tales*; Chernaik, Landow, Lanham, McGillivray, and Sanders for general discussions; and the *CTI Centre Resources Guide* for practical information.) Foley's HEURO I ("Editing" 85–89) has already shown the way, with its ability to allow the operator at a computer terminal to experiment among the motifs arranged in the "object text"—a hypertextual transmission of the text to and by the receiver. Electronic versions of print editions, such as the Oxford Shakespeare and the Riverside Chaucer, while not fully reader- or user-manipulable like HEURO I, allow the reader to search the text for lexical and morphological features in a manner not possible in their print counterparts.

These are some of the technological and theoretical alternatives presented to the would-be editor. But what of the practicalities, the actual production of scholarly editions? What guidelines can be offered for the editor in preparing the materials for the reader-user? There are several useful manuals for would-be editors, either for entire disciplines (e.g., Mary-Jo Kline's *Guide to Documentary Editing*, promoted by the historians of the Association for Documentary Editing) or for particular periods (e.g., the Foulet-Speer *On Editing Old French Texts*), and several longstanding editions have manuals developed for the editing of the works of particular authors. The best general practical guide for scholarly editing can be found in the *Guidelines* published by the Committee on Scholarly Editions of the Modern Language Association, and the final part of this chapter reflects the general order and content of this brochure. For details of any of the stages briefly covered in the next few pages, I would strongly suggest that the editor obtain the CSE Guidelines and confer with the Committee, and to consult the historical surveys and research guides in my forthcoming *Scholarly Editing*.

Before any genuine editorial work begins, the textual scholar must have decided exactly what is the work or works to be edited. This may not be as obvious as it seems, for the very definition of work and author can be highly problematical. The issue has been stated in its widest terms by Foucault ("What Is an Author?"):

> Even when an individual has been accepted as an author, we must still ask whether everything that he wrote, said, or left behind is part of his work. The problem is both theoretical and technical. When undertaking the publication of Nietzsche's works, for example, where should one stop? Surely everything must be published, but what is "everything"? Everything that Nietzsche himself published, certainly. And what about rough drafts of his works? Obviously. The plans for his aphorisms? Yes. The deleted passages and the notes at the bottom of the page? Yes. What if, within a workbook filled with aphorisms, one finds a reference, the notation of a meeting or of an address, or a laundry list: Is it a work, or not? Why not? And so on, ad infinitum. How can one define a work

amid the millions of traces left by someone after his death? A theory of the work does not exist, and the empirical task of those who
naively undertake the editing of works often suffers in the absence
of such a theory. (103–104).

At the time Foucault wrote this (1969), editorial theory on the
"work" was indeed much less sophisticated than it is now, but it
is still true that there is a good deal of unresolved argument about
what ought properly to be within the documentary canon of a
given author (e.g., how many variant versions of the "same"
work?), and the editor must at least have confronted the general
questions posed by Foucault before beginning the selection of
materials. The CSE guidelines go even further than Foucault, for
they raise the question of "second-party" textual materials (e.g.,
letters *to* as well as *from* the author, or changes introduced by
persons other than the author: copy-editors, proof-readers and so
on).

Once the basic logic of selection has been determined, the *ontology* of the work or works, the editor must then make sure that every
potentially useful primary document has been located, adequately described, and that arrangements have been made to gain access to this
material. Obviously, any clearly *authoritative* documents must be
included in a bibliography of primary materials (e.g., holograph manuscripts, manuscripts or printed editions personally overseen by the
author, copies made from lost holographs, etc.), but so must all other
witnesses to the text that could have *potential* authority. For example, until a complete genealogy of textual transmission has been determined, any manuscript which carries the text and cannot be easily
demonstrated to be a copy of an extant exemplar (and *only* of that
exemplar) must appear as a primary document. In practice, this
means that in the editing of classical, biblical, and medieval texts, the
great majority (perhaps all) of the primary witnesses will be posthumous copies, and even in the printed age posthumous editions may
need to be considered as potentially authoritative witnesses, for they
may very well depend upon lost authorities not otherwise accessible.
As noted several times in this book, many of Shakespeare's plays appeared for the *first* time in the posthumous First Folio, and others,
while having been published earlier, had their texts significantly
changed in the Folio, possibly representing an authorial revision since
the earlier publication. The date of the document is not, therefore,
automatically an assurance of its authority or otherwise.

For editing with a non-intentionalist purpose, and especially for social textual criticism, the traditional procedures associated with the attempted recovery of intention and therefore for evaluating the potential significance of a witness will not always be relevant. It may be that a demonstrably non-authorial state (e.g., one produced through corrupt transmission or through the constraints of censorship) may have greater social prominence and have contributed more to the social "meaning" of the work than a witness with clearly more substantial claims to represent authorial intention (see the arguments of Pizer and McGann in the previous chapter). In such cases, documents will not be adjudicated according to their relative closeness to a putative authorial original but according to their status in the subsequent reception of the work. In a sense, *all* documents are therefore potentially primary in social textual criticism, and perhaps especially posthumous ones.

Another type of material which also ought to be included in either intentionalist or historical initial bibliography is any source or analogous text which might be able to offer useful information on dubious readings in the first-level authoritative documents. For example, if the work being edited is a translation or compendium, the editor should have the primary sources of the work at hand. This is not to suggest that these sources should automatically be used to offer emendations to the edition as a matter of principle, but rather that patterns of translation or quotation might be established from which choices among a series of non-authoritative witnesses could, with editorial care and discrimination, be determined. In some cases, it is possible to decide exactly which manuscript or edition of a source work was used by the author, but in the editing of older material such fine determinations might not be possible (indeed, as has been mentioned before, the printing of a work in the fifteenth or sixteenth centuries typically entailed the loss of exemplars and other sources upon which the printing depended). The presence of such analogous or collateral texts does not mean that their readings can be accepted as significant for the text being edited, even when the analogue or source is manifestly correct and the derivative text incorrect, for, as Tanselle ("External Fact") and Greetham ("Models") have shown, the relationship between source and derived text is often a highly problematical one, requiring not only that the editor establish the specific route whereby the former might have influenced the latter, but also that the editor critically evaluate each possible link between the two with the same sensitivity brought to the elucidation of any other type of variance. In other words, authority can never be assumed; it must always be tested and explained.

Finally, in the initial bibliography, the editor should make sure that all possibly relevant personal material (letters, memoranda, diaries, etc.) are available for consultation, especially where they might bear upon the publication history of the work. Again, certain qualifications must be raised here, for it would be a mistake to allow intentions expressed in a personal document to modify or even determine the intentions demonstrable in the text of the work itself. An author may claim to have undertaken one sort of work but in fact have produced another, and an author's critical evaluation of that work is not *prima facie* any more reliable or authoritative than any other commentator's. Some authors (like Beckett) are perversely unhelpful about their works, and even some intentionalist textual critics may question and ultimately reject the announced intentions of an author, as in the example cited in the previous chapter (p. 336) of Tanselle's rejection of Melville's expressed views on the text of the second edition of *Typee*.

I have introduced a number of complications into this very early stage—the compilation of the initial bibliography—simply to demonstrate that even the most apparently mechanical of editorial procedures require critical adjudication. Many of these complications (intentionality, influence, social status) are typically not addressed directly until later stages of scholarly editing, but it is my belief that the well-informed editor must be aware of the ramifications of bibliographical decisions from the very beginning, while trying to keep the theoretical and methodological options open.

Thus, throughout the preparation of an initial bibliography, the editor should also attempt wherever possible to establish the provenance of the documents (date, place, history), for while it is the content of the documents which is of prime importance at this early stage, it might be that provenance could be of significant value later (e.g., in determining the relationship of the texts). But, as already suggested, provenance should not necessarily drive the methods and values of the edition, for it can be both helpful or misleading, even in the matter of establishing textual relationships.

This is in fact the next logical stage of editing, and whether it is called filiation, genealogy, recension, stemmatics or textual analysis, it must precede the choice of copy-text (where copy-text theory is used at all) and must depend upon preparation of an adequate bibliography. Obviously, the fixing of these textual relationships will depend upon an appropriate system for charting their similarities and differences, and this will involve a careful collation of the primary documents. Some theorists would claim that a *complete* collation of all documents must be achieved before filiation can be established, but others would require only trial collations at several places in each document, so that a base-text can be selected against which all others can then be collated in full. This two-stage collation is perhaps more common in the editing of ancient texts, where a developed "copy-text" theory has not been thought necessary or even possible, and where the "base-text" established after the trial collations will almost certainly be used as the *de facto* copy-text in the edition itself. Since the choice of a base-text in the editing of early texts typically involves only a consideration of substantive variants, this practice may be quite defensible in this field, although it does leave open the possibility that the base-text selected after the first stage of collation might have to yield to another after the collation of all documents. It is unlikely, however, that most editors of two-stage collation would accept Charles Moorman's whimsical suggestion that initial copy-text is selected "by guess or God" (45).

For printed texts, the collation of representative copies of each edition is no longer felt by most bibliographers or editors to be sufficient to establish filiation, for it has been demonstrated that—perhaps especially in the editing of vernacular texts of the sixteenth and seventeenth centuries—there are often significant variants within editions. In some cases, no two copies of the same edition may be identical. The editors of non-vernacular texts of this period (and some editors of Continental texts in this and other periods) have, however, resisted this new stringency, and for them an "edition" is still an integral, undeviating authority. In these circumstances of editorial disagreement, a reasonable compromise might be to suggest the procedures of the editors of the earlier materials—to collate at sample locations in the text of possibly variant copies of each edition, thereby to establish the likelihood of wider variance, and therefore the degree of complete collation required. At least the editors of printed texts can overcome some of the former drudgery of collation by using a mechanical optical collator, such as the Hinman or McLeod, for copies of the same edition.

As has already been shown in Chapter 8, the charting of relationships (after or during collation) has engendered some very complex technical systems of analysis—Greg's *calculus of variants*, Quentin's *positive critical apparatus*, Dearing's *rings* and *principle of parsimo-*

ny—and the complexity of the systems in part reflects the obvious complexity of the possible relationships, where contamination (the remembered influence of another, more familiar, text in the scribe's copying) and conflation (the actual combining of readings from two or more exemplars into the new copy) may often be the norm in certain textual transmissions. In general, it can be observed that the editors of printed texts have been much more likely to find a monogeneous transmission than a heterogeneous (i.e., a straight line of direct descent from one edition to another, rather than a stage of the transmission generating several different descendants and/or itself depending upon different exemplars). For this reason, it is the editors of manuscript works who have tended to formulate the complex systems for describing such heterogeneous traditions, whereas the editors of printed texts have tended to develop the science of the technical analysis and description of books (analytical and descriptive bibliography) to a greater extent than their colleagues working on manuscripts.

Ideally an editor should be competent in both fields, for while the physical and textual nature of a work might not always coincide, and while some theorists (Dearing "Textual Analysis") have declared that the two characteristics must be considered *separately*, the editor must have the expertise to interpret the evidence of both sub-disciplines at some point during the establishment of filiation. As noted in the previous chapter, however, editing from the evidence of recension or filiation has often been rejected by recent editors, who may deny either that filiation is particularly valuable in what it can tell us about the social history of the text's reception or that filiation can even be established. As mentioned earlier, "deep editing" of the type most famously practised by Kane and Donaldson in their edition of *Piers Plowman* falls into this latter persuasion, when they argue that recension cannot be consistently demonstrated in the highly conflated and contaminated manuscripts of Langland. The practical editorial results of such a rejection of filiation theory are that, without the "residual authority" of a copy-text derived from filiation, the editor must treat each variation independently, and thus analyze and edit each variant without recourse to documentary authority. The work must therefore be constructed piece by piece according to some other procedure, principle, or belief (the ontology of the text, the conception the editor might have of the author's composition methods, the editorial characterization of typical scribal idiosyncrasies and their putative relationship to authorial originals). The weight placed upon editorial decisions is thus particularly onerous in deep editing carried out rigorously and comprehensively.

The next stage (if not already completed during the collation itself) is the selection of copy-text, given that a copy-text method is being employed. Enough has been said on this matter in the chapter on textual criticism to give the usual alternatives possible (e.g., whether an authorial manuscript, a first or later edition is considered to bear the greatest authority), and here it should suffice to emphasize that the choice of copy-text will be perhaps the most significant stage of the editorial process and will have a wide-ranging effect on the accidental features of the edited text. While copy-text ideology has dominated Anglo-American scholarly editing for most of the twentieth century, there are signs that, under the influence of structuralism, post-structuralism, and other non-intentionalist, versionist dispensations, it may gradually be ceding to one or other of the various fragmentalist, revisionist methods already discussed in the previous chapter. Thus, the text of the Gabler edition of Joyce's *Ulysses* does not follow copy-text principles, but instead weaves together a seamless series of lections from various witnesses, without recourse to the "residual authority" that a fixed copy-text would provide—the reliance on copy-text readings where there is "indifferent variation" among the witnesses, and thus no critical means of making an authoritative distinction. Moreover, the "divided authority" of accidentals and substantives, on which classic Greg-Bowers copy-text theory was dependent, has similarly been the subject of much interrogation in recent years, as both the logic and the historical validity of Greg's distinction have been challenged.

However, given that a copy-text theory is being used, and that a single copy-text has been selected according to one or other of the principles discussed earlier in this book, this copy-text will have to be transcribed according to clear and consistent principles, which should be presented in the textual introduction and made manifest on the textual page. Is the edition to attempt *any* degree of normalization (e.g., according to apparent authorial preferences) or modernization and if so, how is the normalization rationalized and practiced? Furthermore, the editor must decide how any transcriptional changes (even if they are only such conventions as the regularizing of "u"/"v" and "i"/"j" practice) are to be recorded (i.e., only as a general principle in the introduction, or for each change in the apparatus?). How are such features as word-division, abbreviations, and speech-heads to be handled (for example, are abbreviations to be silently expanded, or expanded with italics, or with a note in the apparatus)? Furthermore, on what principles are emendations to be introduced into the text, by what authority, and how recorded? Is it the intention of the editor that *all* features of the copy-text should be recoverable from the readings in the apparatus? What about variant readings in other witnesses? Are they also to be included in the apparatus, or are they to be relegated to a separate historical collation, leaving the apparatus reserved for rejected readings from the copy-text?

The answers to many of these questions will obviously affect the actual *appearance* of the textual page, and in particular the degree to which apparatus is to be incorporated into the text itself, rather than listed elsewhere. The choices here are between a "clear-text" reading version (which in its purest state, would contain no editorial "flags" to the reader that something has been introduced into the text) and an "inclusive" text (where, by means of brackets, italics, diacritics or other devices, the editor symbolically demonstrates to the reader exactly what changes occurred between copy-text and edited text). A "genetic text" might go even further, attempting to insert on the textual page all features of every stage of the text's transmission, either in the constitution of a specific document or for the total history of the text. As has been shown already, a genetic text might be particularly useful where there are several different authorial versions or stages of composition in the work and the editor wishes the reader to have access to all these versions or stages without editorial prejudice. But if there *is* a demonstrable final intention to the work, and if critical judgments can or have been made between variants, then a clear-text edition is probably best suited to the requirements of a critical edition that it display the editor's decisions on the author's intentions regarding the "perfected" state of the text. Such clear-text representations of final intentions have most usually been associated with literary works intended for publication (novels, poems, published versions of plays), whereas inclusive-text display is often connected with documents under continual revision and not necessarily intended for publication (diaries, journals, letters).

Once the text itself has been edited, the textual scholar may turn to the annotations (textual and otherwise) and the introduction, glossary, index, and other ancillary materials. Some editors (indeed some disciplines) seem to regard the establishment of the text as a comparatively trivial matter preceding the real purpose of the edition—the writing of annotations. But a genuine critical edition will obviously have its focus on the text: in fact, some critical editions may place the annotations in a separate volume, or may not even include them at all.

However, for textual purposes, it is usually thought necessary that the reader of a textual edition must have at the very least some account of the publication history of the work, of the copies consulted for the edition, of the relative authority of these copies, of the principles of transcription and emendation (usually augmented by textual notes on specifically troublesome "cruces" in the text), and of all deviations from copy-text. In editions of prose printed texts, it has also become common practice to include in scholarly editions a hyphenation list (showing the reader how to quote from the text where hyphens occur at the end of a line), but since hyphens are virtually unknown (in their modern usage, anyway) in manuscripts of the medieval and Renaissance periods, it can normally be assumed that any hyphens are editorial not authorial or scribal in editions of works from these periods.

Beyond these basic requirements, the scholarly edition may include explanatory or historical notes, often written by a scholar other than the textual editor. Until recently, the nature and methods of annotation had not been subjected to the sort of rigorous theoretical interrogation accorded copy-text or emendation in Anglo-American editing, but recent work by, for example, Spevack ("Editor as Philologist"), Hanna, and Middleton, has made clear that annotation is as conceptually problematical as any other branch of editing, and is not merely a mechanical provision of historical, cultural, linguistic, or critical "facts" to fill out the bare text. Thus, an annotator now has to consider whether annotation is perhaps a series of "guerrilla raids" upon the text, whether it does not substitute a "vertical" alignment of reference for the "horizontal" alignment (the momentum of narrative) of the text, and what are the political connotations of living in another's "space" and acknowledging the text's *alterity* (Middleton). On a more practical level, the annotator must steer a very careful course between, on the one hand, confusing the reader by giving too little information, and, on the other, patronizing the reader by giving too much. It is possible to argue (though more difficult now than it was ten or twenty years ago) that a text can be definitive, fixed for all time; but annotation is always contingent and local, for the relationship between text and audience is always changing.

Beyond formal elucidatory annotation—bridging the cultural and temporal gap between author and reader—there are other means of editorial intervention. For example, if presenting a work in a particularly difficult or historically removed dialect or stage in the language's development, a glossary or even a complete lexicon might be necessary. The complete lexicon or concordance may often be published separately, of course, and has obvious critical value for the charting of authorial preferences even where the language of the work is not particularly inaccessible. Concordances must be used with some care, however, for they can be as accurate as the text on which they are based and they can only provide linguistic or stylistic information within the context of the subject of the work, as already shown in the example of *Pearl* and *Cleanness*. Thus, the Spevack Shakespeare concordance can give no information on contemporary accidentals usage, for it is based on a modern-spelling edition.

Finally, the edition may include an index (usually of proper nouns—persons, places, etc.—but sometimes of topics too), but this latter type is more likely to be a *desideratum* in historical works than in literary. Just as in all other stages of scholarly editing, the computer has changed both the methods and results of indexing, and while there are still some authors and editors who fervently cling to their 3" x 5" cards, the utility of such programs as CINDEX has removed much of the drudgery formerly associated with preparing an index. The same caveats as expressed elsewhere (e.g., about concordances and collation programs) still apply, however. While entering indexing commands as the text is established will ensure that a complete electronic record is available (and, especially in camera-ready editions, will allow continual revision of pagination reference as the edition progresses), it will still be necessary for the indexer to be aware of related but differently alphabetized forms of the same word, particularly in editions of texts in periods before spelling became standardized, and to be alert to suffix and prefix removal procedures and lemmatization, as discussed in the section on computer collation. And for the topical index there is finally no substitute for the judgment of the individual editor.

The frequent mention of computers in this chapter emphasizes that, perhaps more than any other activity in the humanities, scholarly editing has changed most and benefited most from the use of electronic storage and retrieval. But while this reliance on technology might appear to reinforce the argument of those who have always thought editing to be merely a mechanical procedure, ironically it might have the opposite implications. Removing a large part of the drudgery from traditional textual scholarship has served to highlight the special role of critical intervention in the most significant moments in the production of edited texts. The machines can provide the data, and can even present us with the options possible, but editing is ultimately, like every other aspect of textual scholarship covered in this book,

finally a critical activity, and this is as true in collation as it is in selecting variants, as true in bibliographical description as it is in filiation. It is also true in the very last stage of scholarly editing—the
publication of the edition. For with increasingly sophisticated desk-
top typesetting equipment and with the replacement of movable type
by photoreproduction, the editor is now in a position to exert much
greater personal control over the actual form of the scholarly edition
than was possible in the days when a ragged typescript was gingerly
handed over to the mercies of an often unlearned and unsympathetic
compositor and publisher. One of the suggestions in the CSE guidelines is that the editor should alert the publisher to the fact that a
scholarly edition may very well contain what look like misprints, and
that these should not be "corrected." While it is impossible to pre-
dict exactly what form scholarly editions will take in the next few
decades, one thing seems certain: that individual editors will come to
have a greater involvement in all stages of technical production, and
that the old, basically antagonistic relationship between scholar and
publisher will be replaced by one in which the editor takes over more
and more of the functions formerly assigned to the publisher (only the
reader or user is likely to have an even greater role). With this power, however, comes ever more responsibility and ever more opportunity for the exercise of critical judgment.

  This brief narrative of the stages in putting together a scholarly
edition cannot cover each of the procedures in the sort of detail that an
editor should consider them. Fuller aids to the planning of editions
can be found not only in the textual introductions to major editions
themselves (many of which have been cited in this book), but also in
the guides and manuals mentioned in the text or listed in the bibliography. In addition to the consultation services offered by the CSE, a
beginning editor can also make use of the professional groups mentioned earlier, especially the Toronto conferences on editorial methods, the Association for Documentary Editing, and the Society for
Textual Scholarship, all of which hold meetings on matters of interest
to textual scholars and at which editors in the planning stage of an edition may be able to meet formally or informally to discuss procedures.

  The account of editorial procedures is necessarily simplified. For
example, in the discussion of the glossary, there was no discussion of
how each glossary entry should be related to the text or what form it
should take (e.g., first occurrence only, normalized headword/key-
word, recording of all variant spellings?). Nonetheless, this chapter
does show how the procedures are related to each other, how one de-

pends upon another, and more important, how textual scholarship involves an enormously wide range of skills and critical decisions. This range has been demonstrated in part during the previous chapters of this book—from enumerative bibliography to analytical bibliography to textual bibliography—but it is in editing that the full scholarly dispensation comes into play. It is therefore natural that we should close with editing, for it is this activity of textual scholars which, despite the demurrals of the "anti-editing" school of McLeod, Warren, et al., will put them most on their mettle and which will have the greatest effect on their surrounding (and following) culture. Editions are extremely powerful vehicles of thought and expression: they determine how an author will be approached, and often how valued. It is a major responsibility when textual scholars become editors, and one which will give the widest currency to their theories and practices.

Appendix I

Pages from the Shakespeare First Folio

The following pages illustrate the problems of casting off copy discussed in Chapter 7 on textual bibliography. Refer to pages 285–88 above.

Thou might'ft haue fooner got another Seruice :
For many fo arriue at fecond Mafters,
Vpon their firft Lords necke. But tell me true,
(For I muft euer doubt, though ne're fo fure)
Is not thy kindneffe fubtle, couetous,
If not a Vfuring kindneffe,and as rich men deale Guifts,
Expecting in returne twenty for one ?
  Stew. No my moft worthy Mafter,in whofe breft
Doubt, and fufpect (alas) are plac'd too late :
You fhould haue fear'd falfe times, when you did Feaft.
Sufpect ftill comes, where an eftate is leaft.
That which I fhew, Heauen knowes, is meerely Loue,
Dutie, and Zeale, to your vnmatched minde ;
Care of your Food and Liuing,and beleeue it,
My moft Honour'd Lord,
For any benefit that points to mee,
Either in hope, or prefent, I'de exchange
For this one wifh, that you had power and wealth
To requite me, by making rich your felfe.
  Tim. Looke thee, 'tis fo : thou fingly honeft man,
Heere take : the Gods out of my miferie
Ha's fent thee Treafure. Go, liue rich and happy.
But thus condition'd : Thou fhalt build from men:
Hate all, curfe all, fhew Charity to none,
But let the famifht flefh flide from the Bone,
Ere thou releeue the Begger. Giue to dogges
What thou denyeft to men. Let Prifons fwallow 'em,
Debts wither 'em to nothing, be men like blafted woods
And may Difeafes licke vp their falfe bloods,
And fo farewell, and thriue.
  Stew. O let me ftay,and comfort you, my Mafter.
  Tim. If thou hat'ft Curfes
Stay not : flye,whil'ft thou art bleft and free :
Ne're fee thou man, and let me ne're fee thee.   *Exit*

Enter *Poet, and Painter.*
  Pain. As I tooke note of the place, it cannot be farre
where he abides.
  Poet. What's to be thought of him ?¡
Does the Rumor hold for true,
That hee's fo full of Gold ?
  Painter. Certaine.
  Alcibiades reports it : *Phrinica* and *Timandylo*
Had Gold of him. He likewife enrich'd
Poore ftragling Souldiers, with great quantity.
'Tis faide, he gaue vnto his Steward
A mighty fumme.
  Poet. Then this breaking of his,
Ha's beene but a Try for his Friends ?
  Painter. Nothing elfe :
You fhall fee him a Palme in Athens againe;
And flourifh with the higheft :
Therefore, 'tis not amiffe, we tender our loues
To him, in this fuppos'd diftreffe of his :
It will fhew honeftly in vs,
And is very likely, to loade our purpofes
With what they trauaile for,
If it be a iuft and true report, that goes
Of his hauing.
  Poet. What haue you now
To prefent vnto him ?
  Painter. Nothing at this time
But my Vifitation : onely I will promife him
An excellent Peece.
  Poet. I muft ferue him fo too ;
Tell him of an intent that's comming toward him.

  Painter. Good as the beft.
Promifing, is the verie Ayre o'th'Time;
It opens the eves of Expectation.
Performance. is euer the duller for his acte,
And but in the plainer and fimpler kinde of people,
The deede of Saying is quite out of vfe.
To Promife, is moft Courtly and fafhionable ;
Performance, is a kinde of Will or Teftament
Which argues a great fickneffe in his iudgement
That makes it.

Enter *Timon from his Caue*

  Timon. Excellent Workeman,
Thou canft not paint a man fo badde
As is thy felfe.
  Poet. I am thinking
What I fhall fay I haue prouided for him :
It muft be a perfonating of himfelfe :
A Satyre againft the foftneffe of Profperity,
With a Difcouerie of the infinite Flatteries
That follow youth and opulencie.
  Timon. Muft thou needes
Stand for a Villaine in thine owne Worke ?
Wilt thou whip thine owne faults in other men?
Do fo, I haue Gold for thee.
  Poet. Nay let's feeke him.
Then do we finne againft our owne eftate,
When we may profit meete, and come too late.
  Painter. True :
When the day ferues before blacke-cornet'd night ;
Finde what thou want'ft, by free and offer'd light.
Come.
  Tim. Ile meete you at the turne :
What a Gods Gold, that he is worfhipt
In a bafer Temple, then where Swine feede?
'Tis thou that rigg'ft the Barke,and plow'ft the Fome,
Setleft admired reuerence in a Slaue,
To thee be worfhipt, and thy Saints for aye :
Be crown'd with Plagues, that thee alone obay.
Fit I meet them.
  Poet. Haile worthy *Timon.*
  Pain. Our late Noble Mafter.
  Timon. Haue I once liu'd
To fee two honeft men ?
  Poet. Sir :
Hauing often of your open Bounty tafted,
Hearing you were retyr'd, your Friends falne off,
Whofe thankeleffe Natures (O abhorred Spirits)
Not all the Whippes of Heauen,are large enough.
What, to you,
Whofe Starre-like Nobleneffe gaue life and influence
To their whole being ? I am rapt, and cannot couer
The monftrous bulke of this Ingratitude
With any fize of words.
  Timon. Let it go,
Naked men may fee't the better :
You that are honeft, by being what you are,
Make them beft feene,and knowne.
  Pain. He,and my felfe
Haue trauail'd in the great fhowre of your guifts,
And fweetly felt it.
  Timon. I, you are honeft man.
  Painter. We are hither come
To offer you our feruice.
  Timon. Moft honeft men :

                                              Why

Fig. 129. *Timon of Athens* (First Folio, p. 95).

That could haue better fow'd then *Philomel*.
Oh had the monſter ſeene thoſe Lilly hands,
Tremble like Aſpen leaues vpon a Lute,
And make the ſilken ſtrings delight to kiſſe them,
He would not then haue toucht them for his life.
Or had he heard the heauenly Harmony,
Which that ſweet tongue hath made :
He would haue dropt his knife and fell aſleepe,
As *Cerberus* at the Thracian Poets feete.
Come, let vs goe, and make thy father blinde,
For ſuch a ſight will blinde a fathers eye.
One houres ſtorme will drowne the fragrant meades,
What, will whole months of teares thy Fathers eyes ?
Doe not draw backe, for we will mourne with thee:
Oh could our mourning eaſe thy miſery.   *Exeunt*

Actus Tertius.

Enter the Iudges and Senatours with Titus two ſonnes bound,
paſſing on the Stage to the place of execution, and Titus going
before pleading.

Ti. Heare me graue fathers, noble Tribunes ſtay,
For pitty of mine age, whoſe youth was ſpent
In dangerous warres, whilſt you ſecurely ſlept:
For all my blood in Romes great quarrell ſhed,
For all the froſty nights that I haue watcht,
And for theſe bitter teares, which now you ſee,
Filling the aged wrinkles in my cheekes,
Be pittifull to my condemned Sonnes.
Whoſe ſoules is not corrupted as 'tis thought :
For two and twenty ſonnes I neuer wept,
Becauſe they died in honours lofty bed.
   Andronicus lyeth downe, and the Iudges paſſe by him.
For theſe, Tribunes, in the duſt I write
My harts deepe languor, and my ſoules ſad teares :
Let my teares ſtanch the earths drie appetite.
My ſonnes ſweet blood, will make it ſhame and bluſh:
O earth ! I will be friend thee more with raine   *Exeunt*
That ſhall diſtill from theſe two ancient ruines,
Then youthfull Aprill ſhall with all his ſhowres
In ſummers drought: Ile drop vpon thee ſtill,
In Winter with warme teares Ile melt the ſnow,
And keepe eternall ſpring time on thy face,
So thou refuſe to drinke my deare ſonnes blood.

Enter Lucius, with his weapon drawne.

Oh reuerent Tribunes, oh gentle aged men,
Vnbinde my ſonnes, reuerſe the doome of death,
And let me ſay (that neuer wept before)
My teares are now preuailing Oratours.
   Lu. Oh noble father, you lament in vaine,
The Tribunes heare not, no man is by,
And you recount your ſorrowes to a ſtone.
   Ti. Ah *Lucius* for thy brothers let me plead,
Graue Tribunes, once more I intreat of you.
   Lu. My gracious Lord, no Tribune heares you ſpeake.
   Ti. Why 'tis no matter man, if they did heare
They would not marke me: oh if they did heare
They would not pitty me.
Therefore I tell my ſorrowes bootles to the ſtones.

Who though they cannot anſwere my diſtreſſe,
Yet in ſome ſort they are better then the Tribunes,
For that they will not intercept my tale ;
When I doe weepe, they humbly at my feete
Receiue my teares, and ſeeme to weepe with me,
And were they but attired in graue weedes,
Rome could afford no Tribune like to theſe.
A ſtone is as ſoft waxe,
Tribunes more hard then ſtones:
Aſtone is ſilent, and offendeth not,
And Tribunes with their tongues doome men to death.
But wherefore ſtand'ſt thou with thy weapon drawne ?
   Lu. To reſcue my two brothers from their death,
For which attempt the Iudges haue pronounc'ſt
My euerlaſting doome of baniſhment.
   Ti. O happy man, they haue befriended thee :
Why fooliſh *Lucius*, doſt thou not perceiue
That Rome is but a wildernes of Tigers ?
Tigers muſt pray, and Rome affords no prey
But me and and mine : how happy art thou then,
From theſe deuourers to be baniſhed ?
But who comes with our brother *Marcus* heere ?

Enter Marcus and Lauinia.

   Mar. Titus, prepare thy noble eyes to weepe,
Or if not ſo, thy noble heart to breake :
I bring conſuming ſorrow to thine age.
   Ti. Will it conſume me ? Let me ſee it then.
   Mar. This was thy daughter.
   Ti. Why *Marcus* ſo ſhe is.
   Luc. Aye me this obiect kils me.
   Ti. Faint-harted boy, ariſe and looke vpon her,
Speake *Lauinia*, what accurſed hand
Hath made thee handleſſe in thy Fathers ſight ?
What foole hath added water to the Sea ?
Or brought a faggot to bright burning Troy ?
My griefe was at the height before thou cam'ſt,
And now like *Nylus* it diſdaineth bounds :
Giue me a ſword, Ile chop off my hands too,
For they haue fought for Rome, and all in vaine :
And they haue nur'ſt this woe,
In feeding life :
In booteleſſe prayer haue they bene held vp,
And they haue ſeru'd me to effectleſſe vſe.
Now all the ſeruice I require of them,
Is that the one will helpe to cut the other :
'Tis well *Lauinia*, that thou haſt no hands,
For hands to do Rome ſeruice is but vaine.
   Luci. Speake gentle ſiſter, who hath martyr'd thee ?
   Mar. O that delightfull engine of her thoughts,
That blab'd them with ſuch pleaſing eloquence,
Is torne from forth that pretty hollow cage,
Where like a ſweet mellodius bird it ſung,
Sweet varied notes inchanting euery eare.
   Luci. Oh ſay thou for her,
Who hath done this deed ?
   Mare. Oh thus I found her ſtraying in the Parke,
Seeking to hide herſelfe as doth the Deare
That hath receiude ſome vnrecuring wound.
   Tit. It was my Deare,
And he that wounded her,
Hath hurt me more, then had he kild me dead :
For now I ſtand as one vpon a Rocke,
Inuiron'd with a wilderneſſe of Sea.
Who markes the waxing tide,
Grow waue by waue,
                Expecting

Fig. 130. *Titus Andronicus* (First Folio, p. 40).

The Tragedie of Hamlet.   257

What does this meane my Lord ?   (rouse,

Ham. The King doth wake to night, and takes his
Keepes wassels and the swaggering vpspring reeles,
And as he dreines his draughts of Renish downe,
The kettle Drum and Trumpet thus bray out
The triumph of his Pledge.

Horat. Is it a custome ?

Ham. I marry ist;
And to my mind, though I am natiue heere,
And to the manner borne: It is a Custome
More honour'd in the breach, then the obseruance.

Enter Ghost.

Hor. Looke my Lord, it comes.

Ham. Angels and Ministers of Grace defend vs:
Be thou a Spirit of health, or Goblin damn'd,
Bring with thee ayres from Heauen, or blasts from Hell,
Be thy euents wicked or charitable,
Thou com'st in such a questionable shape
That I will speake to thee. Ile call thee *Hamlet*,
King, Father, Royall Dane: Oh, oh, answer me,
Let me not burst in Ignorance; but tell
Why thy Canoniz'd bones Hearsed in death,
Haue burst their cerments, why the Sepulcher
Wherein we saw thee quietly enurn'd,
Hath op'd his ponderous and Marble iawes,
To cast thee vp againe? What may this meane?
That thou dead Coarse againe in compleat steele,
Reuisits thus the glimpses of the Moone,
Making Night hidious? And we fooles of Nature,
So horridly to shake our disposition,
With thoughts beyond the reaches of our Soules,
Say, why is this? wherefore? what should we doe?

Ghost beckens Hamlet.

Hor. It beckons you to goe away with it,
As if it some impartment did desire
To you alone.

Mar. Looke with what courteous action
It wafts you to a more remoued ground:
But doe not goe with it.

Hor. No, by no meanes.

Ham. It will not speake: then will I follow it.

Hor. Doe not my Lord.

Ham. Why, what should be the feare?
I doe not set my life at a pins fee;
And for my Soule, what can it doe to that?
Being a thing immortall as it selfe:
It waues me forth againe; Ile follow it.

Hor. What if it tempt you toward the Floud my Lord?
Or to the dreadfull Sonnet of the Cliffe,
That beetles o're his base into the Sea,
And there assumes some other horrible forme,
Which might depriue your Soueraignty of Reason,
And draw you into madnesse thinke of it?

Ham. It wafts me still: goe on, Ile follow thee.

Mar. You shall not goe my Lord.

Ham. Hold off your hand.

Hor. Be rul'd, you shall not goe.

Ham. My fate cries out,
And makes each petty Artire in this body,
As hardy as the Nemian Lions nerue:
Still am I cal'd? Vnhand me Gentlemen:
By Heau'n, Ile make a Ghost of him that lets me:
I say away, goe on, Ile follow thee.

Exeunt Ghost & Hamlet.

Hor. He waxes desperate with imagination.

Mar. Let's follow; 'tis not fit thus to obey him.

Hor. Haue after, to what issue will this come?

Mar. Something is rotten in the State of Denmarke.

Hor. Heauen will direct it.

Mar. Nay, let's follow him.   *Exeunt.*

Enter Ghost and Hamlet.   (ther.

Ham. Where wilt thou lead me? speak; Ile go no fur-

Gho. Marke me.

Ham. I will.

Gho. My hower is almost come,
When I to sulphurous and tormenting Flames
Must render vp my selfe.

Ham. Alas poore Ghost.

Gho. Pitty me not, but lend thy serious hearing
To what I shall vnfold.

Ham. Speake, I am bound to heare.

Gho. So art thou to reuenge, when thou shalt heare.

Ham. What?

Gho. I am thy Fathers Spirit,
Doom'd for a certaine terme to walke the night;
And for the day confin'd to fast in Fiers,
Till the foule crimes done in my dayes of Nature
Are burnt and purg'd away? But that I am forbid
To tell the secrets of my Prison-House;
I could a Tale vnfold, whose lightest word
Would harrow vp thy soule, freeze thy young blood,
Make thy two eyes like Starres, start from their Spheres,
Thy knotty and combined locks to part,
And each particular haire to stand an end,
Like Quilles vpon the fretfull Porpentine:
But this eternall blason must not be
To eares of flesh and blood; list *Hamlet*, oh list,
If thou didst euer thy deare Father loue.

Ham. Oh Heauen!

Gho. Reuenge his foule and most vnnaturall Murther.

Ham. Murther?

Ghost. Murther most foule, as in the best it is;
But this most foule, strange, and vnnaturall.

Ham. Hast, hast me to know it,
That with wings as swift
As meditation, or the thoughts of Loue,
May sweepe to my Reuenge.

Ghost. I finde thee apt,
And duller should'st thou be then the fat weede
That rots it selfe in ease, on Lethe Wharfe,
Would'st thou not stirre in this. Now *Hamlet* heare:
It's giuen out, that sleeping in mine Orchard,
A Serpent stung me: so the whole eare of Denmarke,
Is by a forged processe of my death
Rankly abus'd: But know thou Noble youth,
The Serpent that did sting thy Fathers life,
Now weares his Crowne.

Ham. O my Propheticke soule: mine Vncle?

Ghost. I that incestuous, that adulterate Beast
With witchcraft of his wits, hath Traitorous guifts.
Oh wicked Wit, and Gifts, that haue the power
So to seduce? Won to to this shamefull Lust
The will of my most seeming vertuous Queene:
Oh *Hamlet*, what a falling off was there,
From me, whose loue was of that dignity,
That it went hand in hand, euen with the Vow
I made to her in Marriage; and to decline
Vpon a wretch, whose Naturall gifts were poore
To those of mine. But Vertue, as it neuer wil be moued,
Though Lewdnesse court it in a shape of Heauen:
So Lust, though to a radiant Angell link'd,
Will sate it selfe in a Celestiallbed, & prey on Garbage.

O o   But

Fig. 131. *Hamlet* (First Folio, p. 257).

Much adoe about Nothing. 121

Then this for whom we rendred vp this woe.   *Exeunt.*
Enter Leonato,Bene. Marg.Vrsula,old man,Frier,Hero.
Frier. Did I not tell you she was innocent?
Leo. So are the *Prince* and *Claudio* who accus'd her,
Vpon the errour that you heard debated:
But *Margaret* was in some fault for this,
Although againft her will as it appeares,
In the true courfe of all the queftion.
Old. Well,I am glad that all things fort fo well.
Bene. And fo am I,being elfe by faith enforc'd
To call young *Claudio* to a reckoning for it.
Leo. Well daughter,and you gentlewomen all,
Withdraw into a chamber by your felues,
And when I fend for you,come hither mask'd:
The *Prince* and *Claudio* promis'd by this howre
To vifit me,you know your office Brother,
You muft be father to your brothers daughter,
And giue her to young *Claudio.*   *Exeunt Ladies.*
Old. Which I will doe with confirm'd countenance.
Bene. Frier,I muft intreat your paines,I thinke.
Frier. To doe what Signior?
Bene. To binde me,or vndoe me,one of them:
Signior *Leonato*,truth it is good Signior,
Your neece regards me with an eye of fauour.
Leo. That eye my daughter lent her, 'tis moft true.
Bene. And I doe with an eye of loue requite her.
Leo. The fight whereof I thinke you had from me,
From *Claudio*,and the *Prince*,but what's your will?
Bened. Your anfwer fir is Enigmaticall,
But for my will, my will is, your good will
May ftand with ours, this day to be conioyn'd,
In the ftate of honourable marriage,
In which(good Frier)I fhall defire your helpe.
Leon. My heart is with your liking.
Frier. And my helpe.
     Enter Prince and Claudio, with attendants.
Prin. Good morrow to this faire affembly.
Leo. Good morrow *Prince*,good morrow *Claudio*:
We heere attend you,are you yet determin'd,
To day to marry with my brothers daughter?
Claud. Ile hold my minde were fhe an Ethiope.
Leo. Call her forth brother,heres the Frier ready.
Prin. Good morrow *Benedike*,why what's the matter?
That you haue fuch a Februarie face,
So full of froft, of ftorme,and clowdineffe.
Claud. I thinke he thinkes vpon the fauage bull:
Tufh, feare not man, wee'll tip thy hornes with gold,
And all *Europa* fhall reioyce at thee,
As once *Europa* did at lufty *Ioue*,
When he would play the noble beaft in loue.
Ben. Bull *Ioue* fir, had an amiable low,
And fome fuch ftrange bull leapt your fathers Cow,
A got a Calfe in that fame noble feat,
Much like to you,for you haue iuft his bleat.
     Enter brother,Hero, Beatrice,Margaret, Vrfula.
Cla. For this I owe you:here comes other recknings.
Which is the Lady I muft feize vpon?
Leo. This fame is fhe, and I doe giue you her.
Cla. Why then fhe's mine,fweet let me fee your face.
Leon. No that you fhal not, till you take her hand,
Before this Frier,and fweare to marry her.
Clau. Giue me your hand before this holy Frier,
I am your husband if you like of me.
Hero. And when I liu'd I was your other wife,
And when you lou'd, you were my other husband.
Clau. Another *Hero*?

Hero. Nothing certainer.
One *Hero* died, but I doe liue,
And furely as I liue, I am a maid.
Prin. The former *Hero*, *Hero* that is dead. .
Leon. Shee died my Lord,but whiles her flander liu'd.
Frier. All this amazement can I qualifie,
When after that the holy rites are ended,
Ile tell you largely of faire *Heroes* death:
Meane time let wonder feeme familiar,
And to the chappell let vs prefently.
Ben. Soft and faire Frier,which is *Beatrice*?
Beat. I anfwer to that name, what is your will?
Bene. Doe not you loue me?
Beat. Why no,no more then reafon.
Bene. Why then your Vncle,and the Prince, & *Clau-
dio*, haue beene deceiued, they fwore you did.
Beat. Doe not you loue mee?
Bene. Troth no, no more then reafon.
Beat. Why then my Cofin *Margaret* and *Vrfula*
Are much deceiu'd,for they did fweare you did.
Bene. They fwore you were almoft ficke for me.
Beat. They fwore you were wel-nye dead for me.
Bene. Tis no matter,then you doe not loue me?
Beat. No truly,but in friendly recompence.
Leon. Come Cofin,I am fure you loue the gentlemã.
Clau. And Ile be fworne vpon't, that he loues her,
For heres a paper written in his hand,
A halting fonnet of his owne pure braine,
Fafhioned to *Beatrice.*
Hero. And heeres another,
Writ in my cofins hand, ftolne from her pocket,
Containing her affeddtion vnto *Benedicke.*
Bene. A miracle, here's our owne hands againft our
hearts: come I will haue thee, but by this light I take
thee for pittie.
Beat. I would not denie you,but by this good day,I
yeeld vpon great perfwafion, & partly to faue your life,
for I was told, you were in a confumption.
Leon. Peace I will ftop your mouth.
Prin. How doft thou *Benedicke* the married man?
Bene. Ile tell thee what Prince: a Colledge of witte-
crackers cannot flout mee out of my humour, doft thou
think I care for a Satyre or an Epigram? no, if a man will
be beaten with braines,a fhall weare nothing handfome
about him: in briefe,fince I do purpofe to marry, I will
thinke nothing to any purpofe that the world can fay a-
gainft it, and therefore neuer flout at me, for I haue faid
againft it: for man is a giddy thing, and this is my conclufion: for thy part *Claudio*, I did thinke to haue beaten
thee,but in that thou art like to be my kinfman, liue vn-
bruis'd, and loue my coufin.
Cla. I had well hop'd ʒ wouldft haue denied *Beatrice*,ÿ
I might haue cudgel'd thee out of thy fingle life,to make
thee a double dealer, which out of queftiõ thou wilt be,
if my Coufin do not looke exceeding narrowly to thee.
Bene. Come,come, we are friends, let's haue a dance
ere we are married,that we may lighten our own hearts,
and our wiues heeles.
Leon. We'll haue dancing afterward.
Bene. Firft,of my vvord,therfore play mufick.*Prince*,
thou art fad, get thee a vvife,get thee a vvife, there is no
ftaff more reuerend then one tipt with horn. *Enter.Mef.*
Meffen. My Lord,your brother *Iohn* is tane in flight,
And brought with armed men backe to *Meffina.*
Bene. Thinke not on him till to morrow, ile deuife
thee braue punifhments for him: ftrike vp Pipers.*Dance.*
L   *FINIS.*

Fig. 132. *Much Ado About Nothing* (First Folio, p. 121).

about Nothing.

Bene. Why then your vncle, and the prince, and Claudio,
Haue beene deceiued, they fwore vou did.

Beat. Do not you loue me?

Bene. Troth no,no more then reafon.

Beat. Why then my cofin Margaret and Vrfula
Are much deceiu'd,for they did fweare you did.

Bene. They fwore that you were almoft ficke for me.

Beat. They fwore that you were welnigh dead for me.

Bene. Tis no fuch matter,then you do not loue me.

Beat. No truly,but in friendly recompence.

Leon. Come cofin,I am fure you loue the gentleman.

Clau. And ile befworne vpon't, that he loues her,
For heres a paper written in his hand,
A halting fonnet of his owne pure braine,
Fafhioned to Beatrice.

Hero And heres another,
Writ in my cofins hand,ftolne from her pocket,
Containing her affeftion vnto Benedicke.

Bene. A miracle,heres our owne hands againft our hearts:
come,I will haue thee,but by this light I take thee for pittie.

Beat. I would not denie you,but by this good day, I yeeld
vpon great perfwafion, and partly to faue your life , for I was
told, you were in a confumption.

Leon. Peace I will ftop your mouth.

Prince How doft thou Benedicke the married man?

Bene. Ile tel thee what prince:a colledge of witte-crackers
cannot flout me out of my humour, doft thou think I care for
a Satyre or an Epigramme? no, if a man will be beaten with
braines, a fhall weare nothing hanfome about him: in briefe,
fince I doe purpofe to marrie,I will think nothing to anie purpofe that the world can faie againft it, and therfore neuer flout
at me,for what I haue faid againft it: for man is a giddie thing,
and this is my conclufion : for thy part Claudio, I did thinke
to haue beaten thee,but in that thou art like to be my kinfman,
liue vnbruifde,and loue my coufen.

Clau. I had wel hopte thou wouldft haue denied Beatrice,
that I might haue cudgelld thee out of thy fingle life,to make
thee

Fig. 133. Much Ado About Nothing (Quarto I4ʳ)

M uch adoe

thee a double dealer,which out of queſtion thou wilt be,if my
cooſin do not looke exceeding narrowly to thee,

Bene. Come, come,we are friends,lets haue a dance ere we
are maried,that we may lighten our own hearts,and our wiues
heeles.

Leon. Weele haue dancing afterward,

Bene. Firſt,of my worde, therefore plaie muſicke, Prince,
thou art ſad,get thee a wife,get thee a wife , there is no ſtaffe
more reuerent then one tipt with horne,

Enter Meſſenger.

Meſſ. My Lord,your brother Iohn is tane in flight,
And brought with armed men backe to Meſſina.

Bene. Thinke not on him till to morrow , ile deuiſe thee
braue puniſhments for him:ſtrike vp Pipers.　　　　*dance.*

F I N I S.

Fig. 134. *Much Ado About Nothing* (Quarto I4^v)

364   *The Tragedie of*

The Souldiers pole is falne : young Boyes and Gyrles
Are leuell now with men : The odds is gone,
And there is nothing left remarkeable
Beneath the visiting Moone.
  Char. Oh quietnesse, Lady.
  Iras. She's dead too, our Soueraigne.
  Char. Lady.
  Iras. Madam.
  Char. Oh Madam, Madam, Madam,
  Iras. Royall Egypt : Empresse.
  Char. Peace, peace, *Iras.*
  Cleo. No more but in a Woman, and commanded
By such poore passion, as the Maid that Milkes,
And doe's the meanest chares. It were for me,
To throw my Scepter at the iniurious Gods,
To tell them that this World did equall theyrs,
Till they had stolne our Iewell. All's but naught :
Patience is sottish, and impatience does
Become a Dogge that's mad : Then is it sinne,
To rush into the secret house of death,
Ere death dare come to vs. How do you Women?
What, what good cheere? Why how now *Charmian?*
My Noble Gyrles? Ah Women, women! Looke
Our Lampe is spent, it's out. Good sirs, take heart,
Wee'l bury him : And then, what's braue, what's Noble,
Let's doo't after the high Roman fashion,
And make death proud to take vs. Come, away,
This case of that huge Spirit now is cold.
Ah Women, Women! Come, we haue no Friend
But Resolution, and the breefest end.
                    Exeunt, bearing of Anthonies body.

    *Enter Cæsar, Agrippa, Dollabella, Menas, with
           his Counsell of Warre.*

Cæsar. Go to him *Dollabella*, bid him yeeld,
Being so fruftrate, tell him,
He mockes the pawses that he makes.
  Dol. Cæsar, I shall.
         Enter Decretas with the sword of Anthony.
  Cæf. Wherefore is that? And what art thou that dar'st
Appeare thus to vs?
  Dec. I am call'd *Decretas,*
Marke Anthony I seru'd, who best was worthie
Best to be seru'd : whil'st he stood vp, and spoke
He was my Master, and I wore my life
To spend vpon his haters. If thou please
To take me to thee, as I was to him,
Ile be to Cæsar : if ŷ pleasest not, I yeild thee vp my life.
  Cæsar. What is't thou say'st?
  Dec. I say (Oh Cæsar) *Anthony* is dead.
  Cæsar. The breaking of so great a thing, should make
A greater cracke. The round World
Should haue shooke Lyons into ciuill streets,
And Citizens to their dennes. The death of *Anthony*
Is not a single doome, in the name lay
A moity of the world.
  Dec. He is dead Cæsar,
No by a publike minister of Iustice,
Nor by a hyred Knife, but that selfe-hand
Which writ his Honor in the Acts it did,
Hath with the Courage which the heart did lend it,
Splitted the heart. This is his Sword,
I robb'd his wound of it : behold it stain'd
With his most Noble blood.
  Cæf. Looke you sad Friends,

The Gods rebuke me, but it is Tydings
To wash the eyes of Kings.
  Dol. And strange it is,
That Nature must compell vs to lament
Our most persisted deeds.
  Mec. His taints and Honours, wag'd equal with him.
  Dol. A Rarer spirit neuer
Did steere humanity : but you Gods will giue vs
Some faults to make vs men. Cæsar is touch'd.
  Mec. When such a spacious Mirror's set before him,
He needes must see himselfe.
  Cæsar. Oh *Anthony,*
I haue followed thee to this, but we do launch
Diseases in our Bodies. I must perforce
Haue shewne to thee such a declining day,
Or looke on thine : we could not stall together,
In the whole world. But yet let me lament
With teares as Soueraigne as the blood of hearts,
That thou my Brother, my Competitor,
In top of all designe ; my Mate in Empire,
Friend and Companion in the front of Warre,
The Arme of mine owne Body, and the Heart
Where mine his thoughts did kindle ; that our Starres
Vnreconciliable, should diuide our equalnesse to this.
Heare me good Friends,
But I will tell you at some meeter Season,
The businesse of this man lookes out of him,
Wee'l heare him what he sayes.
                    Enter an Ægyptian.
Whence are you?
  Ægyp. A poore Egyptian yet, the Queen my mistris
Confin'd in all, she has her Monument
Of thy intents, desires, instruction,
That she preparedly may frame her selfe
To'th'way shee's forc'd too.
  Cæsar. Bid her haue good heart,
She soone shall know of vs, by some of ours,
How honourable, and how kindely Wee
Determine for her. For Cæsar cannot leaue to be vngentle
  Ægyp. So the Gods preserue thee.   *Exit.*
  Cæf. Come hither *Proculeius.* Go and say
We purpose her no shame : giue her what comforts
The quality of her passion shall require ;
Least in her greatnesse, by some mortall stroke
She do defeate vs. For her life in Rome,
Would be eternall in our Triumph : Go,
And with your speediest bring vs what she sayes,
And how you finde of her.
  Pro. Cæsar I shall.   *Exit Proculeius,*
  Cæf. *Gallus,* go you along : where's *Dolabella,* to se-
cond *Proculeius?*
  All. *Dolabella.*
  Cæf. Let him alone : for I remember now
How hee's imploy'd : he shall in time be ready.
Go with me to my Tent, where you shall see
How hardly I was drawne into this Warre,
How calme and gentle I proceeded still
In all my Writings. Go with me, and see
What I can shew in this.   *Exeunt.*

    Enter Cleopatra, Charmian, Iras, and Mardian.

  Cleo. My desolation does begin to make
A better life : Tis paltry to be Cæsar :
Not being Fortune, hee's but Fortunes knaue,
A minister of her will : and it is great

                                         To

Fig. 135. *Anthony and Cleopatra* (First Folio, p. 364).

Anthony and Cleopatra.   365

T do that thing that ends all other deeds,
Which fhackles accedents, and bolts vp change;
Which fleepes, and neuer pa'lates more the dung,
The beggers Nurfe, and Cafars.

Enter Proculeius.

Pro. Cafar fends greeting to the Queene of Egypt,
And bids thee ftudy on what faire demands
Thou mean'ft to haue him grant thee.

Cleo. What's thy na:ie ?

Pro. My name is Proculeius.

Cleo. Anthony
Did tell me of you, bad me truft you, but
I do not greatly eare to be deceiu'd
That haue no vfe for truiting. If your Mafter
Would naue a Queece his begger, you muft tell him,
That Maiefty to keepe *decorum*, muft,
No leffe begge then a Kingdome : If he pleafe
To giue me conquer'd Egypt for my Sonne,
He giues me fo much of mine owne, as I
Will kneele to him with thankes.

Pro. Be of good cheere :
Y'are falne into a Princely hand, feare nothing,
Make your full reference freely to my Lord,
Who is fo full of Grace, that it flowes ouer
On all that neede. Let me report to him
Your fweet dependacie, and you fhall finde
A Conqueror that will pray in ayde for kindneffe,
Where he for grace is kneel'd too.

Cleo. Pray you tell him,
I am his Fortunes Vaffall, and I fend him
The Greatneffe he has got. I hourely learne
A Doctrine of Obedience, and would gladly
Looke him i'th'Face.

Pro. This Ile report (deere Lady)
Haue comfort, for I know your plight is pittied
Of him that caus'd it.

Pro. You fee how eafily fhe may be furpriz'd :
Guard her till Cafar come.

Iras. Royall Queene.

Char. Oh Cleopatra, thou art taken Queene.

Cleo. Quicke, quicke, good hands.

Pro. Hold worthy Lady, hold :
Doe not your felfe fuch wrong, who are in this
Releeu'd, but not betraid.

Cleo. What of death too that rids our dogs of languifh

Pro. Cleopatra, do not abufe my Mafters bounty, by
Th'vndoing of your felfe : Let the World fee
His Nobleneffe well acted, which your death
Will neuer let come forth.

Cleo. Where art thou Death?
Come hither come ; Come, come, and take a Queene
Worth many Babes and Beggers.

Pro. Oh temperance Lady.

Cleo. Sir, I will eate no meate, Ile not drinke fir,
If idle talke will once be neceffary
Ile not fleepe neither. This mortall houfe Ile ruine,
Do Cafar what he can. Know fir, that I
Will not waite pinnion'd at your Mafters Court,
Nor once be chaftic'd with the fober eye
Of dull Octauia. Shall they hoyft me vp,
And fhew me to the fhowting Varlotarie
Of cenfuring Rome ? Rather a ditch in Egypt.
Be gentle graue vnto me, rather on Nylus mudde
Lay me ftarke-nak'd, and let the water-Flies
Blow me into abhorring; rather make
My Countries high pyramides my Gibbet,

And hang me vp in Chaines.

Pro. You do extend
Thefe thoughts of horror further then you fhall
Finde caufe in Cafar.

Enter Dolabella.

Dol. Proculeius,
What thou haft done, thy Mafter Cafar knowes,
And he hath fent for thee : for the Queene,
Ile take her to my Guard.

Pro. So Dolabella,
It fhall content me beft : Be gentle to her,
To Cafar I will fpeake, what you fhall pleafe,
If you'l imploy me to him.   *Exit Proculeius*

Cleo. Say, I would dye.

Dol. Moft Noble Empreffe, you haue heard of me.

Cleo. I cannot tell.

Dol. Affuredly you know me.

Cleo. No matter fir, what I haue heard or knowne :
You laugh when Boyes or Women tell their Dreames,
Is't not your tricke?

Dol. I vnderftand not, Madam.

Cleo. I dreampt there was an Emperot Anthony.
Oh fuch another fleepe, that I might fee
But fuch another man.

Dol. If it might pleafe ye.

Cleo. His face was as the Heau'ns, and therein ftucke
A Sunne and Moone, which kept their courfe, & lighted
The little o'th'earth.

Dol. Moft Soueraigne Creature.

Cleo. His legges beftrid the Ocean, his rear'd arme
Crefted the world : His voyce was propertied
As all the tuned Spheres, and that to Friends :
But when he meant to quaile, and fhake the Orbe,
He was as rating Thunder. For his Bounty,
There was no winter in't. An Anthony it was,
That grew the more by reaping : His delights
Were Dolphin-like, they fhew'd his backe aboue
The Element they liu'd in : In his Liuery
Walk'd Crownes and Crownets: Realms & Iflands were
As plates dropt from his pocket.

Dol. Cleopatra.

Cleo. Thinke you there was, or might be fuch a man
As this I dreampt of?

Dol. Gentle Madam, no.

Cleo. You Lye vp to the hearing of the Gods :
But if there be, nor euer were one fuch
It's paft the fize of dreaming : Nature wants ftuffe
To vie ftrange formes with fancie, yet t'imagine
An Anthony were Natures peece, 'gainft Fancie,
Condemning fhadowes quite.

Dol. Heare me, good Madam :
Your loffe is as your felfe, great ; and you beare it
As anfwering to the waight, would I might neuer
Ore-take purfu'de fucceffe : But I do feele
By the rebound of yours, a greefe that fuites
My very heart at roote.

Cleo. I thanke you fir :
Know you what Cafar meanes to do with me ?

Dol. I am loath to tell you what, I would you knew.

Cleo. Nay pray you fir.

Dol. Though he be Honourable.

Cleo. Hee'l lende me then in Triumph.

Dol. Madam he will. I know't.   *Flourifh.*

*Enter Proculeius, Cafar, Gallus, Mecenas,
and others of his Traine.*

All. Make way there Cafar.

z z   Cafar

Fig. 136. *Anthony and Cleopatra* (First Folio, p. 365).

Appendix II

Some Types of Scholarly Edition

The following pages illustrate different options in scholarly editing, from single-document transcription to multiple-witness eclectic and genetic texts. Each alternative is described fully in Chapter 9 on scholarly editing.

Type Facsimile Edition: John Heywood. *The Pardoner and the Friar* (Malone Society Edition). Ed. G. R. Proudfoot, Figs. 137–39.

Diplomatic Transcript Edition: *The Captive Lady* (Malone Society Edition). Ed. A. R. Braunmuller, Figs. 140–42.

Critical Edition with Inclusive Text: William Langland. *Piers Plowman. The A Version.* (Athlone Edition). Ed. George Kane, Fig. 143.

Eclectic Clear-Text Edition with Multiple Apparatus: Stephen Crane, *Maggie* (Virginia Edition). Ed. Fredson Bowers, Figs. 144–49.

Parallel Text Edition: William Wordsworth, *The Prelude: 1799, 1805, 1850* (Norton Edition). Ed. Jonathan Wordsworth, M. H. Abrams, and Stephen Gill, Figs. 150–51.

Old and Modern-Spelling Parallel Text Edition with Commentary: Wiliam Shakespeare, *Sonnets* (Yale Edition). Ed. Stephen Booth, Figs. 152–54.

Genetic Edition: Ralph Waldo Emerson, *Journals* (Harvard Edition) and *Sermons* (Missouri Edition). Ed. William Gilman (*Journals*) and Albert J. von Frank, Jr. (*Sermons*), Figs. 155–56.

Critical and Synoptic Edition: James Joyce, *Ulysses* (Garland Edition). Ed. Hans Walter Gabler, Figs. 157–59.

Variorum Edition: William Shakespeare, *Measure for Measure* (Variorum Edition, MLA). Ed. Mark Eccles, Fig. 160.

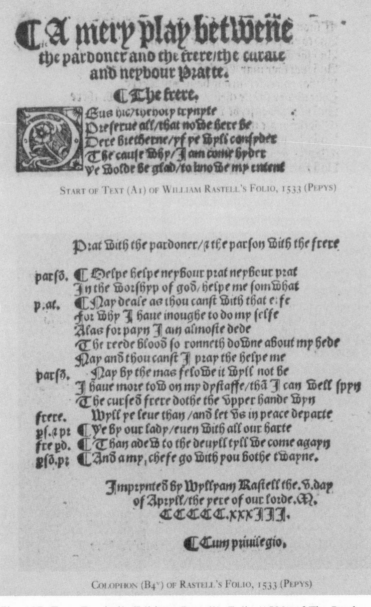

<small>START OF TEXT (A1) OF WILLIAM RASTELL'S FOLIO, 1533 (PEPYS)</small>

<small>COLOPHON (B4ᵛ) OF RASTELL'S FOLIO, 1533 (PEPYS)</small>

Fig. 137. Type Facsimile Edition: Rastell's Folio (1533) of *The Pardoner and the Friar* (Malone Society Edition).

Press Variant

	HN	PEPYS
B4, l. 616	weneth	wenoth

List of Irregular and Doubtful Readings

editor has looked at other editions

8 Jcom
33 no ꝛſoꝛ
34 luche
71 colacyou
72 pꝛeſe (? for pꝛeſence)
88 good (for god)
108 ſcoꝛne (? for no ſcoꝛne)
129 ſoule (? for ſaule = fallen)
148 Ge (for He)
160 Hf (for Of)
172 ueuer
226 Lacks (at end of line before turnunder (cf. 354, 438, 464).
275 Lacks speech prefix pardo. (added in MS; HN, Pepys in very dissimilar hands).
a curſt
294 ❡ does not start new speech.
295 eareſt
310 gydes (? for gyde, gyder)
313 thon
315 de ſpyſeſt
326 ſwewed
329 Lacks ❡ (also 331, 349, 385, 387, 393, 441, 481, 555, 624, 648, 651).
330 tkynge
331–6 Speech prefixes all one line too high.
331 Lacks speech prefix pardo.
398 woꝛdly
418 ihou
450 lyuyuge
496 /ſo ſhulde/
508 aud
522 kuaue
539 frere· (. turned)
587 egoteles (? for couteles = knives: cugelles)
588 ſyuge
621 Speech prefix pardo. (? for frere.; cf. l. 617)

Fig. 138. *The Pardoner and the Friar*: List of Variants and Doubtful Readings.

ℭ A mery play betwene

the pardoner and the frere/the curate
and neybour Platte.

ℭ The frere.

Eus hic/the holy trynyte
Pꝛeſerue all/that nowe here be
Dere bꝛetherne/yf ye wyll conſyder
The cauſe why/J am come hyder
Ye wolde be glad/to knowe my entent
Foꝛ J com not hyther/foꝛ monye noꝛ foꝛ rent
Jcom not hyther/foꝛ meate noꝛ foꝛ meale
But J com hyther/foꝛ your ſoules heale
J com not hyther/to poll noꝛ to ſhaue   10
J com not hyther to begge noꝛ to craue
J com not hyther/to gloſe noꝛ to flatter
J com not hyther to bable noꝛ to clatter
J com not hyther/to fable noꝛ to lye
But J come hyther/your ſoules to edyfye
Foꝛ we freres/are bounde the people to teche
The goſpell of Chꝛyſt/openly to pꝛeche
As dyd the appoſtels/by Chꝛyſt theyꝛ mayſter ſent
To turne the people/and make them to repent
But ſyth the appoſtels/fro heuen wolde not come   20
We freres now/muſt occupy theyꝛ rome
We freres are bounde/to ſerche mennes conſcyens
We may not care foꝛ grotes/noꝛ foꝛ pens
We freres haue pꝛofeſſed/wylfull pouerte
No peny in our purſe/haue may we
Knyfe noꝛ ſtaffe/may we none cary
Ercepte we ſhulde/from the goſpell vary
Foꝛ woꝛldly aduerſyte/may we be in no ſoꝛowe
We may not care to day/foꝛ our meate to moꝛowe
Bare fote and bare legged/muſt we go alſo   30
We may not care/foꝛ froſt noꝛ ſnowe
We may haue/no maner care ne thynke
Nother foꝛ our meate/no ꝛfoꝛ our dꝛynke
But let our thoughtes/fro luche thynges be as free
As be the byꝛdes/that in the ayꝛe flee
Foꝛ why our loꝛde/clyped ſwete Jeſus
Jn the goſpell/ſpeketh to vs thus

A.i.

Fig. 139. *The Pardoner and the Friar*: Type Facsimile of A.1.

Type Facsimile Edition
(John Heywood. *The Pardoner and the Friar*. Ed. G. R. Proudfoot. Oxford: Malone Society, 1984.)
Commentary: The type facsimile editions prints an unemended but reset text, using the same typeface as the original printing. The photo-facsimile of the beginning of the text and the colophon is included only as a sample, and the rest of the edition is in the modern typesetting. As the list of press variants and doubtful readings notes, there is only one variant between the two extant copies in the Pepys and Huntington Libraries, a minor accidentals variation on "weneth." Such problematic readings as "luche" (line 34) are retained in the type facsimile, though noted in the list of doubtful readings. There is, however, some regularization, for variant sorts of certain letters (e.g., the looped ascender form of "d") are mentioned in the textual introduction but not recorded in the text. Nonetheless, the lower case "w" used at the beginning of lines toward the end of the text (indicating a shortage of upper-case "W" when the forme was set) are reproduced.

young Master is fortunate: if he had not t'wou'd ha' binn all my fault   600

Per.   Heaven hath acknowledged me for yrs, and hath givn'n me the
                                        victorye,   (He reades ye letter
I must desire yr leave to enjoy it, the content it may bring to you I shall
not find my selfe, If I am not as happye in the affection I have for
                                        Arabella: (Ha!)
I understand w^n I first went out the reason was I might be from her, &
therefore privatelye dispatch'd this Messenger, to Know whether y^e
                                        same reason
will not Keepe me here. y'are pleasd' to thinke this absence a Remedye,
                                        & t'is
indeed a favour, for if I can't be with her, It will be my choise, to be so
farr away, and present my dutye at this distance. so long as I must
my love, y^r sonne Richardo. — How, I'le dispatch you presently: (to ye seaman.
in the mean while doe you entertaine him Servanto.   Exit Per.

Serv.   Why ffreind I shou'd have binne at sea with him, but I came too late,   611
The wind outwent me. though I may thanke my selfe for't. such haste
I made, such puffing, and blowing, as did fill yr sayles questionlesse.
you never heard him speake of me did you? — Sea: No.

Serv.   why freind to tell you ye truth, when my M^r tooke shipping last,
I Knowing ye danger _ of it, stood upon the shoare praying for him,
sea-sicke I have binn formerlye, and nere cou'd like it since, there
t'was for lacke of any thing else to come up, after a greate deal of heaving
[courage casting] I cast up my courage. Rid me of that greate stomack I had
against enemyes. but cause you say my M^r is not so mindfull of me,   620
and partlye for excuse, I care not If I venture a letter of mine to sea.

Seam.   I'le carrye it.

Serv.   Well then let's see, Victorious Master. Wou'nt that tickle him?
Now y^r enemyes are runne away, pray will you heare something of
your servant. who did not run away, † Sea: but only stayd behind.

Serv.   I perform'd one part of a souldier, and Kept my ground:

Seam.   you'd faine I see mince yr Cowardice, as much as you cou'd. though

Fig. 140. Diplomatic Transcript Edition: *The Captive Lady* (Malone Society
Edition), p. 20.

let me tell you there's as little difference t'wixt yr running away, &
staying behind, as there is twixt yr Halfe quarter pointe & the pointe
it selfe, come, come, playnelye tell him, that Knowing yr owne   630
infirmitye, and that, that morning you found yr heart very heavye,
so yt you were a ffrayd you shou'd have bin a burthern to ye shipp,

Serv.   so, Lets see what's here: Most victorious Master, Now yr enemyes
are run away, pray will you hear something of yr servant, who
did not run away, but performed one part of a souldier, and Kept
my ground, nor cou'd any thing have parted us. but ye sea which parts lands
and countryes, I thought besides a stiffe coward might raise tempests & drown
a ship as well as a dead bodye. The last time I was there It made me reach &
reach, I Knew't had a mind to have my soule out, I made bold to Remember
my selfe to you, for you have valour enough of y^r owne, If you lacke a   640
Coward I can helpe you to one. y^r Terrestriall animal,_Servanto.
How like it you, this is o^r land way of expressing o^r selves.

Seam.   Methinkes you don't much commend yr selfe, though.
Serv.   what 'cause I call my selfe Coward. why T'is ye Greatest complement,
not but I have heart enough, but it be comes my humility to give it up all
to my Mr Here, — but prethee who were those fellows you beate?
Seam.   pyrats, a Kind of Water rats, the sharkes of ye Northerne sea. you'l see 'um
Serv.   Lord Had I his courage now, I cou'd vapour Ten times better then   (Aside)
this fellow; what freind hast thee noe hurt in thy sterne, is thy   649
maine yarde safe,   Enter Peralto.
Per.   Here ffreind, deliver this to Richardo, and tell him I expecte him
   home,   gives him money
Here's for you __ __ seam. I shall s^r   Exit seaman
Per.   I fear'd this, my sonne Knows too well ye Advantages he hath over o^r
affections, T'is rash this, never to returne but send his victoryes to us, I did
intend to have alter'd my sonnes love, had it not binne so strongely rooted
But he must be obey'd, if he can't be woonne
To chuse a daughter I'le ne're loose a sonne.   Exeunt.

---

628 *you*] *o* altered from *e*   634 *yr*] *r* altered from *e*   638 *reach*] *r* mended   640 *selfe*] ²*e* mended
645 *heart*] *a* altered from *e*   651 *expecte*] *p* altered from *sp*; two descenders remain   652 *seaman*]
²*a* mended   656 *woonne*] ²*o* mended

21

Fig. 141. Diplomatic Transcript Edition: *The Captive Lady* (Malone Society Edition), p. 21.

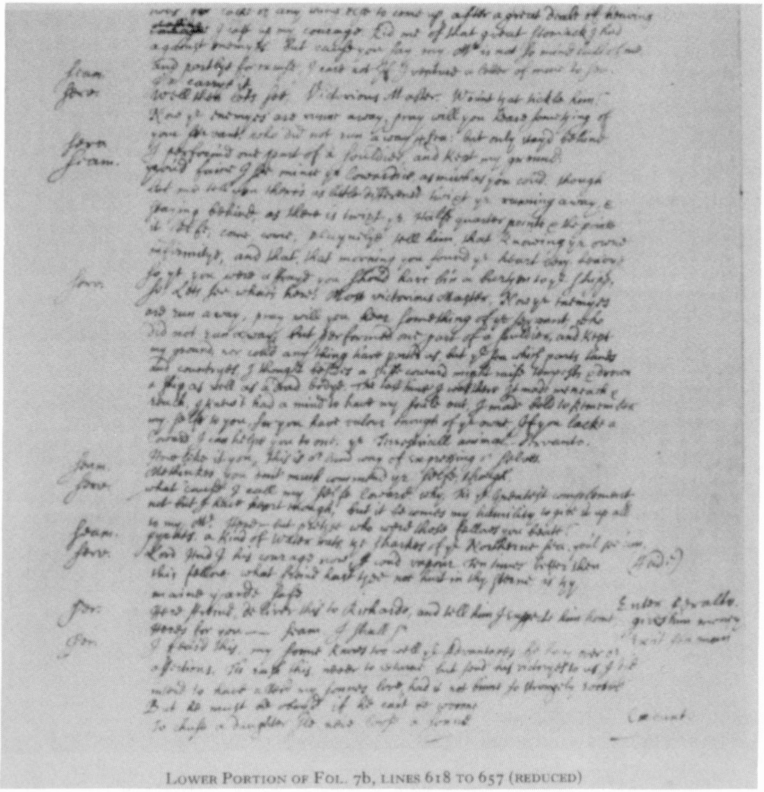

LOWER PORTION OF FOL. 7b, LINES 618 TO 657 (REDUCED)

Fig. 142. Diplomatic Transcript Edition: *The Captive Lady* (Malone Society Edition). Manuscript photocopy.

Diplomatic Transcript Edition
(*The Captive Lady.* Ed. A. R. Braunmuller. Oxford: Malone Society, 1982.)
Commentary: This is not a parallel-text edition, and the photofacsimile of the manuscript is included only as a sample. (For an example of such a facing-page edition of manuscript and transcript with annotations, see Fig. 127 in Chapter 7, of the *Beowulf* manuscript.) The diplomatic transcript reproduces as many of the features of the manuscript as possible in a modern typesetting, including exact lineation, spelling, and abbreviations, which are not expanded. Where features of the manuscript cannot be clearly reproduced (e.g., the deletion of "courage casting" at line 619 and the superscript "casting"), these are recorded in the apparatus. Thus, all mended, blotted, deleted, decorated, or altered letter-forms are mentioned in the apparatus. Where it might not be clear which letter is referred to in the lemma, a superscript number gives the appropriate reference (e.g., "652 *seaman*] [2]*a* mended" showing that it is the second, not the first, "a" of "seaman" that is mended). Lineation reference is added to the transcript, and is not present in the manuscript.

The textual introduction to the edition contains detailed analyses of such matters as the provenance, paper, watermarks, format, handwriting, ink, and so on.

PROLOGUE

IN a somer sesoun whanne softe was the sonne   *fol.* xxiiij *a*
I shop me into a shroud as I a shep were;
In abite as an Ermyte, vnholy of werkis,
Wente wyde in þis world wondris to here.
But on a may morwenyng on maluerne hilles   5
Me befel a ferly, of fairie me þou3te:
I was wery [for]wandrit ⁊ wente me to reste
Vndir a brood bank be a bo*ur*n[e] side,
And as I lay ⁊ lenide ⁊ lokide on þe watris
I slomeride into a slepyng, it swi3ede so merye.   10

1 sesoun] sesyn J; season K.   whanne]
whenne R; when ChHL; whon V; as
UE.   softe . . . sonne] I south wente RUE.
2 shop] schaped L.   into] in UEM; to D;
vndur H; *om* R.   a shroud] schroudes
DH²L; a shrowedes W; schrubbes K;
þe schropbys J; schregges Ch.   as . . .
shep] a schep as y M; a schepe as I J;
A scheep as I V.   shep] schepe ChHEK;
scheep UH².
3 abite] an abyte DH; whit M.   as] of
ChVHJK.   Ermyte] *after a* k H²; herment
E.   vnholy] von holy R; my holy E;
vnworthy L.   of] *om* UE.   werkis] workes
DCh; warkus H.
4 Wente] Y wente RUHJEKW; wente I
M; wende I V.   wyde] wydene V.   in]
into L.   þis] þe ChWM.   world] wordle
R; werlde JE.   wondris] wonderys EM;
wondres ChUH²VLW; wonderes D;
wonders JK.   here] heare K; hure R; wayte
L. *Here* K *adds a line like* C I 5.
5 on(1)] vpon R; apon E; in DChV.
a] *om* L. may] Mayes VHJ.   morwenyng]
Morwnynge V; mornynge UDChHJ
KWM; morwe RH²; morn LE.   on(2)]
RUVHJLEKWM; vpon TDChH².   mal-
uerne] maluarne ChL; malueron J.   hilles]
hulles DVL; hullis H; hellys M.
6 befel] byfeol L.   ferly] farly H; farley
case K.   of . . . þou3te] ⁊ fayre me it

thowte J.   of] A V.   fairie] fayre D;
feirey Ch; ferrom E.
7 *line om*; *supplied marginally in another
hand* W.   wery] weori V.   forwandrit]
forwandryd UJM; forwandred RH²L;
for wandryng D; for wanderyng E; of
wandringe VHW; of wandrit T; of
wandred ChK.   ⁊] I RUE; *om* H².   reste]
rist E.
8 Vndir] Vnderneth J; Opon W.   bourne]
burne RDChVHLKWM; bournis TU
H²E (*a caret below* ur T); broke J.   side]
brymme L.
9 And] But RE; *om* ChW.   as] als J.
lenide] lenyd K; lenede RH²W; lenedde
D; lened ChLM; leonede V; leoned H;
laynyd J; lened me UE.   ⁊] *twice* M;
I J.   lokide] lokyd EK; lokede UH²VM;
loked DChHLW; luked R; kokyd J.
on] in H.   watris] water ChJLW.
10 slomeride] slomeryd DE; slomered
LW; slomerde M; slomerd Ch; slombride
U; slombryd R; slomberyd J; slombred
H²H; slumberde V; sclombrid K.   into a]
into J; in a RVH; on a UH²LEM; a KW.
slepyng] slepe W; sclepe K.   it] I RUE;
and J.   swi3ede] swyed H²LW; swyyd K;
swede Ch; sweiued E; sweuedyn J;
sweuenede R; sweuenyd U; semede M;
sownede VH; schewed D.   so] ful J; os E;
me M.   merye] myrie UH; murie VL.

Fig. 143. Critical Edition with Inclusive Text: *Piers Plowman* A-Text (Athlone Edition).

Critical Edition with Inclusive Text
(William Langland. *Piers Plowman: The A Version*. Ed. George Kane. London: Athlone, 1960.)
Commentary: The edition is eclectic in that it is based on a single manuscript and reads into this manuscript variants from other witnesses plus emendations made by the editors without any manuscript authority. The transcription preserves manuscript accidentals, including such special signs as thorn [Þ], yogh [ȝ], and the symbol for the ampersand. Punctuation is modern. The editors indicate all changes to manuscript accidentals (for example, the expansion of abbreviations) by italics (as in line 1, "som*er*," where the manuscript presumably reads "som̃" and line 5 "malu*er*ne," where the manuscript presumably reads "malũne." Emendations of copy-text readings are shown in square brackets, thus "[for]wandrit," where the manuscript reads "wandrit." Foliation of the manuscript is recorded marginally, e.g., *fol. xxiiij a.*

The apparatus is included on the text-page and lemmata are keyed to lineation in the text. Where a word in a lemma occurs twice in a line, the one referred to is shown by a following number: thus "5 on(1)" shows that the first, not the second "on" in line 5 is the referent for the lemma. Editorial comments within the apparatus are shown in italics: thus "*om.*" = "omit(s)" and the comment in the note for line 7, indicating that the line is "*supplied marginally in another hand.*" All witnesses to the text are assigned sigla in the apparatus, usually a single letter (e.g. J, K, Y) or sometimes a letter with a supralinear number (e.g., H^2). All substantive variants are recorded, together with accidentals variants of possible significance; after the line reference, the head-word and the square bracket to signal the end of the lemma, variant readings are listed before the sigla showing their source. Note that these variants range from comparatively minor forms (e.g., J's "sesyn" for copy-text "sesoun" in line 1) to major rewritings (e.g., M's "whit" for copy-text "abite" in line 3, and the wide range of forms for copy-text "swiȝede" in line 10).

eclectic

392

no witness behind this reading — authorial intent in question

22 · Maggie

the police were always actuated by malignant impulses and the rest of the world was composed, for the most part, of despicable creatures who were all trying to take advantage of him and with whom, in defense, he was obliged to quarrel on all possible occasions. He himself occupied a down-trodden position which had a private but distinct element of grandeur in its isolation.

The greatest cases of aggravated idiocy were, to his mind, rampant upon the front platforms of all of the street cars. At first his tongue strove with these beings, but he eventually became superior. In him grew a majestic contempt for those strings of street cars that followed him like intent bugs.

He fell into the habit, when starting on a long journey, of fixing his eye on a high and distant object, commanding his horses to start and then going into a trance of observation. Multitudes of drivers might howl in his rear, and passengers might load him with opprobrium, but he would not awaken until some blue policeman turned red and began to frenziedly seize bridles and beat the soft noses of the responsible horses.

When he paused to contemplate the attitude of the police toward himself and his fellows, he believed that they were the only men in the city who had no rights. When driving about, he felt that he was held liable by the police for anything that might occur in the streets, and that he was the common prey of all energetic officials. In revenge, he resolved never to move out of the way of anything, until formidable circumstances, or a much larger man than himself forced him to it.

Foot passengers were mere pestering flies with an insane disregard for their legs and his convenience. He could not comprehend their desire to cross the streets. Their madness smote him with eternal amazement. He was continually storming at them from his throne. He sat aloft and denounced their frantic leaps, plunges, dives and straddles.

When they would thrust at, or parry, the noses of his champing horses, making them swing their heads and move their feet, and thus disturbing a stolid dreamy repose, he swore at the men as fools, for he himself could perceive that Providence had caused it clearly to be written, that he and his team had the unalienable right to stand in the proper path of the sun chariot, and if they so minded, obstruct its mission or take a wheel off.

Fig. 144. Eclectic Clear-Text Edition with Multiple Apparatus: Stephen Crane, *Maggie* (Virginia Edition). Text-Page.

no editorial presence

TEXTUAL NOTES

11.25 denounced . . . consumed] At first sight the A2 change of the A1 in-
finitive series might appear to be a sophistication, probably by the Appleton
editor; and indeed the possibility cannot be ruled out. But it is equally possible that Crane saw that the 'heroic endeavors' more properly applied only
to the baby trying to keep his equilibrium. Certainly, the relative clause
'which he chewed between the times of his infantile orations' does not jibe
with a 'heroic endeavor' to eat the orange peeling.

13.25 at] That A1 'look out at the window' was not inadvertent is indicated
by the appearance of the same phrase later at 43.22, where A2 once again
sophisticates, editorially no doubt, to 'look out of'. The same phrase with
'at' in 19.17–18 was repeated without change in A2.

14.21 infant] The addition in A2 of the possessive (infant's) would seem
to be the same editorial interference found in the A2 alteration at 18.17 of
'panther' to 'panther's'.

19.7 into] Despite 26.23 'Maggie leaned back in the shadow', the phrase
'into shadows' at 28.8 suggests that the A2 change of A1 'in' to 'into' was
here authoritative.

22.14 observation] Demonstrable common errors in A1 and A2 that are
not simple misprints like 'smoked-filled' at 52.12 are hard to find, unless
the present be an example. Follett emended 'observation' to 'oblivion',
which is tempting. Nevertheless, the odds favor the authority of 'observation'. For example, Jimmie is described as 'fixing his eye on a high and
distant object' and 'then going into a trance of observation', which makes
sense if the 'observation' consists of the 'fixing' of the eye that induces a
trancelike state resulting from this selection of an object to observe fixedly.
It would be odd if Crane missed an error here since for the A2 revision he
altered A1 'begin' to 'start' at 22.14, and at 22.14 deleted 'sort of' before
'trance'.

23.14 swearing for the half of an hour] That A2 'for half an hour' is an
editorial alteration is indicated by A1 (and A2) 'ran up and down the
avenue for the half of a block' at 49.17–18. If the editor's hand is to be
seen here, then it is very likely that the A2 substitution of 'storming' for
A1 'swearing' is part of the editorial censorship of Crane's language and
is to be rejected.

81

Fig. 145. Eclectic Clear-Text Edition: Crane, *Maggie*. Textual Notes.

at end

84 · Maggie

20.14–15 Once. . . . What?] A2; omit A1

20.28 tourists] A2; gentlemen A1

21.17 nothing] A2; neither the devil nor the leader of society A1

21.22 There was given to him] A2; He was given A1

21.26 punch] A2; beat A1

21.34 If . . . became the] A2; If in the front and the A1

21.35 which] A2; that A1

22.5 which] A2; that A1

22.7 greatest] A2; most complete A1

22.9–10 became superior.] A2; was superior. He became immured like an African cow. A1

22.14 start‸] A2; begin, A1

22.14 trance] A2; sort of a trance A1

*22.14 observation] stet A1-E2

22.16 but] A2; omit A1

22.17 seize] A2; tear A1

22.22 that he] A2; omit A1

22.28–29 comprehend their desire] A2; conceive their maniacal desires A1

22.35 and thus] A2; omit A1

22.35 stolid] A2; solid A1

23.1 And] A2; And, perhaps, A1

23.1 had had a] A2; had an ungovernable A1

23.4 hard] A2; very hard A1

23.10 struck] A2; would strike A1

*23.14–15 swearing for the half of] stet A1

23.18 a street car] A2; street-cars A1

24.12 er] A2; or A1

24.18 with a name which might have been] A2; the name of whose brand could be A1

24.19 connected] A2; in connection A1

24.25 such a] A2; that A1

24.30 courts] A2; a court A1

25.1 a] A2; a sort of A1

25.13 pugged] A2; rather pugged A1

25.16 was] A2; omit A1

25.17 weapons] A2; murder-fitted weapons A1

25.22 Rats!] A2; Fudge. A1

25.24 "elegant"] A2; elegant and graceful A1

25.29 dey] V; deh A1; d' A2-E2

26.12 outa sight] A2; great A1

26.35 ideal] A2; beau ideal of a A1

27.13 which] A2; that A1

27.28 er somethin'] A2; an' all A1

28.3 of a] A2; omit a A1

28.14 which] A2; omit A1

29.1–2 wore a different suit] A2; had different suits on A1

29.3 prodigious] A2; prodigally extensive A1

29.12 as endowed] A2; omit A1

29.17 It would be] A2; omit A1

29.37 ghastly,] A2; ghastly, like dead flesh, A1

29.37 mother] A2; red mother A1

30.14 drudging] A2; trudge A1

30.16 men] A2; kid-gloved men A1

31.6 visited] A2; been to A1

32.4 enthusiasm] A2; stereotyped enthusiasm A1

32.8 diversions] A2; phantasies A1

32.10 is] A2; it A1

32.17 set down] A2; omit A1

32.18 which] A2; that A1

32.22 they] A2; the duettists A1

32.28 harrowing] A2; the most harrowing A1

32.32 the kind] A2; that kind A1

32.35 annihilated] A2; being annihilated A1

32.36 climax] A2; crisis A1

32.37 when] A2; where A1

32.39 this] A2; the A1

32.39–33.1 most of them of foreign birth] A2; omit A1

33.4 noisily] A2; crashingly A1

33.7 silk] A2; glossy silk A1

33.7 leers] A2; leers, or smiles, A1

33.8 devil] A2; pictured devil A1

33.17 With . . . orchestra‸] A2; When the orchestra crashed finally, A1

Fig. 146. Eclectic Clear-Text Edition: Crane, *Maggie*. Substantive Variants.

EDITORIAL ACCIDENTALS EMENDATIONS
IN THE COPY-TEXT

[NOTE: Except for such silent typographical alterations as are remarked in the prefatory "Text of the Virginia Edition," every editorial change made in the accidentals from the 1893 copy-text is listed here. The wavy dash ∼ represents the same word that appears before the bracket and is used in recording punctuation variants. An inferior caret ∧ indicates the absence of a punctuation mark.]

7.7 git yehs!] A2; get yehs A1
8.19 interest.] V; ∼ , A1-E2
8.24 d'] A2; deh A1
8.32 d'] V; deh A1 (*omit* A2-E2)
8.34 t'] V; teh A1-E2
8.36 forward] A2; foward A1
9.8 d'] A2; deh A1
9.12 d'] V; deh A1 (*omit* A2-E2)
9.12 d'] V; deh A1-E2
9.22 d'] A2; deh A1
9.30 Jimmie] E1; Jimmy A1-2
9.36 dinner-pail] E2; ∼ ∧ ∼ A1-2
11.31 disdainfully] A2; distain-fully A1
12.1 d'] A2; deh A1
12.2 him.] A2; ∼ , A1
12.7 d'] V; deh A1 (*omit* A2-E2)
13.20 t'] A2; teh A1
13.33 The ragged (*no* ⦅)] A2; ⦅ A1
13.37 d'] A2; deh A1
14.1 I———"] A2; ∼ "——— A1
14.12 d'] A2; deh A1
14.17 t'] A2; teh A1
14.28–29 sleep, . . . doubled,] A2; ∼ ∧ . . . ∼ ∧ A1
16.10 music∧ box] A2; ∼ - ∼ A1
17.5 d'] V; deh A1-E2
17.7 t'] V; teh A1-E2
17.17 d'] V; deh A1-E2
17.17 D'] V; Deh A1-E2
17.37 d' . . . t'] V; deh . . . teh A1-E2

18.1 d'] V; deh A1 (*omit* A2-E2)
18.5 t'] V; teh A1 (*omit* A2-E2)
18.9 shrieks—] A2; ∼ , A1
18.13 doorways] A2; ∼ - ∼ A1
18.17 up stairs] V; upstairs A1-E1; up-stairs E2
19.14 doorway] A2; ∼ - ∼ A1
20.14 you's] V; yous A1-E2
20.16 ⦅ While] A2; no ⦅ A1
21.8 it.] A2; ∼ ∧ A1
21.15 chrysanthemums] A2; chris-anthemums A1
21.25 breathe] A2; breath A1
21.31; 22.27 foot∧ passengers] A2; ∼ - ∼ A1
23.2 flame-colored] A2 (-coloured); ∼ ∧ ∼ A1
23.8 sidewalk] A2; ∼ - ∼ A1
23.16 fire∧ engine] A2; ∼ - ∼ A1
23.18 street∧ car] A2; ∼ - ∼ A1
23.33 D'] V; Deh A1-E2
24.5,22 up stairs] V; upstairs A2-E1; ∼ - ∼ A1, E2
24.5 down stairs] V; downstairs A2-E1; ∼ - ∼ A1, E2
24.12 t'] A2; teh A1
24.12 t' hell] V; teh hell A1 (*omit* A2-E2)
25.2 Island] V; island A1-E2
25.17 shoes∧] A2; ∼ , A1
25.29 t' . . . d'] A2; teh . . . deh A1

87

Fig. 147. Eclectic Clear-Text Edition: Crane, *Maggie*. Editorial Accidentals Emendations.

WORD-DIVISION

1. *End-of-the-Line Hyphenation in the Virginia Edition*

[NOTE: No hyphenation of a possible compound at the end of a line in the Virginia text is present in the 1893 copy-text except for the following readings, which are hyphenated within the line in the 1893 edition. Hyphenated compounds in which both elements are' capitalized are not included.]

10.11	apple-|wood	29.18	mouse-|colored
18.18	door-|panels	30.2	green-|hued
21.3	street-|corners	39.26	dinner-|pail
25.16	patent-|leather	53.3	half-|closed
28.4	brass-|clothed	61.35	up-|town

2. *End-of-the-Line Hyphenation in the 1893 Copy-Text*

[NOTE: The following compounds, or possible compounds, are hyphenated at the end of the line in the 1893 copy-text. The form in which they have been transcribed in the Virginia Edition, as listed below, represents the practice of the 1893 edition as ascertained by other appearances or by parallels within the edition. Crane manuscripts have been consulted when evidence was not available in the 1893 edition.]

23.26	barroom	49.35	coat-tails
31.32	reappeared	51.12	overwhelming
33.6	foot-lights	55.22	re-echoed
33.33	lamp-post	60.27	cock-tails
35.2	pocketbook	61.17	cobwebs
42.9	forefinger	68.10	eye-brows
49.25	sidewalk		

Fig. 148. Eclectic Clear-Text Edition: Crane, *Maggie*. Word-Division List.

Historical Collation · 93

16.4   and] mingled with A1

16.21   almost kicked the stomach] kicked the breath A2-E2

16.23   damn] d—n A2-E2

16.24   cursed] a A2-E2

17.1   to] and A1

17.5   man] man, threateningly A1

17.10   throat] hairy throat

17.18   raisin' hell] trowin' fits A2-E2

17.19   man] old man E1–2

17.20   toward] towards E1–2

17.21   club hell outa] paste A2-E2

17.25,27   hell] h—l A2-E2

17.25   Damndes' place! Reg'lar hell!] omit A2-E2

18.1–2   wha' d' hell.] W'ats bitin' yeh? A2-E2

18.3   damn] omit A2-E2

18.5   t' hell,] chase yerself! A2-E2

18.8   yell] howl A1

18.10   a confused] confusingly in A1

18.10   it] omit A1

18.10   there] omit A1

18.12   his] omit A1

18.14   raisin' hell] playin' horse A2-E2

18.17   panther] panther's A2-E2

18.33–34   an attitude . . . that] positions . . . those A1

18.36   bended] bent A2-E2

19.2   an] that A1

19.7   into] in A1

19.9   his eyes] the eyes from out his drawn face A1

19.16   in uneasy] in an uneasy A2-E2

19.21   with] from A1

19.25   the] omit A1

20.1   an insignificant] a white, insignificant A1

20.10   for] from E1–2

20.14–15   Once. . . . What?"] omit A1

20.20   of words] of the words A2-E2

20.28   tourists] gentlemen A1

21.1   meet God] go to heaven A2-E2

21.3   on] at E1–2

21.9   toward] towards E1–2

21.11   order] orders E1–2

21.17   nothing] neither the devil nor the leader of society A1

21.22   There was given to him] He was given A1

21.26   punch] beat A1

21.34   If . . . became the] If in the front and the A1

22.5   which] that A1

22.7   greatest] most complete A1

22.9–10   became superior.] was superior. He became immured like an African cow. A1

22.14   start] begin A1

22.14   trance] sort of a trance A1

22.16   but] omit A1

22.17   policeman] policemen E1–2

22.17   to frenziedly] frenziedly to A2-E2

22.17   seize] tear A1

22.20   toward] towards E1–2

22.22   that he] omit A1

22.28–29   comprehend their desire] conceive their maniacal desires A1

22.35   and thus] omit A1

22.35   stolid] solid A1

22.39   obstruct] to obstruct A2-E2

23.1   And] And, perhaps, A1

23.1   had had a] had an ungovernable A1

23.4   hard] very hard A1

23.8   toward] towards E1–2

23.10   struck] would strike E1

23.14   swearing] storming A2-E2

23.15   the half of] half A2-E2

23.18   a street car]' street-cars A2-E2

23.33   hell] h—l A2-E2

24.10   disguised] disgusted E1–2

24.12   t' hell] on d' toif A2-E2

24.12   er] or A1

24.13   of going to hell] to the alternative A2-E2

24.18   with . . . been] the name of whose brand could be A1

24.19   connected] in connection A1

24.25   such a] that A1

Fig. 149. Eclectic Clear-Text Edition: Crane, *Maggie*. Historical Collation.

Eclectic Clear-Text Edition with Multiple Apparatus
(Stephen Crane. *The Works of Stephen Crane.* Ed. Fredson Bowers.
Charlottesville: UP of Virginia, 1969–75, 10 vols.)
Commentary: The text-page is entirely free of signs of editorial intervention, providing a clear reading text separate from the various types
of apparatus. To preserve this feature, unlike the inclusive text there
is no lineation to key the apparatus to the text. Unless the reader specifically looks into the apparatus, there is thus no sign of any changes
to copy-text accidentals or substantives made by the editor.

The apparatus is divided into several sections. The textual notes
give the rationale for emendation, or for rejecting emendation, as in
22.14, where the editor argues in favor of the retention of copy-text
"observation" over "oblivion" suggested by another critic. Here, as
throughout the apparatus, the variant editions are referred to by sigla
(A1, A2). The list of variants in the substantives variants list for this
page shows a wide range, including an entire sentence ("He became
immured like an African cow" at 22.9–10) not included in A1 and
rejected from the clear-text, and substantial variants like "conceive
their maniacal desires" for the copy-text "comprehend their desire" at
22.28–29. The list of accidentals emendations shows no changes for
this page, but significant changes elsewhere (e.g., "chrysanthemums"
for "chrisanthemums" at 21.15). The list of word-division forms is
normal (indeed expected) in CEAA/CSE editions and reflects the
dominance of editions from the post-Renaissance periods. The purpose of the list is to clarify which line-end hyphens should be retained
in quoting from the edition. The historical collation lists all variants
from every edition recorded in the transmission and is not limited to
authorial variants. It does not include editorial emendations unless
these emendations are derived from one of the editions cited. Thus
the historical collation inevitably contains much of the same information as the list of substantives variants (e.g., the entries for 22.9–10
and 22.28–29 are identical in both), but the historical collation also
includes variants such as "22.17 policeman] policemen," which is
derived from the non-authorial editions E1–2 and thus not cited in the
substantives list.

394-400
eclectic
clear text

Parallel-Text Edition
(William Wordsworth. *The Prelude: 1799, 1805, 1850.* Ed. Jonathan Wordsworth, M. H. Abrams, and Stephen Gill. New York: Norton, 1979.)
Commentary: While the edition also includes the 1799 two-book version of *The Prelude*, this version is printed separately before the parallel-text 1805 and 1850 versions. This arrangement reflects the fact that 1799 is very much shorter than the other two and that a parallel-text edition of all three would be visually awkward, though very illuminating. The edition prints basically a clear-text of each version on facing pages, with some but not all of the parallel lines aligned. There is no attempt to signal to the reader where major variations occur between the two versions, either by editorial symbols or by the placement of lines, so that "Make ceaseless music" at the top of each page is aligned, but "Oh, many a time" (288/292 and 288 respectively) is not. This presentation encourages each version to be read separately (i.e., vertically). The only interruptions to the clear-text are the supralinear numbers keying lines to the notes at the foot of each page. These notes are explanatory rather than textual, and comment on variance between the two texts only when this has some historical or personal significance (e.g., note 1 on Wordsworth's age, before 9 in 1805 and before 10 in 1850).

402 - 403

44 · 1805. Book First

Make ceaseless music through the night and day,
Which with its steady cadence tempering   280
Our human waywardness, composed my thoughts
To more than infant softness, giving me
Among the fretful dwellings of mankind,
[280] A knowledge, a dim earnest, of the calm
Which Nature breathes among the hills and groves?   285
When, having left his mountains, to the towers
Of Cockermouth that beauteous river came,
Behind my father's house he passed, close by,
[286] Along the margin of our terrace walk.
He was a playmate whom we dearly loved: 290
Oh, many a time have I, a five years' child,
A naked boy, in one delightful rill,
A little mill-race severed from his stream,
[290] Made one long bathing of a summer's day,
Basked in the sun, and plunged, and basked again,   295
Alternate, all a summer's day, or coursed
Over the sandy fields, leaping through groves
Of yellow grunsel; or, when crag and hill,
[295] The woods, and distant Skiddaw's lofty height,[7]
Were bronzed with a deep radiance, stood alone   300
Beneath the sky, as if I had been born
On Indian plains,[8] and from my mother's hut
Had run abroad in wantonness to sport,
[300] A naked savage, in the thunder-shower.

      Fair seed-time had my soul, and I grew up   305
Fostered alike by beauty and by fear,
Much favored in my birthplace, and no less
In that beloved vale to which erelong
[305] I was transplanted.[9] Well I call to mind—

      'Twas at an early age, ere I had seen   310
Nine summers —when upon the mountain slope
The frost and breath of frosty wind had snapped
The last autumnal crocus, 'twas my joy
To wander half the night among the cliffs
And the smooth hollows where the woodcocks ran   315
Along the open turf. In thought and wish
[310] That time, my shoulder all with springes[2] hung,
I was a fell destroyer. On the heights

7. Skiddaw, nine miles due east of Cockermouth, is the fourth highest peak in the Lake District (3,053 feet). "Grunsel" (*1805*, 298): ragwort—i.e., ragweed —(as in *1850*), not the modern groundsel.
8. Wordsworth's reference is to the American Indian.
9. The experiences that follow take place after Wordsworth has been "transplanted" to Hawkshead Grammar School, thirty-five miles from Cockermouth, in May 1779.
2. Snares.

Fig. 150. Parallel-Text Edition: Wordsworth, *The Prelude* (Norton Edition). 1805 Text (verso pages).

Make ceaseless music that composed my thoughts
To more than infant softness, giving me
Amid the fretful dwellings of mankind
A foretaste, a dim earnest, of the calm   280
That Nature breathes among the hills and groves.
When he had left the mountains and received
On his smooth breast the shadow of those towers
That yet survive, a shattered monument
Of feudal sway,[6] the bright blue river passed   285
Along the margin of our terrace walk;
A tempting playmate whom we dearly loved.
Oh, many a time have I, a five years' child,
In a small mill-race severed from his stream,
Made one long bathing of a summer's day;   290
Basked in the sun, and plunged and basked again
Alternate, all a summer's day, or scoured
The sandy fields, leaping through flowery groves
Of yellow ragwort; or when rock and hill,
The woods, and distant Skiddaw's lofty height,[7]   295
Were bronzed with deepest radiance, stood alone
Beneath the sky, as if I had been born
On Indian plains,[8] and from my mother's hut
Had run abroad in wantonness, to sport
A naked savage, in the thunder shower.   300

    Fair seed-time had my soul, and I grew up
Fostered alike by beauty and by fear:
Much favoured in my birth-place, and no less
In that beloved Vale to which erelong
We were transplanted[9]—there were we let loose   305
For sports of wider range. Ere I had told
Ten birth-days,[1] when among the mountain slopes
Frost, and the breath of frosty wind, had snapped
The last autumnal crocus, 'twas my joy
With store of springes[2] o'er my shoulder hung   310
To range the open heights where woodcocks ran
Along the smooth green turf. Through half the night,
Scudding away from snare to snare, I plied
That anxious visitation;—moon and stars

---

6. Cockermouth Castle.   1. The right number (Wordsworth was
                                          nine years old), as against that in *1805.*

Fig. 151. Parallel Text Edition: Wordsworth, *The Prelude*. 1850 Text (recto
pages).

Sonnets.

Might I not then fay now I loue you beſt,
When I was certaine ore in-certainty,
Crowning the preſent,doubting of the reſt:
  Loue is a Babe , then might I not ſay ſo
  To giue full growth to ſhat which ſtill doth grow.

119

Et me not to the marriage of true mindes
Admit impediments,loue is not loue
Which alters when it alteration findes,
Or bends with the remouer to remoue.
O no,it is an euer fixed marke
That lookes on tempeſts and is neuer ſhaken;
It is the ſtar to euery wandring barke,
Whoſe worths vnknowne,although his higth be taken.
Lou's not Times foole,though roſie lips and cheeks
Within his bending ſickles compaſſe come,
Loue alters not with his breefe houres and weekes,
But beares it out euen to the edge of doome:
  If this be error and vpon me proued,
  I neuer writ,nor no man euer loued.

117

Ccufe me thus,that I haue ſcanted all,
Wherein I ſhould your great deſerts repay,
Forgot vpon your deareſt loue to call,
Whereto al bonds do tie me day by day,
That I haue frequent binne with vnknown mindes,
And giuen to time your owne deare purchaſ'd right,
That I haue hoyſted ſaile to al the windes
Which ſhould tranſport me fartheſt from your ſight.
Booke both my wilfulneſſe and errors downe,
And on iuſt proofe ſurmiſe,accumilate,
Bring me within the leuel of your frowne,
But ſhoote not at me in your wakened hate:
  Since my appeale ſaies I did ſtriue to prooue
  The conſtancy and virtue of your loue

H   118

Fig. 152. Parallel Old and Modern Spelling Edition: Shakespeare, *Sonnets*
(Booth Edition). Facsimile of Quarto (verso pages).

100

Might I not then say, now I love you best,
When I was certain o'er incertainty,
12   Crowning the present, doubting of the rest?
   Love is a babe; then might I not say so,
   To give full growth to that which still doth grow.

116

Let me not to the marriage of true minds
Admit impediments. Love is not love
Which alters when it alteration finds,
4   Or bends with the remover to remove.
O no, it is an ever-fixèd mark
That looks on tempests and is never shaken;
It is the star to every wand'ring bark,
8   Whose worth's unknown, although his height be taken.
Love's not time's fool, though rosy lips and cheeks
Within his bending sickle's compass come.
Love alters not with his brief hours and weeks,
12   But bears it out ev'n to the edge of doom.
   If this be error and upon me proved,
   I never writ, nor no man ever loved.

117

Accuse me thus: that I have scanted all
Wherein I should your great deserts repay,
Forgot upon your dearest love to call,
4   Whereto all bonds do tie me day by day;
That I have frequent been with unknown minds,
And giv'n to time your own dear purchased right;
That I have hoisted sail to all the winds
8   Which should transport me farthest from your sight.
Book both my wilfulness and errors down,
And on just proof surmise accumulate;
Bring me within the level of your frown,
12   But shoot not at me in your wakened hate,
   Since my appeal says I did strive to prove
   The constancy and virtue of your love.

Fig. 153. Parallel Old and Modern-Spelling Edition: Shakespeare, *Sonnets*.
Modernized Text (recto pages).

in the implications of the definition: Cupid, who never grows up, is a baby *still*, "forever."

The ramifications of the couplet and their contradictions of one another might be continued indefinitely. The logical conclusion the sonnet reaches is not expressed in the particular assertion embodied in its last sentence; the point the couplet makes is not in what its words express in relation to one another but in what is demonstrated about all human assertions by its syntactic completeness, its sound of finality, its position at the end of the poem, and its ultimate incapacity to make a final, a definitive, an ultimate, statement. It is impossible to make an absolute statement at any moment in—or about anything that exists in—time.

SONNET 116

See the headnotes to 115 and 117.

In twelve of the thirteen surviving copies of Q, sonnet 116 comes between 115 and 117 but is numbered 119, presumably as a result of an easy confusion by which a *9* was misplaced in sorting and put with the *6*'s in the printer's font. The Folger-Mildmay copy numbers 116 correctly (see 89.11, note).

Some glosses are omitted from the line-by-line commentary because they occur in the final general note on the poem.

1–2. In context of *marriage, Admit impediments* evokes a strong specific echo of the marriage service: "I require and charge you (as you will answer at the dreadful day of judgment, when the secrets of all hearts shall be disclosed) that if either of you do know any impediment why ye may not be lawfully joined together in matrimony, that ye confess it." Note that, although both the marriage service and this sonnet are principally concerned with truth—being true, being faithful, being constant—this first sentence of the sonnet and the section of the marriage service it echoes are concerned with speaking the truth, confessing what is true (see lines 13–14).

1. *Let me not* May I never. (The tone is that of a vow, but the imperative use of *Let* also suggests prayerful beseeching and gives the poem psalm-like overtones; compare Psalms 31:17–18: "Let me not be confounded, o Lord: for I have called upon thee: let the wicked be put to confusion, & to silence in the grave / Let the lying lippes be made dumme . . .").

2. *Admit* (1) concede the existence of, acknowledge; (2) permit consideration of. (The idiomatic implications of the construction "admit to the marriage" give the sentence overtones of a metaphor in which the speaker is like a doorkeeper or usher admitting or not admitting wedding guests, allowing or impeding their passage; compare *Measure* IV.iii.116: "You shall not be admitted to his sight.") *Love is not love* that so-called love is not true love, is not real love. Note that, although the word "true" is not physically present here, this phrase implies the idea of genuineness—an idea expressible in the word "true." See the note on lines 1–2 above; the substance of this phrase relates to a third sense of "true."

2–12. Compare the proverbs "A perfect love does last eternally" and "Love without end has no end [i.e. has no ulterior motive]" (Tilley, L539, L533).

Fig. 154. Parallel Old and Modern Spelling Edition: Shakespeare, *Sonnets*. Textual/Critical Commentary on Sonnet 116 (beginning).

Parallel Old and Modern-Spelling Edition with Commentary
(William Shakespeare. *Shakespeare's Sonnets*. Ed. Stephen Booth.
New Haven: Yale UP, 1977. Repr. with corrections, 1980.)
Commentary: This is an unusual format and presentation, with parallel texts of both the original quarto edition of the sonnets (in facsimile) and a modernized version. The commentary is keyed to the modern-spelling version. While there is some textual information in the
commentary (e.g., on the misnumbering of sonnet 116 as 119 in
twelve of the thirteen extant copies of the quarto), the bulk of the
commentary is critical and explanatory, citing sources and discussing
critical readings and reception. In this sense, the edition combines the
features of a classical commentary edition and a critical variorum (see
below). The commentary is arranged by line-order but is concluded
by a general critical article on the sonnet as a whole.

404 – 406

I find a kindling excitement in the thought that the feeling which prompts ⟨me⟩ ↑a child↓ to an act of ⟨honesty⟩ ↑generosity↓ is the same which guides ⟨the⟩ ↑an↓ archangel to his awful duties; that in the humblest transaction in which we can engage we can introduce these stupendous laws which make the sovereignty of the ⟨Universe⟩ ↑Creation↓ the Character of God. It seems to me in obeying them[,] in squaring my conduct by them I part with the weakness of ⟨my nature⟩ ↑humanity↓. I exchange ↑the rags of↓ my nature for ↑a portion of↓ the majesty of my maker. I am backed by ⟨Divine strength⟩ ↑the Universe of beings↓. I lean on ⟨the Universe.⟩ omnipotence.

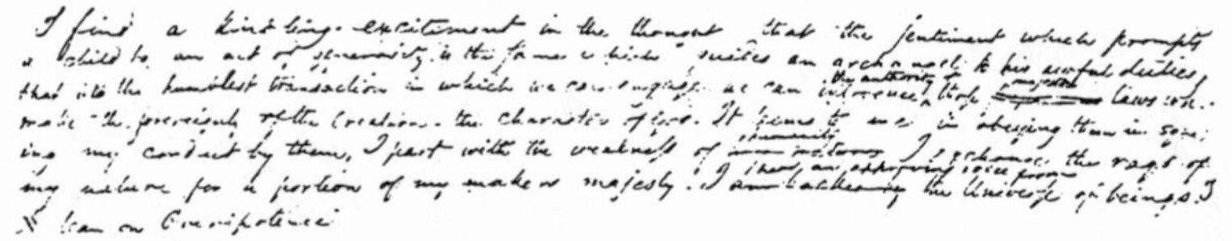
I find a kindling excitement in the thought that the sentiment which prompts a child to an act of generosity is the same which guides an archangel to his awful duties; that into the humblest transaction in which we can engage we can introduce those laws which make the provinces of the Creation the Character of God. It seems to me in obeying them in squaring my conduct by them, I part with the weakness of humanity. I exchange the rags of my nature for a portion of my maker's majesty. I am backed by the Universe of beings. I lean on Omnipotence

Fig. 155. Genetic Edition: Emerson Journal Entry (Harvard Edition) and Facsimile of Sermon Manuscript.

```
     I find a kindling excitement in the thought that the
     sentiment which prompts a child to an act of generosity
     is the same which guides an archangel to his awful
     duties; that in+to* the humblest transaction in which
5    we can engage we can introduce +the authority of* those
     <stupendous> +majestic* laws wh. make the sovereignty
     of the Creation--the character of God.  It seems to me
     in obeying them in squaring my conduct by them, I part
     with the weakness of <my nature> +humanity*  I exchange
10   the rags of my nature for a portion of my makers
     majesty.  I <am backed by> +hear an approving voice
     from* the Universe of beings.  +I* <I> lean on
     Omnipotence
```

```
     I find a kindling excitement in the thought that the
     sentiment which prompts a child to an act of generosity
     is the same which guides an archangel to his awful
     duties; that into the humblest transaction in which we
5    can engage we can introduce the authority of those
     majestic laws which make the sovereignty of the
     Creation--the character of God.  It seems to me in
     obeying them, in squaring my conduct by them, I part
     with the weakness of humanity.  I exchange the rags of
10   my nature for a portion of my maker's majesty.  I hear
     an approving voice from the Universe of beings.  I lean
     on Omnipotence.
```

Fig. 156. Genetic Edition: Transcription (above) and Clear-Text Transcription (below) of Emerson Sermon Passage (Missouri Edition).

Genetic Edition

Ralph Waldo Emerson. *Journals and Miscellaneous Notebooks of Ralph Waldo Emerson.* Ed. William H. Gilman et al. Cambridge: Harvard UP, 1969–82.

Ralph Waldo Emerson. *The Complete Sermons of Ralph Waldo Emerson.* Ed. Albert J. von Frank, Jr., et al. Columbia: U of Missouri P, 1989– .

Commentary: The journal entry made by Emerson on May, 8, 1828 (as published in the Harvard edition) shows by special symbols the various levels of composition, the "hypergrammar" or syntax of construction, whereby an original "me" is replaced by the generic "a child" and "honesty" by "generosity" etc., through the cancelling pointed brackets " < me > " and the arrow keys ↑ ↓. As Albert von Frank (see bibliography to Chapter 9) points out, through the hypergrammar of genetic text, both "me" and "a child" are simultaneously encoded as objects of the verb "prompts," in a manner not possible in clear texts. The passage from the manuscript of Sermon XIX, read in conjunction with the genetic text of the journals, from which it derives, shows a similar series of equivocations, which the clear-text transcription of the sermon obscures by having to choose only the final reading. In the genetic transcription of the Sermon, von Frank sees the operation of a "poetics" of editing, whereby the reader is made visually aware that the levels of revision are related to each other: with an original "stupendous" linking back to the "kindling excitement" of the earlier journal entry, and its substitute "majestic" linking forward with "sovereignty of the Creation" and "the character of God."

408 - 409

Critical and Synoptic Edition
James Joyce. *Ulysses: A Critical and Synoptic Edition.* Ed. Hans
Walter Gabler, with Wolfhard Steppe and Claus Melchior. New
York: Garland, 1984. 3 vols.
Commentary: The left-hand (verso) pages contain the synoptic apparatus and the right-hand (recto) pages a clear-text rendering. These two
methods of presentation have different aims and different editorial
procedures: the synoptic apparatus is not concerned with final intention but with showing the various levels of composition of which final
intention is just one part, whereas the clear-text reading page produces
a text driven by intentionality.

Within the synoptic apparatus, which attempts to tabulate spatially
(synchronically) the temporal (diachronic) construction of the text,
there are two basic types of revision, one within a single document
("intra-document") and the other among different documents ("inter-
document"). The list of symbols in the textual introduction shows
how this distinction works out. For example, the exclamation mark
after "Kinch" (line 8) is retained after the period in the same document is deleted, as it is when the comma after "barracks" is deleted in
line 19. Levels of overlay addition within the same document are indicated by the direction of the carets marking the addition. Thus,
"christine" in line 21 is an overlay at the first level, with upward ($^\wedge$)
carets. The reading "Three" (enclosed within square brackets—the
sign for deletion—on line 26) derives from a document different from
the "Two" which replaces it. The half square brackets in which the
"variation area" is contained are used to show such inter-document
replacement, within which the deletion can be marked with the full
square brackets. There are layers of addition that can be signalled,
and in this case the whole of the rest of the sentence down to "through
the calm" is an addition at the fourth level of composition after the
first type-setting, and within this the further deletion/addition (at the
fifth level of composition after the type-setting) of "Three" into
"Two" takes place. The raised $^\circ$ at various points in the synoptic
apparatus alerts the reader to a "single-word emendation note" in the
critical apparatus below. So, the form "Stately,$^\circ$" in line 1 is keyed
to the note explaining that the word (and line) are not indented in the
Rosenbach manuscript (R). These symbols can take some time to
master, but once learned they allow the reader to follow Joyce's composition process not only within a single document, as was the case
with the Emerson genetic text, but from one document to another, in
an extension of genetic method from text to work.

412 - 415

SYMBOLS

1. Synopsis

Revisions within one document (intra-document changes):
The extent of additions and replacements is indicated by pairs of carets. These are rotated for successive levels of revision within one document. *Currente calamo* cancellations and deletions in revision are enclosed in pointed brackets.

⟨text cancelled⟩	deletion only within one document (*currente calamo* cancellation)
^text new^	revision (addition) within one document at overlay level
^⟨text old⟩ text new^	revision (deletion and replacement) within one document at overlay level
⟨^text old⟩	deletion only within one document at overlay level
^() . . . . ()^	revision, positioning inferred
^ . . . . . ^	revision implied by other changes and editorially construed
|^|	paragraph separation at overlay level
← ^ →	paragraph cancellation at overlay level
^ . . . . ^	first overlay level
> . . . . <	second overlay level
v v	third overlay level
< . . . . >	fourth overlay level
\ . . . . / and " . . . . "	pseudo-overlay at first and second levels, e.g., interlinear addition of text already present in extant early draft

Revisions in the progression of documents (inter-document changes):
The extent of additions and replacements is indicated by pairs of half-brackets. The levels of revision are indexed by letters of the alphabet before the first type-setting in proof (1st *placards*) and by rising numbers thereafter. Deletions are enclosed in square brackets.

⌐B text new B⌐	revision (addition) at level B
⌐B[text old] text new B⌐	revision (deletion and replacement) at level B
[B text old]	deletion only at level B
⌐(B) . . . . (B)⌐	revision (addition) at level B, document of entry lost
⌐B() . . . . ()B⌐	revision (addition) at level B, positioning inferred
⌐*B . . . . B*⌐	revision (addition) at level B, implied by other changes and editorially construed
|B|	paragraph separation at level B
←B→	paragraph cancellation at level B

Fig. 157 (a). Critical and Synoptic Edition: Joyce, *Ulysses* (Gabler Edition). Editorial Symbols.

Index letter A generally indicates changes between a holograph and a typescript typed from it.

Index letters B, C and D indicate the stages of revision belonging to the typescripts extant or lost (i.e., their reproduction of a lost revised final working draft and/or their revisional autograph overlay).

Index letter R indicates collateral revisions uniquely present in the fair copy (Rosenbach Manuscript) and editorially admitted.

Index letter V indicates collateral revisions uniquely present in the fair copy and editorially not admitted (NB: the unique fair-copy reading is bracketed {. . . . .}).

Index letter W in episode 15 ("Circe") only indicates collateral revisions present in the typescript in a brief mid-chapter section.

Index letter S indicates the entry of a revision in a scribal hand.

Index letters S and A in episode 10 ("Wandering Rocks") only distinguish the strata of scribal inscription and overlay and of authorial overlay in the Rosenbach Manuscript.

Index numbers 1 to 12 indicate the levels of revision at the successive proof stages; an independent series begins for each chapter.

$^{\ulcorner}$). . . . .$^{\urcorner}$ in episode 15 ("Circe") only: missing section in the autograph

$^{\ulcorner}$+. . . . .+$^{\urcorner}$ in episode 17 ("Ithaca") only: addition of complete question-and-answer segments in the final working draft

Further symbols:

Ø	space reserved in the autograph
◻	word or words illegible
▯	letter, letter sequence or mark of punctuation illegible
▨	erasure
Δ	insert indicated but missing
||	turn of leaf in the autograph
-|	word division at line-break in the autograph, hyphenated
|	word division at line-break in the autograph, not hyphenated
-|-	word division at line-break in the autograph, doubly hyphenated
°	reference to a single-word emendation note or footnote
⸨	reference to a phrase-extension emendation note or footnote
⸩	end of phrase extension
⊞	reference to a notable change in the document situation (footnoted)
~	identical text in roman to text italicized in revision
*	in episode 15 ("Circe") only: emendation without specification of source in direction-text surroundings (upper- or lower case initial letters supplied, full stops and parentheses supplied or deleted)
*	in episode 18 ("Penelope") only: revision without specification of level (marks of punctuation and apostrophes eliminated)

Fig. 157 (b). Critical and Synoptic Edition: Joyce, *Ulysses*. Editorial Symbols.

Jenetic side

Stately,° plump Buck Mulligan came from the stairhead, bearing a bowl of lather on which a mirror and a razor lay crossed. A yellow dressinggown, ungirdled, was sustained gently behind him ⌐(B)⌐[by] on°(B)⌐ the mild morning air. He held the bowl aloft and intoned:

5 —*Introibo ad altare Dei.*

Halted, he peered down the dark winding stairs and called out° coarsely:

—Come up, Kinch⟨.⟩!° Come up, you fearful jesuit!°

Solemnly he came forward and mounted the round gunrest. He faced
10 about and blessed gravely thrice the tower, the surrounding land° and the awaking mountains. Then, catching sight of Stephen Dedalus, he bent towards him and made rapid crosses in the air, gurgling in his throat and shaking his head. Stephen Dedalus, displeased and sleepy, leaned his arms on the top of the staircase and looked coldly at the shaking gurgling face
15 that blessed him, equine in its length, and at the light untonsured hair, grained and hued like pale oak.

Buck Mulligan peeped an instant under the mirror and then covered the bowl smartly.

—Back to barracks⟨,⟩! he said sternly.
20 He added in a preacher's tone:

—For this, O dearly beloved, is the genuine ^⟨Ø⟩ christine^: body and soul and blood and ouns. Slow music, please. Shut your eyes, gents. One moment. A little trouble about those white corpuscles. Silence, all.

He peered sideways up and gave a long slow° whistle of call,° then
25 paused awhile in rapt attention, his even white teeth glistening here and there with gold points. Chrysostomos. ⌐⁵[Three] Two⌐ strong shrill whistles answered through the calm.⌐

—Thanks, old chap, he cried briskly. That will do nicely. Switch off the current, will you?

PRECEDING PAGE I] CF Faire préceder par une page vide marquée au milieu ainsi I a1
GENERAL NOTE →TN 1 Stately,] (tB); NOT INDENTED aR 3 on] LR,Eg; by (aC) PCU; CF
892.23 6 out] STET aR; TD: up (tB) (ANTICIPATION) 8 Kinch!] STET aR; TD: Kinch (tB);

Fig. 158. Critical and Synoptic Edition: Joyce, *Ulysses*. Synoptic Apparatus (verso pages).

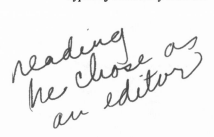

Stately, plump Buck Mulligan came from the stairhead, bearing a bowl of lather on which a mirror and a razor lay crossed. A yellow dressinggown, ungirdled, was sustained gently behind him on the mild morning air. He held the bowl aloft and intoned:
—*Introibo ad altare Dei.*   5
Halted, he peered down the dark winding stairs and called out coarsely:
—Come up, Kinch! Come up, you fearful jesuit!
Solemnly he came forward and mounted the round gunrest. He faced about and blessed gravely thrice the tower, the surrounding land and the   10
awaking mountains. Then, catching sight of Stephen Dedalus, he bent towards him and made rapid crosses in the air, gurgling in his throat and shaking his head. Stephen Dedalus, displeased and sleepy, leaned his arms on the top of the staircase and looked coldly at the shaking gurgling face that blessed him, equine in its length, and at the light untonsured hair,   15
grained and hued like pale oak.
Buck Mulligan peeped an instant under the mirror and then covered the bowl smartly.
—Back to barracks! he said sternly.
He added in a preacher's tone: 20
—For this, O dearly beloved, is the genuine christine: body and soul and blood and ouns. Slow music, please. Shut your eyes, gents. One moment. A little trouble about those white corpuscles. Silence, all.
He peered sideways up and gave a long slow whistle of call, then paused awhile in rapt attention, his even white teeth glistening here and   25
there with gold points. Chrysostomos. Two strong shrill whistles answered through the calm.
—Thanks, old chap, he cried briskly. That will do nicely. Switch off the current, will you?

Kinch. LR,a4   8 jesuit!] *STET* aR; *TD:* jesuit. (tB); Jesuit. 1; jesuit. aE   10 land] *STET* aR; *TD:*
country (tB)   24 slow] *STET* aR; *TD:* low (tB)   24 call,] *STET* aR,aE; call a4

EPISODE 1   3

Fig. 159. Critical and Synoptic Edition: Joyce, *Ulysses*. Clear-Text (recto pages).

3.2.184-95   *Measure for Measure*

vngenitur'd Agent will vn-people the Prouince with   1660
Continencie. Sparrowes must not build in his house-
eeues, because they are lecherous: The Duke yet would
haue darke deeds darkelie answered, hee would neuer
bring them to light: would hee were return'd. Marrie
this *Claudio* is condemned for vntrussing. Farwell good   1665
Friar, I prethee pray for me: The Duke (I say to thee
againe) would eate Mutton on Fridaies. He's now past
it, yet (and I say to thee) hee would mouth with a beg-
gar, though she smelt browne-bread and Garlicke: say

1667–8 now past it, yet] not past it yet; HAN1, WARB, JOHN, SING2, COL3,
CAM1-DYCE2, DYCE3, HUD2, WH2, CAM2, ARD1, CAM3-ALEX, PEL1, PEN2; now
past it: yea, CAP; not past it; COL4
1668 say] say't v1773, NLSN
1669 smelt] smelt of ROWE1-v1773 (−CAP)

1660 vngenitur'd] CAPELL (1779, 1:glossary, 73): "Unfurnish'd with the Organs of Geniture or Generation." RICHARDSON (1837): *"Ungenerated. Ungenitured.*
Not begotten, or borne into existence; not procreated." HUDSON (ed. 1851): *"Unfa-
thered,* not begotten after the ordinary course of nature." SCHMIDT (1875): "Impotent." BALD (ed. 1956): "Sexless." LEVER (ed. 1965): "Sterile, seedless; or without
genitals." Cf. *vnseminar'd, Ant.* 1.5.11 (537), and *vnpaued Eunuch, Cym.* 2.3.34 (992).
        1661–2 Sparrowes . . . lecherous] TILLEY (S715) and WILSON (p. 497): "As
lustful as sparrows." Cf. Chaucer, *C.T. Prol.* 626, "lecherous as a sparwe."
        1663 darke deeds] Cf. *Per.* 4.6.32, *Lr.* 3.4.90 (1867). See n. 2250.
        darkelie] SCHMIDT (1874): "Secretly" (*OED, adv.* 1), as in *AWW* 4.3.13
(2117). ONIONS (1911): "S. is earliest for 'secretly'." Again in 2657.
        1664 would] See *OED* (Will *v.* 1 36): "With ellipsis of 1st pers. pron. as an
expression of longing = 'I wish'." Cf. 2303.
        1665 vntrussing] HALLIWELL (ed. 1854): "To untruss was to untie the tags
which united the doublet and hose" (*OED, v.* 3 and *vbl. sb.*).
        1667 eate . . . Fridaies] THEOBALD (ed. 1733) compares *lac'd-Mutton* in *TGV*
1.1.102 (101), and a note on that passage quotes *1 Promos,* 1.3 (p. 312 below), "he
lou'd lase mutton well." STEEVENS (Var. 1778) quotes Marlowe's *Dr. Faustus* (1604,
708–10). NARES (1822): *Mutton,* "A loose woman" (*OED,* 4). TILLEY (M1338) and
WILSON (p. 552): "He loves laced mutton." Lucio means that "The Duke would not
give up women, fast-day or no fast-day, law or no law." See n. 1545.
        now] JOHNSON (Var. 1773): Hanmer's emendation *not* "was received in the
former edition, but seems not necessary. It were to be wished, that we all explained
more, and amended less." HART (ed. 1905): "I agree with M. Mason [1785, p. 40]
that 'Hanmer's amendment appears absolutely necessary'. Otherwise there is no force
in the previous sentence, or rather there would be contradiction." RIDLEY (ed.
1935): "There is an additional insult in the picture of the now *impotent* old lecher."
LEISI (ed. 1964): "Most edd. emend to *not,* putting a semicolon after *yet.* Cf. the
present tense in *he's a better woodman,* [2255]."
        past] See *OED* (*prep.* 1): "Beyond the age for."
        1668 mouth] *OED* (*v.* 6): "Join lips," first quotation in this sense.
        1669 smelt] HALLIWELL (ed. 1854): "We should now write, *smelt of,* but a

172

Fig. 160. Variorum Edition: Shakespeare, *Measure for Measure* (Shakespeare Variorum).

Variorum Edition
(William Shakespeare. *Measure for Measure*. Ed. Mark Eccles. *New Variorum Edition*. New York: MLA, 1980.)
Commentary: The text-page of the Variorum is divided into three sections. The upper section presents an old-spelling reprint of the copy-text. It does not attempt to construct a critical text. The middle section records the textual emendations to the copy-text made by previous editors of Shakespeare, and the lower section lists the commentary on the text by editors and critics. Cumulatively, a variorum can therefore present a cultural and critical history of the transmission and reception of a text, but it does not usually try to create a new text. The critical commentary includes definitions (e.g., of "vngenitur'd" line 1660 and "darkelie" line 1663), from both *OED* and earlier editions, the citation of parallel or similar passages (e.g., 1667, "eate . . . Fridaies"), and reference to critical and textual disagreements. It is particularly appropriate that Johnson's comment "It were to be wished, that we all explained more, and amended less" should be cited in a variorum (line 1667, "now"), whose purpose is to explain rather than emend. Note that a substantial number of editors have accepted Hanmer's emendation of "now" to "not" (see the listing in the textual section), as the editor admits, by quoting Leisi.

← 416

top : clear text

middle: variants

bottom: history
of critical
response

Selected Bibliography

General Note: The selected bibliography is arranged under Chapter topics, with further subdivisions in Chapters 1, 8, and 9 for ease of reference. There is no attempt to cover the bibliography of the entire field of textual scholarship, but only to suggest further readings to the student. Items with a good introductory coverage, or with other features likely to be of value to the beginner, are marked with an asterisk (*). Each section of the bibliography is intended to be free-standing, and while I have tried to avoid duplicating entries, certain titles are inevitably cited more than once (e.g., the Williams and Abbott *Introduction to Bibliographical and Textual Studies* and the Gaskell *New Introduction to Bibliography*, both of which are essential for the study of analytical, descriptive, and textual bibliography and thus appear in the reading for all these areas).

Introduction: Definitions and the Bibliographical Debate

*Blum, Rudolf. *Bibliographia: An Inquiry Into Its Definitions and Designations*. Trans. Mathilde V. Rovelstad. Chicago: American Library Association / Folkestone: Wm. Dawson, 1980.
*Bowers, Fredson. "The Bibliographical Way." *Essays in Bibliography, Text, and Editing*. Charlottesville: UP of Virginia, 1975: 3–108.
—. "The Function of Bibliography." *Library Trends* 7, No. 4 (1959): 497–510.
—. *Bibliography and Textual Criticism*. Oxford: Clarendon, 1964.
—. *Textual and Literary Criticism*. Cambridge: Cambridge UP, 1966.
—. "Bibliography." *Encyclopaedia Britannica*. Chicago: Benton, 1968: vol. 3: 588–92.
Darnton, Robert. "What Is the History of Books?" *Books and Society in History*. Ed. Kenneth E. Carpenter. New York: Bowker: 3–26.
Dearing, Vinton. "Methods of Textual Editing." *Williams Andrews Clark Memorial Library Seminar Papers*. 1962: 1–34. Repr. in Brack and Barnes: 73–101.
Du Rietz, Rolf. "What Is Bibliography?" *Text* (Sweden) 1 (1974): 6–40.
Fish, Stanley. *Is There a Text in This Class? The Authority of Interpretive Communities*. Cambridge: Harvard UP, 1980.

Greetham, D. C. "Textual and Literary Theory: Redrawing the Matrix." *Studies in Bibliography* 42 (1989): 1–24.

—. "[Textual] Criticism and Deconstruction." *Studies in Bibliography* 44 (1991): 1–30.

—. *Theories of the Text.* Oxford: Oxford UP. Forthcoming.

Greg, W. W. "What Is Bibliography?" *Bibliographical Society Transactions* 12, pt. 1 (1911–12): 10–12.

—. "The Present Position of Bibliography." *The Library* Fourth Series, 11 (1930): 211–62.

—. "Bibliography—A Retrospect." *The Bibliographical Society 1892–1942: Studies in Retrospect.* London: Bibliographical Society, 1945: 23–31.

Shaw, David. *"La bibliologie* in France." *The Book Encompassed.* Ed. Peter Davison. Cambridge: Cambridge UP, 1992: 206–214.

Tanselle, G. Thomas. "Textual Criticism and Deconstruction." *Studies in Bibliography* 43 (1990): 1–33.

—. "Issues in Bibliographical Studies since 1942." *The Book Encompassed.* Ed. Peter Davison: Cambridge: Cambridge UP, 1992: 24–36.

Vinaver, Eugène. "Principles of Textual Emendation." *Studies in French Language and Medieval Literature Presented to Professor M. K. Pope.* Manchester: U of Manchester P, 1930: 351–69.

Willis, James. *Latin Textual Criticism.* Urbana: U of Illinois P, 1972.

Chapter 1: Enumerative Bibliography

History of Libraries (See also history of textual criticism bibliography in Chapter 8.)

Becker, G. *Catalogi bibliothecarum antiqui: I, Catalogi sæculo XIII vetustiores; II, Catalogus catalogorum posterioris ætatis.* Bonn: Cohen, 1885.

Blum, Rudolf. *Kallimachos: The Alexandrian Library and the Origins of Bibliography.* Trans. Hans H. Wellisch. Madison: U of Wisconsin P, 1991.

Bury, Richard de. *Philobiblon.* Cologne: Printer of Augustinus *de Fide,* 1473. Ed. and transl. E. G. Thomas. Oxford: Blackwell, 1959 / New York: Barnes and Noble, 1970.

Burton, M. *Famous Libraries of the World.* 1937.

Chartier, Roger. "Libraries without Walls." *Representations* 42 (Spring 1993): 38–52. Repr. *The Order of Books.* Stanford: Stanford UP, 1994.

Clark, J. W. *Libraries in the Medieval and Renaissance Periods.* Cambridge: Macmillan and Bowes, 1894. Repr. Chicago: Argonaut, 1968.

—. *The Care of Books.* Cambridge: Cambridge UP, 1901. Repr. Cambridge: Cambridge UP, 1970, London: Variorum, 1975, New York: Gordon, 1976.

Esdaile, Arundel. *National Libraries of the World: Their History, Administration and Public Services.* Rev. R. J. Hill. London: Library Association, 1957. 2nd ed.

Fehrenbach, R. J., ed. *Private Libraries in Renaissance England.* Binghamton: Medieval and Renaissance Texts, 1992– .

*Irwin, R. *The English Library: Sources and History.* London: Allen and Unwin, 1966.

James, M. R. *The Wanderings and Homes of Manuscripts.* London: SPCK, 1919.

Jayne, Sears. *Library Catalogues of the English Renaissance.* Berkeley: U of California P, 1956.

Kenyon, F. G. *Books and Readers in Ancient Greece and Rome.* Oxford: Clarendon, 1951.

Ker, N. R. *Medieval Libraries of Great Britain: A List of Surviving Books.* London: Royal Historical Society, 1964.

Knowles, Dom David. *The Religious Orders of England.* Cambridge: Cambridge UP, 1948–59. 3 vols.

Kristeller, Paul Oskar. *Latin Manuscript Books before 1600: A List of the Printed Catalogues and Unpublished Inventories of Extant Collections.* New York: Fordham UP, 1965. 3rd ed.

—. "In Search of Renaissance Manuscripts." *The Library* Sixth Series 10 (1988): 291–303.

Parsons, Eduard Alexander. *The Alexandrian Library, Glory of the Hellenic World. Its Rise, Antiquities, and Destruction.* Amsterdam: Elsevier, 1952.

*Pfeiffer, Rudolph. *History of Classical Scholarship from the Beginnings to the End of the Hellenistic Age.* Oxford: Oxford UP, 1968.

*—. *History of Classical Scholarship from 1300 to 1850.* Oxford: Oxford UP, 1976.

Putnam, G. H. *Books and Their Makers During the Middle Ages.* New York: Hillary H, 1962 (Repr. of 1896–97 ed.). 2 vols.

Rashdall, H. *Universities of Europe in the Middle Ages.* Ed. F. M. Powicke and A. B. Emden. Oxford: Clarendon, 1936. 3 vols.

*Sandys, J. E. W. *A History of Classical Scholarship.* Cambridge: Cambridge UP, 1906–8. Repr. New York: Hafner, 1964. 2nd ed. 3 vols.

*Thompson, James W. *The Medieval Library.* Chicago: U of Chicago P, 1939. Repr. with supplement by B. B. Boyer, New York: 1957.

—. *Ancient Libraries.* Hamden: 1962. Repr. of 1940 ed.

Vorstius, J. *Grundzüge der Bibliotheksgeschichte.* 1954. 5th ed.

Weiss, Roberto. *Humanism in England in the Fifteenth Century.* 1957. 2nd ed.

—. *The Spread of Italian Humanism.* London: Hutchinson, 1964.

—. *The Renaissance Discovery of Classical Antiquity.* Oxford: Blackwell, 1969.

*Wormald, R. and C. E. Wright, eds. *The English Library before 1700: Studies in its History.* London: Athlone, 1958.

History and Practice of Systematic Bibliography

Bale, John. *Illustrium majoris brittanniæ scriptorum summarium.* [Wesel: D. van den Staten], 1548.

Bell, David N., ed. *The Libraries of the Cistercians, Gilbertines and Premonstratensians.* London: British Library / British Academy, 1993.

Blum, Rudolf. *Kallimachos: The Alexandrian Library and the Origins of Bibliography.* Trans. Hans H. Wellisch. Madison: U of Wisconsin P, 1991.

*Bowers, Fredson. "Bibliography." *Encyclopaedia Britannica.* Chicago: Benton, 1968. vol. 3. 588–92.

Brunet, J. C. *Manuel du librairie et de l'amateur des livres.* Paris: Brunet, 1814.

Burger, Konrad. *Ludwig Hain repertorium bibliographicum: Register.* Leipzig: Harrassowitz, 1891.

—. *Monumenta Germaniæ et Italiæ typographica.* Berlin, 1892–1913.

*Collison, Robert L. *Bibliographies, Subject and National: A Guide to Their Contents, Arrangements and Use.* New York: Haffner / London: Lockwood, 1968. 3rd ed.

Corpus christianorum. Turnolti: Typograph / Brepols, 1951– .

Corpus scriptorum ecclesiasticorum latinorum. New York: Johnson Reprint, 1962– . Repr. of 1866– .

Darlow, T. H. and H. F. Moule. *Historical Catalogue of the Printed Editions of Holy Scripture.* London: Bible House, 1903–11. 4 vols.

Dibdin, T. F. *Typographical Antiquities. Begun by Joseph Ames, augmented by William Herbert.* London: W. Miller, 1810–19. 4 vols.

Duff, E. Gordon. *Early English Printing . . . Facsimiles of All Types Used in England During the XV Century.* London: Kegan Paul, 1896. Repr. New York: B. Franklin, 1970.

422   Selected Bibliography

Edwards, A. S. G. "Some Problems in Modern Enumerative Bibliography." *Text* 1 (1984): 327–336.

Fabricius, Johann. *Bibliotheca latina.* Venice: S. Coleti, 1697.

—. *Bibliotheca græca.* Hamburg: C. Leibezeit, 1705–26.

—. *Bibliotheca antiquaria.* Hamburg: C. Leibezeit, 1713.

—. *Bibliotheca latinæ mediæ et infimæ ætatis.* Hamburg: 1734–36.

Gesamtkatalog der Wiegendrucke. Stuttgart: Hiersemann, 1968. New York: Kraus, 1972– . 2nd ed.

Gesner, Konrad von. *Bibliotheca universalis.* Froschauer, 1545–55; Osnabrück: Zeller, 1966 (facs. repr.).

Guppy, Henry. *Rules for the Cataloguing of Incunabula.* London: Library Association, 1932. Repr. 1947.

Haebler, Konrad. *Typenrepertorium der Wiegendrucke.* Leipzig: Haupt, 1905–24. 6 vols.

—. *Tipografía ibérica.* La Haye-Leipzig, 1901.

Hain, Ludwig. *Repertorium bibliographicum, in quo libri omnes ab arte typographica inventa usque ad annum MD.* Stuttgart: Cotta / Paris: Lutetiae, 1826–38. *Supplement* by W. A. Copinger. Berlin: Altmann, 1926. *Index* by Konrad Burger.

Hellinga, Lotte. *Incunabula Short-Title Catalogue.* London: British Library. In progress.

Holtrop, J. W. *Monuments typographiques des Pays-Bas au quinzième siècle.* Paris, 1857–68. 24 pts.

—. *Catalogus . . . bibliotheca regia Hagana.* Hagae Comitum, 1856.

Maunsell, Andrew. *Catalogue of English Printed Books.* London: Maunsell, 1595.

Migne, J. P. *Patrologiæ cursus completus. Series latinæ.* Paris: Migne, 1844–64. 221 vols. *Indexes.* 1862–64. 4 vols. Repr. *Index alphabeticus.* Farnborough: Gregg, 1965. Electronic edition: Chadwyck-Healey, 1991.

—. *Patrologiæ cursus completus. Series græca.* Paris: Petit-Montrouge / Migne, 1857–66. 166 vols. *Indexes.* 1912–39. 3 vols. Electronic Edition: Chadwyck-Healey, 1991.

Monumenta Germaniæ historica (MGH): Scriptores rerum germanicorum in usum scholarum ex monumentis Germaniæ historicis recusi. Hanover: Reichsinstitut für ältere deutsche Geschichtskunde, 1840– .

Naudé, Gabriel. *Avis pour dresser une bibliothèque.* Paris: Tarya, 1627.

Panzer, Georg Wolfgang Franz. *Annales typographici ab artis inventæ origine ad annum MD.* Nuremberg: Zeh, 1793–97.

Pits, John. *Relationum historicarum de rebus anglicis.* Paris: Rolinum Thierry and Sebastianum, 1619. Repr. Farnborough: Gregg, 1969.

*Pollard, Alfred W. and G. R. Redgrave, comps. *A Short-Title Catalogue of Books Printed in England, Scotland, and Ireland, and of English Books Printed Abroad, 1475–1640.* Rev. Katharine F. Pantzer, W. A. Jackson, and F. S. Ferguson, London: Bibliographical Society, 1976–89. 2nd ed. 3 vols. *Index:* 1991.

Proctor, Robert. *An Index to the Early Printed Books in the British Museum: From the Invention of Printing to the Year 1500. With Notes of Those in the Bodleian Library.* London: Holland, 1960. Repr. of 1898–1906 ed.

Reichling, Dietrich. *Appendices ad Hainii-Copingeri repertorium bibliographicum: Additiones et emendationes.* Munich: Rosenthal, 1905–11.

Rerum britannicorum medii ævi scriptores or Chronicles and Memorials of Great Britain and Ireland during the Middle Ages (Rolls Series). London: 1858–91.

Rerum gallicarum et francicarum scriptores (Recueil des historiens des Gaules et de la France). Paris: 1738–1904. Repr. Farnborough: Gregg, 1967–68. 24 vols.

Scholars and Research Libraries in the 21st Century. New York: American Council of Learned Societies, 1990.

Smith, Eldred. *The Librarian, the Scholar, and the Future of the Research Library.* New York: Greenwood, 1990.

Tanner, Thomas. *Bibliotheca britannico-hibernica*. London: Bowyer, 1748.
Tanselle, G. Thomas. *Libraries, Museums, and Reading*. Sixth Sol M. Malkin Lecture
in Bibliography. New York: Book Arts Press, Columbia U, 1991.
Thierry-Poux, J. *Premiers monuments de l'imprimerie en France au xvme siècle*. Paris, 1890.
Van Hoesen, Henry Bartlett. *Bibliography: Practical, Enumerative, Historical*. New
York: B. Franklin, 1971. Repr. of 1928 ed.
Who's Who: An Annual Biographical Dictionary. London: Black, 1849– .
World Guide to Libraries / Internationale Bibliotheks-Handbuch. Handbook of International Documentation and Information / Handbuch der Internationalen Dokumentation und Information. Munich: Saur, 1966– .

Resources for Scholarly Research: General Guides

Altick, Richard D. and Andrew Wright. *Selective Bibliography for the Study of English and American Literature*. New York: Macmillan, 1979. 6th ed.
*—. *The Art of Literary Research*. Rev. John J. Fenstermaker. New York: Norton,
1993. 4th ed.
—. *The Scholar Adventurers*. Columbus: Ohio State UP, 1987.
American Archivist. Cedar Rapids: Society of American Archivists, 1943– .
American Book Collector. 1950– .
American Reference Books Annual (1970–). Littleton: Libraries Unlimited, 1970– .
L'année philologique. Paris: 1928– .
Antiquarian Book Monthly Review. 1974– .
Archives. Journal of the British Records Association. London: The Association,
1949– .
Archivum: Revue internationale des archives. Paris: Presses universitaires, 1951– .
Barzun, Jacques and Henry F. Graff. *The Modern Researcher*. San Diego: Harcourt,
1985. 4th ed.
Bateson, F. W. *The Scholar-Critic: An Introduction to Literary Research*. London:
Routledge, 1972.
—. and Harrison T. Meserole, *A Guide to English and American Literature*. London:
Longman, 1976. 3rd ed.
*Beasley, David. *How To Use a Research Library*. New York: Oxford UP, 1988.
Bell, Marion V. and Mary Neill Barton. *Reference Books: A Brief Guide for Students*. Baltimore: Pratt, 1970. 7th ed.
Besterman, Theodore. *A World Bibliography of Bibliographies, and of Bibliographical Catalogues, Calendars, Abstracts, Digests, Indexes, and the Like*. Lausanne:
Societas Bibliographica, 1965–66. 5 vols. 4th ed.
—. *Literature English and American: A Bibliography of Bibliographies*. Totowa:
Rowman, 1971.
Bibliographic Index: A Cumulative Bibliography of Bibliographies. New York: Wilson, 1937– .
Bibliographische Berichte / Bibliographical Bulletin. Frankfurt: Klostermann,
1959– .
Bibliographie der Buch- und Bibliotheksgeschichte (1980–). Bad Iburg: Meyer,
1982– .
Bibliography of British Newspapers. Gen. Ed. Charles A. Toase. London: British Library, 1975– .
*Blanck, Jacob, comp. *Bibliography of American Literature*. Completed by Michael
Winship and Virginia L. Smyers. New Haven: Yale UP / London: Oxford UP,
1955–91.
Bodleian Library Record. Oxford: 1938– .
Bond, Donald F. *A Reference Guide to English Studies*. Chicago: U of Chicago P,
1971. 2nd ed.

Book Collector. 1952– .

Brooks, Philip C. *Research in Archives: The Use of Unpublished Primary Sources.* Chicago: U of Chicago P, 1969.

Bruccoli, Matthew, ed. *First Printings of American Authors: Contributions toward Descriptive Checklists.* Detroit: Gale, 1977–87. 5 vols.

Bulletin of Bibliography. Westwood, MA: Faxon, 1897–1981; Westport, CT: Meckler, 1982– .

Bulletin of the John Rylands Library. Manchester: 1903– .

Bulletin of the New York Public Library (later *Bulletin of Research in the Humanities*): 1897–1987.

Cheney, Frances and Wiley Williams. *Fundamental Reference Sources.* Chicago: American Library Association, 1971.

Choice: Current Reviews for College Libraries. 1964– .

College and Research Libraries. Fulton: Association of College and Research Libraries, 1939– .

Comprehensive Dissertation Index, 1861–1972. Ann Arbor: Xerox, 1973.

Dissertation Abstracts International. Ann Arbor: University Microfilms International, 1938– .

*Gibaldi, Joseph, ed. *Introduction to Scholarship in Modern Languages and Literatures.* New York: MLA, 1981. 2nd ed. 1991.

Gohdes, Clarence and Sanford E. Marovitz. *Bibliographical Guide to the Study of the Literature of the U.S.A.* Durham: Duke UP, 1984.

*Harner, James L. *Literary Research Guide: A Guide to Reference Sources for the Study of Literatures in English and Related Topics.* New York: MLA, 1989. Rev. ed. 1993.

Harrod, Leonard Montague. *The Librarians' Glossary . . . and Reference Book.* London: Deutsch, 1971. 3rd ed.

Harvard Library Bulletin. Cambridge: 1947– .

Havlice, Patricia V. *Index to American Author Bibliographies.* Metuchen: Scarecrow, 1971.

Hede, Agnes Ann. *Reference Readiness: A Manual for Librarians and Students.* Hamden: Shoe String, 1984. 3rd ed.

Hibberd, Lloyd. "Physical and Reference Bibliography." *The Library* Fifth Series 20 (1965): 124–34.

*Howard-Hill, T. H. *Index to British Literary Bibliography.* Oxford: Clarendon, 1969– .

Huntington Library and Art Gallery. *Guide to Literary Manuscripts.* San Marino: Huntington, 1979.

Huntington Library Quarterly. San Marino: 1937– .

Journal of the Society of Archivists. London: The Society, 1947–

Kehler, Dorothea. *Problems in Literary Research: A Guide to Selected Reference Works.* Metuchen: Scarecrow, 1981. 2nd ed.

Kennedy, Arthur G. and Donald F. Bond. *A Concise Bibliography for Students of English.* Stanford: Stanford UP, 1972. Rev. William E. Colborn. 5th ed.

Literary Research: A Journal of Scholarly Method and Technique. Ed. Michael Marcuse. College Park: 1976– .

Malclès, Louise-Noëlle. *Les sources du travail bibliographique.* Geneva: Droz, 1950–58. 3 vols.

*Marcuse, Michael J. *A Reference Guide for English Studies.* Berkeley: U of California P, 1990.

*Mann, Thomas. *A Guide to Library Research Methods.* New York: Oxford UP, 1986.

McKitterick, David. "Book Catalogues: Their Varieties and Uses." *The Book Encompassed.* Ed. Peter Davison. Cambridge: Cambridge UP, 1992: 161–175.

Milkau, Fritz and Georg Leyh. *Handbuch der Bibliothekswissenschaft.* Wiesbaden:

Harrossowitz, 1965. 2nd ed. 2 vols.

*Modern Humanities Research Association. *Annual Bibliography of English Language and Literature*. London: MHRA., 1921- .

MLA Directory of Periodicals: A Guide to Journals and Series in Languages and Literatures (1978-). New York: MLA, 1979- .

MLA International Bibliography of Books and Articles on the Modern Languages and Literatures, New York: MLA, 1922- .

New Cambridge Bibliography of English Literature. Ed. George Watson and I. R. Willison. Cambridge: Cambridge UP, 1969-77. 5 vols. Rev. ed. in preparation.

Nilon, Charles H. *Bibliography of Bibliographies in American Literature*. New York: Bowker, 1970.

Oxford History of English Literature. Ed. F. P. Wilson et al. Oxford: Clarendon, 1945- .

Patterson, Margaret. *Literary Research Guide*. New York: MLA, 1984. 2nd ed.

Reader's Adviser: A Layman's Guide to Literature. Series eds. Barbara A. Chernow and George A. Vallasi. New York: Bowker, 1986-88. 13th ed.

Schweik, Robert C. and Dieter Riesner. *Reference Sources in English and American Literature*. New York: Norton, 1977.

*Sheehy, Eugene P., ed. *Guide to Reference Books*. Chicago: American Library Association, 1986. 10th ed.

Spiller, Robert C., et al. eds. *Literary History of the United States: History*. New York: Macmillan / London: Collier, 1974. *Bibliography*. Ed. Thomas H. Johnson and Richard M. Ludwig.

Thorpe, James, ed. *The Aims and Methods of Scholarship in Modern Languages and Literatures*. New York: MLA, 1970. 2nd ed.

—. *The Use of Manuscripts in Literary Research: Problems of Access and Literary Property Rights*. New York: MLA, 1979.

*Walford, A. J. and L. J. Taylor, eds. *Walford's Guide to Reference Material*. London: Library Association, 1980-87. 4th ed.

Watson, George. *The Literary Thesis: A Guide to Research*. London: Longman, 1970.

—. *The Study of Literature*. London: Penguin, 1969.

Wortman, William A. *A Guide to Serial Bibliographies for Modern Literatures*. New York: MLA, 1982.

Year's Work in Archives London: British Records Association, 1934- .

Year's Work in English Studies. London: Murray / Atlantic Highlands: Humanities for the English Association, 1921- .

Zeitschrift für Bibliothekswesen und Bibliographie. Frankfurt-am-Main: 1954- .

Zentralblätt für Bibliothekswesen. Leipzig: 1884-1944; 1947- .

Library Catalogues and Library Access

Aberdeen University Library. *Catalogue of the Mediaeval Manuscripts*. Ed. M. R. James. Aberdeen, 1932.

American Antiquarian Society. *Catalogue of the Manuscript Collections*. Boston: Hall, 1979. 4 vols.

—. *Dictionary Catalog of American Books Pertaining to the Seventeenth through Nineteenth Centuries*. Westport: Greenwood, 1971. 20 vols.

American Library Directory. New York: Bowker, 1923- .

Arts and Humanities Citation Index, (1976-). Philadelphia: Institute for Scientific Information, 1978- .

Beinecke Library [Yale]. *Guide to the Collections*. New Haven: Yale U Library, 1974.

—. *Catalogue of Medieval and Renaissance Manuscripts in the Beinecke Rare Book and Manuscript Library*. Ed. Barbara Shailor. Binghamton: Medieval & Renais-

sance Texts & Studies, 1984– .
Bibliographic Index: A Cumulative Bibliography of Bibliographies. New York: Wilson, 1937– .
Bibliothèque Nationale. *Les catalogs du département des imprimés.* Ed. Lydia Mériogot. Paris: Bibliothèque Nationale, 1970.
—. *Les catalogs du département des manuscrits: Manuscrits occidentales.* Paris: Bibliothèque Nationale, 1974.
—. *Catalogue général des livres imprimés: Auteurs [1897–1959].* Paris: Bibliothèque Nationale, 1897–1981. 231 vols.
—. *Catalogue général des livres imprimés: Auteurs-collectivités-auteurs-anonymes.* Paris: Bibliothèque Nationale, 1965– .
—. *Nouveau catalog général 1960–1969.* Paris: Bibliothèque Nationale, 1972–75.
BLAISE-LINE. British Library, Bibliographic Services Division, 2 Sheraton St., London W1V 4BH.
*Bodleian Library. Madan, Falconer, H. E. Craster, Noel Denholm-Young et al. *Summary Catalogue of Western Manuscripts in the Bodleian Library.* Oxford: Clarendon, 1895–1953. 7 vols.
—. *Summary Catalogue of Post-Medieval Western Manuscripts in the Bodleian Library: Acquisitions 1916–1975.* Ed. Mary Clapinson and T. D. Rogers. Oxford: Oxford UP, 1992.
Book Review Index. Detroit: Gale, 1965–69, 1972– .
Books in Print. New York: Bowker, 1948– .
Boston Athenæum. *Catalogue of the Library 1807–1871.* Boston: Athenæum, 1874–82. 5 vols.
Boston Public Library. *American Literary Manuscripts.* Boston: Boston Public Library, 1973.
—. *English Literary Manuscripts: A Check List.* Boston: Boston Public Library, 1966.
Boyle, Leonard E. *A Survey of the Vatican Archives and of its Medieval Holdings.* Toronto: Pontifical Institute of Medieval Studies, 1972.
British Books in Print. London: Whitaker, 1874– .
British Library General Catalogue of Printed Books to 1975. London: Bingley / New York: Saur, 1979–87. 360 vols. *Supplement 1976 to 1982.* 1983. 50 vols; *1982 to 1985.* 1986. 26 vols. London: British Library, 1986.
British Library General Subject Catalogue 1881–. London: British Library, 1902– .
British Library Guide to the Catalogues and Indexes of the Department of Manuscripts. London: British Library, 1978.
—. *Short-Title Catalogue of Books Printed in France . . . 1470 to 1600.* London: British Library, 1924.
—. *Short-Title Catalogue of French Books 1601–1700.* London: British Library, 1973.
—. *Short-Title Catalogue of Books Printed in the German-Speaking Countries . . . 1455 to 1600.* London: British Library, 1962.
—. *Short-Title Catalogue of Books Printed in Italy . . . 1465 to 1600.* London: British Library, 1958.
—. *Short-Title Catalogue of Books Printed in the Netherlands and Belgium . . . 1470 to 1600.* London: British Library, 1965.
—. *Short-Title Catalogue of Spanish, Spanish-American and Portuguese Books Printed before 1601.* London: British Library, 1966.
British Museum Guide to the Processes and Schools of Engraving. London: British Museum, 1933. 3rd ed.
John Carter Brown Library. *Bibliotheca Americana: A Catalogue of the John Carter Brown Library.* Providence: Brown UP, 1919–31. 5 vols.
—. *Short-Title List of Additions: Books Printed 1471–1700.* Providence: Brown UP, 1973.

BRS / SEARCH. BRS Information Technologies. 1200 Rte. 7, Latham, NY 12110. 800-345-4277.

Cambridge University Library. *Catalogue of the Western Manuscripts.* Cambridge: Cambridge UP, 1856-57. 5 vols.

—. *Early English Printed Books in the University Library.* Cambridge: Cambridge UP, 1900-07. 4 vols.

Catalog of Books Represented by Library of Congress Printed Cards Issued to July 31, 1942. Ann Arbor: Edwards, 1942-46.

Catalogue of Books Printed in the XVth Century Now in the British Museum. London: British Library, 1908.

*Collison, Robert. *Published Library Catalogues: An Introduction to Their Contents and Use.* London: Mansell, 1973.

Columbia University Library. *Manuscript Collections . . . : A Descriptive List.* New York: Columbia, 1959.

*Crum, Margaret, ed. *First-Line Index Of English Poetry, 1500-1800, in Manuscripts of the Bodleian Library, Oxford.* Oxford: Clarendon / New York: MLA, 1969.

Darnay, Brigitte T. *Directory of Special Libraries and Information Centers.* Detroit: Gale, 1987. 10th ed. 3 vols.

Delisle, L. *Le cabinet des manuscrits de la Bibliothèque Nationale.* Paris: 1868-81. 4 vols.

DIALOG. Dialogue Information Services, Inc. 3460 Hillview Ave., Palo Alto, CA 94304. 415-858-3810.

Dictionary Catalogue of the History of Printing from the John M. Wing Foundation in the Newberry Library. Boston: Hall, 1961, 1970.

Dublin. Trinity College. *Catalogue of the Manuscripts.* Ed. T. K. Abbott. Dublin, 1900.

Ellis, Henry J. and Francis B. Bickley, eds. *Index to the Charters and Rolls in the Department of Manuscripts, British Museum.* London: British Library, 1900-12. 2 vols.

Folger Shakespeare Library. *Catalog of Manuscripts.* Boston: Hall, 1971. 3 vols.

—. *Catalog of Printed Books.* Boston: Hall, 1970. *Supplements* 1976, 1981.

—. *Catalog of the Shakespeare Collection.* Boston: Hall, 1972.

Galbraith, V. H. *An Introduction to the Use of Public Records.* Oxford: Clarendon, 1963. 2nd ed.

Goff, Frederick R., comp. and ed. *Incunabula in American Libraries: A Third Census of Fifteenth-Century Books Recorded in North American Collections.* New York: Bibliographical Society of America, 1964.

Guide to the Contents of the Public Record Office. London: HMSO, 1963-68.

Guide to Microforms in Print. Westport: Meckler, 1978- .

Gwinn, Nancy E., ed. *Preservation Microfilming: A Guide for Librarians and Archivists.* Chicago: American Library Association, 1987.

Hardwick, Charles and H. R. Luard. *Catalogue of the [Western] Manuscripts Preserved in the Library of the University of Cambridge.* Cambridge: Cambridge UP, 1856-67. 5 vols.

Harvard. *A Catalogue of Fifteenth-Century Printed Books in the Harvard University Library.* Binghamton: Medieval Texts & Studies, 1991- .

Hill Monastic Manuscript Library (Collegeville, Minn.). *Descriptive Inventories of Manuscripts Microfilmed for the Hill Monastic Library: Austrian Libraries, I (Geras—Schwaz).* Ed. D. Yates. Collegeville, Minn.: 1981.

Houghton Library [Harvard]. *Catalogue of Manuscripts.* Cambridge [England]: Chadwyck-Healey, 1986. 8 vols.

Humanities Index. New York: Wilson, 1975- .

Huntington Library and Art Gallery. *Guide to Literary Manuscripts.* San Marino: Huntington, 1979.

—. *Guide to American Historical Manuscripts*. San Marino: Huntington, 1979.

—. *Guide to Medieval and Renaissance Manuscripts*. Ed. Consuelo Wager Dutschke and Richard H. Rouse. San Marino: Huntington, 1989. 2 vols.

—. *Guide to British Historical Manuscripts*. San Marino: Huntington, 1982.

Index of Christian Art. Princeton University.

INFOTRAC. Foster City: Information Access, 1985– . CD-ROM.

Lambeth Palace Library. *Catalogue of Manuscripts 1–1906*. Cambridge: Cambridge UP, 1930–32.

Lambeth Palace Library. *Catalogue of Manuscripts 1907–2340*. London: Oxford UP, 1976.

Library of Congress and National Union Catalog Author Lists, 1942–1962: A Master Cumulation. Detroit, Gale, 1969–71.

Library of Congress Author Catalog: A Cumulative List of Works Represented by Library of Congress Printed Cards, 1948–52. Ann Arbor: Edwards, 1953.

Library of Congress. Main Catalog of the Library of Congress: Titles Cataloged through December 1980. Munich: Saur, 1984– .

Library of Congress Catalogs. Subject Catalog. Washington: Library of Congress, 1950– .

Library of Congress. *Manuscripts on Microfilm: A Checklist of the Holdings in the Manuscript Division*. Washington: Library of Congress, 1975.

List of Catalogues of English Book Sales, 1676–1900, Now in the British Museum. London: British Museum, 1915.

London Library. *Subject Index of the London Library . . . with Appendix and Synopsis of Headings*. London: Williams and Norgate, 1909–55. 4 vols.

—. *Catalogue of the London Library*. London: 1913–14. 2 vols. *Supplements* 1920, 1928. 1953.

London. University College Library. *Manuscript Collection in the Library*. London: 1978.

London. University of London. *Catalogue of Manuscripts and Autograph Letters*. Ed. R. A. Raye. London: U of London P, 1921.

Maryland Historical Society. *Manuscript Collections*. Baltimore: The Society, 1968.

Massachusetts Historical Society. *Catalog of Manuscripts*. Boston: Hall, 1969. 7 vols. *Supplement*. 1980. 2 vols.

Morgan, Paul. *Oxford Libraries outside the Bodleian: A Guide*. Oxford: Bodleian, 1980. 2nd ed.

Pierpont Morgan Library. *Major Acquisitions 1924–1974*. New York: Morgan Library, 1974.

Munby, A. N. L. *Cambridge College Libraries: Aids for Research Students*. Cambridge: Heffer, 1962. 2nd ed.

National Library of Scotland. *Catalogue of Manuscripts Acquired since 1925*. Edinburgh: 1938–80. 4 vols.

—. *Summary Catalogue of the Advocates Manuscripts*. Edinburgh: 1970.

—. *Accessions of Manuscripts 1959–1964*. Edinburgh: 1964.

—. *Accessions of Manuscripts 1965–1970*. Edinburgh: 1971.

—. *British Literary Manuscripts . . . Microform Series*. Brighton: Harvester, 1986–1987. 4 parts.

National Library of Wales. *Handlist of Manuscripts . . . 1940–42 [annual]*.

National Union Catalog, Pre-1956 Imprints. London: Mansell, 1968–81. 685 vols, plus supplements. Microfiche ed. Chicago: American Library Association, 1983.

National Union Catalog . . . 1953–57. Ann Arbor: Edwards, 1958.

National Union Catalog: A Cumulative Author List Representing Library of Congress Printed Cards and Titles Reported by Other American Libraries. Washington: Library of Congress, 1958– .

Newberry Library [Chicago]. *Dictionary Catalogue*. Boston: 1961. 16 vols. *Supplement*. 1970. 3 vols.

—. *A Catalogue of the Pre-1500 Western Manuscripts at the Newberry Library*. Ed. Paul Saenger. Chicago: U of Chicago P, 1989.
New York Public Library. *Dictionary Catalog of the Manuscript Division*. Boston: Hall, 1967. 2 vols.
—. *Dictionary Catalog of American History*. Boston: Hall, 1961. 28 vols.
*—. *Dictionary Catalog of the Berg Collection*. Boston; Hall, 1969-75. 5 vols. plus *Supplements*.
—. *Catalog of the Theatre and Drama Collection*. Boston: Hall, 1967-76. 51 vols.
—. *Schomburg Collection of Negro Literature and History*. Boston: Hall, 1962. 9 vols. *Supplements* 1967, 1972.
—. *Dictionary Catalog of Local History and Genealogy*. Boston: Hall, 1974. 18 vols.
—. *Catalog of the Dance Collection*. Boston: Hall, 1974. 10 vols.
—. *Dictionary Catalog of the Rare Book Division*. Boston: Hall, 1971. 21 vols.
*—. *Dictionary Catalog of the Research Libraries 1911-71*. Boston: Hall, 1983. 800 vols.
*—. *Dictionary Catalog of the Research Libraries 1971-81*.
NUC: Books. Washington: Library of Congress, 1983- .
Peabody Institute [Baltimore]. *Catalogue of the Library*. Baltimore, 1883-1905. 13 vols.
Peddie, R. A. *Subject Index of Books Published up to and Including 1880*. London: Grafton, 1933-48. 4 vols.
Princeton University Library. *Manuscript Collections . . . : An Introductory Survey*. Princeton: Princeton UP, 1958.
Reader's Guide to Periodical Literature: An Author and Subject Index. New York: Wilson, 1901- .
Research Libraries Information Network (RLIN). Research Libraries Group, Jordan Quadrangle, Stanford, CA 94305.
Ricci, Seymour de. *Census of Medieval and Renaissance Manuscripts in the United States and Canada*. New York: Wilson, 1935-40.
Roberts, Julian and Andrew G. Watson. *John Dee's Library Catalogue*. Oxford: Oxford UP / Bibliographical Society, 1990.
John Rylands Library [Manchester]. *Handlist of English Manuscripts*. Ed. Moses Tyson. Manchester: Manchester UP, 1929. *Supplements* 1935, 1951.
—. *Handlist of Additions to the Collection of English Manuscripts . . . 1952-1970*. Manchester: Library, 1977.
—. *Catalogue of the Printed Books and Manuscripts*. Manchester: 1899. 3 vols.
Skeat, T. C. *British Museum: The Catalogues of the Manuscript Collections*. London: British Museum, 1962.
Taylor, Archer. *Book Catalogues: Their Varieties and Uses*. Rev. Wm. P. Barlow, Jr. New York: Beil, 1987. 2nd ed.
Thomas, Daniel H. and Lynn M. Case, eds. *Guide to the Diplomatic Archives of Western Europe*. Philadelphia: U of Pennsylvania P, 1959.
Victoria and Albert Museum. *Forster and Dyce Manuscript Collections [Microform]*. Brighton: Harvester, 1987. 4 parts.
WILSONLINE. H. W. Wilson and Co., 950 University Ave., Bronx, NY 10452. 800-367-6770.

National Bibliography

Accessing Early English Books, 1641-1700: A Cumulative Index to Units 1-32 of the Microfilm Collection. Ann Arbor: University Microfilms International, 1981-82.
Adams, H. M. *Catalogue of Books Printed on the Continent of Europe, 1501-1600*. Cambridge: 1967. 2 vols.
Allison, A. F. and V. F. Goldsmith. *Titles of English Books (and of Foreign Books*

Printed in England): An Alphabetical Finding-List by Title of Books Published under the Author's Name, Pseudonym, or Initials. Hamden: Archon-Shoe String, 1977.

*Arber, Edward. *Transcript of the Registers of the Company of Stationers of London, 1554-1640 A.D.* London and Birmingham: Privately printed, 1875-94.

—. *The Term Catalogues, 1668-1709 A.D.; with a Number for Easter Term, 1711 A.D.* London: Privately printed, 1903-06.

Ash, Lee and William G. Millet, comps. *Subject Collections: A Guide to Special Book Collections and Subject Emphases as Reported by University, College, Public, and Special Libraries and Musuems in the United States and Canada.* New York: Bowker, 1985. 6th ed.

Aslib Directory of Information Sources in the United Kingdom. London: Aslib, 1982-84. 5th ed.

*Beaudiquez, Marcelle, ed. *Inventaire général des bibliographies nationales rétrospectives / Retrospective National Bibliographies: An International Bibliography.* Munich: Saur, 1986.

*Bell, Barbara L. *An Annotated Guide to Current National Bibliographies.* Alexandria: Chadwyck-Healey, 1986.

Billington, Ray Allen. *Guides to American History Manuscript Collections in Libraries of the United States.* New York: P. Smith, 1952.

Books in Print. New York: Bowker, 1948- .

Born, Lester K. *British Manuscripts Project: A Checklist of the Microfilms Prepared in England and Wales for the American Council of Learned Societies 1941-1945.* Washington: Library of Congess, 1955.

Bowers, Fredson. *A Bibliography of the English Printed Drama, 1660-1770.* In progress.

British Books in Print. London: Whitaker, 1874- .

British National Bibliography. London: British Library, Bibliographic Services Division, 1950- .

British Union-Catalogue of Periodicals: A Record of the Periodicals of the World, from the Seventeenth Century to the Present Day, in British Libraries. Ed. James D. Stewart. New York: Academic / London: Butterworths, 1955-58. *Supplement to 1960*: 1962.

Bruccoli, Matthew, ed. *First Printings of American Authors: Contributions toward Descriptive Checklists.* Detroit: Gale, 1977-87. 5 vols.

Christianson, C. Paul. *A Directory of London Stationers and Book Artisans 1300-1500.* New York: Bibliographical Society of America, 1991.

Courtney, William P. *Register of [British] National Bibliography, with a Selection of the Chief Bibliographical Books and Articles Printed in Other Countries.* London: Constable, 1905-12. 3 vols.

Croft, P. J., Theodore Hofmann, Peter Beal, and John Horden. *Index of English Literary Manuscripts.* London: Mansell / New York: Bowker, 1980- . 5 vols.

Cumulative Book Index: A World List of Books in the English Language. New York: Wilson, 1898- .

Directory of Archives and Manuscript Repositories in the United States. Phoenix, Oryx, 1988. 2nd ed.

Directory of Rare Book and Special Collections in the United Kingdom and the Republic of Ireland. Ed. Moelwyn I. Williams. London: Library Association, 1985.

*Domay, Friedrich. *Bibliographie der nationalen Bibliographien / Bibliographie des bibliographies nationales / A World Bibliography of National Bibliographies.* Stuttgart: Hiersemann, 1987.

*Downs, Robert B. *American Library Resources: A Bibliography Guide.* Chicago: American Library Association, 1951. *Supplements* 1962, 1972, 1981. *Cumulative Index* 1981.

*—. *British and Irish Library Resources: A Bibliographical Guide.* London: Mansell,

1981. 2nd ed.

Eighteenth-Century Short-Title Catalogue. Ed. Robin Alston. London: British Library / Baton Rouge: Louisiana State U. In progress.

English Catalogue of Books (1801–1968). London: Publishers Circular, 1858–1969.

Evans, Charles. *American Bibliography: A Chronological Dictionary of All Books, Pamphlets, and Periodical Publications Printed in the United States of America from the Genesis of Printing in 1639 down to and Including the Year 1820 [i.e. 1800].* Chicago: Privately printed, 1903–34; Worcester: American Antiquarian Society, 1955–59.

Eyre, George Edward Briscoe, Charles Robert Rivington, and Henry Robert Plomer, eds. *A Transcript of the Registers of the Worshipful Company of Stationers from 1640–1708 A.D.* London: privately printed, 1913–14. 3 vols.

Goff, Frederick R., comp. and ed. *Incunabula in American Libraries: A Third Census of Fifteenth-Century Books Recorded in North American Collections.* New York: Bibliographical Society of America, 1964.

Greg, W. W. and E. Boswell, eds. *Records of the Court of the Stationers' Company, 1576 to 1602, from Register B.* London: Bibliographical Society, 1930.

—. *Dramatic Documents from the Elizabethan Playhouses.* Oxford: Clarendon, 1931. 2 vols.

—. *A Bibliography of the English Printed Drama to the Restoration.* London: Bibliographical Society, 1939–59. 4 vols.

—. *A Companion to Arber: Being a Calendar of Documents in Edward Arber's Transcript.* Oxford: Clarendon, 1967.

Guide to the Accessibility of Local Records of England and Wales. London: Institute for Historical Research, 1932–34. 2 vols.

Hamer, Philip. *A Guide to Archives and Manuscripts in the United States.* New Haven: Yale UP, 1961.

Lathem, Edward Connery. *Chronological Tables of American Newspapers, 1690–1820: Being a Tabular Guide to Holdings of Newspapers Published in America through the Year 1820.* Barre: American Antiquarian Society, 1972.

Lewanski, Richard C. *Subject Collections in European Libraries: A Directory and Bibliographical Guide.* New York: Bowker, 1978. 2nd ed.

Lewanski, Rudolf J. *Guide to Italian Libraries and Archives.* New York: Council for European Studies, 1979.

Linder, LeRoy Harold. *The Rise of Current Complete National Bibliography.* New York: Scarecrow, 1959.

Location Register of English Literary Manuscripts and Letters. The Library, P. O. Box 223, U of Reading, Whiteknights, Reading, England RG6 2AE.

McKay, George L., comp. *American Book Auction Catalogues, 1713–1934: A Union List.* Detroit: Gale, 1967.

Morrison, Paul G. *Index of Printers, Publishers, and Booksellers in Donald Wing's Short-Title Catalogue.* Charlottesville: U of Virginia P, 1955.

Munby, A. N. L. and Lenore Caral, comps. and eds. *British Book Sale Catalogues, 1676–1800: A Union List.* London: Mansell, 1977.

National Historical and Public Records Commission. Directory of Archives and Manuscript Repositories. Washington: NHPRC, 1978.

National Inventory of Documentary Sources in the United Kingdom. Cambridge: Chadwyck-Healey, 1958– . [microfiche]

National Inventory of Documentary Sources in the United States. Cambridge: Chadwyck-Healey, 1984– . [microfiche]

National Newspaper Index. Belmont: Information Access, 1979– .

National Register of Archives. *List of Accessions to Repositories* London: 1958– .

National Union Catalog, Pre-1956 Imprints. London: Mansell, 1968–81. 685 vols, plus supplements. Microfiche ed. Chicago: American Library Association, 1983.

National Union Catalog of Manuscript Collections. Library of Congress Catalogs.

Washington: Library of Congress, 1962– .

National Union Catalog . . . 1953–57. Ann Arbor: Edwards, 1958.

National Union Catalog: A Cumulative Author List Representing Library of Congress Printed Cards and Titles Reported by Other American Libraries. Washington: Library of Congress, 1958– .

Nelson, Carolyn W. and Matthew Seccombe, eds. *British Newspapers and Periodicals, 1641–1700.* New York: MLA, 1988.

Nineteenth Century Short Title Catalogue. Newcastle-upon-Tyne: Avero, 1984– .

North American Imprints Program. American Antiquarian Society, 185 Salisbury St. Worcester, MA 01609.

*Pollard, Alfred W. and G. R. Redgrave, comps. *A Short-Title Catalogue of Books Printed in England, Scotland, and Ireland, and of English Books Printed Abroad, 1475–1640.* Rev. Katharine F. Pantzer, W. A. Jackson, and F. S. Ferguson, London: Bibliographical Society, 1976–1989. 2nd ed. 3 vols. *Index,* 1991.

Ramage, David. *A Finding-List of English Books to 1640 in Libraries in the British Isles.* Durham: Bailes, 1958.

Records of the Worshipful Company of Stationers and Newspaper Makers. Stationers' Hall, London EC4M 7DD.

Ricci, Seymour de. *Census of Medieval and Renaissance Manuscripts in the United States and Canada.* New York: Wilson, 1935–40.

Richardson, E. C. *A Union World Catalog of Manuscript Books, III: A List of Printed Catalogs of Manuscript Books.* New York: Wilson, 1935. Repr. New York: Franklin, 1972.

Robbins, J. Albert, et al. *American Literary Manuscripts: A Checklist of Holdings in Academic, Historical, and Public Libraries, Museums, and Authors' Homes in the United States.* Athens: U of Georgia P, 1977.

Roberts, Stephen, Alan Cooper, and Leslie Gilder. *Research Libraries and Collections in the United Kingdom: A Selective Inventory and Guide.* Hamden: Linnet, 1978.

Rollins, Hyder E., comp. *An Analytical Index to the Ballad-Entries (1557–1709) in the Registers of the Company of Stationers of London.* Chapel Hill: U of North Carolina P, 1924. Repr. Hatboro, PA: Tradition, 1967.

Sabin, Joseph, Wilberforce Eames, and R. W. G. Vail, eds. *Bibliotheca Americana: A Dictionary of Books Relating to America from Its Discovery to the Present Time.* New York: Sabin. 1868–1936. *Index,* 1974.

Sheppard's Book Dealers in North America: A Directory of Antiquarian and Second-hand Book Dealers in the U.S.A. and Canada. London: Europa, 1954– .

Sheppard's Book Dealers in the British Isles: A Directory of Antiquarian and Second-hand Book Dealers in the United Kingdom, the Channel Islands, the Isle of Man, and the Republic of Ireland. London: Europa, 1954– .

Subject Guide to Books in Print. New York: Bowker, 1957– .

Sullivan, Alvin, ed. *British Literary Magazines.* Westport: Greenwood, 1983–86.

Tanselle. G. Thomas. *Guide to the Study of United States Imprints.* Cambridge: Belknap-Harvard UP, 1971.

Thompson, Lawrence S. *The New Sabin: Books Described by Joseph Sabin and His Successors, Now Described Again on the Basis of Examination of Originals, and Fully Indexed by Title, Subject, Joint Authors, and Institutions and Agencies.* Troy: Whitston, 1974–86.

Vann, J. Donn, ed. *Victorian Novels in Serial.* New York: MLA, 1985.

—. and Rosemary T. VanArsdel, eds. *Victorian Periodicals: A Guide to Research.* New York: MLA, 1978–1989. 2 vols.

Watt, Robert. *Bibliotheca Britannica; or, A General Index to British and Foreign Literature.* Edinburgh: Constable, 1824.

Wehefritz, Valentin, ed. *International Loan Services and Union Catalogues.* Frankfurt: Klostermann, 1980. 2nd ed.

Weil, Gerald E., ed. *International Directory of Manuscript Collections, Libraries, Private Collections, Repositories and Archives.* Paris: Berger-Lerault, 1978– .

Welsch, Erwin K. *Libraries and Archives in Germany.* Pittsburgh: Council for European Studies, 1975.

—. *Libraries and Archives in France: A Handbook.* New York: Council for European Studies, 1979. 2nd ed.

Williams, William Proctor, ed. *Index to the Stationers' Register, 1640–1708: Being an Index to A Transcript of the Registers of the Worshipful Company of Stationers from 1640–1708 A.D.* Edited by Eyre, Rivington, and Plomer (1913–14). La Jolla: McGilvery, 1980.

Winans, Robert B. *A Descriptive Checklist of Book Catalogues Separately Printed In America, 1693–1800.* Worcester: American Antiquarian Society, 1981.

Wing, Donald. *A Gallery of Ghosts: Books Published between 1641–1700 Not Found in the Short-Title Catalogue.* New York: Index Committee of the MLA, 1967.

—. Short-Title Catalogue of Books Printed in England, Scotland, Ireland, Wales, and British America and of English Books Printed in Other Countries, 1641–1700. New York: MLA, 1972–1988. 3 vols. 2nd ed.

Young, William C. *American Theatrical Arts: A Guide to Manuscripts and Special Collections in the United States and Canada.* Chicago: American Library Association, 1971.

Zempel, Edward N., and Linda A. Verkler, eds. *First Editions: A Guide to Identification: Statements of Selected North American, British Commonwealth, and Irish Publishers on Their Methods of Designating First Editions.* Peoria: Spoon River, 1989. 2nd ed.

Literary Research (British): Some Representative Sources (see also General Research Guides and National Bibliography.)

Arber, Edward. *Transcript of the Registers of the Company of Stationers of London, 1554–1640 A.D.* London and Birmingham: Privately printed, 1875–1894.

—. *The Term Catalogues, 1668–1709 A.D.; with a Number for Easter Term, 1711 A.D.* London: Privately printed, 1903–06.

Bailey, Richard W., ed. *Early Modern English: Additions and Antedatings to the Record of English Vocabulary 1475–1700.* Hildesheim: Olms, 1978.

—., et al. *Michigan Early Modern English Materials.* Ann Arbor: Xerox University Microfilms, 1975.

Beale, Walter H. *Old and Middle English Poetry to 1500: A Guide to Information Sources.* Detroit: Gale, 1976.

Beasley, Jerry C., comp. *A Check List of Prose Fiction Published in England, 1740–1749.* Charlottesville: UP of Virginia, 1972.

Bessinger, J. B., Jr., ed. *A Concordance to The Anglo-Saxon Poetic Records.* Ithaca: Cornell UP, 1978.

Bibliographic Index: A Cumulative Bibliography of Bibliographies. New York: Wilson, 1937– .

Biggs, Frederick M., Thomas D. Hill, and Paul E. Szarmach, eds. *Sources of Anglo-Saxon Literary Culture: A Trial Version.* Binghamton: Medieval and Renaissance Texts and Studies, 1990.

British Books in Print. London: Whitaker, 1874– .

British National Bibliography. London: British Library, Bibliographic Services Division, 1950– .

Brown, Carleton and Rossell Hope Robbins. *The Index of Middle English Verse.* New York: Columbia UP, for Index Society, 1943. With Supplement.

Brown, Christopher and William B. Thesing. *English Prose and Criticism, 1900–1950: A Guide to Information Sources.* Detroit: Gale, 1983.

Cameron, Angus. "A List of Old English Texts." *A Plan for the Dictionary of Old*

English. Ed. Roberta Frank and Angus Cameron. Toronto: U of Toronto P in association with Centre for Medieval Studies, U of Toronto, 1973.

Cameron, Kenneth Neill and Donald H. Reiman, eds. *Shelley and His Circle 1772-1822*. Cambridge: Harvard UP, 1961- .

Carpenter, Charles A., comp. *Modern British Drama*. Arlington Heights: AHM, 1979.

—. *Modern Drama Scholarship and Criticism, 1966-1980: An International Bibliography*. Toronto: U of Toronto P, 1986.

Cassis, A. F. *The Twentieth-Century English Novel: An Annotated Bibliography of General Criticism*. New York: Garland, 1977.

Croft, P. J., Theodore Hofmann, and John Horden. *Index of English Literary Manuscripts*. London: Mansell / New York: Bowker, 1980- .

DeLaura, David, ed. *Victorian Prose: A Guide to Research*. New York: MLA, 1973.

Dictionary of Old English. Ed. Angus Cameron et al. Toronto: Pontifical Institute of Mediaeval Studies for Dictionary of Old English Project, Centre for Medieval Studies, U of Toronto, 1987- .

Donohue, Joseph, and James Ellis, eds. *The London Stage, 1800-1900: A Documentary Record and Calendar of Performances*. In progress.

Early Modern English Dictionary, 1475-1700. In progress (see Bailey).

Faverty, Frederic E., ed. *The Victorian Poets: A Guide to Research*. Cambridge: Harvard UP, 1968.

Foxon, D. F. *English Verse, 1701-1750: A Catalogue of Separately Printed Poems with Notes on Contemporary Collected Editions*. Cambridge: Cambridge UP, 1975.

Fulton, Richard D. and C. M. Colee, gen. eds. *Union List of Victorian Serials: A Union List of Selected Nineteenth-Century British Serials Available in United States and Canadian Libraries*. New York: Garland, 1985.

Ganzl, Kurt. *The British Musical Theatre*. New York: Oxford UP, 1986.

Gingerich, Martin E. *Contemporary Poetry in America and England, 1950-1975*. Detroit: Gale, 1983.

Greg, W. W. *English Literary Autographs 1550-1650*. London: Oxford UP, 1925-32.

Grimes, Janet and Diva Daims. *Novels in English by Women, 1891-1920: A Preliminary Checklist*. New York: Garland, 1981.

Harbage, Alfred. *Annals of English Drama 975-1700*. Philadelphia: U of Pennsylvania P / London: Methuen, 1964. Rev. by S. Schoenbaum.

Harris, Richard H. *Modern Drama in America and England, 1950-1970: A Guide to Information Sources*. Detroit: Gale, 1982.

Houghton, Walter E., Esther Rhoads Houghton, and Jean Harris Slingerland, eds. *Wellesley Index to Victorian Periodicals, 1824-1900*. Toronto: U of Toronto P / London: Routledge, 1966- .

Howard-Hill, T. H. *Index to British Literary Bibliography*. Oxford: Clarendon, 1969- .

Index of Middle English Prose. Gen. Ed. A. S. G. Edwards. Cambridge: Boydell and Brewer, 1977- .

Jackson, J. R. de J. *Annals Of English Verse, 1770-1835: A Preliminary Survey of the Volumes Published*. New York: Garland, 1985.

Jackson, William A., ed. *Records of the Court of the Stationers' Company, 1602 to 1640*. London: Bibliographical Society, 1957.

Jordan, Frank, ed. *The English Romantic Poets: A Review of Research and Criticism*. New York: MLA, 1985. 4th ed.

Ker, N. R. *Fragments of Medieval Manuscripts used as Pastedowns in Oxford Bindings, c. 1515-1620*. Oxford: Oxford Bibliographical Society, 1954.

—. *Catalogue of Manuscripts Containing Anglo-Saxon*. Oxford: Clarendon, 1957. *Supplement* in *Anglo-Saxon England* 5 (1976): 121-31.

—. *English Manuscripts in the Century after the Norman Conquest.* Oxford: Clarendon, 1960.

—. *Medieval Libraries of Great Britain: A List of Surviving Books.* London: Royal Historical Society, 1964.

—. *Medieval Manuscripts in British Libraries.* Oxford: Clarendon, 1969.

King, Kimball. *Twenty Modern British Playwrights: A Bibliography, 1956–1976.* New York: Garland, 1977.

Leclaire, Lucien. *A General Analytical Bibliography of the Regional Novelists of the British Isles, 1800–1950.* Paris: Belles Lettres, 1969.

Location Register of English Literary Manuscripts and Letters. The Library, P. O. Box 223, U of Reading, Whiteknights, Reading, England RG6 2AE.

Location Register of Twentieth-Century English Literary Manuscripts and Letters: A Union List of Papers of Modern English, Irish, Scottish, and Welsh Authors in the British Isles. London: British Library, 1988.

London Stage, 1660–1800: A Calendar of Plays, Entertainments, and Afterpieces Together with Casts, Box-Receipts, and Contemporary Comment: Compiled from the Playbills, Newspapers, and Theatrical Diaries of the Period. Carbondale: Southern Illinois UP, 1960–79.

Mayo, Robert D. "A Catalogue of Magazine Novels and Novelettes, 1740–1815." *The English Novel in the Magazines, 1740–1815: With A Catalogue of 1375 Novels and Novelettes.* Evanston: Northwestern UP / London: Oxford UP, 1962.

McBurney, William Harlin, comp. *A Check List of English Prose Fiction, 1700–1739.* Cambridge: Harvard UP, 1960.

McIntosh, Angus et al. *A Linguistic Atlas of Late Medieval English.* Aberdeen: Aberdeen UP, 1987.

Mellown, Elgin W. *A Descriptive Catalogue of the Bibliographies of Twentieth Century British Poets, Novelists, and Dramatists.* Troy: Whitston, 1978.

Middle English Dictionary. Ed. Hans Kurath et al. Ann Arbor: U of Michigan P, 1952– .

Milhous, Judith and Robert D. Hume, comps. *A Register of English Theatrical Documents, 1660–1737.* Carbondale: Southern Illinois UP, 1990.

Nineteenth Century Readers' Guide to Periodical Literature 1890–1899: With Supplementary Indexing 1900–1922. New York: Wilson, 1944. 2 vols.

Oxford English Dictionary. Ed. J. A. Simpson and E. S. C. Weiner. Oxford: Clarendon 1989. 2nd ed.; CD-ROM edition. Oxford: Oxford UP, 1989.

Oxford English Dictionary. Ed. James A. H. Murray et al. Oxford: Clarendon, 1933.

Palmer, H. R. *List of English Editions and Translations of Greek and Latin Classics Printed Before 1641.* Oxford: Bibliographical Society, 1911.

Poetry Index Annual: A Title, Author, First Line, and Subject Index to Poetry in Anthologies. Great Neck: Poetry Index, 1982– .

Raven, James. *British Fiction, 1750–1770: A Chronological Check-List of Prose Fiction Printed in Britain and Ireland.* Newark: U of Delaware P / London: Associated U Presses, 1987.

Records of Early English Drama (REED). Gen. Ed. A. F. Johnston. Toronto: U of Toronto P, 1979– .

Reiman, Donald H. *English Romantic Poetry, 1800–1835: A Guide to Information Sources.* Detroit: Gale, 1979.

Ricci, Seymour de. *Census of Medieval and Renaissance Manuscripts in the United States and Canada.* New York: Wilson, 1935–40.

Rice, Thomas Jackson. *English Fiction, 1900–1950: A Guide to Information Sources.* Detroit: Gale, 1979–83.

Ringler, W. A., Jr. *A Bibliography and Index of English Verse Printed 1476–1558.* London / New York: Mansell, 1988.

Rouse, Richard H. *Serial Bibliographies for Medieval Studies.* Berkeley: U of California P, 1969.

Sadleir, Michael. *XIX Century Fiction: A Bibliographical Record Based on His Own Collection.* London: Constable / Berkeley: U of California P, 1951.

Severs, J. Burke and Albert E. Hartung, gen. eds. *A Manual of the Writings in Middle English, 1050–1500.* New Haven: Archon-Shoestring, for Connecticut Acad. of Arts and Sciences, 1967– .

Stanton, Robert J. *A Bibliography of Modern British Novelists.* Troy: Whitston, 1978.

Stevenson, Lionel. *Victorian Fiction: A Guide to Research.* Cambridge: Harvard UP, 1964.

Stratman, Carl J., C.S.V. *Bibliography of Medieval Drama.* New York: Ungar, 1972. 2nd ed. 2 vols.

Vann, J. Don. *Victorian Novels in Serial.* New York: MLA, 1985.

Venezky, Richard and Sharon Butler. *A Microfiche Concordance to Old English: The High Frequency Words.* Newark: U of Delaware, 1983. Microfiche.

— and Antonette dePaolo Healey, comps. *A Microfiche Concordance to Old English.* Newark: U of Delaware, 1980.

Vinson, James and D. L. Kirkpatrick. *Contemporary Dramatists.* New York: St. Martin's, 1982.

—. *Contemporary Poets.* New York: St. Martin's, 1985.

Ward, William S., comp. *Index and Finding List of Serials Published in the British Isles, 1789–1832.* Lexington: U of Kentucky P, 1953.

—. comp. *Literary Reviews in British Periodicals, 1798–1820 . . . 1821–1826: A Bibliography: With a Supplementary List of General (non-Review) Articles on Literary Subjects.* New York: Garland, 1972, 1977. 3 vols.

Wearing, J. P. *The London Stage, 1890–1899: A Calendar of Plays and Players.* Metuchen: Scarecrow, 1976. *The London Stage, 1900–1909: A Calendar of Plays and Players.* 1981. *The London Stage, 1910–1919: A Calendar of Plays and Players.* 1982. *The London Stage, 1920–1929: A Calendar of Plays and Players.* 1984.

Wiley, Paul L., comp. *The British Novel: Conrad to the Present.* Northbrook: AHM, 1973.

Wilson, Harris W. and Diane Long Hoeveler. *English Prose and Criticism in the Nineteenth Century: A Guide to Information Sources.* Detroit: Gale, 1979.

Wolff, Michael, John S. North, and Dorothy Deering. *The Waterloo Directory of Victorian Periodicals, 1824–1900: Phase I.* Waterloo: Wilfrid Laurier UP, for U of Waterloo, 1976.

Wolff, Robert Lee. *Nineteenth-Century Fiction: A Bibliographical Catalogue Based on the Collection Formed by Robert Lee Wolff.* New York: Garland, 1981–86. 5 vols.

Literary Research (American): Some Representative Sources (see also General Research Guides and National Bibliography)

Adkins, Nelson F. *Index to Early American Periodicals to 1850.* New York: Readex, 1964.

Afro-American Novel Project. Database. Maryemma Graham, director. Dept. of English, U of Mississippi, University, MS 38677.

Alden, John and Dennis C. Landis, eds. *European Americana: A Chronological Guide to Works Printed in Europe Relating to the Americas, 1493–1776.* New York: Readex, 1980– .

American Book Prices Current (1894–). Washington: Bancroft-Parkman, 1895– .

American Book Publishing Record. New York: Bowker, 1960– .

American Book Trade Directory. New York: Bowker, 1915– .

American Fiction, 1901–1925: A Contribution toward a Bibliography, a database located at the William Charvat Collection of American Fiction. Ohio State U Libraries, 1858 Neil Ave. Mall, Columbus 43210–1286.

American Literary Scholarship: An Annual. Durham: Duke UP, 1965– .

Annals of American Literature, 1602-1983. Ed. Richard M. Lug and Clifford A. Nault. New York: Oxford UP, 1986.

Archer, Stephen M. *American Actors and Actresses: A Guide to Information Sources.* Detroit: Gale, 1983.

Arksey, Laura, Nancy Pries, and Marcia Reed. *American Diaries: An Annotated Bibliography of Published American Diaries and Journals 1492-1980.* Detroit: Gale, 1983-87.

Bakish, David and Edward Margolies. *Afro-American Fiction, 1853-1976: A Guide to Information Sources.* Detroit: Gale, 1979.

Baugham, Ronald. *Contemporary Authors: Bibliographical Series; American Poets.* Detroit: Gale, 1986.

Bell, Marion V. and Jean C. Bacon. *Poole's Index Date and Volume Key.* ACRL Monographs 19. Chicago: Association of College and Reference Libraries, 1957.

Bibliography of United States Literature. New York: Facts on File. In progress, 1990-.

Blanck, Jacob, comp. *Bibliography of American Literature.* Completed by Michael Winship and Virginia L. Smyers. New Haven: Yale UP / London: Oxford UP, 1955-1991.

Books in Print. New York: Bowker, 1948- .

Books out of Print. New York: Bowker, 1983- .

Brier, Peter A. and Anthony Arthur. *American Prose and Criticism, 1900-1950: A Guide to Information Sources.* Detroit: Gale, 1981.

Brigham, Clarence S. *History and Bibliography of American Newspapers, 1690-1820.* Worcester: American Antiquarian Society, 1947.

—. "Additions and Corrections to History and Bibliography of American Newspapers, 1690-1820," *Proceedings of the American Antiquarian Society* 71 (1961): 15-62.

Brignano, Russell C. *Black Americans in Autobiography: An Annotated Bibliography of Autobiographies and Autobiographical Books Written since the Civil War.* Durham: Duke UP, 1984.

Briscoe, Mary Louise, ed. *American Autobiography, 1945-1980: A Bibliography.* Madison: U of Wisconsin P, 1982.

Brumble, H. David, III. *An Annotated Bibliography of American Indian and Eskimo Autobiographies.* Lincoln: U of Nebraska P, 1981.

—. "A Supplement to An Annotated Bibliography of American Indian and Eskimo Autobiographies." *Western American Literature* 17 (1982): 243-60.

Cannon, Carl L. *American Book Collectors and Collecting.* New York: Wilson, 1941.

Cheung, King-Kok and Stan Yogi. *Asian American Literature: An Annotated Bibliography.* New York: MLA, 1988.

Chielens, Edward E. *The Literary Journal in America, 1900-1950: A Guide to Information Sources.* Detroit: Gale, 1977.

Contemporary Authors: Bibliographical Series. Detroit: Gale, 1986- . Vol. 1: *American Novelists.* Ed. James J. Martine. 1986. Vol. 2: *American Poets.* Ed. Ronald Baughman. 1986.

Contemporary Theatre, Film, and Television: A Biographical Guide Featuring Performers, Directors, Writers, Producers, Designers, Managers, Choreographers, Technicians, Composers, Executives, Dancers, and Critics in the United States and Great Britain. Detroit: Gale, 1984- .

Cripe, Helen and Diane Campbell, comps. and eds. *American Manuscripts, 1763-1815: An Index to Documents Described in Auction Records and Dealers' Catalogues.* Wilmington: Scholarly Resources, 1977.

Davis, Lloyd and Robert Irwin. *Contemporary American Poetry: A Checklist.* Metuchen: Scarecrow, 1975. Rev. 1984.

Dearing, Vinton. *Transfer Vectors for Poole's Index to Periodical Literature: Number One: Titles, Volumes, and Dates.* Los Angeles: Pison, 1967.

Dictionary Catalog of the Schomburg Collection of Negro Literature and History. Boston: Hall, 1962.

Dictionary of American English on Historical Principles. Ed. William A. Craigie and James R. Hulbert. Chicago: U of Chicago P, 1938–44.

Dictionary of American Regional English. Ed. Frederic G. Cassidy. Cambridge: Belknap / Harvard, 1985– .

Dictionary of Americanisms on Historical Principles. Ed. Mitford M. Mathews. Chicago: U of Chicago P, 1951.

Dramatic Compositions Copyrighted in the United States, 1870 to 1916. Washington: GPO, 1918.

Eger, Ernestina N. *A Bibliography of Criticism of Contemporary Chicano Literature.* Berkeley: Chicano Library Publication, U of California, 1982.

Evans, Charles. *American Bibliography: A Chronological Dictionary of All Books, Pamphlets, and Periodical Publications Printed in the United States of America from the Genesis of Printing in 1639 down to and Including the Year 1820 [i.e. 1800].* Chicago: Privately printed, 1903–34; Worcester: American Antiquarian Society, 1955–59.

French, William P., et al. *Afro-American Poetry and Drama, 1760–1975: A Guide to Information Sources.* Detroit: Gale, 1979.

Gerstenberger, Donna and George Hendrick. *The American Novel, 1789–1959: A Checklist of Twentieth-Century Criticism.* Denver: Swallow, 1961.

—. *The American Novel: A Checklist of Twentieth Century Criticism on Novels Written since 1789.* Chicago: Swallow, 1979.

Gingerich, Martin E. *Contemporary Poetry in America and England, 1950–1975.* Detroit: Gale, 1983.

Gohdes, Clarence and Sanford E. Marovitz. *Bibliographical Guide to the Study of the Literature of the U.S.A.* Durham: Duke UP, 1984.

Harris, Richard H. *Modern Drama in America and England, 1950–1970: A Guide to Information Sources.* Detroit: Gale, 1982.

Hill, Frank Pierce, comp. *American Plays Printed, 1714–1830: A Bibliographical Record.* Stanford: Stanford UP / London: Oxford UP, 1934.

Hinding, Andrea and Ames Sheldon Bower. *Women's History Sources: A Guide to Archives and Manuscript Collections in the United States.* New York: Bowker, 1979. 2 vols.

Houghton, Walter E., Esther Roads Houghton, and Jean Harris Slingerland. *Wellesley Index to Victorian Periodicals 1824–1900.* Toronto: U of Toronto P / London: Routlege, 1966– . 5 vols.

Index of American Periodical Verse: (1971–). Metuchen: Scarecrow, 1971– .

Jantz, Harold S. "The First Century of New England Verse." *Proceedings of the American Antiquarian Society* 53 (1944): 219–508. Worcester: American Antiquarian Society, 1944.

Kallenbach, Jessamine S., comp. *Index to Black American Literary Anthologies.* Boston: Hall, 1979.

Kaplan, Louis, comp. *A Bibliography of American Autobiographies.* Madison: U of Wisconsin P, 1961.

Katz, Joseph, ed. *Calendars of American Literary Manuscripts.* Columbus: Ohio State UP, 1967– .

Kelly, James, comp. *The American Catalogue of Books (Original and Reprints) Published in the United States from Jan., 1861, to Jan., 1871, with Date of Publication, Size, Price, and Publisher's Name.* New York: Wiley, 1866–71.

Larson, Carl F. W., comp. *American Regional Theatre History to 1900: A Bibliography.* Metuchen: Scarecrow, 1979.

Leiter, Samuel L., ed. *The Encyclopedia of the New York Stage, 1920–1930.* Westport: Greenwood, 1985.

Lemay, J. A. Leo. *A Calendar of American Poetry in the Colonial Newspapers and Magazines and in the Major English Magazines through 1765.* Worcester: American Antiquarian Society, 1972.

Lepper, Gary M. *A Bibliographical Introduction to Seventy-Five Modern American Authors.* Berkeley: Serendipity, 1976.

Levernier, James A. and Douglas R. Wilmes, eds. *American Writers before 1800: A Biographical and Critical Dictionary.* Westport: Greenwood, 1983.

Littlefield, Daniel F., Jr. and James W. Parins, eds. *A Biobibliography of Native American Writers, 1772-1924.* Metuchen: Scarecrow, 1981.

—, eds. *American Indian and Alaska Native Newspapers and Periodicals, (1826-1985).* Westport: Greenwood, 1984-86.

Martine, James J. *Contemporary Authors: Bibliographical Series. American Novelists.* Detroit: Gale, 1986.

Martinez, Julio A. and Francisco A. Lomeli, eds. *Chicano Literature: A Reference Guide.* Westport: Greenwood, 1985.

McGill, Raymond D. *Notable Names in the American Theatre.* Clifton: White, 1976.

McPheron, William. *The Bibliography of Contemporary American Poetry, 1945-1985: An Annotated Checklist.* Westport: Meckler, 1986.

— and Jocelyn Sheppard. *The Bibliography of Contemporary American Fiction, 1945-1988: An Annotated Checklist.* Westport: Meckler, 1989.

Meserve, Walter J. *An Emerging Entertainment: The Drama of the American People to 1828.* Bloomington: Indiana UP, 1977.

—. *American Drama to 1900: A Guide to Information Sources.* Detroit: Gale, 1980.

—. *Heralds of Promise: The Drama of the American People during the Age of Jackson, 1829-1849.* New York: Greenwood, 1986.

Nadel, Ira Bruce. *Jewish Writers of North America: A Guide to Information Sources.* Detroit: Gale, 1981.

Nilon, Charles H. *Bibliography of Bibliographies in American Literature.* New York: Bowker, 1970.

Odell, George C. D. *Annals of the New York Stage.* New York: Columbia UP, 1927-49.

Parker, Patricia L. *Early American Fiction: A Reference Guide.* Boston: Hall, 1984.

Partridge, Elinore Hughes. *American Prose and Criticism, 1820-1900: A Guide to Information Sources.* Detroit: Gale, 1983.

Pearce, Roy Harvey. *The Continuity of American Poetry.* Princeton: Princeton UP, 1965.

Perry, Margaret. *The Harlem Renaissance: An Annotated Bibliography and Commentary.* New York: Garland, 1982.

Pitcher, E. W. *Fiction in American Magazines before 1800: An Annotated Catalogue.* In progress.

Poole's Index to Periodical Literature. By William Frederick Poole et al. Boston: Houghton, 1888-1908.

Raimo, John., ed. *A Guide to Manuscripts Relating to America in Great Britain and Ireland.* Westport: Mackler, British Association for American Studies, 1979.

Reardon, Joan and Kristine A. Thorsen. *Poetry by American Women, 1900-1975: A Bibliography.* Metuchen: Scarecrow, 1979.

Robinson, Barbara J. and J. Cordell Robinson. *The Mexican American: A Critical Guide to Research Aids.* Greenwich: JAI, 1980.

Roorbach, O. A. *Bibliotheca Americana: Catalogue of American Publications, Including Reprints and Original Works, from 1820 to 1852, Inclusive.* New York: Roorbach, 1852. *Supplements* (to January, 1861). New York: Roorbach / London: Trubner, 1861.

Sabin, Joseph, Wilberforce Eames, and R. W. G. Vail, eds. *Bibliotheca Americana: A Dictionary of Books Relating to America from Its Discovery to the Present Time.* New York: Sabin. 1868-1936. *Index*, 1974.

Schatz, Walter, ed. *Directory of Afro-American Resources.* New York: Bowker, 1970.

Scheick, William H. and JoElla Doggett. *Seventeenth-Century American Poetry: A*

440   *Selected Bibliography*

Reference Guide. Boston: Hall, 1977.
Shaw, Ralph R. and Richard H. Shoemaker. *American Bibliography: A Preliminary Checklist for 1801-1819*. New York: Scarecrow, 1958-66. 22 vols.
Shoemaker, Richard H., Gayle Cooper, Scott Bruntjen, and Carl Rinderknecht, comps. *A Checklist of American Imprints for 1820-86*. Metuchen: Scarecrow, 1964- .
Stratman, Carl J., C.S.V. *Bibliography of the American Theatre Excluding New York City*. Chicago: Loyola UP, 1965.
—. *American Theatrical Periodicals, 1798-1967: A Bibliographical Guide*. Durham: Duke UP, 1970.
Turner, Darwin T., comp. *Afro-American Writers*. New York: Appleton, 1970.
Wall, C. Edward, comp. and ed. *Cumulative Author Index for Poole's Index to Periodical Literature, 1802-1906*. Ann Arbor: Pierian, 1971.
Webster's Second. Ed. William Allan Neilson. Springfield: Merriam, 1934.
Webster's Third New International Dictionary of the English Language Unabridged. Ed. Philip Babcock Gove. Springfield: Merriam, 1961.
Wegelin, Oscar. *Early American Poetry: A Compilation of the Titles of Volumes of Verse and Broadsides by Writers Born or Residing in North America North of the Mexican Border (1650-1820)*. New York: Smith, 1930.
Wells, Daniel A. *The Literary Index to American Magazines, 1815-1865*. Metuchen: Scarecrow, 1980.
Wildbihler, Hubert and Sonja Volklein. *The Musical: An International Annotated Bibliography / Eine internationale annotierte Bibliographie*. Munich: Saur, 1986.
Wilmeth, Don B. *The American Stage to World War I: A Guide to Information Sources*. Detroit: Gale, 1978.
Woodress, James. *American Fiction. 1900-1950: A Guide to Information Sources*. Detroit: Gale, 1974.
Wright, Lyle H. *American Fiction, 1851-1875: A Contribution toward a Bibliography*. Repr. with additions and corrections. San Marino: Huntington Library, 1965.
—. *American Fiction, 1876-1900: A Contribution toward a Bibliography*. San Marino: Huntington Library, 1966.
—. *American Fiction, 1774-1850: A Contribution toward a Bibliography*. San Marino: Huntington Library, 1969. 2nd ed.
Yannella, Donald and John H. Roch. *American Prose to 1820: A Guide to Information Sources*. Detroit: Gale, 1979.

Ancillary Materials

American Historical Assocation's Guide to Historical Literature. Ed. George Frederick Howe et al. New York: Macmillan, 1961.
American Humanities Index. Troy: Whitston, 1976- .
Annual Bibliography of the History of the Printed Book and Libraries: (1970-). Dordrecht: Nijhoff, 1973- .
Barricelli, Jean-Pierre and Joseph Gibaldi, eds. *Interrelations of Literature*. New York: MLA, 1982.
Besterman, Theodore. *Early Printed Books: A Bibliography of Bibliographies*. London: Quaritch, 1940 / Geneva: Societas bibliographica, 1961. 2nd ed.
Book Auction Records: A Priced and Annotated Annual Record of International Book Auctions (1902-). Folkestone: Dawson, 1903- .
Bookman's Price Index: A Guide to the Value of Rare and Other Out-of-Print Books. Ed. Daniel F. McGrath. Detroit: Gale, 1964- .
Bookman's Price Index: Subject Series. Ed. Daniel F. McGrath. Detroit: Gale, 1987- .
Bordin, Ruth B. and Robert M. Wagner. *Modern Manuscript Library*. New York: Scarecrow, 1966.

British Humanities Index. London: Library Association, 1963– .

Cannon, Carl L. *American Book Collectors and Collecting from Colonial Times to the Present.* New York: Bowker, 1941.

Chicago Guide to Preparing Electronic Manuscripts for Authors and Publishers. Chicago: U of Chicago P, 1987.

Chicago Manual of Style for Authors, Editors, and Copywriters. Rev. and expanded. Chicago: U of Chicago P, 1982. 13th ed.

Datrix Direct. University Microfilms International, 300 North Zeeb Rd., Ann Arbor, MI 48106.

Dickinson, Donald C. *Dictionary of American Book Collectors.* New York: Greenwood, 1986.

Dictionary of American Biography. Ed. Allen Johnson and Dumas Malone. New York: Scribner, 1964.

Dictionary of Literary Biography. Detroit: Gale, 1978– .

Dictionary of National Biography from the Earliest Times to 1900. Ed. Leslie Stephen and Sidney Lee. London: Oxford UP, 1885–1900. 63 parts. Repr. London: Oxford UP, 1967–68. 22 vols. with ten-year supplements.

Dictionary of the Old Spanish Language. Madison: Hispanic Seminary of Medieval Studies, 1982– .

English Dialect Dictionary: Being the Complete Vocabulary of All Dialect Words Still in Use, or Known to Have Been in Use during the Last Two Hundred Years. Ed. Joseph Wright. London: Frowde / New York: Putnam, 1898–1905.

Essay and General Literature Index. New York: Wilson, 1931– .

Gray, Richard A. *Serial Bibliographies in the Humanities and Social Sciences.* Ann Arbor: Pierian P, 1969.

Historian's Handbook: A Descriptive Guide to Reference Works. Ed. Helen J. Poulton. Norman: U of Oklahoma P, 1972.

Historical Manuscripts Commission. *Guide to the Reports [1870–1911] on Collections of Manuscripts of Private Families, Corporations, and Institutions in Great Britain and Ireland.* London: HMSO, 1914–1938. 2 vols.

—. *Record Repositories in Great Britain: A Geographical Directory.* London: HMSO, 1979. 6th ed.

Historical Thesaurus of English. Ed. M. L. Samuels et al. London: Oxford UP. Forthcoming.

Humanities Index. New York: Wilson, 1975– .

Index to Reviews of Bibliographical Publications: An International Annual (1976–). Troy: Whitston, 1977– .

Index to Theses with Abstracts Accepted for Higher Degrees by the Universities of Great Britain and Ireland and the Council for National Academic Awards. London: Aslib, 1953– .

Internationale Bibliographie der Zeitschriftenliteratur aus allen Gebieten des Wissens / International Bibliography of Periodical Literature Covering All Fields of Knowledge / Bibliographie internationale de la littérature periodique dans tous domaines de la connaissance (1965–). Osnabrück: Dietrich, 1965– .

Internationale Jahresbibliographie der Festschriften / International Annual Bibliography of Festschriften / Bibliographie internationale annuelle des mélanges (1980–). Osnabrück: Dietrich, 1982– .

International Library Directory. Ed. A. P. Wales. London: Wales, 1969–70. 3rd ed.

McNamee, Lawrence F. *Dissertations in English and American Literature: Theses Accepted by American, British, and German Universities, 1865–1964.* New York: Bowker, 1968.

New Cambridge Bibliography of English Literature. Ed. George Watson and I. R. Willison. Cambridge: Cambridge UP, 1969–77. 5 vols.

New Cambridge History of American Literature. Ed. Sacvan Bercovitch. Cambridge: Cambridge UP, 1990. 5 vols. Rev. ed. in preparation.

New History of Literature. New York: Bedrick, 1987– .

New Pelican Guide to English Literature. Ed. Boris Ford. Harmondsworth: Penguin, 1982–84. 9 vols.

New Serial Titles: A Union List of Serials Held by Libraries in the United States and Canada . . . after Dec. 31, 1949. Washington: Library of Congress: 1953– .

New York Review of Books. New York: 1963– .

New York Times Index. Current Series. New York: New York Times, 1913– .

NEXIS. Mead Data Central, Inc. 9443 Springboro Pike, Miamisburg, OH 45342. 800–227–9597.

Oxford History of England. Ed. George N. Clark. Oxford: Clarendon, 1936–86.

Oxford History of English Literature. Ed. F. P. Wilson et al. Oxford: Clarendon, 1945– .

Paetow, L. J. *Guide to the Study of Medieval History.* New York: Crofts / Medieval Academy, 1931/60. 2nd ed.

Palfrey, Thomas R., Joseph C. Fucilla, and William C. Holbrook. *Bibliographical Guide to the Romance Languages and Literatures.* Evanston: Chandler's, 1971. 8th ed.

Poulton, Helen J. *Historian's Handbook: A Descriptive Guide to Reference Works.* Norman: U of Oklahoma P, 1972.

Proctor, Robert. *An Index to the Early Printed Books in the British Museum: From the Invention of Printing to the Year 1500. With Notes of Those in the Bodleian Library.* London: Holland, 1960. Repr. of 1898–1906 ed.

Prucha, Francis Paul. *Handbook for Research in American History: A Guide to Bibliographies and Other Reference Works.* Lincoln: U of Nebraska P, 1987.

Quaritch, Bernard, ed. *Contributions towards a Dictionary of English Book-Collectors: As Also of Some Foreign Collectors Whose Libraries Were Incorporated in English Collections or Whose Books Are Chiefly Met with in England.* London: Quaritch, 1892–1921.

Reader's Guide to Periodical Literature: An Author and Subject Index. New York: Wilson, 1901– .

Reynolds, Michael M. *A Guide to Theses and Dissertations: An International Bibliography of Bibliographies.* Phoenix: Oryx, 1985.

Ricci, Seymour de. *English Collectors of Books and Manuscripts (1530–1930) and Their Marks of Ownership.* Cambridge: Cambridge UP, 1930 / Bloomington: Indiana UP, 1960.

Richardson, R. C., comp. *The Study of History: A Bibliographical Guide.* Manchester: Manchester UP, 1988.

Rigdon, Walter, ed. *The Biographical Encyclopaedia and Who's Who of the American Theatre.* New York: Heineman, 1966.

Royal Commission on Historical Manuscripts / Historical Manuscripts Commission. Quality House, Quality Court, Chancery Lane, London WC2A 1HP.

Serials Directory: An International Reference Book. Birmingham: Ebsco, 1986– .

Social Sciences and Humanities Index. New York: Wilson, 1966–74.

Social Sciences Index. New York: Wilson, 1974– .

Standard Periodical Directory. New York: Oxbridge, 1965– .

Stubbs, John and Frank Wm. Tompa. "Waterloo and the *New Oxford English Dictionary." Editing, Publishing and Computer Technology.* Ed. Sharon Butler and William P. Stoneman. New York: AMS, 1988: 19–44.

Tennyson, Alfred, Lord. *The Poems of Tennyson.* Ed. Christopher Ricks. Berkeley: U of California P / Harlow: Longman, 1987. 2nd ed. 3 vols.

Times Index (1906–). Reading: Research Publications, 1907– .

TLS: Times Literary Supplement. London: 1902– .

Trésor de la langue française: Dictionnaire de la langue du XIXe siècle et du XXe siècle 1789–1960. Ed. Paul Imbs. Paris: Centre National de la Recherche Scientifique, 1971– .

Trevisa, John. *Trevisa's Translation of Bartholomaeus Anglicus De Proprietatibus Rerum.* Ed. M. C. Seymour et al. Oxford: Clarendon, 1975-88. 3 vols.
Ulrich's International Periodicals Directory: A Classified Guide to Current Periodicals, Foreign and Domestic. New York: Bowker, 1932- .
Ulrich's Irregular Serials and Annuals: An International Directory. 1967- .
Wilford, John Noble. "Monopoly Over Dead Sea Scrolls Is Ended." *New York Times.* 22 September 1991 A19-20.

Textual Research

Analytical and Enumerative Bibliography. Ed. William P. Williams. De Kalb: Bibliographical Society of Northern Illinois, 1977- .
Brack, O M Jr. and Warner Barnes, eds. *Bibliography and Textual Criticism: English and American Literature, 1700 to the Present.* Chicago: U of Chicago P, 1969.
Bowers, Fredson. "Textual Criticism." *Encyclopaedia Britannica.* Chicago: Benton, 1968: vol. 21: 918-23.
—. "Textual Criticism." *The Aims and Methods of Scholarship in Modern Languages and Literatures.* Ed. James Thorpe. New York: MLA, 1970. 2nd ed.
Center for Editions of American Authors. *Statement of Editorial Principles and Procedures.* Rev. ed. New York: MLA, 1972.
Center / Committee for Scholarly Editions. *An Introductory Statement.* New York: MLA, 1977.
Documentary Editing (formerly *Newsletter of the Association for Documentary Editing*). Ed. Thomas A. Mason. Association for Documentary Editing. 1979- .
Falconer, Graham and David H. Sanderson. "Bibliographie des études génétiques littéraires." *Texte* 7 (1988): 287-352.
Gottesman, Ronald and Scott Bennett, eds. *Art and Error: Modern Textual Editing.* Bloomington: Indiana UP, 1970.
Greetham, D. C. "Textual Scholarship." *Introduction to Literary Scholarship in the Modern Languages and Literatures.* Ed. Joseph Gibaldi. New York: MLA, 1991.
—, ed. *Scholarly Editing: A Guide to Research.* New York: MLA, 1994.
Kline, Mary-Jo. *A Guide to Documentary Editing.* Baltimore: Johns Hopkins UP, 1987.
The Library. Transactions of the Bibliographical Society. London: Bibliographical Society, 1892- .
Luey, Beth. *Editing Documents and Texts: An Annotated Bibliography.* Madison: Madison House, 1990.
Papers of the Bibliographical Society of America. New York: Bibliographical Society of America. 1906- .
Studies in Bibliography. Ed. Fredson Bowers and David Vander Meulen. Charlottesville: Bibliographical Society of the U of Virginia / UP of Virginia, 1948/49- .
Tanselle. G. Thomas. "Textual Scholarship." *Introduction to Literary Scholarship in the Modern Languages and Literatures.* Ed. Joseph Gibaldi. New York: MLA, 1981. 29-52.
—. *Selected Studies in Bibliography.* Charlottesville: UP of Virginia, 1979.
—. *Textual Criticism Since Greg, A Chronicle, 1950-1985.* Charlottesville: UP of Virginia, 1988.
Text: Transactions of the Society for Textual Scholarship. Eds. D. C. Greetham and W. Speed Hill. New York: AMS, 1984- .
Toronto, U of. Conferences on Editorial Problems. Toronto: U of Toronto Press, A. M. Hakkert / New York: Garland, AMS, 1966- .
Williams, William Proctor and Craig S. Abbott. *An Introduction to Bibliographical and Textual Studies.* New York: MLA, 1989. 2nd ed.

Some Specific Research Tools

Annals of English Literature, 1475–1950: The Principal Publications of Each Year Together with an Alphabetical Index of Authors with Their Works. Ed. R. W. Chapman and W. K. Davin. Oxford: Clarendon, 1965.

Brown, Carleton and Rossell Hope Robbins. *The Index of Middle English Verse*. New York: Columbia UP, for Index Society, 1943.

Crum, Margaret, ed. *First-Line Index Of English Poetry, 1500–1800, in Manuscripts of the Bodleian Library, Oxford*. Oxford: Clarendon / New York: MLA, 1969.

English Poetry Full-Text Database. Alexandria, VA: Chadwyck-Healey. Forthcoming.

MLA International Bibliography of Books and Articles on the Modern Languages and Literatures. New York: MLA, 1922– .

New Oxford English Dictionary. Electronic Edition. Ed E. S. C. Weiner. Oxford: Clarendon / Waterloo: U of Waterloo. In progress.

Oxford English Dictionary. Ed. J. A. Simpson and E. S. C. Weiner. Oxford: Clarendon 1989. 2nd ed.; CD-ROM edition. Oxford: Oxford UP, 1989. *OED Additions Series*. Ed. E. S. C. Weiner. Oxford: Oxford UP, 1994.

Tanselle. G. Thomas. *Guide to the Study of United States Imprints*. Cambridge: Belknap-Harvard UP, 1971.

Wing, Donald. *Short-Title Catalogue of Books Printed in England, Scotland, Ireland, Wales, and British America and of English Books Printed in Other Countries, 1641–1700*. New York: MLA, 1972. Rev. ed. in progress.

The Rewards

Blau, Eleanor. "Declaration of Independence Sells for $2.4 Million." *New York Times* 14 June 1991: C3.

Marchand, Leslie A., ed. *Byron's Letters and Journals*. London: Murray / Cambridge: Harvard UP, 1973–82. 12 vols.

Whitney, Craig. "Two More T. S. Eliot Poems Found Amid Hundreds of His Letters." *New York Times* 2 November, 1991: A13.

Chapter 2: Bibliography and History of Manuscript Books

Alexander, J. G., gen ed. *A Survey of Manuscripts Illuminated in the British Isles*. London: Miller / New York: Graphic Society, 1975–76.

— and M. T. Gibson, eds. *Medieval Learning and Literature: Essays Presented to Richard William Hunt*. Oxford: Oxford UP, 1976.

—. *Medieval Illuminators and Their Methods of Work*. New Haven: Yale UP, 1992.

Archiv für Diplomatik, Schriftgeschichte, Siegel- und Wappenkunde. Munich / Cologne: 1955– .

Archiv für Geschichte des Buchwesens. Frankfurt-am-Main: 1956– .

Arnold, Thomas W. and Adolf Grohmann. *The Islamic Book: A Contribution to Its Art and History from VII to XVIII Centuries*. London: Pegasus, 1929.

Avrin, Leila. *Scribes, Script and Books: The Book Arts from Antiquity to the Renaissance*. London: British Library, 1991

Barrow, W. J. *Manuscripts and Documents: Their Deterioration and Restoration*. Charlottesville: UP of Virginia, 1972. 2nd ed.

Bell, H. E. "The Price of Books in Medieval England," *The Library* 4th Series 17 (1936–37): 312–32.

Bennett, H. S. "The Production and Dissemination of Vernacular Manuscripts in the Fifteenth Century." *The Library* 5th Series (1947): 16–78.

—. *English Books and Readers 1475 to 1557*. Cambridge: Cambridge UP, 1969.

Repr. 1989. 2nd ed. 3 vols.
*Bischoff, Bernhard. *Latin Palaeography: Antiquity and the Middle Ages*. Trans. Daibhí Ó Cróinín and David Ganz. Cambridge: Cambridge UP, 1990.
—. *Manuscripts and Libraries in the Age of Charlemagne*. Trans. Michael M. Gorman. Cambridge: Cambridge UP, 1994.
Blake, N. F. "Manuscript to Print." Griffiths and Pearsall: 403–432.
Boffey, Julia and John J. Thompson. "Anthologies and Miscellanies: Production and Choice of Texts." Griffiths and Pearsall: 279–316.
*Boyle, Leonard E. *Medieval Latin Palaeography: A Bibliographical Introduction*. Toronto: U of Toronto P, 1984.
Brassington, W. Salt, ed. *A History of the Art of Bookbinding*. London: Stock, 1894.
*Braswell, Laurel Nichols. *Western Manuscripts from Classical Antiquity to the Renaissance: A Handbook*. New York: Garland, 1981.
Bühler, Curt F. "The Margins in Medieval Books." *Papers of the Bibliographical Society of America* 40 (1946): 34–42.
Calkins, Robert G. "Distribution of Labor: The Illuminators of the Hours of Catherine of Cleves and Their Workshop," *Transactions of the American Philosophical Society* 69, Pt. 5 (1979): 1–83.
Cambridge History of the Book in Britain. Ed. D. F. McKenzie, David McKitterick, Ian Willison. Cambridge: Cambridge UP. 7 vols. In progress.
Camille, Michael. *Image on the Edge: The Margins of Medieval Art*. Cambridge: Harvard UP, 1992.
Carlson, David R. *English Humanist Books: Writers and Patrons, Manuscript and Print, 1475–1525*. Toronto: U of Toronto P, 1993.
*Chaytor, H. J. *From Script to Print: An Introduction to Medieval Vernacular Literature*. Cambridge: Heffer, 1945.
Christianson, C. Paul. "Evidence for the Study of London's Late Medieval Manuscript Book Trade." Griffiths and Pearsall: 87–108.
Clanchy, M. T. *From Memory to Written Record: England, 1066–1307*. London: Edward Arnold / Cambridge: Harvard UP, 1979.
Clark, A. C. *The Descent of Manuscripts*. Oxford: Oxford UP, 1918. Repr. Oxford: Clarendon, 1969.
Clark, J. W. *Libraries in the Medieval and Renaissance Periods*. Cambridge: Macmillan and Bowes, 1894. Repr. Chicago: Argonaut, 1968.
—. *The Care of Books*. Cambridge: Cambridge UP, 1901. Repr. Cambridge: Cambridge UP, 1970, London: Variorum, 1975, New York: Gordon, 1976.
Constable, Giles. *Medieval Monasticism: A Select Bibliography*. Toronto: Toronto UP, 1976.
Contreni, John J. *Carolingian Learning, Masters and Manuscripts*. Aldershot: Variorum, 1992.
Dain, Alphonse. *Les manuscrits*. Paris: Belles Lettres, 1975. 3rd ed.
David, Martin and B. A. van Groningen. *Papyrological Primer*. Leiden: Brill, 1952.
De Hamel, Christopher. *A History of Illuminated Manuscripts*. Boston: Godine / London: Phaidon, 1986.
—. "Medieval Manuscript Studies." *The Book Encompassed*. Ed. Peter Davison. Cambridge: Cambridge UP, 1992: 37–45.
Destrez, J. "La 'pecia' dans les manuscrits du moyen âge." *Revue des sciences philosophiques et théologiques* 13 (1924): 182–97.
—. *La pecia dans les manuscrits universitaires du XIII et du XIV siècle*. Paris: Vautrain, 1935.
Diringer, David. *The Book before Printing: Ancient, Medieval and Oriental*. New York: Dover, 1982. Repr. of *The Hand-Produced Book*. New York: Philosophical Library, 1953.
—. *The Illuminated Book, Its History and Production*. New York: Philosophical Library, 1967.

Doughtie, Edward. "John Ramsey's Manuscript as a Personal and Family Document." *New Ways of Looking at Old Texts*. Ed. W. Speed Hill. Binghamton: Medieval & Renaissance Texts & Studies / Renaissance English Text Society, 1993: 281-288.

Doyle, A. I. "Publication by Members of the Religious Orders." Griffiths and Pearsall: 109-124.

—, E. Rainey, and C. B. Wilson. *Manuscript to Print: Tradition and Innovation in the Renaissance Book*. Durham: Durham U Library, 1975.

— and Malcolm B. Parkes. "The Production of Copies of the *Canterbury Tales* and *Confessio Amantis* in the Early Fifteenth Century." Parkes and Watson.

Edwards, A. S. G. and Derek Pearsall. "The Manuscripts of the Major English Poetic Texts." Griffiths and Pearsall: 257-278.

Egbert, Virginia Wylie. *The Medieval Artist at Work*. Princeton: Princeton UP, 1967.

English Manuscript Studies 1100-1700. Oxford: Blackwell, 1988- .

Fehrenbach, R. J., gen. ed. *Private Libraries in Renaissance England*. Binghamton: Medieval & Renaissance Texts & Studies, 1992- .

Foot, Mirjam M. "English Decorated Book Bindings." Griffiths and Pearsall: 65-86.

Gameson, Richard, ed. *The Early Medieval Bible: Its Production, Decoration, and Use*. Cambridge: Cambridge UP, 1994.

Gaur, Albertine. *The Writing Materials of the East*. London: British Library, 1979.

Gillespie, Vincent. "Vernacular Books of Religion." Griffiths and Pearsall: 317-344.

Goldschmidt, E. P. *Gothic and Renaissance Bookbinding*. London: Benn, 1928. 2 vols.

*Griffiths, Jeremy and Derek Pearsall. *Book Production and Publishing in Britain 1375-1475*. Cambridge: Cambridge UP, 1989.

Gumbert, J. P. and M. J. M. Haan, eds. *Litteræ Testuales: A Series on Manuscripts and Their Texts: Essays Presented to G. I. Lieftinck*. Amsterdam: van Gendt, 1972-76. 4 vols.

— and A. Gruys, eds. *Codicologica*. Leiden: Brill, 1976- .

Harris, Kate. "Patrons, Buyers and Owners: The Evidence for Ownership, and the Role of Book Owners in Book Production and the Book Trade." Griffiths and Pearsall: 163-200.

Harris, William V. *Ancient Literacy*. Cambridge: Harvard UP, 1989.

Haselden, R. B. *Scientific Aids for the Study of Manuscripts*. Oxford: Oxford UP, 1934.

Hellinga, Lotte. "Manuscripts in the Hands of Printers." Trapp: 3-11.

Hoccleve, Thomas. *The Regement of Princes*. Ed. Frederick J. Furnivall. EETS ES 53 (1897).

Hudson, Anne. "Lollard Book Production." Griffiths and Pearsall: 125-142.

Illich, Ivan. *In the Vineyard of the Text: A Commentary to Hugh's Didascalion*. Chicago: U of Chicago P, 1993.

Jenkinson, Hilary. "The Representation of Manuscripts in Print." *The London Mercury* 30 (1934): 429-38.

Kirchner, Joachim, ed. *Lexicon des Buchwesens*. Stuttgart: Hiersemann, 1952-56. 4 vols.

Leclercq, Jean. *The Love of Learning and the Desire for God: A Study of Monastic Culture*. Trans. Catharine Misrahi. New York: Fordham UP, 1961.

Lesne, Émile. *Les livres, scriptoria et bibliothèques du commencement du VIIIe à la fin du XIe siècles*. Lille: 1938.

Levarie, Norma. *The Art and History of Books*. New York: Heineman, 1968.

Loubier, Hans. *Der Bucheinband von seinem Anfängen bis zum Ende des 18 Jahrhunderts*. Leipzig: Klinkhardt and Biermann, 1926. 2nd ed.

Lucas, Peter J. "The Growth and Development of English Literary Patronage in the Later Middle Ages and the Early Renaissance." *The Library* Sixth Series 4 (1982): 219-48.

Lutz, Cora E. *Essays on Manuscripts and Rare Books*. Hamden: Archon, 1975.
Lyall, R. J. "Materials: The Paper Revolution." Griffiths and Pearsall: 11–30.
—. "Books and Book Owners in Fifteenth-Century Scotland." Griffiths and Pearsall: 239–256.
Madan, Falconer. *Books in Manuscript: A Short Introduction to Their Study and Use*. London: Kegan Paul, 1920. 2nd ed. Repr. New York: Empire, 1927.
Manion, Margaret M. and Bernard J. Muir, eds. *Medieval Texts and Images: Studies of Manuscripts from the Middle Ages*. Reading: Harwood, 1991.
Manuscripta. St. Louis: St. Louis Univ. Lib., 1957– .
Manuscripts. Newton, MA: Manuscript Society, 1948– .
May, Steven W. "Manuscript Circulation at the Elizabethan Court." *New Ways of Looking at Old Texts*. Ed. W. Speed Hill. Binghamton: Medieval & Renaissance Texts & Studies / Renaissance English Text Society, 1993: 273–280.
Mazal, Otto. *Buchkunst der Gotik*. Graz: Akadem. Druck, 1975.
McKitterick, Rosamond. *The Carolingians and the Written Word*. Cambridge: Cambridge UP, 1989.
—. "Carolingian Book Production: Some Problems." *The Library* Sixth Series 12 (1990): 1–33.
—, ed. *The Uses of Literacy in Early Medieval Europe*. Cambridge: Cambridge UP, 1992.
Meale, Carol. "Patrons, Buyers and Owners: Book Production and Social Status." Griffiths and Pearsall: 201–238.
Miner, D., ed. *The History of Bookbinding 525–1950 A.D.* Baltimore: Walters Art Gallery, 1957.
Mumby, Frank A. *Publishing and Bookselling from the Earliest Times to the Present*. London: Cape / New York: Bowker, 1974. 5th ed.
*Needham, P. *Twelve Centuries of Bookbinding: 400–1600*. New York: Pierpont Morgan Library / London: Oxford UP, 1979.
Netzer, Nancy. *Cultural Interplay in the Eighth Century: The Trier Gospels and the Makings of a Scriptorium at Echternach*. Cambridge: Cambridge UP, 1994.
Ogilvy, J. D. A. *Books Known to the English 597–1066*. Cambridge: Mediaeval Academy, 1967.
—. "Books Known to the English A.D. 597–1066. Addenda et Corrigenda." *Mediaevalia* 7 (1984): 281–325.
Olmert, Michael. *The Smithsonian Book of Books*. Washington: Smithsonian, 1992.
Parkes, M. B. "The Influence of the Concepts of *Ordinatio* and *Compilatio* on the Development of the Book." *Medieval Learning and Literature: Essays Presented to Richard William Hunt*. Ed. J. J. G. Alexander and M. T. Gibson. Oxford: Clarendon, 1976: 115–141.
—. *Scribes, Scripts and Readers*. London: Hambledon, 1991.
*—. *Pause and Effect: An Introduction to the History of Punctuation in the West*. Berkeley: U of California P, 1993.
*—. and Andrew G. Watson, eds. *Medieval Scribes, Manuscripts and Libraries: Essays Presented to N. R. Ker*. London: Oxford UP, 1978.
Pearsall, Derek, ed. *Manuscripts and Readers in Fifteenth-Century England*. Cambridge: Brewer, 1983.
Pebworth, Ted-Larry. "John Donne, Coterie Poetry, and the Text as Performance." *Studies in English Literature* 29 (1989): 61–75.
—. "Manuscript Transmission and the Selection of Copy-Text in Renaissance Coterie Poetry." *Text* 7 (1994).
Pedersen, J. *The Arabic Book*. Trans. G. French. Princeton: Princeton UP, 1984.
Pickering, F. P. *Literature and Art in the Middle Ages*. Coral Gables: U of Miami P, 1970.
*Plant, M. *The English Book Trade, or Economic History of the Making and Sale of Books*. London: Allen and Unwin, 1974. 3rd ed.

Pliny the Elder. *Naturalis historia* [on papyrus] IV, 139–53; XIII, xxi. 68 - xxvii. 89. Ed. H. Rackham. London: Loeb, 1945.

Pollard, G. "The University and the Book Trade in Mediaeval Oxford." *Beiträge zum Berufsbewusstsein des mittelalterlichen Menschen.* Ed. P. Wilpert and W. Eckert. Berlin: 1964.

—. "The *Pecia* System in the Medieval Universities." Parkes and Watson.

*Putnam, G. H. *Books and Their Makers During the Middle Ages.* New York: Hillary H, 1962. Repr. of 1896–97 ed. 2 vols.

Rand, E. K. *A Survey of the Manuscripts of Tours.* Cambridge: Mediaeval Academy, 1929.

Rashdall, H. *Universities of Europe in the Middle Ages.* Ed. F. M. Powicke and A. B. Emden. Oxford: Clarendon, 1936. 3 vols.

Reed, R. *Ancient Skins, Parchments and Leathers.* London / New York: Seminar P, 1972.

—. *The Nature and Making of Parchment.* Leeds: Elmete, 1975.

Reiman, Donald H. *The Study of Modern Manuscripts: Public, Confidential, and Private.* Baltimore: Johns Hopkins UP, 1993.

Roberts, Colin H. "The Codex," *Proceedings of the British Academy* 40 (1954): 169–204.

—. *Manuscript, Society and Belief in Early Christian Egypt.* London: Oxford UP for the British Academy, 1977.

—. and T. C. Skeat. *The Birth of the Codex.* London: Oxford UP, 1983.

Samaran, Charles and Robert Marichal. *Catalogue des manuscrits en écriture latine portant des indications de date, lieu ou de copiste.* Paris: CNRS, 1959- .

Santiffaler, Leo. *Beiträge zur Geschichte der Beschreibstoffe im Mittelalter.* Graz-Cologne: Mitteilungen des Instituts für Osterreichische Geschichtsforschung, 1953.

Savage, E. *Old English Libraries: The Making, Collection, and Use of Books during the Middle Ages.* London: Methuen, 1912. Repr. Detroit: Gale, 1968; New York: Barnes and Noble, 1970.

Schulz, H. C. "Thomas Hoccleve, Scribe." *Speculum* 12 (1937): 71–81.

Scott, Kathleen L. "Design, Decoration and Illustration." Griffiths and Pearsall: 31–64.

Scriptorium: Revue international des études relatives aux manuscrits / International Review of Manuscript Studies. Antwerp / Brussels / Paris: 1946/7- . Ghent: 1969- .

Sezgin, F. *Geschichte des arabischen Schrifttums.* Leiden: Brill, 1967- .

*Shailor, Barbara. *The Medieval Book.* Toronto: U of Toronto P, 1991.

Shakespeare, William. *The Norton Facsimile: The Shakespeare First Folio.* Ed. Charlton Hinman. New York: Norton, 1968.

Smalley, Beryl. *English Friars and Antiquity.* Oxford: Blackwell, 1960.

Steele, R. "The Pecia." *The Library* 4th Series 11 (1931): 230–34.

Stegmüller, F. *Repertorium biblicum medii ævi.* Madrid: Inst. Francisco Suarez, 1950–61. 7 vols.

Stevens, Martin. "The Towneley Plays Manuscript (HM1): *Compilatio* and *Ordinatio.*" *Text* 5 (1991): 157–174.

Stoll, Jakob. "Zur Psychologie der Schreibfehler." *Fortschritte der Psychologie und ihrer Ahwendung* 2 (1914): 1–133.

Stratford, Jenny. "English Literary Manuscripts of the Twentieth Century." *The Book Encompassed.* Ed. Peter Davison. Cambridge: Cambridge UP, 1992: 46–56.

Studia papyrologica. Rome: 1962- .

Studies in the Age of Chaucer. Norman: 1979- .

Sullivan, Ernest W., II. "The Renaissance Manuscript Verse Miscellany: Private Party, Private Text." *New Ways of Looking at Old Texts.* Ed. W. Speed Hill. Binghamton: Medieval & Renaissance Texts & Studies / Renaissance English Text Society, 1993: 289–298.

Thompson, James W. *The Medieval Library*. Chicago: U of Chicago P, 1939. Repr. with supplement by B. B. Boyer, New York: 1957.
—. *Ancient Libraries*. Hamden: 1962. Repr. of 1940 ed.
Trapp, J. B., ed. *Manuscripts in the Fifty Years after the Invention of Printing*. London: Warburg Institute, 1983.
Trevisa, John. *Trevisa's Translation of Bartholomaeus Anglicus De Proprietatibus Rerum*. Ed. M. C. Seymour et al. Oxford: Clarendon, 1975–88. 3 vols.
Turner, Eric G. *Athenian Books in the Fifth and Sixth Centuries B.C.* London: Lewis, 1952.
—. *Greek Manuscripts of the Ancient World*. Princeton: Princeton UP, 1971. 2nd ed.
—. *The Typology of the Early Codex*. Philadelphia: U of Pennsylvania P, 1972, 1977.
—. *Greek Papyri: An Introduction*. Oxford: Clarendon / Princeton: Princeton UP, 1968, 1980.
Vervliet, H. D. L. *The Book Through Five Thousand Years*. London: Phaidon, 1972.
Voigts, Linda Ehrsam. "Scientific and Medical Books." Griffiths and Pearsall: 345–402.
Wathey, Andrew. "The Production of Books of Liturgical Polyphony." Griffiths and Pearsall: 143–161.
Webber, Teresa. *Scribes and Scholars at Salisbury Cathedral. c. 1075–c. 1125*. Oxford: Clarendon P, 1992.
Weiterkampf, Frank. *The Illustrated Book*. Cambridge: Harvard UP, 1938.
Weitzmann, Kurt, gen. ed. *Studies in Manuscript Illumination*. Princeton: Princeton UP, 1940– .
—. *Illustrations in Roll and Codex: A Study of Origins and Methods of Text Illustration*. Princeton: Princeton UP, 1947.
—. *Ancient Book Illumination*. Cambridge: Harvard UP, 1959.
—. *Studies in Classical and Byzantine Manuscript Illumination*. Chicago: Chicago UP, 1971.
—. *Late Antique and Early Christian Book Illumination*. New York: Braziller, 1977.
Westwood, J. O. *The Art of Illuminated Manuscripts*. New York: Arch Cape, 1988. Repr. of *Palæographia sacra pictoria*. London: William Smith, 1843–45.
Williams, John. *Early Spanish Manuscript Illumination*. New York: Braziller, 1977.
Zimmermann, E. Heinrich. *Vorkarolingische Miniaturen*. Berlin: Deutsche Verein für Kunstwissenschaft, 1916.

Chapter 3: History and Bibliography of Printed Books

Alston, Robin C. "Books and Electronics." *Politics of the Electronic Text*. Ed. Warren Chernaik et al. Oxford: Oxford U Computing Services, 1993: 81–90.
Anderson, Patricia. *The Printed Image and the Transformation of Popular Culture, 1790–1860*. Oxford: Clarendon P, 1991.
Archives of British and American Publishers on Microform with Indexes. Cambridge: Chadwyck-Healey, 1973–1988.
Barolini, Helen. *Aldus and His Dream Book*. New York: Italica P, 1992.
Baym, Nina. *At Home with History: History Books and Women's Sphere Before the Civil War*. James Russell Wiggins Lectures in the History of the Book in American Culture. Worcester: American Antiquarian Society, 1991.
Berry, W. T. and A. F. Johnson. *Catalogue of Specimens of Printing Types by English and Scottish Printers 1665–1830*. Oxford: Oxford UP, 1935.
—. and A. F. Johnson. *The Encyclopaedia of Type Faces*. London: Blandford, 1953. 4th ed. 1970.

—. and H. E. Poole. *Annals of Printing: A Chronological Encyclopaedia from the Earliest Times to 1950.* London: Blandford, 1966.

Bibliofilia: Rivista di storia del libro e delle arti grafiche. Florence: 1899– .

Bidwell, John. "The Study of Paper as Evidence, Artefact, and Commodity." *The Book Encompassed.* Ed. Peter Davison. Cambridge: Cambridge UP, 1992: 69–82.

*Bigmore, E. C. and C. W. H. Wyman. *A Bibliography of Printing.* London: Quaritch, 1884–86. Repr. London: Holland P, 1969. 3 vols.

Binns, Norman E. *An Introduction to Historical Bibliography.* London: Association of Assistant Librarians, 1953.

Black, Michael. *A Short History of Cambridge University Press.* Cambridge: Cambridge UP, 1992.

*Blades, William. *The Biography and Typography of William Caxton.* London: Trübner, 1877. Rev. ed. New York: Scribner and Welford, 1882.

Blagden, C. *The Stationers' Company: A History 1403–1959.* London: Allen and Unwin / Cambridge: Harvard UP, 1960.

Blake, N. F. *Caxton: England's First Publisher.* New York: Harper & Row, 1976.

Bland, David. *A Bibliography of Book Illustration.* London: Cambridge UP, 1955.

—. *A History of Book Illustration.* Berkeley: U of California P, 1969. Rev. ed.

Blegen, Theodore, et al. *Book Collecting and Scholarship.* Minneapolis: U of Minnesota P, 1954.

Bliss, Douglas P. *A History of Wood Engraving.* London: Spring, 1964.

Blissett, William, ed. *Editing Illustrated Books.* New York: Garland, 1980.

Bloy, C. H. *A History of Printing Ink, Balls and Rollers, 1440–1850.* London: Wynkyn de Worde Society / New York: Sandstone P., 1980.

Blum, Andre. *On the Origin of Paper.* Trans. H. M. Leydenberg. New York: Bowker, 1934.

—. *The Origins of Printing and Engraving.* New York: Scribner, 1940.

Bond, William H. "Imposition by Half-Sheets." *The Library* Fourth Series 22 (1941–42): 163–67.

Bove, Tony, Cheryl Rhodes, and Wes Thomas. *The Art of Desktop Publishing.* New York: Bantam, 1987.

Bowers, Fredson. "The Headline in Early Books." *English Institute Annual* (1941): 185–205. Repr. *Essays*: 199–211.

—. "Elizabethan Proofing." *Joseph Quincy Adams Memorial Studies.* Ed. J. G. McManaway (1948): 571–86. Repr. *Essays*: 240–53.

—. "Bibliographical Evidence from the Printer's Measure." *Studies in Bibliography* 2 (1949–50): 153–67. Repr. *Essays*: 258–68.

—. *Essays in Bibliography, Text, and Editing.* Charlottesville: UP of Virginia, 1975.

Brassington, W. Salt, ed. *A History of the Art of Bookbinding.* London: Stock, 1894.

Bühler, Curt F. "Aldus Manutius: The First Five Hundred Years." *Papers of the Bibliographical Society of America* 44 (1950): 205–15.

*—. *The Fifteenth-Century Book: The Scribes, the Printers, the Decorators.* Philadelphia: U of Pennsylvania P, 1960.

Butler, Pierce. *The Origins of Printing in Europe.* Chicago: U of Chicago P, 1940.

Cambridge History of the Book in Britain. Ed. D. F. McKenzie, David McKitterick, Ian Willison. Cambridge: Cambridge UP. 7 vols. In progress.

Cannon, Carl L. *American Book Collectors and Collecting from Colonial Times to the Present.* New York: Wilson, 1941.

Carlson, David R. *English Humanist Books: Writers and Patrons, Manuscript and Print, 1475–1525.* Toronto: U of Toronto P, 1993.

Carpenter, Kenneth, ed. *Books and Society in History.* New York: Bowker, 1983.

Carter, Harry. *Publishers' Cloth: An Outline History of Publishers' Bindings in England 1820–1900.* New York: Bowker / London: Constable, 1938. Repr. Ann Arbor: U Microfilms, 1970.

— and P. H. Muir, eds. *Printing and the Mind of Man: A Descriptive Catalogue Illus-*

trating The Impact of Print on the Evolution of Western Civilization During Five Centuries. London: Cassell / New York: Holt, Rinehart, 1967.

Carter, John. *Taste and Technique in Book Collecting*. London: Private Libraries Association, 1970.

*—. *ABC for Book Collectors*. Corrections and additions by Nicolas Barker. London: Granada, 1980. 6th ed.

Carter, T. F. *The Invention of Printing in China and Its Spread Westward*. Rev. L. Carrington Goodrich. New York: Ronald P, 1955. 2nd ed.

Cave, Roderick. *The Private Press*. New York: Watson-Guptill, 1971.

*Chappell, Warren. *A Short History of the Printed Word*. New York: Knopf, 1970. Repr. Boston: Godine, 1980. Repr. New York: Dorset, 1990.

*Chartier, Roger. *The Cultural Uses of Print in Early Modern France*. Trans. Lydia G. Cochrane. Princeton: Princeton UP, 1987.

*—. *The Culture of Print: Power and the Uses of Print in Early Modern Europe*. Trans. Lydia G. Cochrane. Princeton: Princeton UP, 1987.

—. *Frenchness in the History of the Book: From the History of Publishing to the History of Reading*. James Russell Wiggins Lecture in the History of the Book in American Culture. Worcester: American Antiquarian Society, 1988.

—. "Texts, Printing, Reading." *The New Cultural History*. Ed. Lynn Hunt. Berkeley: U of California P, 1989.

*—. *The Order of Books: Readers, Authors and Libraries in Europe between the 14th and 18th Centuries*. Trans. Lydia Cochrane. Stanford: Stanford UP, 1994.

—. "From Codex to Screen." *Common Knowledge*. Forthcoming.

Charvat, Wiliam. *The Profession of Authorship in America, 1800–1870*. Ed. Matthew J. Bruccoli. New York: Columbia UP, 1992.

—. *Literary Publishing in America, 1790–1850*. Afterword Michael Winship. Amherst: U of Massachusetts P, 1993.

Chaytor, H. J. *From Script to Print: An Introduction to Medieval Vernacular Literature*. Cambridge: Heffer, 1945.

Christianson, C. Paul. *A Directory of London Stationers and Book Artisans 1300–1500*. New York: Bibliographical Society of America, 1991.

Churchill, W. A. *Watermarks in Paper in Holland, England, France etc. in the XVII and XVIII Centuries and Their Interconnection*. Amsterdam: Hertzberger, 1935/1965.

Clair, Colin. *Christopher Plantin*. London: Cassell, 1960.

*—. *A History of Printing in Britain*. London: Cassell, 1965.

Clapperton, R. H. and W. Henderson. *Modern Papermaking*. Oxford: Blackwell, 1947. 3rd ed.

Cockerell, D. *Bookbinding, and the Care of Books*. London: Pitman, 1925. 4th ed. Repr. New York: Lyons and Burford, 1991.

Coleman, D. C. *The British Paper Industry, 1495–1860*. Oxford: Clarendon, 1958.

Copinger, W. A. *Incunabula Biblica, or The First Half Century of the Latin Bible*. London: Quaritch, 1892.

Coser, Lewis A., Charles Kadushin, and Walter W. Powell. *Books: The Culture and Commerce of Publishing*. Chicago: U of Chicago P, 1985.

Crotch, W. J. B. *The Prologues and Epilogues of William Caxton*. Early English Text Society 176. London: Oxford UP, 1928.

Curwen, H. *Processes of Graphic Reproduction in Printing*. Rev. Charles Mayo. London: Faber, 1966. 4th ed.

Darlow, T. H. and H. F. Moule. *Historical Catalogue of the Printed Editions of Holy Scripture*. London: Bible House, 1903–11. 4 vols.

Darnton, Robert.

Darnton, Robert. *The Business of Enlightenment: A Publishing History of the Encyclopédie 1775-1800*. Cambridge: Belknap / Harvard UP, 1979.

—. *The Literary Underground of the Old Regime*. Cambridge: Harvard UP, 1982.

—. "What Is the History of Books?" *Daedalus* 111 (1982): 65-83. Repr. Carpenter: 3-26.

—. *The Great Cat Massacre and Other Episodes in French Cultural History.* New York: Vintage, 1984.

— and Daniel Roche, eds. *Revolution in Print: The Press in France 1775-1800.* Berkeley: U of California P / New York: New York Public Library, 1989.

Davenport, Cyril J. H. *Thomas Berthelet, Royal Printer and Bookbinder.* Chicago: Caxton Club, 1901. Repr. New York: B. Franklin, 1969.

Davidson, Cathy N. *Ideology and Genre: The Rise of the Novel in America.* James Russell Wiggins Lecture in the History of the Book in American Culture. Worcester: American Antiquarian Society, 1987.

—, ed. *Reading in America: Literature and Social History.* Baltimore: Johns Hopkins UP, 1989.

Davies, David W. *The World of the Elseviers 1580-1712.* The Hague: Nijhoff, 1954.

Dictionary Catalogue of the History of Printing from the John M. Wing Foundation in the Newberry Library. Boston: Hall, 1961, 1970.

Didot, A. F. *Alde Manuce.* Paris: Didot, 1875.

*Diehl, E. *Bookbinding: Its Background and Technique.* New York: Rinehart, 1946. 2 vols. Repr. New York: Dover, 1980. 1 vol.

*Dooley, Allan C. *Author and Printer in Victorian England.* Charlottesville: UP of Virginia, 1992.

*Duff, E. Gordon. *A Century of the English Book Trade . . . from the Issue of the First Dated Book in 1458 to the Incorporation of the Company of Stationers in 1557.* London: Blades, East and Blades, 1905.

—. *The Printers, Stationers and Book Binders of Westminster and London from 1476 to 1535.* Cambridge: Cambridge UP, 1906.

—. *The English Provincial Printers, Stationers and Booksellers to 1557.* Cambridge, 1912.

—. *Fifteenth-Century English Books.* Oxford: Bibliographical Society, 1917.

Eder, J. M. *History of Photography.* Trans. E. Epstean. New York: Columbia UP, 1945.

*Eisenstein, Elizabeth L. *The Printing Press as an Agent of Change.* 2 vols. Cambridge: Cambridge UP, 1979.

—. *The Printing Revolution in Early Modern Europe.* Cambridge: Cambridge UP, 1983.

—. *Print Culture and Enlightenment Thought.* Sixth Hanes Lecture. Chapel Hill, Hanes Foundation / U of N Carolina P, 1986.

—. *Grub Street Abroad: Aspects of the French Cosmopolitan Press from the Age of Louis XIV to the French Revolution.* Oxford: Clarendon P, 1992.

Exman, Eugene. *The House of Harper: 150 Years of Publishing.* New York: Harper, 1967.

Feather, John. "British Publishing in the Eighteenth Century: A Preliminary Subject Analysis." *The Library* Sixth Series 8 (1986): 32-46.

*—. *A Dictionary of Book History.* New York: Oxford UP, 1986.

—. *A History of British Publishing.* London: Croom Helm, 1988.

*Febvre, Lucien, and Henri-Jean Martin. *The Coming of the Book: The Impact of Printing 1450-1800.* Trans. David Gerard. London & New York: Verso, 1990.

Fletcher, Harry George. *New Aldine Studies: Documentary Essays on the Life and Work of Aldus Manutius.* San Francisco: Rosenthal, 1989.

Fletcher, W. Y. *English Bookbindings in the British Museum.* London: Kegan Paul, 1895.

—. *Foreign Bookbindings in the British Museum.* London: Kegan Paul, 1896.

Flodr, M. *Incunabula classicorum. Wiegendrucke der griechischen und römische Literatur.* Amsterdam: Hakkert, 1973.

Foot, Mirjam M. "The Future of Bookbinding Research." *The Book Encompassed.*

Ed. Peter Davison. Cambridge: Cambridge UP, 1992: 99–106.

—. *Studies in the History of Book-Binding*. Aldershot: Scolar, 1993.

Foxon, David. *Pope and the Early Eighteenth-Century Book Trade*. Rev. and ed. James McLaverty. New York: Oxford UP, 1991.

Franklin, Colin. *The Private Presses*. London: Studio Vista, 1969.

French, Hannah. *Bookbinding in Early America*. Charlottesville: UP of Virginia, 1986.

Gaskell, Philip, G. Barber, and G. Warrilow. "An Annotated List of Printers' Manuals to 1850." *Journal of the Printing Historical Society* 4 (1968): 11–32.

— New Introduction to Bibliography. Oxford: Oxford UP, 1972. Repr. with corrections, 1985.

Geduld, Harry M. *Prince of Publishers: Work and Career of Jacob Tonson*. Bloomington: Indiana UP, 1969.

Gernsheim, H. and A. *The History of Photography from the Camera Obscura to the Beginning of the Modern Era*. New York: McGraw-Hill, 1969. 2nd ed.

*Glaister, Geoffrey Ashall. *Glaister's Glossary of the Book: Terms Used in Papermaking, Printing, Bookbinding, and Publishing, with Notes on Illuminated Manuscripts and Private Presses*. London: Allen and Unwin / Berkeley: U of California P, 1979.

Goldschmidt, E. P. *Gothic and Renaissance Bookbinding*. London: Benn, 1928. 2 vols.

—. *Medieval Texts and their First Appearance in Print*. London: Bibliographical Society / Oxford: Oxford UP, 1943. Repr. 1965.

—. *The Printed Book of the Renaissance*. Amsterdam: van Heusden, 1974. 2nd ed.

Green, R. *The Iron Hand Press in America*. Privately printed, 1948.

*Greenfield, Howard. *Books From Writer to Reader*. New York: Crown, 1989.

Greg, W. W. *Some Aspects and Problems of London Publishing between 1550 and 1650*. Oxford: Oxford UP, 1956.

Grevel, H., ed. *The Book: Its Printers, Illustrators, and Binders to the Present Time*. New York: 1890. Repr. Detroit: Gale, 1971.

Griffiths, Jeremy and Derek Pearsall, eds. *Book Production and Publishing in Britain 1375-1475*. Cambridge: Cambridge UP, 1989.

The Grolier Club 1884-1984: Its Library, Exhibitions, & Publications. New York: Grolier Club, 1984.

Gross, Robert A. *Printing, Politics and the People*. James Russell Wiggins Lecture in the History of the Book in American Culture. Worcester: American Antiquarian Society, 1990.

Growoll, A. *Three Centuries of English Book Trade Bibliography*. New York: Dibdin Society / Greenhalgh, 1903.

Gutenberg-Jahrbuch. 1926– .

*Haebler, Konrad. *The Study of Incunabula*. Trans. Lucy Eugenia Osborne. New York: Grolier, 1933. Repr. Kraus, 1967.

Hall, Basil. *The Great Polyglot Bibles*. San Francisco: Book Club of California, 1966.

Hall, David. "On Native Ground: From the History of Printing to the History of the Book." *Proceedings of the American Antiquarian Society* 93 (1983): 313–336.

—. and John B. Hench, eds. *Needs and Opportunities in the History of the Book: America, 1639-1876*. Charlottesville: UP of Virginia, 1987.

Handover, Phyllis. *Printing in London from 1476 to Modern Times*. London: Allen and Unwin, 1960.

Hansel, Johannes. *Bücherkunde für Germanisten: Studienausgabe*. Berlin: Schmidt, 1978. Rev. Lydia Tschakert. 7th ed.

Hanson, L. W. *Government and the Press 1695-1763*. London: Oxford UP, 1936. Repr. 1967.

Hartman, John. *The History of the Illustrated Book: The Western Tradition*. London:

Thames and Hudson, 1981.

Hartz, S. L. *The Elseviers and Their Contemporaries*. Amsterdam: Elsevier, 1955.

Hellinga, Lotte. "Manuscripts in the Hands of Printers." Trapp: 3–11.

—. "Incunabula, 1942–1992: From Type to Text." *The Book Encompassed*. Ed. Peter Davison. Cambridge: Cambridge UP, 1992: 107–115.

Herring, R. *Paper and Paper-making*. London: Longman, 1855.

Hesse, Carla. *Publishing and Cultural Politics in Revolutionary Paris 1789–1810*. Berkeley: U of California P, 1991.

*Hind, Arthur M. *A History of Engraving and Etching*. Boston: Houghton Mifflin, 1923. Repr. New York: Dover, 1963.

*—. *An Introduction to a History of Woodcut*. Boston: Houghton Mifflin, 1935. Repr. New York: Dover, 1963. 2 vols.

Hindman, Sandra L., ed. *Printing the Written Word: The Social History of Books c. 1450–1520*. Ithaca: Cornell UP, 1991.

*Hinman, Charlton. *The Printing and Proof-reading of the First Folio of Shakespeare*. Oxford: Clarendon, 1963. 2 vols.

Hirsch, R. *Printing, Selling, and Reading 1450–1550*. Wiesbaden: Harrasowits, 1967. Rev. 1974.

Hobson, Anthony. *The Literature of Bookbinding*. London: Cambridge UP, 1954.

— *Humanists and Bookbinders: The Origins and Diffusion of the Humanistic Bookbinding 1459–1559*. Cambridge: Cambridge UP, 1989.

Hobson, Geoffrey D. *English Binding Before 1500*. Cambridge: Cambridge UP, 1925.

Hodnett, E. *English Woodcuts, 1480–1535*. Oxford: Bibliographical Society, 1935.

Hofer, P. *Baroque Book Illustration*. Cambridge: Harvard UP, 1951.

Holme, Charles, ed. *The Art of the Book*. London: Studio, 1914. Repr. New York: Dorset, 1990.

Hughes, Linda K. and Michael Lund. *The Victorian Serial*. Charlottesville: UP of Virginia, 1991.

*Hunter, Dard. *Papermaking: The History and Technique of an Ancient Craft*. New York: Knopf, 1943. Repr. New York: Dover, 1978.

Isaac, Peter and Michael Perkin. "The British Provincial Book Trade." *The Book Encompassed*. Ed. Peter Davison. Cambridge: Cambridge UP, 1992: 176–181.

Jackson, Holbrook. *The Printing of Books*. London: Cassell, 1947. 2nd ed.

Jenkinson, Hilary. "The Representation of Manuscripts in Print." *The London Mercury* 30 (1934): 429–38.

Johnson, Alfred F. *A Catalogue of Engraved and Etched English Title-Pages*. London: Oxford UP for the Bibliographical Society, 1934.

Johnson, J. and S. Gibson. *Print and Privilege at Oxford to the Year 1700*. London: Oxford UP, 1946. Repr. 1966.

Johnson, Julie Greer. *The Book in the Americas: The Role of Books and Printing in the Development of Culture and Society in Colonial Latin America*. Providence: John Carter Brown Library, 1988.

Journal of the Printing Historical Society. London: 1965– .

Judge, C. B. *Elizabethan Book-Pirates*. Cambridge: Harvard UP, 1934.

Kirschbaum, L. *Shakespeare and the Stationers*. Columbus, Ohio: Ohio State UP, 1955.

Labarre, E. J. *Dictionary and Encyclopaedia of Paper and Paper Making*. Amsterdam: Swets and Zeitlinger / London: Oxford UP, 1952. Repr. Amsterdam: 1969. *Supplement*. Amsterdam: 1967.

Lanham, Richard A. *The Electronic Word: Democracy, Technology, and the Arts*. Chicago: U of Chicago P, 1993.

Lehmann-Haupt, Hellmut. *Bookbinding in America*. New York: Portland, ME: Southworth-Anthochsen, 1941. Repr. New York: Bowker, 1967.

—. *Peter Schoeffer of Gernsheim and Mainz*. Rochester, NY: Hart, 1950.

—, Rollo Silver, and Laurence C. Wroth. *A History of the Making and Selling of Books in the U.S.* New York: Bowker, 1951. 2nd ed.

—. *The Book in America.* New York: Bowker, 1952. 2nd ed.

—. *Gutenberg and the Master of the Playing Cards.* New Haven: Yale UP, 1966.

Leif, I. P. *An International Sourcebook of Paper History.* Hamden: Archon / Folkestone: Dawson, 1978.

Leighton, D. *Modern Bookbinding, a Survey and a Prospect.* London: Dent, 1935.

Lenhart, John M. *Pre-Reformation Printed Books: A Study in Statistical and Applied Bibliography.* Franciscan Studies 14. New York: 1935.

Lepschy, Anna Laura, John Took, and Dennis E. Rhodes, eds. *Book Production and Letters in the Western European Renaissance: Essays in Honour of Conor Fahy.* London: Modern Humanities Research Association, 1986.

Levarie, Norma. *The Art and History of Books.* New York: Heineman, 1968.

Lilien, Otto M. *An Outline of the History of Industrial Gravure Printing up to 1920.* London: Lund Humphries, 1972.

Loubier, Hans. *Der Bucheinband von seinem Anfängen bis zum Ende des 18 Jahrhunderts.* Leipzig: Klinkhardt and Biermann, 1926. 2nd ed.

Love, Harold. "Manuscript versus Print in the Transmission of English Literature, 1600-1700." *Bibliographical Society of Australia and New Zealand Bulletin* 9 (1985): 95-107.

—. *Scribal Publication in Seventeenth-Century England.* New York: Oxford UP, 1993.

Lowry, Martin. *The World of Aldus Manutius.* London, 1979.

—. *Nicholas Jenson and the Rise of Venetian Publishing in Renaissance Europe.* Oxford: Blackwell, 1991.

Lucas, Peter J. "The Growth and Development of English Literary Patronage in the Later Middle Ages and the Early Renaissance." *The Library* Sixth Series 4 (1982): 219-48.

Lutz, Cora E. *Essays on Manuscripts and Rare Books.* Hamden: Archon, 1975.

McAleer, Joseph. *Popular Reading and Publishing in Britain, 1914-1950.* Oxford: Clarendon P, 1992.

McCusker, John J. "The Business Press in England before 1775." *The Library* Sixth Series 8 (1986): 205-31.

McKenzie, D. F. *The Cambridge University Press 1696-1712.* Cambridge: Cambridge UP, 1966. 2 vols.

*—. "Printers of the Mind: Some Notes on Bibliographical Theories and Printing-House Practices." *Studies in Bibliography* 22 (1969): 1-75.

McKerrow, R. B. *A Dictionary of Printers and Booksellers in England, Scotland and Ireland, and of Foreign Printers of English Books, 1557-1640.* London: Bibliographical Society, 1910. Repr. 1968.

*—. *An Introduction to Bibliography for Literary Students.* Oxford: Oxford UP, 1927.

McKitterick, David. *A History of Cambridge University Press (vol. I: Printing and the Book Trade in Cambridge, 1534-1698).* Cambridge: Cambridge UP, 1992.

McLean, Ruari. *Modern Book Design, from William Morris to the Present Day.* London: Faber, 1958. 2nd ed.

Middleton, Bernard C. *A History of English Craft Bookbinding Technique.* New York: Hafner, 1963. Rev. with supplement, 1978.

Millgate, Jane. *Scott's Last Edition: A Study in Publishing History.* Edinburgh: U of Edinburgh P, 1987.

Miner, D., ed. *The History of Bookbinding 525-1950 A.D.* Baltimore: Walters Art Gallery, 1957.

Moran, J. *Wynkyn de Worde, Father of Fleet Street.* London: Wynkyn de Worde Society, 1960. Rev. 1976.

—. *The Composition of Reading Matter.* London: Wace, 1965.

*—. *Printing Presses*. London: Oxford UP / Berkeley: U of California P, 1973.

Moxon, Joseph. *Mechanick Exercises on the Whole Art of Printing*. London: 1683. Ed. Herbert Davis and Harry Carter. London: Oxford UP, 1962. Repr. New York: Dover, 1978. 2nd ed.

*Mumby, Frank A. *Publishing and Bookselling from the Earliest Times to the Present*. London: Cape / New York: Bowker, 1974. 5th ed.

Myers, Robin. *The British Book Trade from Caxton to the Present Day: A Bibliographical Guide Based on the Libraries of the National Book League and St. Bride Institute*. London: Deutsch, 1973.

—. "Stationers' Company Bibliography, 1892-1992." *The Book Encompassed*. Ed. Peter Davison. Cambridge: Cambridge UP, 1992: 116-121.

*Needham, P. *Twelve Centuries of Bookbinding: 400-1600*. New York: Pierpont Morgan Library / London: Oxford UP, 1979.

—. "The Bradshaw Method: Henry Bradshaw's Contributions to Bibliography." Chapel Hill: Hanes Foundation / U of North Carolina U Library, 1988.

Nixon, Howard, ed. *Studies in the Book Trade in Honour of Graham Pollard*. Oxford: Oxford Bibliographical Society, 1975.

—. "Caxton, His Contemporaries and Successors." *The Library* Fifth Series 31 (1976): 305-26.

—, ed. *Five Centuries of English Bookbinding*. London: Scolar, 1978.

— and Mirjam M. Foot. *The History of Decorated Book Binding in England*. New York: Oxford UP, 1992.

Nordlunde, C. V. *Sir Emery Walker and the Revival of Printing*. Cophenhagen: Nordlunde, 1959.

Olmert, Michael. *The Smithsonian Book of Books*. Washington: Smithsonian, 1992.

One Book/Five Ways: The Publishing Procedures of Five University Presses. Los Altos: Kaufmann, 1978.

Ong, Walter J. *Orality and Literacy: The Technologizing of the Word*. London: Methuen, 1982.

Oswald, John Clyde. *Printing in the Americas*. New York: Hacker, 1968. Repr. of 1937 ed.

Painter, George. *William Caxton: A Quincentenary Biography*. London: Chatto and Windus, 1976.

Papermaking, Art and Craft. Washington: Library of Congress, 1968.

Pedersen, J. *The Arabic Book*. Trans. G. French. Princeton: Princeton UP, 1984.

Perkins, Maxwell. *Editor to Author: The Letters of Maxwell E. Perkins*. Ed. John Hall Wheelock. New York: Scribner, 1987.

Peters, Jean. *The Bookman's Glossary*. New York: Bowker, 1983.

*Plant, M. *The English Book Trade, or Economic History of the Making and Sale of Books*. London: Allen and Unwin, 1974. 3rd ed.

Plomer, H. R. *A Dictionary of the Printers and Booksellers Who Were at Work in England, Scotland and Ireland from 1668 to 1725*. London: Bibliographical Society, 1922.

—. *Wynkyn de Worde and His Contemporaries from the Death of Caxton to 1535*. London: Grafton / New York: Wilson, 1925. Repr. London: Dawson, 1974.

—., G. H. Bushnell, and E. R. Mc. Dix. *A Dictionary of the Printers and Booksellers Who Were at Work in England, Scotland and Ireland from 1726 to 1775*. London: Bibliographical Society, 1932.

Pollard, Alfred W. *Records of the English Bible*. London: Oxford UP, 1911.

—. *Fine Books*. London: Methuen / New York: Putnam, 1912. Repr. 1973.

Pollard, H. G. and A. Ehrman. *The Distribution of Books by Catalogue to 1800*. Cambridge: Privately printed, 1965.

Pottinger, D. T. *The French Book Trade in the Ancien Régime 1500-1791*. Cambridge: Harvard UP, 1958.

The Publishers' Circular 1837-1900 and The English Catalogue of Books. Ed. Simon

Eliot and John Sutherland. Cambridge: Chadwyck-Healey, 1992.

Publishing, The Booktrade and the Diffusion of Knowledge. Ed. R. C. Alston and H. Fellner. Cambridge: Chadwyck-Healey, 1992.

Ransom, Will. *Private Presses and Their Books*. New York: Bowker, 1929.

Ray, Gordon N. *The Art of the French Illustrated Book: 1700–1914*. New York: Pierpont Morgan / Ithaca: Cornell UP, 1982. 2 vols. Repr. New York: Dover, 1986.

Records of the Worshipful Company of Stationers and Newspaper Makers. Stationers' Hall, London EC4M 7DD.

Reidy, Denis V., ed. *The Italian Book, 1465–1800: Studies Presented to Dennis E. Rhodes*. London: British Library, 1993.

Renouard, A. *Annales de l'imprimerie des Aldes*. Paris: Renouard, 1834. 3rd ed.

Richardson, Brian. *Print Culture in Renaissance Italy: The Editor and the Vernacular Text*. Cambridge: Cambridge UP, 1994.

Rider, Philip, Paul Werstine, William P. Williams, and O M Brack, Jr., "Research Opportunities in the Early English Book Trade." *Analytical and Enumerative Bibliography* 3 (1979): 165–200.

Rogers, Bruce. *Paragraphs on Printing*. New York: Rudge, 1943. Repr. New York: Dover, 1979.

Rosner, C. *The Growth of the Book-Jacket*. Cambridge: Harvard UP, 1954.

Saint Bride Foundation Catalogue of the Technical Reference Library of Works on Printing and the Allied Arts. London: Saint Bride, 1919.

Sale, William M. *Samuel Richardson, Master Printer*. Ithaca: Cornell UP, 1950.

Savage, W. A. *A Dictionary of the Art of Printing*. London: Longman, 1841. Repr. London: Gregg, 1966.

Schreiber, Fred. *The Hanes Collection of Estienne Publications: From Book Collecting to Scholarly Resource*. Chapel Hill: Hanes Foundation / U of North Carolina U Library, 1984.

Schwab, Richard N. et al. "Cyclotron Analysis of the Ink in the Forty-Two Line Bible." *Papers of the Bibliographical Society of America*. 77 (1983): 285–315.

—. "Ink Patterns in the Gutenberg New Testament: The Proton Milliprobe Analysis of the Lilly Library Copy." *Papers of the Bibliographical Society of America* 80:(1986): 305–31.

—. "The Proton Milliprobe Ink Analysis of the Harvard B42, Volume II." *Papers of the Bibliographical Society of America* 81: (1987): 403–32.

Sheavyn, Phoebe. *The Literary Profession in the Elizabethan Age*. Manchester: Manchester UP, 1909. Rev. ed. Manchester: Manchester UP / New York: Barnes and Noble, 1967.

Shillingsburg, Peter L. *Pegasus in Harness: Victorian Publishing and W. M. Thackeray*. Charlottesville: UP of Virginia, 1992.

Short, Sir Frank. *Etchings and Engravings*. Rev. M. Osborne. London: Print Collectors' Club, 1952. 3rd ed.

Shorter, Alfred H. *Paper-Mills in England 1495–1860*. Hilversum: Paper Publications Society, 1957. Repr. Newton Abbott: David and Charles, 1971.

—. *Studies on the History of Paper-Making in Britain*. Ed. Richard L. Hills. Aldershot: Variorum, 1993.

Silver, Rollo G. *Typefounding in America 1787–1825*. Charlottesville: UP of Virginia, 1965.

—. *The American Printer 1787–1825*. Charlottesville: UP of Virginia, 1967.

*Simpson, Percy. *Proof-Reading in the Sixteenth, Seventeenth and Eighteenth Centuries*. Oxford: Clarendon, 1935. Repr. 1970.

Southward, J. *Practical Printing*. London: Printers' Register Office, 1892. 4th ed. Repr. New York: Garland, 1980 (of 1882 ed).

Sparling, Henry H. *The Kelmscott Press and William Morris, Mastercraftsman*. London: Macmillan, 1924.

*Steinberg, S. H. *Five Hundred Years of Printing*. Harmondsworth: Penguin, 1961.

2nd ed. (3rd ed. 1968).

Stokes, Roy. ed. *Esdaile's Manual of Bibliography*. New York: Scarecrow, 1981. 5th ed.

Stower, C. *The Printer's Grammar*. London: Crosby, 1808. Repr. London: Gregg, 1965.

Straus, Ralph. *The Unspeakable Curll*. London: Chapman and Hall, 1927.

Tanis, James and John Dooley. *Bookbinding in America 1680–1910 from the Collection of Frederick E. Maser*. Charlottesville: UP of Virginia, 1983.

Tanselle, G. Thomas. "The Historiography of American Literary Publishing." *Studies in Bibliography* 18 (1965): 3–39.

—. "Copyright Records and the Bibliographer." *Studies in Bibliography* 22 (1969): 77–124.

—. "The Latest Forms of Book-Burning." *Common Knowledge*. Forthcoming.

(See also items under Tanselle in Chapters 4 and 7.)

Tebbel, John. *A History of Book Publishing in the United States*. New York: Bowker, 1972–81.

Thomas, Alan G. *Great Books and Book Collectors*. New York: Excalibur, 1975.

Trapp, J. B., ed. *Manuscripts in the Fifty Years after the Invention of Printing*. London: Warburg Institute, 1983.

Tribble, Evelyn B. *Margins and Marginality: The Printed Page in Early Modern England*. Charlottesville: UP of Virginia, 1993.

Turner, Mary C. *The Bookman's Glossary*. New York: Bowker, 1961. 4th ed.

*Vervliet, H. D. L. *The Book Through Five Thousand Years*. London: Phaidon, 1972.

Wallis, L. W. *A Concise Chronology of Typesetting Development 1889–1986*. London: Wynkyn de Worde Society, 1988.

Walters, Gwyn. "Developments in the Study of Book Illustration." *The Book Encompassed*. Ed. Peter Davison. Cambridge: Cambridge UP, 1992: 142–150.

Warner, Michael. *The Letters of the Republic: Publication and the Public Sphere in Eighteenth-Century America*. Cambridge: Harvard UP, 1992.

Watt, Alexander. *The Art of Paper-Making*. London: Lockwood, 1890.

Watt, Tessa. *Cheap Print and Popular Piety, 1550–1640*. Cambridge: Cambridge UP, 1991.

Weiterkampf, Frank. *The Illustrated Book*. Cambridge: Harvard UP, 1938.

West, James L. W., III. *American Authors and the Literary Marketplace since 1900*. Philadelphia: U of Pennsylvania P, 1988.

—. "The Chace Act and Anglo-American Literary Relations." *Studies in Bibliography* 45 (1992): 303–311.

Wiborg, Frank B. *Printing Ink: A History*. New York: Harper, 1926.

Williams, George Walton. "Setting by Formes in Quarto Printing." *Studies in Bibliography* 11 (1958): 39–53.

*Williams, William Proctor and Craig S. Abbott. *An Introduction to Bibliographical and Textual Studies*. New York: MLA, 1989. 2nd ed.

Willis, J. H., Jr. *Leonard and Virginia Woolf as Publishers: The Hogarth Press, 1917–41*. Charlottesville: UP of Virginia, 1992.

Willison, Ian. *The History of the Book in Twentieth-Century Britain and America*. James Russell Wiggins Lecture in the History of the Book in American Culture. Worcester: American Antiquarian Society, 1992.

Willoughby, Edwin E. *A Printer of Shakespeare: The Books and Times of William Jaggard*. London: Allen and Unwin, 1934. Repr. New York: Haskell H, 1970.

Wilson, Adrian. *The Design of Books*. New York: Reinhold, 1967 / Salt Lake City: Peregrine Smith, 1976.

Winterich, John T. *Early American Books and Printing*. Boston: Houghton Mifflin, 1935. Repr. New York: Dover, 1981.

Won-Young, Kim. *Early Moveable Type in Korea*. Seoul: Eul-Yu, 1954.

Wroth, L. C., ed. *A History of the Printed Book, Being the Third Number of the Dolphin*. New York: Limited Editions Club, 1938.

—. *The Colonial Printer*. Portland, ME: Southworth-Anthoensen, 1938. Charlottesville: Dominion, 1964. 2nd ed.

Zaehnsdorf, J. W. *The Art of Bookbinding*. London: Bell, 1890. 2nd ed. Repr. Farnborough: Gregg, 1967.

Chapter 4: Descriptive Bibliography

Bartlett, Henrietta C. and Alfred W. Pollard. *A Census of Shakespeare's Plays in Quarto 1594–1709*. New Haven: Yale UP, 1939. Rev. Bartlett.

Bloomfield, B. C. and Edward Mendelson. *W. H. Auden: A Bibliography 1924–1969*. Charlottesville: UP of Virginia, 1972. 2nd ed.

Bowers, Fredson. "Certain Basic Problems in Descriptive Bibliography." *Papers of the Bibliographical Society of America* 42 (1948): 211–28.

*—. *Principles of Bibliographical Description*. Princeton: Princeton UP, 1949. Repr. New York: Russell, 1962.

*—. "Purposes of Descriptive Bibliography, with Some Remarks on Methods." *The Library* Fifth Series 8 (1953): 1–22. Repr. *Essays*: 111–34.

—. *Essays in Bibliography, Text, and Editing*. Charlottesville: UP of Virginia, 1975.

*Briquet, C. M. *Les Filigranes: Dictionnaire historique des marques du papier des leur apparition vers 1282 jusqu'en 1600*. Paris: Picard, 1923. Repr. New York: Hacker, 1966, Amsterdam: Paper Publications Society, 1968. 4 vols.

Bruccoli, Matthew. *F. Scott Fitzgerald: A Descriptive Bibliography*. Pittsburgh: U of Pittsburgh P, 1972.

Bühler, Curt F., J. G. McManaway, and L. C. Wroth. *Standards of Bibliographical Description*. Philadelphia: U of Pennsylvania P, 1949. Repr. High Wycombe: Univ. Microfilms, 1971 and Westport: Greenwood, 1973.

Carpenter, Kenneth. "The Bibliographical Description of Translations." *Papers of the Bibliographical Society of America* 76 (1982): 253–71.

Carter, John. *Binding Variants in English Publishing 1820–1900*. London: Constable / New York: Lang and Smith, 1932.

Chapman, R. W. *Cancels*. London: Constable, 1930.

Churchill, W. A. *Watermarks in Paper in Holland, England, France etc. in the XVII and XVIII Centuries and Their Interconnection*. Amsterdam: Hertzberger, 1935/1965.

Davies, Hugh W. *Devices of the Early Printers 1457–1560: Their History and Development*. London: Grafton, 1935. Repr. Hildesheim: G. Olms, 1969, London: Dawsons, 1974.

Duff, E. Gordon. *Early English Printing . . . Facsimiles of All Types Used in England During the XV Century*. London: Kegan Paul, 1896. Repr. New York: B. Franklin, 1970.

Ford, H. L. *Shakespeare 1700–1740: A Collation of the Editions and Separate Plays*. New York: B. Bloom, 1968.

Foxon, D. F. *Thoughts on the History and Future of Bibliographical Description*. Berkeley: U of California P, 1970.

Gaskell, Philip. *Bibliography of the Foulis Press*. London: Hart–Davis, 1964.

*—. *New Introduction to Bibliography*. Oxford: Oxford UP, 1972. Repr. with corrections, 1985.

Gerritsen, Johann. "The Thorkelin Transcripts of *Beowulf*: A Codicological Description, with Notes on Their Genesis and History." *The Library* Sixth Series 13 (1991): 1–22.

Gilson, David. *A Bibliography of Jane Austen*. Oxford: Clarendon, 1892.

Grimshaw, James A., Jr. *Robert Penn Warren: A Descriptive Bibliography*

1922-1979. Charlottesville: UP of Virginia, 1981.

Heawood, E. *Watermarks Mainly in the 17th and 18th Centuries*. Hilversum: Paper Publications Society, 1950. Repr. Amsterdam: Paper Publications Society / Edward Arnold, 1970.

Howard-Hill, T. H. "Enumerative and Descriptive Bibliography." *The Book Encompassed*. Ed. Peter Davison. Cambridge: Cambridge UP, 1992: 122–129.

Jackson, William A. *Records of a Bibliographer: Selected Papers of William Alexander Jackson*. Ed. William H. Bond. Cambridge: Belknap / Harvard UP, 1967.

Johnson, Alfred F. *A Catalogue of Engraved and Etched English Title-Pages*. London: Oxford UP for the Bibliographical Society, 1934.

Jones, John B., ed. *Readings in Descriptive Bibliography*. Kent: Kent State UP, 1974.

Madan, Falconer, "Degressive Bibliography: A Memorandum." *Transactions of the Bibliographical Society* 9 (1906–08): 53–65.

Maynard, Joe and Barry Miles. *William S. Burroughs: A Bibliography, 1953–73*. Charlottesville: UP of Virginia, 1978.

*McKerrow, R. B. *A Dictionary of Printers and Booksellers in England, Scotland and Ireland, and of Foreign Printers of English Books, 1557–1640*. London: Bibliographical Society, 1910. Repr. 1968.

*—. *Printers' and Publishers' Devices in England and Scotland, 1485–1640*. Oxford: Bibliographical Society, 1913. Repr. 1949.

*—. *An Introduction to Bibliography for Literary Students*. Oxford: Oxford UP, 1927.

— and F. S. Ferguson. *Title-Page Borders Used in England and Scotland, 1485–1640*. Oxford: Bibliographical Society, 1932. (See also *The Library*, Fourth Series, 17 (1936): 264–311.)

Meriwether, James B. and Joseph Katz. "A Redefinition of 'Issue'." *Proof* 2 (1972): 61–70.

Mosley, James. "Introduction," *Catalogue of Specimens of Printing Types*. New York: Garland, 1983.

Myerson, Joel. *Ralph Waldo Emerson: A Descriptive Bibliography*. Pittsburgh: U of Pittsburgh P, 1982.

—. *Walt Whitman: A Descriptive Bibliography*. Pittsburgh: Pittsburgh UP, 1993.

Peters, Jean. *The Bookman's Glossary*. New York: Bowker, 1983.

Pollard, Alfred W. *Shakespeare Folios and Quartos: A Study in the Bibliography of Shakespeare's Plays 1594–1685*. New York: Cooper Square, 1970. Repr. of 1909 ed.

Pouncey, Lorene. "The Fallacy of the Ideal Copy." *The Library* Fifth Series 33 (1978): 108–18.

Povey, Kenneth. "A Century of Press Figures." *The Library* Fifth Series 14 (1959): 251–73.

—. "Working to Rule, 1600–1800: A Study of Pressmen's Practice." *The Library* Fifth Series 20 (1965): 13–54.

Sadleir, Michael. *The Evolution of Publishers' Binding Styles 1770–1900*. London: Constable / New York: R. R. Smith, 1930.

Sayce, R. A. "Compositorial Practices and the Localization of Printed Books 1530–1800." *The Library* Fifth Series 21 (1966): 1–45.

Scholderer, V. *Fifty Essays in Fifteenth- and Sixteenth-Century Bibliography*. Amsterdam: Menno Hertzberger, 1967.

Simpson, Percy. *Proof-Reading in the Sixteenth, Seventeenth and Eighteenth Centuries*. Oxford: Clarendon, 1935. Repr. 1970.

Spector, Stephen. "Symmetry in Watermark Sequences." *Studies in Bibliography* 31 (1978): 162–78.

Stokes, Roy, ed. *Esdaile's Manual of Bibliography*. New York: Scarecrow, 1981. 5th ed.

Tanselle, G. Thomas. "Press Figures in America: Some Preliminary Observations." *Studies in Bibliography* 19 (1966): 123–60.

—. "The Recording of Press Figures." *The Library* Fifth Series 21 (1966): 318–25.

—. "A System of Color Identification for Bibliographical Description." *Studies in Bibliography* 20 (1967): 203–34.

—. "The Identification of Type Faces in Bibliographical Description." *The Library* Fifth Series 26 (1968): 1–12.

—. "The Descriptive Bibliography of American Authors." *Studies in Bibliography* 21 (1968): 1–24.

—. "Tolerances in Bibliographical Description." *The Library* Fifth Series 23 (1968): 1–12.

—. "The Use of Type Damage as Evidence in Bibliographical Description." *The Library* Fifth Series 23 (1968): 328–51.

—. "Copyright Records and the Bibliographer." *Studies in Bibliography* 22 (1969): 77–124.

—. "The Bibliographical Description of Patterns." *Studies in Bibliography* 23 (1970): 71–102.

—. "The Bibliographical Description of Paper." *Studies in Bibliography* 24 (1971): 27–67.

—. "Book Jackets, Blurbs and Bibliographers." *The Library* 26 (1971): 91–134.

—. "The Bibliographical Concept of 'Issue' and 'State'." *Papers of the Bibliographical Society of America* 69 (1975): 17–66.

—. "Descriptive Bibliography and Library Cataloguing." *Studies in Bibliography* 30 (1977): 1–56.

*—. "The Concept of Ideal Copy." *Studies in Bibliography* 33 (1980): 18–53.

—. "The Description of Non-Letterpress Material in Books." *Studies in Bibliography* 35 (1982): 1–42.

*—. "The Arrangement of Descriptive Bibliographies." *Studies in Bibliography* 37 (1984): 1–38.

*—. "Title-Page Transcription and Signature Collation Reconsidered." *Studies in Bibliography* 38 (1985): 45–81.

*—. "A Sample Bibliographical Description, with Commentary." *Studies in Bibliography* 40 (1987): 1–30.

*—. "A Description of Descriptive Bibliography." *Studies in Bibliography* 45 (1992): 1–30. Repr. as pamphlet, Washington: Library of Congress / Center for the Book, 1992.

Todd, William B. "Observations on the Incidence and Interpretation of Press Figures." *Studies in Bibliography* 3 (1950–51): 171–205.

—. "On the Use of Advertisements in Bibliographical Studies." *The Library* Fifth Series 8 (1953): 174–87.

—. *A Bibliography of William Burke.* London: Hart-Davis, 1964.

Turner, Mary C. *The Bookman's Glossary.* New York: Bowker, 1961. 4th ed.

Tyacke, Sarah. "Describing Maps." *The Book Encompassed.* Ed. Peter Davison. Cambridge: Cambridge UP, 1992: 130–141.

Vander Meulen, David. "The Identification of Paper without Watermarks." *The Library* Fifth Series 37 (1984): 58–81.

—. "The History and Future of Bowers's *Principles.*" *Papers of the Bibliographical Society of America* 79 (1985): 197–219.

—. "*The Dunciad in Four Books* and the Bibliography of Pope." *Papers of the Bibliographical Society of America* 83 (1989): 293–310.

Van Hoesen, Henry Bartlett. *Bibliography: Practical, Enumerative, Historical.* New York: B. Franklin, 1971. Repr. of 1928 ed.

West, James L. W., III. "The Bibliographical Concept of Plating." *Studies in Bibliography* 36 (1983): 252–66.

*Williams, William Proctor and Craig S. Abbott. *An Introduction to Bibliographical* and Textual Studies. New York: MLA, 1989. 2nd ed.

Working Group on the International Standard Bibliographical Description. London: IFLA Committee on Cataloguing, 1971.

Chapter 5: Paleography

Archiv für Diplomatik, Schriftgeschichte, Siegel- und Wappenkunde. Munich / Cologne: 1955– .

Arndt, Wilhelm. Schrifttafeln zur Erlernung der lateinischen Paläographie. Berlin: Grote, 1904–29. 4th ed. 3 vols.

Autenrieth, Johanne, ed. Datierte Handschriften in Bibliotheken der Bundesrepublik Deutschland. Stuttgart: Powitz, 1984.

Avrin, Leila. Scribes, Script and Books: The Book Arts from Antiquity to the Renaissance. London: British Library, 1991.

Barber, Peter. Diplomacy. London: British Library, 1979.

Battelli, Giulio. Lezioni di paleografia. Rome: Vatican Library, 1949. 3rd ed.

Bergh, B. Palaeography and Textual Criticism. Lund: Laromede / Gleerup, 1979–80.

Bergkamp, Joseph U. Dom Jean Mabillon and the Benedictine Historical School of Saint-Maur. Diss. Catholic U of America. Washington: 1928.

Bieler, L. "Insular Palaeography: Present State and Problems." Scriptorium 3 (1949): 267–94.

*Bischoff, Bernhard. Latin Palaeography: Antiquity and the Middle Ages. Trans. Daibhí Ó Cróinín and David Ganz. Cambridge: Cambridge UP, 1990.

Bishop, T. A. M. English Caroline Minuscule. Oxford: Clarendon P, 1971.

Boyle, Leonard E. "The Emergence of Gothic Handwriting." Journal of Typographical Research 4 (1970): 307–16.

*—. Medieval Latin Palaeography: A Bibliographical Introduction. Toronto: U of Toronto P, 1984.

Bridges, M. M. A New Handwriting for Teachers. London: 1898.

Bruckner, Albert and Robert Marichal, eds. Chartæ latinæ antiquiores. Facsimile Editions of the Latin Charters Prior to the Ninth Century. Dietikon / Zürich: Urs Graf, 1969– . 7 vols.

Burnell, Arthur C. Elements of South-Indian Palaeography from the Fourth to the Seventeenth Century A.D., Being an Introduction to the Study of South-Indian Inscriptions and MSS. London: Trübner, 1878. 2nd ed.

Cagnat, René L. V. Cours d'epigraphie latine. Rome: Bretschneider, 1964. 4th ed.

*Capelli, Adriano. The Elements of Abbreviation in Medieval Latin Paleography. Trans. David Heimann and Richard Kay. Lawrence: U of Kansas Libraries, 1982.

Catalogo dei manoscritti latina datati o databili. Ed. Viviana Jemolo and Francesca di Cesare. Turin: 1971–82. 2 vols.

Catalogue of the Dated Manuscripts Written in the Latin Script from the Beginnings of the Middle Ages to 1550 in the Libraries of Switzerland. Dietikon-Zürich: 1977.

Chassant, Alphonse Antoine Louis. Dictionnaire des abréviationes latines et françaises usitées dans les inscriptions lapidaires et metalliques, les manuscrits et les chartes du moyen âge. Paris: Martin, 1884. 5th ed.

Chatelain, É. La paléographie des classiques latins. Paris: Hachette, 1884–1900.

Chroust, Anton. Monumenta palaeographica, Denkmäler der Schreibkunst des Mittelalters. Munich 1902–17 (Series 1 and 2); Leipzig: 1931–40 (Series 3).

Clemoes, Peter et al., eds. Early English Manuscripts in Facsimile. Copenhagen: Rosenkilde and Baggar / Baltimore: Johns Hopkins UP, 1951– .

Codices Manuscripti: Zeitschrift für Handschriftkunde. Vienna: 1974– .

Codices Selecti. Graz: Akademische Druck- und Verlangsanstalt, 1960– .

Coulmas, Florian. The Writing Systems of the World. Oxford: Blackwell, 1989.

*Croft, P. J. Autograph Poetry in the English Language: Facsimiles of Original

Manuscripts from the Fourteenth to Twentieth Centuries. London: Cassell, 1973. 2 vols.

Crous, E. and J. Kirchner. *Die gotischen Schriftarten*. Leipzig: Klinkhardt and Biermann, 1928.

Davis, Tom. "The Analysis of Handwriting: An Introductory Survey." *The Book Encompassed*. Ed. Peter Davison. Cambridge: Cambridge UP, 1992: 57–68.

Dawson, G. E. and L. Kennedy-Skipton. *Elizabethan Handwriting 1500–1650*. Toronto: McLeod / New York: Norton, 1966.

Day, Lewis F. *Penmanship of the XVI, XVII & XVIIIth. Centuries*. New York: Pentalic / Taplinger, 1979.

De la Mare, A. C. *The Handwriting of Italian Humanists*. Oxford: Oxford UP, 1973.

Degering, Hermann. *Die Schrift. Atlas der Schriftformen des Abendlandes vom Altertum bis zum Ausgang des 18. Jahrhunderts*. Tübingen: Wasmuth, 1952. 3rd ed. Trans. as *Lettering: Modes of Writing in Western Europe from Antiquity to the Eighteenth Century*. London: Benn, 1929. Repr. New York: Pentalic, 1965.

Delisle, L. *Le cabinet des manuscrits de la Bibliothèque Nationale*. Paris: 1868–81. 4 vols.

*Denholm-Young, Noel. *Handwriting in England and Wales*. Cardiff: U of Wales P, 1964.

Doane, A. N. and Philip Pulsiano, eds. *Anglo-Saxon Manuscripts in Microfiche Facsimile*. Binghamton: Medieval & Renaissance Texts and Studies, 1993- .

*Drogin, Marc. *Medieval Calligraphy: Its History and Technique*. Montclair: Allanheld & Schram / London: Prior, 1980.

Elliott, Ralph W. V. *Runes: An Introduction*. Manchester: Manchester UP, 1963.

Evetis, L. C. *Roman Lettering: A Study of . . . the Trajan Column [and] . . . Lettering in Britain*. New York: Pentalic / Taplinger, 1979.

*Fairbank, A. *A Book of Scripts*. Harmondsworth: King Penguin Books, 1949. Rev. 1960.

—. *A Handwriting Manual*. London: Faber, 1954.

— and R. W. Hunt. *Humanistic Script of the Fifteenth and Sixteenth Centuries*. Oxford: Bodleian Library, 1960.

— and Berthold. L. Wolpe. *Renaissance Handwriting: An Anthology of Italic Scripts*. London: Faber / Cleveland: World, 1960.

—. *The Story of Handwriting: Origins and Development*. London: Faber, 1970.

Facsimiles of Ancient Manuscripts. Ed. J. P. Gilson, E. M. Thompson, and G. F. Warner. *First Series*. London: New Palaeographical Society, 1903–12; *Second Series*. 1913–32; *Indices*. 1914, 1932.

Facsimiles of Manuscripts and Inscriptions. Ed. E. A. Bond, E. M. Thompson, and G. F. Warner. *First Series*. London: Clowes / Palaeographical Society, 1873–83; *Second Series*. London: 1884–94; *Indices*. 1901.

Fichtenau, Heinrich. *Mensch und Schrift im Mittelalter*. Vienna: Universum, 1946.

*Foerster, Hans. *Abriss der lateinischen Paläographie*. Stuttgart: Hiersemann, 1963. 2nd ed.

Gaur, Albertine. *A History of Writing*. London: British Library, rev. ed. 1993.

Goldberg, Jonathan. *Writing Matter: From the Hands of the English Renaissance*. Stanford: Stanford UP, 1990.

Gordon, A. E. and J. S. Gordon. *Contributions to the Palaeography of Latin Inscriptions*. Berkeley: U of California P, 1957.

Gordon, Cyrus H. *Forgotten Scripts: Their Ongoing Discovery and Decipherment*. New York: Basic Books. Rev. ed. 1982.

Gourdie, T. *Italic Handwriting*. London / New York: Studio, 1955.

Greetham, D. C. "Normalisation of Accidentals in Middle English Texts: The Paradox of Thomas Hoccleve." *Studies in Bibliography* 38 (1985): 121–50.

Grieve, Hilda E. P. *Examples of English Handwriting 1150–1750, with Transcripts and Translations*. Chelmsford: Essex Record Office, 1954.

Groningen, Bertrand A. *Short Manual of Palaeography*. Leyden: Sijthoff, 1967. 2nd ed.

Heal, A. *The English Writing-Masters and Their Copy-Books 1570–1800*. Cambridge: Cambridge UP, 1931.

Healey, John F. *The Early Alphabet*. Berkeley: U of California P / British Museum, 1990.

Hector, L. C. *The Handwriting of English Documents*. London: 1966.

Heinemeyer, Walter. *Studien zur Geschichte der gotischen Urkundenschrift*. Cologne: Böhlau, 1962.

Hill, G. F. *The Development of Arabic Numerals in Europe Exhibited in Sixty-Four Tables*. Oxford: Clarendon, 1915.

Hofstadter, Douglas R. *Metamagical Themas: Questing for the Essence of Mind and Pattern*. New York: Basic Books, 1985. Repr. New York: Bantam, 1986.

Honemann, Volker and Nigel F. Palmer, eds. *Deutsche Handschriften 1100–1400*. Oxford Colloquium 1985. Tübingen: Niemeyer, 1988.

Hübner, Emil. *Exempla scripturæ epigraphicæ latinæ*. Berlin: Reimerus, 1885.

*Jackson, Donald. *The Story of Writing*. New York: Taplinger, 1981.

Ingram, William H. "The Ligatures of Early Printed Greek." *Greek, Roman, & Byzantine Studies* 7 (1966): 371–89.

Jenkinson, Hilary. *The Later Court Hands in England from the Fifteenth to the Seventeenth Century: Illustrated from the Common Paper of the Scrivener's Company of London, the English Writing Masters, and the Public Records*. Cambridge: Cambridge UP, 1927.

—. *Palaeography and the Practical Study of Court Hand*. Cambridge: Cambridge UP, 1915.

Jessen, Peter. *Masterpieces of Calligraphy 1500–1800*. New York: Dover, 1981.

John, James J. "Latin Palaeography." *Medieval Studies, An Introduction*. Ed. James M. Powell. Syracuse, NY: 1976: 1–68.

*Johnson, Charles and Hilary Jenkinson. *English Court Hand, A.D. 1066 to 1500, Illustrated Chiefly from the Public Records*. Oxford: Clarendon, 1915. Repr. New York: Ungar, 1967. 2 vols.

*Johnston, Edward. *Writing, & Illuminating, & Lettering*. London: Pitman, 1906. Repr. New York: Taplinger, 1977.

— and Eric Gill. *Manuscript and Inscription Letters for Schools and Classes and for the Use of Craftsmen*. London: Hogg, 1909. Repr. London: Pitman, 1950.

Judge, C. B. *Specimens of Sixteenth-Century English Handwriting*. Cambridge: Harvard UP, 1935.

Katalog der datierten Handschriften in lateinischer Schrift in Österreich. Vienna: 1969– .

Killough, George B. "Middle English Verse Punctuation: A Sample Survey." *Text* 4 (1988): 163–188.

Kirchner, Joachim. *Scriptura latina libraria a sæculo primo usque ad finem medii ævi*. Munich: Oldenbourg, 1955. Repr. 1970.

—. *Scriptum gothica libraria a sæculo 12 usque ad finem medii ævi*. Munich / Vienna: Oldenbourg, 1970.

Kirkham, E. Kay. *Handwriting of American Records for a Period of 300 Years*. Logan, UT: Everton, 1973.

Knight, Stan. *Historical Scripts: A Handbook for Calligraphers*. New York: Taplinger, 1986.

Koehler, Wilhelm. *Die karolingischen Miniaturen*. Berlin: 1930–60. 3 vols.

Lindsay, W. M. *Contractions in Early Latin Minuscule Manuscripts*. Oxford: Parker, 1908.

—. *Early Irish Minuscule Script*. Oxford: Parker, 1910.

*—. *Notæ Latinæ, An Account of Abbreviation in Latin Manuscripts of the Early Minuscule Period (ca. 700–850): Supplement*, by D. Bains. Hildesheim: Olm, 1965.

2nd ed.

Lowe, E. A. *The Beneventan Script: A History of the South Italian Minuscule*. Oxford: Clarendon, 1914.

*—. *Codices latini antiquiores*. Oxford: Oxford UP, 1934–71, 11 vols. plus supplement.

—. *Handwriting: Our Medieval Legacy*. Rome: Edizioni di storia e litteratura, 1969.

—. *Palaeographical Papers, 1907–1965*. Ed. L. Bieler. Oxford: Oxford UP, 1972. 2 vols.

Mabillon, Jean. *De re diplomatica libri sex in quibus quidquid ad veterum instrumentorum antiquitatem, materiam, scripturam et stilum: quidquid ad sigilla, monogrammata, subscriptiones ac notas chronologicas; quidquid inde ad antiquariam, historicam, forensemque disciplinam pertinet, explicatur et illustratur*. Paris: Robustel, 1681. 2nd ed. 1709.

Mallon, Jean, Robert Marichal, and Carolus Silva-Tarouca. *L'écriture latine de la capitale romaine à la minuscule*. Paris: Arts et métiers, 1939.

—. *De l'écriture, receuil d'études*. Paris: 1982.

Manitius, M. *Handschriften antiker Autoren in mittelalterlichen Bibliothekskatalogen, Zentralblatt für Bibliothekswesen*. Leipzig: Harrossowitz, 1935.

Martin, Charles Trice. *Record Interpreter: A Collection of Abbreviations, Latin Words, and Names Used in English Historical Manuscripts and Records*. London: Stevens, 1910. 2nd ed.

Medieval and Renaissance Manuscripts. New York: Pierpont Morgan Library, 1974.

Merkelbach, Reinhold. *Lateinisch Lesehaft zur Einführung in Paläographie und Textkritik*. Göttingen: Vandenhoeck and Ruprecht, 1969.

Metzger, Bruce M. *Manuscripts of the Greek Bible, an Introduction to Greek Palaeography*. New York and Oxford: Oxford UP, 1981.

Millares Carlo, Agustín. *Tratado de paleografía española*. Madrid: Espasa-Calpe, 1983. 3rd ed.

Morison, Stanley. *The Calligraphic Models of Ludovico degli Arrighi*. Paris: Frederic Warde, 1926.

—. *Notes on the Development of the Latin Script from Early to Modern Times*. Cambridge: Cambridge UP, 1949.

—. *American Copybooks*. Philadelphia: Fell, 1951.

—. *Politics and Script*. Oxford: Clarendon, 1972.

Nash, Ray. *American Penmanship 1800–1850: A History of Writing and a Bibliography of Copybooks from Jankins to Spencer*. Worcester: American Antiquarian Society, 1969.

—. *American Writing Masters and Copybooks: History and Bibliography through Colonial Times*. Boston: Colonial Society of Massachusetts, 1959.

Ogg, D. *Three Classics of Italian Calligraphy: An Unabridged Reissue of the Writing Books of Arrighi, Tagliente, Palatino*. New York: Dover, 1953.

Ohlgren, Thomas H., ed. *Insular and Anglo-Saxon Illuminated Manuscripts: An Iconographic Catalogue ca. A.D. 625 to 1100*. New York: Garland, 1986.

Paap, A. H. R. E. *Nomina Sacra in the Greek Papyri of the First Five Centuries A.D.: The Sources and Some Deductions*. Leiden: Brill, 1959.

Pächt, O. and J. G. Alexander. *Illuminated Manuscripts in the Bodleian Library, Oxford*. Oxford: Clarendon, 1973. 3 vols.

Page, R. I. *An Introduction to English Runes*. London: Methuen / New York: Harper, 1973.

Palaima, Thomas G. "Secondary Criteria for Identifying Scribal Hands: Interdisciplinary Considerations," *Text* 2 (1985): 55–68.

*Parkes, M. B. *English Cursive Book Hands, 1250–1500*. Berkeley: U of California P, 1980.

—. *Scribes, Scripts and Readers*. London: Hambledon, 1991.

*—. *Pause and Effect: An Introduction to the History of Punctuation in the West*.

Berkeley: U of California P, 1993.

*Petti, Anthony G. *English Literary Hands from Chaucer to Dryden*. London: Arnold, 1977.

Petzet, Erich. *Deutsche Schrifttafeln des IX bis XV Jahrhunderts*. Hildesheim: Olms, 1975.

Poulle, Emmanuel. *Paléographie des écritures cursives en France du XVe au XVIIe siècle*. Geneva: Droz, 1966.

*Preston, Jean F. and Laetitia Yeandle. *English Handwriting 1400–1650: An Introductory Manual*. Binghamton: Pegasus, 1991.

Prou, M. *Manuel de paléographie latine et française du VIe au XVIIe siècle*. Paris: Picard, 1892–1904. 3 vols.

*Reusens, E. *Eléments de paléographie*. Louvain: Privately printed, 1899. Repr. Brussels: Moorthamus, 1963.

Robb, David M. *The Art of the Illuminated Manuscript*. Cranbury: Barnes / Philadelphia Art Alliance, 1973.

Robinson, Fred C. and E. G. Stanley, eds. *Old English Verse from Many Sources: A Comprehensive Collection*. Early English Manuscripts in Facsimile 23. Copenhagen: Rosenkilde, 1990.

Samaran, Charles and Robert Marichal. *Catalogue des manuscrits en écriture latine portant des indications de date, lieu ou de copiste*. Paris: CNRS, 1959- .

Sattler, P. and G. von Selle. *Bibliographie zur Geschichte der Schrift bis in das Jahr 1930*. Linz: Winkler, 1935.

Saunders, O. E. *English Illumination*. Florence: Pantheon, 1928. 2 vols.

Schimmel, A. *Calligraphy and Islamic Culture*. New York: NYU P, 1984.

Schools of Illumination: Reproductions from Manuscripts in the British Museum. London: British Museum, 1914–22. 4 vols.

Seider, Richard. *Paläographie der lateinischen Papyri*. Stuttgart: Hiersemann, 1972–78.

Senner, Wayne M., ed. *The Origins of Writing*. Lincoln: U of Nebraska P, 1989.

Steffens, F. *Lateinische Paläographie. 100 Tafeln mit einer systematischen Darstellung der lateinischen Schrift*. Berlin / Leipzig: De Gruyter, 1929. 2nd ed. Repr. 1964.

*Stiennon, Jacques and G. Hasenohr. *Paléographie du moyen âge*. Paris: A. Colin, 1973.

Stockwell, Robert P. and C. Westbrook Barritt. "Scribal Practice: Some Assumptions." *Language* 37 (1961): 75–82.

*Tannenbaum, S. A. *The Handwriting of the Renaissance*. New York: F. Ungar, 1967.

*Thompson, E. M. *An Introduction to Greek and Latin Palaeography*. Oxford: Clarendon, 1912. Repr. Chicago: Ares, 1966.

Thompson, Samuel H. *Latin Bookhands of the Later Middle Ages 1100–1500*. Cambridge: Cambridge UP, 1969.

Traube, Ludwig. *Vorlesungen und Abhandlungen*. Ed. F. Boll. Munich: Beck, 1902–20. Repr. 1965. 3 vols.

*—. *Nomina sacra: Versuch einer Geschichte der christlichen Kürzung*. Munich: Beck, 1907. Rev. Darmstadt: Wissenschaftliche Buchgesellschaft, 1967.

Tschichold, Jan. *An Illustrated History of Writing and Lettering*. London: Zwemmer, 1947.

*Ullman, Berthold L. *The Origin and Development of Humanistic Script*. Rome: Edizioni di storia e letteratura, 1960.

*—. *Ancient Writing and its Influence*. London: Harrap / New York: Longman, 1932; Cambridge: MIT, 1969. Repr. Toronto: U of Toronto P, 1980. 2nd ed.

Ullmann, S. O. A. "Dating through Calligraphy: The Example of 'Dover beach'." *Studies in Bibliography* 26 (1973): 19–36.

Van Hoesen, Henry Bartlett. *Roman Cursive Writing*. Princeton: Princeton UP, 1915.

Walker, C. B. F. *Reading the Past: Cuneiform.* Berkeley: U of California P / London: British Library, 1987.

Walter, Johann L. *Lexicon diplomaticvm VIII–XVI C.* Göttingen: Schmidlos, 1745–47. Repr. New York: B. Franklin, 1966.

Wardrop, James. *The Script of Humanism: Some Aspects of Humanistic Script 1460–1560.* Oxford: Clarendon, 1963.

Warner, G. *Illuminated Manuscripts in the British Museum.* London: British Museum, 1899–1903.

—. *British Museum Reproductions of Illuminated Manuscripts.* London: British Museum, 1923.

Wasson, John M. *Early Drama, Art, and Music Documents: A Palaeography Handbook.* Kalamazoo: Medieval Institute Publications, 1993.

*Watson, Andrew G. *Catalogue of Dated and Datable Manuscripts in the Department of Manuscripts in the British Library.* London: British Library, 1979.

*—. *Catalogue of Dated and Datable Manuscripts ca. 435–1600 in Oxford Libraries.* Oxford / New York: Clarendon, 1984.

*Wattenbach, Wilhelm. *Anleitung zur lateinischen Palaeographie.* Leipzig: Hirzel, 1886. Repr. Hildesheim: Gerstenberg, 1971. 4th ed.

—. *Das Schriftwesen im Mittelalter.* Leipzig: 1896. Repr. Graz: Akademische Druck- und Verlangsanstalt, 1958. 3rd ed.

Whalley, J. I. *English Handwriting 1540–1853: An Illustrated Survey.* London: HMSO, 1969.

Wilks, John and A. D. Lacey. *Catalogue of Works Dealing with the Study of Western Palaeography in the Libraries of the University of London.* London: U of London P, 1921.

Woodcock, John. *A Book of Formal Scripts.* Boston: Godine, 1992.

*Wright, C. E. *English Vernacular Hands from the Twelfth to the Fifeenth Centuries.* Oxford: Clarendon, 1960.

Chapter 6: Typography

Barker, Nicolas. *Stanley Morison.* Cambridge: Harvard UP, 1972.

—. "Typography and the Meaning of Words: The Revolution in the Layout of Books in the Eighteenth Century." *Buch und Buchhandel in Europa im achtzehnten Jahrhundert.* Ed. Giles Barber and Bernhard Fabian. Hamburg: Hauswedell, 1981: 126–65.

—. *Aldus Manutius and the Development of Greek Script and Type in the Fifteenth Century.* Sandy Hook: Chiswick, 1985.

—. "Typographic Studies." *The Book Encompassed.* Ed. Peter Davison. Cambridge: Cambridge UP, 1992: 83–92.

Barolini, Helen. *Aldus and His Dream Book.* New York: Italica P, 1992.

Bennett, W. *John Baskerville, The Birmingham Printer.* Birmingham: City of Birmingham School of Printing, 1937–39. 2 vols.

Benton, J. H. *John Baskerville, Typefounder and Printer, 1706–1775.* Boston: Privately printed, 1914.

Berry, W. T. and A. F. Johnson. *Catalogue of Specimens of Printing Types by English and Scottish Printers 1665–1830.* Oxford: Oxford UP, 1935. Rev. with introduction by James Mosley, New York: Garland, 1983.

— and A. F. Johnson. *The Encyclopaedia of Type Faces.* London: Blandford, 1953. 4th ed. 1970.

Blades, William. *The Biography and Typography of William Caxton.* London: Trübner, 1877. Rev. ed. New York: Scribner and Welford, 1882.

*Blumenthal, Joseph. *The Art of the Printed Book.* New York: Pierpont Morgan Library / Boston: Godine, 1973.

*—. *The Printed Book in America*. Boston: Godine, 1977.

Briggs, R. *The Typographical Adventure of William Morris*. London: Chiswick P / Eyre and Spottiswoode, 1957.

Bromwich, John. "The First Book Printed in Anglo-Saxon Type." *Transactions of the Cambridge Bibliographical Society* 3 (1962): 265–71.

Carter, Harry. *A View of Early Typography*. Oxford: Clarendon P, 1969.

Cave, Roderick. *The Private Press*. New York: Watson-Guptill, 1971.

Day, K. *Book Typography 1815–1965 in Europe and the United States of America*. Chicago: U of Chicago P, 1966.

Dibdin, T. F. *Typographical Antiquities. Begun by Joseph Ames, augmented by William Herbert*. London: W. Miller, 1810–19. 4 vols.

Dreyfus, J. G. *Type Specimen Facsimiles*. London: Bowes and Bowes / Putnam, 1963– .

*Duff, E. Gordon. *Early English Printing . . . Facsimiles of All Types Used in England During the XV Century*. London: Kegan Paul, 1896. Repr. New York: B. Franklin, 1970.

Fine Print: A Review for the Arts of the Book. Ed. Sandra Kirschenbaum. 1975– .

Fournier, Pierre S. *Fournier on Typefounding*. Trans. of *Manuel typographique* by Harry Carter. London: Soncino / Fleuron, 1930.

Gill, Eric and René Hague. *Hague and Gill on Printing*. Aylesford: Upton, 1993.

Goudy, Frederic W. *Typologia: Studies in Type Design and Type Making*. Berkeley: U of California P, 1940. Repr. 1977.

—. *A Half-Century of Type-Design and Typography 1895–1945*. Typophiles Chap Book no. 13–14. New York: Typophiles, 1946. 2 vols.

—. *The Alphabet and Elements of Lettering*. Berkeley: U of California P, 1952. Repr. New York: Dover, 1963.

Hofstadter, Douglas R. *Metamagical Themas: Questing for the Essence of Mind and Pattern*. New York: Basic Books, 1985. Repr. New York: Bantam, 1986.

Jaspert, W. P., W. T. Berry, and A. F. Johnson. *The Encyclopaedia of Type Faces*. London: Blandford / New York: Barnes and Noble, 1970. 4th ed.

Johnson, A. F. *Type Designs: Their History and Development*. London: Deutsche, 1966, 3rd ed.

Jones, Herbert. *Stanley Morison Displayed*. London: Muller, 1976.

Koch, Rudolf. *The Little ABC Book of Rudolf Koch*. Boston: Godine, 1976.

Legros, L. A. and J. C. Grant. *Typographical Printing Surfaces*. London: 1916.

Lawson, Alexander. *Anatomy of a Typeface*. Boston: Godine, 1990.

Lowry, Martin. *The World of Aldus Manutius*. London, 1979.

—. *Nicholas Jenson and the Rise of Venetian Publishing in Renaissance Europe*. Oxford: Blackwell, 1991.

Macrae, John F. *Two Centuries of Typefounding: Annals of the Letter Foundry Established by William Caslon in . . . 1720*. London: G. W. Jones, 1920.

Mores, E. R. *A Dissertation upon English Typographical Founders and Founderies*. (1788). Ed. Harry Carter and C. Ricks. Oxford: Oxford Bibliographical Society Pub. New Series 9, 1961.

Morison, Stanley. *On Type Design, Past and Present*. London: Fleuron, 1926. Rev. 1962.

—. *A Tally of Types Cut for Machine Composition and Introduced at the University Press, Cambridge 1922–32*. Privately printed, Cambridge: 1953.

*—. *The Typographic Book 1450–1935*. Chicago: U of Chicago P, 1963.

— and H. G. Carter. *John Fell, the University Press and the Fell Types*. Oxford: Clarendon, 1967.

Nelson, Roy Paul. *The Design of Advertising*. Dubuque: Brown, 1973. 2nd ed.

Nordlunde, C. V. *Sir Emery Walker and the Revival of Printing*. Copenhagen: Nordlunde, 1959.

Nunberg, Geoffrey. "The Places of Books in the Age of Electronic Reproduction."

Representations 42 Spring 1993: 13–37.

Olschki, L. S. *Incunables illustré imitant les manuscrits. Le passage du manuscrits au livre imprimé*. Florence: Olschki, 1914.

Peterson, William S. *The Kelmscott Press: A History of William Morris's Typographical Adventure*. Oxford: Clarendon, 1991.

Proctor, Robert. *The Printing of Greek in the Fifteenth Century*. Oxford: Oxford UP for the Bibliographical Society, 1900.

Reed, Talbot Baines. *A History of the Old English Letter Foundries*. Rev. A. F. Johnson. London: Faber and Faber, 1952. Repr. London: Dawson, 1974.

Rosen, Ben. *Type and Typography: The Designer's Type Book*. New York: Van Nostrand Reinhold, 1976.

Scholderer, V. *Greek Printing Types 1465–1927*. London: British Museum, 1927.

Sparling, Henry H. *The Kelmscott Press and William Morris, Mastercraftsman*. London: Macmillan, 1924.

*Steinberg, S. H. *Five Hundred Years of Printing*. Harmondsworth: Penguin, 1961. 2nd ed. (3rd ed. 1968).

Straus, Ralph and R. K. Dent. *John Baskerville: A Memoir*. Cambridge: Cambridge UP / London: Chatto and Windus 1907. Repr. New York: B. Franklin, 1970.

*Sutton, James and Alan Bartram. *An Atlas of Typeforms*. Secaucus: Chartwell, 1988.

—. *Typefaces for Books*. London: British Library, 1990.

Type Specimen Book. New York: Van Nostrand Reinhold, 1974 et seq.

*Updike, Daniel Berkeley. *Printing Types: Their History, Forms, and Use*. Cambridge: Harvard UP, 1937. 2nd ed. Repr. New York: Dover, 1980. 2 vols.

Vervliet, H. D. L. *Sixteenth-Century Printing Types of the Low Countries*. Amsterdam: Menno Hertzberger, 1968.

—. and Harry Carter. *Type Specimen Facsimiles: Plantin and Le Bé-Moretus*. Toronto: U of Toronto P, 1972.

Wallis, L. W. *A Concise Chronology of Typesetting Development 1889–1986*. London: Wynkyn de Worde Society, 1988.

—. *Typomania: Selected Essays on Typesetting and Related Subjects*. Lund Humphries, 1993.

Chapter 7: Textual Bibliography

Since textual bibliography is founded upon the research done in codicology and analytical and descriptive bibliography, see also the suggested readings for Chapters 2, 3, and 4.

Barnard, John. "Bibliographic Context and the Critic," *Text* 3 (1987): 27–46.

Beowulf: Facsimile. Ed. Norman Davis. EETS 245. London: Oxford UP, 1959. 2nd ed.

Bond, William H. "Casting Off Copy by Elizabethan Printers." *Papers of the Bibliographical Society of America* 42 (1948): 281–91.

—. "Imposition by Half-Sheets." *The Library* Fourth Series 22 (1941–42): 163–67.

Bowers, Fredson. "Running-Title Evidence for Determining Half-Sheet Imposition." *Studies in Bibliography* 1 (1948–49): 199–202.

—. "Bibliographical Evidence from the Printer's Measure." *Studies in Bibliography* 2 (1949–50): 153–67.

Boyle, Leonard E. "'Epistulae Venerant Patrum Dulces': The Place of Codicology in the Editing of Medieval Latin Texts." *Editing and Editors: A Retrospect*. Ed. Richard Landon. New York: AMS, 1988: 29–46.

Cárdenas, Anthony J. "The Florentine Version of Alfonso X's *Libro del Saber de As-*

trologia: The Case of the Tell-Tale Lacunae." Conference paper, Society for Textual Scholarship. New York: April, 1983.

Carter, J. W. and H. G. Pollard. *An Enquiry into the Nature of Certain Nineteenth-Century Pamphlets*. London: Constable, 1934. Rev. London: Scolar, 1983. Ed. Nicholas Barker and John Collins.

Cole, George Watson. "The Photostat in Bibliographical and Research Work—A Symposium." *Papers of the Bibliographical Society of America* 15 (1921): 1–16.

Flood, John L. and Conor Fahy. "Analytical and Textual Bibliography in Germany and Italy." *The Book Encompassed*. Ed. Peter Davison. Cambridge: Cambridge UP, 1992: 258–269.

*Gaskell, Philip. *New Introduction to Bibliography*. Oxford: Oxford UP, 1972. Repr. with corrections, 1985.

Gerritsen, Johann. "The Thorkelin Transcripts of *Beowulf*: A Codicological Description, with Notes on Their Genesis and History." *The Library* Sixth Series 13 (1991): 1–22.

*Glaister, Geoffrey Ashall. *Glaister's Glossary of the Book: Terms Used in Papermaking, Printing, Bookbinding, and Publishing*. London: Allen and Unwin / Berkeley: U of California P, 1979.

Hedges, Chris. "Re-creating U.S. First Editions, Typos and All." *New York Times* 9 July 1991: C 13, 18.

Hibberd, Lloyd. "Physical and Reference Bibliography." *The Library* Fifth Series 20 (1965): 124–34.

Hill, W. Speed. "Casting off Copy and the Composition of Hooker's Book V." *Studies in Bibliography* 33 (1980): 144–61.

*Hinman, Charlton. *The Printing and Proof-reading of the First Folio of Shakespeare*. Oxford: Clarendon, 1963. 2 vols.

Jackson, William A. *Records of a Bibliographer: Selected Papers of William Alexander Jackson*. Ed. William H. Bond. Cambridge: Belknap / Harvard UP, 1967.

Katz, Joseph. "Analytical Bibliography and Literary History: The Writing and Printing of *Wieland*." *Proof* 1 (1977): 8–34.

Kiernan, Kevin. *Beowulf and the Beowulf Manuscript*. New Brunswick: Rutgers UP, 1981.

McKenzie, D. F. "Typography and Meaning: The Case of William Congreve." *Buch und Buchhandel in Europa im achtzehnten Jahrhundert*. Ed. Giles Barber and Bernhard Fabian. Hamburg: Hauswedell, 1981: 81–125.

—. "Speech-Manuscript-Print." in *New Directions in Textual Studies*. Ed. Dave Oliphant and Robin Bradford. Austin: Harry Ransom Humanities Research Center / U of Texas P, 1990: 87–110.

*McKerrow, R. B. *An Introduction to Bibliography for Literary Students*. Oxford: Oxford UP, 1927.

McLaverty, James. "The Mode of Existence of Literary Works of Art: The Case of the *Dunciad* Variorum." *Studies in Bibliography* 37 (1984): 82–105.

McLeod, Randall (Random Cloud). "Spellbound." *Play-Texts in Old Spelling*. Ed. G. B. Shand and Raymond C. Shady. New York: AMS, 1984: 81–96.

—. "The Psychopathology of Everyday Art." *The Elizabethan Theatre* 9 (1986): 100–168.

—. "Information upon Information," *Text* 5 (1991): 241–86.

—. "Tranceformations in the Text of *Orlando Furioso*. *New Directions in Textual Studies*. Ed. Dave Oliphant and Robin Bradford. Austin: Harry Ransom Humanities Research Center / U of Texas P, 1990: 61–86.

Mosley, James. "Introduction." *Catalogue of Specimens of Printing Types*. New York: Garland, 1983.

Needham, Paul. "The Compositor's Hand in the Gutenberg Bible: A Review of the Todd Thesis." *Papers of the Bibliographical Society of America* 77 (1983): 341–71.

—. "Johann Gutenberg and the Catholicon Press." *Papers of the Bibliographical Society of America* 76 (1982): 395-456.

—. "The Paper Supply of the Gutenberg Bible." *Papers of the Bibliographical Society of America* 79 (1985): 303-74.

Peters, Jean. *The Bookman's Glossary*. New York: Bowker, 1983.

Sayce, R. A. "Compositorial Practices and the Localization of Printed Books 1530-1800." *The Library* Fifth Series 21 (1966): 1-45.

Scholderer, V. *Fifty Essays in Fifteenth- and Sixteenth-Century Bibliography*. Amsterdam: Menno Hertzberger, 1967.

Schwab, Richard N., et al. "Cyclotron Analysis of the Ink in the Forty-Two Line Bi ble." *Papers of the Bibliographical Society of America* 77 (1983): 285-315.

—. "Ink Patterns in the Gutenberg New Testament: The Proton Milliprobe Analysis of the Lilly Library Copy." *Papers of the Bibliographical Society of America* 80 (1986): 305-31.

—. "The Proton Milliprobe Ink Analysis of the Harvard B42, Volume II." *Papers of the Bibliographical Society of America* 81 (1987): 403-32.

Shakespeare, William. *The Norton Facsimile: The Shakespeare First Folio*. Ed. Charlton Hinman. New York: Norton, 1968.

Spector, Stephen. "Symmetry in Watermark Sequences." *Studies in Bibliography* 31 (1978): 162-78.

Stevenson, A. H. *The Problem of the Missale Speciale*. London: Bibliographical Society, 1967.

Stevenson, Allan. "Paper as Bibliographical Evidence." *The Library* Fifth Series 17 (1962): 285-315.

Stockwell, Robert P. and C. Westbrook Barritt. "Scribal Practice: Some Assumptions." *Language* 37 (1961): 75-82.

Stoll, Jakob. "Zur Psychologie der Schreibfehler." *Fortschritte der Psychologie und ihrer Ahwendung* 2 (1914): 1-133.

Tanselle, G. Thomas. "The Bibliographical Concept of 'Issue' and 'State'." *Papers of the Bibliographical Society of America* 69 (1975): 17-66.

—. "Book Jackets, Blurbs and Bibliographers." *The Library* 26 (1971): 91-134.

—. "Reproductions and Scholarship." *Studies in Bibliography* 42 (1989): 25-54.

—. *A Rationale of Textual Criticism*. Philadelphia: Pennsylvania UP, 1989.

Taylor, Gary. "Revising Shakespeare." *Text* 3 (1987): 285-304.

Todd, William B. *The Gutenberg Bible: New Evidence of the Original Printing*. 3rd Hanes Lecture. Chapel Hill: Hanes Foundation / U of North Carolina P, 1982.

Turner, Mary C. *The Bookman's Glossary*. New York: Bowker, 1961. 4th ed.

Turner, Robert K., Jr. "Reappearing Types as Bibliographical Evidence." *Studies in Bibliography* 19 (1966): 198-209.

Van Hoesen, Henry Bartlett. *Bibliography: Practical, Enumerative, Historical*. New York: B. Franklin, 1971. Repr. of 1928 ed.

Vinaver, Eugène. "Principles of Textual Emendation." *Studies in French Language and Medieval Literature Presented to Professor M. K. Pope*. Manchester: U of Manchester P, 1930: 351-69.

Walker, Alice. "Compositor Determination and Other Problems in Shakespearian Texts." *Studies in Bibliography* 7 (1955): 3-16.

Walton, J. K. *The Quarto Copy for the First Folio of Shakespeare*. Dublin: Dublin UP, 1971.

Wells, Stanley. "Narratives about Printed Shakespeare Texts: 'Foul Papers' and 'Bad' Quartos." *Shakespeare Quarterly* 41 (1990): 65-86.

*Williams, William Proctor and Craig S. Abbott. *An Introduction to Bibliographical and Textual Studies*. New York: MLA, 1989. 2nd ed.

Willis, James. *Latin Textual Criticism*. Urbana: U of Illinois P, 1972.

Woshinsky, Barbara. "La Bruyère's *Caractères*: A Typographical Reading," *Text* 2 (1985): 229-43.

Chapter 8: Textual Criticism

Note: In order to save space and prevent duplication, most of the specific *editions* cited in the text of this chapter are given full bibliographical reference in the bibliography to chapter 9, on scholarly editing, and are not included here unless they are also a significant part of the history of textual criticism. Readers should thus consult the bibliographies for both chapters for access to research in these fields. To ease reference to the text, a separate list of works cited precedes the general bibliography for this chapter.

Works Cited in Text

Bateson, F. W. "Modern Bibliography and the Literary Artifact." *English Studies Today*. Ed. Georges A. Bonnard. Bern: 1961: 67–77. 2nd ed.

Bédier, Joseph, "La Tradition manuscrite du *Lai du l'Ombre*: réflexions sur l'art d'éditer les anciens textes," *Romania* 54 (1928): 161–196, 321–356. Repr. as pamphlet, 1970.

Bennett, Betty. "Feminism and Editing: The Mary Shelley Letters." Bornstein and Williams: 67–96.

Berger, Thomas L. "The New Historicism and the Editing of English Renaissance Texts." *New Ways of Looking at Old Texts: Papers of the Renaissance English Text Society, 1985–1991*. Ed. W. Speed Hill. Binghamton: Medieval & Renaissance Texts & Studies / Renaissance English Text Society, 1993: 195–198.

Bornstein, George. "Remaking Himself: Yeats's Revisions of His Early Canon," *Text* 5 (1991): 341–60.

— and Ralph Williams, eds. *Palimpsest: Editorial Theory in the Humanities*. Ann Arbor: U of Michigan P, 1993.

Bowers, Fredson. *Principles of Bibliographical Description*. Princeton: Princeton UP, 1949. Repr. New York: Russell, 1962.

—. "Some Principles for Scholarly Editions of Nineteenth-Century American Authors." *Studies in Bibliography* 17 (1964): 223–28.

—. "Greg's 'Rationale of Copy-Text' Revisited." *Studies in Bibliography* 31 (1970): 90–161.

—. "Multiple Authority: New Problems and Concepts of Copy-Text." *The Library* 5th Series 27 (1972): 81–115. Repr. *Essays in Bibliography, Text, and Editing*. Charlottesville: UP of Virginia, 1975: 447–87.

Boydston, Jo Ann, ed. *The [Early/Middle/Later] Works of John Dewey 1892–1953*. Carbondale: Southern Illinois UP, 1967–90. 36 vols.

—. "*The Collected Works of John Dewey* and the CEAA/CSE: A Case History." *Papers of the Bibliographical Society of America* 85 (1991): 119–144.

Braudel, Fernand. *The Mediterranean and the Mediterranean World in the Age of Philip II*. Trans. Sîan Reynolds. New York: Harper & Row, 1972. 2 vols.

Center for Editions of American Authors. *Statement of Editorial Principles and Procedures*. Rev. ed. New York: MLA, 1972.

Center / Committee for Scholarly Editions. *An Introductory Statement*. New York: MLA, 1977.

Cohen, Philip, ed. *Devils and Angels: Textual Editing and Literary Theory*. Charlottesville: UP of Virginia, 1991.

Dearing, Vinton. *Principles and Practice of Textual Analysis*. Berkeley: U of California P, 1974.

De Robertis, Domenico. "Per l'edizione critica del 'Dolore' di Giuseppe Ungaretti." *Studi di filologia italiana* 38 (1980): 309–23.

Donaldson, E. T. *Speaking of Chaucer*. London: Athlone / New York: Norton, 1970.

Duff, E. Gordon. *Early English Printing . . . Facsimiles of All Types Used in Eng-*

land During the XV Century. London: Kegan Paul, 1896. Repr. New York: B. Franklin, 1970.

Eisenstein, Elizabeth L. *The Printing Press as an Agent of Change*. 2 vols. Cambridge: Cambridge UP, 1979.

Emerson, Ralph Waldo. *The Collected Works of Ralph Waldo Emerson*. Ed. Alfred R. Ferguson. Cambridge: Belknap-Harvard UP, 1971- .

—. *Journals and Miscellaneous Notebooks of Ralph Waldo Emerson*. Ed. William H. Gilman et al. Cambridge: Harvard UP, 1969–82.

—. *The Complete Sermons of Ralph Waldo Emerson*. Ed. Albert J. von Frank, Jr., et al. Columbia: U of Missouri P, 1989- .

Febvre, Lucien, and Henri-Jean Martin. *The Coming of the Book: The Impact of Printing 1450–1800*. Trans. David Gerard. London & New York: Verso, 1990.

Foley, John Miles. "Editing Yugoslav Epics: Theory and Practice." *Text* 1 (1981): 75–96.

Ford, J. Massyngberde, ed. Revelation. *The Anchor Bible*. Garden City: Doubleday, 1975.

Furnivall, F. J., ed. *Hoccleve's Works: The Regement of Princes*. EETS ES 72. London: Kegan Paul, 1897.

Gaskell, Philip. *New Introduction to Bibliography*. Oxford: Oxford UP, 1972. Repr. with corrections, 1985.

—. *From Writer to Reader: Studies in Editorial Method*. Oxford: Clarendon P, 1978.

— and Clive Hart, eds. Ulysses: *A Review of Three Texts*. New York: Barnes and Noble, 1989.

Greetham, D. C. "Textual and Literary Theory: Redrawing the Matrix." *Studies in Bibliography* 42 (1989): 1–24.

—. "[Textual] Criticism and Deconstruction." *Studies in Bibliography* 44 (1991): 1–30.

—. *Theories of the Text*. Oxford: Oxford UP. Forthcoming.

Greg, W. W. *A Calculus of Variants: An Essay on Textual Criticism*. Oxford: Clarendon P, 1927.

—, ed. *Marlowe's The Tragicall History of the Life and Death of Doctor Faustus, 1604–1616. Parallel Texts*. Oxford: Clarendon, 1950.

—, ed. *Jonson's Masque of Gipsies in the Burley, Belvoir, and Windsor Versions: An Attempt at Reconstruction*. London: British Academy, 1952.

—. "The Rationale of Copy-Text." *Studies in Bibliography* 3 (1950–51): 19–36.

Hancher, Michael. "Three Kinds of Intention." *Modern Language Notes* 87 (1972): 827–51.

Hartman, Geoffrey, et al. *Deconstruction and Criticism*. New York: Continuum, 1979.

Hill, Archibald. "Some Postulates for Distributional Study of Texts." *Studies in Bibliography* 3 (1950–51): 63–95.

Hirsch, E. D., Jr. *Validity in Interpretation*. New Haven: Yale UP, 1967.

—. *The Aims of Interpretation*. Chicago: U of Chicago P, 1978.

Housman, A. E. *Selected Prose*. Ed. John Carter. Cambridge: Cambridge UP, 1961.

Jack, Ian. "A Choice of Orders: The Arrangement of 'The Poetical Works'." *Textual Criticism and Literary Interpretation*. Ed. Jerome J. McGann. Chicago: U of Chicago P, 1985: 144–61.

Kane, George, ed. *Piers Plowman: The A Version*. London: Athlone, 1960.

— and E. Talbot Donaldson, eds. *Piers Plowman: The B Version* London: Athlone, 1975.

Kenney, E. J. *The Classical Text: Aspects of Editing in the Age of the Printed Book*. Berkeley: U of California P, 1974.

King, Katie. "Bibliography and a Feminist Apparatus for Literary Production." *Text* 5 (1991): 91–104.

Ladurie, Emmanuel Le Roy. *Montaillou: The Promised Land of Error.* Trans. Barbara Bray. New York: Braziller, 1978.

Lafuma, Louis, ed. *Œuvres complètes.* By Blaise Pascal. Paris: Éditions du Seuil, 1963.

Lixacev, Dmitrij. *Tekstologija russkoj literatury X-XVII vekov.* Leningrad: Nauka, 1983.

Maas, Paul. *Textual Criticism.* Trans. Barbara Flower. Oxford: Clarendon, 1958.

Mabillon, Jean. *De re diplomatica libri sex in quibus quidquid ad veterum instrumentorum antiquitatem, materiam, scripturam et stilum: quidquid ad sigilla, monogrammata, subscriptiones ac notas chronologicas; quidquid inde ad antiquariam, historicam, forensemque disciplinam pertinet, explicatur et illustratur.* Paris: Robustel, 1709. 2nd ed.

Mailloux, Steven. *Interpretive Conventions: The Reader in the Study of American Fiction.* Ithaca: Cornell UP, 1982.

McGann, Jerome J. *A Critique of Modern Textual Criticism.* Chicago: U of Chicago P, 1983. Repr. Charlottesville: UP of Virginia, 1992.

—. "What Is Critical Editing?" *Text* 5 (1991): 15-30.

—. *The Textual Condition.* Princeton: Princeton UP, 1991.

McKenzie, D. F. *The Cambridge University Press 1696-1712.* Cambridge: Cambridge UP, 1966. 2 vols.

—. "Printers of the Mind: Some Notes on Bibliographical Theories and Printing-House Practices." *Studies in Bibliography* 22 (1969): 1-75.

—. "Typography and Meaning: The Case of William Congreve." *Buch und Buchhandel in Europa im achtzehnten Jahrhundert.* Ed. Giles Barber and Bernhard Fabian. Hamburg: Hauswedell, 1981: 81-125.

—. "The Sociology of a Text: Orality, Literacy, and Print in Early New Zealand." *The Library* Sixth Series 6 (1984): 333-65.

—. *Bibliography and the Sociology of Texts.* London: The British Library, 1986.

—, et al, eds. *Cambridge History of the Book in Britain.* Cambridge: Cambridge UP. In preparation.

McKerrow, R. B., ed. *The Works of Thomas Nashe.* London: Bullen / Sidgwick and Jackson, 1904-10. Repr. with corrections and supplementary notes. Ed. F. P. Wilson. Oxford: Blackwell, 1958. 5 vols.

—. *An Introduction to Bibliography for Literary Students.* Oxford: Oxford UP, 1927.

—. *Prolegomena for the Oxford Shakespeare.* Oxford: Clarendon, 1939. Repr. 1969.

McLaverty, James. "The Concept of Authorial Intention in Textual Criticism." *The Library,* Sixth Series 6 (June, 1984): 121-38.

—. "The Mode of Existence of Literary Works of Art: The Case of the *Dunciad* Variorum." *Studies in Bibliography* 37 (1984): 82-105.

Metz, G. Harold. "Disputed Shakespearean Texts and Stylometric Analysis," *Text* 2 (1985): 149-72.

Modern Language Association of America. *Professional Standards and American Editions: A Response to Edmund Wilson.* New York: MLA, 1969.

Oliphant, Dave and Robin Bradford, eds. *New Directions in Textual Studies.* Austin: Harry Ransom Humanities Research Center / U of Texas P, 1990.

Parker, Hershel. *Flawed Texts and Verbal Icons: Literary Authority in American Fiction.* Evanston: Northwestern UP, 1984.

—. "'The New Scholarship': Textual Evidence and Its Implications for Criticism, Literary Theory, and Aesthetics." *Studies in American Fiction* 9 (1984): 181-97.

Pasquali, Giorgio. *Storia della tradizione e critica del testo.* Florence: Le Monnier, 1934.

Patterson, Lee. "The Logic of Textual Criticism and the Way of Genius: The Kane-Donaldson *Piers Plowman* in Historical Perspective." *Textual Criticism and Literary Interpretation.* Ed. Jerome J. McGann. Chicago: U of Chicago P, 1985: 55-91.

Pearsall, Derek. "Editing Medieval Texts." *Textual Criticism and Literary Interpretation*. Ed. Jerome J. McGann. Chicago: U of Chicago P, 1985: 92–106.

Pizer, Donald. "Self-Censorship and Textual Editing." *Textual Criticism and Literary Interpretation*. Ed. Jerome J. McGann. Chicago: U of Chicago P, 1985: 144–61.

Pollard, Alfred W. *Shakespeare Folios and Quartos: A Study in the Bibliography of Shakespeare's Plays 1594–1685*. New York: Cooper Square, 1970. Repr. of 1909 ed.

— and G. R. Redgrave, comps. *A Short-Title Catalogue of Books Printed in England, Scotland, and Ireland, and of English Books Printed Abroad, 1475–1640*. Rev. Katharine F. Pantzer, and F. S. Ferguson. London: Bibliographical Society, 1976–89. 2nd ed. 3 vols. *Index*, 1991.

Proctor, Robert. *An Index to the Early Printed Books in the British Museum: From the Invention of Printing to the Year 1500. With Notes of Those in the Bodleian Library*. London: Holland, 1960. Repr. of 1898–1906 ed.

Quentin, Dom Henri. *Essai de critique textuelle*. Paris: Picard, 1926.

Reeve, Michael D. "*Eliminatio codicum descriptorum*: A Methodological Problem." *Editing Greek and Latin Texts*. Ed. John N. Grant. New York: AMS, 1989: 1–36.

Reiman, Donald H. "The Four Ages of Editing and the English Romantics." *Text* 1 (1984): 231–55. Repr. *Romantic Texts and Contexts*. Columbia: U of Missouri P, 1987: 17–32.

—. "'Versioning': The Presentation of Multiple Texts." *Romantic Texts and Contexts*. Columbia: U of Missouri P, 1987: 167–80.

Rossi, Aldo, ed. *Il Decameron*. By Giovanni Boccaccio. Bologna: Capelli, 1977.

Saussure, Ferdinand de. *Course in General Linguistics*. Ed. Charles Bally and Albert Sechehaye. Trans. Roy Harris. La Salle, IL: Open Court, 1986.

Sellier, Philippe, ed. *Pensées*. By Blaise Pascal. Paris: Mercure de France, 1976.

Shillingsburg, Peter L. "The Limits of the Editor's Responsibility." Conference paper. Society for Textual Scholarship, New York City. April, 1987.

—. "Text as Matter, Concept, and Action." *Studies in Bibliography* 44 (1991): 31–82.

—. "Polymorphic, Polysemic, Protean, Reliable, Electronic Texts." Bornstein and Williams: 29–44.

Silver, Brenda R. "Textual Criticism as Feminist Practice: Or, Who's Afraid of Virginia Woolf Part II." *Representing Modernist Texts: Editing as Interpretation*. Ed. George Bornstein. Ann Arbor: U of Michigan P, 1991: 193–222.

Smith, M. W. A. "The Authorship of *Timon of Athens*." *Text* 5 (1991) 195–240.

Sutherland, John. "Publishing History: A Hole at the Centre of Literary Sociology." *Critical Inquiry* 14 (1988): 574–89.

Tanselle, G. Thomas. "Greg's Theory of Copy-Text and the Editing of American Literature." *Studies in Bibliography* 28 (1975): 167–229.

—. "The Editorial Problem of Final Authorial Intention." *Studies in Bibliography* 29 (1976): 167–211.

—. "The Editing of Historical Documents." *Studies in Bibliography* 31 (1978): 1–56.

—. "External Fact as an Editorial Problem." *Studies in Bibliography* 32 (1979): 1–47.

—. *The History of Books as a Field of Study*. Second Hanes Lecture, Hanes Foundation. Chapel Hill: U of North Carolina, 1981.

—. "Recent Editorial Discussion and the Central Questions of Editing." *Studies in Bibliography* 34 (1981): 23–65.

—. "Textual Scholarship." *Introduction to Literary Scholarship in the Modern Languages and Literatures*. Ed. Joseph Gibaldi. New York: MLA, 1981. 29–52.

—. "Historicism and Critical Editing." *Studies in Bibliography* 39 (1986): 1–46.

—. *Textual Criticism Since Greg, A Chronicle, 1950–1985*. Charlottesville: UP of Virginia, 1988.

—. *A Rationale of Textual Criticism*. Philadelphia: Pennsylvania UP, 1989.

—. "Textual Criticism and Literary Sociology" *Studies in Bibliography* 44 (1991):

83–143.

Taylor, Gary. "Revising Shakespeare." *Text* 3 (1987): 285–304.

Textual Scholarship and Literary Theory. Special issue of *Critical Exchange* 24 (Fall, 1989).

Thorpe, James. *Principles of Textual Criticism.* San Marino: Huntington Library, 1972.

Timpanaro, S. *La genesi del metodo del Lachmann.* Florence: Bibliotechina del saggiatore, 1963. Trans. as *Die Entstehung der Lachmannschen Methode.* Hamburg: Buske.

—. "Recentiores e deteriores, codices descripti e codices inutiles." *Filologia e critica* 10 (1985): 164–92.

Urkowitz, Steven. *Shakespeare's Revision of "King Lear".* Princeton: Princeton UP, 1980.

Vieth, David M., ed. *The Complete Poems of John Wilmot, Earl of Rochester.* New Haven: Yale UP, 1968.

Vinaver, Eugène. "Principles of Textual Emendation." *Studies in French Language and Medieval Literature Presented to Professor M. K. Pope.* Manchester: U of Manchester P, 1930: 351–69.

Warren, Michael, ed. *The Complete "King Lear" 1608–1623.* Berkeley: U of California P, 1989. 4 pts.

White, Patricia S. "Black and White and Read All Over: A Meditation On Footnotes." *Text* 5 (1991): 81–90.

Willison, Ian. "Editorial Theory and Practice and the History of the Book." Oliphant and Bradford: 111–26.

Wilson, Edmund. *The Fruits of the MLA.* New York: New York Review of Books, 1968.

John Dover Wilson, ed. *The New Cambridge Shakespeare.* Cambridge: Cambridge UP, 1921–66. 42 vols. *Love's Labour's Lost* 1962.

Wolf, F. A. *Prolegomena ad Homerum.* 1795.

Wordsworth, William. *The Cornell Wordsworth.* Gen. Ed. Stephen Parrish. Ithaca: Cornell UP, 1975– .

General Introductions to the Field

Bowers, Fredson. *Bibliography and Textual Criticism.* Oxford: Clarendon, 1964.

—. Textual and Literary Criticism. Cambridge: Cambridge UP, 1966.

*—. "Textual Criticism." *The Aims and Methods of Scholarship in Modern Languages and Literatures.* Ed. James Thorpe. New York: MLA, 1970: 29–54. 2nd ed.

*—. "Textual Criticism." *Encyclopaedia Britannica.* Chicago: Benton, 1968. vol. 21: 918–23.

*Falconer, Graham and David H. Sanderson. "Bibliographie des études génétiques littéraires." *Texte* 7 (1988): 287–352.

Greetham, D. C. "A Suspicion of Texts." *Thesis* 2, no. 1 (Fall, 1987): 18–25.

*—. "Textual Scholarship." *Introduction to Literary Scholarship in the Modern Languages and Literatures.* Ed. Joseph Gibaldi. New York: MLA. 2nd ed. 1992.

Hockey, Susan. *A Guide to Computer Applications in the Humanities.* Baltimore: Johns Hopkins UP, 1980.

Housman, A. E. "The Application of Thought to Textual Criticism," *Proceedings of the Classical Association* 18 (1921): 67–84. Repr. *Selected Prose*: 131–50. Repr. *Collected Poems and Selected Prose*: 325–39.

*Kenney, E. J. "Textual Criticism." *Encyclopaedia Britannica, Macropaedia* XVIII. New York: 1974–5: 189–95.

Kline, Mary-Jo. *A Guide to Documentary Editing.* Baltimore: Johns Hopkins UP, 1987.

Luck, Georg. "Textual Criticism Today." *American Journal of Philology* 102 (1981): 164-94.
Maas, Paul. *Textual Criticism.* Trans. Barbara Flower. Oxford: Clarendon, 1958.
Maxwell, James C., P. G. Zamberg, and F. W. Bateson. "Textual Criticism and Its Problems." *Essays in Criticism* 18, no. 1 (1968): 87-100.
McClelland, John. "Critical Editing in the Modern Languages." *Text* 1 (1984): 201-16.
Oakman, Robert. *Computer Methods for Literary Research.* Athens: U of Georgia P, rev. 1984.
*Tanselle, G. Thomas. "Textual Scholarship." *Introduction to Literary Scholarship in the Modern Languages and Literatures.* Ed. Joseph Gibaldi. New York: MLA, 1981. 29-52.
Textual Criticism. Special Issue of *Romance Philology* 45 (August, 1991).
Thorpe, James. *Principles of Textual Criticism.* San Marino: Huntington Library, 1972.
*Williams, William Proctor and Craig S. Abbott. *An Introduction to Bibliographical and Textual Studies.* New York: MLA, 1989. 2nd ed.
Willis, James. "The Science of Blunders: Confessions of a Textual Critic." *Text* 6 (1993): 63-80.

Surveys, Histories, Collections

*Barney, Stephen, ed. *Annotation and Its Texts.* New York: Oxford UP, 1991.
Benson, Charles and Mary Pollard. "The Silken Purse: Bibliography in Ireland." *The Book Encompassed.* Ed. Peter Davison. Cambridge: Cambridge UP, 1992: 200-205.
Børch, Marianne, Andreas Haarder, and Julia McGrew, eds. *The Medieval Text: Editors and Critics.* 1990.
Bornstein, George, ed. *Representing Modernist Texts: Editing as Interpretation.* Ann Arbor: U of Michigan P, 1991.
— and Ralph Williams, ed. *Palimpsest: Editorial Theory in the Humanities.* Ann Arbor: U of Michigan P, 1993.
*Bowers, Fredson. *Essays in Bibliography, Text, and Editing.* Charlottesville: UP of Virginia, 1975.
Brack, O M Jr. and Warner Barnes, eds. *Bibliography and Textual Criticism: English and American Literature, 1700 to the Present.* Chicago: U of Chicago P, 1969.
Brink, C. O. *English Classical Scholarship: Historical Reflections on Bentley, Porson and Housman.* Cambridge: Clark / New York: Oxford UP, 1986.
Cambridge History of the Book in Britain. Ed. D. F. McKenzie, David McKitterick, Ian Willison. Cambridge: Cambridge UP. 7 vols. In progress.
Cerquiglini, Bernard. *Éloge de la variante: histoire critique de la philologie.* Paris: Seuil, 1989.
Cohen, Philip, ed. *Devils and Angels: Textual Editing and Literary Theory.* Charlottesville: UP of Virginia, 1991.
—, ed. *Texts and Textuality: Textual Instability, Theory, Interpretation, and Pedagogy.* New York: Paragon H. Forthcoming.
Cosenza, M. E. *Biographical and Bibliographical Dictionary of the Italian Humanists and the World of Classical Scholarship.* Oxford: Oxford UP, 1934-71. 6 vols.
Dain, Alphonse, ed. *Geschichte der Textüberlieferung der antiken und mittelalterlichen Literatur.* Zürich: Atlantis, 1961.
*Davison, Peter, ed. *The Book Encompassed: Studies in Twentieth-Century Bibliography.* Cambridge: Cambridge UP, 1992.
Douglas, D. C. *English Scholars 1660-1730.* London: Eyre and Spottiswoode, 1951. 2nd ed.

Doyle, A. E., E. Rainey, and C. B. Wilson. *Manuscript to Print: Tradition and Innovation in the Renaissance Book.* Durham: Durham U Library, 1975.

Eisenstein, Elizabeth L. *The Printing Press as an Agent of Change.* 2 vols. Cambridge: Cambridge UP, 1979.

Erdman, David V. and Ephim G. Fogel, eds. *Evidence for Authorship: Essays on Problems of Attribution.* Ithaca: Cornell UP, 1966.

Fahy, Conor. "The Bowers Legacy in Italian Studies." *Text* 8. Forthcoming.

*Faulhaber, Charles B. "Textual Criticism in the 21st Century." *Romance Philology* 45 (1991): 123–148.

*—, ed. *Textual Criticism.* Special Issue of *Romance Philology* 45 (1991).

*Febvre, Lucien, and Henri-Jean Martin. *The Coming of the Book: The Impact of Printing 1450–1800.* Trans. David Gerard. London & New York: Verso, 1990.

Flood, John L. and Conor Fahy. "Analytical and Textual Bibliography in Germany and Italy." *The Book Encompassed.* Ed. Peter Davison. Cambridge: Cambridge UP, 1992: 258–269.

Geanakoplos, Deno J. *Greek Scholars in Venice: Studies in the Dissemination of Greek Learning from Byzantium to Western Europe.* Cambridge: Harvard UP, 1962.

*Gottesman, Ronald and Scott Bennett, eds. *Art and Error: Modern Textual Editing.* Bloomington: Indiana UP, 1970.

Grafton, Anthony. *Joseph Scaliger: A Study in the History of Classical Scholarship.* Oxford: Clarendon, 1983, 1993. 2 vols.

—. "Quattrocento Humanism and Classical Scholarship." *Renaissance Humanism: Foundations, Forms and Legacy. III. Humanism and the Disciplines.* Ed. Albert Rabil, Jr. 1988: 23–66.

—. *Forgers and Critics: Creativity and Duplicity in Western Scholarship.* Princeton: Princeton UP, 1990.

—. *Defenders of the Text.* Cambridge: Harvard UP, 1991.

—. *New Worlds, Ancient Texts: The Power of Tradition and the Shock of Discovery.* Cambridge: Harvard UP, 1992.

Greetham, D. C. *From Texts to Texualities.* New York: Garland. Forthcoming.

—, ed. *The Margins of the Text.* In preparation.

Greg, W. W. *Collected Papers.* Ed. J. C. Maxwell. Oxford: 1966.

Hay, Louis and Péter Nagy, eds. *Avant-texte, texte, après-texte.* 1982.

Hill, W. Speed, ed. *New Ways of Looking at Old Texts.* Binghamton: Medieval & Renaissance Texts & Studies / Renaissance English Text Society, 1993.

Hillyard, Brian. "Scottish Bibliography for the Period Ending 1801." *The Book Encompassed.* Ed. Peter Davison. Cambridge: Cambridge UP, 1992: 182–192.

Housman, A. E. *Selected Prose.* Ed. John Carter. Cambridge: Cambridge UP, 1961.

—. *Collected Poems and Selected Prose.* Ed. Christopher Ricks. London: Allen Lane, The Penguin Press, 1988.

Hunt, R. W. and A. C. de la Mare. *Duke Humfrey and English Humanism in the Fifteenth Century.* Oxford: Bodleian Library, 1970.

Jardine, Lisa. *Erasmus, Man of Letters: The Construction of Charisma in Print.* Princeton: Princeton UP, 1993.

Jaszi, Peter and Martha Woodhouse, eds. *Intellectual Property and the Construction of Authorship.* Special issue of *Cardozo Arts & Entertainment Law Journal* 10.2 (1992).

Jones, R. F. *Lewis Theobald: His Contribution to English Scholarship.* New York: Columbia UP, 1919.

*Kenney, E. J. *The Classical Text: Aspects of Editing in the Age of the Printed Book.* Berkeley: U of California P, 1974.

Kirsop, Wallace. "Tradition and Innovation: Bibliography in Australia and New Zealand." *The Book Encompassed.* Ed. Peter Davison. Cambridge: Cambridge UP,

1992: 227-235.

Kleinhenz, Christopher, ed. *Medieval Manuscripts and Textual Criticism*. Chapel Hill: U of North Carolina Department of Romance Languages, 1976.

Lathrop, H. B. *Translations from the Classics into English from Caxton to Chapman (1477-1620)*. Madison: U of Wisconsin P, 1933.

Lemerle, P. *Byzantine Humanism. The First Phase*. Trans. H. Lindsay and A. Moffatt. Byzantina Australiensia 3 Canberra: Australian Association for Byzantine Studies, 1986.

*Machan, Tim William, ed. *Medieval Literature: Texts and Interpretation*. Binghamton: Medieval & Renaissance Texts & Studies, 1991.

—. "Late Middle English Texts and the Higher and Lower Criticisms." Machan *Medieval Literature*: 3-16.

*—. *Textual Criticism and Middle English Texts*. Charlottesville: UP of Virginia. Forthcoming.

*McGann, Jerome J, ed. *Textual Criticism and Literary Interpretation*. Chicago: U of Chicago P, 1985.

—. *The Textual Condition*. Princeton: Princeton UP, 1991.

McKenzie, D. F. "'What's Past Is Prologue': The Bibliographical Society and the History of the Book." Bibliographical Society Centenary Lecture 1992. London: Hearthstone, 1993.

McKerrow, R. B. *McKerrow: A Selection of His Essays*. Ed. John P. Immroth. Metuchen: Scarecrow, 1974.

*Minnis, A. J. and Charlotte Brewer, eds. *Crux and Controversy in Middle English Textual Criticism*. Cambridge: Brewer, 1992.

*Oliphant, Dave and Robin Bradford, eds. *New Directions in Textual Studies*. Austin: Harry Ransom Humanities Research Center / U of Texas P, 1990.

Pearsall, Derek, ed. *Manuscripts and Texts: Editorial Problems in Later Middle English Literature*. Cambridge: Brewer, 1987.

*Pfeiffer, Rudolph. *History of Classical Scholarship from the Beginnings to the End of the Hellenistic Age*. Oxford: Oxford UP, 1968.

*—. *History of Classical Scholarship from 1300 to 1850*. Oxford: Oxford UP, 1976.

Prete, S. *Observations on the History of Textual Criticism in the Medieval and Renaissance Periods*. Collegeville, MN: 1970.

Rees, Eiluned. "From Autograph to Automation: Welsh Bibliography." *The Book Encompassed*. Ed. Peter Davison. Cambridge: Cambridge UP, 1992: 193-199.

Reiman, Donald H. "The Four Ages of Editing and the English Romantics." *Text* 1 (1984): 231-55. Repr. *Romantic Texts and Contexts*. Columbia: U of Missouri P, 1987: 17-32.

—. "Textual Criticism in Nineteenth-Century Studies." *Nineteenth-Century Contexts* 11 (1987): 9-21.

*Sandys, J. E. W. *A History of Classical Scholarship*. Cambridge: Cambridge UP, 1906-8. Repr. New York: Hafner, 1964. 2nd ed. 3 vols.

Shand, G. B. and Raymond C. Shady, eds. *Play-Texts in Old Spelling*. New York: AMS, 1984.

Shaw, David. "*La bibliologie* in France." *The Book Encompassed*. Ed. Peter Davison. Cambridge: Cambridge UP, 1992: 206-214.

*Small, Ian and Marcus Walsh, eds. *The Theory and Practice of Text-Editing*. Cambridge: Cambridge UP, 1991.

Smalley, Beryl. *English Friars and Antiquity*. Oxford: Blackwell, 1960.

Tanselle, G. Thomas. *Selected Studies in Bibliography*. Charlottesville: UP of Virginia, 1979.

*—. *Textual Criticism Since Greg, A Chronicle, 1950-1985*. Charlottesville: UP of Virginia, 1988.

—. "Classical, Biblical, and Medieval Textual Criticism and Modern Editing." *Studies in Bibliography* 36 (1983): 21-68.

*—. *Textual Criticism and Scholarly Editing.* Charlottesvillle: UP of Virginia, 1991.
—. "The Life and Work of Fredson Bowers." *Studies in Bibliography* 46 (1993): 1–154. Repr. as monograph, 1993.
*Toronto, U of. Conferences on Editorial Problems. Toronto: U of Toronto Press, A. M. Hakkert / New York: Garland, AMS, 1966– .
Treadgold, W., ed. *Renaissances before the Renaissance. Cultural Revivals of Late Antiquity and the Middle Ages.* Stanford: Stanford UP, 1984.
Uitti, Karl D., ed. "The Poetics of Textual Criticism: The Old French Example." *L'Ésprit Créateur* 27.1 (Spring 1987): 1–128.
Vogt, George L. and John Bush Jones, eds. *Literary and Historical Editing.* Lawrence: U of Kansas Libraries, 1981.
Weiss, Roberto. *The Spread of Italian Humanism.* London: Hutchinson, 1964.
—. *The Renaissance Discovery of Classical Antiquity.* Oxford: Blackwell, 1969.
Wellek, René and Alvaro Ribeiro, eds. *Evidence in Literary Scholarship: Essays in Memory of James Marshall Osborn.* Oxford: Clarendon P, 1979.
Wilamowitz-Moellendorff, U. von. *History of Classical Scholarship.* Ed. Hugh Lloyd-Jones, trans. Alan Harris. Baltimore: Johns Hopkins UP, 1982.
Wilson, N. G. *From Byzantium to Italy: Greek Studies in the Italian Renaissance.* London: Duckworth, 1993.
Yamada, Akihiro. "Bibliographical Studies in Japan." *The Book Encompassed.* Ed. Peter Davison. Cambridge: Cambridge UP, 1992: 270–275.

Journals

Analytical and Enumerative Bibliography. Ed. William P. Williams. De Kalb, Ill.: Bibliographical Society of Northern Illinois, 1977– .
L'année philologique: Bibliographie critique et analytique de l'antiquité greco-latine. Gen. Eds. Jules Marouzeau, Juliette Ernst et al. Paris: Société d'Edition "Les Belles Lettres." 1927– .
Bibliographical Society of Australia and New Zealand Bulletin. 1976– .
Center for Editing Early Canadian Texts Newsletter. Ed. Mary Jane Edwards. 1982– .
Computers and the Humanities. 1966– .
Documentary Editing (formerly *Newsletter of the Association for Documentary Editing*). Ed. Thomas A. Mason. Association for Documentary Editing. 1979– .
Editio: Internationales Jahrbuch für Editionswissenschaft. Ed. Winfried Woesler et al. Tübingen: Max Niemeyer, 1987– .
Editorial Quarterly. Tallahassee: 1975–77.
**The Library.* Transactions of the Bibliographical Society.* London: Bibliographical Society, 1892– .
Literary and Linguistic Computing: Journal of the Association for Literary and Linguistic Computing. Oxford: Oxford UP, 1986– .
Literary Research: A Journal of Scholarly Method and Technique. Ed. Michael Marcuse. College Park: 1976– .
New England Book and Text Studies. Ed. C. Deirdre Phelps. Cambridge, MA: 1994– .
Papers of the Bibliographical Society of Canada. 1961– .
Papers of the Bibliographical Society of America. New York: Bibliographical Society of America. 1906– .
Philologus: Zeitschrift für das klassische Altertum. Stolberg: 1846–1944; 1954– .
Proof: Yearbook of American Bibliographical and Textual Studies. Columbia, SC: 1971–77.
Research in Humanities Computing. Ed. Susan Hockey and Nancy Ide. Oxford: Oxford UP, 1991– .
Resources for American Literary Study. Ed. Jackson R. Bryer and Carla Mulford. University Park: Penn State UP. 1974– .
Review. Ed. James O. Hoge and James L. W. West, III. Charlottesville: UP of Vir-

ginia, 1979– .
Revue des études latines. Paris: 1888– .
Revue d'histoire des textes. Paris: 1971– .
Revue d'histoire diplomatique. Paris: 1887– .
Revue du moyen âge latin, études, textes, chronique, bibliographie. Lyon / Strasbourg: 1945– .
Speculum. Cambridge, MA: 1934– .
Studies in the Age of Chaucer. Norman: 1979– .
*Studies in Bibliography. Eds. Fredson Bowers and David Vander Meulen. Charlottesville: Bibliographical Society of the U of Virginia / UP of Virginia, 1948/49– .
*Text: Transactions of the Society for Textual Scholarship. Eds. D. C. Greetham and W. Speed Hill. New York: AMS, 1984– .
Traditio: Studies in Ancient and Mediaeval History, Thought, and Religion. New York: 1942– .

Biblical Textual Criticism

**Aland, Kurt and Barbara. *The Text of the New Testament.* Grand Rapids: Eerdmans / Leiden: Brill, 1989. 2nd ed.
Albrektson, B. "Reflections on the Emergence of a Standard Text of the Hebrew Bible." *Vetus Testamentum Supplement* 29: 49–65.
Andersen, Francis I. "Computer-Assisted Investigation of Textual Transmission through the Study of Orthography," *Text* 2 (1985): 25–54.
Barthélemy, Dominique. *Études d'histoire du texte de l'ancien testament.* Orbis Biblicus et Orientalis 21. Göttingen: Vandenhoeck and Ruprecht, 1978.
Brock, Sebastian P. "Developments in Editing Biblical Texts." *The Book Encompassed.* Ed. Peter Davison. Cambridge: Cambridge UP, 1992: 227–235.
Cross, Frank More. "The History of the Biblical Text in the Light of Discoveries in the Judaean Desert." *Harvard Theological Review* 57 (1964): 281–99.
—. "Problems of Method in the Textual Criticism of the Hebrew Bible." *The Critical Study of Sacred Texts.* Ed. Wendy Doniger O'Flaherty. Berkeley: Graduate Theological Union, 1979: 31–54.
—. "New Directions in Dead Sea Scroll Research. Part I: The Text Behind the Text of the Hebrew Bible." *Bible Review* 1.
Eisenman, Robert H. and Michael Wise, eds. *The Dead Sea Scrolls Uncovered.* Harmondsworth: Penguin, 1993.
Finegan, Jack. *Encountering New Testament Manuscripts: A Working Introduction to Textual Criticism.* Grand Rapids: Eerdmans, 1974.
Freedman, David Noel. "Editing the Editors: Translation and Elucidation of the Text of the Bible." *Palimpsest: Editorial Theory in the Humanities.* Ed. George Bornstein and Ralph Williams. Ann Arbor: U of Michigan P, 1993: 227–256.
Goodwin, Donald Watson. *Text-Restoration Methods in Contemporary USA Biblical Scholarship.* Pubblicazioni del Seminario di Semistica a cura di Giovanni Garbini. Richerche V. Naples: Instituto Orientale di Napoli, 1969.
Gordis, Robert. *The Biblical Text in the Making.* Ph.D. Thesis. Philadelphia: Drupsie College for Hebrew and Cognate Learning, 1937.
Greenlee, J. Harold. *An Introduction to New Testament Textual Criticism.* Grand Rapids: Eerdmans, 1964.
—. *Scribes, Scrolls, and Scriptures: A Student's Guide to New Testament Criticism.* Grand Rapids: Eerdmans, 1985.
Kenyon, F. G. *The Text of the Greek Bible.* London: Duckworth, 1937. Rev. A. W. Adams, 1975.
—. *Books and Readers in Ancient Greece and Rome.* Oxford: Clarendon, 1951.
Metzger, Bruce M. *Annotated Bibliography of the Textual Criticism of the New Tes-*

tament, 1914–1939. Copenhagen: 1955.

—. *Chapters in the History of New Testament Textual Criticism.* Grand Rapids: Eerdmans, 1963.

—. *The Early Versions of the New Testament: Their Origin, Transmission, and Limitations.* Oxford: Clarendon, 1977.

*—. *The Text of the New Testament: Its Transmission, Corruption, and Restoration.* New York: Oxford UP, 1992. 3rd ed.

—. *The Canon of the New Testament, Its Origin, Development, and Significance.* Oxford: Clarendon, 1987. 2nd ed.

Orlinsky, Harry M. "The Textual Criticism of the Old Testament." *The Bible and the Ancient Near East: Essays in Honor of William Foxwell Albright.* Ed. George Ernest Wright. London: Routledge, 1961: 113–32.

—. "The Masoretic Text: A Critical Evaluation." Prolegomenon to Christian David Ginsburg. *Introduction to the Massoretico-critical Edition of the Hebrew Bible.* New York: KTAV, 1986: i–xlv.

Roberts, B. J. *The Old Testament Text and Versions.* Cardiff: U of Wales P, 1951.

Shanks, Hersel, ed. *Understanding the Dead Sea Scrolls: A Reader from the Biblical Archaeological Review.* New York: Vintage, 1993.

Souter, Alexander. *The Text and Canon of the New Testament.* London: Duckworth, 1954. 2nd ed.

Tanselle, G. Thomas. "Classical, Biblical, and Medieval Textual Criticism and Modern Editing." *Studies in Bibliography* 36 (1983): 21–68.

Taylor, Vincent. *The Text of the New Testament: A Short Introduction.* London and New York: 1961.

Tov, Emanuel. *The Text-Critical Use of the Septuagint in Biblical Research.* Jerusalem: Simor, 1981.

*—. "The Text of the Old Testament." *The World of the Bible.* Ed. A. S. van der Woude. Grand Rapids: Eerdmans, 1986: 156–190.

*—. *The Textual Criticism of the Bible: An Introduction.* 1992.

Twilley, L. D. *The Origin and Transmission of the New Testament: A Short Introduction.* Edinburgh: 1957.

Würthwein, Ernst. *The Text of the Old Testament: An Introduction to the Biblica Hebraica.* Trans. Erroll F. Rhodes. Grand Rapids: Eerdmans, 1979.

Zeitlin, S. *A Historical Study of the Canonization of the Hebrew Scriptures.* New York: Amer. Acad. for Jewish Research, 1933.

Classical Textual Criticism

Bagnall, Roger S. "Restoring the Text of Documents." *Text* 4 (1988): 109–19.

Brink, C. O. *English Classical Scholarship: Historical Reflections on Bentley, Porson and Housman.* Cambridge: Clark / New York: Oxford UP, 1986.

Cosenza, M. E. *Biographical and Bibliographical Dictionary of the Italian Humanists and the World of Classical Scholarship.* Oxford: Oxford UP, 1934–71. 6 vols.

Dain, Alphonse, ed. *Geschichte der Textüberlieferung der antiken und mittelalterlichen Literatur.* Zürich: Atlantis, 1961.

Geanakoplos, Deno J. *Greek Scholars in Venice: Studies in the Dissemination of Greek Learning from Byzantium to Western Europe.* Cambridge: Harvard UP, 1962.

*Hall, F. W. *A Companion to Classical Texts.* Oxford: Clarendon, 1913.

Havet, L. *Manuel de critique verbale appliquée aux textes latins.* Paris: Hachette, 1911. Repr. Rome: Bretschneider, 1967.

*Housman, A. E. "The Application of Thought to Textual Criticism," *Proceedings of the Classical Association* 18 (1921): 67–84. Repr. *Selected Prose*: 131–50. Repr. *Collected Poems and Selected Prose*: 325–39.

—. *Selected Prose.* Ed. John Carter. Cambridge: Cambridge UP, 1961.

—. *Collected Poems and Selected Prose.* Ed. Christopher Ricks. London: Allen Lane, The Penguin Press, 1988.
Hunt, R. W., ed. *The Survival of Ancient Literature.* Oxford: Bodleian Library, 1975.
Kennedy, George A., ed. *Classical Criticism*, vol. 1 of *The Cambridge History of Literary Criticism.* Cambridge: Cambridge UP, 1989.
*Kenney, E. J. *The Classical Text: Aspects of Editing in the Age of the Printed Book.* Berkeley: U of California P, 1974.
McGuire, Martin R. P. *Introduction to Classical Scholarship: A Syllabus and Bibliographical Guide.* Washington: Catholic U of America, 1961.
—. and H. Dressler. *Introduction to Medieval Latin Studies: A Syllabus and Bibliographical Guide.* Washington: Catholic U of America, 1977. 2nd ed.
Pack, Roger. *The Greek and Latin Literary Texts from Graeco-Roman Egypt.* Ann Arbor: U of Michigan P, 1965.
*Pfeiffer, Rudolph. *History of Classical Scholarship from the Beginnings to the End of the Hellenistic Age.* Oxford: Oxford UP, 1968.
*—. *History of Classical Scholarship from 1300 to 1850.* Oxford: Oxford UP, 1976.
Renehan, Robert. *Greek Textual Criticism: A Reader.* Cambridge: Harvard UP, 1969.
*Reynolds, L. D. and N. G. Wilson. *Scribes and Scholars: A Guide to the Transmission of Greek and Latin Literature.* Oxford: Oxford UP, 1974. 2nd ed.
—, ed. *Texts and Transmissions: A Survey of the Latin Classics.* Oxford: Clarendon P, 1983.
*Sandys, J. E. W. *A History of Classical Scholarship.* Cambridge: Cambridge UP, 1906–8. Repr. New York: Hafner, 1964. 2nd ed. 3 vols.
Tanselle, G. Thomas. "Classical, Biblical, and Medieval Textual Criticism and Modern Editing." *Studies in Bibliography* 36 (1983): 21–68.
Timpanaro, S. *La genesi del metodo del Lachmann.* Florence: Bibliotechina del saggiatore, 1963. Trans. as *Die Entstehung der Lachmannschen Methode.* Hamburg: Buske.
*West, M. L. *Textual Criticism and Editorial Technique Applicable to Greek and Latin Texts.* Stuttgart: Teubner, 1973.
Wilamowitz-Moellendorff, U. von. *History of Classical Scholarship.* Ed. Hugh Lloyd-Jones, trans. Alan Harris. Baltimore: Johns Hopkins UP, 1982.
Willis, James. *Latin Textual Criticism.* Urbana: U of Illinois P, 1972.
Zetzel, James. "Religion, Rhetoric, and Editorial Technique: Reconstructing the Classics." *Palimpsest: Editorial Theory in the Humanities.* Ed. George Bornstein and Ralph Williams. Ann Arbor: U of Michigan P, 1993: 99–120.

Anglophone Textual Criticism: Methods and Problems

Arn, Mary-Jo. "On Punctuating Medieval Literary Texts" *Text* 7 (1994).
Baender, Paul. "The Meaning of Copy-Text." *Studies in Bibliography* 22 (1969): 311–18.
Barber, Giles and Bernhard Fabian, eds. *Buch und Buchhandel in Europa im achtzehnten Jahrhundert.* Hamburg: Hauswedell, 1981.
Barnard, John. "Bibliographic Context and the Critic," *Text* 3 (1987): 27–46.
Barnes, Warner and James T. Cox, eds. "Textual Studies in the Novel." *Studies in the Novel* 7 (1975): 317–471.
Beal, Peter. "Notions in Garrison: The Seventeenth-Century Commonplace Book." *New Ways of Looking at Old Texts.* Ed. W. Speed Hill. Binghamton: Medieval & Renaissance Texts & Studies / Renaissance English Text Society, 1993: 131–148.
Becker, Robert Stephen. "Challenges in Editing Modern Literary Correspondence: Transcription," *Text* 1 (1984): 257–70.
Bennett, Betty T. "The Editor of Letters as Critic: A Denial of Blameless Neutrality"

Text 6 (1993): 213–224.

Bibliographical Society of America. *Fredson Bowers at Eighty*. New York: BSA, 1985.

Bowers, Fredson. "Current Theories of Copy-Text with an Illustration from Dryden." *Modern Philology* 68 (1950): 12–20.

—. "Greg's 'Rationale of Copy-Text' Revisited." *Studies in Bibliography* 31 (1970): 90–161.

—. "Multiple Authority: New Problems and Concepts of Copy-Text." *The Library* 5th Series 27 (1972): 81-115. Repr. *Essays*: 447–87.

*—. *Essays in Bibliography, Text, and Editing*. Charlottesville: UP of Virginia, 1975.

—. "Mixed Texts and Multiple Authority," *Text* 3 (1987): 63–90.

—. "Unfinished Business: Presidential Address, Society for Textual Scholarship." *Text* 4 (1988): 1–12.

—. "Regularization and Normalization in Modern Critical Texts." *Studies in Bibliography* 42 (1989): 79–102.

—. "Authorial Intention and Editorial Problems," *Text* 5 (1991): 49–62.

Bronson, Bertrand H. "Printing as an Index of Taste in Eighteenth-Century England." *Bulletin of the New York Public Library* 62 (1958): 373–87; 443–62. Repr. as pamphlet. New York: New York Public Library, 1958.

Cappon, Lester J. "The Historian as Editor." *In Support of Clio: Essays in Memory of Herbert A. Kellar*. Ed. William B. Hesseltine and Donald R. McNeil. Madison: State Historical Society of Wisconsin, 1958, 173–93.

*Chartier, Roger. "Livres bleus et lectures populaires." *L'histoire de l'édition française*. Ed. Henri-Jean Martin, Roger Chartier, and Jean-Pierre Vivet. Paris: Promodis, 1984.

*—. *The Cultural Uses of Print in Early Modern France*. Princeton: Princeton UP, 1987.

*—. *The Culture of Print: Power and the Uses of Print in Early Modern Europe*. Trans. Lydia G. Cochrane. Princeton: Princeton UP, 1987.

—. "Texts, Printing, Reading." *The New Cultural History*. Ed. Lynn Hunt. Berkeley: U of California P, 1989: 154–175.

—. "Meaningful Forms." *Liber* 1 (October, 1989): 8–9.

*—. *The Order of Books: Readers, Authors and Libraries in Europe between the 14th and 18th Centuries*. Trans. Lydia G. Cochrane. Stanford: Stanford UP, 1994.

Chaytor, H. J. "The Medieval Reader and Textual Criticism." *Bulletin of the John Rylands Library* 26 (1941–42): 49–56.

Cook, Don L. "The Short, Happy Thesis of G. Thomas Tanselle." *Newsletter of the Association for Documentary Editing* 3.1 (1981): 1–4.

—. "Some Considerations in the Concept of Pre-Copy-Text." *Text* 4 (1988): 79–91.

Darnton, Robert. "What Is the History of Books?" *Books and Society in History*. Ed. Kenneth E. Carpenter. New York: Bowker: 3–26.

— and Daniel Roche, eds. *Revolution in Print: The Press in France 1775–1800*. Berkeley: U of California P / New York: New York Public Library, 1989.

Davis, Tom. "The CEAA and Modern Textual Editing." *The Library* Fifth Series 32 (1977): 61–74.

—. "Substantives? Accidentals?" *Library* 6th Series 3 (1981): 149–151.

—. "Textual Criticism: Philosophy and Practice." *Library* 6th Series 6 (1984): 386–397.

Davison, Peter. "Science, Method, and the Textual Critic." *Studies in Bibliography* 25 (1972): 1–28.

—. "The Selection and Presentation of Bibliographical Evidence." *Analytical and Enumerative Bibliography* 1 (1977): 101–36.

Dearing, Vinton. "Concepts of Copy-Text Old and New." *The Library* Fifth Series 28 (1973): 281–93.

—. Principles and Practice of Textual Analysis. Berkeley: U of California P, 1974.

—. "Textual Analysis: A Kind of Textual Criticism," *Text* 2 (1985): 13–24.

*Dooley, Allan C. *Author and Printer in Victorian England.* Charlottesville: UP of Virginia, 1992.

Eisenstein, Elizabeth L. *The Printing Revolution in Early Modern Europe.* Cambridge: Cambridge UP, 1983.

—. *Print Culture and Enlightenment Thought.* Sixth Hanes Lecture. Chapel Hill, Hanes Foundation / U of N Carolina P, 1986.

Elsky, Martin. *Authorizing Words: Speech, Writing, and Print in the English Renaissance.* Ithaca: Cornell UP, 1989.

Erdman, David V. and Ephim G. Fogel, eds. *Evidence for Authorship: Essays on Problems of Attribution.* Ithaca: Cornell UP, 1966.

Gibson, William M. and George R. Petty, Jr. "Project OCCULT: The Ordered Computer Collation of Unprepared Literary Text." *Art and Error: Modern Textual Editing.* Ed. Ronald Gottesman and Scott Bennett. Bloomington: Indiana UP / London: Methuen, 1970: 279–300.

Glavin, John. "Bulgakov's Lizard and the Problem of Playwright's Authority," *Text* 4 (1988): 385–406.

Gorman, David. "The Wordly Text: Writing as Social Action, Reading as Historical Reconstruction." *Literary Theory's Future.* Ed. Joseph Natoli. Urbana: U of Illinois P, 1989: 181–220.

Greetham, D. C. "Politics and Ideology in Current Anglo-American Textual Scholarship." *Editio* 4 (1990): 1–20.

Greg, W. W. *A Calculus of Variants: An Essay on Textual Criticism.* Oxford: Clarendon P, 1927.

*—. "The Rationale of Copy-Text." *Studies in Bibliography* 3 (1950–51): 19–36.

Harkness, Bruce. "Bibliography and the Novelistic Fallacy." *Studies in Bibliography* 12 (1959): 59–74.

Hay, Louis. "Genetic Editing, Past and Present: A Few Reflections of a User." *Text* 3 (1987): 117–34.

Higgins, Brian and Hershel Parker. "The Chaotic Legacy of the New Criticism and the Fair Augury of the New Scholarship." *Ruined Eden of the Present: Hawthorne, Melville, and Poe.* Ed. G. R. Thompson and Virgil L. Lokke. 1981: 27–45.

*Hill, Archibald. "Some Postulates for Distributional Study of Texts." *Studies in Bibliography* 3 (1950–51): 63–95.

Hirsch, E. D., Jr. *Validity in Interpretation.* New Haven: Yale UP, 1967.

Howard-Hill, T. H. "Playwrights' Intentions and the Editing of Plays." *Text* 4 (1988): 269–278.

—. "Modern Editorial Theories and the Editing of Plays." *The Library* Sixth Series 11 (1989): 89–115.

—. "Theory and Praxis in the Social Approach to Editing." *Text* 5 (1991): 31–46.

Hruby, Antonín. "A Quantitative Solution to the Ambiguity of Three Texts." *Studies in Bibliography* 18 (1965): 147–82.

—. "Statistical Methods in Textual Criticism." *General Linguistics* 5 (1961–62): 77–138.

Hudson, Anne. "The Variable Text." Minnis and Brewer: 49–60.

Jack, Ian. "A Choice of Orders: The Arrangement of 'The Poetical Works'." *Textual Criticism and Literary Interpretation.* Ed. Jerome J. McGann. Chicago: U of Chicago P, 1985: 144–61.

Jacobs, Nicolas. "Regression to the Commonplace in Some Vernacular Textual Traditions." Minnis and Brewer: 61–70.

*Kane, George. "Conjectural Emendation." *Medieval Literature and Civilization: Studies in Memory of G. N. Garmonsway.* Ed. Derek Pearsall and R. A. Waldron. London: Athlone, 1969: 155–69.

—. "'Good' and 'Bad' Manuscripts: Texts and Critics." *Studies in the Age of Chaucer.*

supp. 2 (1985): 137–145.

Knight, Stephen. "Textual Variants: Textual Variance." *Southern Review* [Adelaide] 16 (1983): 44–54.

*Kristeller, Paul Oskar. "The Lachmann Method: Merits and Limitations," *Text* 1 (1984): 11–20.

*—. "Textual Scholarship and General Theories of History and Literature." *Text* 3 (1987): 1–9.

Long, William B. "Stage Directions: A Misinterpreted Factor in Determining Textual Provenance," *Text* 2 (1985): 121–38.

Machan, Tim William. "Middle English Text Production and Modern Textual Criticism." Minnis and Brewer: 1–18.

MacLean, Gerald M. "What Is a Restoration Poem? Editing a Discourse, Not an Author." *Text* 3 (1987): 319–47.

—. "Literacy, Class, and Gender in Restoration England." *Text* 7 (1994).

Madden, David and Richard Powers. *Writers' Revisions: An Annotated Bibliography of Articles and Books about Writers' Revisions and Their Comments on the Creative Process.* Metuchen: Scarecrow, 1991.

Marotti, Arthur. "Malleable and Fixed Texts: Manuscript and Printed Miscellanies and the Transmission of Lyric Poetry in the English Renaisance." *New Ways of Looking at Old Texts.* Ed. W. Speed Hill. Binghamton: Medieval & Renaissance Texts & Studies / Renaissance English Text Society, 1993: 159–174.

—. "Manuscript, Print, and the English Renaissance Lyric." *New Ways*: 223–228.

McAdam, E. L. "The Textual Approach to Meaning." *English Institute Essays* 1946: 191–201

McGann, Jerome J. "The Text, the Poem, and the Problem of Historical Method." *New Literary History* 12 (1981): 269–88.

*—. *A Critique of Modern Textual Criticism.* Chicago: U of Chicago P, 1983. Repr. Charlottesville: UP of Virginia, 1992.

—. "Shall These Bones Live?" *Text* 1 (1984): 21–40.

(See also entries under Textual Theory)

McLeod, Randall. "The Marriage of Good and Bad Quartos." *Shakespeare Quarterly* 33 (1982): 421–431.

—. (Random Cloud). "The Psychopathology of Everyday Art." *The Elizabethan Theatre* 9 (1986): 100–168.

—. "Information upon Information," *Text* 5 (1991): 241–86.

*Minnis, A. J. and Charlotte Brewer, eds. *Crux and Controversy in Middle English Textual Criticism.* Cambridge: Brewer, 1992.

Modern Language Association of America. *Professional Standards and American Editions: A Response to Edmund Wilson.* New York: MLA, 1969.

Neumann, Frederick. "Text and Interpretation in Eighteenth-Century Music." *Text* 2 (1985): 251–256.

Parker, Hershel. "Regularizing Accidentals: The Latest Form of Infidelity." *Proof* 3 (1973): 1–20.

—. "The 'New Scholarship': Textual Evidence and Its Implications for Criticism, Literary Theory, and Aesthetics." *Studies in American Fiction* 9 (1981): 181–197.

Pearsall, Derek. "Texts, Textual Criticism, and Fifteenth-Century Manuscript Production." *Fifteenth-Century Studies: Recent Essays.* Ed. Robert F. Yeager. Hamden: Archon, 1984: 121–136.

—. "Authorial Revision in Some Late-Medieval English Texts." Minnis and Brewer: 39–48.

Peckham, Morse. "Reflections on the Foundations of Modern Textual Editing." *Proof* 1 (1971): 122–55.

Pizer, Donald. "On the Editing of Modern American Texts." *Bulletin of the New York Public Library* 75 (1971): 147–53; 504–05.

—. "Self-Censorship and Textual Editing." *Textual Criticism and Literary Interpreta-*

tion. Ed. Jerome J. McGann. Chicago: U of Chicago P, 1985: 144–161.

Quentin, Dom Henri. *Essai de critique textuelle.* Paris: Picard, 1926.

*Reiman, Donald H. *The Study of Modern Manuscripts: Public, Confidential, and Private.* Baltimore: Johns Hopkins UP, 1993.

*Robinson, Peter M. W. "Collation, Textual Criticism, Publication and the Computer." *Text* 7 (1994).

Rosenberg, Robert. "Technological Artifacts as Historical Documents." *Text* 3 (1987): 393–407.

Severs, J. Burke. "Quentin's Theory of Textual Criticism." *English Institute Annual* 1941 (New York 1942): 65–93.

Shaw, David. "A Sampling Theory for Bibliographical Research." *The Library* Fifth Series 27 (1972): 310–19.

Simon, John Y. "Editors and Critics." *Newsletter of the Association for Documentary Editing* 3 (Dec. 1981): 1–4.

Speer, Mary B. "Textual Criticism Redivivus." *L'Ésprit Créateur* 23 (1983): 38–48.

Stillinger, Jack. "Multiple Authorship and the Question of Authority," *Text* 5 (1991): 285–96.

—. *Multiple Authorship and the Myth of Solitary Genius.* New York: Oxford UP, 1991.

Sullivan, Ernest W., II. "The Problem of Text in Familiar Letters." *Papers of the Bibliographical Society of America* 75 (1981): 115–126.

Tanselle, G. Thomas. "Textual Study and Literary Judgment." *Papers of the Bibliographical Society of America* 65 (1971): 109–22.

—. "The Periodical Literature of English and American Bibliography." *Studies in Bibliography* 26 (1973): 167–91.

—. "Bibliography and Science." *Studies in Bibliography* 27 (1974): 55–89.

*—. "Greg's Theory of Copy-Text and the Editing of American Literature." *Studies in Bibliography* 28 (1975): 167–229.

—. "Bibliographers and the Library." *Library Trends* 25 (1976–77): 745–62.

*—. "External Fact as an Editorial Problem." *Studies in Bibliography* 32 (1979): 1–47.

—. *The History of Books as a Field of Study.* Second Hanes Lecture, Hanes Foundation. Chapel Hill: U. of North Carolina, 1981.

*—. "Recent Editorial Discussion and the Central Questions of Editing." *Studies in Bibliography* 34 (1981): 23–65.

—. "The Bibliography and Textual Study of American Books." *Proceedings of the American Antiquarian Society* 95 (1985): 113–151.

—. "Historicism and Critical Editing." *Studies in Bibliography* 39 (1986): 1–46.

—. "Bibliographical History as a Field of Study." *Studies in Bibliography* 41 (1988): 33–63.

—. "Reproductions and Scholarship." *Studies in Bibliography* 42 (1989): 25–54.

—. *Libraries, Museums, and Reading.* Sixth Sol. M. Malkin Lecture in Bibliography (Book Arts Press Occasional Publication No. 10). New York: Book Arts P, 1991.

*—. "Textual Criticism and Literary Sociology" *Studies in Bibliography* 44 (1991): 83–143.

*Taylor, Gary. "The Rhetoric of Textual Criticism." *Text* 4 (1988): 39–56.

Taylor, Robert. "Editorial Practices — An Historian's View." *Newsletter of the Association for Documentary Editing* 3.1 (1981): 4–8.

Thompson, John. "Textual Instability and the Late Medieval Reputation of Some Middle English Religious Literature." *Text* 5 (1991): 175–194.

Thorpe, James. "Literary and Historical Editing: The Values and Limits of Diversity." *Literary and Historical Editing.* Ed. George L. Vogt and John Bush Jones. Lawrence: U of Kansas Libraries, 1981: 13–22.

—. "The Practice of Our Craft." *Text* 6 (1993): 1–10.

Velz, John W. "From Authorization to Authorship, Orality to Literature: The Case of

Medieval and Renaissance Drama." *Text* 6 (1993): 197-212.

Weiss, Adrian. "Reproductions of Early Dramatic Texts as a Source of Bibliographical Evidence." *Text* 4 (1988): 237-268.

Weitzman, Michael. "The Analysis of Open Traditions." *Studies in Bibliography* 38 (1985): 82-120.

Wellek, René and Alvaro Ribeiro, eds. *Evidence in Literary Scholarship.* Oxford: Clarendon P, 1979.

West, James L. W., III. "Fair Copy, Authorial Intention, and 'Versioning'." *Text* 6 (1993): 81-92.

—. *Creating American Authors: The Language of Editing.* Ann Arbor: U of Michigan P. Forthcoming.

Willis, James. "The Science of Blunders: Confessions of a Textual Critic." *Text* 6 (1993): 63-80.

*Wilson, Edmund. *The Fruits of the MLA.* New York: New York Review of Books, 1968.

*Zeller, Hans. "A New Approach to the Critical Constitution of Literary Texts." *Studies in Bibliography* 28 (1975): 231-63.

Selected Anglophone Textual Criticism of Individual Authors or Works

Alspach, Russell K. "Some Textual Problems in Yeats." *Studies in Bibliography* 9 (1957): 51-67. Repr. *Art and Error: Modern Textual Editing.* Ed. Ronald Gottesman and Scott Bennett. Bloomington: Indiana UP / London: Methuen, 1970.

Barker, Nicholas. *A Sequel to* An Enquiry . . . ; *The Forgeries of H. Buxton Forman and T. J. Wise Re-Examined.* London: Scolar, 1983. (See Carter and Pollard).

Bates, Robin. "Reflections on the Kidd Era." *Studies in the Novel* 22 (1990): 119-41.

Beadle, Richard. "The York Cycle: Texts, Performances, and the Bases for Critical Enquiry." Tim W. Machan, ed. *Medieval Literature: Texts and Interpretations.* Binghamton: Medieval & Renaissance Texts & Studies, 1991: 105-120.

Bennett, Betty T. "Feminism and Editing Mary Wollstonecraft Shelley: The Editor And? / Or? the Text." *Palimpsest: Editorial Theory in the Humanities.* Ed. George Bornstein and Ralph Williams. Ann Arbor: U of Michigan P, 1993: 67-96.

Bentley, G. E., Jr. "William Blake's Protean Text." *Editing Eighteenth-Century Texts.* Ed. D. I. B. Smith. Toronto: Hakkert, 1972: 44-58.

—. "Blake's Works as Performances: Attentions and Inattentions," *Text* 4 (1988): 319-42.

Boffey, Julia. "Middle English Lyrics: Texts and Interpretation." Tim W. Machan, ed. *Medieval Literature: Texts and Interpretations.* Binghamton: Medieval & Renaissance Texts & Studies, 1991: 121-138.

Bornstein, George. "Remaking Himself: Yeats's Revisions of His Early Canon," *Text* 5 (1991): 341-60.

—. "What Is the Text of a Poem by Yeats?" *Palimpsest: Editorial Theory in the Humanities.* Ed. George Bornstein and Ralph Williams. Ann Arbor: U of Michigan P, 1993: 167-194.

Bowers, Fredson. "Shakespeare's Text and the Bibliographical Method." *Studies in Bibliography* 6 (1954): 71-91.

—. "The Text of Johnson." *Modern Philology* 61 (1964): 298-309.

Bowers, John M. "Hoccleve's Two Copies of *Lerne To Dye*: Implications for Textual Critics." *Papers of the Bibliographical Society of America* 83 (1989): 437-472.

Bradford, Curtis B. *Yeats at Work.* New York: Ecco, 1978.

Brewer, Charlotte. "Authorial vs. Scribal Writing in *Piers Plowman.* Tim W. Machan, ed. *Medieval Literature: Texts and Interpretations.* Binghamton: Medieval & Renaissance Texts & Studies, 1991: 59-90.

Bruccoli, Matthew. *The Composition of* Tender Is the Night: *A Study of the Manuscripts.* Pittsburgh: U of Pittsburgh P, 1963.

Bush, Ronald. "'Unstill, Ever Turning': The Composition of Ezra Pound's *Drafts and Fragments*." *Text* 7 (1994).

Cameron, Sharon. *Choosing Not Choosing: Dickinson's Fascicles*. Chicago: U of Chicago P, 1993.

Carter, Harry and Graham Pollard. *An Enquiry into the Nature of Certain Nineteenth-Century Pamphlets*. London: Constable, 1934. Rev. 1983.

Cohen, Philip. *Texts and Textuality: Textual Instability, Theory, Interpretation, and Pedagogy*. New York: Paragon H. Forthcoming.

—. "'The Key to the Whole Book': Faulkner's *The Sound and the Fury*, the Compson Appendix, and Textual Instability." Cohen *Texts and Textuality*.

Crane, Elaine Forman. "Gender Consciousness in Editing: The Diary of Elizabeth Drinker," *Text* 4 (1988): 375–84.

Dane, Joseph A. "The Notions of Text and Variant in the Prologue to Chaucer's *Legend of Good Women*. *Papers of the Bibliographical Society of America*. 87 (1993): 65–80.

De Grazia, Margreta. *Shakespeare Verbatim: The Reproduction of Authenticity and the 1790 Apparatus*. New York: Oxford UP, 1991.

Dobson, Michael. *The Making of the National Poet: Shakespeare, Adaptation and Authorship, 1660–1769*. New York: Oxford UP, 1992.

Donaldson, E. T. *Speaking of Chaucer*. London: Athlone / New York: Norton, 1970.

Doyno, Victor A. *Writing Huck Finn: Mark Twain's Creative Process*. Philadelphia: U of Pennsylvania P, 1991.

Eggert, Paul. "The Literary Work of a Readership: *The Boy in the Bush* in Australia, 1924–1926." *Bibliographical Society of Australia and New Zealand Bulletin* 12 (1988): 149–166.

—. "An Editorial Commitment to History: Tracking the Agent and Moment of Composition in D. H. Lawrence's *The Rainbow* and *Twilight in Italy*." Cohen *Texts and Textuality*.

Feehan, Michael. "Multiple Editorial Horizons in the Study of *Leaves of Grass*." Cohen *Texts and Textuality*.

Finkelstein, David. "Breaking the Thread: The Authorial Reinvention of John Hanning Speke in his *Journal of the Discovery of the Nile*." *Text* 8. Forthcoming.

Fisher, John H. "Historical and Methodological Considerations for Adopting 'Best Text' or 'Usus Scribendi' for Textual Criticism of Chaucer's Poems." *Text* 6 (1993): 165–180.

Foxon, D. F. *Thomas J. Wise and Pre-Restoration Drama*. London: Bibliographical Society, 1959.

*Gabler, Hans Walter. "The Synchrony and Diachrony of Texts: Practice and Theory of the Critical Edition of James Joyce's *Ulysses*." *Text* 1 (1984): 305–26.

—. "A Response to John Kidd, 'Errors of Execution in the 1984 *Ulysses*.'" Conference paper, Society for Textual Scholarship, New York City, April 26, 1985. *Studies in the Novel* 22 (1990): 250–56.

—. "On Textual Criticism and Editing: The Case of Joyce's *Ulysses*." *Palimpsest: Editorial Theory in the Humanities*. Ed. George Bornstein and Ralph Williams. Ann Arbor: U of Michigan P, 1993: 195–224.

Gaskell, Philip. "*Night and Day*: Development of a Play Text." *Textual Criticism and Literary Interpretation*. Ed. Jerome J. McGann. Chicago: U of Chicago P, 1985: 162–79.

— and Clive Hart, eds. Ulysses: *A Review of Three Texts*. New York: Barnes and Noble, 1989.

Geduld, Harry M. "*Back to Methuselah*: Textual Problems in Shaw." *Art and Error: Modern Textual Editing*. Ed. Ronald Gottesman and Scott Bennett. Bloomington: Indiana UP /London: Methuen, 1970: 208–218.

Goodheart, Eugene. "Censorship and Self-Censorship in the Fiction of D. H. Lawrence." *Representing Modernist Texts*. Ed. George Bornstein. Ann Arbor: U of

Michigan P, 1991: 223-240.

Hanna, Ralph, III. "Representing Chaucer as Author." Tim W. Machan, ed. *Medieval Literature: Texts and Interpretations*. Binghamton: Medieval & Renaissance Texts & Studies, 1991: 17-40.

Hewitt, David S. "Burns and the Argument for Standardisation," *Text* 1 (1984): 217-30.

—. "Scott and Textual Multipoinding." *Text* 4 (1988): 361-73.

Higdon, David Leon and Mark C. Harper. "Auden 'Abandons' a Poem: Problems of Eclectic Texts." *Text* 7 (1994).

Hobson, Christopher Z. "Richard Wright's Communisms: Textual Variance, Intentionality, and Socialization in Wright's *American Hunger* and *I Tried to Be a Communist*." *Text* 6 (1993): 307-344.

Holdeman, David. "Interpreting Textual Processes: The Case of Yeats's *In the Seven Woods*." *Text* 8. Forthcoming.

Honigmann, Ernest A. J. *The Stability of Shakespeare's Text*. London: Edward Arnold, 1965.

—. "Shakespeare as a Reviser." *Textual Criticism and Literary Interpretation*. Ed. Jerome J. McGann. Chicago: U of Chicago P, 1985: 1-22.

Horne, Philip. *Henry James and Revision: The New York Edition*. New York: Oxford UP, 1991.

Howard-Hill, T. H. "The Author as Scribe or Reviser? Middleton's Intentions in *A Game at Chess*." *Text* 3 (1987): 305-318.

Hunt, Tim. "Double the *Axe*, Double the Fun: Is There a Final Version of Jeffers' *The Double Axe*?" *Text* 7 (1994).

Ioppolo, Grace. "'Old' and 'New' Revisionists: Shakespeare's Eighteenth-Century Editors." *Huntington Library Quarterly* 52 (1989): 347-61.

—. *Revising Shakespeare*. Cambridge: Harvard UP, 1991.

Jackson, Donald. "The Papers of George Washington." *Manuscripts* 22 (1970): 3-11.

Jefferson, Judith A. "The Hoccleve Holographs and Hoccleve's Metrical Practice." *Manuscripts and Texts*. Ed. Derek Pearsall. Cambridge: Brewer, 1987: 95-109.

Johnson, Linck C. *Thoreau's Complex Weave: The Writing of* A Week on the Concord and Merrimack Rivers *with the Text of the First Draft*. Charlottesville: UP of Virginia, 1986.

Jones, Steven. "Material Intertextuality: The Case of Shelley's Rough-Draft Notebooks." *Text* 8. Forthcoming.

Jordan, Heather Bryant. "*Ars Vos Prec*: A Rescued Volume." *Text* 7 (1994).

Jowett, John. "Jonson's Authorization of Type in *Sejanus* and Other Early Quartos." *Studies in Bibliography* 44 (1991): 254-265. Repr. *New Ways of Looking at Old Texts*. Ed. W. Speed Hill. Binghamton: Medieval & Renaissance Texts & Studies / Renaissance English Text Society, 1993: 175-186.

*Kane, George. "The Text." *A Companion to Piers Plowman*. Ed. John A. Alford. Berkeley: U of California P, 1988: 175-200.

*—. *Chaucer and Langland: Historical and Textual Approaches*. London: Athlone / Berkeley: U of California P, 1989.

Kappel, Andrew. "Complete with Omissions: The Text of Marianne Moore's *Complete Poems*." *Representing Modernist Texts*. Ed. George Bornstein. Ann Arbor: U of Michigan P, 1991: 125-156.

Kelly, Birte. "The Formative Stages of *Beowulf* Textual Scholarship." *Anglo-Saxon England* 11 (1983): 247-274.

Kidd, John. "Errors of Execution in the 1984 *Ulysses*." Conference paper, Society for Textual Scholarship, New York City, April 26, 1985. *Studies in the Novel* 22 (1990): 243-49.

—. "The Scandal of *Ulysses*." *New York Review of Books* 30 June, 1988: 32-39.

*—. "An Inquiry into *Ulysses: The Corrected Text*." *Papers of the Bibliographical Society of America* 82.4 (Dec., 1988): 411-584.

Kroll, Richard W. F. "Mise-en-Page, Biblical Criticism, and Inference During the Restoration." *Studies in Eighteenth-Century Culture* 16 (1986): 3–40.

Laurence, Dan H. "A Bibliographical Novitiate: In Search of Henry James." *Papers of the Bibliographical Society of America* 52 (1958): 23–33.

Machan, Tim W. "Speght's *Works* and the Invention of Chaucer." *Text* 8. Forthcoming.

McDermott, Anne and Marcus Walsh. "Editing Johnson's *Dictionary*: Some Editorial and Textual Considerations." *Theory and Practice of Text-Editing*. Ed. Ian Small and Marcus Walsh. Cambridge: Cambridge UP, 1991: 35–61.

McGann, Jerome J. "The Case of *The Ambassadors* and the Textual Condition." *Palimpsest: Editorial Theory in the Humanities*. Ed. George Bornstein and Ralph Williams. Ann Arbor: U of Michigan P, 151–166.

McKenzie, D. F. "Typography and Meaning: The Case of William Congreve." *Buch und Buchhandel in Europa im achtzehnten Jahrhundert*. Ed. Giles Barber and Bernhard Fabian. Hamburg: Hauswedell, 1981: 81–125.

McKerrow, R. B. *Prolegomena for the Oxford Shakespeare*. Oxford: Clarendon, 1939. Repr. 1969.

McLeod, Randall (Random Cloud). "Tranceformations in the Text of *Orlando Furioso*." Oliphant and Bradford: 61–86.

Mendelson, Edward. "The Fading Coal vs. The Gothic Cathedral or What to Do about an Author Both Forgetful and Deceased." *Text* 3 (1987): 409–16.

—. "The Two Audens and the Claims of History." *Representing Modernist Texts*. Ed. George Bornstein. Ann Arbor: U of Michigan P, 1991: 157–170.

Menikoff, Barry. *Robert Louis Stevenson and "The Beach at Falesá": A Study in Victorian Publishing with the Original Text*. Stanford: Stanford UP, 1984.

Meriwether, James B. "Notes on the Textual History of *The Sound and the Fury*." *Papers of the Bibliographical Society of America* 56 (1962): 285–316. Repr. *Art and Error: Modern Textual Editing*. Ed. Ronald Gottesman and Scott Bennett. Bloomington: Indiana UP / London: Methuen, 1970: 219–252.

Metz, G. Harold. "Disputed Shakespearean Texts and Stylometric Analysis," *Text* 2 (1985): 149–72.

Moon, Michael. *Disseminating Whitman: Revision and Corporeality in Leaves of Grass*. Cambridge: Harvard UP, 1991.

Morris, Tim. "'Thought Undressed': Some Theoretical Implications of the Texts of Dickinson's Poems." Cohen *Texts and Textuality*.

*Mumford, Lewis. "Emerson Behind Barbed Wire." *New York Review of Books*, 18 January, 1968: 3–5.

Murphy, James. "Henry James and the Dance of Intention: Towards an Unstructuring of Authorial Intention." Cohen *Texts and Textuality*.

Nicholson, Peter. "Poet and Scribe in the Manuscripts of Gower's *Confessio Amantis*." *Manuscripts and Texts*. Ed. Derek Pearsall. Cambridge: Brewer, 1987: 130–142.

Oberg, Barbara. "Benjamin Franklin's Correspondence: Whose Intent? What Text? I Don't Know's the Author." *Palimpsest: Editorial Theory in the Humanities*. Ed. George Bornstein and Ralph Williams. Ann Arbor: U of Michigan P, 1993: 271–284.

Oliphant, Dave and Robin Bradford, eds. *New Directions in Textual Studies*. Austin: Harry Ransom Humanities Research Center / U of Texas P, 1990.

Parker, Hershel. "Melville and the Concept of 'Author's Final Intentions.'" *Proof* 1 (1971): 156–68.

Parrish, Stephen M. "The Whig Interpretation of Literature." *Text* 4 (1988): 343–50.

*Patterson, Lee. "The Logic of Textual Criticism and the Way of Genius: The Kane-Donaldson *Piers Plowman* in Historical Perspective." *Textual Criticism and Literary Interpretation*. Ed. Jerome J. McGann. Chicago: U of Chicago P, 1985: 55–91.

Pebworth, Ted-Larry. "John Donne, Coterie Poetry, and the Text as Performance."

Studies in English Literature 29 (1989): 61–75.

— and Ernest W. Sullivan II. "Rational Presentation of Multiple Textual Traditions." *Papers of the Bibliographical Society of America* 83 (1989): 43–60.

—. "Manuscript Transmission and the Selection of Copy-Text in Renaissance Coterie Poetry." *Text* 7 (1994).

Peters, Julie Stone. *Congreve, the Drama, and the Printed Word*. Stanford: Stanford UP, 1990.

Phelps, C. Deirdre. "The Edition as Art Form: Social and Authorial Readings of Wil liam Cullen Bryant's *Poems*." *Text* 6 (1993): 249–286.

Pollard, Alfred W. *Shakespeare's Fight with the Pirates and the Problems of the Transmission of His Text*. Sandars Lectures in Bibliography 1915. London: Moring, 1917.

Rainey, Lawrence S. "Canon, Gender, and Text: The Case of H.D." *Representing Modernist Texts*. Ed. George Bornstein. Ann Arbor: U of Michigan P, 1991: 99–124.

—. "The Letters and the Spirit: The Correspondence of Ezra Pound." *Text* 7 (1994).

Rasmussen, Eric. "Rehabilitating the A-Text of Marlowe's *Dr. Faustus*." *Studies in Bibliography* 46 (1993): 221–238.

Reddick, Allen. *The Making of Johnson's Dictionary*. Cambridge: Cambridge UP, 1991.

Ross, Charles L. *The Composition of The Rainbow and Women in Love: A History*. Charlottesville: UP of Virginia, 1979.

Rossman, Charles. "The New *Ulysses*: The Hidden Controversy." *New York Review of Books* December 8, 1988: 53–58.

—. "The Critical Reception of the "Gabler *Ulysses*": Or, Gabler's *Ulysses* Kidd-Napped." *Studies in the Novel* 21 (1989): 154–81.

—, ed. *Studies in the Novel: Special Issue on Editing* Ulysses. 22 (1990): 113–269.

Rubey, Daniel. "Howells's *Venetian Life* as a Vertical Text: Authors/Writers, Text(s), and Copy-Text Theory." *Text* 5 (1991): 315–338.

Saatkamp, Herman J. "Final Intentions, Social Context, and Santayana's Autobiography," *Text* 4 (1988): 93–108.

Shillingsburg, Peter L. *Pegasus in Harness: Victorian Publishing and W. M. Thackeray*. Charlottesville: UP of Virginia, 1992.

Silver, Brenda R. "Textual Criticism as Feminist Practice: Or, Who's Afraid of Virginia Woolf Part II." *Representing Modernist Texts*. Ed. George Bornstein. Ann Arbor: U of Michigan P, 1991: 193–222.

—. "Fighting Over 'A Room of One's Own'." Greetham *Margins of the Text*. In preparation.

Smith, Johanna. "'Hideous Progenies': The Texts of *Frankenstein*." Cohen *Texts and Textuality*.

Spear, Gary. "Reading Before the Lines: Typography, Iconography, and the Author in Milton's 1645 Frontispiece." *New Ways of Looking at Old Texts*. Ed. W. Speed Hill. Binghamton: Medieval & Renaissance Texts & Studies / Renaissance English Text Society, 1993: 187–197.

Stallworthy, Jon. *Between the Lines: W. B. Yeats's Poetry in the Making*. Oxford: Clarendon P, 1963.

Stillinger, Jack. *Coleridge and Textual Instability: The Multiple Versions of the Major Poems*. New York: Oxford UP, 1994.

Stuber, Florian. "On Original and Final Intentions, or Can There Be an Authoritative *Clarissa*?" *Text* 2 (1985): 229–44.

Sullivan, Ernest W., II. "*1633* Vndone." *Text* 7 (1994).

*Taylor, Gary. "Revising Shakespeare." *Text* 3 (1987): 285–304.

*—. "The Renaissance and the End of Editing." *Palimpsest: Editorial Theory in the Humanities*. Ed. George Bornstein and Ralph Williams. Ann Arbor: U of Michigan P, 121–150.

*— and Michael Warren, eds. *The Division of the Kingdoms: Shakespeare's Two Versions of King Lear.* Oxford: Clarendon, 1983.

— and John Jowett. *Shakespeare Reshaped 1606-1623.* New York: Oxford UP, 193.

Todd, William B. "Bibliography and the Editorial Problem in the Eighteenth Century." *Studies in Bibliography* 4 (1951): 41-56.

*Urkowitz, Steven. *Shakespeare's Revision of King Lear.* Princeton: Princeton UP, 1980.

—. "'Well Said, Old Mole': Burying Three *Hamlets* in Modern Editions." *Shakespeare Study Today.* Ed. Georgiana Ziegler. New York: AMS, 1986: 37-70.

Vander Meulen, David. "*The Dunciad in Four Books* and the Bibliography of Pope." *Papers of the Bibliographical Society of America* 83 (1989): 293-310.

*Von Frank, Albert, Jr. "Genetic versus Clear Texts: Reading and Writing Emerson." *Documentary Editing* 9 (1987): 5-9.

Walsh, Marcus. "Text, 'Text', and Swift's *A Tale of a Tub.*" *Modern Language Review* 85 (1990): 290-303.

—. "Bentley Our Contemporary: Or, Editors Ancient and Modern." Small and Walsh *The Theory and Practice of Text-Editing.* Cambridge: Cambridge UP, 1991: 157-185.

Wells, Stanley. *Modernizing Shakespeare's Spelling.* Oxford: Clarendon / New York: Oxford UP, 1979.

—. "Revision in Shakespeare's Plays." *Editing and Editors: A Retrospect.* Ed. Richard Landon. New York: AMS, 1988: 67-97.

*— and Gary Taylor, with John Jowett and William Montgomery. *William Shakespeare: A Textual Companion.* Oxford: Clarendon, 1987.

Woodring, Carl. "Recording from Coleridge's Voice." *Text* 3 (1987): 367-376.

Woshinsky, Barbara. "La Bruyère's *Caractères*: A Typographical Reading," *Text* 2 (1985): 229-43.

Zitner, S. P. "Four Feet in the Grave: Some Stage Directions in *Hamlet*, V.i," *Text* 2 (1985): 139-48.

Textual Theory

Barnard, John. "Bibliographic Context and the Critic." *Text* 3 (1987): 27-46.

Bate, Jonathan and Sonia Massai. "Adaptation as Edition." Greetham *Margins of the Text.*

Bateson, F. W. "Modern Bibliography and the Literary Artifact." *English Studies Today.* Ed. Georges A. Bonnard. Bern: 1961: 67-77. 2nd ed.

Bloch, R. Howard. "New Philology and Old French." Nichols: 38-58.

Bolter, Jay David. "Hyperbaton and Hypertext: The Rhetoric of the Electronic Writing Space." Cohen *Texts and Textuality.*

*Bornstein, George and Ralph Williams, eds. *Palimpsest: Editorial Theory in the Humanities.* Ann Arbor: U of Michigan P, 1993.

Brockbank, Philip. "Towards a Mobile Text." Small and Walsh: 90-106.

Camille, Michael. "Gloss, Graffiti and Grotesque on the Scholastic Page." Greetham *Margins of the Text.*

Chartier, Roger. "Meaningful Forms." *Liber* 1 (October, 1989): 8-9.

*Cohen, Philip, ed. *Devils and Angels: Textual Editing and Literary Theory.* Charlottesville: UP of Virginia, 1991.

—, ed. *Texts and Textuality: Textual Instability, Theory, Interpretation, and Pedagogy.* New York: Paragon H. Forthcoming.

— and David H. Jackson. "Notes on Emerging Paradigms in Editorial Theory." Cohen *Devils*: 103-123.

Currie, Gregory. "Work and Text." *Mind* 100 (1991): 325-341.

Dane, Joseph A. "The Lure of Oral Theory in Medieval Criticism: From Edited 'Text' to Critical 'Work'." *Text* 7 (1994).

Darnton, Robert. *The Business of Enlightenment: A Publishing History of the Encyclopédie 1775-1800*. Cambridge: Belknap / Harvard UP, 1979.

—. *The Literary Underground of the Old Regime*. Cambridge: Harvard UP, 1982.

*—. "What Is the History of Books?" *Daedalus* 111 (1982): 65-83.

—. *The Great Cat Massacre and Other Episodes in French Cultural History*. New York: Vintage, 1984.

Davis, Robert Murray. "Writing as Process: Beyond Hershel Parker." *Literary Research* 12 (1987): 179-86.

De Grazia, Margreta. "Sanctioning Voice: Quotation Marks, the Abolition of Torture, and the Fifth Amendment." Jaszi and Woodhouse: 545-566.

—. "What Is a Work? What Is a Document?" *New Ways of Looking at Old Texts*. Ed. W. Speed Hill. Binghamton: Medieval & Renaissance Texts & Studies / Renaissance English Text Society, 1993: 199-208.

Delery, Clayton. "The Subject Presumed to Know: Implied Authority and Editorial Apparatus." *Text* 5 (1991): 63-80.

Derrida, Jacques. "This Is Not an Oral Footnote." *Annotation and Its Texts*. Ed. Stephen A. Barney. New York: Oxford UP, 1991: 192-206.

Eggert, Paul. "Textual Product or Textual Process: Procedures and Assumptions of Critical Editing." Cohen *Devils*: 57-77.

—. "Document and Text: The 'Life' of the Literary Work and the Capacities of Editing." *Text* 7 (1994).

Felker, Christopher. "'The Tongues of the Learned Are Insufficient'." Cohen *Texts and Textuality*.

Feltes, N. N. *Modes of Production of Victorian Novels*. Chicago: U of Chicago P, 1986.

Fleischmann, Suzanne. "Philology, Linguistics, and the Discourse of the Medieval Text." Nichols: 19-37.

Flint, Kate. *The Woman Reader 1837-1914*. Oxford: Clarendon P, 1993.

Foley, John Miles. "Oral Tradition and Textuality." Cohen *Texts and Textuality*.

Gabler, Hans Walter. "The Text as Process and the Problem of Intentionality," *Text* 3 (1987): 107-16.

—. "Textual Studies and Criticism." Oliphant and Bradford: 151-66.

—. "Unsought Encounters." Cohen *Devils*: 152-166.

Gill, Stephen. "The Question of Text." *Review of English Studies* 34 (1983): 172-190.

Ginsburg, Jane C. "Copyright without Walls?: Speculations on Literary Property in the Library of the Future." *Representations* 42 (Spring 1993): 53-73.

Ginzburg, Carlo. *Clues, Myths, and the Historical Method*. Trans. Anne and John Tedeschi. Baltimore: Johns Hopkins UP, 1989.

Goldberg, Jonathan. "Textual Properties." *Shakespearean Quarterly* 37 (1986): 213-217.

*—. *Writing Matter: From the Hands of the English Renaissance*. Stanford: Stanford UP, 1990.

—. "Under the Covers with Caliban." Greetham *Margins of the Text*.

Gorman, David. "The Wordly Text: Writing as Social Action, Reading as Historical Reconstruction." *Literary Theory's Future*. Ed. Joseph Natoli. Urbana: U of Illinois P, 1989: 181-220.

*Greetham, D. C. "Textual and Literary Theory: Redrawing the Matrix." *Studies in Bibliography* 42 (1989): 1-24.

—. "[Textual] Criticism and Deconstruction." *Studies in Bibliography* 44 (1991): 1-30.

—. "The Manifestation and Accommodation of Theory in Textual Editing." Cohen *Devils*: 78-102.

—. "Editorial and Critical Theory: From Modernism to Post-modernism." Bornstein and Williams: 9-28.

—. *Theories of the Text*. Oxford: Oxford UP. Forthcoming.

—, ed. *The Margins of the Text*. In preparation.

Grigely, Joseph. "The Textual Event." Cohen *Devils*: 167–194.

—. "Textual Criticism and the Arts: The Problem of Textual Space." *Text* 7 (1994).

—. *Textualterity: Art, Theory, and Textual Criticism*. Ann Arbor: U of Michigan P. Forthcoming.

*Groden, Michael. "Contemporary Textual and Literary Theory." *Representing Modernist Texts: Editing as Interpretation*. Ed. George Bornstein. Ann Arbor: U of Michigan P, 1991: 259–86.

Hancher, Michael. "Three Kinds of Intention." *Modern Language Notes* 87 (1972): 827–51.

Hay, Louis. "Does Text Exist?" *Studies in Bibliography* 41 (1988): 64–76.

Hill, W. Speed. "Commentary upon Commentary upon Commentary." Greetham *Margins of the Text*.

—. "Text as Scripture, Scripture as Text." *Text* 8. Forthcoming.

Howard-Hill, T. H. "Theory and Praxis in the Social Approach to Editing." *Text* 5 (1991): 31–46.

Hurlebusch, Klaus. "Conceptualisations for Procedures of Authorship." *Studies in Bibliography* 41 (1988): 100–35.

Jaszi, Peter. "On the Author Effect: Contemporary Copyright and Collective Creativity." Jaszi and Woodhouse: 293–320.

—. and Martha Woodhouse, eds. *Intellectual Property and the Construction of Authorship*. Special issue of *Cardozo Arts & Entertainment Law Journal* 10.2 (1992).

Kenyon, Nicholas. *Authenticity and Early Music: A Symposium*. New York: Oxford UP, 1989.

King, Katie. "Bibliography and a Feminist Apparatus for Literary Production." *Text* 5 (1991): 91–104.

*Landow, George P. *Hypertext: The Convergence of Contemporary Critical Theory and Technology*. Baltimore: Johns Hopkins UP, 1992. Electronic edition, 1994.

Lang, Susan. "Hypertext and Literary Studies: Implications of Using Electronic Technology in the Study of Printed Texts." Cohen *Texts and Textuality*.

Lanham, Richard A. *The Electronic Word: Democracy, Technology, and the Arts*. Chicago: U of Chicago P, 1993.

Lebrave, Jean-Louis. "Rough Drafts: A Challenge to Uniformity in Editing," *Text* 3 (1987): 135–42.

Long, William B. "On Stage Directions." Greetham *Margins of the Text*.

MacLean, Gerald M. "What's Class Got To Do With It?" Greetham *Margins of the Text*.

Mailloux, Steven. *Interpretive Conventions: The Reader in the Study of American Fiction*. Ithaca: Cornell UP, 1982.

McClelland, John. "Text, Rhetoric, Meaning," *Text* 3 (1987): 11–26.

McGann, Jerome J. "The Text, the Poem, and the Problem of Historical Method." *New Literary History* 12 (1981): 269–88.

*—. *A Critique of Modern Textual Criticism*. Chicago: U of Chicago P, 1983. Repr. Charlottesville: UP of Virginia, 1992.

—. "Shall These Bones Live?" *Text* 1 (1984): 21–40.

—. *The Beauty of Inflections: Literary Investigations in Historical Method and Theory*. Oxford: Clarendon, 1985.

*—. "The Monks and the Giants: Textual and Bibliographical Studies and the Interpretation of Literary Works." *Textual Criticism and Literary Interpretation*. Ed. Jerome J. McGann. Chicago: U of Chicago P, 1985: 180–99.

—. "*Ulysses* as a Postmodernist Text: The Gabler Edition." *Criticism* 27 (1985): 283–305. Repr. as "*Ulysses* as a Postmodern Work." McGann. *Social Values and Poetic Acts: The Historical Judgment of Literary Work*. Cambridge: Harvard UP, 1988: 173–94.

—. "Interpretation, Meaning, and Textual Criticism: A Homily." *Text* 3 (1987):

55-62.
—. "The Textual Condition." *Text* 4 (1988): 29-38.
—. "Theories of Texts." *London Review of Books* 18 February 1988: 20-21.
—. "How to Read a Book." Oliphant and Bradford: 13-38.
—. "The Socialization of Texts." *Documentary Editing* 12 (1990): 56-61.
*—. "What Is Critical Editing?" *Text* 5 (1991): 15-30.
*—. *The Textual Condition*. Princeton: Princeton UP, 1991.
—. "Literary Pragmatics and the Editorial Horizon." Cohen *Devils*: 1-21.
McGillivray, Murray. "Towards a Post-Critical Edition: Theory, Hypertext, and the Presentation of Middle English Works." *Text* 7 (1994).
McKenzie, D. F. "The Sociology of a Text: Orality, Literacy, and Print in Early New Zealand." *The Library* Sixth Series 6 (1984): 333-65.
*—. *Bibliography and the Sociology of Texts*. London: The British Library, 1986.
—. "Speech-Manuscript-Print." Oliphant and Bradford: 87-110.
*—. "History of the Book." *The Book Encompassed*. Ed. Peter Davison. Cambridge: Cambridge UP, 1992: 290-301.
*McLaverty, James. "The Concept of Authorial Intention in Textual Criticism." *The Library*, Sixth Series 6 (1984): 121-38.
*—. "The Mode of Existence of Literary Works of Art: The Case of the *Dunciad* Variorum." *Studies in Bibliography* 37 (1984): 82-105.
—. "Issues of Identity and Utterance: An Intentionalist Response to 'Textual Instability'." Cohen *Devils*: 134-151.
—. "Titling in Eighteenth-Century Books." Greetham *Margins of the Text*.
Miller, R. H. "The Place of the Received Text in Editorial Theory." *Analytical and Enumerative Bibliography* n.s. 3 (1989): 89-95.
Minnis, A. J. *Medieval Theory of Authorship: Scholastic Literary Attitudes in the Later Middle Ages*. Philadelphia: U of Pennsylvania P, 1987. 2nd ed.
*— and Charlotte Brewer, eds. *Crux and Controversy in Middle English Textual Criticism*. Cambridge: Brewer, 1992.
Nadel, Ira Bruce. "Textual Criticism, Literary Theory, and the New *Ulysses*." *Assessing the 1984 Ulysses*. Ed. George C. Sandulescu and Clive Hart. London: Colin Smyth / New York: Barnes and Noble, 1986: 122-39.
Neufeldt, Leonard N. "Neopragmatism and Conventions in Textual Editing, with Examples from the Editing of Thoreau's Autograph Journal." *Analytical and Enumerative Bibliography* New Series 1 (1987): 237-46.
Nichols, Stephen G., ed. *The New Philology*. Special Issue of *Speculum* 65 (1990): 1-108.
*Oliphant, Dave and Robin Bradford, eds. *New Directions in Textual Studies*. Austin: Harry Ransom Humanities Research Center / U of Texas P, 1990.
Orgel, Stephen. "What Is a Text?" *Research Opportunities in Renaissance Drama* 24 (1981): 3-7.
—. "What Is a Character?" *Text* 8. Forthcoming.
Parker, Hershel. "The Determinacy of the Creative Process and the 'Authority' of the Author's Textual Decisions." *College Literature* 10 (1983): 99-125.
*—. *Flawed Texts and Verbal Icons: Literary Authority in American Fiction*. Evanston: Northwestern UP, 1984.
—. "'The New Scholarship': Textual Evidence and Its Implications for Criticism, Literary Theory, and Aesthetics." *Studies in American Fiction* 9 (1984): 181-97.
—. "'The Text Itself'—Whatever That Is." *Text* 3 (1987): 47-54.
Parrish, S. M. "The Whig Interpretation of Literature." *Text* 4 (1988): 343-350.
*Patterson, Lee. "On the Margin: Postmodernism, Ironic History, and Medieval Studies." Nichols: 87-108.
Pebworth, Ted-Larry and Ernest W. Sullivan, II. "Rational Presentation of Multiple Textual Traditions." *Papers of the Bibliographical Society of America* 83 (1989): 43-60.

Phelps, C. Deirdre. "The Edition as Art-Form in Textual and Interpretative Criticism." *Text* 7 (1994).

—. "Where's the Book? The Text in the Development of Literary Sociology." *Text* 8. Forthcoming.

Rajan, Tilottama. "Is There a Romantic Ideology? Some Thoughts on Schleiermacher's Hermeneutic and Textual Criticism," *Text* 3 (1988): 57-76.

*Reiman, Donald H. "'Versioning': The Presentation of Multiple Texts." *Romantic Texts and Contexts*. Columbia: U of Missouri P, 1987: 167-80.

—. "Gender and Documentary Editing: A Diachronic Perspective," *Text* 4 (1988): 351-60.

Rose, Mark. *Authors and Owners: The Invention of Copyright*. Cambridge: Harvard UP, 1993.

Rubinstein, E. "What Is the Text of a Film?" *Text* 3 (1987) 417-26.

Saunders, David and Ian Hunter. "Lessons from the 'Literatory': How to Historicise Authorship." *Critical Inquiry* 7 (1991): 479-509.

Saussure, Ferdinand de. *Course in General Linguistics*. Ed. Charles Bally and Albert Sechehaye. Trans. Roy Harris. La Salle, IL: Open Court, 1986.

Scholz, Bernhard F. "From Illustrated Epigram to Emblem: The Canonization of a Typographical Arrangement." *New Ways of Looking at Old Texts*. Ed. W. Speed Hill. Binghamton: Medieval & Renaissance Texts & Studies / Renaissance English Text Society, 1993: 149-158.

Shillingsburg, Peter L. "Key Issues in Editorial Theory." *Analytical and Enumerative Bibliography* 6 (1982): 3-16.

*—. *Scholarly Editing in the Computer Age: Lectures in Theory and Practice*. U of New South Wales Department of English Occasional Papers No. 3 (1984), rev. ed. Athens: U of Georgia P, 1986.

—. "The Limits of the Editor's Responsibility." Conference paper. Society for Textual Scholarship, New York City. April, 1987.

—. "An Inquiry into the Social Status of Texts and Modes of Textual Criticism." *Studies in Bibliography* 42 (1989): 55-79.

*—. "Text as Matter, Concept, and Action." *Studies in Bibliography* 44 (1991): 31-82.

—. "Textual Variants, Performance Variants, and the Concept of Work." *Bibliographical Society of Australia and New Zealand Bulletin* 15 (1991): 60-72. Repr. *Editio* 7 (1993): 221-234.

—. "The Autonomous Author, the Sociology of Texts, and the Polemics of Textual Criticism." Cohen *Devils*: 22-43.

Slights, William W. E. "The Cosmopolitics of Reading: Navigating the Margins of John Dee's *General and Rare Memorials*. Greetham *Margins of the Text*.

*Small, Ian and Marcus Walsh, eds. *The Theory and Practice of Text-Editing*. Cambridge: Cambridge UP, 1991.

Spiegel, Gabrielle M. "History, Historicism, and the Social Logic of the Text in the Middle Ages." Nichols: 59-86.

Sturges, Robert S. "Textual Scholarship: Ideologies of Literary Production." *Exemplaria* 3 (1991): 109-31.

*Sutherland, John. "Publishing History: A Hole at the Centre of Literary Sociology." *Critical Inquiry* 14 (1988): 574-89.

*Tanselle, G. Thomas. "The Editorial Problem of Final Authorial Intention." *Studies in Bibliography* 29 (1976): 167-211.

*—. *A Rationale of Textual Criticism*. Philadelphia: Pennsylvania UP, 1989.

—. "Textual Criticism and Deconstruction." *Studies in Bibliography* 43 (1990): 1-33.

*Taylor, Gary. "The Rhetoric of Textual Criticism." *Text* 4 (1988): 39-57.

Textual Scholarship and Literary Theory. Special issue of *Critical Exchange* 24 (Fall, 1989).

Timpanaro, S. *Il Lapsus Freudiano: Psicanalisi e critica testuale*. Florence: 1974. Trans. by Kate Soper as *The Freudian Slip: Psychoanalysis and Textual Criticism*. London: Verso, 1976.

Tribble, Evelyn B. *Margins and Marginality: The Printed Page in Early Modern England*. Charlottesville: UP of Virginia, 1993.

—. "Managing the Past: From Margins to Footnotes." Greetham *Margins of the Text*.

Wenzel, Siegfried. "Reflections on (New) Philology." Nichols: 11–18.

West, James L. W., III. *American Authors and the Literary Marketplace since 1900*. Philadelphia: U of Pennsylvania P, 1988.

—. "Editorial Theory and the Act of Submission." *Papers of the Bibliographical Society of America* 83 (1989): 169–85.

Wheatley, Phyllis. "Publishing Objectives and Personal Liberty." Cohen *Texts and Textuality*.

White, Patricia S. "Black and White and Read All Over: A Meditation On Footnotes." *Text* 5 (1991): 81–90.

Williams, Ralph. "I Shall Be Spoken: Textual Boundaries, Authors, and Intent." Bornstein and Williams: 45–66.

Willison, Ian. "Editorial Theory and Practice and the History of the Book." Oliphant and Bradford: 111–26.

Woodhouse, Martha. "On the Author Effect: Recovering Collectivity." Jaszi and Woodhouse: 279–292.

Yen, Alfred C. "The Interdisciplinary Future of Copyright Theory." Jaszi and Woodhouse: 423–438.

Ziolkowski, Jan, ed. *On Philology*. U Park: Pennsylvania State UP, 1990.

Selected Contemporary Non-Anglophone Textual Criticism

Alberti, Giovan Battista. *Problemi di critica testuale*. 1979.

Antonelli, Roberto. "Interpretazione e critica del testo." *Letteratura italiana*. Ed. Alberto Asor Rosa. Turin: Einaudi, 1985. vol. 4: 141–243.

Aguilecchia, Giovanni. "Trelemma of Textual Criticism (Author's Alterations, Different Versions, Autonomous Works): An Italian View." *Book Production and Letters in the Western European Renaissance: Essays in Honour of Conor Fahy*. Ed. Anna Laura Lepschy, John Took, and Dennis E. Rhodes. London: Modern Humanities Research Association, 1986.

Balduine, Armando. *Manuale di filologia italiana*. Florence: Sansoni, 1989. 3rd ed.

Barbi, Michele. *La nuova filologia e l'edizione dei nostri scrittori da Dante al Manzoni*. 1938.

Blacker, Jean. "Will the Real *Brut* Please Stand Up?" *Text* 8. Forthcoming.

Blecua, Alberto. "Medieval Castilian Texts and Their Editions." *Scholarly Editing*. Ed. D. C. Greetham. New York: MLA, 1994.

Bloomfield, B. C. "Bibliography and Oriental Literature." *The Book Encompassed*. Ed. Peter Davison. Cambridge: Cambridge UP, 1992: 215–226.

Branca, Vittore and J. Starobinski. *La filologia e la critica letteraria*. Milan: Rizzoli, 1977.

Chiarini, Giorgio. "Prospetti translachmanniane dell'ecdoctica." *Ecdoctica e testi ispanici. Atti del convegno nazionale della associazione ispanici italiani*. Verona: Università degli studi di Verona, 1982: 45–64.

De Robertis, Domenico. "Per l'edizione critica del 'Dolore' di Giuseppi Ungaretti." *Studi di filologia italiana* 38 (1980): 309–23.

Eixenbaum, B. "O tekstax Lermontova." *Literaturnoe nasledstvo* vols. 19–21. Moscow: Zurnal'no-gazetnoe ob'edinenie, 1935: 485–501.

Faris, James C. "Navajo Nightway Texts." *Texts and Textuality*. Ed. Philip Cohen. New York: Paragon H. Forthcoming.

Fennell, John L. I. "Textology as a Key to the Study of Old Russian Literature and

History." *Text* 1 (1981): 157–66.

Fischer, W., ed. *Grundriss der arabischen Philologie.* Vol. I. Sprachwissenschaft. Wiesbaden: 1982.

Flood, John L. "Schwarze Kunst—graue Theorie? Some Reflections on Textual Bibliography and German Literature." *London German Studies* 2 (1983): 18–30.

Gätje, H. *Grundriss der arabischen Philologie.* Vol. II. Literaturwissenschaft. Wiesbaden: Reichert, 1987.

Gorni, Guglielmo. "Le gloriose pompe (e i fieri ludi) della filologia italiana." *Rivista di letteratura italiana* 4 (1986): 391–412.

Heinemann, Edward A. "Textual Criticism or Literary Criticism? Echo (Or Is It Redundancy?) and the Shifting Text of the Old French Epic." *Text* 4 (1988): 121–133.

Jambeck, Karen K. "The *Fables* of Marie de France: Base Text and Critical Text." *Text* 2 (1985): 83–92.

Katre, Sumitra M. *Introduction to Indian Textual Criticism.* Poona: Deccan College, 1954. 2nd ed.

*Lixacev, Dmitrij. *Tekstologija russkoj literatury X–XVII vekov.* Leningrad: Nauka, 1983.

*Martens, Gunter. "Textdynamik und Edition." Martens and Zeller: 165–201.

—. "Texte ohne Varianten?" *Zeitschrift für Deutsche Philologie* 101 (1982): 43–64.

—. "'Historisch,' 'kritisch,' und die Rolle des Herausgebers bei der Textkonstitution." *Editio* 5 (1991): 12–27.

*—. and H. Zeller, eds. *Texte und Varianten: Probleme ihrer Edition und Interpretation.* Munich: Beck, 1971.

*McClelland, John. "Critical Editing in the Modern Languages." *Text* 1 (1984): 201–16.

Norman, Buford. "Editing and Interpreting Fragmentary Texts: A Justification of Pascal's Text in MSL 527–Br 40," *Text* 2 (1985): 197–208.

Orduna, Germán. "Hispanic Textual Criticism and the Stemmatic Value of the History of the Text." *Scholarly Editing.* Ed. D. C. Greetham. New York: MLA, 1994.

*Pasquali, Giorgio. *Storia della tradizione e critica del testo.* Florence: Le Monnier, 1934.

Piksanov, N. K. "Novyj put' literanoj nauki. Izucnie tvorceskoj istoriii šedevra. (Principy i metody)." *Iskusstvo* (1923): 94–113.

Quaglio, Antonio Enzo. "Rassegna di studi filologia italiana e romanza." *Lettere italiane* 15 (1963): 348–69.

Sabbadini, R. *Le scoperte dei codici latini e greci ne'secoli xiv e xv.* Florence: Sansoni. 1905–19. 2 vols.

Scheibe, Siegfried and Christel Laufer, eds. *Zu Werk und Text: Beiträge zur Textologie.* Berlin: Akademie, 1991.

Seidel, Gerhard. "Intentionswandel in der Entstehungsgeschichte. Ein Gedicht Bertolt Brechts über Karl Kraus historisch-kritisch ediert." *Zeitschrift für Deutsche Philologie* 101 (1982): 163–88.

Shaw, David. "*La bibliologie* in France." *The Book Encompassed.* Ed. Peter Davison. Cambridge: Cambridge UP, 1992: 206–214.

Speer, Mary B. "Wrestling with Change: Old French Textual Criticism and Mouvance." *Olifant* 7 (1980): 311–326.

Stussi, Alfredo. *La critica del testo.* Bologna: Il Mulino, 1985.

Weigel, Harald. *"Nur was du nie gesehn wird ewig dauern": Carl Lachmann und die Entstehung der wissenschaftlichen Edition.* Freiburg: Rombach, 1989.

Winters, Margaret E. "Manuscript Variation and Syntactic Change." *Text* 5 (1991): 131–143.

Yamada, Akihiro. "Bibliographical Studies in Japan." *The Book Encompassed.* Ed. Peter Davison. Cambridge: Cambridge UP, 1992: 270–275.

Zeller, Hans. "Textologie und Textanalyse." *Editio* 1 (1987): 145–158.

Chapter 9: Scholarly Editing

Some Representative Scholarly Editions

As in the rest of this book, the emphasis is on English-language editions, from Old English to the present, but representative scholarly editions in some other languages are included (e.g., French, German, Italian, and Russian). The list is alphabetical by order of author, or title for anonymous works; in multiple listings, complete editions are listed first, then individual works, both in chronological order. Also included are non-scholarly editions mentioned in the text (e.g., the two editions of Fowles's *The Magus*).

Abailard, Peter. *Sic et Non*. Ed. Blanche B. Boyer and Richard C. McKeon. Chicago: U of Chicago P, 1987.

The Adams Papers. Ed. Lyman H. Butterfield. Cambridge: Belknap / Harvard UP, 1961– .

Addison, Joseph. *The Spectator*. Ed. Donald H. Bond. Oxford: Clarendon, 1965. 5 vols.

Ælfred. *King Alfred's West-Saxon Version of Gregory's Pastoral Care*. Ed. Henry Sweet, rev. N. R. Ker. EETS 45, 50, 1871. London: Oxford UP, 1973.

Ælfric. *Homilies: Supplementary Collection*. Ed. John C. Pope. EETS 259–60. London: Oxford UP, 1967–68.

—. *Catholic Homilies: The Second Series*. Ed. Malcolm Godden. EETS SS 5. London: Oxford UP, 1979.

—. *Colloquy*. Ed. G. N. Garmonsway. London: Methuen, 1947. 2nd ed.

—. *Lives of Three English Saints* (Oswald, Edmund, Swithin). Ed. G. I. Needham. London: Methuen / New York: Appleton, 1966.

The English Text of the Ancrene Riwle (BL MS Cleopatra C. vi). Ed. E. J. Dobson. EETS 267. London: Oxford UP, 1972.

—. (Magdalene College Cambridge MS Pepys 2498). Ed. Arne Zettersten. EETS 274. London: Oxford UP, 1976.

Anglo-Saxon Chronicle: Two of the Saxon Chronicles Parallel. Ed. Charles Plummer. Oxford: 1892–99. 2 vols.

The Anglo-Saxon Poetic Records. Ed. George Philip Krapp and Elliott Van Kirk Dobbie. New York: Columbia UP, 1931–53. 6 vols.

The Arabian Nights. Ed. H. Haddawy. New York / London, 1990.

Ariosto, Ludovico. *L'Orlando furioso*. Ed. Santorre Debenedetti. Bari: Laterza, 1928.

—. *L'Orlando furioso*. Ed. Santorre Debenedetti and Cesare Segre. Bologna: Commissione per i testi di lingua, 1960.

Arnold, Matthew. *The Complete Prose Works*. Ed. R. H. Super. Ann Arbor: U of Michigan P, 1960–77.

—. *Matthew Arnold*. Ed. Miriam Allott and Robert H. Super. Oxford: Oxford UP, 1986.

*Austen, Jane. *The Novels of Jane Austen*. Ed. R. W. Chapman. Oxford: Oxford UP, 1923. 3rd ed. 1933. 5 vols.

The Awntyrs of Arthure at the Terne Wathelyne: A Critical Edition. Ed. Robert J. Gates. Philadelphia: U of Pennsylvania P, 1969.

—. Ed. Ralph Hanna, III. Manchester: Manchester UP, 1974.

Bacon, Francis. *The Essayes or Counsels, Civill and Morall*. Ed. Michael Kiernan. Cambridge: Harvard UP / Oxford: Oxford UP, 1985.

Barberino, Andrea da. *I reali di Francia*. Ed. Giovanni Vandelli. Bologna: Romagnoli, 1892–1900.

The Battle of Brunanburh. Ed. Alistair Campbell. London: Heinemann, 1938.

The Battle of Maldon. Ed. E. V. Gordon. London: Methuen, 1937.

*Beaumont and Fletcher. *The Dramatic Works in the Beaumont and Fletcher Canon.* Ed. Fredson Bowers. Cambridge: Cambridge UP, 1966–89. 7 vols.

Beckett, Samuel. *The Theatrical Notebooks of Samuel Beckett.* Ed. James Knowlson et al. New York: Grove, 1992– .

Bede, Venerable. *The Old English Version of Bede's Ecclesiastical History of the Eng lish People.* Ed. Thomas Miller. EETS 95, 96, 110, 111. London: Oxford UP, 1890–98. 4 vols.

Beowulf, the Travellers Song and The Battle of Finnesburh. Ed. John M. Kemble. London: 1835. 2nd ed.

Beowulf with the Finnsburg Fragment. Ed. R. W. Chambers. Cambridge: Cambridge UP, 1914. Rev. A. J. Wyatt.

Beowulf and the Fight at Finnsburg. Ed. Fr. Klaeber. Boston: Heath, 1950. 3rd ed. with Supplements.

Beowulf with the Finnesburg Fragment. Ed. C. L. Wrenn. London: Harrap, 1958. Rev. ed.

Beowulf: Facsimile. Ed. Norman Davis. EETS 245. London: Oxford UP, 1959. 2nd ed.

Béroul. *The Romance of Tristran.* Ed. Alfred Ewert. Oxford: Blackwell, 1939–70. 2 vols.

Blake, William. *William Blake's Writings.* Ed. G. E. Bentley, Jr. Oxford: Clarendon, 1978. 2 vols.

*—. *The Complete Poetry and Prose.* Ed. David V. Erdman. Berkeley: U of California P, 1982. Rev. ed.

Boccaccio, Giovanni. *Il Decameron.* Ed. Vittore Branca. Florence: Le Monnier, 1960. 2nd ed.

—. *Decameron: edizione critica secondo l'autografo Hamiltoniano.* Ed. Vittore Branca. Florence: Accademia della Crusca, 1976.

—. *Il Decameron.* Ed. Aldo Rossi. Bologna: Cappelli, 1977.

Boswell, James. *Life of Johnson.* Ed. G. B. Hill. Oxford: Clarendon, 1887.

—. *Yale Edition of the Private Papers of James Boswell.* Gen. Ed. Frederick W. Pottle. New Haven: Yale UP, 1950– .

Bronte, Charlotte. *An Edition of the Early Writings.* Ed. Christine Alexander. Oxford: Shakespeare Head, 1987– . 3 vols.

Brown Women Writers Project 1330–1830. Providence: Brown U, 1988– .

Browning, Robert. *The Complete Works.* Ed. Roma A. King, Jr. et al. Athens: Ohio UP, 1969– .

—. *The Poems.* New Haven: Yale UP, 1981.

—. *The Poetical Works.* Ed. Ian Jack and Margaret Smith. Oxford: Clarendon, 1983– .

—. *The Brownings' Correspondence.* Ed. Philip Kelley and Ronald Hudson. Winfield: Wedgestone P, 1984– .

—. *The Poems of Browning.* Ed. John Woolford and Daniel Karlin. London: Longman, 1991. 2 vols.

Burke, Edmund. *Correspondence of Edmund Burke.* Ed. Thomas Copeland. London: Cambridge UP, 1958–70. 9 vols.

Burney, Fanny. *The Early Journals and Letters of Fanny Burney.* Ed. Lars E. Troide. Kingston and Montreal: McGill-Queen's UP, 1988– .

Burton, Robert. *The Anatomy of Melancholy.* Ed. Thomas C. Faulkner, Nicolas K. Kiessling, and Rhonda L. Blair. Oxford: Clarendon, 1989–1994.

Byron, George Gordon, Lord. *Byron's "Don Juan": A Variorum Edition.* Ed. Truman Guy Steffan and William W. Pratt. Austin: U of Texas P, 1971. 2nd ed.

*—. *Lord Byron: The Complete Poetical Works.* Ed. Jerome J. McGann. Oxford: Clarendon, 1980–1993.

*—. *Byron's Letters and Journals.* Ed. Leslie A. Marchand. London: Murray / Cam-

bridge: Harvard UP, 1973–82. 12 vols.

—. *Lord Byron: The Complete Miscellaneous Prose.* Ed. Andrew Nicholson. New York: Oxford UP, 1991.

Carey, Lady Elizabeth. *The Tragedy of Mariam (1613).* Ed. A. C. Dunstan. Oxford: Malone Society, 1992.

Carlyle, Thomas and Jane. *The Collected Letters.* Ed. Charles Richard Sanders and Kenneth J. Fielding. Durham: Duke UP, 1971– .

Cather, Willa. *Willa Cather Scholarly Edition.* Gen. Ed. Susan J. Rosowski. Lincoln: U of Nebraska P, 1992– .

Cavalcanti, Guido. *Le rime.* Ed. Guido Favati. Milan / Naples: Ricciardi, 1957.

Cervantes, Miguel de. *Works (Alcalá Edition).* Ed. Daniel Eisenberg et al. In preparation.

La chanson de Roland, publiée d'après le manuscrit d'Oxford et traduite. Ed. Joseph Bédier. Paris: Piazza, 1937.

—. Ed. Cesare Segre. Geneva: Droz, 1989. 2 vols.

Chapman, George. *Plays of George Chapman.* Ed. Allan Holaday. Urbana: U of Illinois P, 1970–87. 2 vols.

Chatterton, Thomas. *The Complete Works.* Ed. Donald S. Taylor. Oxford: Clarendon, 1971. 2 vols.

*Chaucer, Geoffrey. *The Text of the Canterbury Tales.* Ed. J. M. Manly and Edith Rickert. Chicago: U of Chicago P, 1940. 8 vols.

—. *The Works of Geoffrey Chaucer.* Ed. F. N. Robinson. Boston: Houghton Mifflin / London: Oxford UP, 1957. 2nd ed.

*—. *The Variorum Chaucer.* Ed. Paul G. Ruggiers. Norman: U of Oklahoma P / Folkestone: Wm. Dawson, 1979– . 8 vols. to date.

—. *A Facsimile and Transcription of the Hengwrt Manuscript, with Variants from the Ellesmere Manuscript.* Ed. Paul G. Ruggiers. Norman: U of Oklahoma P / Folkestone: Wm. Dawson, 1979.

—. *The Riverside Chaucer.* Ed. Larry Benson. Boston: Houghton Mifflin, 1987; Electronic Edition. Oxford: Oxford UP, 1991.

*—. *The Canterbury Tales Project (Electronic Edition).* Ed. Peter M. W. Robinson, Norman Blake, Elizabeth Solopova et al. Cambridge: Cambridge UP Electronic Editions. In preparation.

Chester Cycle. Ed. R. M. Lumiansky and D. Mills. EETS SS 3, 9. London: Oxford UP, 1974, 1986. 2 vols.

Chrétien de Troyes. *Sämtliche Werke nach allen bekannten Handschriften.* Ed. Wendelin Foerster. Halle: Niemeyer, 1884–89. Amsterdam: Rodopi, 1965. 4 vols.

—. *Le chevalier au lion (Yvain).* Ed. Mario Roques. Paris: Champion, 1960.

—. *Le chevalier de la charrete.* Ed. Mario Roques. Paris: Champion, 1958.

—. *Cligés.* Ed. Alexandre Micha. Paris: Champion, 1957.

—. *Le conte du graal (Perceval).* Ed. Félix Lecoy. Paris: Champion, 1973–75. 2 vols.

—. *Erec et Enide.* Ed. Mario Roques. Paris: Champion, 1952.

—. *Le roman de Perceval ou le conte du graal.* Ed. William Roach. Geneva: Droz, 1959. 2nd ed.

Cleanness. Ed. Israel Gollancz. Oxford: Oxford UP, 1921, 1933. Repr. Cambridge: Brewer, 1974.

Coleridge, Samuel Taylor. *The Collected Works of Samuel Taylor Coleridge.* Gen. Ed. Kathleen Coburn. London: Routledge / Princeton: Princeton UP, Bollingen series LXXV, 1971– .

Conrad, Joseph. *The Collected Letters.* Ed. Frederick R. Karl and Laurence Davies. Cambridge: Cambridge UP, 1983– .

—. *The Works of Joseph Conrad.* Gen. Eds. Bruce Harkness and S. W. Reid. Cambridge: Cambridge UP, 1990– .

Corneille, Pierre. *Œuvres complètes*. Ed. Charles Marty-Laveaux. Paris: Hachette, 1862–93. 12 vols.

—. *Œuvres complètes*. Ed. Georges Couton. Paris: Gallimard, 1980. 3 vols.

—. *Le Cid*. Ed. Milorad R. Margitic. Amsterdam: John Benjamins, 1989.

Cowper, William. *The Letters and Prose Writings*. Ed. James King and Charles Ryskamp. Oxford: Clarendon, 1979– .

—. *The Poems*. Ed. John D. Baird and Charles Ryskamp. Oxford: Clarendon, 1980. 2 vols.

*Crane, Stephen. *The Works of Stephen Crane*. Ed. Fredson Bowers. Charlottesville: UP of Virginia, 1969–75, 10 vols.

—. *Red Badge of Courage: Facsimile Edition of the Manuscript*. Ed. Fredson Bowers. Washington: Microcard, 1973.

—. *Red Badge of Courage*. Ed. Henry Binder. New York: Norton, 1982.

Cynewulf. *Andreas and the Fates of the Apostles*. Ed. George Philip Krapp. Boston: Ginn, 1906.

—. *Christ: An Eighth-Century English Epic*. Ed. Israel Gollancz. London: 1892.

—. *Christ*. Ed. Albert S. Cook. Freeport: Books for Libraries P, 1970. Repr. of 1900 ed.

—. *Elene*. Ed. P. O. E. Gradon. New York: Appleton, 1966.

Dante Alighieri. *La divina commedia*. in M. Barbi et al. *Le opere di Dante. Testo critico della Società Dantesca Italiana*. Florence: Bemporad, 1921.

—. *La divina commedia secondo l'antica vulgata*. Ed. Giorgio Petrocchi. Milan: Mondadori, 1966–67.

—. *La vita nuova*. Ed. Michele Barbi. Florence: Società Dantesca Italiana, 1907.

Darwin, Charles. *The Origin of Species: A Variorum Edition*. Ed. Morse Peckham. Philadelphia: U of Pennsylvania P, 1959.

Defoe, Daniel. *Letters of Daniel Defoe*. Ed. G. H. Healey. Oxford: Clarendon, 1955.

Dekker, Thomas. *The Dramatic Works of Thomas Dekker*. Ed. Fredson Bowers. Cambridge: Cambridge UP, 1953–61, 4 vols.

*Dewey, John. *The [Early / Middle / Later] Works of John Dewey 1892–1953*. Ed. Jo Ann Boydston. Carbondale: Southern Illinois UP, 1967–90. 37 vols.

Dickens, Charles. *Clarendon Edition*. Gen. Ed. K. Tillotson. Oxford: Clarendon, 1966– .

—. *Bleak House*. Ed. Sylvère Monod and George H. Ford. New York: Norton, 1977.

—. *Great Expectations*. Ed. Margaret Cardwell. Oxford: Clarendon P, 1993.

—. *Hard Times*. Ed. Sylvère Monod and George H. Ford. New York: Norton, 1966.

—. *Dickens' Working Notes for His Novels*. Ed. Harry Stone. Chicago: U of Chicago P, 1986.

Dickinson, Emily. *Poems: Including Variants Critically Compared with All Known Manuscripts*. Ed. Thomas H. Johnson. Cambridge: Belknap / Harvard UP, 1955.

—. *The Manuscript Books of Emily Dickinson: A Facsimile Edition*. Ed. Ralph Franklin. Cambridge: Belknap / Harvard UP, 1981.

Diderot, Denis. *Œuvres complètes*. Paris: Hermann, 1975– .

*Donne, John. *The Poems of John Donne*. Ed. H. J. C. Grierson. Oxford: Clarendon, 1912. Repr. 1929–66.

—. *Variorum Edition of the Poetry of John Donne*. Ed. Gary Stringer, Ted-Larry Pebworth, and Ernest W. Sullivan, II. Bloomington: Indiana UP, 1994– .

*Dreiser, Theodore. *The University of Pennsylvania Dreiser Edition*. Ed. James L. W. West, III. Philadelphia: U of Pennsylvania P, 1981– .

Dryden, John. *The Works of John Dryden*. Ed. H. T. Swedenberg, Jr., et al. Berkeley and Los Angeles: U of California P, 1956– .

—. *Four Comedies*. Ed. Fredson Bowers and L. A. Beaurline. Chicago: U of Chicago P, 1967.

—. *Four Tragedies.* Ed. Fredson Bowers and L. A. Beaurline. Chicago: U of Chicago P, 1967.

Eliot, George. *The George Eliot Letters.* Ed. Gordon S. Haight. New Haven: Yale UP, 1954–78. 9 vols.

—. *The Mill on the Floss.* Ed. Gordon Haight. Oxford: Clarendon, 1980.

*Eliot, T. S. *The Waste Land: A Facsimile and Transcript.* Ed. Valerie Eliot. New York: Harcourt, 1971.

Emerson, Ralph Waldo. *The Collected Works of Ralph Waldo Emerson.* Ed. Alfred R. Ferguson. Cambridge: Belknap / Harvard UP, 1971– .

*—. *Journals and Miscellaneous Notebooks of Ralph Waldo Emerson.* Ed. William H. Gilman et al. Cambridge: Harvard UP, 1969–82.

—. *The Complete Sermons of Ralph Waldo Emerson.* Ed. Albert J. von Frank, Jr., et al. Columbia: U of Missouri P, 1989– .

English and Scottish Popular Ballads. Ed. F. J. Child. Boston: Little, Brown, 1857.

English Poems Commemorating the Stuart Restoration. Ed. Gerald M. MacLean. In preparation.

Exodus and Daniel. Ed. Francis A. Blackburn. Boston: Heath, 1907.

Fielding, Henry. *The Wesleyan Edition of the Works of Henry Fielding.* Ed. William B. Coley et al; textual editor Fredson Bowers. Middletown: Wesleyan UP / Oxford: Clarendon, 1967– .

Fitzgerald, F. Scott. *Tender Is the Night: A Romance.* Ed. Malcolm Cowley. New York: Scribner, 1951.

—. *Manuscripts.* Ed. Matthew J. Bruccoli and Alan Margolies. New York: Garland, 1990– . 18 vols.

—. *The Cambridge Edition of the Works of F. Scott Fitzgerald.* Ed. Matthew J. Bruccoli. Cambridge: Cambridge UP, 1991– .

*Flaubert, Gustave. *Corpus flaubertianum. Un coeur simple.* Ed. Giovanni Bonnacorso, Maria Francesca Davi-Trimarchi, Simonetta Micale, Eliane Contaz-Sframeli. Paris: Belles Lettres, 1983.

—. —. *Hérodias.* Ed. Giovanni Bonnacorso, Claudia Napoli, Rosa Maria Palermo Di Stefano, and Enzo Liberale. Paris: Nizet, 1991.

Ford, John. *The Nondramatic Works of John Ford.* Ed. L. E. Stock, G. D. Monsarrat, J. Kennedy, and D. Danielson. Binghamton: Medieval & Renaissance Texts & Studies / Renaissance English Text Society, 1991.

Four Middle English Mystery Cycles. Ed. Martin Stevens. Princeton: Princeton UP, 1987.

Fowles, John. *The Magus.* Boston: Little, Brown, 1965. Rev. ed. Boston: Little, Brown, 1978.

Franklin, Benjamin. *The Papers of Benjamin Franklin.* Ed. Leonard W. Labaree et al. New Haven: Yale UP, 1959– .

—. *The Autobiography of Benjamin Franklin: A Genetic Text.* Ed. J. A. Leo Lemay and P. M. Zall. Knoxville: U of Tennessee P, 1981.

Frost, Robert. *The Poetry of Robert Frost.* Ed. Edward Connery Lathem. New York: Holt, 1969.

Genesis A: A New Edition. Ed. A. N. Doane. Madison: U of Wisconsin P, 1978.

Gibbon, Edward. *The Letters of Edward Gibbon.* Ed. J. E. Norton. New York: Macmillan, 1965. 3 vols.

Goethe, Johann Wolfgang von. *Werke.* Vollständiger Ausgabe letzter Hand. Stuttgart / Tübingen: Cotta, 1827–30.

—. *Werke.* Ed. in Auftrag der Grossherzogin Sophie von Sachsen. Weimar: Böhlau, 1887–1919.

—. *Werke Goethes.* Ed. Deutsche Akademie der Wissenschaften zu Berlin. Berlin [DDR]: Akademie, 1952–66.

Gogol, N. V. *Socinenija.* Ed. B. M. Èjxenbaum and K. I. Xalabaev. Moscow / Len-

Scholarly Editing (Representative Editions) 505

—. *Polnoe sobranie socinenij.* Moscow / Leningrad: Akademija Nauk SSR, Institut Russkoj Literatury, 1937–52. 14 vols.
—. *Sobranie socinenij v šesti tomax.* Ed. A. L. Slonimskij. Moscow: Goslitizdat, 1952–53. 6 vols.
Goldsmith, Oliver. *Collected Works.* Ed. Arthur Friedman. Oxford: Clarendon, 1966. 5 vols.
Gorkij, M. *Sobranie socinenij.* Moscow: Goslitizdat, 1949–55. 30 vols.
Gower, John. *English Works.* EETS 1900–01. 2 vols. Repr. 1957.
—. *Confessio Amantis.* Ed. Russell A. Peck. Toronto: U of Toronto P, 1980. Repr. of 1966.
Grandes heures of Jean, Duke of Berry. New York: Braziller, 1972.
Grant, Ulysses S. *The Papers of Ulysses S. Grant.* Ed. John Y. Simon. Carbondale: Southern Illinois UP, 1967– .
Gray, Thomas. *Complete Poems.* Ed. H. W. Starr and J. R. Hendrickson. Oxford: Clarendon, 1966.
Handel, George Frideric. *Messiah.* Philharmonia Baroque Orchestra / Nicholas McGegan. Harmonia Mundi HMU90 7050 / 2.
Hardy, Thomas. *The Complete Poems.* Ed. James Gibson. New York: Macmillan, 1976.
—. *New Wessex Edition.* Gen. Ed. P. N. Furbank. London: 1974–77. 19 vols.
—. *The Collected Letters of Thomas Hardy.* Ed. Richard Little Purdy and Michael Millgate. Oxford: Clarendon, 1978–88. 7 vols.
—. *The Thomas Hardy Archive.* Gen. Ed. Kristen Brady. New York: Garland, 1986– .
—. *The Return of the Native: A Facsimile of the Manuscript.* Ed. Simon Gattrell. New York: Garland, 1986.
—. *Tess of the d'Urbevilles.* Ed. Juliet Grindle and Simon Gattrell. Oxford: Clarendon, 1983.
—. *Tess of the d'Urbevilles: A Facsimile of the Manuscript.* Ed. Simon Gattrell. New York: Garland, 1986.
The Harleian Miscellany. Ed. Thomas Park. London: White and Murray, 1808–13. Repr. New York: AMS, 1965.
Hawthorne, Nathaniel. *The Centenary Edition of the Works of Nathaniel Hawthorne.* Ed. William Charvat et al. Columbus: Ohio State UP, 1963– .
Heine, Heinrich. *Säkularausgabe. Werke - Briefwechsel - Lebenszeugnisse.* Ed. Nationale Forschungs- und Gedenkstätten der klassischen deutschen Literatur (Weimar) / Centre National de la Recherche Scientifique (Paris). Berlin [DDR]: Akademie / Paris: CNRS, 1970– .
Henryson, Robert. *The Poems of Robert Henryson.* Ed. Denton Fox. Oxford: Clarendon, 1981.
Heywood, John. *The Pardoner and the Friar.* Ed. G. R. Proudfoot. Oxford: Malone Society, 1984.
Hoccleve, Thomas. *The Regement of Princes.* Ed. Frederick J. Furnivall. EETS ES 53 (1897).
—. *The Regement of Princes.* Ed. Charles R. Blyth. In preparation.
—. *The Minor Works.* Ed. F. J. Furnivall and Israel Gollancz. Rev. Jerome Mitchell and A. I. Doyle. EETS ES 61 and 73. London: Oxford UP, 1970.
—. *Selections from Hoccleve.* Ed. M. C. Seymour. Oxford: Clarendon, 1981.
*Hölderlin, Friedrich. *Sämtliche Werke.* Ed. Friedrich Beissner. Stuttgart: Gr. Stuttgart Ausgabe, 1943.
—. *Sämtliche Werke.* Ed. D. E. Sattler. Frankfurt: Roter Stern, 1975– .
*Hooker, Richard. *The Folger Library Edition of the Works of Richard Hooker.* Gen. Ed. W. Speed Hill. Cambridge: Harvard UP, 1978– .
Hopkins, Gerard Manley. *Gerard Manley Hopkins.* Ed. Catherine Phillips. Oxford:

Oxford UP, 1986.
—. *Gerard Manly Hopkins: The Early/Later Poetic Manuscripts.* Ed. Norman H.
MacKenzie. New York: Garland, 1989, 1990.
—. *The Poetical Works.* Ed. Norman H. MacKenzie. Oxford: Clarendon. Forth-
coming.
Howells, W. D. *A Selected Edition of W. D. Howells.* Ed. Edwin H. Cady, Don L.
Cook, Ronald Gottesman, David J. Nordloh et al. Bloomington: Indiana UP,
1968– .
Hugo, Victor. *Œuvres complètes.* Gen. Ed. Jean Massin. Paris: Club français du
livre, 1967–70. 18 vols.
The Intelligencer. Ed. James Woolley. Oxford: Clarendon, 1992.
James, William. *The Works of William James.* Ed. Fredson Bowers. Cambridge:
Harvard UP / New York: ACLS, 1975– .
*Jefferson, Thomas. *The Papers of Thomas Jefferson.* Ed. Julian P. Boyd, Charles
T. Cullen et al. Princeton: Princeton UP, 1950– .
*Johnson, Samuel. *The Yale Edition of the Works of Samuel Johnson.* Gen. Ed. John
H. Middendorf. New Haven: Yale UP, 1958– .
—. *The Letters of Samuel Johnson.* Ed. R. W. Chapman. Oxford: Clarendon, 1952.
3 vols.
—. *The Letters of Samuel Johnson: The Hyde Edition.* Ed. Bruce Redford. Princeton:
Princeton UP, 1992–1994. 5 vols.
*Jonson, Benjamin. *Ben Jonson.* Ed. C. H. Herford and Percy and Evelyn Simpson.
Oxford: Clarendon, 1925–52. 11 vols.
—. *Jonson's Masque of Gipsies in the Burley, Belvoir, and Windsor Versions: An At-
tempt at Reconstruction.* Ed. W. W. Greg. London: British Academy, 1952.
—. *Ben Jonson: The Complete Masques.* Ed. Stephen Orgel. New Haven: Yale UP,
1969.
—. *Epicoene, or The Silent Woman.* Ed. L. A. Beaurline. Lincoln: U of Nebraska P,
1966.
—. *Every Man in His Humour: A Parallel-Text Edition of the 1601 Quarto and the
1616 Folio.* Ed. J. W. Lever. Lincoln: U of Nebraska P, 1971.
Joyce, James. *The James Joyce Archive.* Gen. Ed. Michael Groden. New York: Gar-
land, 1978–79. 63 vols.
—. *Ulysses.* New York: Random H, 1934, rev. 1961.
*—. *Ulysses: A Critical and Synoptic Edition.* Ed. Hans Walter Gabler, with Wolf-
hard Steppe and Claus Melchior. New York: Garland, 1984. 3 vols.
—. *Ulysses: Corrected Text.* Ed. Hans Walter Gabler. New York: Random H, 1986.
—. *Ulysses: The 1922 Text.* Ed. Jeri Johnson. Oxford: Oxford UP, 1993.
—. *Joyce's Notes and Early Drafts for Ulysses: Selections from the Buffalo Collection.*
Ed. Phillip F. Herring. Charlottesville: UP of Virginia, 1977.
—. *Joyce's Ulysses Notesheets in the British Museum.* Ed. Phillip F. Herring. Char-
lottesville: UP of Virginia, 1972.
—. *The Dublin Edition of the Works of James Joyce.* Ed. John Kidd. New York:
Norton. Forthcoming.
Judith. Ed. Albert S. Cook. Boston: 1888.
Kafka, Franz. *Schriften, Tagebücher, Briefe.* Ed. Jürgen Born, Gerhard Neumann,
Malcolm Pasley, and Jost Schillemeit. Frankfurt: S. Fischer, 1982– .
*Keats, John. *The Poems of John Keats.* Ed. Jack Stillinger. Cambridge: Belknap /
Harvard UP, 1978.
—. *Poetry Manuscripts at Harvard: A Facsimile Edition.* Ed. Jack Stillinger. Cam-
bridge: Belknap / Harvard UP, 1990.
Kempe, Margery. *The Book of Margery Kempe.* Ed. Sanford Brown Meech. EETS
212. London: Oxford UP, 1940.
Kern, Jerome and Oscar Hammerstein, II. *Show Boat.* London Sinfonietta, McGlinn.
EMI CDS 7 49108 2.

King Horn. Ed. Rosamund S. Allen. New York: Garland, 1984.

Klopstock, Friedrich Gottlieb. *Werke und Briefe.* Ed. Adolf Beck, Karl-Ludwig Schneider, Hermann Tiemann, Horst Gronemeyer, Elisabeth Höpker-Herberg, Klaus Hurlebusch, and Rosa-Maria Hurlebusch. Berlin: De Gruyter, 1974– .

Kyd, Thomas. *The Works of Thomas Kyd.* Ed. Frederick S. Boas. Oxford: Clarendon, 1901. Repr. with Supplement. Oxford: Clarendon, 1955.

*Langland, William. *The Vision of William Concerning Piers the Plowman, in Three Parallel Texts.* Ed. W. W. Skeat. Oxford: Clarendon P, 1886. Rev. J. A. W. Bennett, 1954.

*—. *Piers Plowman: The A Version.* Ed. George Kane. London: Athlone, 1960.

*—. *Piers Plowman: The B Version.* Ed. George Kane and E. Talbot Donaldson. London: Athlone, 1975.

—. *Piers Plowman. An Edition of the C-text.* Ed. Derek Pearsall. Berkeley: U of California P, 1978.

—. *Piers Plowman: The Z Version.* Ed. Charlotte Brewer and A. G. Rigg. Toronto: Pontifical Institute of Medieval Studies, 1983.

—. *Piers Plowman Archive: Diplomatic-Critical Edition.* Ed. Hoyt N. Duggan et al. In preparation.

—. *Piers Plowman: The C Version.* Ed. G. H. Russell. London: Athlone. Forthcoming.

Lawrence, D. H. *The Works of D. H. Lawrence.* Gen. Eds. James T. Boulton and Warren Roberts. Cambridge: Cambridge UP, 1981– .

—. *Letters.* Gen. Ed. James T. Boulton. Cambridge: Cambridge UP, 1979– .

Layamon. *Brut.* Ed. G. L. Brook and R. F. Leslie. EETS 250. London: Oxford UP, 1963.

Lermontov, M. Ju. *Polnoe sobranie socinenij.* Ed. B. M. Èjxenbaum. Moscow / Leningrad: Academia, 1935–37. 5 vols.

Life of Machutus: The Old English Life of Machutus. Ed. David Yerkes. Toronto: U of Toronto P, 1984.

Lorris, Guillaume de and Jean de Meun. *Le roman de la rose.* Ed. Ernest Langlois. Paris: Firmin Didot and Champion, 1914–24. 5 vols.

—. *Le roman de la rose.* Ed. Félix Lecoy. Paris: Champion, 1965–70. 3 vols.

Lydgate, John. *Poems.* Ed. John Norton-Smith. Oxford: Clarendon, 1966.

Lyndsay, Sir David. *Ane Satyre of the Thrie Estatis.* Ed. J. Kinsley. London: 1954.

Mahabharata: The Adiparvan. Ed. Vishnu S. Sukthankar. Poona: Bhandarkar Oriental Research Institute, 1983.

Mailer, Norman. *An American Dream: (Esquire Version).* January-August 1964.

—. *An American Dream.* New York: Dial, 1965.

Majaz al-Qur'an. Ed. F. Sezgin. Cairo: Maktabat al-Kheanjei, 1954–62. 2 vols.

*Malory, Sir Thomas. *The Works of Sir Thomas Malory.* Ed. Eugène Vinaver. Oxford: Clarendon, 1967. 2nd ed. 3 vols.

Mandeville, Sir John. *Mandeville's Travels.* Ed. M. C. Seymour. Oxford: Clarendon, 1967.

—. *The Metrical Version of Mandeville's Travels.* Ed. M. C. Seymour. EETS 269. London: Oxford UP, 1973.

Manzoni, Alessandro. *Tutte le opere.* Ed. Alberto-Ghislberti Chiari. Milan: Mondadori, 1954–70.

Marie de France. *Lais.* Ed. Alfred Ewert. Oxford: Blackwell, 1944.

Marlowe, Christopher. *The Complete Works of Christopher Marlowe.* Ed. Fredson Bowers. Cambridge: Cambridge UP, 1973. 2nd ed. 1981. 2 vols.

—. *Complete Works of Christopher Marlowe.* Ed. Roma Gill. Oxford: Clarendon, 1989– .

*—. *Marlowe's The Tragicall History of the Life and Death of Doctor Faustus, 1604-1616. Parallel Texts.* Ed. W. W. Greg. Oxford: Clarendon, 1950.

—. *Dr. Faustus: The A-Text.* Ed. David Ormerod and Christopher Wortham. Western

Australia: U of Western Australia. 1985.

—. *Dr. Faustus: A 1604-Version Edition.* Ed. Michael Keefer. Peterborough, Ontario: Broadview P, 1991.

Massinger, Philip. *Plays and Poems.* Ed. Philip Edwards and Colin Gibson. Oxford: Clarendon, 1976.

*Melville, Herman. *The Writings of Herman Melville.* Ed. Harrison Hayford, Hershel Parker, and G. Thomas Tanselle. Evanston: Northwestern UP / Chicago: The Newberry Library, 1968– .

—. *Typee: A Peep at Polynesian Life.* Ed. Harrison Hayford, Hershel Parker, and G. Thomas Tanselle. Evanston: Northwestern UP / Chicago: Newberry Library, 1968.

Milton, John. *Works of John Milton.* Ed. Frank A. Patterson et al. New York: Columbia UP, 1931–38. 18 vols.

—. *Poetical Works.* Ed. Helen Darbishire. Oxford: Clarendon, 1952–55. 2 vols.

—. *Poems.* Ed. John Carey and Alastair Fowler. London: Longman, 1968.

—. *A Variorum Commentary on the Poems of John Milton.* Ed. Merritt Y. Hughes et al. New York: Columbia UP, 1970–75. 6 vols.

—. *Milton's Paradise Lost: A New Edition.* Ed. Richard Bentley. London: 1732.

Molière. *Œuvres complètes.* Ed. Georges Couton. Paris: Gallimard, 1971. 2 vols.

Montaigne, Michel de. *Essais.* Ed. Pierre Villey. Paris: Alcan, 1922–23. 3 vols.

—. *Essais.* Ed. Fortunat Strowski. Bordeaux: Pech, 1906–33. 5 vols.

Morris, William. *The Letters of William Morris.* Ed. Norman Kelvin. Princeton: Princeton UP, 1984– .

Nabokov, Vladimir. *Lectures on Don Quixote.* Ed. Fredson Bowers. New York: Harcourt Brace / Bruccoli Clark, 1983.

—. *Lectures on Literature.* Ed. Fredson Bowers. New York: Harcourt, Brace / Bruccoli Clark, 1980.

—. *Lectures on Russian Literature.* Ed. Fredson Bowers. New York: Harcourt, Brace / Bruccoli Clark, 1981.

*Nashe, Thomas. *The Works of Thomas Nashe.* Ed. R. B. McKerrow. London: Bullen / Sidgwick and Jackson, 1904–10. Repr. with corrections and supplementary notes. Ed. F. P. Wilson. Oxford: Blackwell, 1958. 5 vols.

The New Mermaids. Gen. Ed. Philip Brockbank. London: Benn, 1965–76.

The N-Town Play (Cotton MS Vespasian D.8). Ed. Stephen Spector. Oxford: EETS SS 11, 1992.

Orwell, George. *The Complete Works of George Orwell.* Gen. Ed. Peter Davison. London: Secker and Warburg / New York: Harcourt, 1986– .

The Owl and the Nightingale. Ed. J. E. Wells. Boston and London: Belles Lettres, 1907. Repr. New York: AMS, 1972.

—. Ed. J. H. G. Grattan and G. F. H. Sykes. EETS 119. London: Oxford UP, 1935. Repr. 1959.

—. Facsimile of Jesus College Oxford 29 and BM Cotton Caligula A. IX. Ed. N. R. Ker. EETS 251. London: Oxford UP, 1963.

The Parker Chronicle 832–900. Ed. A. H. Smith. London: Methuen, 1935.

*Pascal, Blaise. *Œuvres complètes.* Ed. Louis Lafuma. Paris: Éditions du Seuil, 1963.

*—. *Pensées.* Ed. Philippe Sellier. Paris: Mercure de France, 1976.

Pearl, Cleanness, Patience, and Sir Gawain Facsimile of BL Cotton Nero A.X. Ed. Israel Gollancz. EETS 162. Oxford: Oxford UP, 1923.

Pearl. Ed. E. V. Gordon. Oxford: Clarendon, 1953.

The Poems of the Pearl Manuscript. Ed. Malcolm Andrew and Ronald Waldron. Berkeley: U of California P, 1978.

Peele, George. *Dramatic Works.* Gen. Ed. Charles Tyler Pouty. New Haven. Yale UP, 1961–70. 2 vols.

Penn, William. *The Papers of William Penn.* Gen. Eds. Mary Maples Dunn and Richard S. Dunn. Philadelphia: U of Pennsylvania P, 1981–86. 5 vols.

Pepys, Samuel. *The Diary of Samuel Pepys*. Ed. Robert Latham and William Matthews. Berkeley: U of California P, 1970–1983. 11 vols.

Petrarch, Francesco. *Il canzoniere*. Ed. Gianfranco Contini. Turin: Einaudi, 1964.

Physiologus; The Middle English Physiologus. Ed. Hanneke Wirtjes. Oxford: EETS OS 299, 1991.

*Pope, Alexander. *The Twickenham Edition of the Poems of Alexander Pope*. Gen. Ed. John Butt. London: Methuen / New Haven: Yale UP, 1939–69.

—. *Correspondence of Alexander Pope*. Ed. George Sherburn. Oxford: Clarendon, 1956. 5 vols.

Pound, Ezra. *Ezra Pound's Poetry and Prose: Contributions to Periodicals*. Ed. Lea Baechler, A. Waltton Litz, and James Longenbach. New York: Garland, 1991. 11 vols.

—. *Variorum Edition of 'Three Cantos' by Ezra Pound: A Prototype*. Ed. Richard Taylor. Bayreuth: Boomerang P, 1991.

Proust, Marcel. *Matinée chez la Princesse de Guermantes, Cahiers du temps retrouvé*. Ed. Henri Bonnet and Bernard Brun. Paris: Gallimard, 1972.

—. *À la recherche du temps perdu*. Ed. Bernard Brun, Henri Bonnet, Eliane Dezon-Jones, Antoine Compagnon et al. Paris: Flammarion, 1987– .

Puškin, A. S. *Polnoe sobranie socinenij*. Ed. B. V. Tomaševskij. Moscow / Leningrad: AN SSSR, 1949: 10 vols.

—. *Polnoe sobranie socinenij*. Moscow / Leningrad: AN SSSR, 1937–59. 17 vols.

Racine, Jean. *Andromaque*. Ed. R. C. Knight and H. T. Barnwell. Geneva: Droz, 1977.

Records of Early English Drama. Gen. Ed. Alexandra F. Johnston. Toronto: U of Toronto P, 1979– .

Regents Renaissance Drama Series. Gen. Ed. Cyrus Hoy. Lincoln: U of Nebraska P, 1963–72.

Renard, Jean. *Le lai de l'Ombre*. Ed. Joseph Bédier. Paris: Firmin Didot, 1913.

Revelation. Ed. J. Massyngberde Forde. *The Anchor Bible*. Garden City: Doubleday, 1975.

Revels Plays. Ed. Clifford Leech, F. David Hoeniger et al. London: Methuen, 1958–74; Manchester: Manchester UP, 1975– .

Rolle, Richard. *English Writings*. Ed. H. E. Allen. Oxford: 1931.

—. *Prose and Verse*. Ed. S. J. Ogilvie-Thomson. EETS 293. Oxford: Oxford UP, 1988.

Roman de Thèbes. Ed. Gaston Raynaud. Paris: Champion, 1966–68. 2 vols.

Ronsard, Pierre de. *Œuvres complètes*. Ed. Charles Marty-Laveaux. Paris: A. Lemerre, 1887–93. 6 vols.

—. *Œuvres complètes*. Ed. Paul Laumonier, Raymond Lebègue, and Isidore Silver. Paris: Hachette, Didier, and Droz, 1914–59. 17 vols.

—. *Œuvres*. Ed. Isidore Silver. Chicago: U of Chicago P, 1966–70. 8 vols.

*Rossetti, Dante Gabriel. *Complete Writings and Pictures of Dante Gabriel Rossetti: A Hypermedia Research Archive*. Ed. Jerome J. McGann. In preparation.

Rousseau, Jean-Jacques. *Œuvres complètes*. Ed. Bernard Gagnebin and Marcel Raymond. Paris: Gallimard, 1959–69. 4 vols.

—. *Correspondance complète*. Ed. R. A. Leigh. Oxford: Voltaire Foundation, 1965–89. 49 vols.

St. Katherine, St. Margaret, St. Juliana, Hali Meidhad, Sawles Warde. Facsimile of MS Bodley 34. Ed. N. R. Ker. EETS 247. London: Oxford UP, 1960.

Santayana, George. *The Works of George Santayana*. Ed. Herman J. Saatkamp et al. Cambridge: MIT P, 1986– .

Savile, George. *The Works of George Savile Marquis of Halifax*. Ed. Mark N. Brown. Oxford: Oxford UP, 1989. 3 vols.

Schiller, Friedrich. *Sämmtliche Schriften. Historische-critische Ausgabe*. Ed. Karl

Goedeke. Stuttgart: Cotta, 1867-76.
—. *Werke. Nationalausgabe*. Ed. Julius Petersen, Gerhard Fricke, Hermann Schneider, Lieselotte Blumenthal, Benno von Wiese, Norbert Oellers. Weimar: Böhlau, 1943- .
Shakespeare, William. *Works*. Ed. Alexander Pope. London: 1723-25. 6 vols. 2nd ed, London: 1728. 10 vols.
—. *Works*. Ed. Lewis Theobald. London: 1740. 2nd ed. 8 vols.
—. *Works*. Ed. Samuel Johnson. London: 1765. 8 vols. 2nd ed. 1765; 3rd ed. 1768.
—. *Plays and Poems*. Ed. Edmond Malone. London: 1790. 10 vols.
—. *The Works: Globe Edition*. Eds. William G. Clark and W. Aldis Wright. Rev. ed. with John Glover. London: Macmillan, 1864. 9 vols. Further rev. 1891-95.
*—. *A New Variorum Edition of Shakespeare*. Ed. Robert. K. Turner, Richard Knowles et al. New York: MLA, 1930- . Rev. ed. of Philadelphia (later New York): 1871- . ed. H. H. Furness Sr., H. H. Furness Jr. et al. (Repr. New York: 1963- .)
—. *The New Arden Shakespeare*. Gen. Ed. Una Ellis-Fermor. London: 1951- .
—. *The New Cambridge Shakespeare*. Ed. John Dover Wilson and Arthur Quiller-Couch. Cambridge: Cambridge UP, 1921-66. 42 vols.
*—. *The Norton Facsimile: The Shakespeare First Folio*. Ed. Charlton Hinman. New York: Norton, 1968.
—. *The Riverside Shakespeare*. Ed. Gwynne Blakemore Evans. Boston: Houghton Mifflin, 1974.
—. *The Annotated Shakespeare*. Ed. A. L. Rowse. New York: C. N. Potter, 1978.
—. *Shakespeare's Plays in Quarto*. Ed. Michael J. B. Allen and Kenneth Muir. Berkeley: U of California P, 1981.
—. *The Complete Works*. Eds. Stanley Wells and Gary Taylor. Oxford: Clarendon, 1986.
*—. *The Complete Works: Original-Spelling Edition*. Eds. Stanley Wells and Gary Taylor. Oxford: Clarendon, 1988.
—. *The Complete Works: Electronic Edition*. Oxford: Oxford UP, 1989.
—. *The Three-Text Hamlet*. Ed. Paul Bertram and Bernice W. Kliman. New York: AMS, 1991.
*—. *The Parallel "King Lear" 1608-1623*. Ed. Michael Warren. Berkeley: U of California P, 1989.
*—. *The Complete "King Lear" 1608-1623*. Ed. Michael Warren. Berkeley: U of California P, 1990. 4 pts.
—. *Measure for Measure*. Ed. Mark Eccles. *New Variorum Edition*. New York: MLA, 1980.
—. *Shakespeare's Sonnets*. Ed. Stephen Booth. New Haven: Yale UP, 1977. Repr. with corrections, 1980.
Shaw, George Bernard. *Bernard Shaw: Texts: Play Manuscripts in Facsimile*. Ed. Dan H. Laurence. New York: Garland, 1981. 12 vols.
Shelley, Mary. *The Letters of Mary Wollstonecraft Shelley*. Ed. Betty Bennett. Baltimore: Johns Hopkins UP, 1980-88. 3 vols.
—. *Frankenstein, or The Modern Prometheus*. Ed. James Rieger. Chicago: U of Chicago P, 1982.
—. *The Journals of Mary Shelley*. Ed. Paula R. Felman and Diana Scott-Kilvert. Oxford: Clarendon, 1987.
Shelley, Percy Bysshe. *Shelley and his Circle 1773-1822*. Ed. Kenneth Neill Cameron and Donald H. Reiman. Cambridge: Harvard UP, 1961- .
—. *Shelley's Poetry and Prose*. Ed. Donald H. Reiman and Sharon B. Powers. New York: Norton, 1977.
—. *Shelley's "The Triumph of Life": A Critical Study, Based on a Text Newly Edited from the Bodleian Manuscript*. Ed. Donald H. Reiman. Urbana: U of Illinois P,

1965.

—. *The Prose Works of Percy Bysshe Shelley.* Ed. E. B. Murray. Oxford: Clarendon P, 1993– .

Sibelius, Jan. *Violin Concerto in D Major, Op. 47: Original (1903–04) Version and Final (1905) Version.* Leonidas Kavakos (vln); Lahti Symphony Orchestra / Osmo Vänskä. BIS / Conifer CD500.

Sidney, Sir Philip. *The Countess of Pembrokes Arcadia.* [Ed. M. Gwinne and F. Greville?] London: J. Windet for W. Ponsonbie, 1590.

—. *The Countess of Pembrokes Arcadia.* [Ed. H. S(anford)]. London: [J. Windet] for W. Ponsonbie, 1593. 2nd ed.

—. *The Countess of Pembroke's Arcadia (The Old Arcadia).* Ed. Jean Robertson. Oxford: Clarendon, 1973.

—. *The Countess of Pembroke's Arcadia (The New Arcadia).* Ed. Victor Skretowicz. Oxford: Clarendon, 1987.

The Simonie: A Parallel-Text Edition. Ed. Dan Embree and Elizabeth Urquhart. Middle English Texts 24. Heidelberg: Carl Winter U, 1991.

Sir Gawain and the Green Knight. Ed. Israel Gollancz. EETS 210. Oxford: Oxford UP, 1940.

—. Ed. J. R. R. Tolkien and E. V. Gordon. Oxford: Clarendon, 1967. 2nd ed. Rev. Norman Davis.

—. *The Works of the Gawain Poet.* Ed. Charles Moorman. Jackson, MS: 1977.

Smart, Christopher. *Poetical Works.* Ed. Karina Williamson. Oxford: Clarendon, 1980.

Smollett, Tobias. *The Works of Tobias Smollett.* Gen. Ed. Jerry Beasley. Athens: U of Georgia P, 1988– .

The Spectator. Ed. Donald F. Bond. Oxford: Clarendon P, 1965.

Spenser, Edmund. *The Faerie Queene Books I and II.* Ed. Robert Kellogg and Oliver Steele. New York: Odyssey, 1965. Repr. New York: Macmillan, 1988.

—. *The Faerie Queene.* Ed. A. C. Hamilton. London: Longman, 1977.

—. *The Yale Edition of the Shorter Poems of Edmund Spenser.* Ed. William A. Oram, Einar Bjorvand, Ronald Bond, Thomas H. Cain, Alexander Dunlop, and Richard Schell. New Haven: Yale UP, 1989.

Sterne, Laurence. *The Florida Edition of the Works of Laurence Sterne.* Ed. Melvyn New et al. Gainesville: UP of Florida, 1978.

Swift, Jonathan. *Correspondence.* Ed. Sir Harold Williams. Oxford: Clarendon, 1941.

—. *Journal to Stella.* Ed. Sir Harold Williams. Oxford: Clarendon, 1948.

Swinburne, Algernon. *The Swinburne Letters.* Ed. Cecil Y. Lang. New Haven, Yale UP, 1959–62.

The Tatler. Ed. Donald F. Bond. Oxford: Clarendon P, 1987.

Tennyson, Alfred, Lord. *The Tennyson Archive.* Ed. Christopher Ricks and Aidan Day. New York: Garland, 1987– .

—. *The Poems of Tennyson.* Ed. Christopher Ricks. Berkeley: U of California P / Harlow: Longman, 1987. 2nd ed. 3 vols.

—. *The Letters of Alfred Lord Tennyson.* Ed. Cecil Y. Lang and Edgar F. Shannon. Cambridge: Harvard UP, 1981–90. 3 vols.

Thackeray, W. M. *The Thackeray Edition Project.* Gen. Ed. Peter L. Shillingsburg. New York: Garland, 1989– .

Thoreau, Henry D. *The Writings of Henry D. Thoreau.* Ed. William L. Howarth, Walter Harding, Elizabeth Witherell, et al. Princeton: Princeton UP, 1969– .

The Thousand and One Nights . . . from the Earliest Known Sources. Ed. M. Mahdi. Leiden: Brill, 1984– .

Tolstoj, L. N. *Polnoe sobranie socinenij.* Ed. G. Culkov. Moscow / Leningrad: Gos. izdat'stvo xudozestvennoj literatury, 1928–58. 90 vols.

Tottel's Miscellany 1557–1587. Ed. Hyder Edward Rollins. Cambridge: Harvard UP,

1928-29. Rev. 1965.

Tourneur, Cyril. *Works of Cyril Tourneur*. Ed. Allardyce Nicoll. London: Fanfrolico P, 1930.

Towneley Cycle. Ed. George England and A. W. Pollard. EETS ES 71. London: Oxford UP, 1897.

—. *A Facsimile of Huntington MS HM1*. Ed. A. C. Cawley and Martin Stevens. Leeds Texts and Monographs, Medieval Drama Facsimiles 2. Leeds: U of Leeds P, 1976.

Très riches heures of Jean, Duke of Berry. New York: Braziller, 1969.

Trevisa, John. *Trevisa's Translation of Bartholomaeus Anglicus De Proprietatibus Rerum*. Ed. M. C. Seymour et al. Oxford: Clarendon, 1975-88. 3 vols.

Turgenev, I. S. *Socinenija*. Ed. B. M. Èjxenbaum and K. I. Xalabaev. Moscow / Leningrad: GIZ, 1928-34. 12 vols.

—. *Polnoe sobranie socinenij i pisem v 28-tomax*. Leningrad: Akademia Mauk, 1960-68. 28 vols.

Twain, Mark (Samuel Clemens). *The Mark Twain Project*. Ed. Frederick Anderson, Robert Hirst, et al. Berkeley: U of California P, 1966- .

Vercelli Homilies and Related Texts. Ed. Donald G. Scragg. Oxford: EETS OS 300, 1993.

Verdi, Giuseppe, Joseph Méry, and Camille Du Locle. *Don Carlos*. (1867 / 1882-83 / 1886). La Scala Orchestra / Claudio Abbado. DGG 415316 2, 1985.

— and Antonio Somma. *A Masked Ball (Un Ballo in Maschera)*. Naples 1857—Rome 1859.

Villon, François. *Œuvres complètes*. Ed. Auguste Longnon. Paris: Lemerre, 1892.

Voltaire. *Œuvres complètes*. Ed. Louis Moland. 52 vols. Paris: Garnier Frères, 1877-85.

—. *Œuvres complètes*. Ed. Theodore Besterman et al. Oxford: Voltaire Foundation, 1968- .

Wagner, Richard. *Tannhäuser*. Dresden, 1845 / Paris, 1861.

*Walpole, Horace. *The Yale Edition of Horace Walpole's Correspondence*. Ed. Wilmarth S. Lewis et al. New Haven: Yale UP, 1937-81. 42 vols.

The Wanderer. Ed. T. P. Dunning and A. J. Bliss. London: Methuen, 1969.

The Wars of Alexander. Ed. Hoyt N. Duggan and Thorlac Turville-Petre. EETS SS 10. Oxford: Oxford UP, 1989.

Webster, John. *Complete Works*. Ed. F. L. Lucas. London: Chatto and Windus, 1927. 4 vols.

The Welles Anthology: A Critical Edition. Ed. Sharon L. Jansen and Kathleen H. Jordan. Binghamton: Medieval & Renaissance Texts & Studies, 1991.

Wharton, Edith. *Fast and Loose and The Buccaneers*. Ed. Viola Hopkins Winner. Charlottesville: UP of Virginia, 1993.

Whitman, Walt. *The Collected Writings of Walt Whitman*. Ed. Gay Wilson Allen, Sculley Bradley, et al. New York: New York UP, 1961- .

—. *Whitman's Manuscripts: Leaves of Grass (1860): A Parallel Text*. Ed. Fredson Bowers. Chicago: U of Chicago P, 1955.

—. *Daybooks and Notebooks*. Ed. William White. New York: NYU P, 1978. 2 vols.

—. *Leaves of Grass*. Ed. Sculley Bradman and Harold W. Blodgett. New York: Norton, 1973.

Widsith. Ed. Kemp Malone. Copenhagen: Rosenkilde, 1962. 2nd ed.

Wilde, Oscar. *The Letters of Oscar Wilde*. Ed. Rupert Hart-Davis. New York: Harcourt, 1962.

Williams, William Carlos. *The Collected Poems*. Ed. A. Walton Litz and Christopher MacGowan. New York: New Directions, 1986-88. 2 vols.

Wilmot, John. *The Complete Poems of John Wilmot, Earl of Rochester*. Ed. David M. Vieth. New Haven: Yale UP, 1968.

Winner and Waster. Ed. Israel Gollancz. London: Oxford UP, 1921. Repr. Cambridge: Brewer, 1974.

—. Ed. Stephanie Trigg. EETS 290. Oxford: Oxford UP, 1990.
*Wordsworth, William. *The Cornell Wordsworth*. Gen. Ed. Stephen Parrish. Ithaca: Cornell UP, 1975– .
—. *The Prelude; or, Growth of a Poet's Mind*. Ed. Ernest de Selincourt. Oxford: Clarendon, 1959. 2nd ed., rev. Helen Darbishire.
—. *The Prelude: 1799, 1805, 1850*. Ed. Jonathan Wordsworth, M. H. Abrams, and Stephen Gill. New York: Norton, 1979.
Wyatt, Sir Thomas. *The Canon of Sir Thomas Wyatt's Poetry*. Ed. Richard C. Harrier. Cambridge: Harvard UP, 1975.
Wycherley, William. *Plays*. Ed. Arthur Friedman. Oxford: Clarendon, 1979.
Wycliff, William. *English Wycliffite Sermons*. Ed. Anne Hudson (vol. 1) and Pamela Gradon (vol. 2). Oxford: Clarendon P, 1983, 1988.
Yeats, W. B. *The Poems of W. B. Yeats*. Ed. Richard J. Finneran. New York: Macmillan, 1983. Rev. 1989.
*—. *The Cornell Yeats: Poems*. Gen. Ed. Richard J. Finneran. Ithaca: Cornell UP, 1987– .
—. *Yeats's Vision Papers*. Ed. George Mills Harper et al. Iowa City: U of Iowa P, 1992. 3 vols.

Studies of Scholarly Editing

(Since works on scholarly editing overlap significantly with textual criticism, see also the bibliography for Chapter 8.)

*Adams, Robert. "Editing *Piers Plowman*: The Imperative of an Intermittently Critical Edition." *Studies in Bibliography* 45 (1992): 31–68
Allen, Rosamund. "Some Sceptical Observations on the Editing of *The Awntyrs off Arthure*." Pearsall *Manuscripts*: 5–25.
Alspach, Russell K. "Some Textual Problems in Yeats." *Studies in Bibliography* 9 (1957): 51–67. Repr. Gottesman and Bennett: 186–207.
Alston, Robin. "Bibliography in the Computer Age." *The Book Encompassed*. Ed. Peter Davison. Cambridge: Cambridge UP, 1992: 276–289.
Amos, Ashley Crandell. "Computers and Lexicography: *The Dictionary of Old English*." *Editing, Publishing and Computer Technology*. Eds. Sharon Butler and William P. Stoneman. New York: AMS, 1988: 45–64.
Andersen, Francis I. "Scholarly Editing of the Hebrew Bible / Old Testament." Greetham *Scholarly Editing*.
Andrews, William. "Editing 'Minority' Literature." Greetham *Margins of the Text*.
Antush, John V. "Editing the Bi-Lingual Text at Cross-Cultural Purposes." *Text* 6 (1993): 345–358.
Baird, W. J. B. *Editing Texts of the Romantic Period*. Toronto: Hakkert, 1972.
*Bald, R. C. "Editorial Problems: A Preliminary Survey." *Studies in Bibliography* 3 (1950–51): 3–17. Repr. Gottesman and Bennett: 37–53.
Barnes, Warner. "Eighteenth- and Nineteenth-Century Editorial Problems: A Selective Bibliography." *Papers of the Bibliographical Society of America* 62 (1968), 59–67.
Barney, Stephen, ed. *Annotation and Its Texts*. Oxford: Oxford UP, 1991.
Basler, Roy P. "Collecting the 'Collected Works'." *Autograph Collector's Journal* 5 (1953): 37–38.
Bates, Robin. "Reflections on the Kidd Era." *Studies in the Novel* 22 (1990): 119–141.
Battestin, Martin. "A Rationale of Literary Annotation: The Example of Fielding's Novels." *Studies in Bibliography* 34 (1981) 1–22. Repr. Vogt and Jones.
Becker, Robert Stephen. "Challenges in Editing Modern Literary Correspondence:

Transcription," *Text* 1 (1984): 257-70.

*Bédier, Joseph, "La tradition manuscrite du *Lai du l'Ombre*: réflexions sur l'art d'éditer les anciens textes," *Romania* 54 (1928): 161-196, 321-356. Repr. as pamphlet, 1970.

Bennett, Philip and Graham Runnalls, eds. *The Editor and the Text*. 1990.

Bentley, G. E., Jr., ed. *Editing Eighteenth-Century Novels*. Toronto: Hakkert, 1975.

—. "Final Intention or Protean Performance: Classical Editing Theory and the Case of William Blake." Eggert *Editing in Australia*: 169-178.

Berger, Thomas L. "'Opening Titles Miscreate': Literary Theory and the 'Titling' of Shakespeare's Plays." Greetham *Margins of the Text*.

Bestermann, Theodore. "Twenty Thousand Voltaire Letters." Smith: 7-24.

Bevington, David. "Editorial Indications of Stage Business in Old-Spelling Editions." Shand and Shady: 105-112.

Blake, N. F. "The Editorial Process." *The English Language in Medieval Literature*. London: Dent / Totowa: Rowman, 1977: 55-79; 175-76.

—. "Geoffrey Chaucer: Textual Transmission and Editing." *Crux and Controversy in Middle English Textual Criticism*. Ed. A. J. Minnis and Charlotte Brewer. Cambridge: Brewer, 1992: 19-38.

Blecua, Alberto. *Manual de crítica textual*. 1983.

—. "Medieval Castilian Texts and Their Editions." Greetham *Scholarly Editing*.

Boddy, Gillian. "Editing the Notebooks of Katherine Mansfield: Some Preliminary Observations." Eggert *Editing in Australia*: 191-197.

*Bornstein, George, ed. *Representing Modernist Texts: Editing as Interpretation*. Ann Arbor: U of Michigan P, 1991.

*— and Ralph Williams, eds. *Palimpsest: Editorial Theory in the Humanities*. Ann Arbor: U of Michigan P, 1993.

*Bowers, Fredson. "The Method for a Critical Edition." *On Editing Shakespeare and the Elizabethan Dramatists*. Philadelphia: U of Pennsylvania Library, 1955: 67-101.

—. "Established Texts and Definitive Editions." *Philological Quarterly* 41 (1962): 1-17. Repr. *Essays*: 359-74.

*—. "Some Principles for Scholarly Editions of Nineteenth-Century American Authors." *Studies in Bibliography* 17 (1964): 223-28. Repr. Gottesman and Bennett: 54-61.

—. "Today's Shakespeare Texts, and Tomorrow's." *Studies in Bibliography* 19 (1966): 39-66.

*—. "Practical Texts and Definitive Editions." *Two Lectures on Editing: Shakespeare and Hawthorne*. Ed. Charlton Hinman and Fredson Bowers. Columbus: Ohio State UP, 1969: 21-70. Repr. *Essays*: 412-39.

—. *Essays in Bibliography, Text, and Editing*. Charlottesville, UP of Virginia, 1975.

—. "Scholarship and Editing." *Papers of the Bibliographical Society of America* 70 (1976): 161-88.

—. "Greg's 'Rationale of Copy-Text' Revisited." *Studies in Bibliography* 31 (1978): 90-161.

—. "Editing a Philosopher: The Works of William James." *Analytical and Enumerative Bibliography* 4 (1980): 3-36.

—. "Notes on Editorial Apparatus." *Historical and Editorial Studies in Medieval and Early Modern English, for Johann Gerritsen*. Ed. Mary-Jo Arn and Hanneke Wirtjes, with Hans Jensen. Groningen: Wolters-Nordhoff, 1985: 147-62.

—. "Readability and Regularization in Old-Spelling Texts of Shakespeare." *Huntington Library Quarterly* 50 (1987): 199-227.

—. "Regularization and Normalization in Modern Critical Texts." *Studies in Bibliography* 42 (1989): 79-102.

—. "Notes on Theory and Practice in Editing Texts." *The Book Encompassed*. Ed. Peter Davison. Cambridge: Cambridge UP, 1992: 244-257.

—. "Why Apparatus?" *Text* 6 (1993): 11–20.

Boydston, Jo Ann. "Editing the Library of America." *Scholarly Publishing* 16 (1984–85): 121–32.

—. "Editing the Poems of John Dewey." *Documentary Editing* 7 (March 1985): 1–6.

—. "In Praise of Apparatus," *Text* 5 (1991): 1–14.

—. "Standards for Scholarly Editing: The CEAA and the CSE." *Text* 6 (1993): 21–34.

—. *"The Collected Works of John Dewey* and the CEAA/CSE: A Case History." *Papers of the Bibliographical Society of America* 85 (1991): 119–144.

Boyle, Leonard E. "'Epistulae Venerant Patrum Dulces': The Place of Codicology in the Editing of Medieval Latin Texts." Landon: 29–46.

Brack, O M Jr. and Warner Barnes, eds. *Bibliography and Textual Criticism: English and American Literature, 1700 to the Present.* Chicago: U of Chicago P, 1969.

Brandt, Kathleen Weil-Garris. "The Grime of the Centuries Is a Pigment of the Imagination: Michelangelo's Sistine Ceiling." Bornstein and Williams: 257–270.

Braunmuller, A. R. "Editing Elizabethan Letters." *Text* 1 (1984): 185–199.

—. "Accounting for Absence: The Transcription of Space." Hill *New Ways*: 47–56.

Brett, Philip. "Text, Context, and the Early Music Editor." *Authenticity and Early Music: A Symposium.* Ed. Nicholas Kenyon. New York: Oxford UP, 1988: 83–114.

Brewer, Charlotte. "The Textual Principles of Kane's A-Text." *Yearbook of Langland Studies* 3 (1989): 67–90.

—. "George Kane's Processes of Revision." *Crux and Controversy in Middle English Textual Criticism.* Ed. A. J. Minnis and Charlotte Brewer. Cambridge: Brewer, 1992: 71–96.

Brock, Sebastian P. "Developments in Editing Biblical Texts." *The Book Encompassed.* Ed. Peter Davison. Cambridge: Cambridge UP, 1992: 236–243.

Broude, Ronald. "When Accidentals Are Substantive: Applying Methodologies of Textual Criticism to Scholarly Editions of Music." *Text* 5 (1991): 105–20.

—. "Establishing Texts in Improvisatory Traditions." *Text* 7 (1994).

Brown, Arthur. "Editorial Problems in Shakespeare." *Studies in Bibliography* 8 (1956): 15–26.

—. "The Rationale of Old-Spelling Editions of the Plays of Shakespeare and His Contemporaries: A Rejoinder." *Studies in Bibliography* 13 (1960): 69–76.

Brown, John Russell. "The Rationale of Old-Spelling Editions of the Plays of Shakespeare and His Contemporaries." *Studies in Bibliography* 13 (1960): 49–68.

Burkhardt, Frederick. "Editing the Correspondence of Charles Darwin." *Studies in Bibliography* 41 (1988): 149–159.

Bush, Ronald. "Excavating the Ideological Faultlines of Modernism: Editing Ezra Pound's *Cantos.*" Bornstein: 67–98.

Butler, Sharon and William P. Stoneman, eds. *Editing, Publishing and Computer Technology.* New York: AMS, 1988.

Butt, John. "Editing a Nineteenth-Century Novelist (Proposals for an Edition of Dickens)." *English Studies Today* 2nd Series (1961): 187–195. Repr. Gottesman and Bennett: 155–166.

Caldwell, John. *Editing Early Music.* New York: Oxford UP, 1985.

Campion, Edmund J. "Scholarly Editing of Early Modern French Literature." Greetham *Scholarly Editing.*

Carlson, Clayborne. "Editing Martin Luther King: Political and Scholarly Issues." Bornstein and Williams: 305–316.

Carroll, John. "On Annotating *Clarissa.*" Bentley: 49–66.

Carter, Michael. "Scholarly Editing of Arabic Literature." Greetham *Scholarly Editing.*

Center for Editions of American Authors. *Statement of Editorial Principles and Procedures.* Rev. ed. New York: MLA, 1972.

Center / Committee for Scholarly Editions. *An Introductory Statement.* New York:

MLA, 1977.

Cherchi, Paolo. *Scholarly Editing of Italian Literature*. Greetham *Scholarly Editing*.

*Chernaik, Warren, Caroline Davis and Marilyn Deegan, eds. *The Politics of the Electronic Text*. Oxford: Oxford U Computing Services, 1993.

Chicago Guide to Preparing Electronic Manuscripts for Authors and Publishers. Chicago: U of Chicago P, 1987.

*Committee on Scholarly Editions. *Guidelines for Scholarly Editions*. New York: MLA, 1991.

Conklin, E. Jeffrey. "Hypertext: An Introduction and Survey." *IEEE Computer* 20.9 (1987): 17–41.

*Cook, Don L. "The Short, Happy Thesis of G. Thomas Tanselle." *Newsletter of the Association for Documentary Editing* 3.1 (1981): 1–4.

*—. "Preparing Scholarly Editions." *Humanities* 9, no. 3 (May / June 1988): 14–17.

Coombs, James H., Allen H. Renear, and Steven J. Derose. "Markup Systems and the Future of Scholarly Text Processing." *Communications of the Association for Computing Machinery* 30.11 (1988): 933–947.

Cosgrove, Peter W. "Undermining the Text: Edward Gibbon, Alexander Pope, and the Anti-Authenticating Footnote." Barney *Annotation*: 130–151.

Cowen, Janet M. "Metrical Problems in Editing *The Legend of Good Women*." Pearsall *Manuscripts*: 26–33.

Crane, Elaine Forman. "Gender Consciousness in Editing: The Diary of Elizabeth Drinker." *Text* 4 (1988): 375–384.

Crow, John. "Editing and Emending." *Essays and Studies* 1955: 1–20.

**CTI Centre for Textual Studies: Resources Guide March 1992*. Ed. Caroline Davis, Marilyn Davies, and Stuart Lee. Oxford: Oxford U Computing Services, 1992.

Cullen, Charles T. "Principles of Annotation in Editing Historical Documents: Or, How To Avoid Breaking the Butterfly on the Wheel of Scholarship." Vogt and Jones: 81–95.

Dainard, J. A., ed. *Editing Correspondence*. New York: Garland, 1979.

Dane, Joseph A. "The Reception of Chaucer's Eighteenth-Century Editors." *Text* 4 (1988): 217–236.

Davis, Tom. "The CEAA and Modern Textual Editing." *Library* 5th Series 32 (1977): 61–74.

Davison, Peter. "Editing Orwell: Eight Problems." *Library* 6th Series 6 (1984): 217–228.

De Quehen, A. H., ed. *Editing Poetry from Spenser to Dryden*. New York: Garland, 1981.

De Robertis, Domenico. "Per l'edizione critica del 'Dolore' di Giuseppi Ungaretti." *Studi di filologia italiana* 38 (1980): 309–23.

De Tienne, André. "Selecting Alterations for Apparatus." *Text* 8. Forthcoming.

*Dearing, Vinton. "Methods of Textual Editing." *Williams Andrews Clark Memorial Library Seminar Papers*. 1962: 1–34. Repr. Brack and Barnes: 73–101.

—. "Computer Aids to Editing the Text of Dryden." Gottesman and Bennett: 254–278.

—. *Principles and Practice of Textual Analysis*. Berkeley: U of California P, 1974.

—. "Textual Analysis: A Kind of Textual Criticism," *Text* 2 (1985): 13–24.

*Delany, Paul and George Landow, eds. *Hypermedia and Literary Studies*. Cambridge: MIT P, 1991.

Derrida, Jacques. "This Is Not an Oral Footnote." Barney *Annotation*: 192–206.

Dictionary of American Regional English. Ed. Frederic G. Cassidy. Cambridge : Belknap / Harvard, 1985– .

Dictionary of Old English. Ed. Angus Cameron et al. Toronto: Pontifical Institute of Mediaeval Studies for Dictionary of Old English Project, Centre for Medieval Studies, U of Toronto, 1987– .

Diller, George T. "Editing Froissart's *Chronicles*." *Text* 8. Forthcoming.

Dilts, Mervyn R. "Scholarly Editing of Classical Greek Literature." Greetham *Scholarly Editing*.

Domville, Eric W. *Editing British and American Literature, 1880–1920*. New York: Garland, 1976.

Donaldson, E. T. *Speaking of Chaucer*. London: Athlone / New York: Norton, 1970.

Doyle, Jeff. "McLeoding the Issue: The Printshop and Heywood's *Iron Ages*." Eggert *Editing in Australia*: 151–168.

Duggan, Hoyt N. "Scribal Self-Correction and Editorial Theory." *Neuphilologische Mitteilungen* 91 (1990): 215–227.

*—. "The Electronic *Piers Plowman B*: A New Diplomatic-Critical Edition." *Æstel* 1 (1993): 55–75.

Edwards, A. S. G. "Observations on the History of Middle English Editing." Pearsall *Manuscripts*: 34–48.

—. "Middle English Romance: The Limits of Editing, the Limits of Criticism." Tim W. Machan, ed. *Medieval Literature: Texts and Interpretations*. Binghamton: Medieval & Renaissance Texts and Studies, 1991: 91–104.

—. "Scholarly Editing of Middle English Literature." Greetham *Scholarly Editing*.

Edwards, Mary Jane. "CEECT: Progress, Procedures, and Problems." *Papers of the Bibliographical Society of Canada* 26 (1987): 13–26.

—. "Angles from the Margin: Editing Early English-Canadian Literature." Eggert *Editing in Australia*: 85–102.

—. "Views from 'The Attic': The Publication of Canadian Works in Canada and Abroad." *Text* 5 (1991): 295–306.

Edwards, Philip. "The Function of Commentary." Shand and Shady: 97–104.

Eggert, Paul, ed. *Editing in Australia*. Canberra: New South Wales University Press, 1990 (Occasional Paper No. 17, English Department, University College ADFA).

Eisenberg, Daniel. "On Editing *Don Quixote*." *Cervantes* 3 (1983): 18–30.

Elias, Robert H. "Eighteenth-Century Thorns, Twentieth-Century Secretaries, & Other Prickly Matters." *Text* 3 (1987): 347–353.

Embree, Dan and Elizabeth Urquhart. "*The Simonie*: The Case for a Parallel-Text Edition." Pearsall *Manuscripts*: 49–59.

Erdman, David V. and Ephim G. Fogel, eds. *Evidence for Authorship: Essays on Problems of Attribution*. Ithaca: Cornell UP, 1966.

Fifer, C. N. "Editing Boswell: A Search for Letters." *Manuscripts* 6 (1953): 2–5.

Finneran, Richard J. *Editing Yeats's Poems: A Reconsideration*. London: Macmillan, 1990. Rev. ed.

—. "Text and Interpretation in the Poems of W. B. Yeats." Bornstein: 17–48.

Fitzmaurice, James. "Some Problems in Editing Margaret Cavendish." Hill *New Ways*: 253–262.

Foley, John Miles. "Editing Yugoslav Epics: Theory and Practice." *Text* 1 (1981): 75–96.

—. "Scholarly Editing of Folk Literature." Greetham *Scholarly Editing*.

Foucault, Michel. "What Is an Author?" Trans. Josué V. Harari. *The Foucault Reader*. Ed. Paul Rabinow. New York: Pantheon, 1984: 101–20.

*Foulet, Alfred and Mary Blakeley Speer. *On Editing Old French Texts*. Lawrence: Regents P of Kansas, 1979.

Fowler, David C. "A New Edition of the B Text of *Piers Plowman*." *Yearbook of English Studies* 7 (1977): 23–42.

Foxon, D. F. "Greg's 'Rationale' and the Editing of Pope." *Library* 5th Series 33 (1978): 119–124.

Frank, Roberta, ed. *The Politics of Editing Medieval Texts*. New York: AMS, 1993.

Franklin, Wayne. "The 'Library of America' and the Welter of American Books." *Iowa Review* 15 (1985): 176–94.

Freedman, David Noel. "Editing the Editors: Translation and Elucidation of the Text of the Bible." Bornstein and Williams: 227–256.

Friedman, Arthur. "Principles of Historical Annotation in Critical Editions of Modern Texts." *English Institute Annual* 1941. Ed. Rudolf Kirk. New York: Columbia UP, 1942.

Gabler, Hans Walter. "A Response to John Kidd, 'Errors of Execution in the 1984 *Ulysses*.'" Conference paper, Society for Textual Scholarship, New York City, April 26, 1985. *Studies in the Novel* 22 (1990): 250–56.

Gaines, Barry. "Textual Apparatus: Rationale and Audience." Shand and Shady: 65–72.

Gair, Reavley. "In Search of 'the Mustie Fopperies of Antiquity'." Shand and Shady: 123–130.

Galloway, Patricia. "Dearth and Bias: Issues in the Editing of Ethnohistorical Materials." *Newsletter of the Association for Documentary Editing* 3.2 (May 1981): 1–6.

*Gaskell, Philip. *From Writer to Reader: Studies in Editorial Method*. Oxford: Clarendon P, 1978.

Girling, Harry Knowles. "A Toot of the Trumpet Against the Scholarly Regiment of Editors." *Bulletin of Research in the Humanities* 81 (1978): 297–323.

Giunta, Mary A. and Beverly S. Hacker. "Using Computer Technology to 'Read' Documents: the Optiram Example." *Documentary Editing* 13 (1991): 65–67.

Gossett, Philip. "Translations and Adaptations of Operatic Texts." Bornstein and Williams: 285–304.

—. "Knowing the Score: Italian Opera as Work and Play." *Text* 8. Forthcoming.

Gottesman, Ronald and Scott Bennett, eds. *Art and Error: Modern Textual Editing*. Bloomington: Indiana UP / London: Methuen, 1970.

Graff, Henry F. and A. Simone Reagor. *Documentary Editing in Crisis: Some Reflections and Recommendations*. Washington: NHPRC, 1981.

Grant, John N., ed. *Editing Greek and Latin Texts*. New York: AMS, 1989.

Graves, Robert and Laura Riding. "A Study in Original Punctuation and Spelling [of Shakespeare's Sonnet 129]." *The Common Asphodel*. London: Hamilton, 1949: 84–95.

Greetham, D. C. "Models for the Textual Transmission of Translation: The Case of John Trevisa." *Studies in Bibliography* 37 (1984): 131–55.

—. "Challenges of Theory and Practice in the Editing of Hoccleve's *Regement of Princes*." Pearsall, *Manuscripts*: 60–86.

—. "The Place of Fredson Bowers in Mediaeval Editing." *Papers of the Bibliographical Society of America* 82 (1988): 53–69.

*—, ed. *Scholarly Editing: A Guide to Research*. New York: MLA, 1994.

—, ed. *The Margins of the Text*. In preparation.

Greg, W. W. *A Calculus of Variants: An Essay on Textual Criticism*. Oxford: Clarendon P, 1927.

—. "Principles of Emendation in Shakespeare." *Proceedings of the British Academy* 14 (1928): 147–216.

*—. "The Rationale of Copy-Text." *Studies in Bibliography* 3 (1950–51): 19–36.

—. *The Editorial Problem in Shakespeare: A Survey of the Foundations of the Text*. Oxford: Clarendon, 1965. 3rd ed.

Grigsby, John L. "Editing Medieval Texts." *Romance Philology* 34 (1981): 64–73.

Guffey, George. "Standardization of Photographic Reproductions for Mechanical Collation." *Papers of the Bibliographical Society of America* 62 (1968): 237–240.

Hageman, Elizabeth H. "*Did* Shakespeare Have Any Sisters? Editing Texts by Englishwomen of the Renaissance and Reformation." Hill *New Ways*: 103–110.

Hagen, Waltraud, Inge Jensen, Edith Nahler, and Horst Nahler, eds. *Handbuch der Editionen: Deutschsprachige Schriftsteller Ausgang des 15. Jahrhunderts bis zur Gegenwart*. Berlin: Volk und Wissen, 1983. 2nd ed.

Haight, Gordon S. "The Reader's Convenience." Hall *Browning*: 137–140.

Hall, J. R. "Scholarly Editing of Old English Literature." Greetham *Scholarly Editing*.

Hall, N. John, ed. *Browning Institute Studies.* Special Issue on Editing. 9 (1981).

Halpenny, Francess G., ed. *Editing Twentieth-Century Texts.* Toronto: U of Toronto P, 1972.

—, ed. *Editing Canadian Texts.* Toronto: Hakkert, 1975.

Halsband, Robert. "Editing the Letters of Letter-Writers." *Studies in Bibliography* 11 (1958): 25–37. Repr. Gottesman and Bennett: 124–139.

Hanna, Ralph, III. "Problems of 'Best Text' Editing and the Hengwrt Manuscript of *The Canterbury Tales.*" Pearsall *Manuscripts*: 87–94.

—. "A la Recherche du Temps Bien Perdu: The Text of *The Awyntyrs off Arthure.*" *Text* 4 (1988): 189–206.

—. "Editing Middle English Prose Translations: How Prior Is the Source?" *Text* 4 (1988): 207–216.

—. "Annotation as Social Practice." Barney *Annotation*: 178–184.

—. "Producing Manuscripts and Editions." *Crux and Controversy in Middle English Textual Criticism.* Ed. A. J. Minnis and Charlotte Brewer. Cambridge: Brewer, 1992: 109–130.

—. "Annotating *Piers Plowman.*" *Text* 6 (1993): 153–164.

Hay, Louis and Winfried Woesler, eds. *Die Nachlassedition: La publication des manuscrits inédits.* Bern: P. Lang, 1979.

— and Winfried Woesler, eds. *Edition und Interpretation: Edition et interprétation des manuscrits littéraires.* Bern: P. Lang, 1981.

Hedges, Chris. "Re-creating U.S. First Editions, Typos and All." *New York Times* 9 July 1991: C 13, 18.

Heideking, Jürgen. "A Troubled Past and a Few Great Men: Historical Editing in Germany." *Documentary Editing* 12 (1990): 66–69.

Hergenhein, Laurie. "Some Comments on the Editing of Australian Literary Texts." Eggert *Editing in Australia*: 179–184.

Hewitt, David S. "Burns and the Argument for Standardisation." *Text* 1 (1984): 217–229.

Hill, W. Speed. "The Calculus of Error, or Confessions of a General Editor." *Modern Philology* 75 (1978): 247–60. ·

—, ed. *New Ways of Looking at Old Texts: Papers of the Renaissance English Text Society, 1985–1991.* Binghamton: Medieval & Renaissance Texts & Studies / Renaissance English Text Society, 1993.

—. "The Theory and Practice of Transcription." Hill *New Ways*: 25–32.

—. "Scholarly Editing of English Non-Dramatic Renaissance Literature." Greetham *Scholarly Editing.*

Hinman, Charlton. "Mechanized Collation at the Houghton Library." *Harvard Library Bulletin* 9 (1955): 132–134.

Hobbs, Mary. "Early Seventeenth-Century Verse Miscellanies and Their Value for Textual Editors." *English Manuscript Studies 1100–1700* 1 (1989): 182–210.

Hockey, Susan. *A Guide to Computer Applications in the Humanities.* Baltimore: Johns Hopkins UP, 1980.

— and Ian Marriot. *Oxford Concordance Program.* Version 2.0. Oxford: Oxford U Computing Service, 1987.

Holland, Peter. "Authorship and Collaboration: The Problem of Editing Shakespeare." Chernaik: 17–23.

Howard. Wm. J., ed. *Editor, Author, and Publisher.* Toronto: U of Toronto P, 1969.

Howard-Hill, T. H. "A Practical Scheme for Editing Critical Texts with the Aid of a Computer." *Proof* 3 (1973): 335–56.

—. "Computer and Mechanical Aids to Editing." *Proof* 5 (1975): 217–35.

—. *Literary Concordances: A Guide to the Preparation of Manual and Computer Concordances.* Oxford: Pergamon, 1979.

—. "Playwrights' Intentions and the Editing of Plays." *Text* 4 (1988): 269–278.

—. "Modern Editorial Theories and the Editing of Plays." *The Library* Sixth Series 11

(1989): 89-115.

—. "Scholarly Editing of English Non-Shakespearean Dramatic Literature." Greetham *Scholarly Editing*.

Hult, David F. "Reading It Right: The Ideology of Text Editing." *Romanic Review* 79 (1988): 74-88.

Hurlebusch, Klaus. "'Relic' and 'Tradition': Some Aspects of Editing Diaries," *Text* 3 (1987): 143-54.

Hussey, S. S. "Editing *The Scale of Perfection*: Return to Recension." *Crux and Controversy in Middle English Textual Criticism*. Ed. A. J. Minnis and Charlotte Brewer. Cambridge: Brewer, 1992: 97-108.

Iversen, Gunilla. "Problems in the Editing of Tropes." *Text* 1 (1984): 95-132.

Jack, Ian. "'Commented It Must Be': Browning Annotating." Hall *Browning*: 59-78.

Jackson, H. J., ed. *Editing Polymaths: Erasmus to Russell.* Toronto: Committee for Conference on Editorial Problems, 1983.

Jackson, Russell. "Victorian Editors of *As You Like It* and the Purposes of Editing." Small and Walsh: 142-156.

Janzen, Henry D. "Preparing a Diplomatic Edition: Heywood's *The Escapes of Jupiter*." Shand and Shady: 73-80.

Jarman, Douglas. *Alban Berg: Lulu.* Cambridge: Cambridge UP, 1991.

Jenkins, Reese V. and Thomas E. Jeffrey. "Worth a Thousand Words: Nonverbal Documents in Editing." *Documentary Editing* 6.3 (1984): 1-8.

Johnson, Thomas H. "Establishing a Text: The Emily Dickinson Papers." *Studies in Bibliography* 5 (1952-53): 21-32. Repr. Gottesman and Bennett: 140-154.

Johnston, A. F., ed. *Editing Early English Drama: Special Problems and New Directions.* New York: AMS, 1987.

Jones, John Bush. "Editing Victorian Playwrights: Some Problems, Priorities, and Principles." *Theatre Survey* 17 (1976): 106-123.

Kallberg, Jeffrey. "Are Variants a Problem? 'Composer's Intentions' in Editing Chopin." *Chopin Studies* 4 (1990): 257-67.

Kasinec, Edward and Robert Whittaker. "Scholarly Editing of Russian Literature." Greetham *Scholarly Editing*.

Kelley, Philip and Ronald Hudson. "Editing the Brownings' Correspondence: An Editorial Manual." Hall *Browning*: 141-160.

Kenyon, Nicholas. "'Messiah' Meets the Millennium." *New York Times*. 24 November 1991: H29.

Kidd, John. "Errors of Execution in the 1984 *Ulysses*." Conference paper, Society for Textual Scholarship, New York City, April 26, 1985. *Studies in the Novel* 22 (1990): 243-49.

—. "The Scandal of *Ulysses*." *New York Review of Books* 30 June, 1988: 32-39.

—. "An Inquiry into *Ulysses: The Corrected Text*." *Papers of the Bibliographical Society of America* 82 (1988): 411-584.

Kiernan, Kevin. *Beowulf and the Beowulf Manuscript*. New Brunswick: Rutgers UP, 1981.

—. *The Thorkelin Transcript of Beowulf*. Anglistica 25. Copenhagen: Rosenkilde, 1986.

Kipling, Gordon. "*The Receyt of the Ladie Kateryne* and the Practice of Editorial Transcription." Hill *New Ways*: 33-46.

Kirby, Carol Bingham. "Editing Spanish Golden Age Dramatic Texts: Past, Present, and Future Models." *Text* 8. Forthcoming.

Kirsop, Wallace. "The Australian Bookselling and Publishing History Project and Editing in Australia." Eggert *Editing in Australia*: 185-190.

—. "Bowers and the French Connection." *Text* 8. Forthcoming.

Klene, Jean. "Recreating the Letters of Lady Anne Southwell." Hill *New Ways*: 239-252.

*Kline, Mary-Jo. *A Guide to Documentary Editing*. Baltimore: Johns Hopkins UP,

1987.

Knight, Alan E. "On Editing Early Printed French Plays." *Romance Philology* 40 (1986): 65–74.

—. "Editing the Unique Manuscript: The Case of the Lille Plays." *Text* 5 (1988): 145–155.

Knowles, Richard. "Variorum Commentary." *Text* 6 (1993): 35–48.

Kristeller, Paul Oskar. "The Editing of Fifteenth-Century Texts: Tasks and Problems." *Italian Culture* 4 (1983): 115–122.

Lancashire, Anne, ed. *Editing Renaissance Dramatic Texts: English, Italian, and Spanish.* New York: Garland, 1976.

*Landon, Richard, ed. *Editing and Editors: A Retrospect.* New York: AMS, 1988.

*Landow, George. *Hypertext: The Convergence of Contemporary Critical Theory and Technology.* Baltimore: Johns Hopkins UP, 1992. Electronic Edition, 1994.

*Lanham, Richard A. *The Electronic Word: Democracy, Technology, and the Arts.* Chicago: U of Chicago P, 1993.

Lau, Beth. "Editing Keats's Marginalia." *Text* 7 (1994).

Lavagnino, John. "Reading, Scholarship, and Hypertext Editions." *Text* 8. Forthcoming.

Lavazzi, Tom. "Editing Schwerner: Versions of Armand Schwerner's 'Design Tablet'." *Text* 8. Forthcoming.

Lawler, Traugott. "Medieval Annotation: The Example of the Commentaries on Walter Map's *Dissuasio Valerii*." Barney *Annotation*: 94–107.

Lennox, John and Janet M. Paterson, eds. *Challenges, Projects, Texts: Canadian Editing / Défis, projets et textes dans l'édition critique au Canada.* New York: AMS, 1993.

Leslie, Michael. "Electronic Editions and the Hierarch of Texts." Chernaik: 41–51.

Levere, Trevor H., ed. *Editing Texts in the History of Science and Medicine.* New York: Garland, 1982.

Lewis, Wilmarth S. "Editing Familiar Letters." *Daedalus* 86 (1955): 71–77.

Lindstrand, Gordon. "Mechanized Textual Collation and Recent Designs." *Studies in Bibliography* 24 (1971): 204–14.

Litz, A. Walton and Christopher MacGowan. "Editing William Carlos Williams." Bornstein: 49–66.

Logan, George M., David T. Barnard, and Robert G. Crawford. "Computer-Based Publication of Critical Editions: Some General Considerations and a Prototype." *Computers and the Humanities.* Toronto: U of Toronto P, 1986: 318–326.

Love, Harold. "Standards for Scholarly Editions of Australian and New Zealand Writers." *Bibliographical Society of Australia and New Zealand Bulletin* 5 (1981): 1–4.

—. "The Ranking of Variants in the Analysis of Moderately Contaminated Manuscript Traditions." *Studies in Bibliography* 37 (1984): 39–57.

—. "The Editing of Restoration Scriptorial Satire." Eggert *Editing in Australia*: 65–84.

*Luey, Beth. *Editing Documents and Texts: An Annotated Bibliography.* Madison: Madison House, 1990.

Machan, Tim William. "Editorial Method and Medieval Translations: The Examples of Chaucer's *Boece*." *Studies in Bibliography* 41 (1988): 188–196.

Machuta, Daniel J. and William F. Lawrence. *The Complete Desktop Publisher.* Greensboro: Compute Pub., 1986.

MacLean, Gerald M. "What Is a Restoration Poem? Editing a Discourse, not an Author." *Text* 3 (1987): 319–346.

*Mahaffey, Vicki. "Intentional Error: The Paradox of Editing Joyce's *Ulysses*." Bornstein: 171–192.

Martens, Gunter and Hans Zeller, eds. *Texte und Varianten: Probleme ihrer Edition und Interpretation.* Munich: Beck, 1971.

Martin, Henri-Jean, Roger Chartier, and Jean-Pierre Vivet, eds. *Histoire de l'édition française.* Paris: Promodis, 1982–86.

Matthews, John. "The Hunt for Disraeli Letters." Dainard: 81–92.
Mayali, Laurent. "For a Political Economy of Annotation." Barney *Annotation*: 185–191.
Mays, J. C. C. "Editing Coleridge in the Historicized Present." *Text* 8. Forthcoming.
McCarran, Vincent P. and Douglas Moffat, eds. *Guide to Editing Middle English*. Ann Arbor: U of Michigan P. Forthcoming.
McClelland, John. "Critical Editing in the Modern Languages." *Text* 1 (1984): 201–216.
McCutcheon, Elizabeth. "Life and Letters: Editing the Writing of Margaret Roper." Hill *New Ways*: 111–118.
McElrath, Joseph R., Jr. "Tradition and Innovation: Recent Developments in Literary Editing." *Documentary Editing* 10, no. 4 (December, 1988): 5–10.
McFarland, Thomas. "Who Was Benjamin Whichcote? or, The Myth of Annotation." Barney *Annotation*: 152–177.
McGaha, Michael and Frank P. Casa, eds. *Editing the Comedia*. Michigan Romance Studies 5, 11 (1985, 1991).
McGann, Jerome J. "*Ulysses* as a Postmodernist Text: The Gabler Edition." *Criticism* 27 (1985): 283–305. Repr. as "*Ulysses* as a Postmodern Work." McGann. *Social Values and Poetic Acts: The Historical Judgment of Literary Work*. Cambridge: Harvard UP, 1988: 173–94.
*—. "The Complete Writings and Pictures of Dante Gabriel Rossetti: A Hypermedia Research Archive." *Text* 7 (1994).
McGerr, Rosemarie Potz. "Editing the Self-Conscious Medieval Translator: Some Issues and Examples." *Text* (1988): 147–161.
McGillivray, Murray. "Towards a Post-Critical Edition: Theory, Hypertext, and the Presentation of Middle English Works" *Text* 7 (1994).
McLeod, Randall. "Editing Shak-speare." *Sub-Stance* 33/34 (1982): 26–55.
—, ed. *Crisis in Editing: Texts of the English Renaissance*. New York: AMS. Forthcoming.
Metzger, Bruce M. "Scholarly Editing of the Greek New Testament." Greetham *Scholarly Editing*.
Middendorf, John H. "Scholarly Editing of English Eighteenth-Century Literature." Greetham *Scholarly Editing*.
Middleton, Anne. "Life in the Margins, or What's an Annotator to Do?" *New Directions in Textual Studies*. Ed. Dave Oliphant and Robin Bradford. Austin: Harry Ransom Humanities Research Center / U of Texas P, 1990: 167–83.
Miller, Leo. "Establishing the Text of Milton's State Papers." *Text* 2 (1985): 181–186.
Millgate, Jane, ed. *Editing Nineteenth-Century Fiction*. New York: Garland, 1978.
—. "The Limits of Editing: The Problem of Scott's *The Siege of Malta*." *Bulletin of Research in the Humanities* 82 (1979): 190–212.
Mills, David. "Theories and Practices in the Editing of the Chester Cycle." Pearsall *Manuscripts*: 110–121.
Moggridge, D. E., ed. *Editing Modern Economists*. New York: AMS, 1988.
Moorman, Charles. *Editing the Middle English Manuscript*. Jackson, MS: UP of Mississippi, 1975.
—. "One Hundred Years of Editing the *Canterbury Tales*." *Chaucer Review* 24 (1989): 99–114.
Morrison, Elizabeth. "Editing a Newspaper Novel for the Colonial Texts Series: *A Woman's Friendship*." Eggert *Editing in Australia*: 113–124.
Morse, Charlotte C. "The Value of Editing the *Clerk's Tale* for the *Variorum Chaucer*." Pearsall *Manuscripts*: 122–129.
Morton, Richard. "How Many Revengers in *The Revengers Tragedy*?" Shand and Shady: 113–122.
*Mosser, Daniel W. "Reading and Editing *The Canterbury Tales*: Past, Present, and Future(?)." *Text* 7 (1994).

Moyles, R. G. *The Text of Paradise Lost: A Study in Editorial Procedure*. Toronto: U of Toronto P, 1985.

Myerson, Joel. "Scholarly Editing of American Colonial and Nineteenth-Century Literature." Greetham *Scholarly Editing*.

New Oxford English Dictionary. Electronic Edition. Ed E. S. C. Weiner. Oxford: Clarendon / Waterloo: U of Waterloo. In progress.

Nichols, Stephen G. "On the Sociology of Medieval Manuscript Annotation." Barney *Annotation*: 43–73.

Nida, Eugene A. "Editing Translated Texts." *Text* 4 (1988): 13–27.

Nohrnberg, James C. "Justifying Narrative: Commentary within Biblical Storytelling." Barney *Annotation*: 3–42.

Oakman, Robert. *Computer Methods for Literary Research*. Athens: U of Georgia P, rev. 1984.

Oberg, Barbara. "Interpretation in Editing: The Gallatin Papers." *Newsletter of the Association for Documentary Editing* 4.2 (May 1982): 7–9.

Orduna, Germán. "Hispanic Textual Criticism and the Stemmatic Value of the History of the Text." Greetham *Scholarly Editing*.

Owen, W. J. B. "Annotating Wordsworth." Baird: 47–71.

Oxford English Dictionary. Ed. J. A. Simpson and E. S. C. Weiner. Oxford: Clarendon 1989. 2nd ed.; CD-ROM edition. Oxford: Oxford UP, 1989.

Parker, Hershel. "Conjectural Emendations: An Illustration from the Topography of Pierre's Mind." *Literary Research Newsletter* 3 (1978): 62–66.

Pearsall, Derek. "Editing Medieval Texts." *Textual Criticism and Literary Interpretation*. Ed. Jerome J. McGann. Chicago: U of Chicago P, 1985: 92–106.

—, ed. *Manuscripts and Texts: Editorial Problems in Later Middle English Literature*. Cambridge: Brewer, 1987.

—. "Theory and Practice in Middle English Editing." *Text* 7 (1994).

— and R. A. Cooper. "The *Gawain* Poems: A Statistical Approach to the Question of Common Authorship." *Review of English Studies*. New Series 39, No. 155 (Aug. 1988): 365–85.

Pebworth, Ted-Larry. *Editing Literary Texts on the Microcomputer: The Example of John Donne's Poetry*. 1988.

—. "Manuscript Transmission and the Selection of Copy-Text in Renaissance Coterie Poetry." *Text* 7 (1994).

—. and Gary A. Stringer. *Scholarly Editing on the Micro-Computer*. New York: MLA. Forthcoming (available from Gary A. Stringer, University of Southern Mississippi, Box 10044, Hattiesburg, MS 39406–0044).

Perkins, Maxwell. *Editor to Author: The Letters of Maxwell E. Perkins*. Ed. John Hall Wheelock. New York: Scribner, 1987.

Pettit, Alexander, ed. *Editing the Novel: Current Series, Current Problems, Current Discoveries*. Special Issue of *Studies in the Novel* 27 (Fall, 1995). Forthcoming.

Pitcher, John. "Editing Daniel." Hill *New Ways*: 57–76.

Plachta, Bodo. "Scholarly Editing of German Literature." Greetham *Scholarly Editing*.

Polk, Noel. "Where the Comma Goes: Editing William Faulkner." Bornstein: 241–258.

Proudfoot, Richard. "Richard Johnson's *Tom a' Lincoln* Dramatized: A Jacobean Play in British Library MS. Add. 61745." Hill *New Ways*: 75–102.

Quentin, Dom Henri. *Essai de critique textuelle*. Paris: Picard, 1926.

Reiman, Donald H. "Scholarly Editing of British Nineteenth-Century Poetry and Non-Fiction Prose." Greetham *Scholarly Editing*.

Renear, Allen. "Representing Text on the Computer: Lessons for and from Philosophy." *Bulletin of the John Rylands University Library* 74 (1992): 221–248.

Rigg, A. G., ed. *Editing Medieval Texts: English, French, and Latin Written in England*. New York: Garland, 1977.

Roberts, Josephine A. "Lady Mary Wroth's *Urania*: A Response to Jacobean Censorship." Hill *New Ways*: 125–129.
Robinson, Peter M. W. "Manuscript Politics." Chernaik: 9–15.
*—. "Collation, Textual Criticism, Publication, and the Computer." *Text* 7 (1994).
Robson, John M. "A Mill for Editing." Hall *Browning*: 1–14.
Rocher, Ludo. "Scholarly Editing of Sanskrit Literature." Greetham *Scholarly Editing*.
Rosenberg, Edgar. "Last Words on *Great Expectations*: A Textual Brief on the Six Endings." *Dickens Studies Annual* 9 (1981): 87–116.
*Rossman, Charles, ed. *Studies in the Novel: Special Issue on Editing Ulysses*. 22 (1990): 113–269.
Ruggiers, Paul G., ed. *Editing Chaucer: The Great Tradition*. Norman: Pilgrim, 1984.
*Sanders, Arnold. "Hypertext, Learning, and Memory: Some Implications from Manuscript Tradition." *Text* 8. Forthcoming.
Sanders, Charles Richard. "Carlyle and Wordsworth." Hall *Browning*: 115–122.
Sandulescu, George and Clive Hart, eds. *Assessing the 1984 Ulysses*. London: Colin Smyth / New York: Barnes and Noble, 1986.
Scheibe, Siegfried. "Some Notes on Letter Editions: With Special Reference to German Writers." *Studies in Bibliography* 41 (1988): 136–48.
Schoeck, R. J., ed. *Editing Sixteenth-Century Texts*. Toronto: U of Toronto P, 1966.
Schoenbaum, Samuel. "Old-Spelling Editions: The State of the Art." Shand and Shady: 9–26.
Schuchard, Ronald. "Yeats's Letters, Eliot's Lectures: Toward a New Focus on Annotation." *Text* 6 (1993): 287–306.
Schweik, Robert C. and Michael Piret. "Editing Hardy." Hall *Browning*: 15–42.
Scott, P. G. "The Editorial Problem in Clough's *Adam and Eve*." Hall *Browning*: 79–104.
Seary, Peter. *Lewis Theobald and the Editing of Shakespeare*. Oxford: Oxford UP, 1990.
Shand, G. B. and Raymond C. Shady, eds. *Play-Texts in Old Spelling: Papers from the Glendon Conference*. New York: AMS P, 1984.
Shawcross, John T. "Scholarly Editions: Composite Editorial Principles of Single Copy-Texts, Multiple Copy-Texts, Edited Copy-Texts," *Text* 4 (1988): 297–318.
Shillingsburg, Peter L. "Critical Editing and the Center for Scholarly Editions." *Scholarly Publishing* 9 (1977–78): 31–40.
—. "Textual Problems in Editing Thackeray." Millgate *Editing*: 41–59.
—. "The Computer as Research Assistant in Scholarly Editing." *Literary Research Newsletter* 5 (1980): 31–45.
—. "The Printing, Proof-Reading, and Publishing of Thackeray's *Vanity Fair*: The First Edition." *Studies in Bibliography* 34 (1981): 118–45.
—. "Editorial Problems Are Readers' Problems." Hall *Browning*: 43–58.
—. *Computer Assisted Scholarly Editing (CASE)*. P. Shillingsburg, Department of English, Mississippi State University, MS 39762. 601-325-3644.
—. "The Meanings of a Scholarly Edition." *Bibliographical Society of Australia and New Zealand Bulletin* 13 (1989): 41–50.
*—. "Polymorphic, Polysemic, Protean, Reliable, Electronic Texts." Bornstein and Williams: 29–44.
—. "Scholarly Editing of British Nineteenth-Century Fiction." Greetham *Scholarly Editing*.
Simon, John Y. "Editors and Critics." *Newsletter of the Association for Documentary Editing* 3.4 (December 1981): 1–4.
*Small, Ian. "The Editor as Annotator as Ideal Reader." Small and Walsh: 186–209.
—. "Text-Editing and the Computer: Facts and Values." Chernaik: 25–30.
*— and Marcus Walsh, eds. *The Theory and Practice of Text-Editing*. Cambridge:

Cambridge UP, 1991.

Smith, D. I. B., ed. *Editing Eighteenth-Century Texts*. Toronto: U of Toronto P, 1968.

—. *Editing Seventeenth-Century Prose*. Toronto: Hakkert, 1972.

Spadacini, Nicholas and Jenaro Talens, eds. *The Politics of Editing*. Minneapolis: U of Minnesota P, 1992.

Speer, Mary B. "Editing Old French Texts in the Eighties: Theory and Practice." *Romance Philology* 45 (1991): 7–43.

—. "Scholarly Editing of Old French Literature." Greetham *Scholarly Editing*.

Sperberg-McQueen, C. M. *Guidelines for the Encoding and Interchange of Machine-Readable Texts*. Text Encoding Initiative: August, 1990.

Spevack, Marvin. *Complete and Systematic Concordance to the Works of Shakespeare*. Hildesheim: G. Ohms, 1968–70. 6 vols.

—. *The Harvard Concordance to Shakespeare*. Cambridge: Belknap / Harvard, 1973.

—. "The Editor as Philologist," *Text* 3 (1987): 91–106.

Stallworthy, Jon. "Old-Spelling Editions: The State of the Business." Shand and Shady: 141–152.

Statement of Editorial Principles and Procedures: A Working Manual for Editing Nineteenth-Century American Texts. New York: MLA, 1972.

Steen, Sara Jayne. "Behind the Arras: Editing Renaissance Women's Letters." Hill *New Ways*: 229–238.

Storey, Mark. "'Creeping into Print': Editing the Letters of John Clare." Small and Walsh: 62–89.

Stubbs, John and Frank Wm. Tompa. "Waterloo and the *New Oxford English Dictionary*." Butler and Stoneman: 19–44.

Sutherland, Kathryn. "Challenging Assumptions: Women Writers and New Technology." Chernaik: 53–67.

*Tanselle, G. Thomas. "Some Principles for Editorial Apparatus." *Studies in Bibliography* 25 (1972): 41–88. Repr. *Selected Studies*: 403–50.

—. "Editorial Apparatus for Radiating Texts." *The Library* Fifth Series 29 (1974): 330–37.

—. "The Editing of Historical Documents." *Studies in Bibliography* 31 (1978): 1–56. Repr. *Selected Studies*: 451–506.

—. *Selected Studies in Bibliography*. Charlottesville: UP of Virginia, 1979.

—. "External Fact as an Editorial Problem." *Studies in Bibliography* 32 (1979): 1–47.

*—. "Textual Scholarship." *Introduction to Literary Scholarship in the Modern Languages and Literatures*. Ed. Joseph Gibaldi. New York: MLA, 1981. 29–52.

*—. "The Varieties of Scholarly Editing." Greetham *Scholarly Editing*.

Tarrant, R. H. "Scholarly Editing of Classical Latin Literature." Greetham *Scholarly Editing*.

Taylor, Robert. "Editorial Practices — An Historian's View." *Newsletter of the Association for Documentary Editing* 3.1 (1981): 4–8.

Teague, Frances. "Provenance and Propaganda as Editorial Stumbling Blocks." Hill *New Ways*: 119–124.

Theobald, Lewis. *Shakespeare Restored*. London: 1726.

Thompson, Ann. "Feminist Theory and the Editing of Shakespeare: *The Taming of the Shrew* Revisited." Greetham *Margins of the Text*.

Thorpe, James and Claude M. Simpson, Jr. *The Task of the Editor*. Los Angeles: Clark Library, 1969.

Thorson, John L. "Authorial Duplicity: A Warning to Editors." *Analytical and Enumerative Bibliography* 3 (1979): 79–96.

Tiffin, Chris. "Final Intention, Revision and the Genetic Text: Editing Rosa Praed's *My Australian Girlhood*." Eggert *Editing in Australia*: 125–136.

Toon, Thomas E. "Dry-Point Annotations in Early English Manuscripts: Understanding Texts and Establishing Contexts." Barney *Annotation*: 74–93.

Toronto, U of. Conferences on Editorial Problems. Toronto: U of Toronto Press, A. M. Hakkert / New York: Garland, AMS, 1966– .

Trésor de la langue française: Dictionnaire de la langue du XIXe siècle et du XXe siècle 1789–1960. Ed. Paul Imbs. Paris: Centre National de la Recherche Scientifique, 1971– .

Trigg, Stephanie. "Speaking with the Dead." Eggert *Editing in Australia*: 137–150.

Turner, Robert Kean. "Accidental Evils." Shand and Shady: 27–34.

Turville-Petre, Thorlac. "Editing *The Wars of Alexander.*" Pearsall *Manuscripts*: 143–160.

Uitti, Karl D. and Gina Greco. "Computerization, Canonicity and the Old French Scribe: The Twelfth and Thirteenth Centuries." *Text* 6 (1993): 133–152.

Velz, John W. "Giving Voices to the Silent: Editing the Private Writings of Women." Hill, *New Ways*: 263–272.

Vieth, David M. "A Textual Paradox: Rochester's 'To a Lady in a Letter'." *Papers of the Bibliographical Society of America* 54 (1960): 147–162; addendum 55 (1961): 130–133. Repr. Gottesman and Bennett: 102–123.

Vogt, George L. and John Bush Jones, eds. *Literary and Historical Editing.* Lawrence: U of Kansas Libraries, 1981.

Walker, Alice. "Principles of Annotation: Some Suggestions for Editors of Shakespeare." *Studies in Bibliography* 9 (1957): 95–105.

Walsh, Marcus. "Bentley Our Contemporary; Or, Editors Ancient and Modern." Small and Walsh: 157–185.

—. "The Fluid Text and the Orientations of Editing." Chernaik: 31–39.

Welland, Dennis. "Samuel Clemens and His English Publishers: Biographical and Editorial Problems." Gottesman and Bennett: 167–185.

Wells, Stanley. *Modernizing Shakespeare's Spelling.* Oxford: Clarendon / New York: Oxford UP, 1979.

*— and Gary Taylor, eds. with John Jowett and William Montgomery. *William Shakespeare: A Textual Companion.* Oxford: Clarendon, 1987.

Werstine, Paul. "The Editorial Usefulness of Printing House and Compositor Studies." Shand and Shady: 35–64.

—. "Scholarly Editing of Shakespeare." Greetham *Scholarly Editing*.

West, James L. W., III. *A Sister Carrie Portfolio.* Charlottesville: UP of Virginia, 1985.

—. "Scholarly Editing of British and American Twentieth-Century Literature." Greetham *Scholarly Editing*.

Whitesell, David R. "Bowers and the Editing of Spanish Golden Age Drama." *Text* 8. Forthcoming.

Whittaker, John. "The Practice of Manuscript Collation." *Text* 5 (1991): 121–130.

Whitworth, Charles. "Rectifying Shakespeare's *Errors*: Romance and Farce in Bardeditry." Small and Walsh: 107–141.

Williams, William P., ed. "Special Issue on the New Oxford Shakespeare." *Analytical and Enumerative Bibliography* n.s.4 (1990): 1–97.

Wilson, Frank P. "The Malone Society: The First Fifty Years, 1906–56." Malone Society. *Collections* 4 (1956): 1–16.

Worthen, John. "D. H. Lawrence: Problems with Multiple Texts." Small and Walsh: 14–34.

Wyatt, Diana. "Editing for *REED [Records of Early English Drama].*" Pearsall *Manuscripts*: 161–170.

Yamashita, Hiroshi. "Bowers and the Editing of Modern Japanese." *Text* 8. Forthcoming.

Zitner, S. P. "Excessive Annotation, or Piling Pelion on Parnassus." Shand and Shady: 131–140.

Index

To save space, short titles of works are occasionally used. Bold-face indicates the main discussion in multiple entries, and italic indicates an illustration or figure.